LETTERS OF DELEGATES 1774 ☆ 1789 TO CONGRESS

14

October 1, 1779–March 31, 1780

Paul H. Smith, Editor

Gerard W. Gawalt and Ronald M. Gephart
Associate Editors

LIBRARY OF CONGRESS   WASHINGTON   1987

Library of Congress Cataloging-in-Publication Data
(Revised for volume 14)

Letters of delegates to Congress, 1774–1789.

Includes bibliographical references and indexes.
Supt. of Docs. no.: LC 1.34:14
1. United States. Continental Congress—History—
Sources—Collected works. I. Smith, Paul Hubert, 1931–
JK1033.L47   973.3'12   76–2592
ISBN 0-8444-0177-3 (set)
ISBN 0-8444-0562-0 (v. 14)

For sale by the Superintendent of Documents, U.S. Government Printing Office
Washington, D.C. 20402

Editorial Method and Apparatus

In its treatment of documents this edition of delegate letters strives to achieve a middle ground between facsimile reproduction and thorough modernization. The original spelling and grammar are allowed to stand except where editorial changes or insertions are required to make the text intelligible. For example, when a badly misspelled word is misleading, the correct spelling is inserted in roman type in brackets after the word. Moreover, words omitted through oversight have been supplied at appropriate places in italic type in brackets. Obvious slips of the pen and inadvertent repetitions are usually silently corrected. Capitalization and punctuation have been standardized according to certain conventions. Each sentence begins with a capital letter, as do all proper and geographic names as well as days of the week and months of the year. Doubtful cases have been resolved in favor of modern usage; otherwise the usage of the original texts has been followed. Generally, abbreviations, contractions, and monetary signs are preserved as they appear in manuscript except when they are ambiguous or misleading. On the other hand, the thorn and the tilde are consistently expanded. "Ye" always appears as "The," for instance, and "rec̃vd" as "received." Likewise, "pr." and tailed *p*'s are always expanded to "per," "pre," or "pro," as the case demands. Finally, superscript letters are always lowered to the line.

Gaps in the text are indicated by ellipses in brackets for missing words and by blank spaces in brackets for missing numbers. Conjectural readings are supplied in roman type in brackets, and editorial insertions in italic type in brackets. Material canceled in manuscript but restored to the printed text is included in italic type in angle brackets ("square parentheses"). Marginalia in letters are treated as postscripts if not obviously keyed to the body of the document, and postscripts which appear without explicit designation are supplied with a *P.S.* in brackets. Documents are arranged chronologically, with more than one document of the same date arranged alphabetically according to writer. Documents dated only by the month or by the year are placed at the end of the respective month or year. Place-and-date lines always appear on the same line with the salutation regardless of their position in the manuscript.

A descriptive note at the foot of each entry provides abbreviations indicating the nature and location of the document when it was copied for this project, except for privately owned manuscripts whose

iii

ownership is explained. The descriptive note also contains information on the document's authorship if explanation is necessary, and endorsements or addresses are quoted when they contain more than routine information. Other editorial practices employed in this work are explained in the sections on editorial apparatus which follow.

TEXTUAL DEVICES

The following devices will be used in this work to clarify the text.

[. . .], [. . . .]	One or two words missing and not conjecturable.
[. . .]^1, [. . . .]^1	More than two words missing; subjoined footnote estimates amount of material missing.
[ ]	Number or part of a number missing or illegible.
[ ]^1	Blank space in manuscript; explanation in subjoined footnote.
[roman]	Conjectural reading for missing or illegible matter; question mark inserted if reading is doubtful.
[*italic*]	Editorial insertion in the text.
⟨*italic*⟩	Matter crossed out in manuscript but restored.

DESCRIPTIVE SYMBOLS

The following symbols are used in this work to describe the kinds of documents drawn upon. When more than one symbol is used in the descriptive note, the first to appear is that from which the main text is taken.

RC	recipient's copy
FC	file copy
LB	letterbook copy
MS	manuscript
Tr	transcript (used to designate not only contemporary and later handwritten copies of manuscripts, but also printed documents)

LOCATION SYMBOLS

The following symbols, denoting institutions holding the manuscripts printed in the present volume, are taken from *Symbols of American Libraries*, 13th ed. (Washington: Library of Congress, 1985). Each volume of this edition will contain a revised list.

CSmH	Henry E. Huntington Library, San Marino, Cal.
Ct	Connecticut State Library, Hartford
CtHi	Connecticut Historical Society, Hartford
CtHWa	Wadsworth Atheneum, Hartford
CtY	Yale University, New Haven
DLC	Library of Congress
DLC(ESR)	Library of Congress, Early State Records Collection
DNA	National Archives and Records Administration
DNLM	National Library of Medicine, Bethesda, Md.
DSoC	Society of the Cincinnati, Washington, D.C.
De–Ar	Delaware Public Archives Commission, Dover
ICHi	Chicago Historical Society
IU–HS	University of Illinois, Urbana, Illinois Historical Survey
In	Indiana State Library, Indianapolis
M–Ar	Massachusetts Archives, Boston
MB	Boston Public Library, Boston
MDaAr	Danvers Historical Society, Danvers, Mass.
MH–H	Harvard University, Houghton Library, Cambridge, Mass.
MHi	Massachusetts Historical Society, Boston
MSaE	Essex Institute, Salem, Mass.
MdAA	Maryland Hall of Records, Annapolis
MdHi	Maryland Historical Society, Baltimore
MeHi	Maine Historical Society, Portland
MiDbEI	Edison Institute, Henry Ford Museum and Greenfield Village Library, Dearborn, Michigan
MiU–C	William L. Clements Library, Ann Arbor, Mich.
N	New York State Library, Albany
NHi	New-York Historical Society, New York
NN	New York Public Library, New York
NNC	Columbia University, New York
NNPM	Pierpont Morgan Library, New York
NbO	Omaha Public Library, Omaha, Neb.
Nc–Ar	North Carolina State Department of Archives and History, Raleigh
NcU	University of North Carolina, Chapel Hill
Nh–Ar	New Hampshire Division of Archives and Records Management, Concord
NhD	Dartmouth College, Hanover, N.H.
NhHi	New Hampshire Historical Society, Concord
Nj	New Jersey State Library, Trenton
NjHi	New Jersey Historical Society, Newark
NjMoHP	Morristown National Historical Park, Morristown, N.J.
NjP	Princeton University, Princeton, N.J.
NjR	Rutgers University, New Brunswick, N.J.
PHC	Haverford College, Haverford, Pa.

PHarH	Pennsylvania Historical and Museum Commission, Harrisburg
PHi	Historical Society of Pennsylvania, Philadelphia
PPAmP	American Philosophical Society, Philadelphia
PPIn	Independence National Historical Park, Philadelphia
PPL	Library Company of Philadelphia
PPRF	Rosenbach Foundation, Philadelphia
PSC	Swarthmore College, Swarthmore, Pa.
PU	University of Pennsylvania, Philadelphia
PWcHi	Chester County Historical Society, West Chester, Pa.
R–Ar	Rhode Island State Archives, Providence
RHi	Rhode Island Historical Society, Providence
RNHi	Newport Historical Society, Newport, R.I.
ScC	Charleston Library Society, Charleston, S.C.
ScHi	South Carolina Historical Society, Charleston
Vi	Virginia State Library, Richmond
ViHi	Virginia Historical Society, Richmond
ViU	University of Virginia, Charlottesville
Vt–PR	Vermont Public Records Library, Montpelier

ABBREVIATIONS AND SHORT TITLES

Adams, *Family Correspondence* (Butterfield)
Butterfield, Lyman H., et al., eds. *Adams Family Correspondence.* Cambridge: Harvard University Press, Belknap Press, 1963–.
Adams, *Works* (Adams)
Adams, John. *The Works of John Adams, Second President of the United States* .... Edited by Charles Francis Adams. 10 vols. Boston: Charles C. Little and James Brown, 1850–56.
Adams, *Writings* (Cushing)
Adams, Samuel. *The Writings of Samuel Adams.* Edited by Harry A. Cushing. 4 vols. Boston: G. P. Putnam's Sons, 1904–8.
Austin, *Life of Gerry*
Austin, James T. *The Life of Elbridge Gerry, with Contemporary Letters to the Close of the American Revolution.* 2 vols. Boston: Wells and Lilly, 1828–29.
Bartlett, *Papers* (Mevers)
Bartlett, Josiah. *The Papers of Josiah Bartlett.* Edited by Frank C. Mevers. Hanover, N.H.: Published for the New Hampshire Historical Society by the University Press of New England, 1979.
Bio. Dir. Cong.
U.S. Congress. *Biographical Directory of the American Congress, 1774–1971.* Washington: U.S. Government Printing Office, 1971.
Burnett, *Letters*
Burnett, Edmund C., ed. *Letters of Members of the Continental Con-*

gress. 8 vols. Washington: Carnegie Institution of Washington, 1921–36.

Clinton, *Papers* (Hastings)
Clinton, George. *Public Papers of George Clinton, First Governor of New York, 1777–1795, 1801–1804.* Edited by Hugh Hastings and J. A. Holden. 10 vols. New York and Albany: Wynkoop Hallenbeck Crawford Co. et al., 1899–1914.

DAB
Dictionary of American Biography. Edited by Allen Johnson and Dumas Malone.

Evans, *Am. Bibliography*
Evans, Charles. *American Bibliography.* 12 vols. Chicago: Privately printed, 1903–34.

Freeman, *Washington*
Freeman, Douglas S. *George Washington, a Biography.* 7 vols. New York: Charles Scribner's Sons, 1948–57.

Jay, *Papers* (Morris)
Jay, John. *John Jay, the Making of a Revolutionary: Unpublished Papers, 1745–1780.* Edited by Richard B. Morris et al. New York: Harper & Row, 1975.

Jefferson, *Papers* (Boyd)
Jefferson, Thomas. *The Papers of Thomas Jefferson.* Edited by Julian P. Boyd et al. Princeton: Princeton University Press, 1950–.

JCC
U.S. Continental Congress. *Journals of the Continental Congress, 1774–1789.* 34 vols. Edited by Worthington C. Ford et al. Washington: Library of Congress, 1904–37.

Lafayette, *Papers* (Idzerda)
Idzerda, Stanley J., et al., eds. *Lafayette in the Age of the American Revolution: Selected Letters and Papers, 1776–1790.* Ithaca: Cornell University Press, 1977–.

Lee, *Letters* (Ballagh)
Lee, Richard Henry. *The Letters of Richard Henry Lee.* Edited by James C. Ballagh. 2 vols. New York: Macmillan Co., 1911–14.

Madison, *Papers* (Hutchinson)
Madison, James. *The Papers of James Madison.* Edited by William T. Hutchinson and William M. E. Rachal. Chicago: University of Chicago Press, 1962–.

Md. Archives
Archives of Maryland. Edited by William H. Browne et al. Baltimore: Maryland Historical Society, 1883–.

Mason, *Papers* (Rutland)
Mason, George. *The Papers of George Mason, 1725–1792.* Edited by Robert A. Rutland. 3 vols. Chapel Hill: University of North Carolina Press, 1970.

Morgan, *Captains to the Northward*
Morgan, William J. *Captains to the Northward: The New England*

Captains in the Continental Navy. Barre, Mass.: Barre Publishing Co., 1959.

N.C. State Records

North Carolina. *The State Records of North Carolina.* Edited by Walter Clark. Vols. 11–26. Winston and Goldsboro, N.C.: N. I. and J. C. Stewart et al., 1895–1914.

N. H. State Papers

New Hampshire. *Provincial and State Papers.* 40 vols. Concord, 1867–1943.

NYHS Collections

Collections of the New-York Historical Society.

Pa. Archives

Pennsylvania Archives. 9 series, 119 vols. in 120. Philadelphia: J. Severns & Co., 1852–56; Harrisburg: State printer, 1874–1935.

Pa. Council Minutes

Pennsylvania. *Minutes of the Supreme Executive Council of Pennsylvania, from Its Organization to the Revolution.* 6 vols. [Colonial Records of Pennsylvania, vols. 11–16]. Harrisburg: Theo. Fenn & Co., 1852–53.

Paullin, *Marine Committe Letters*

Paullin, Charles O., ed. *Out-Letters of the Continental Marine Committee and Board of Admiralty, 1776–1780.* 2 vols. New York: Printed for the Naval History Society by the De Vinne Press, 1914.

PCC

Papers of the Continental Congress. National Archives and Records Administration. Washington, D.C.

PRO

Public Record Office. London.

Public Records of Connecticut

Hoadly, Charles J., et al., eds. *The Public Records of the State of Connecticut.* 11 vols. Hartford: Case, Lockwood & Brainard Co., 1894–1967.

Rodney, *Letters* (Ryden)

Rodney, Caesar. *Letters to and from Caesar Rodney, 1756–1784.* Edited by George H. Ryden. Philadelphia: University of Pennsylvania Press, 1933.

Shipton, *Harvard Graduates*

Shipton, Clifford K. *Biographical Sketches of Those Who Attended Harvard College.* Sibley's Harvard Graduates. Boston: Massachusetts Historical Society, 1873–.

Staples, *Rhode Island*

Staples, William R. *Rhode Island in the Continental Congress, 1765–1790.* Providence: Providence Press Co., 1870.

Sullivan, *Letters* (Hammond)

Sullivan, John. *Letters and Papers of Major-General John Sullivan.* Edited by Otis G. Hammond. 3 vols. Collections of the New Hampshire Historical Society, vols. 13–15. Concord: New Hampshire Historical Society, 1930–39.

Trumbull, *Papers* (MHS Colls.)
Trumbull, Jonathan, Sr. *The Trumbull Papers*. 4 vols. Massachusetts Historical Society Collections, 5th ser., vols. 9–10; 7th ser., vols. 2–3. Boston: Massachusetts Historical Society, 1885–1902.

Warren-Adams Letters
Warren-Adams Letters, Being Chiefly a Correspondence among John Adams, Samuel Adams, and James Warren. 2 vols. Massachusetts Historical Society Collections, vols. 72–73. Boston: Massachusetts Historical Society, 1917–25.

Washington, *Writings* (Fitzpatrick)
Washington, George. *The Writings of George Washington*. Edited by John C. Fitzpatrick. 39 vols. Washington: U.S. Government Printing Office, 1931–44.

Wharton, *Diplomatic Correspondence*
Wharton, Francis, ed. *The Revolutionary Diplomatic Correspondence of the United States*. 6 vols. Washington: U.S. Government Printing Office, 1889.

Wright, *The Continental Army*
Wright, Robert K., Jr. *The Continental Army*. Washington: Center of Military History, United States Army, U.S. Government Printing Office, 1983.

Acknowledgments

This edition began in 1970 as a project of the Library of Congress' American Revolution Bicentennial Office, now incorporated into the Library's Manuscript Division as the Historical Publications Office. The Library has had a long tradition of publishing scholarship on the period of the American Revolution. Its monumental edition of the *Journals of the Continental Congress, 1774–1789* (34 vols., Washington, 1904–37) is a predecessor, and will be a companion, of the present work. The editors wish to thank the Ford Foundation for a substantial gift which has been indispensable to the progress of the edition. Our appreciation is also extended to the innumerable individuals who have contributed to enriching the holdings of the Library of Congress to make it the premier institution for conducting research on the American Revolution.

The photocopies of the more than twenty-two thousand documents that have been collected for this project have been assembled through the cooperation of several hundred institutions and private individuals devoted to preserving the documentary record upon which the history and traditions of the American people rest, and it is to their work that a documentary publication of this nature should ultimately be dedicated. Unfortunately, the many individual contributors to this collecting effort cannot be adequately recognized, but for permission to print documents appearing in the present volume we are especially grateful to the following institutions: the American Philosophical Society, Archives du ministère des affaires étrangères (Paris), Archivo General de Indias (Seville), Boston Public Library, Charleston Library Society, Chester County Historical Society, Chicago Historical Society, Society of the Cincinnati, William L. Clements Library, Columbia University, Connecticut Historical Society, Connecticut State Library, Danvers Historial Society, Dartmouth College, Delaware Public Archives Commission, Donaldson, Lufkin & Jenrette, Essex Institute, Greenfield Village and Henry Ford Museum, Harvard University, Haverford College, Henry E. Huntington Library, University of Illinois, Independence National Historical Park, Indiana State Library, Maine Historical Society, Maryland Hall of Records, Maryland Historical Society, Massachusetts Archives Division, Massachusetts Historical Society, Pierpont Morgan Library, Morristown National Historical Park, National Archives, National Library of Medicine, New Hampshire Division of Archives and Records Management, New Hampshire Historical Society, New Jersey Historical Society, New Jersey State Library, Newport Historical

Society, New-York Historical Society, New York Public Library, New York State Library, North Carolina State Department of Archives and History, University of North Carolina, Omaha Public Library, Pennsylvania Historical and Museum Commission, Historical Society of Pennsylvania, University of Pennsylvania, Library Company of Philadelphia, Princeton University, Public Record Office (London), Rhode Island Historical Society, Rhode Island State Archives, Rosenbach Foundation, Rutgers University, South Carolina Historical Society, Swarthmore College, Virginia Historical Society, Virginia State Library, University of Virginia, Wadsworth Atheneum, and Yale University. And in addition we express our thanks and appreciation to the following persons: Mr. Joseph G. Deering, Mr. Sol Feinstone, Mr. Herbert E. Klingelhofer, Capt. J. G. M. Stone, Mr. Robert J. Sudderth, Jr., and Mrs. Aileen Moore Topping.

This work has benefited not only from Edmund C. Burnett's pathfinding 8-volume edition of *Letters of Members of the Continental Congress* but also from the generous cooperation of the editors of several other documentary publications with a common focus on the revolutionary era. From them the Library has borrowed heavily and to them it owes a debt it can never adequately acknowledge. It is a pleasure to give special thanks to the editors of the papers of John Adams, Benjamin Franklin, Thomas Jefferson, Henry Laurens, James Madison, and George Washington. Finally we owe thanks to the historians who served on the Advisory Committee on the Library's American Revolution Bicentennial Program, and especially to Mr. Julian P. Boyd, Mr. Lyman H. Butterfield, and Mr. Merrill Jensen, who generously acted as an advisory committee for the *Letters* project.

Paul H. Smith
Historical Publications Office
Manuscript Division

Chronology of Congress

October 1   Orders preparation of a plan for reorganizing the conduct of naval affairs.

October 2   Requests Vermont claimants to authorize Congress to settle Vermont claims.

October 4   Adopts instructions for minister to Spain (John Jay).

October 6   Admonishes Benedict Arnold on treatment of Pennsylvania officials.

October 7   Calculates and apportions 1780 state fiscal quotas.

October 9   Adopts circular letter to the states on meeting fiscal quotas.

October 13   Authorizes Arthur Lee to return to America.

October 14   Commends John Sullivan for conduct of expedition against the Indians; resolves to emit an additional $5 million; sets day of thanksgiving.

October 15   Adopts instructions for minister to Spain; resolves to seek a loan in Holland.

October 20   Adopts thanksgiving day proclamation.

October 21   Appoints Henry Laurens to negotiate Dutch loan.

October 22   Rejects appeal for Continental intervention against state taxation of Continental quartermasters.

October 26   Adopts instructions for negotiation of Dutch loan and treaty of amity and commerce.

October 28   Creates Board of Admiralty, ending management of naval affairs by congressional committee.

October 30   Urges Virginia to reconsider decision to open land office for sale of unappropriated lands.

November 1   Appoints Henry Laurens to negotiate Dutch treaty of amity and commerce.

November 2–3   Adjourns because of expiration of President Huntington's credentials as Connecticut delegate.

November 5   Notified of evacuation of Rhode Island; appoints committee to plan an executive board to supervise Continental officials.

November 8   Requests correspondence files of former presidents of Congress.

November 9   Elects Treasury officers.

November 10   Orders deployment of three frigates to South Carolina.

November 11   Orders reinforcement of southern department; observes funeral of Joseph Hewes.

November 13   Rejects resignation of Gen. John Sullivan; approves parole of Gens. William Phillips and Baron Riedesel of the Convention Army.

November 16   Undertakes care of Spanish prisoners held at New York; rejects Massachusetts' appeal to retain Continental taxes to defray Penobscot expedition costs; recommends that states compel persons to give testimony at Continental courts-martial.

November 17   Holds audience with the newly arrived French minister, the chevalier de La Luzerne; resolves to emit an additional $10 million.

November 18   Gives General Washington free hand to coordinate operations with the French armed forces.

November 19   Recommends state adoption of price regulations.

November 23   Resolves to draw bills of exchange to £100,000 sterling each on John Jay and Henry Laurens.

November 25   Adopts new regulations for clothing Continental Army; discharges committee for superintending the commissary and quartermaster departments.

November 26   Appoints Admiralty commissioners.

November 29   Commemorates General Pulaski's death; resolves to emit an additional $10 million; accepts resignation of commissary general Jeremiah Wadsworth.

November 30   Appoints committee to confer with Washington at headquarters; accepts resignation of Gen. John Sullivan.

December 2   Receives notification of Spanish declaration of war against Britain; appoints Ephraim Blaine commissary general of purchases.

December 3   Resolves to move Congress from Philadelphia at the end of April 1780; appoints Admiralty commissioners.

December 6   Reinforces armed forces in southern department.

December 9   Observes day of thanksgiving.

December 15   Recommends that states extend provisions embargo to April 1780.

December 16   Authorizes Gen. Benjamin Lincoln to coordinate southern operations with Spanish officers at Havana.

December 20–24   Debates proposal to borrow $20 million abroad.

December 24   Authorizes use of depositions of witnesses at courts-martial in noncapital cases.

December 27   Recommends moratorium on granting lands in region of Pennsylvania-Virginia boundary dispute; orders Post Office to institute twice-weekly in place of weekly deliveries.

December 28   Authorizes Continental reimbursement of militia expenses incurred defending Connecticut against invasion.

December 31   Endorses Board of War plan to employ greater secrecy to reduce procurement expenses.

January 3   Postpones decision on selecting 'a new site for Congress.

January 4–8   Debates plan for creating a court of appeals.

January 8   Reorganizes Georgia's Continental regiments.

January 10   Dismisses Charles Lee, second ranking Continental general; debates plan for reducing the army to curtail expenses.

January 12   Sends emergency appeal to the states for provisioning the army; abolishes mustermaster's department.

January 13   Adopts new regulations for negotiation of prisoner exchanges.

January 14   Recommends that states make provision for guaranteeing the privileges and immunities of French citizens recognized in the Franco-American treaty of amity and commerce.

January 15   Creates Court of Appeals in admiralty cases.

January 17   Endorses export of grain to French forces by the French agent of marine.

January 18   Resolves to print the journals of Congress monthly, but ends practice of printing the yeas and nays.

January 20   Orders investigation into the expenses of the staff departments; abolishes barrackmaster's department.

January 22   Elects judges to Court of Appeals.

January 24   Adopts new measures for recruitment of Continental troops.

January 25   Halts pay of inactive naval officers.

January 26   Appoints committee to confer with the French minister on joint Franco-American operations.

January 27   Authorizes inflation adjustment in the salaries of Continental officials.

January 31   Pledges to wage a vigorous campaign in conjunction with French forces during 1780.

February 4–5   Debates Continental Army quotas for 1780.

February 9   Sets state quotas and adopts recruitment measures for an army of 35,000 by April 1, 1780.

February 11   Affirms commitment to the reconquest of Georgia.

February 12   Confirms sentence in the court-martial of Gen. Benedict Arnold.

February 16–24   Debates proposals for a system of in-kind requisitions from the states.

February 22   Debates congressional privilege issue arising from the complaint of Elbridge Gerry.

February 25   Adopts system of in-kind requisitions from the states.

February 28   Postpones decision on selecting a new site for Congress.

March 2   Postpones debate on Vermont controversy.

March 3   Sets "day of fasting, humiliation and prayer."

March 4   Commends John Paul Jones and crew of *Bonhomme Richard* for victory over *Serapis.*

March 8   Orders reinforcements for the southern department.

March 13–18   Debates proposals for fiscal reform.

March 18   Repudiates Continental dollar, adopting measures for redeeming bills in circulation at the ratio of 40 to 1.

March 20   Recommends state revision of legal tender laws.

March 21   Postpones debate on Vermont controversy.

March 24   Observes Good Friday.

March 26   Observes funeral of James Forbes.

March 27   Rejects proposals for a new site for Congress; receives plan for reorganizing quartermaster department.

March 29–31   Debates proposals for adjusting Continental loan office certificates for inflation.

List of Delegates to Congress

This section lists both the dates on which delegates were elected to terms falling within the period covered by this volume and the inclusive dates of their attendance. The former are generally ascertainable from contemporary state records, but the latter are often elusive bits of information derived from the journals of Congress or extrapolated from references contained in the delegates' correspondence, and in such cases the "facts" are inevitably conjectural. It is not possible to determine interruptions in the attendance of many delegates, and no attempt has been made to record interruptions in service caused by illness or brief trips home, especially of delegates from New Jersey, Delaware, Maryland, and Pennsylvania living within easy access of Congress. For occasional references to such periods of intermittent service as survive in the correspondence and notes of various delegates, see the index under individual delegates. Until fuller information is provided in a consolidated summary of delegate attendance in the final volume of this series, the reader is advised to consult Burnett, *Letters*, 4:lix–lxvi, 5:lv–lxiv, for additional information on conjectural dates of attendance. Brief biographical sketches of all the delegates are available in the *Biographical Directory of the American Congress, 1774–1971*, and fuller sketches of more than half of the delegates can be found in the *Dictionary of American Biography*.

CONNECTICUT

Eliphalet Dyer
Elected: October 21, 1778; October 14, 1779; January 6, 1780
Did not attend October 1779 to March 1780
Oliver Ellsworth
Elected: October 21, 1778; October 14, 1779; January 6, 1780
Attended: December 16, 1779, to March 31, 1780
Titus Hosmer
Elected: October 21, 1778; October 14, 1779
Did not attend October 1779 to March 1780
Benjamin Huntington
Elected: January 6, 1780
Did not attend January to March 1780
Samuel Huntington
Elected: October 21, 1778; October 14, 1779; January 6, 1780
Attended: October 1, 1779, to March 31, 1780

Jesse Root
  Elected: October 21, 1778; October 14, 1779; January 6, 1780
  Attended: October 1 to November 26, 1779
Roger Sherman
  Elected: October 21, 1778; October 14, 1779; January 6, 1780
  Attended: October 1, 1779, to March 31, 1780
Joseph Spencer
  Elected: January 7, 1779; October 14, 1779
  Did not attend October 1779 to March 1780
Oliver Wolcott
  Elected: January 6, 1780
  Did not attend January to March 1780

DELAWARE

John Dickinson
  Elected: January 18, 1779; December 22, 1779
  Attended: October 21? to November 18, 1779
Thomas McKean
  Elected: January 18, 1779; December 24, 1779
  Attended: November 5?–22; December 2? 1779, to March 25, 1780
George Read
  Elected: December 22, 1779
  Declined
Nicholas Van Dyke
  Elected: January 18, 1779; December 22, 1779
  Attended: October 4–11? 1779; January 27–February 11? 1780

GEORGIA

Georgia was not represented during the period October 1779 to March 1780. The invasion of the state in December 1778 had thrown civil government into chaos and obstructed the routine election of delegates. The credentials of delegates chosen in 1778 had expired early in 1779, and although as many as three slates of delegates were appointed by rump conventions, councils, and assemblies during the year, none ever reached Philadelphia. The state was not again represented in Congress until May 15, 1780, when three of the five delegates elected by the Georgia assembly in January 1780 presented their credentials.

MARYLAND

William Carmichael
  Elected: November 13, 1778
  Did not attend October 1779 to March 1780

James Forbes
  Elected: November 13, 1778; December 22, 1779
  Attended: October 1, 1779, to March 7? 1780 (died March 25, 1780)
John Hall
  Elected: December 22, 1779
  Did not attend October 1779 to March 1780
John Hanson
  Elected: December 22, 1779
  Did not attend October 1779 to March 1780
John Henry
  Elected: November 13, 1778; March 31, 1780
  Did not attend October 1779 to March 1780
Daniel of St. Thomas Jenifer
  Elected: November 13, 1778
  Attended: October 1–30, 1779
Thomas Johnson
  Elected: December 22, 1779
  Did not attend October 1779 to March 1780
Edward Lloyd
  Elected: December 22, 1779
  Did not attend October 1779 to March 1780
William Paca
  Elected: November 13, 1778
  Attended: October 1–30, 1779
George Plater
  Elected: November 13, 1778; December 22, 1779
  Attended: October 11, 1779, to March 31, 1780
Stephen West
  Elected: March 31, 1780
  Declined

MASSACHUSETTS

Samuel Adams
  Elected: October 8, 1778; November 18, 1779
  Did not attend October 1779 to March 1780
Francis Dana
  Elected: October 8, 1778
  Did not attend October 1779 to March 1780
Elbridge Gerry
  Elected: October 8, 1778; November 18, 1779
  Attended: October 1, 1779, to February 17, 1780
John Hancock
  Elected: October 8, 1778; November 18, 1779
  Did not attend October 1779 to March 1780

Samuel Holten
  Elected: October 8, 1778; November 18, 1779
  Attended: October 1, 1779, to March 31, 1780
James Lovell
  Elected: October 8, 1778; November 18, 1779
  Attended: October 1, 1779, to March 31, 1780
George Partridge
  Elected: June 29, 1779; November 18, 1779
  Attended: October 1, 1779, to March 31, 1780
Artemas Ward
  Elected: June 4, 1779; November 18, 1779
  Did not attend October 1779 to March 1780

NEW HAMPSHIRE

Nathaniel Folsom
  Elected: March 24, 1779; November 3, 1779
  Attended: December 30, 1779, to March 31, 1780
George Frost
  Elected: August 18, 1778
  Did not attend October 1779 to March 1780
Woodbury Langdon
  Elected: April 3, 1779; November 3, 1779
  Attended: October 1 to November 20, 1779
Samuel Livermore
  Elected: January 1, 1780
  Attended: February 7–28, 1780
Nathaniel Peabody
  Elected: March 25, 1779; November 3, 1779
  Attended: October 1, 1779, to March 31, 1780
William Whipple
  Elected: August 18, 1778; November 3, 1779
  Did not attend October 1779 to March 1780

NEW JERSEY

Abraham Clark
  Elected: May 25, 1779; December 25, 1779
  Attended: January 25 to March 31, 1780
John Fell
  Elected: November 6, 1778; November 17, 1779
  Attended: October 1, 1779, to March 31, 1780
Thomas Henderson
  Elected: November 17, 1779
  Did not attend Congress

William C. Houston
Elected: May 25, 1779; November 17, 1779
Attended: October 1, 1779, to March 31, 1780
Nathaniel Scudder
Elected: November 6, 1778
Attended: October 21 to November 25, 1779
John Witherspoon
Elected: November 6, 1778
Attended: October 8? to November 1, November 16–23, 1779

NEW YORK

James Duane
Elected: October 1, 1779
Attended: Did not attend October 1779 to March 1780
William Floyd
Elected: October 1, 1779
Attended: December 2, 1779, to March 31, 1780
John Jay
Elected: October 1, 1779
Did not attend October 1779 to March 1780
Francis Lewis
Elected: October 16, 1778
Attended: October 1 to November 19? 1779
Ezra L'Hommedieu
Elected: October 1, 1779
Attended: December 2, 1779, to March 31, 1780
Robert R. Livingston
Elected: October 18, 1779; February 24, 1780
Attended: November 20, 1779, to March 31, 1780
Gouverneur Morris
Elected: October 16, 1778
Attended: October 6 to November 19? 1779
Philip Schuyler
Elected: October 18, 1779
Attended: November 16 to December 8? 1779 (on mission to
  headquarters, ca. December 3–8, 1779); March 7–31, 1780
John Morin Scott
Elected: October 1, 1779
Attended: March 6–31, 1780

NORTH CAROLINA

Thomas Burke
Elected: August 12, 1778; October 26, 1779
Attended: December 8, 1779, to March 31, 1780

Cornelius Harnett
  Elected: May 8, 1779
  Attended: October 1 to December 8, 1779
Joseph Hewes
  Elected: February 4, 1779
  Attended: October 1–29, 1779 (died November 10, 1779)
Whitmell Hill
  Elected: August 12, 1778; October 26, 1779
  Did not attend October 1779 to March 1780
Allen Jones
  Elected: October 26, 1779
  Attended: December 8, 1779, to March 31, 1780
John Penn
  Elected: May 8, 1779
  Attended: December 14, 1779, to March 4? 1780
William Sharpe
  Elected: February 4, 1779
  Attended: October 1 to December 8? 1779

PENNSYLVANIA

John Armstrong, Sr.
  Elected: November 20, 1778; November 12, 1779
  Attended: October 1–14, 1779
Samuel Atlee
  Elected: November 20, 1778
  Attended: October 1 to November 12, 1779
James McLene
  Elected: March 2, 1779; November 12, 1779
  Attended: November 20, 1779, to March 23? 1780
Frederick A. Muhlenberg
  Elected: March 2, 1779; November 12, 1779
  Attended: October 1 to December 15? 1779; January 1 to March 31, 1780
James Searle
  Elected: November 20, 1778; November 12, 1779
  Attended: October 22? 1779, to March 31, 1780
William Shippen, Sr.
  Elected: November 20, 1778; November 12, 1779
  Attended: November 15? 1779, to March 31, 1780
Henry Wynkoop
  Elected: March 2, 1779
  Attended: October 1 to November 12, 1779

RHODE ISLAND

John Collins
  Elected: May 5, 1779
  Attended: October 1–4, 1779; February 4 to March 31, 1780

William Ellery
Elected: May 5, 1779
Attended: November 30, 1779, to March 31, 1780
Stephen Hopkins
Elected: May 5, 1779
Did not attend October 1779 to March 1780
Henry Marchant
Elected: May 5, 1779
Attended: October 1 to December 8? 1779 (on mission to head-
quarters, ca. December 3–8, 1779)

SOUTH CAROLINA

Thomas Bee
Elected: February 1, 1780
Did not attend October 1779 to March 1780
Francis Kinloch
Elected: February 1, 1780
Attended: March 25–31, 1780
Henry Laurens
Elected: February 5, 1779; February 1, 1780
Attended: October 1 to November 8, 1779
Rawlins Lowndes
Elected: February 17, 1779
Did not attend Congress
John Mathews
Elected: February 5, 1779; February 1, 1780
Attended: October 1, 1779, to March 31, 1780
Arthur Middleton
Elected: February 5, 1779; February 1, 1780
Did not attend October 1779 to March 1780

VIRGINIA

William Fitzhugh
Elected: June 18, 1779
Attended: October 1–30, 1779
Cyrus Griffin
Elected: June 18, 1779
Attended: October 1, 1779, to March 31, 1780
James Henry
Elected: December 14, 1779
Did not attend October 1779 to March 1780
Patrick Henry
Elected: June 18, 1779
Did not attend October 1779 to March 1780

Gabriel Jones
  Elected: June 18, 1779
  Did not attend Congress
Joseph Jones
  Elected: December 14, 1779
  Did not attend October 1779 to March 1780
James Madison, Jr.
  Elected: December 14, 1779
  Attended: March 20–31, 1780
James Mercer
  Elected: June 18, 1779
  Attended: October 1–30, 1779
Edmund Randolph
  Elected: June 18, 1779
  Did not attend October 1779 to March 1780
Meriwether Smith
  Elected: June 18, 1779
  Did not attend October 1779 to March 1780
John Walker
  Elected: December 14, 1779
  Did not attend October 1779 to March 1780

Illustrations

View of Philadelphia   endpapers

"An East Prospect of the City of Philadelphia; taken by George Heap from the Jersey Shore, under the Direction of Nicholas Scull Surveyor General of the Province of Pennsylvania." This detail is from an engraving by Thomas Jeffreys based on an etching of the city published in Thomas Jeffreys, *A General Topography of North America and the West Indies. Being a Collection of All the Maps, Charts, Plans, and Particular Surveys, That Have Been Published of That Part of the World, Either in Europe or America* (London: R. Sayer, 1768).

Samuel Huntington   4

Huntington had little formal education, but he served as a cooper's apprentice before turning to the study of law and opening a law practice in Norwich, Conn., in 1758. Success in this profession led him into public life. In 1765 he was appointed king's attorney for Connecticut and he was subsequently elected as justice of the peace and judge of the superior court of Connecticut, a position he held from 1773 to 1783, when he was appointed chief justice. During the same period, he also served in the Connecticut General Assembly and as an assistant in the upper house of the legislature, from which he was elected a delegate to Congress annually from 1775 to 1783. There he served on many committees, was a signer of the Declaration of Independence, and, upon the appointment of John Jay as minister to Spain, was elected president in September 1779, serving until July 1781. He was second only to John Hancock in length of service as president of Congress. Following his return to Connecticut and appointment as chief justice, Huntington was elected lieutenant-governor in 1785 and governor the following year. He was reelected as governor annually the next eleven years until his death in 1796 at age 64.

Portrait by Charles Willson Peale. Independence National Historical Park Collection.

Nathaniel Scudder   198

The place and date of Scudder's birth are uncertain, but he was raised in Monmouth County, N.J., graduated from the College of New Jersey, and turned to the study of medicine as a young man. He apparently had developed a large and flourishing practice before he was drawn into the current of public life at the onset of the Revolution. He was elected to the first provincial congress in 1774 and after election to the New Jersey legislature was named speaker in 1776. He also served as lieutenant colonel and colonel of Monmouth County militia, in which capacity he had several opportunities to engage the enemy during 1776–77. Scudder served as delegate to Congress in 1778–79 and was appointed to numerous committees, most conspicuously the Medical Committee and the committee for superintending the commissary and quartermaster departments, where his training and experience were of great benefit. As a friend of Richard Henry Lee he was often identified with causes associated with the Lee interest in Congress, such as preventing the recall of Arthur Lee, and his correspondence with Richard Henry is an important source of information on congressional affairs. Upon retiring from Congress, Scudder resumed his duties as a militia officer, primarily repelling Loyalist raiding parties, in the course of which he was killed, at the age of 48, near Shrewsbury, N.J., just three days before the American victory at Yorktown in October 1781. He was the only delegate to Congress to fall in battle during the American Revolution.

Nathaniel Scudder to George Washington, November 15, 1779, from the Washington Papers, Manuscript Division, Library of Congress.

Anne-César, Chevalier de La Luzerne   208

La Luzerne succeeded Conrad-Alexandre Gérard as French minister to the United States in September 1779, and he immediately set about gaining congressional confidence in his ability to avoid the partisan politics in which Gérard had become embroiled. His diplomatic experience before coming to America was of short duration but included a post at the Bavarian Court in Munich before and during the crisis of the Bavarian Succession in 1777–78. La Luzerne, a comparatively young man of 37 when he reached Boston in August 1779, journeyed slowly to Philadelphia, visiting numerous officials and dignitaries en route, and delayed his formal audience with Congress for nearly six weeks. He made an excellent impression nearly everywhere he was received and generally succeeded in distancing himself from the overtly partisan maneuvers of his predecessor. He was markedly more subtle in working with the delegates, benefiting from the presence of Francophiles who often informed him of major policy debates, and he eventually secured court approval to pay retainers to some, such as John Sullivan, to forward French interests. He worked to limit American calls on French funds, urged ratification of the Articles of Confederation to preserve American unity, and sought to limit American claims to Florida and the Mississippi

River so as to secure greater Spanish commitment to military cooperation in North America. He also encouraged Congress to instruct its
minister plenipotentiary in Paris to work closely with the comte de
Vergennes in planning negotiations with Britain and generally
enjoyed good relations with such key officials as the American secretary of foreign affairs, Robert R. Livingston. In June 1784, he
returned to France, ostensibly on leave of absence, but he studiously
avoided returning to America and in 1787 secured the more presti-
gious post of ambassador to London.

Portrait by Charles Willson Peale. Independence National Historical Park Collection.

William Ellery   238

Ellery, a Newport lawyer, had graduated from Harvard College
and briefly tried his hand as a merchant before taking up the law
and stepping onto the stage of public life during the Stamp Act
crisis. Elected to succeed Samuel Ward in Congress in 1776, Ellery
quickly became identified with efforts to create a strong Continental
Navy, in part because of his state's early advocacy of a naval build
up. He was elected to Congress seven times from 1776 to 1784,
signed the Declaration of Independence, and repeatedly served on
the Marine Committee and Committee of Commerce in recognition
of his abilities in those fields. Service on the Committee of Appeals
also added to his experience in maritime cases and, upon its creation
in 1779, he was appointed to the new Board of Admiralty, to which
he was also appointed as a noncongressional commissioner following
his failure to be reelected as a delegate in 1780. He was reelected to
Congress in 1781 and 1783–84, however, after which he returned to
Rhode Island permanently, holding the positions of Continental
Loan Office commissioner for Rhode Island from 1786 to 1790 and
collector of customs for the district of Newport from 1790 until his
death in 1820 at age 92.

Portrait by James Reid Lambdin after a work by John Trumbull.
Independence National Historical Park Collection.

George Plater   354

Born and reared at "Sotterley," the family estate in St. Mary's
County, Md., Plater graduated from the College of William and
Mary in 1753 and turned to the legal profession. He began his
public career as justice of the peace of St. Mary's County, served as a
delegate in the lower house of the Maryland Assembly, 1757–66,
and held appointments as naval officer of the Patuxent district and
as a member of the Executive Council before the Revolution. In
1776 he was elected to the Maryland Council of Safety and in 1778
to Congress, where he served three terms, until 1780. His committee

assignments were less numerous than those of many delegates, although he was a member of the standing Marine Committee. He and his wife were warm friends of Gouverneur Morris, who received their nurturing care after he lost a leg in a carriage accident in Philadelphia in 1780. They corresponded regularly with him when not in Pennsylvania. Plater was elected to the Maryland Senate from St. Mary's County after the Revolution and was active in the movement to obtain ratification of the new federal Constitution in 1787–88. He was elected governor of Maryland in 1791 but occupied that post less than a year before his death in 1792 at the age of 66.

Gratz Collection, the Historical Society of Pennsylvania.

James Lovell's instructions
in use of diplomatic ciphers   442

From the creation of a network of American agents and correspondents abroad in 1775–76, Congress experimented with invisible ink and various diplomatic codes and ciphers, often successfully but not without considerable frustration. Lovell's interest in cryptography, his position on the Committee for Foreign Affairs, and his unequaled continuous attendance at Congress from 1777 to 1782 made him the key figure in the use of such systems, which repeatedly led him to undertake the education of the American commissioners abroad in the use of ciphers. His polyalphabetic grid system was transparently simple in conception but frustrating to use in practice, often leading John Adams and Benjamin Franklin to despair when attempting to decipher Lovell's letters. The February 24, 1780, letter from Lovell to Franklin illustrated here contains one of the fullest and clearest expositions of the use of his system.

From the Benjamin Franklin Papers, American Philosophical Society.

Samuel Livermore   499

Little is known of Livermore's early life, which was spent in Massachusetts, where he taught school briefly before attending the College of New Jersey to prepare himself for the ministry. He subsequently turned to the study of law and opened a practice in Waltham, Mass., before moving to Portsmouth, N.H., and becoming connected to Gov. John Wentworth, whose patronage brought him an appointment as attorney general in 1769. Thereafter he was seldom out of public office, although he soon moved to the wilderness village of Holderness, N.H., and for a time subordinated his public career to the acquisition of a vast landed estate. It was perhaps this facet of his activities that led New Hampshire to appoint him commissioner and a special delegate to Congress in 1779 to represent the state's claims in the New Hampshire Grants controversy with the Vermont settlers. But Congress was unable to get the parties to the dispute together during the brief time he attended in February 1780. Hearings on the case were postponed until May, by which time Livermore's credentials had expired and he returned home. He returned to Congress as a delegate in 1781–82 and 1785–86, during which terms he was appointed to many committees, particularly those relating to western lands and Indian affairs. He served several years as chief justice of the superior court of New Hampshire, represented the state in the first two federal Congresses, and was elected twice to the United States Senate, from which he resigned in 1801 because of ill health. He died in 1803 a few days before his 71st birthday.

Prints and Photographs Division, Library of Congress. LC-USZ62-54687.

Congressional resolution of March 18, 1780,
devaluing the Continental dollar   522

Following numerous unsuccessful attempts to curb the catastrophic depreciation of the Continental dollar that had destroyed the credibility of its financial system, Congress yielded to the inevitable and officially devalued the dollar at the ratio of 40 to 1 on March 18, 1780. Retirement of the bills in circulation was left to the states, which were to collect them in taxes and return them to the Continental Treasury in payment of their fiscal quotas, set at a $15 million monthly total. One-twentieth of the bills destroyed were to be reissued in new bills bearing interest at the rate of 5 percent per annum to be redeemed in six years, ostensibly "in sterling bills of exchange, drawn by the United States on their commissioners in Europe," who had no prospects whatever of defraying such expenses. The exhortation contained in the preamble of the resolves embodying this decision had little effect on the establishment of the "appropriate funds" required to "ensure the punctual redemption of the bills," and in the meantime Congress proceeded with plans for in-kind requisitions from the states to provision and supply the Continental Army in 1780.

From the Continental Congress Miscellany, Manuscript Division, Library of Congress.

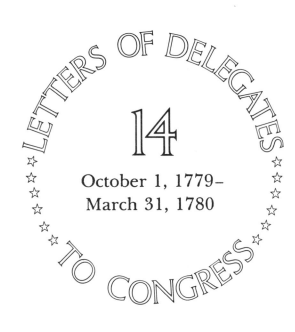

October 1, 1779–
March 31, 1780

John Fell's Diary

Friday October 1st [1779].

Coml Committee. Congress.

Several Letters &c Read. Genl Arnolds Accts. of his Expences for 9 Mo. Extravigant indeed. Committed to 5 vizt.[1]

Moved for the thanks of the House to be given our late President Mr Jay. Agreed.

MS (DLC).

[1] Fell left the remainder of the line blank and never filled in the names of the committee—Samuel Holten, Henry Laurens, James Mercer, William Paca, and Nathaniel Peabody.

Samuel Holten's Diary

[October 1–2, 1779]

Octr. 1. Friday. We have Accounts this evening, that, Capt. Tayler has taken another lode of Hissians.

2. Saturday. I dined with the honl. Mr. Root, & drank tea with the secy.[1]

MS (MDaAr).

[1] That is, Charles Thomson.

Samuel Huntington to George Clinton

Sir   Philadelphia Octor 1st. 1779

You will herewith receive enclosd an Act of Congress of the 29th ultimo among other things directing Mr John Bradford Continental Agent at Boston to Sell and deliver out of the stores of these United States there, to such person or persons as the State of N. York Shall Authorise for that purpose, any quantity of Rum & sugar not Exceedg. five hundred Hogsheads of the former & fifty of the latter, within a limitted time. And recommending to the Legislative or Executive powers of the State to sell and distribute the same for the benefit of the people as therein Expressd.[1]

I gives me pleasure to have an Opportunity in the begining of my Correspondence with your Excy. in the public Character with which Congress have been pleasd to honour me to transmit an Act of theirs which I trust will be acceptable; & beneficial to the good people of your State in their peculiar Situation.

I have the honour to be with Sentiments of Esteem, Your Excelys humble Servt.   Saml. Huntington President

3

Samuel Huntington

RC (MH–H: Sparks Manuscripts).
[1] This resolve, which was actually passed on September 30, was reluctantly adopted at the recommendation of the committee for superintending the commissary and quartermaster departments. *JCC*, 15:1130–31. Although some delegates were concerned that such a transaction might have "an ill influence on the credit of our money," the majority were obviously moved by the plea of New Yorkers that the British occupation of New York City the past three years had left them "wholly dependant on the other States for supplies of salt and other foreign commodities." For Congress' reluctance to endorse such barter transactions—i.e., "making purchases in Ordinary Cases otherwise than for money"—see also Huntington to Jeremiah Wadsworth, this date.

In writing this letter to Clinton, Huntington seriously distorted the resolve herewith enclosed. Congress had authorized the sale of "sugar and rum not exceeding five hundred hogsheads of the former, and fifty hogsheads of the latter," not "Rum & Sugar" as Huntington carelessly wrote. In the letterbook copy of Huntington's brief October 1 letter transmitting this resolve to John Bradford, however, the passage properly reads "sugar and rum." PCC, item 14, fol. 197.

Samuel Huntington to John Jay

Sir,   Philadelphia 1st October 1779
It is with real pleasure I do myself the honour of transmitting the enclos'd resolution containing the thanks of Congress and testimony of their Approbation of your conduct in the Chair and in the execution of public business as President of the great Council of these United States.[1]
I am with much esteem, your humble Servant,   S. H. President[2]

LB (DNA: PCC, item 14).
[1] See *JCC*, 15:1134. Jay's October 4 reply acknowledging this expression of "the approbation of Congress" is in PCC, item 78, 13:113.
[2] This day Huntington also wrote the following brief letter to Lt. Col. François-Louis Teissèdre de Fleury in consequence of a•recommendation by the Board of War.

"You will receive enclosed an Act of Congress of this date expressing the high Sense they entertain of your military merit and the deserved esteem and reputation you have acquired during your services in the Armies of these United States.

"Be assured Sir that with pleasure I transmit such ample testimony of the merits of a brave and gallant Officer."

Although Fleury had been granted leave of absence to return to France, he abruptly canceled his plans to return home upon learning of d'Estaing's arrival in Georgia. He went instead, as Washington explained to Lafayette, to the southern department "in pursuit of fresh laurels." See PCC, item 14, fol. 196; *JCC*, 15:1111, 1129–30, 1134; and Washington, *Writings* (Fitzpatrick), 16:327, 491. See also John Jay to Fleury, July 27, 1779.

Samuel Huntington to Jesse Root

Sir   Philadelphia 1st Octor 1779
I have this moment receivd the enclosd Act of Assembly from their Speaker, with his Information that the Committee of their

Assembly are ready to confer with the Committee of Congress at
Such time as they Shall appoint, & notify the Committee of the
Assembly.[1]

I am Sir with Esteem, your humble Servant,

Saml. Huntington

RC (DNA: PCC, item 19). Addressed: "For the Honble Mr Root &c, Committee in the
Case Sloop Active &c."

[1] In response to a memorial from Gideon Olmsted, Congress appointed a committee on September 29, consisting of Jesse Root, William Paca, and Henry Laurens,
"relative to carrying into execution the decree of the court of appeals concerning the
sloop Active." *JCC*, 15: 1122.

When Huntington communicated this information to Pennsylvania, the assembly
immediately appointed Joseph Gardner, John Smilie, and Thomas Smith to confer
with Root's committee, but this gesture represented no capitulation on the part of
Pennsylvania to Continental authority in admiralty appeals. The state's position had
been forcefully presented in a series of assembly resolves on March 10, 1779, and the
assemblymen appointed to confer with Root's committee were strictly instructed "that
they observe the former Resolutions of the House on this subject as the rule of their
conduct." The September 30 "Act of Assembly" instructing the Pennsylvania conferees,
which Huntington enclosed with this note to Root, is in PCC, item 19, 4:499. For the
background and other aspects of this case, see also these *Letters*, 11:341–43, 516–17,
525–26; and William Churchill Houston to Caleb Camp, November 12, 1779, note 2.

Henry Laurens' duties on this committee may also have been the occasion for his
drafting the following undated motion concerning prize shares, which survives among
his papers.

"Resolved, that from & after this day the Captors of all prizes made by any Ship or
other Vessel in Continental service shall be entitled to & enjoy the whole amount or
value of such prizes without deduction any Resolve of Congress to the contrary
notwithstanding." Laurens Papers, no. 20, ScHi.

Samuel Huntington to Jeremiah Wadsworth

Sir   Philadelphia Octor 1st. 1779

You will herewith receive an Act of Congress, directing, (among
other thing) that the Marine Committee give the Necessary Orders
to enable the Commissary General to perform his engagments Actually made with the people, for sugar &c.[1]

You will observe this measure is Justified from Necessity alltho'
Congress cannot approve of making purchases in Ordinary Cases
otherwise than for money.

I am with Esteam, Your humble Servt,

Saml. Huntington President

RC (CtHWa: James Wadsworth Collection).

[1] See *JCC*, 15:1130–32; and Huntington to George Clinton, this date. Although
Congress hereby endorsed Wadsworth's "engagement" to exchange flour from New
York for sugar and rum from Massachusetts, it simultaneously declared this barter
transaction to be a special exception to Continental policy and announced disapproval
of "any purchases in ordinary cases, otherways than for money."

James Lovell to John Adams

[October 1, 1779]
The Resolve of the 26th of Sepr. for appointing a *Minister plenipotentiary* for Spain was reconsidered on the 27th and the words *in lieu of a Commissioner* were added, by the urgency of Brother Gerry least our State should appear to be against an Alliance with Spain, on this Mass. was div'd & S'th Carolina all the rest stood as the day before.[1]

On the 28th Order for Tomorrow for appointing Secretaries & a Person to examine accounts in Europe agreable to the Resolve of Augst. 6th.

The Nominations you know except in the last Case Mr. Joshua Johnston Brother to Govr. Johnston of Maryland.[2]

A Comtee. to draught a Commissn. for Spain and Commissns. for the Secretaries.

Another Comtee. to report Salaries, Mathews, Gerry, Root.

                                   29th
Carmichael for Spain. Mr. Searles name being previously withdrawn. I wish therefore you would blot it from my former letter as it is blotted from our Journals.

Mr. Dana for Peace.

Col. John Laurens for France.

Mr. Joshua Johnstone for Accounts.

Comtee. reported Salaries.

                                   Oct. 1
Report of the Comtee.[3] recommitted upon my Suggestions as to *unde derivetur*.

Your Return in the Frigate which brought you must be more agreable than even one of ours with a new set of Faces. If Dana does not consent, the answer shod be immediate. For though I do not think the Door for yr. Business is yet opening, the Delay of the Frigate is to be considered, notwithstanding Mr. G——d[4] has kept ours more than two Months.

I wish heartily I could render you such Service as I think Dana can. It is tripping no Man to become *your* Secy. though in a former Case I should have been charged with putting my foot against the *faithful* Bancroft.

Pray miss no possible Chance to inform A L[5] of what has happened. It may reach him before an Authenticated account by Mr. Jay; and be a warning to take his measures. I was [wish] him immediately here to see to his Suit which was commenced 3 or 4 days ago. He can have no Accounts to cause Delay. And as he has Power to borrow Money; he cannot be obliged to apply to F——[6]. I will suggest the Thought of empowering you to make sure of a Loan if possible. I am persuaded the English would many of them seize the Opportunity of serving us & themselves all under one.

You will have a decent Commission *this Time*. I wish I could see yr. old one; as do the Secretary and Mr. Laurens between whom there have been formal Proceedings *in doors* respecting some Indecencies of the former.[7]   Yr. affectte,

                                                                       JL

RC (MHi: Adams Papers). Endorsed by Adams: "Mr. Lovell Octr. 1. 1779."

[1] For more detailed accounts of the voting in Congress for commissioners and ministers, see Lovell to John Adams, September 28, and Elbridge Gerry to John Adams, September 29, 1779.

[2] In his October 25 reply to Lovell, Adams indicated that when in France he had been honored with many "civilities" by Joshua Johnson, who was conducting his mercantile affairs at Nantes during this period. Adams, *Works* (Adams), 9:501.

[3] That is, the report on salaries of commissioners and their secretaries. *JCC*, 15:1135.

[4] That is, Conrad Alexandre Gérard, who had been postponing his departure since July and thereby kept the Continental frigate *Confederacy* standing-by for courier duty.

[5] Arthur Lee.

[6] Benjamin Franklin.

[7] Henry Laurens had charged Charles Thomson with refusing to recopy Adams' commission, which Laurens considered unsuitable for Adams' use as commissioner to France. Adams later replied, however, that "Upon the whole, I think [my commission] . . . a very decent, respectable and honorable commission. It was treated with great respect at Versailles, and I see no reason to object to it." See Adams, *Works* (Adams), 9:503; and the letters of Henry Laurens and Charles Thomson to a Committee of Congress, September 1 and 6, 1779, respectively.

James Mercer to the Virginia House of Delegates

Honble. Sir   Philadelphia. Oct 1st. 1779.

The singular Honour done me by the General Assembly, by their appointment to Congress at a time when Matters of Importance were said to be before them, induced my acceptance, in hopes that Integrity & Diligence might render some Service to my Country.[1] But the experience I have allready had, convinces me that a still greater change must happen in Men & Measures, to make it either Honble. or Safe to continue in Congress. I must therefore beg leave to decline the appointment for the year ensuing after the first day of November next.[2] As a Friend to *a* Congress I think it my Duty to recommend it to the General Assembly of Virginia to reduce the Number of Delegates to three, let these be Men of *Integrity* and *Diligence*, and abilities too if to be had. The Idea of Rotation is totally improper, as a member must be here near a month before he can be acquainted with the business on Hand & Rules of Congress, and if he is to be allowed to go home every quarter upon the plan of the present Act, he must ever remain a stranger to the business and an useless member—& when more than three members do attend you may rest assured that a great deal of time is wasted in needless debate—moreover the example of Virginia may influence other States & thereby occasion the recall of certain old members who have been

too long here allready. As this is intended for the General Assembly
& not for the Gallery—I hope it will not be read in public. I have the
Honour to be—Honble. Sir, Your most respectfull & very huble.
Servt.   Js. Mercer

RC (NjMoHP: Lloyd W. Smith Collection).

[1] Mercer, who had taken his seat in Congress on September 9, had been named to
the Virginia delegation in a special election the previous June to serve "until the first
Monday in November next." See *JCC*, 14:861–62, 15:1038, 1048; and Richard Henry
Lee to the Virginia House of Delegates, May 4, 1779, note.

[2] Mercer's request to resign from Congress after such a brief period of service was
symptomatic of a more general decline in the Virginia delegation. Mercer, William
Fitzhugh, Cyrus Griffin, and Meriwether Smith had been chosen as delegates for the
ensuing year in the regular June election. Fitzhugh and Smith, however, had already
obtained leaves of absence on September 28 and Smith departed for Virginia almost
immediately. Fitzhugh and Mercer attended Congress for the last time on October
30, the end of the terms for which they had been specially elected, leaving only Cyrus
Griffin to represent the state. See the *Journal of the House of Delegates of the Commonwealth of Virginia; Begun . . . on Monday, the Third Day of May [1779]* (Richmond: Printed
by Thomas W. White, 1827), pp. 54–55; *JCC*, 15:1115, 1229; and the letters of the
Virginia Delegates, Cyrus Griffin, and Meriwether Smith to the Virginia House of
Delegates, November 2, 9, and 25, 1779, respectively.

In its fall session the House of Delegates responded to altered conditions in Philadelphia by passing an act increasing delegate living expenses, but limiting the size of
the delegation to five and empowering any one to cast the state's vote. Cyrus Griffin
presented the act to Congress on December 30. Lacking this new authorization,
Virginia had been without a vote in Congress since November 1 for want of a quorum,
as Griffin was the sole Virginia delegate in attendance after that date until James
Madison's arrival in March 1780. See William W. Hening, *The Statutes at Large: Being a
Collection of All the Laws of Virginia*, 13 vols. (Richmond: J. & G. Cochran, 1809–23),
10:163–64; *JCC*, 15:1422; PCC, item 71, 1:295–96; and Griffin to the Virginia House
of Delegates, November 9, 1779.

John Fell's Diary

Saturday Octr. 2d [1779].
Com. Committee. Congress. After reading the Journals went into
the order of the day which was for the house to goe in to a Committee of the whole house on Finance.

MS (DLC).

William Churchill Houston to Robert Morris

Dear Sir,[1]   Philada. 2 Octr. 1779.
Yours of 18 July last I received the 27 of the same Month, and am
unhappy that I cannot, after waiting so long, speak with more Certainty relative to the Subject of it. That the present Plan of Confederation is not in all Parts just and equal, is, in my Opinion, a Proposition

as true as any in Euclid. I am confirmed in it by observing that the most candid People are of that way of Thinking, and those who are interested, particularly in the Mode in which what are called the Crown-lands, are disposed of, seem put to Difficulty in controuling their Consciences when they abet it. I often think that I would not submit to be roasted and basted as the Virginians and our Southern Friends are upon this Subject; for all the Lands will ever produce to their respective States. But like true Statesmen they do and bear any Thing on this Score. The Virginians endeavour to shelter themselves under an Argument which I never heard till I came to Congress, that they disputed the Right of the Crown to any Lands within the Bounds of their Charter, and contended for an Immunity from any Payments whatever claimed in Virtue of such Right; that Nothing but Force could have compelled such Payments from them; and that by joining with their Sister-states to renounce the Power and Jurisdiction of Great-Britain, they have only gained what other States have, — their Bounds. They add moreover, and persist in it, that the Settlement and Sale of these Lands will never be of any Value to their Treasury, or give them any available Assistance in discharging their Quota of the Continental Debt. This is in Part true & in Part problematical. Ingenious Men will speculate and refine up on any Subject, and the Truth or Falsehood of its goes out of Sight in the Multiplicity of Argument and Bluster of Utterance. Two Memorials lately came into Congress, one from the Proprietours of a Tract of Land on the Ohio called Indiana, granted by the Indians to a Company of Traders who had suffered Losses by their Means in the Course of Traffick; and the other from a number of Grantees of a large Tract including the former called Vandalia,[2] and which a little before the Commencement of the present Troubles it was in Contemplation to erect into a new Government. With both these Grants the Virginians have interfered, and the Memorialists complain of the Interference, and pray that they may not be deprived of their Property, and that Vandalia may be erected into, and acknowledged as a free State. This gave Alarm to the Virginians; they object to the Jurisdiction of Congress to receive or take Order on the Memorials, and in this Situation the Matter lies. How it will terminate, I am not able to conjecture. I think Congress are nearly equally divided upon the Question relative to the vacant Lands, and this being the Point to which Maryland most strenuously adheres, others are more out of Sight, but certainly it is not the only one in the Confederation where Justice does not seem to be strictly consulted. There are others little inferiour in my Judgment, though not so much discussed. The Virginians tell me they have made ample Provision to settle the Soldiers of any State, who will come and settle on their Lands without any Expense to the State from which they come;[3] and this would be of some Moment were it not for losing the Inhabitants, which for our Part we shall want at the End of the War. If any Thing relative to the

Confederation moves in Congress, I shall not fail to communicate it, and shall do it with the greater Pleasure, if agreeable to what I take to be your Wishes.

I am sorry to hear you have not attended the Legislature this Sitting, though I know the State of your private Affairs affords a very sufficient Apology. You know our Situation at this Time. Many of our former Men of Business have forsaken us, new Statesmen must be employed, without Experience, sometimes without Knowledge, too late in Life to learn in Season, much Business to be done, difficult in it's Kind, a region unexplored, the Foundations of Government to be laid, the Superstructure to be raised, while every Thing is Hurry and Tumult around. I have a further View in saying this than to express my regret that you have not attended; I hope no private Consideration will have Weight to induce you to make Excuses against being a Member the ensuing year. Capable Men are wanted, and of no Profession more than that of the Law. It is certainly a discouraging reflection that the honest and faithful are sacrificing their Time and Opportunities to the Service of the Publick, while selfish Men are enriching themselves, and without one Thought of the Prosperity of their Country, are engrossed with Projects of private Gain: but Somebody must serve the State, and I hope at least it will be remembered who they are if no other reward is ever offered them.

A Question of no small Importance has lately been decided in Congress by the recal of Mr. Arthur Lee. Much Time has been wasted here, and many Suspicions entertained through the Country, relative to this Matter. The Decision on his Merit, or Demerit must be left to Futurity, I own I am not at a Certainty about it, but I am happy the Matter is ended, as Things of more Consequence call for that Time which has been too much lavished on an idle Dispute. It is with Pleasure I can assure you that Subjects of Contention, and ill Humour are one after another taking their Leave, and that Unanimity returning which once made Congress respectable and useful, and will, I hope, make them so again.

Does it ever lie in your Way to see Philadelphia, or are you ever at Princeton? It would give me particular Pleasure to spend an Hour, and I have Something of Concern, to me more especially, to communicate to you. Your Friendship would be of Use in it, and I flatter myself would not be refused.

We have no Accounts as yet of any Operations of the Count D'Estaing in Georgia. Whether he will be able to effect his Purpose there will depend on many Circumstances, one of which is the Practicablity of doing a great Deal in a little Time. Should he think proper to push his Expedition as far Northward as to visit New-York, it would be A Matter much to be lamented if we should not be in Preparation with Men and Provisions to cooperate. I hear the Legislature have passed a Law for facilitating a Supply to the Army, and I sincerely wish the Execution may be so diligent as to put us in the best possible readiness. It would be a peculiar Misfortune if Count D'Estaing should be discouraged from coming through the Scarcity of Provisions or disappointed when actually come.

How do you approve the Measure of stopping further Emissions of Paper-money? It is a risque, but in my View absolutely necessary; and I am persuaded if any kind of good Economy could be introduced into publick Departments, the War could be amply supported by Taxes, at least with the Assistance of a few Loans, and I would have as few as possible. I hope every Friend of his Country will now put on a double Spirit of Exertion. I know you will not be wanting.

Here the People are bewitched. They seem to have no one Idea of Virtue and Patriotism left. Motives of private gain swallow up every laudable Principle. The Merchant against the Farmer, the Farmer against the Merchant. I wish New-Jersey were not so near them.

You will please to excuse this lengthy Scrawl; if I had time to copy it over and shorten it, I would. It will give me Pleasure to hear from you, and I can venture to promise I shall not again be so long delinquent in advising of the Receipt of Favours.

I am, with much regard, your obedt hble Servt.

William Ch. Houston

RC (NjR: Robert Morris Papers).
[1] Robert Morris, the New Jersey jurist, is identified in these *Letters*, 9:424n.1.
[2] For the introduction of these memorials in Congress, see John Fell's Diary, September 14, 1779, note.
[3] For a discussion of Virginia's offer of bounty lands to the officers and soldiers "of any State" and Maryland's reaction to it, see these *Letters*, 11:538n.1.

Samuel Huntington to John Laurens

Sir,   Philada. 2d Octr 1779
You will herewith enclos'd receive a Commission appointing you Secretary to our Minister Plenipotentiary at the Court of Versailles.[1]

Also a Letter of Credence to his most Christian Majesty for your Introduction in Case of the death of the Minister plenipotentiary, when it will be incumbent upon you to take Charge of our Affairs at that Court agreable to the tenor of your Commission.

The nature and Importance of the business with which you are intrusted evinces the propriety of entering upon the Service without delay.

I am Sir with great Respect, your humble Servant,

S. H. President

LB (DNA: PCC, item 14).
[1] For Congress' September 29 appointment of Laurens to this post, see *JCC*, 15:1127–28. The commission and letter of credence Huntington enclosed with this

letter were returned by Laurens in a December 6 letter to Congress declining the appointment. For the commission and Laurens' letter of refusal, see PCC, item 165, fols. 5–9; and *JCC*, 15:1366. The letter of credence is in PCC, item 25, 1:405–7.

Henry Laurens to John Laurens

My Dear son,   Philadelphia 2d October 1779.
    I have lately written to you by divers opportunities to Charles Town directed in your absence to Colonal Gervais, from an opinion that you would have left that place & I had suggested to my friends the probability of your taking Passage in Count d'Estaing's squadron; this Idea is countenanced by intimations in your Letter of the 3d September which I received three days since. I therefore expect this will meet you at the Head Quarters of His Excellency the Commander in Chief.
    You were put in Nomination in Congress by the Honorable Mr. Gerry the 27th Ulto. For the Office of Secretary to the Minister Plenipotentiary at the Court of Versailles & were on the 28th Unanimously elected by eleven, or twelve, States—the Salary not fixed—£1000 Stg recommended in a Report. I shall oppose every thing above £700.— but from what fund or funds is even that Sum to be paid?—I know not. The appointment is honorable to you in every appearance & will put you in a road leading to the service of your Country. I know you are equal to the task, nor could I forbear my testimony; it was due to a meritorious fellow Citizen, but I could not engage for your acceptance. Therefore you are by no means bound by any promise or even seeming promise on my part. I shall be glad to converse with you before you finally determine aye or no. You may, if you please, receive from me an honest & faithful & I believe accurate state of our affairs foreign & domestic. No attempts will be made on my part to induce or dissuade. You will be left by me to judge for your self. I need say no more but that I long to embrace you. I pray God to direct you in all Things & commend you to his protection,
                                                        Henry Laurens.

[*P. S.*] I might have added one word more. I wait here only to know your resolution, when I receive that from your self my Horses will be put to the vehicle in which I mean to return to my own poor distressed wretched Country.
    Capt. Roberts's conduct towards the Delegates of So. Carolina has not done the highest Credit to your recommendation—this as a hint.[1]

    5th. October. This address remaining on my Table unsealed gives me an opportunity to add—the Salaries of the Ministers Plenipo. are £2500 Stg Per Annum each—of their respective Secretaries

£1000—in full of all expences &c. My protest against both stands on the Book No! Men who are sincerely devoted to the service of their Country will not accept of Salaries which will tend to distress it.

RC (ScHi: Laurens Papers).

[1] For John's recommendation of Capt. Richard Brooke Roberts, see Laurens to John Laurens, September 21, 1779, note 1.

Henry Marchant to John Adams

Dear Sir,   Philadelphia Octr. 2d. 1779

By the last Post I was highly gratified by your kind & very polite Favour of the 10th of Sepr. The Notice & Recollection of my former Letter sufficiently convinces me that You have not forgot an old Friend. In your Absence I had frequent Temptations to write You; but I was affraid of being amongst the Number of troublesome and useless Correspondants.

We have finished Our foreign Affairs that mostly pressed upon Us. Your appointment will convince You, that however awkward Your Situation has been, it was not from any Alteration of Sentiment towards you since your first Appointment as one of Our Commrs. at Paris. I must hope, however hurksome the Task, You will once more be induced to quit the *Rank* of a Citizen to become a Servant of the Publick. We must all look back at Our first setting out; and take Spirit from those Principles which first annimated Our Souls; and which we lament that torpid, base Degeneracy, which hath seized too many, we must not suffer Ourselves to faint, or repine at Our Burthens. Mr. Dana is appointed Secretary, I rather wish for, than expect his Acceptance, Yet I will hope that every Obstacle will give way to the good of his Country. If Mr. Dana goes he will be ready there should another Minister be wanted thro' Death, Sickness or otherwise. I shall rejoice to hear of your safe Arrival at Paris; And shall esteem myself truly happy in your Correspondance; for with great Esteem I am your, sincere Friend & Servt.

                                                              Hy. Marchant

RC (MHi: Adams Papers).

Samuel Huntington to Thomas Johnson

Sir,   Philadelphia Octobr. 3d. 1779.

You will herewith receive enclosed an Act of Congress of the 2d Instant recommending to the Governor & Council of Maryland, to permit as much bread, flour and wheat, to be exported for the State of Virginia, as the said State may want for its public supply.[1]

I have the honor to be, with sentiments of esteem, Your Excellency's Humble servt,   Saml. Huntington President[2]

RC (MdAA: Red Books). In the hand of George Bond and signed by Huntington.
[1] Congress adopted this resolve in response to a recent request from Virginia to the Maryland Council, which had been forwarded to Congress through the Maryland delegates. See *JCC*, 15:1137. Although the correspondence between Viginia and Maryland on this subject has not been found, a Maryland Council letter of October 8 directing Col. Samuel Smith to comply with this resolve is in *Md. Archives*, 21:552. See also Maryland Delegates to Thomas Johnson, October 4, 1779.
[2] Huntington sent a nearly identical letter this day to Virginia governor Thomas Jefferson. See PCC, item 14, fol. 200; and Jefferson, *Papers* (Boyd), 2:100.

Samuel Huntington to Meshech Weare

Sir,   Philadelphia Octobr. 3d. 1779.
You will herewith receive enclosed an Act of Congress of the 2d Instant, repealing a Clause of an Act of Congress passed the 24th of September last, relative to a district of Country called New hampshire grants: and adopting another resolve as more adequate to the purposes intended in the former.[1]
I am, Sir, with sentiments of esteem, Your humble servant,
Saml. Huntington. President

RC (MHi: Weare Papers). In the hand of George Bond and signed by Huntington.
[1] For Congress' "Act" of September 24, which was slightly amended by the October 2 resolve herewith transmitted to New Hampshire, see John Jay's letters to Thomas Chittenden and to George Clinton of September 25, 1779.
By its previous action, Congress had solicited authorization from New Hampshire, Massachusetts, and New York to proceed in determining the "New Hampshire Grants" dispute, "in the mode prescribed for such cases by the articles of confederation." But as the pertinent ninth article of the confederation had been devised to deal simply with interstate disputes, Elbridge Gerry believed that it did not cover "disputes between any State and the grantees of any other State," and he therefore moved this amendment to close what he considered to be a loophole in the resolve of the 24th. *JCC*, 15:1135–36.
President Huntington also sent this October 2 amendment this day to Massachusetts, New York, and Vermont in letters addressed to Jeremiah Powell, George Clinton, and Thomas Chittenden. PCC, item 14, fols. 200–201. For additional information, see also Massachusetts Delegates to the Massachusetts Council, October 4; and John Jay to George Clinton, October 5, 1779.

John Fell's Diary

Monday 4th [October 1779].
Commercial Committee. Congress. This day spent in Reading dispatches, Memorials, Treasury Reports & c.
NB a great tumult in the City and some Lives Lost, several Wounded and several sent to Goal.[1]

MS (DLC).
[1] Philadelphia had experienced several recent outbreaks of violence as extralegal committees established by the city's radical leaders increasingly defied civil authority. This day, in response to a handbill calling upon the militia to "drive off from the city all disaffected persons and those who supported them," a mixed group of militiamen and townspeople attacked the fortified house of lawyer James Wilson, who had recently defended merchants against charges brought by the price-control committee. Several exchanges of musket and pistol fire between the crowd and Wilson's supporters barricaded inside left nearly two dozen killed and wounded. The confrontation ended only with the timely arrival of Pres. Joseph Reed at the head of the city's Light Horse and Baylor's Continental Dragoons. For delegates' comments, see Fell to Robert Morris, and James Lovell to William Whipple, October 5; Jesse Root to Jeremiah Wadsworth, October 6; and William Paca to William Hemsley, October 7, 1779. For analyses of the incident within the context of Philadelphia politics see John K. Alexander, "The Fort Wilson Incident of 1779: A Case Study of the Revolutionary Crowd," *William and Mary Quarterly*, 3d ser., 31 (October 1974): 589–612; and Steven J. Rosswurm, "Arms, Culture, and Class: the Philadelphia Militia and 'Lower Orders' in the American Revolution, 1765 to 1783" (Ph.D. diss., Northern Illinois University, 1979), pp. 430–65.

Samuel Holten's Diary

[October 4–5, 1779]

4. Monday. There has been a mob in this City To-day, & I am informed that several are killed & a number is wounded; & I fear it will not stop here.[1]

5. Tuesday. I wrote to Mr. Avery & Mrs. Holten (No. 78).[2] A rainy day.

MS (MDaAr).
[1] See the preceding entry, note.
[2] Neither letter has been found.

William Churchill Houston to Robert Morris

Dear Sir   Philada 4 Octr. 1779.

Since writing the enclosed[1] Mr. Fell has favoured me with the Sight of a Letter from you, in which you mention that if you consent to be proposed a Candidate at the ensuing Election, it will be for the Assembly rather than the Council. I have advised Mr. Fell to give his warmest Approbation of this Intention for two reasons. One, that there has not been a single Gentleman of the Law in the Assembly, which has been a great Defect, and Business has not been so well and so expeditiously done on that Account; and the other is that I have heard some Gentlemen preposterously [say] that they would not be Members of Assembly after having been Members of Council, because it would be a Degradation. Could wish this absurd Sentiment nipped in the Bud [for] if it should grow into an established Usage the

Inconveniencies to the Publick are obvious. One House certainly is as honourable and useful as the other.

I have also advised Mr. Fell to suffer himself to be put up for Council, which I should not do if it were a Bar to his being elected to Congress. He can have his Election to continue in Council or be a Delegate, and all the Inconvenience will be putting the County to the Trouble of a new Choice which will not be much. The Sufferings and Sacrifices of Mr. Fell entitle him to every Respect from his County and from his Country, not to mention his Merit in other respects.

Be sure to press Mr. Wilson to return to the Assembly. He is a worthy and capable Man, and fully justifies the Character you gave of him to me the first Time I saw [him]. I well recollect it.

Yours with regard,   William Ch. Houston

RC (NjR: Robert Morris Papers).
[1] Possibly Houston's October 2 letter to Morris.

Henry Laurens to John Adams

My Dear Sir.   Philadelphia 4th October 1779.
The receipt & perusal of your favour of 10th Ulto. afforded me a very high satisfaction—the answer with which you honored my Letter of May 1778[1] has not yet reached me. From the earliest intelligence of your return to America I felt a strong disposition to wait on you with a line or two of sincere congratulation on your happy return to your family & American friends, but there were certain irresistible pullbacks to the intended operation. I am not addicted to commonplace Ceremony & I perceived it extremely difficult to compose a palatable address, of blended gratulation & condolence to an exauctorated[2] fellow-Citizen who had deserved well of his Country & who at the same time stood in the most awkward situation that an honest susceptible mind can be reduced to—Sent, without his own desire & probably inconsistently with his Interest & inclination, on an ambassy beyond the Atlantic—kept unemployed— & in the course of a few Months virtually dismissed without censure or applause & without the least intimation when, or in what manner he was to return & report his proceedings. From these & other considerations I found myself constrained to wait future events. These, tho' a little clumsily brought forth, have happened as I wished, & now My Dear Sir, I not only congratulate you on a safe return but I have another opportunity of rejoicing with my Country Men on the judicious choice which Congress have made in their late election of a Minister Plenipotentiary to treat—in *due time* be it understood—with his Britanic Majesty on Peace & Commerce. The determination of Congress in this instance, will be grateful to the People of these

States & may expiate the queernesses of some of the queerest fellows that ever were invested with rays of sovereignty. Let me intreat you Sir, for my Country's sake, to accept the appointment without hesitation or retrospection, you know "whereof we are made." Wisdom & Patriotism forbid exceptions on account of past circumstances. I speak in pure truth & sincerity & will not risque offence by uttering a word respecting your fitness or peculiar or exclusive fitness for the important Office, but I will venture to add, it is necessary you should accept & stand ready to execute it, your determination to do so, will make the true friends of American Independence happy, & will abate their apprehensions from incompetency or negligence in other quarters—not that I believe you will be directly the object of negotiation, the Pride of our haughty Enemy will lead him to manœvre by mediation & my Ideas teach me to suppose, you are for some time to remain behind the Curtain but the moment cannot be far distant, according to present appearances, when you will step on the Stage & act a part, productive of substantial good to your Country, of honorable fame to yourself & to your posterity. My prayers & good wishes for your success will be accompanied by the utmost exertions of my feeble powers to insure it.

I pay no regard to the slanders of stock jobbers, Monopolizers nor any of the various tribes & Classes of the Enemies of our Peace, it gives me some satisfaction however to know that better Men think well of me, but I draw an infinitely more solid consolation from this knowledge, that I have uniformly striven to persevere faithfully & disinterestedly in the service of my Country; this well founded assurance will in every event, however untoward, calm the mind & secure that Peace which neither the great nor the little World can give, or rob me of. I have, now, no hope of embracing you corporeally, on this or the other Continent to which you are going, but as a good Citizen & fellow labourer in the common Cause, my Heart will embrace you at whatever distance we may be from each other, be this as it shall happen, should we be permitted to come within reach, I tell you plainly & I know you will not be displeased, I shall prefer shaking hands in the old American stile.

Should I be detained in Congress the ensuing Winter I mean to ask leave in the Spring to visit Massachusetts & New Hampshire as one of the last of my terrestrial peregrinations; that journey finished I hope the *time* will give me leave to withdraw & learn to die, a science I most devoutly wish to enter upon with a sedulousness which the present day prohibits.

Commodore G's[3] ill success in France may possibly abate a little of his fervor for accomplishing every thing by the force of his own powers, his expences being fruitless will make no inconsiderable deduction from our Carolina finances & I am sorry to hear that when he returns to Charles Town he will be asked unpleasant questions respecting his general conduct & Don Juan de Miralles complains heavily of one of his transactions at Havanna, these are things of no immediate concern to you, nor would it be instructive to say, 'tis difficult to judge of Men from appearances.

I wish I had time to speak of the awful state of our national debt & Credit, the field is too wide for the Compass of a Letter, but believe me Sir, while we are decorating our fabric we are censurably careless of the foundation. Censure if ever it comes, will not light wholly on those whom the pious Duffield[4] calls "the great Council of these States" each State at too late a day will find cause to apply blame to itself. We are at this moment on the brink of a precipice & what I have long dreaded & often intimated to my friends, seems to be breaking forth a convulsion among the People. Yesterday produced a bloody scene in the streets of this City, the particulars you will probably learn from other friends—and from circumstances which have come to my knowledge this Morning there are grounds for apprehending much more confusion. The Enemy has been industriously sapping our fort & we gazing & frolicing—peradventure we, meaning every State, may improve the present alarm to good purpose. But what shall we do by & by & not far distant, for quieting an hungry & naked Army. Shall we call forth a grand Convention in Aid of the great Council?[5] This may become absolutely necessary.

I will presume on your kindness & friendship to trouble you by the next Post with a Packet for my friends in Europe & no further in the meantime but to subscribe with great truth, Dear sir, Your faithful, obliged & affectionate friend & servant,   Henry Laurens

RC (MHi: Adams Papers).
[1] Adams' July 27, 1778, response to Laurens' May 19 letter is in Adams, *Papers* (Taylor), 6:322–23.
[2] From the obsolete verb meaning to dismiss from service or divest of authority. *OED.*
[3] Alexander Gillon's expedition to Europe in behalf of South Carolina, which had previously aroused French apprehension that individual state initiatives abroad might undermine efforts of Congress to speak with a united voice in Europe, see these *Letters,* 11:38n.1
[4] George Duffield, chaplain to Congress.
[5] For Laurens' previous references to such a convention of the states, see Laurens to William Livingston, July 5, 1779, note.

Maryland Delegates to Thomas Johnson

Sir,   Phila. Octr. 4th. 1779.
Your Excellencys Letter of the 28th Ulto. together with the applications from the Executive Council & Board of War of Virga. we laid before Congress, and in consequence thereof, you have an Act recommending the permitting of as much Bread, flour & wheat to be exported for the State of Virginia as may be wanted for its Public supply.[1]

The State of Maryland it is said suppl'd the Baltimore Packet Capt. Reed with 10, 3 or 4 Pounders. On her return to Philadelphia, they were left in the care of the Navy board, and have been delivered to Messr. Morris & Nesbit, who say that they purchased them. The Navy board want these Guns, & would give a great price for them. Be pleased to inform us whether the Guns belong to our State, or to M & N.[2] If to the Former is it your opinion that we may let the Navy board have them at the present prices of Canon.

We are with the greatest respect & Esteem, your Excellencys Obed Servts.   Wm. Paca

James Forbes

Daniel of St Thos Jenifer

P.S. Perhaps you may meet with an oppertunity of Transmitting the Enclosed Act of Congress to your Brother.[3]

RC (MdAA: Red Books). Written by Jenifer and signed by Jenifer, Forbes, and Paca.
[1] See Samuel Huntington to Johnson, October 2, 1779.
[2] For a previous inquiry concerning the ownership of these cannon, see the Marine Committee to Johnson, August 31, 1779. For the Maryland Council's October 8 response informing the delegates that the state had "no Claim" to the cannon, which in fact "belonged to the Congress," see *Md. Archives*, 21:552–53.
[3] Undoubtedly Congress' September 29 resolve electing Joshua Johnson "to examine the accounts of the several commissioners, commercial agents and others in Europe, entrusted with the public money of the United States." *JCC*, 15:1114–15, 1126.

Massachusetts Delegates
to the Massachusetts Council

Sir,   Philadelphia Octr 4th. 1779

The Resolutions of Congress of the 24th of Sepr. last, & of the 2d Instant,[1] respecting the New Hamshire Grants, are so important in their Nature, that We think it our Duty to request You to communicate to the General Assembly, what occurs to Us on the Subject.

It is generally known, that soon after the Declaration of Independence, Part of the People of the Grants, conceiving they had a Right to be a seperate State, refused to submit to the Jurisdiction of any of the united States, & in Consequence thereof, formed a Constitution & appointed a Government for themselves; & that this produced Controversy between them & the State of New Hamshire, & renewed their Disputes with the State of New York.

Frequent Applications from the contending Parties have been made to Congress, & every Measure has been taken on their Part to heat the Divisions, untill the Causes thereof could be adjusted by the Articles of Confederation; but failing on this, & finding that the

State of New York, & the people of the Grants were on the Eve of Hostilities, Congress have unanimously adopted the Resolutions referred to—should the States mentioned in the Resolves conform to the Recommendations thereof, We have every Reason to expect a speedy & equitable Settlement of their Disputes, as well with each other, as with the People of the Grants; Whilst the Claim of these to a seperate independent Jurisdiction, & the contested Titles of their Lands, will be fairly heard & determined. But, from our Knowledge of the Circumstances of the Controversy, We deprecate the Continuance of it as the inevitable Cause of an intestine War; & view this as an Event, the most desirable to our Enemies, discouraging to our Allies, & dangerous to our Liberties.

The Assemblies of New Hamshire & N York having preferred to Congress, their Claims to the Jurisdiction of the Territory in Dispute, & the State of Massachusetts Bay having been silent on the Subject, We thot it our Duty to name it as a Claimant, to be included in the Resolutions mentioned;[2] & are clearly of Opinion, that their Claim will be weakened by a Neglect to appoint their Agents, & support it on this Occasion.

The Delegates of New Hamshire, & N York, to prevent Delays, which may arise from the different Modes in which the States may comply with the Recommendations of Congress, have agreed to transmit to their respective States the Form of a Bill, a Copy of which at their Request, We inclose to the honorable Assembly,[3] remaining sir, with the highest Sentiments of Respect for them & yourself.

Your most obedt. & very humble Sert,

E. Gerry	James Lovell
S. Holten	Geo. Partridge

RC (MH–H: bMS Am 1582). Written by Gerry and signed by Gerry, Holten, Lovell, and Partridge. Addressed: "Hona. Jeremiah Powell Esqr. President of the Council of Massachusetts Bay."

[1] See Samuel Huntington to Meshech Weare, October 3, 1779.

[2] That is, those of September 24 and October 2 discussed above, the second of which was in fact introduced by Gerry. Ibid., note.

Despite similar occasional proddings from her delegates, Massachusetts never formally presented claims of the Vermont territory to Congress. Winn L. Taplin, Jr., "The Vermont Problem in the Continental Congress and in Interstate Relations, 1776–1787" (Ph.D. diss., University of Michigan, 1955), p. 142.

[3] For John Jay's explanation of the origins of this proposed "Bill," see Jay to George Clinton, October 5, 1779. See also Woodbury Langdon to Meshech Weare, October 12; and Nathaniel Peabody to Weare, October 26, 1779.

Nathaniel Scudder to Henry Laurens

Dear Sir,   Monmouth[1] Octobr. 4th. 1779.

I received your kind Letter of the 28th ultimo[2] with the Inclosures, for which I sincerely thank you.

Sunday 26th Septr. seems to me to have been with Congress a Day of strange *Devotion*. If none of the political or commercial Advantages of this Country shall prove to have been *devoted* by that Day's work, I, for my own Part, shall be extremly happy.

What must now become of the mighty Matters of Newyork versus Vermont? for the advantageous Management of which there was a special Delegation of one of their first officers,[3] who boldly declared, that unless certain Process immediatley took Place &c. &c. he would immediately quit his Seat & return to his State &c. &c. Can that gentleman under such special Trust, without the Leave of his State, the Business being unfinished, consent to accept a foreign Mission, and sail with Mr. Gerard? Let me answer yes undoubtedly, if he can aggrandize himself, & serve a P——ty.

I think I clearly perceive from the Paper you were pleased to furnish me with, that there was high Manouvring on that Day in the Prosecution of the Business, and I suppose the Success of the Resolution for appointing a Minister plenipotentiary to Spain must operate as a Supersedeas to Doctor Lee. I hope his Friends have taken Care to place the late Communications from the Honorable R. H. Lee Esqr. on such Ground as may prove advantageous to him, and secure the Honor of his Res—gn—n. I conclude Mr. D——ne[4] must be highly gratified with the Appointment of the Minister to Spain, and if Mr. C——l[5] can be added as his Secretary, he may cry, *all hollow*, more especially if the said Minister should be pitched upon to examine and attest his Accounts in France, which I suspect will be attempted. Can't Mr. Adams with great Propriety be sent on soon, and, in the Interval, which must even before he can enter upon the Business of his Mission, attend to that important Business of Accounts in France? I wish he might. Do you imagine the Instructions for a commercial Treaty with B——n[6] as they now stand will be sent on? I earnestly hope not. I can never consent, that those infernal Butchers of our Brethren shall be immediately (their hands driping with our Blood) be put, in point of Commone, upon the same advantageious Footing with our noble and generous Ally & their Connections.

I shew your Communication to Doctr Witherspoon, which I judged no Infringement of the restrictive hint in your Letter.

I intended when I left Town to have returned by to morrow's Stage, but the ill State of Mrs. Scudder's Health, and the Circumstances of my Family forbid; nor can I determine precisely when I shall be down. We expect the Appearance of the Count at Sandy Hook every hour—as soon as I hear of his Arrival I shall endeavour to pay him another Visit, and perhaps if Heaven succeed him, may have the Pleasure of being in New-York before I return. Pilots are providing for him as fast as possible—two of them lodged with me last Night, and are gone down this Morning.

I heard last Evening the Enemy had evacuated Rhode Island, and ordered all the Troops to New York, if so, they mean to make a desperate Push for the Salvation of that Post—this I the rather think to be their Intention, as they have now a large Number of Men on Sandy-Hook erecting a Fort and Batteries with very heavy Cannon, to prevent if possible the French Fleet from entering the Bay. In this I think however they cannot succeed, as with the Tide and a brisk S. Wester Ships may run by and sustain little Damage.

I earnestly wish to hear what has been their Success to the Southward. I *will* presume it has been compleat.

A Line from you, as often as convenient, will be extremely gratifying. I'll chearfully repay them with Such Scrawls as the current, which I beg youll excuse, as on Account of an urgent Call from the sick, I am not able to copy it.

If it is possible to comply with your Request in purchasing the Articles you mention, I will do it, tho' I wish you had hinted nearly how far I might go in Point of Price, as every Thing is amazingly risen of late. Please to present my most respectfull Complements to all our Friends in Congress, and permit me, Dear Sir, to assure you that I am with the most sincere Esteem and Affection, Your most obedient & very humble Servant.   Nath. Scudder

RC (NNC: Scudder Manuscripts).
[1] Although Scudder did not apply for a leave of absence as he had in July, he had departed for New Jersey shortly after voting on September 17 and did not return to Congress until October 21. See *JCC*, 14:815, 15:1074, 1193; and John Fell's Diary, October 21, 1779.
[2] Not found.
[3] That is, John Jay.
[4] Silas Deane.
[5] William Carmichael.
[6] Britain.

John Fell's Diary

Tuesday 5th [October 1779].
Coml Committee. Congress. A very long Letter from Genl. Sulevan was Read giving and Account of his Expidition in to the Indian Country, destroying 40 Towns &c &c. On the Report from the Committee to ascertain the Sallery Per Annum of the Minister Plenoptentiary and the Secretary.

Motion first for	£3000 Sterlg.	Ayes	3	Noes	3	Divided	4
do	for £2500 do	do	5	do	3	do	3
do for Secretary	1000 do	do	5	do	3	do	3[1]

P.M. Marine Committee.

MS (DLC).
[1] Although Secretary Thomson's entry in the secret journal indicates that the balloting on salaries took place on October 4, Fell's testimony that this balloting took place the following day is corroborated by Henry Laurens. See *JCC*, 15:1143–45; PCC, item

5, 1:344–50; and Laurens to Samuel Adams, this date. Thomson's secret journal was often posted after the event.

John Fell to Robert Morris

Dear sir,   Phila Octr 5t. 1779
I had the honour of writing you last Week supposing you to be at Trenton. Mr Huston inclosed my Letter to the speaker Mr Camp.[1] Yesterday I was favour'd from Pompton with your very oblidging Letter of the 30th ulto. The good opin[ion] which you and other Gentlemen of the County, entertain of my conduct to induce you to Put me in nomination as a Candidate for the Council is a matter which requires my most gratefull thanks, but if I had ever so great an inclination to accept your kind offer, I dare not live at home, therefore if I must continue to be deprived of all Domestick Happyness, the being here on Account of safety, is the most Eligeable. I shall think myself happy to be left out in the next choice of Members for Congress, lett my Collegues be whom they may. The one Principle reason & Objection that I have is being depriv'd of Mrs Fells Company (A circumstance which you cannot be a Proper Judge of). I am exceeding glad of your good intention of going in to the Assembly, give me leave to say without flattery You will be a valuable acquisition in that House, but I do not see how the confinement is less.

Now we have chiefly and to my great satisfaction got through Our foreign affairs; and I hope the Name of Lee will be no more mentiond, that we shall do business [in a] better humour. On Saturday we began with a Committee of the whole house to consider on Finance and ways and means to carry on the War, and in a few days I hope the Public will be made acquainted with what we expect from them so that we shall at least do Our Duty. Yesterday a great Mobb of Militia with their Arms Paraded the Streets under a Pretence of taking up and sending off Tories, they chiefly thretend Mr Wilson, the Lawyer. A number of Gentlemen got in the House with him to defend him, when those in the Street began to grow very Restive and at last fired in the House when the Batle became general. Some I beleave were Killd on Both sides and many wounded. When fortunatly the President (Reed) came up at the head of the Light Horse and his Spirited behaviour Put an end to the affair and a number of them, were sent to Prison. I have just now been told, that this morning has Produc'd fresh trouble, that the Rioters had swore vengence against a Major Lenox who was very Active Yesterday, and that the President had orderd the Light Horse out againe on the Occasion. I am very Respectfully, Your Most H Serv.   John Fell

RC (NjR: Robert Morris Papers).
[1] Not found.

James Forbes to Thomas Sim Lee

Dear Sir,   Philadelphia Octobr 5th 1779
I have the pleasure of yours of the 30th Ulto. Inclosed you have
the papers & a Second Essay on Trade & Finance: it is wrote by a Mr.
Webster of this Town and I think contains many observations worthy the particular attention of the several Legislatures.[1] No accounts
from the southward since my last, every day expected and to hear of
the French Fleet being off NYork—a very large Embarcation was
taking place there said to be for the Southward Commanded by
Lord Cornwalles but now expected to be stopt. The bad effects of
the Committees in this Town has been experienced yesterday by a
very daring & violent Insurrection & Mob, in which several Persons
were Killed & wounded before they were quelled, many are made
Prisoners, this morning they are collecting at Germantown and there
is no judging how this unhappy affair may end. The amazing rise of
every article in this place is truly allarming, Flour at £60 Per Ct, Rum
£20 Per Gall. Adieu & be asshured that I ever am, My Dear Sir,
Yours Sincerely,   James Forbes

RC (MdHi: Lee, Horsey, and Carroll Papers deposit, 1985).
[1] Pelatiah Webster's *Second Essay on Free Trade and Finance* (Philadelphia: Thomas
Bradford, 1779). See Evans, *Am. Bibliography*, no. 16,671.

William Churchill Houston to Caleb Camp

Sir,[1]   Philada. 5 October 1779.
I am sorry that it has not been in my Power to command as much
Time as I should have wished to employ, in giving a distinct Account
to the Legislature of the most material Occurrences in the Progress
of Business since I came to Congress. It is certainly the Duty of every
Person in publick Trust to make those from whom he derives his
Appointment acquainted with the Manner in which he executes it,
that they may be enabled to decide how far he fulfils or deceives
their Expectations, and to form, at any Time, a clear Estimate of his
Character. Next to Want of Fidelity, I look upon the Neglect of
giving due Information to his Constituents, the greatest Crime in a
publick Man.
The principal Intention of this is to point at a Question which
from accidental Circumstances has acquired a Magnitude and Importance above what, simply considered, it was entitled to. A Question
which has excited much Inveteracy and Ill-blood in Congress, and
not a few Speculations and Suspicions abroad. I mean the Recal, or
rather Supersession, of Mr. Arthur Lee, Commissioner of the United
States at the Court of Madrid. I have carefully read over the Papers,
and attended to every feasible Means of unbiassed Information rela-

tive to this Question, and I think have done it with a Temper divested
of Prejudice. The Result is this: I take Mr. Arthur Lee to be a man of
a jealous, suspecting, difficult Disposition; trusty, capable and
industrious. Indefatigable above others in procuring and transmitting Intelligence, accurate and frugal in Expenses and Mony-matters,
simple, severe and republican in his manners; so much so as to be
thought by many sour and cynical. This I take to be his Character;
and in many Essentials I am not afraid to call him equal to any
Person Congress ever employed in a similar Capacity in Europe.
The Story hawked about, that his Indiscretions prevented the Court
of Spain from treating with him, I cannot think believed by those
who propagate it, as that Conduct in the Spanish Ministry is ascrib-
able to very different Reasons which must strike every Person at
once who has the least Knowledge of the State of matters as they
respected that Power. But admitting he were the best-qualified and
most meritorious Man on Earth, is it not my Duty to vote for removing him when the Time of Congress is absolutely wasted, and the
publick Business not only retarded but stopped by unavailing Altercations concerning an Individual? When a General offers up a *forlorn
Hope* to save an *Army*, the Alternative is dreadful; but the Principle is
defensible and the Practice of it often necessary. I confess that in a
republick, where Approbation, Honour and Praise, more than Money
and Emoluments, are the Reward of faithful Services, such Things
ought to be admitted with Reluctance and Caution; yet still they may
not be always avoidable. But further, should it turn out to be a Fact
that France was doubtful of him, and that Spain hesitated, it mat-
tered not how good a Man he was, one every way inferiour, if free
from such Exception, would have been preferable for the Purpose
of treating. The *real* Causes of Delay being now removed, it is to be
hoped the gentleman who succeeds Mr. Lee will be successful. As I
would ever wish to be simply just, but at the same Time to do what is
best, all Things considered, I have no other Request than that this
State of Facts may be remembered another Day, when Time will
throw Light upon what is now dark, Prejudice will be extinct and the
Means of judging fairly will come within the Reach of all. Into what
Course of Conduct, or to what Length of Crimination, Resentment
may impel this unfortunate Man, I am excused from surmising.
Whether, as many have done, he will adhere to the Part he has taken
in Spite of what he may think ill Treatment; or whether, as many
have also done, he will transfer himself to a Situation where he will
expect more Attention; does not belong immediately to the present
Decision; at least, I have taken the Liberty to throw it out of the
Balance. At all Events I am happy this troublesome Affair is ended,
and I hope it will never rise up to disturb the Counsels of America
more. Subjects of Contention and Animosity are retiring one after
another, and Unanimity reviving in Congress where it is so essentially necessary. Trifles have had their Day, and too long a one has it

been; Matters of Moment have now a Claim to their, and that it may not only be longer, but perpetual, I am persuaded is the ardent wish of every honest Man.

Upon reviewing what I have written, a Suspicion occurs that the above Representation may imply a Reflection on the Conduct of some of my Colleagus, which is as far from my Meaning as it would be repugnant to Justice. The Time is not the same, other Circumstances also disagree. On the contrary I must declare that I think their Situaton hard and undeserved. The whole Train of the Transaction I can trace minutely. To the Quarter from whence the Accusations have originated, the Motives which inspired them and the Instruments which have been employed for their Circulation I am not a Stranger, nor am I surprised at any Thing thus far. But that their Fellow-citizens should entertain Impressions unfavourable to those they once thought well of, and not call for an Investigation of their Conduct, or suspend their Opinions till an Explanation should be had, may perhaps be a Matter of some Discouragement. If the Gentlemen know what is alledged to their Charge, I am astonished they do not apply for an Opportunity of Justification. Certainly if I should ever be of Importance enough to be found fault with, I should expect the Liberty of explaining Facts and Motives; after that it is the Part of an honest Man to submit in Silence to the Judgment of those who have a Right to pass upon his Conduct.

I enclose sundry Papers marked from Number 1 to 5[2] which I have met with since I came to this Place, and which I have copied for the Sight of such Gentlemen of the Legislature as may think it worth their Trouble to read them. They relate to a Matter which was before the Legislature at their last Sitting previous to the present. One, if not more of them, is on the Files of the Assembly. They may be of Use on some future Occasion, but my principal Object in copying them is to communicate the noble and dignified Sentiments of the Commander in Chief, and to give some Idea of the Difficulties he has to encounter. If ever any Man deserved Gratitude and Confidence he does, and the more especially as his modesty will never allow him to be elated with the former, nor his goodness of Heart to abuse the latter. His Letter marked No. 2 is an Example of it's Kind.

It is necessary that I give you the Trouble of communicating to the Houses the *Substance* of this lengthened Letter. I have no Idea they will have Patience to go over the whole.

I am, with due Respect, your obedt hble Servt,

William Ch Houston

RC (Nj: State Papers).
[1] The recipient of Houston's first "Account to the legislature" was identified by Edmund Burnett as Gov. William Livingston. Burnett, *Letters*, 4:472. The account, however, was probably addressed to Caleb Camp (1736-1816), of Essex Co., N.J., who

served as a delegate to the New Jersey General Assembly, 1776-82, and was speaker of the House, 1778-80. Livingston, *Papers* (Prince), 1:385. Houston, who had recently served with Camp in the assembly, was apparently writing to him in his official capacity, giving him "the Trouble of communicating to the Houses the *Substance* of this lengthened Letter." Houston also directed his reports of November 12 and 22 to Camp, although he addressed his letter of December 20 to both Camp and Livingston. Thereafter, when Camp was no longer speaker, Houston sent most official letters directly to the governor.

[2] Not identified.

Samuel Huntington to George Washington

Sir   Philadelphia Octor 5th. 1779

I am favourd with the receipt of your Excellencies favours of the 29th & 30th ultimo.[1] In consequence of the latter Congress have directed the North-Carolina Troops to halt at Trenton until further Orders.

You will receive enclosd, the Act of Congress of the 4th Instant and Copy of the Orders to Col. Clarke on that Subject.[2]

I have the honour to be with the highest Sentiments of Esteem & regard your Exys. humble Servant,

Saml. Huntington President

RC (DLC: Washington Papers).

[1] Washington's letters of September 29 and 30 are in PCC, item 152, 8:49–51, 57–60; and Washington, *Writings* (Fitzpatrick), 16:361n.98, 363–64.

[2] In response to a congressional resolve of September 23, Washington had ordered two North Carolina regiments under Col. Thomas Clark to begin a march to South Carolina, but as he learned almost simultaneously that the comte d'Estaing had just been reported off the Carolina coast, he suggested that Congress halt the march of the North Carolinians at Trenton until further intelligence from the southern department was available. Thus on October 4 Congress ordered the North Carolina regiments to remain at Trenton "till farther orders," and when Washington subsequently reported that he had "taken the liberty to countermand the march" of Colonel Clark, Huntington replied at once that Congress approved his decision. See *JCC*, 15:1138; John Jay to Washington, September 23; and Huntington to Washington, October 8, 1779.

Notwithstanding his hopes for an autumn offensive and reluctance to disperse his main army, Washington was disappointed in his expectation that French forces under d'Estaing would arrive in northern waters before the end of the campaigning season, and in November Congress reaffirmed its original decision to send the two North Carolina regiments to the southern department, as ordered on September 23. See Huntington to Washington, November 11, 1779; and Freeman, *Washington*, 5:136–40.

Copies of Huntington's brief October 5 letter to Colonel Clark enclosing the October 4 resolve halting his march at Trenton "until further Orders" are in the Washington Papers, DLC; and PCC, item 14, fol. 203.

John Jay to George Clinton

Dr Sr.   Pha. 5 Octr 1779

In a Conference with some of the Delegates of New Hampshire and Massachusets Bay it was agreed that I shd. draw the Draft of a Bill for carrying into Effect the Resolutions of Congress relative to our Disputes with Vermont & with each other.[1]

The enclosed Draft has been perused and approved of by them, and they have promised to transmit Copy of it to their respective States and to press their immediate Attention to the Subject.[2]

It appeared to me expedient that the Acts to be passed for this Purpose by the three States shd be nearly similar, lest variances which might be deemed important, should create Delay & Dispute. I also thought it most adviseable to be content with the Description of the Powers contained in the Resolutions, & not by New ones hazard Alterations or Deviations that might open other Fields for Discussion. For this Reason the Act in Question is made very general, granting in express Terms the Powers asked for by Congress & referring to the Resolutions for a Description of them.

With very sincere Regard & Esteem, I am Dr Sr, your most obt Servt,   J J

FC (NNC: Jay Papers). In the hand of John Jay.

[1] Jay's draft bill "relative to our Disputes with Vermont," which is in the Jay Papers, NNC, is reprinted here from Jay, *Papers* (Morris), 1:653–54.

"An Act for complying with and carrying into Effect the Recommendations contained in certain Resolutions of the Congress of the united States of America of the   Day of   1779

"Whereas the Congress of the united States of America did on the   Day of   last past, *unanimously* enter into certain Resolutions in the Words following vizt (Here insert Resolutions Verbatim) and whereas the 1st Congress did on the   Day of   unanimously enter into a certain other Resolution in the Words following to wit (here insert reso[lutio]n repealing one and substituting another Clause)

"And whereas the aforesaid Resolutions and Recommendation are founded on equal Justice and true Policy, and have for their Object the Establishment of perpetual Harmony, Friendship and mutual Confidence between the States therein named, which it is no less the Desire than the Interest of this State to promote

"Be it enacted by the   and it is hereby enacted by the Authority of the same, that all the Powers and Authorities which it is recommended to or requested of this State in and by the said Resolutions to vest in or grant to the said Congress 1st shall be and hereby are vested in and granted there to as fully and amply as if the same were here again particularly enumerated and described. 2d, And further that this Act shall be always construed in a Sense most advancive of the Design, true Intent and Meaning of the said Resolutions. And that the Decisions and Determinations which shall be made in the premisses in pursuance of the Powers and Authorities hereby granted shall be obligatory on this State and the People thereof so far as the said Decisions and Determinations or any other of them so far as they shall respect the same or any Part thereof.

"And it is hereby further enacted by the Authority af[oresai]d That no Advantage shall be taken by this State of the non performance of the Conditions in any of the Grants of Land in the said Resolutions referred to, but that further Time be given to

fulfil the same respectively to wit until the Expiration of six Years to be computed
from the Publication of this Act."
    [2] See Massachusetts Delegates to the Massachusetts Council, October 4; and Wood-
bury Langdon to Meshech Weare, October 12, 1779.

Daniel of St. Thomas Jenifer to Thomas Johnson

Dear Sir,   Philadelphia Oct. 5th. 1779
    The Enclosed Letters were delivered to me by Mr. Fox[1] lately
from New York. He was taken coming from the West Indies.
    I have understood that Billy Steward[2] always stood up for the
Rights of America, and therefore I wish that your Excellency &
Council would recommend him to Congress, that he may get to his
Friends.
    I am, Dr Sir, Your Obedt Servt   Daniel of S Thos Jenifer

RC (MdAA: Red Books).
    [1] Edward Fox. See also Maryland Delegates to Johnson, September 25, 1779.
    [2] Not identified.

Henry Laurens to Samuel Adams

                                                            State House,
My Dear & respected friend,   Tuesday 5th October 1779
    I have been honored with your favors by the hands of Monsr. le
Chevalier la Luzerne & Monsr. son Secretaire[1] & thank you for the
several introductions—but I want much, a reply to one part of my
Letter of the   respecting the amount paid by order of His
Most Christian majesty to the Owners of the Hancock & Boston.[2]
The arrival of our worthy friend of Bra[i]ntree will enable you to be
accurate & I think it a matter of consequence.
    We are at this instant on the subject of Salary to our Ministers
Plenipotentiaries, shall £3000 Per Annum stand or £2000 be inserted—for the Secretaries £1000 or £700. But I must attend to
business, you will be better informed from the corner House[3] of
every thing worth your notice than you could be by me, therefore I
shall at present only repeat that I continue with great affection &
respect, Dear sir, Your obliged & obedient servant,
                                                        Henry Laurens

RC (NN: Adams Papers).
    [1] François, marquis de Barbé-Marbois, secretary to the French legation in the United
States. Abraham P. Nasatir and Gary Elwyn Monell, *French Counsuls in the United
States: A Calendar of their Correspondence in the Archives Nationales* (Washington: Library
of Congress, 1967), pp. 565–66.
    [2] This letter to Adams has not been found, but the following undated fragment of a
letter from Laurens in Adams' papers pertains to this issue.

"Don't forget the Account of 400,000 or 450,000 Livres paid for the prizes of the Boston & Hancock on what terms & what was the real & true Exchange on Europe at the time when paid.

"I say nothing of the transmissions received from our friend A. Lee, because you have Letters directly from himself & because I know Mr. Lovel has written copiously on the subject." Adams Papers, NN.

For the payment of 400,000 livres by Jean Holker in October 1778 on behalf of France to the owners of the Massachusetts privateers *Boston* and *Hancock*, see these *Letters*, 10:192n.1, 195n.2.

[3] That is, by Adams' fellow Massachusetts delegates.

James Lovell to John Adams

Dear Sir   [October 5? 1779][1]

I inclose to you the *decent* Fashion in which it was yesterday opinioned to let the World know Mr. Lee has a Successor. Pray strive by Mr. Isaac Smith's Knowledge of the Sailing of Vessels to let Arthur get the paper [2] before his Foes.

The 3 *Ministers* are to have per An[num] £2500 stg. Their Secretary £1000 in full of Services & Expences, to commence at Outset and finish in 3 months after a Recall being notified.[3] So that they may get home as they can But will by seperate Resolution be provided for out.

The funds are to be settled by a recommitment. I judge the Rept will get only the addition of order to the Coml. Comtee. of Produce or *Bills* to be deposited subject to the Officers Draughts. But I have hinted your being Authorized to obtain a Loan as the others are. And I think you will readily obtain more than Pocket Money from either *truly whig* Englishmen or such as are desirous of buying our good Graces in America that they may afterwards pluck us in the Way of Commerce.

Adieu, Dear Sir,   Yrs. J. L.

RC (MHi: Adams Papers).

[1] Although he failed to date this letter, Lovell probably wrote it on October 5. The enclosure that he sent to Adams was undoubtedly the October 5 issue of the *Pennsylvania Packet* (which he also sent to William Whipple this day), containing extracts of congressional resolves of September 28 and October 1 concerning John Jay's appointment as minister plenipotentiary to Spain and Congress' vote of thanks to him "in testimony of their approbation of his conduct in the chair [i.e., as president since December 1778]." The decision to make these public was made by Congress on October 4—hence Lovell's opening comment "it was yesterday opinioned to let the World know Mr. Lee has a Successor." See *JCC*, 15:1114, 1134, 1139; and the following entry.

[2] That is, the enclosed *Pennsylvania Packet* of October 5.

[3] Congress adopted these resolves on October 4. *JCC*, 15:1143–45.

James Lovell to William Whipple

Dear Sir,   Oct. 5th 1779

Your favor from West Point reached me yesterday. You are mistaken as to how much *a* man can do *for* himself. The newspapers of to day will show you what a *body of men* can do *against* themselves.[1] Arthur Lee is recalled by an authenticated newspaper which will reach him accidentally, before any official information can go in the usual and decent course. So that if Jay is taken, or drowned, we shall have a total suspension of negotiations for a time. Will you not think it strange after what I see, that I should have an idea of being willing to go with Mr. J. A. in case D—— refuses?[2] As it is precarious in regard to D——'s Situation, I wish I had been chosen in the first place. I know your idea is for France, but I should have the most implacable enemies there who think they have a right of occupancy in the Secretaryship. Besides the latter is residentiary, the former temporary.[3]

Our Gazette says nothing of the killed and wounded yesterday before Wilson's door and in his house. I am told Capt Campbell of the Invalids, a one handed officer, was killed and General Mifflin's brother wounded in the house—that 4 were killed and several wounded in the street. A party of armed men had some Tory characters on parade through the Streets. Wilson is said to have expected a visit and to have forearmed himself and a collected number. Whether an attack was made from without, or whether provocations indiscretely were made from within, I cannot tell; two stories as usual, are circulated. If you are in Boston you will know all I have written to Mr J & S Adams, Mr Dana or Dr Cooper; if you are not there Peabody will give you at Portsmouth all the manoeuvres of Chesnut St. I have not yet seen the *Tall Boy*;[4] the *Tall Man*[5] good uncle Roger arrived the day after the *Sacrifice*. He is "shocked at the *Ingratitude* of that proceeding."

New Hampshire was the only State for A. L., our's was divided with R. I., Penna. and South Carolina.

I declared openly that I did not approve Mr. J's *conduct* in the Chair—some others followed me in like declarations, but I would not go to the dirty work of Yeas and Nays and urged that, if a *majority* were so disposed, he might receive a *Formality*.

And now let me conceive you at Portsmouth with all your affectations of *indifference* to what has been the object of the wishes of the *bravest Generals* in History to say nothing of the wise King Solomon and the *good* King David. Are you not, even in that State, better off than your friend here brimfull of *Sensibilities*, and in a two pair of stairs chamber *alone*? Need I add to the contrast of our situations, the circumstance of your being where molasses is under £20 per gallon.   Yours J. L.

Tr (DLC: Force Collection).

¹ Lovell's concern was Congress' public announcement of John Jay's appointment as minister plenipotentiary to Spain, which was published in the October 5 issue of the *Pennsylvania Packet*, for which see the preceding entry, note 1.

² That is, John Adams and Francis Dana.

³ Lovell's potential candidacy for the position of secretary to Adams was later suggested by Adams himself in an October 17 letter to Elbridge Gerry. For a discussion of Lovell's interest in the position, see Helen F. Jones, "James Lovell in the Continental Congress, 1777–1782" (Ph.D. diss., Columbia University, 1968), p. 343.

⁴ That is, Gouverneur Morris, who resumed his seat in Congress the next day. *JCC*, 15:1146.

⁵ Roger Sherman, who had resumed his seat in Congress on September 29, *JCC*, 15:1122.

Nathaniel Peabody to Josiah Bartlett

Dear Sir,   No. 10.   Philada. Octo. 5. 1779.
Your obliging favour of the 18th ulto.¹ this moment Came to hand. I am by no means insensible of your friendship, and kind Attention to my interest; and delicacy would forbid Trespassing upon Such a friend. My worthy friend Mr Whipple *departed* this *City* on the 25th ulto. The particular Circumstances of Thorntons Acquital, & the facts proved against him, are unknown to me, but from the opinion I had heretofore formed of that Thornton and the Circumstances attending his being imprisoned, the various reports Concerning his Conduct prior to that period. I must Confess my feelings were not a little Touched by your information upon the Subject—prudence forbids my Going farther.

I informed you in my last if I mistake not all the official accounts we have had respecting Count D. Estaing, his Strength, & Destination. This moment per *Post* we are informed, but not officially, that Count D. Estaing has taken all the Land & Sea forces of our Enemys in Georgia, have Some reason to hope it is true, but am not Sanguine. The Enemy at N York are daily Embarking in Considerable Number but where destined, remains Still with them, as we Can only Conjecture by Some Circumstances, that they Aim either at Virginia, or the West Indias, but I flatter my Self, the intended movement of the Allied fleets And Armies, will point out their Employment.

An unhapy affair happened here last evening, Said to be between whigs & Tories. Several were killd on both Sides & many wounded— the affair is not over, I fear it will be Serious, reports differ exceedingly and I cannot pretend to give particulars, till further Examination. Adieu—for this time.

I am with Sincerity yours, your friend & Humble Servt,
                                                    Nathl Peabody

RC (NhD: Bartlett Papers).
¹ Not found.

Committee of Congress to Jeremiah Wadsworth

Sir,   Philadelphia Octr 6th 1779
    Yours of the 26th ulto. to the Committee. was recd. last Monday.
The Expectation of the French Fleet on our Coast makes it necessary
to provide for them. Our encouragements for flour in this quarter
are at present unpromising, notwithstanding every exertion that has
been used. We have the promise of Eight hundred barrels of flour
from this State ready to be delivered which will be forwarded
immediatly unless prevented by the present Commotions. We have
further prospects of flour from below, & also from this State, but
how Much or how Soon is uncertain, we place Much Dependance, in
this Critical Juncture, on your abilities & unremitting exertions for
the Supplies immediatly wanted.
    Inclosed you have an Order from the Marine Commttee.[1] on our
agent at Boston for any quantity of Sugar not exceeding 100 Hogs. to
enable you to fulfill your engagements for flour—also for 200 Hogs.
of rum for the use of the army.
    The Resolutions of Congress in favour of New York we hope will
have the most Salutary effects.[2] You will know how to make the
proper use of them.
    In behalf of the Commttee. on the Commissary's Departmt. &c, I
am your obedt humble Servant,   Jesse Root Chn.

RC (CtHi: Wadsworth Papers). Written and signed by Root.
    [1] Not found.
    [2] For these resolves, designed to permit Wadsworth to send sugar and rum to New
York in enchange for flour and wheat, see Samuel Huntington to George Clinton,
and to Wadsworth, October 1, 1779; and Jesse Root to Wadsworth, this day.

John Fell's Diary

                              Wednesday October 6 1779
    Coml Committee. Congress. After the dispatches were Read a
Committee of 12 was appointed for the apportening the Quotas for
the Payment of the 15 Million.

MS (DLC).

Samuel Holten's Diary

                                      October 6–7, 1779
    6. Wednesday. General Arnold applied to Congress for a gard,[1] &
Congress informed him that his application shod have been to the
executive of this State.

Octr. 7. Thursday. A Court of inquiry met here this day, respecting the persons killed a few days ago.[2]

MS (MDaAr).
[1] For Arnold's request "for a gard," see the following entry.
[2] Holten is referring to the lives lost at the "Fort Wilson" riot.

Samuel Huntington to Benedict Arnold

Sir,   In Congress Octr 6th 1779
The enclosd act contains the answer of Congress to your letter of this day which I communicated immediately upon the receipt of it.[1]
I am &c.,   S. H. President

LB (DNA: PCC, item 14).
[1] In his October 6 letter to Congress, Arnold had explained that he had been attacked recently by "A Mob of Lawless Ruffians" in the streets of Philadelphia and requested a Continental guard for his protection, as "there is no protection to be expected from the Authority of the State for an honest Man." Arnold's gratuitous remark against Pennsylvania was of course seen as an insult to the state, and in summarily rejecting the general's request Congress added a slap to his wrists by affirming confidence in Pennsylvania officials and expressing disapproval of "the insinuations of every individual to the contrary." He was instead advised, in the resolve Huntington enclosed with his letter, that his application for protection should have been made directly "to the executive authority of the State of Pennsylvania."
In a second letter to Huntington of this date, Arnold immediately offered an apology of sorts, explaining that he had doubted only Pennsylvania's "Abilities" not "Disposition" to protect him, but he could not resist concluding with the feisty warning that should he be attacked again he would defend himself "to the last Extremity" and presumed that Congress would not then hold him "Chargible for the Consequences." See JCC, 15:1147; and PCC, item 162, fols. 185–91.
For Arnold's long feud with Pennsylvania, and the October 4 "Fort Wilson" riot which formed the immediate background to the present incident, see these Letters, 11:522–24, 12:95–96, 143, 152, 178–80, 329–30; and John Fell's Diary, October 4, 1779, note.

Marine Committee to the Eastern Navy Board

Gentlemen   October 6th 1779
This will be forwarded to you from New London by Captain James Nicholson whom we have appointed to take the Command of the Ship Trumbull, and have referred him to the Orders he may receive from your Board in whatever relates to his Ship.[1] We request that you will immediately give him the necessary Instructions on that head, and take measures to have the Trumbull speedily fitted for Sea. Your recommendation of Captain Hinman shall have due weight the first opportunity,[2] but we could not appoint him to the command of this Ship without breaking a general rule which we had

before adopted, viz of paying regard to Seniority in our appointments where merit is equal and to the Ships which our Captains have had. Captain Nicholson has had a ship and so has Captain Hinman but the former is the first Captain on the Navy List and we esteem him a Man of Merit, therefore he could not be passed by.

We are Gentlemen, Your Hble servants

LB (DNA: PCC Miscellaneous Papers, Marine Committee Letter Book).
[1] See the following entry.
[2] In a September 23, 1779, letter to the committee, the board had recommended that Capt. Elisha Hinman remain in command of the *Trumbull*. Eastern Navy Board Letterbook, NN.

Marine Committee to James Nicholson

Sir   October 6th 1779

As you have been appointed to command the Continental frigate Trumbull now at new London in the state of Connecticut, we desire you will immediately proceed to that place and there take the command of the said Frigate which you are to use your best endeavours to fit and man with all expedition. When you arrive there you are to inspect into the State of the Trumbull and give an account thereof to the Commissioners of the Navy Board at Boston who will order everything necessary for equipping her and you are occasionally to inform that Board of your proceedings and be governed by their orders in every matter which they may direct.

We are Sir, Your very Hble Servants

LB (DNA: PCC Miscellaneous Papers, Marine Committee Letter Book).

Jesse Root to Jeremiah Wadsworth

Sir   Philadelphia Octr. 6th 1779

I recd. your favour of the 25th ulto. Supplying the army with bread is & has been a very Serious business, every exertion has been made in these States to procure & forward flour to the army for Some Time past with but little Success & our dependance has been on the Contracts you entered into with the people of New York to exchange Salt, Sugar &c. for flour. You will before this reaches you receive the resolutions of Congress on that head.[1] The Comtte. early reported & urged the necessity of the reports being taken up—but our foreign affairs pressing, it was delayed more than a fortnight. Although Some Members not rightly understanding the business at first blamed the Measure—yet the Committee was able to vindicate your Conduct & I believe you will find by the resolution passed no blame is thrown upon you in this Instance. Our foreign affairs, the business of Finance—& the daily orders necessary to be passed—prevent their attending to the appointment of a Successor in your office, So early as otherways they would.[2] I believe, Sir, your early attachment to the Cause of your Country, the zeal & activity you have shown through the whole of the time—the Signal Services you have rendered in your present Office, being Called to it in the worst of times will not be forgotten by Congress nor rewarded by delivering you up to be Sacrificed. It is the wish of Congress you should Continue to Serve—but it is believed you are in earnest to resign & they Expect to part with you. Your Commissions indeed have a great Sound & may Excite the Envy of Some people, but in reality no more than in A D 1775—yet maybe Considerable Compared with what some other persons who have been engaged in the public Service have got or rather lost—yet this does not go to the Justice of the Commissions you receive. Mr Jay is appointed Minister Plenipo. to negociate a Treaty with the Court of Spain & goes with Mr. Gerard. Mr. Huntington is appointed President of Congress. Some letters from Virginia & Maryland Say, We hear that Count De Estaing has taken Savannah & Made prisoners of all the british Sea & land forces in there path—but this wants Confirmation. Genl Sullivan has sent a long letter to Congress Informing that he has Conquered all the Indians & destroyed their Country & is returning. A terrible mob here last Monday, they attacked Wilson in his house where were assembled a Number of his Friends. They fired Several vollies in to the windows, killed Capt. Campbell & wounded Several others in the house. They fired from the house, killed & wounded Several of the Mob. President Reed Came up at the head of the light horse, as they were entering the house & dispersed them, Seized Several & threw them into Jail. Yesterday the President & Council released those that were put into Jail & Mr Lewis the Lawyer & Several others who were in the house with Wilson were taken by the mob & put into Jail. I cant tell what will be done today. I inclose you a newspaper—& Am, dear Sir, with much Esteem your Most Obedt., humble Servant,

Jesse Root

RC (CtHi: Wadsworth Papers).

[1] See Samuel Huntington to Wadsworth, October 1, 1779.

[2] For Wadsworth's resignation as commissary general of purchases, which was conditional upon the appointment of his successor, see Samuel Huntington to Wadsworth, December 4, 1779.

John Fell's Diary

Thursday 7th [October 1779].

Coml Committee. Congress.
The Committee of 12 brought in a Report as follows. viz

New Hampshire	400,000
Massachusets	2,300,000
Rhode Island	200,000
Connecticut	1,700,000
New York	750,000
New Jersey	900,000
Philadelphia	2,300,000
Delaware	170,000
Maryland	1,580,000
Virginia	2,500,000
No Carolina	1,000,000
So Carolina	1,200,000
	15,000,000

NB the Delegates from New Jersey as well as some other States did all they could to lower their sums but all in vain.
P.M. Marine Committee.

MS (DLC).

John Jay to George Clinton

Dear Sir,   Phil'a, 7th Oct'r 1779.
You will receive this by Mr Phelps, of whose Fidelity to New York I have a good opinion; tho I cannot approve of all his Manoeuvres to serve the State on this occasion.[1] He appears neither to Want Talents or Zeal, but the latter is not always according to knowledge, and the former carry him sometimes into [. . .]. One of the New Hampshire Delegates told me that Phelps, in order to engage him against Vermont, endeavoured to persuade him that New Hampshire had a Right to a number of Townships in it; and he further told me, that on comparing Notes with the Massachusets Delegates, he found that Phelps had been playing the same Game with them. This Story he told me in the Presence of some of the Massachusets Delegates who smiled and were silent. I have never said any thing of this to Phelps because it could have answered no good Purpose; And I mention it to you, as a Circumstance which marks the Man. He has however by talking on the Subject with every body, done good. In my opinion his Expences should be paid without Hesitation, and he should be so treated as to go home in perfect good Humour with the Legislature, for whom he now professes great Regard & Esteem, & I believe he is

sincere in his attachment. Men of his Turn and Talk are always useful when properly directed. It is easily done by encouraging the good opinion he entertains of his own Importance.

The exceeding high opinion entertained here of your Constitution and the wisdom of your Counsels, has made a deep Impression on many People of wealth and Consequence in this State, who are dissatisfied with their own; and unless their opinions should previously be changed, will remove to New York the moment the Enemy leave it. Mr. Gerard, (who seems better acquainted with Republics than almost any man I have ever known) has passed many Encomiums on our Constitution & Government and I am persuaded, no Circumstance will conduce more to the Population of our Country by Migrations from others, than the Preservation of its Vigor and Reputation.

This unhappy City is all in Confusion—the Government wants Nerves, and the public Peace has for some Days been destroyed by Mobs and Riots which seem to defy the authority of the Magistrate. This is one of the Fruits of their whimsical Constitution, and of the Countenance given to Committees & Let Politicians learn from this, to dread the least Deviation from the Line of Constitutional Authority. *Obsta Principiis*, is a good Maxim, but all have not sufficient Decision in their Conduct to observe it. Government once relaxed is not easily braced. And it is far more difficult to reassume Powers than permit them to be taken and executed by those who have no Right by the Constitution to hold them.

Morris is again with us, and I am glad of it. His Constituents must be either infatuated or wretchedly misinformed, if they omit continuing him in the Delegation.[2] But you know my Sentiments on this Subject, and it is unnecessary to dwell on it. For Heaven's Sake, send an able Delegation and preserve the high Rank you hold among the States. I wish Hobart[3] may be sent; at this Season he would be particularly useful, and I am sure until your Vermont Business be over, a special occasion for his being here will clearly exist.

One of the New Hampshire Delegates[4] seems much inclined to make the Ridge of mountains instead of Connecticut River, the Boundary between us; and that the Soil between the Mountains and the River should remain the Property of those to whom it had been granted either under New York or New Hampshire. He observed and I think with Propriety, that this Line by dividing the disaffected between the two States, would render the Reduction of them to good order less difficult, and by interesting both States in their Allegiance prevent their again acting in a Body or easily uniting their Counsell for Purposes injurious to Government. My Reply to this Gentleman was, that I had no Authority to say any thing on this Subject, that I knew the State of New York to be sincerely disposed to cultivate Harmony with her Neighbours, and was persuaded that no Settlement founded in Justice & mutual Convenience will be disagreable to them. To you however I must confess that the Line he proposed does not appear to me to be impolitic. We have unquestionably more Territory than we can govern, and the Loss of that Strip would not in my opinion overballance the Advantages resulting from it. On the contrary, unless I am much mistaken, exclusive of other Considerations, the less our People have to with Connecticut River the better. I would rather see the Productions of our Country go to the Sea by another Rout.

The Country west of Niagara, on the present Ideas which prevail and by the articles of Confederation, belongs to New York. As it lies beyond the convenient Reach of Government, the Retention of it would rather incommode than benefit us. It would always be the object of Envy and Jealousy to the other States, and perhaps the Subject of Dispute. I would therefore be for ceding it to the Continent at a proper Season, or otherwise disposing of it in a way that would conduce to the Credit and Interest of the State. To this Way you can be no Stranger.[5]

There is another Matter which I think deserves Attention—it is the Seat of Government. On this Subject I have bestowed much thought. The Result is a perfect and full Conviction that Snectady is the only proper place in the State, and the sooner the Idea is adopted and carried into Execution the better. Should I have Time and Opportunity before my Departure I shall transmit to you my Reflections on this Subject. Many of them will naturally occur to you. I will just hint however, that it will not be easy to remove the Seat of Governmt. from any Place you may appoint for the Purpose & therefore that great Care should be taken in the Choice. My Sollicitude for the Welfare and Honor of the State prompts me to say many other things interesting to both, but I have no Leisure at present.

I must however recommend to you to appoint Coll. Hughes to be Sherif of the City & County of New York. I should also think it right for the Council of Appointment to provide for Cols. Lamb & Malcolm.

Believe me to be, dear Sir, your affectionate Friend & Serv't,

John Jay.

RC (N: Clinton Papers). Clinton, *Papers* (Hastings), 5:311–15. RC damaged; missing words taken from Tr.

[1] Charles Phelps, of Cumberland County, had delivered the New York Assembly's August 27, 1779, instructions for settling the New Hampshire Grants' dispute. See Jay, *Papers* (Morris), 1:632–33n.1; and Jay to Clinton, September 16, 1779, note 2. Jay's suspicions of Phelps were well founded, because Phelps had in fact been acting as an agent for Massachusetts as well, in recognition of which the Massachusetts General Court on November 27, 1779, granted him £100 "in compensation of the unwearied attention" he had devoted to the state's interest in the Vermont controversy. Massachusetts Council Minutes, p. 151, DLC(ESR).

[2] The New York Assembly had in fact just omitted Gouverneur Morris from the slate of delegates elected on October 1, and in an October 5 letter to Jay, Clinton offered the explanation that "The Imprudence of some of Mr. Morris's friends in voting, occassiond the loss of his Election." Clinton, *Papers* (Hastings), 5:309.

[3] New York Supreme Court justice John Sloss Hobart.

[4] Apparently Woodbury Langdon. For Langdon's views on the New Hampshire Grants, see Langdon to Meshech Weare, October 12; Nathaniel Peabody to Weare, October 26, 1779; and Winn L. Taplin, Jr., "The Vermont Problem in the Continental Congress and in Interstate Relations, 1776–1787" (Ph.D. diss., University of Michigan, 1955), pp. 146–47.

[5] For a discussion of New York's boundary claims within the context of western land claims and the formation of a national government, see Peter S. Onuf, *The Origins of the Federal Republic: Jurisdictional Controversies in the United States, 1775–1787* (Philadelphia: University of Pennsylvania Press, 1983), chaps. 5–6.

Henry Laurens to George Washington

Dear sir.   Philadelphia 7th October 1779.

The day before yesterday I was made very happy by the receipt of Your Excellency's Letter of the 29th Ulto.[1] I had been for some time wishing for a good occasion to pay my respects, nor had subjects been wanting, but such as appeared to me worthy of Your Excellency's attention were of so serious a cast, as to awe me into silence in more than one attempt, nor dare I even upon the present opening expatiate or be explicit. When I had the honor of seeing you in Town I expressed my apprehensions of calamitous events in a short contrast of gain & loss. Your Excellency will also remember my sentiments on the question of appreciation of our Paper Money & the foundation on which I built the opinion which I had then the honor of delivering. I had not been long returned to this City when I discovered there was no solidity in the intelligence alluded to; & our internal circumstances from that time have been descending from bad to worse, referring to the latter I hope we are now at our ne plus ultra.

At length you have seen Sir, a Resolution to "stop the Press," as it is termed, an act which I ardently wished for in Augt 1777, on condition of necessary previos steps of taxation, had we then determined this important point our Public debts foreign & domestic would have been at this day comparatively trifling but when the proposition even at a much later day & when we were overwhelmed with Paper, was, to make that an Harbinger which ought to have been consecutive & secondary, I found my self necessitated to dissent from it. We have pledged our honor that we will emit no more promisary Notes & are reduced to a dependence on contingent circumstances for supplies for carrying on the War & for supporting Public Credit. We are now but beginning to call on the several States for their quota of 15 Million Dollars per Month from the 1st February to the 1st October next inclusive. I doubt the practicability, the possibility of a compliance & my suspicions are strengthned by this observation, that those who were most anxious, most outrageously or blindly pressing for the premature determination, are most reluctant to bearing an equitable proportion of the burthen—'tis impossi-

ble says one—'tis impracticable says another, for my State to raise
such a Sum in one Month. Should we fail in this project & find an
empty Treasury in the Month of March or earlier, which I most
feelingly dread, what will be the consequence?

To reply in the mildest terms, much confusion & derangement of
public affairs, peradventure, commotions & convulsions in the Army,
in the Country, & in the Cities—to repeat Emissions would be infamos
& inefficacios—all Credit would be lost.

For averting these impending evils vigoros Resolutions are absolutely necessary in the several States to comply fully & punctually
with the requisitions of Congress & those must be supported by
virtuos & patriotic exertions of Individuals, nor ought we to lose a
moment or to wait till January for beginning the work. I shall say
every thing I can think of to induce my Country distressed as it is, to
contribute her part for the salvation of our Independence, but alas
we have no fix'd principles for our guide, the requistition is barely
15 Million per Month; our expenditure the lately voted subsistence
to the Army included amounts fully to that Sum & the daily increasing prices of Provisions deprives us of all ground for prospective
calculation.

Your Excellency is too well acquainted with the difficulties of procuring proper supplies of food for the Army, but are you apprized
Sir, of the probability of our deficiency in Cloathing? You may have
been told that ample quantities are expected from France, if you
place any reliance on such information, 'tis high time you should be
undeceived & I esteem it a duty to my Country & an act of friendship to Your Excellency to assure you that our applications to our
Ally for Clothing & Military Stores, which humanity, foresight &
vigilance would have sent forward in March last or earlier, were not
embarked until the latter end of July or beginning of August. From
this improvident delay we cannot, even hope to, receive those articles before January or February next, the application must undergo
the necessary formalities at Court, admitting success there, Orders
are to be issued, Clothing to be provided made,[2] Ships prepared, the
Atlantic to be crossed & a Port to be entered at 3 or 4 hundred Miles
distance from the Army in the very worst season for transportation.
Can the several States supply the necessary wants & in proper time
for saving our brave fellow Citizens from another Valley-forge scene?
or, are we again & again to rely on the Chapter of accidents or the
interposition of Heaven in favor of Men who will not make a proper
use of means. These things unknown to some & unheeded by others
who ought to be attentive & indeed answerable, were they declared
abroad would alarm many an honest & zealos heart now wraped in
profound security. If in this confidential communication I have
offered anything new, Your Excellency who in every view, is peculiarly Interested in the happy existence of the Army & the event of
the War, will make some advantages from the disclosure & in any

case I am perfectly satisfied there will be no unfavorable construction passed upon my motives—what I have said in private can have
no tendency to sounding unnecessary alarms & yet in truth it appears
to me almost time to rouse & call forth that virtuos spirit which led
us into the present War & which is now benumned & motionless—
upon our own virtue our final success depends. I am sure there still
exists virtue enough scattered among us to Insure that success. I
lament the prospect of a convulsion as necessary for collecting &
bringing it into action.

We have chosen Ministers Plenipotentiary for treating with the
Courts of Madrid & London, the former was a necessary appointment, the latter if the Act be not unseasonable, the publicity of it I
am afraid will be attended with pernicious effects, can we expect the
pride of Great Britain will condescend to treat abruptly & directly
with a revolted subject & immediately too after having refused the
mediation of a Crown head. I entertain certain distrusts on the point
which I wish could be communicated without the use of Pen. The
thing however is done & become notorious before this day in the
Garrison at New York from whence I expect to see in a few days
droll strictures & severe animadversions by some of Mr. Rivington's
correspondents.

I must now turn to Your Excellency's Letter from which I have
wandered perhaps too far.

The Proclamation by His Britanic Majesty which has been lately
published,[3] implies an apprehension of a serious attack on his
Kingdom, but neither my depth in Poltics nor in the secrets of the
European Courts reach far enough to determine on the utility of
one step beyond keeping that Kingdom alarmed & acting vigorosly
against its Marine—but it seems to me a joke to say the English Fleet
was blocked up in Torbay, which if I am not mistaken is as accessible
as any part of the British Channel & as undefended except by the
Fleet which may chance to ride there, a little time will enlighten us
on these & other important subjects. I am seldom detected in anticipating events but I must confess that I feel an unusual anxiety to see
our late King's Speech to his Parliament at their Meeting which I
suppose will be early in the present Month. I wish he may have an
opportunity of undeclaring that Georgia is at his Peace. General
Prevost's ill success in South Carolina will however supply him with
an unpalatable spice for the composition & I trust Count d'Estaing
has added a still more bitter ingredient for a subsequent Message.

Your Excellency's Letter to General Lincoln[4] will go forward by an
Express to morrow, 'tis now the 9th. I have been three Mornings on
this performance in scraps.[5] I live at a considerable distance from
the State House, have many Committees to attend & waste much of
my time by a useless habit of punctuality.

Colonel Laurens having intimated to me under the 3d September
a design to return into Your Excellency's service by Sea in Count

d'Estaing's Fleet, I have directed to him at Head Quarters, my Letter will be inclosed with this,[6] & I am persuaded he will tell Your Excellency what I have said on his late appointment. I have not presumed to say, don't go—but I beg the liberty upon second thoughts of leaving the Letter under a flying Seal until Your Excellency shall have perused it if you will be pleased to take that trouble. From the prospect abovementioned I shall also return Your Excellency's Letter for him under the present cover.[7]

I beg pardon Sir, for this long intrusion & subscribe with great truth, Your Excellency's Much obliged & most Obedient servant,

Henry Laurens

RC (DLC: Washington Papers).

[1] Washington's September 29 letter is in Washington, *Writings* (Fitzpatrick), 16:355–56.

[2] Laurens actually interlined "provided" above the word "made," but he let both words stand.

[3] A July 9, 1779, proclamation by George III, issued to prevent the capture of livestock in the event of an invasion of Great Britain, was published in the October 2 issue of the *Pennsylvania Packet* and the October 6 issue of the *Pennsylvania Gazette*.

[4] Washington had enclosed a September 28 letter to Benjamin Lincoln in his September 29 letter to Laurens. See Washington, *Writings* (Fitzpatrick), 16:350–53.

[5] Neither the content nor the physical appearance of Laurens' letter suggests what portion of it he might have penned on October 8.

[6] See Laurens to John Laurens, October 2, 1779.

[7] Undoubtedly Washington's September 28 letter to John Laurens. Washington, *Writings* (Fitzpatrick), 16:347–49.

Gouverneur Morris to George Clinton

Sir,   Public   Phila. 7 Octr. 1779.

Congress yesterday determined to raise 15 Mills. per Month from the 1st Feby to the 1st Octr. inclusive. They did me the Honor to appoint me on the Committee for apportioning this sum.[1] I was unadvised from the State on this Subject but from what I learnt at Kingston deemed it my Duty to endeavor at lowering our Proportion which was effected as well in the Committee as in the House without DisSatisfaction tho' not without Difficulty. Perhaps I may not have thoroughly accorded with the Views of my Constituents if so let me bear the Blame singly and none of it fall on my worthy Colleagues as I am the blameable. If I supposed the weak Voice of their Servant could weigh with those whom I represent amid the loud Calls of public Necessity the risque of public Honor & Safety the Incitements of all good Men & the Weight & Magnitude of the Objects we contend for I would pour out to them my earnest Supplications by speedy, vigorous & repeated Taxation to strike at the Root of a Disease which may prove dangerous if not fatal. I would add one Word to caution agt. those palliative Remedies which under the Name of Regulations and under the Appearance of Patriotism have been at once ineffectual in the Instant, Tyrannous in the Execution and pernicious in the Effect. But I rely on their Wisdom, on their Experience, on the Reason and Nature of things which must at length draw all things into those proper Channels from which temporary Expedients may vainly have forced them. The Attempts which may be made to recover our Capital I wish may prove Successful for so many Reasons that it would be needless to mention (further than to observe that all lesser ones are swallowed up in it) the Consideration that the Legislature as they are in Capacity will exert themselves to replenish the treasury of the Continent with Sums as much greater than those now called for as the Prosperity of the State will be superior to what it now can boast of.

I have the Honor to be most respectfully, Sir, Your Excellency's most obedt. & humble Servant,   Gouv Morris

RC (MHi: Washburn Collection).
[1] New York's share of the $15 million monthly state assessments adopted by Congress on October 6–7 was $750,000. See *JCC*, 15:1147–50.

William Paca to William Hemsley

Dear Sir   7 Octo. 1779
Yours by the Post was just now delivered to me. We have not had yet any intelligence from the Southward except flying reports such as I find you have heard.

On Monday last we have a great riot in this city. A body of two hundred militia assembled for the purpose of expelling all such as they considered Tories: among these they considered Mr. Morris, Mr. Wilson, Gen. Higbee (?) and included all such who had distinguished themselves in opposition to the present Constitution and Code of Pennsylvania. Apprized of the design of the militia those gentlemen collected their friends and armed themselves and took post in Mr. Wilson's House. The militia assembled in the Commons and dismissed their officer (?) not being obedient enough to their orders: they now marched into the City to Mr. Wilson's House where a formal engagement took place. The militia firing in platoons at Wilson's windows & the other Party firing from the windows: four of the militia I hear were killed & ten wounded: one of the other party was killed & four wounded. Happily for both parties Governor Reed headed the light horse of the City and in a lucky moment just as Wilson's doors were broken down charged with drawn swords on the armed militia, wounded several, took many prisoners & put the rest to flight. The next day the militia again assembled but without arms & obliged the Justices to commit to jail several of Wilson's party. Gov. Reed being absent with the lighthorse at Germantown this day. On the Governors return they were released. This day the Governor and Counsel met at the State House to investigate the affair & both parties are to be heard.

Lee is despleased [displaced?]. Mr. Jay is appointed Minister to Spain. Carmichael Secretary. Mr John Adams Minister for the Peace: Francis Dana Secretary. Mr. Franklin continued Minister to France & Col. Laurine [Laurens] (the Delegates son) Secretary. Yr,

Wm Paca

Tr (MdHi: Revolutionary Collection). Dr. L. S. Welty typescript, Denton, Md., 1934.

John Fell's Diary

Friday Octr 8th [1779]

Coml Committee. Congress. Letter from General Washington, relating to .[1] The Memorials of G Morgan and Trent, Respecting the Lands of Indiana and   [Vandalia] Refferd to a Comittee of 5.[2]

Several Reports from the Treasury &c.

Marine Committee.

MS (DLC).

[1] For Washington's October 4 letter concerning measures necessary for cooperating with the comte d'Estaing, see Delaware, Maryland, and South Carolina Delegates to Thomas Johnson, October 9, 1779, note 1.

[2] For the introduction of these memorials and Congress' official response, see John Fell's Diary, September 14; and Samuel Huntington to the States, October 30, 1779.

Samuel Huntington to Jeremiah Wadsworth

Sir   Philadelphia Octor 8th. 1779

You will receive this meerly as a private Letter from an Acquaintance & Friend who wishes to give you the best advice in his power.

Before this comes to hand you will receive an Act of Congress enabling you to perform the Contract you had made for flour by Supplying the people with Sugar &c which will relieve your apprehensions that Congress had wholly disapproved your conduct in that Respect.[1]

I had the honour to recive your Letter of the 4th Instant and laid it before Congress this morning, they are taking the necessary orders without delay to procure flour & rice agreable to your desire.[2]

I Sincerely hope you will content yourself to continue in the department as long as Congress Shall desire it.

Alltho the Events of war are uncertain, yet from the present prospect we have favourable hopes of Important & it may be decisive

Events. Let us all exert ourselves to the best of our abilities & let me add who can surmount difficulties better than your self.

It is with pleasure I assure you that great Harmony & good humour Subsists in Congress with Close attention to business.

I am with Sincerity your humbe Servt,   Saml. Huntington

RC (CtHWa: James Wadsworth Collection).
[1] See Huntington to Wadsworth, October 1, 1779.
[2] Wadsworth's letter to Congress of October 4 and a similar letter from Washington was referred to a committee appointed to assist preparations for provisioning the Continental Army. See *JCC*, 15: 1151; and PCC, item 78, 24:93–96. See also Delaware, Maryland, and South Carolina Delegates to Thomas Johnson, October 9, 1779.

Samuel Huntington to George Washington

Sir   Philadelphia Octor 8th. 1779

I had the honour to receive your Excellencies Letter of the 4th Instant this morning and have laid it before Congress.[1]

Before this comes to hand you will receive the Act of Congress directing the North Carolina Troops to halt at Trenton and a Copy of the orders to Col. Clarke in Consequence of your former Letter.

I have now the pleasure to acquaint your Excellency that Congress fully approve of your Orders, Countermanding the march of those Troops.[2]

I have the honour to be, with Sentiments of the greatest Esteem & Regard, Your Exys humble servant,

Saml. Huntington President[3]

RC (DLC: Washington Papers).
[1] For Congress' response to this letter, see the following entry.
[2] For "the Act of Congress directing the North Carolina Troops to halt at Trenton," see Huntington to Washington, October 5, 1779. Congress' approval of Washington's order "Countermanding the march of those Troops" was not officially recorded in the journals, doubtless because its previous resolve of October 4 had simply provided that their halt was to be observed "till farther Orders."
[3] Huntington also wrote the following personal letter this day to Gov. William Livingston of New Jersey.

"The congratulations your Excellency has been pleasd to honour me with in your favour of the 7th Instant command my most greatfull Acknowledgements.

"At the same time permit me with sincerity to Adopt the Language of the roman ædile [*a subordinate official originally charged with assisting the tribunes in the administration of public buildings*], I call the Gods to witness (Says he) that how honorable soever this dignity seems to me I have too just a Sense of its weight not to have more solicitude & disquiet, than Joy and Pleasure from it.

"If by any Civilities to those of your family in this City I have made my Self agreable it will give me Additional pleasure & Satisfaction.

"Be assured Sir it will be my constant endeavour to pay proper Attention to whatever may relate to Govr Livingston." William Livingston Papers, NN.

Delaware, Maryland, and South Carolina Delegates to Thomas Johnson

Sir,   Phila. Sepr. [i.e. October] 9th. 1779
Your Excellency will be informed by the enclosed Copy of a Letter from the Commander in chief to Congress, that a large quantity of Flour will be immediately wanted for the Army.[1] We have calculated upon the State of Marylands furnishing Ten thousand Barrs. over and above what Mr. Holkers Agents want for the Count D. estaignes Fleet, which we have reason to believe is more than half laid in. The Agent for Virga should suspend his Purchases for that State till the Ten thousand Barrs. for General Washington are procured. Vessels must be had if possible for the Transportation of this Flour to such place or places as his Excellency the General shall hereafter direct.

To enable you to furnish the Purchasers with Money, you will from time to time draw from your Treasury such sums as have, or may come into it from Continental Taxes; and whatever may be further wanted, must be sent from this place of which be pleased to forward an Estimate: But as the Continental Treasury is very low, we beg of you to press as little upon it as possible.

Altho it is well known to the Enemy that the Count D'estaigne may be hourly expected, yet as it is not known that the General & he are to act in Concert, Congress have enjoined its Members to Secrecy, which you & the Council will be pleased to observe.

With the greatest respect and esteem we are, Sir, Your Excellencys, Most Obedient Servts.[2]

Nich. Van Dyke	James Forbes
Wm. Paca	Daniel of St Thos. Jenifer
	Jno. Mathews

RC (MdAA: Red Books). Written by Jenifer and signed by Jenifer, Forbes, Mathews, Paca, and Van Dyke.

[1] Washington's concern stemmed from the anticipated arrival of the French fleet in North American waters and the needs of the troops of Gen. John Sullivan returning from the western expedition. In his October 4 letter to Congress, Washington explained that in anticipation of cooperating with the comte d'Estaing in "an attempt against New York" he had called upon Massachusetts, Connecticut, New York, New Jersey, and Pennsylvania for 12,000 militia. Since Commissary General Jeremiah Wadsworth had informed him that beef was plentiful but flour was in short supply, Washington specifically urged that Gov. Thomas Johnson "be requested to push purchases" in Maryland, its wheat being "in more forwardness for grinding than any other." In a letter of the same date, Wadsworth also informed Congress that he had been ordered by Washington "to Prepare to feed Ten thousand men; more than our present army." And given the difficulty in procuring flour, Wadsworth asked that steps be taken to procure rice from South Carolina as well.

Both letters were read in Congress on October 8 and referred to the delegates of Delaware, Maryland, and South Carolina, who reported this day. Congress thereupon authorized the president of Delaware and the governors of Maryland and

South Carolina to draw on "the several treasurers in those states" to purchase flour and rice from taxes to be levied according to the state quotas adopted on October 7. See *JCC*, 15:1150–51, 1157; PCC, item 152, 8:73–78; and Washington, *Writings* (Fitzpatrick), 16: 406–9, 417n.81.

[2] This day the committee also wrote the following letter to Caesar Rodney, president of Delaware:

"By the inclosed Copy of General Washington's Letter of the 4th Inst, to Congress, your Excellency will perceive the Reasons which induced the General to advise Congress to call on the States therein Mentioned for an immediate large Supply of Flour, for the Army expected to be brought into the Field;

"And altho the State of Delaware is not there Mentioned, as Congress deemed that an Omission in the hurry of Business, and their Duty to supply have included that State in their Requisition.

"The Quantity for Delaware is 5,000 Barrels; Congress judges it prudent to keep this Matter as great a Secret as possible, as well to prevent the wicked Operations of our internal & infernal Enemy called Speculators &c as for other Obvious Reasons.

"As it is absolutely Necessary this Bussiness be immediately set on Foot, with the utmost Industry and Spirit, the Committee have not the least Doubt of your Excellency's vigorous assistance—to enable the Persons you may appoint to this Business to proceed therein sucessfully, inclosed you have a general Order of Congress on the Treasurer of your State for such Sums as may from Time to Time be found to be Necessary—and should that Fund prove insufficient you'l be pleased to give Congress early Intelligence that Provision may be made Accordingly.

"It will be necessary to have the Flour stored at the most proper & Convenient Landings in each County of your State, for Transportation; and when any Considerable Quantity is provided, Information thereof will be proper, that suitable Vessels may be provided to receive the same." FMS Am 1300, MH–H.

The committee undoubtedly prepared a similar letter for Gov. John Rutledge requesting rice from South Carolina, but it apparently has not survived.

John Fell's Diary

Saturday October 9th [1779].

Coml Committee. Congress. After the dispatches were Read the Committee on Ways and mea[n]s brought in the draft of a Letter to be sent to the Governours and President of Each State for the Requisition of the 15 Million &c. The Committee brought in the draught of Commission and Letter of Credence for the Secretary appointed to go to Spain.[1]

MS (DLC).
[1] In his diary for this day Samuel Holten merely recorded that "I dined with Mr. Laurens and about 12 more members of Congress. Mr. Lowell & Mr. Cleveland came to board with us. No news this day." MDaAr.

Cornelius Harnett to Thomas Burke

My Dear Sir   Philadelphia Octr. 9. 1779

I had the pleasure of receiving three letters from you while you was on the Road, which I answered some time ago. I am happy to find by yours of the 16 Septr. you are in your own House & Sincerely wish you every Domestic happiness you can possibly desire. Had Coll Rochester Called upon me according to his promise, you would certainly have heard from me by him. Long before I received yours I had Congratulated Miss Vining on the Brilliant & Successful attempt of Major Lee on Powles' Hook. Her Mamma & herself present their affectionate compts to you, the young Lady promises to write by this Express, I fear she will be worse than her word.

Spains declaration against Britain may as you Conjecture, prolong the war. Mr. Jay is Appointed Minister Plenepotentiary to the Court of Madrid, & Mr. Carmichael his Secretary, John Adams is Appointed Minister Plenipotentiary to Negociate a Peace, Mr. Dana his Secy. and Coll Laurence son of Old Mr. Laurence, Secretary to Docr. Franklin. Fifteen millions per month is Called for from the Sevl. States. Quere will it be paid? I believe not, the Consequences you must know will be distressing indeed. The Quota of Our State is Out of Proportion but this could not be avoided.

We hourly expect good News from Georgia, surely the force the Count has with him, must soon settle Matters in that Quarter, should no unforeseen Accident intervene. He is soon expected here, which will render this a very Active, & I hope Successful Campaign. The No. Carolina Troops were Ordered to the Southward, but this Order has been Countermanded by Genl. Washington,[1] on his hearing of the Arrival of Count DeEstang, many are so Sanguine in their Expectations, as to believe we shall be in Possession of N York & R Island this fall. God send it may so happen. Sullivan has been very Successful in the Indian Country, having destroyd all their Settlements; it is hoped this may prevent the depredations of those Savages for some time. The Press stops at 200 Millions which I believe will be expended in December. Out of the 60 Millions which was heretofore called for from the States, only 3 Million have been recieved. How the war can be carried on after that period (Decr.) I know not, I do not expect the Treasury can possibly be supplied by the States 15 millions per month; North Carolina I am confident cannot supply her Quota Monthly. I dread the Consequences, but as you say "we must take events as they happen."

For Gods sake come on to relieve me in Novr., but at farthest the very beginning of December & make that Domestic creature Whitmil Hill come with you. In fact I can not live here, the prices of every necessary has advanced at 100 per cent since we parted. I shall return indebted to my Country at least 6000 dollars, and you very well know how we lived. Do not mention this Complaint to any person. I am Content to sit down with this loss, & much *more* if my Country requires it. I only mention it to you to guard you against difficulties which you must encounter on your return, unless the Gnl Assembly make suitable provision for yr. *expences at least.* I know they

x

will be Liberal, they always have been in their Allowances to their Servants.

Could not Hooper, Nash, Johnston, or *some such* be sent with you, believe me they will be much wanted. I acknowledge it is cruil in me to wish you to return; you have already suffered more in your private Concerns, than any man who has been in the Delegation for Some time past. But you have this Consolation; that should you fail of receiving your reward in this World, you will no doubt be singing Hallilujas in the Next, to all Eternity—Tho' I acknowlege your Voice is not very well Calculated for that business.

Your Sythes shall be purchased and sent, as soon as any person Applies for them. Remember me to all your friends, I hope they are mine, Send some body or Other to relieve me & let me, for Gods sake, take my leave of this Laborious, disagreeable, & perhaps unthankfull Office for ever. Adieu my Friend, & may you be happy. You will believe me when I assure you that your happiness will be a very great addition to my own. I know you hate professions, so do I. I am, Dr. Sir, Your affectionate & Ob Servt.   Cornl Harnett

[*P.S.*] Mr. Jay Draughted the Circular Letter,[2] Hooper & yourself know his manner.

RC (NcU: Burke Papers).
[1] See Samuel Huntington to Washington, October 8, 1779.
[2] That is, the circular letter of September 12, for which see *JCC*, 15: 1051–62; and John Jay to the States, September 14, 1779, note 3.

Samuel Huntington to
the Continental Loan Office Commissioners

Sir   Philadelphia Octobr. 9th. 1779.
You will receive herewith enclosed an Act of Congress of the 6th Instant extending the resolution of Congress of the 29th of June last for promoting Loans, to all sums which may be paid into the Continental Loan Office on or before the first day of March next, to the amount of the blank loan Office certificates which are Already ordered to be struck by Congress. Also giving certain encouragement to persons who shall subscribe Ten thousand dollars or upwards and make punctual payments as expressed in the Act.[1]

I am with sentiments of Esteem Your Obedient and Very humble servant,   Saml. Huntington President

RC (MHi: Colbourn Collection). In the hand of George Bond and signed by Huntington. Addressed: "Commissioner of the Continental Loan Office, In the State of Massachusetts Bay." LB (DNA: PCC, item 14). Addressed: "Circular."
[1] In its resolve of June 29, Continental loan officers were authorized to pay 6 percent interest on loans to a total of $20 million if subscribed before October 1,

1779. Large investors were also offered an interest bonus, as persons investing $10,000 or more were permitted to open subscriptions with only 50 percent down, earning interest on the full subscription if the balance was paid before October 1. The resolve of October 6 simply extended the period for subscribing this $20 million to March 1, 1780, while persons with $10,000 or more were again offered an interest bonus on one-half their investment if the balance was paid within "two months after the first payment." See *JCC*, 14:783–85, 15:1148.

Samuel Huntington to the States

Sir   Circular   Philadelphia Octr 9th 1779
     I have the honour to transmit your Excellency, Sundry resolutions of Congress of the 6th & 7th instant for supplying the Continental Treasury and to request the earliest Communication of them to the legislative Authority of your State.[1]
     The Money which Congress are at liberty to emit will probably be expended in the beginning of December next and subsequent supplies must be furnished by the States. This evinces the necessity of the punctual payment of their respective Quotas on which their public credit, the existence of their Army, and the support of their Liberties so greatly depend.
     Congress are deeply concerned to find that the sums required are so great but since the emissions are limited, they doubt not that the operation of taxes and other salutary measures in the course of the year will reduce the prices of articles and enable them to lessen the quotas required or apply part thereof to diminish the public debt. To promote so desirable an object Congress on their part will endeavour to observe the strictest Œconomy in their expenditures.
     I have only to add that warrants will be issued on the treasurers of the respective States for the quota to be furnished on the first of January next, and that I remain with the greatest respect, Your Excellency's most obedient and very humble Servt.
                                             S. H. President.

LB (DNA: PCC, item 14).
     [1] See *JCC*, 15:1147–48, 1150. The quota resolves of the sixth and seventh set the quota to be collected from the states from February 1 to October 1, 1780, at $15 million monthly and specified the apportionment of that sum among the twelve states from New Hampshire to South Carolina, "Georgia being invaded." For the loan office resolves of the sixth, see the preceding entry.

Samuel Huntington to George Washington

Sir   Philadelphia October 9th. 1779
     You will herewith receive enclosd an Act of Congress of this day, in Answer to your Excellencys Letter of the 2d Instant.[1]

I have the honour to be, with the greatest Respect, Your Exys. most humble Servant,

Saml. Huntington President

RC (DLC: Washington Papers).
[1] In his letter of October 2, Washington had inquired about the application of an August 18 resolve pertaining to the subsistence of officers and men in the Continental Army. In answer to Washington's query, Congress' October 9 resolve explained that the former resolution did not extend to "the militia who are or may be called out." See *JCC*, 15:1156; PCC, item 152, 8:67–68; and Washington, *Writings* (Fitzpatrick), 16: 388–89.

Henry Laurens to Benjamin Lincoln

Dear Sir.   Philadelphia 9th October 1779.
I had the honor of addressing you under the 24th Ulto. & recommended my Letter to the care of Colonel Malmadi. On the 4th Inst. & no earlier I received your favor of the 20th July together with Doctor Oliphant's return of the state of the Hospital in the southern department. These papers had been detained by Doctor Read who being retarded by sickness was a long time performing his journey from CharlesTown. I shall be particularly attentive to your recommendations, & Doctor Oliphant may rely on my endeavors to obtain an establishment of the Medical department in So. Carolina & Georgia under his direction.[1] The Chairman of the Medical Committee is not yet return'd, consequently no report, on the Commitment spoken of in my last, has been made.[2] I judge it best to hold in my own hands Doctor Oliphant's return 'till that Gentleman shall appear, the presentation will then, act upon him as a stimulous. Public business is exceedingly delayed in Congress by this fluctuatality of its Members, but I will not leave Philadelphia before I see the articles in question determined.

Every Thing practicable is going forward in this quarter for enabling the Commander in Chief to co-operate vigorously & efficaciously with Count d'Estaing. The Frigates & the North Carolina Troops which had been ordered to Charles Town are arrested & Gen. Sullivan with his healthy Troops, who have made great slaughter of Indian Towns & Indian Corn is called to join the Main Army. But a question begins to be now seriously put by every body, what has Count d'Estaing done in Georgia & where is he? We cannot learn either by Land or Sea intelligence of him.

You will receive under cover with this Dunlap's Packet containing Copy of a Letter from Major General Sullivan giving an account of his late Military peregrination.[3] I think it was a little mischievos to print the whole, be that as it may, he has certainly made severe retaliation upon the barbarians who will be driven to the utmost distress the approaching Winter by a deficiency of provisions & by the loss of their "large & elegant Mansions." The General has unluckily displeased by complaints which are said to be groundless, the Commander in Chief, & given high umbrage to the Board of War & to the quarter Master general, but this if you please, inter nos.

Anxious to see the Stores which you had sent for go forward I applied three days ago to the War office, where I was informed by Mr. Peters that the whole were in readiness for departure or very nearly so—but, that it would be impossible to give further aide until large supplies shall be received from France. This cannot possibly be effected earlier than January or February next, in the mean time, I trust a proper use will be made of the authority vested in our State to import.

I have not any thing to add but my repeated assurances of being with very great regard & Esteem, Dear Sir Your obedient & most humble servant, Henry Laurens

P.S. This will be accompanied by a Packet lately received from His Excellency General Washington.

RC (MeHi: Fogg Collection).
[1] For the case of Dr. David Oliphant, director general of hospitals in South Carolina, see Laurens to Lincoln, September 24, 1779, note 3.
[2] For the absence from Congress of medical committee chairman Nathaniel Scudder, see Scudder to Laurens, October 4, 1779, note 1.
[3] John Sullivan's September 30 letter to Congress appeared in the October 9 issue of the *Pennsylvania Packet*.

William Sharpe to Richard Caswell

Sir, Philadelphia Octr. 10th. 1779

On the 26th of June last I had the honor of transmitting, under cover, to your Excellency fifteen copies of the Journals of Congress dated from the 1st January 1779 to the 5th June, by Colo. Longs Waggon.[1] On the 15th July sent 15 copies dated from the 5th to the 19th of June, by an Express.

Mr. Burke took with him 15 copies dated from the 19th June to the 26th of July and I now send by the Express 15 copies dated from the 26th of July to the 20th of August.

I doubt not your Excellency will participate in sending Communications[2] which I have made to Messrs Penn & Burke and to Genl Rutherford & Locke which leaves me nothing to add, but, that I have the honor to be, with the highest esteem and regard, Sir, your mo. ob. huml. Servt. Wm. Sharpe

Tr (Nc–Ar: Governors' Letterbooks). RC (Nc–Ar: Governors' Papers).
[1] Remainder of RC missing; text from this point taken from Tr.
[2] Not found.

John Fell's Diary

Monday, Octor 11th [1779].
Commercial Committee. Sundry Letters, Memorials &c. A Memorial from the Legislature of New Jersey relating to fixing the Price of Produce &c, Committed to a Member from Each State.[1]

MS (DLC).
[1] New Jersey's memorial seeking "a general regulation of prices" immediately revived interest in the previously abandoned device of fixing prices to curb inflation, coinciding with a similar movement in the northern states where delegates were simultaneously preparing to assemble at Hartford to debate solutions to the worsening economic crisis. For the delegates' response to New Jersey's petition and to the similar recommendations of the Hartford Convention that were submitted to Congress on November 10, see Samuel Huntington to the States, November 22, 1779, note. See also these *Letters*, 6:165n.1, 331–32, 9:438n.11, 634n.3, 10:17n.2, 30n.2, 68n.1.

John Fell's Diary

Tuesday 12th [October 1779].
Commercial Committee. Congress. Letter from Col Broadhead giving an Acct. of his Transactions and Expedition against the Indians, &c. Moved that the Commissioners &c for the Board of Treasury hold their Offices during Pleasure.[1]
PM Marine Committee.

MS (DLC).
[1] The debate concerning the terms of office for members of the Board of Treasury who were nominated this day is not mentioned in the journals. Congress approved the report of the treasury committee on October 23, for which see *JCC*, 15:1165, 1190, 1204–6; and Fell's Diary, October 22–23, 1779.

Elbridge Gerry to John Adams

My dear sir,   Philadelphia. Octr 12. 1779
I have received from Mr Lowell your Accounts & Vouchers,[1] & shall deliver them to the Board of Treasury; how far they will be able to comply with the proposition of returning the latter, which is contrary to their usual Practice, I am unable to say, but will use my best Endeavours to accomplish it.
Having lately explained to You some Matters, relative to our internal political Manœuvres, It is needless to trouble You farther on that Subject. I must however acknowledge, that your good Opinion is flattering to the person who is so happy as to enjoy it, & at the same Time that it exceeds his Merit, it cannot fail of increasing his Desires of deserving it. I mentioned in my last, that Doctor Ban-

croft & Sir James Jay will probably be nominated, if Mr Dana declines his appointment to the office of Secretary; since which the Powers thereof are enlarged with the Commission of Charge D'Affairs, in Case of the absence or Death of the principal, & the office is so desirable as to be sought, by others of Influence & abilities.[2] It is uncertain therefore, who will succeed in the new appointment, & it is for the Interest of the publick, to prevail wth. Mr Dana, if he has any Doubts, to annul them on this Occasion, & accept the office.

I am happy to find that the State of Massachusetts has your assistance in forming a Constitution, & am informed, that You are clearly in Favour of giving to the Governor a negative Power, in legislative Matters. This is a great Question, & I am fully persuaded that You have traced it, to its original principles, compared it with the Circumstances of the Times, weighed with Accuracy the advantages & Disadvantages resulting from each Determination thereof, & finally decided in favour of the proposition, but granting, that upon a general Scale, the Measure is wise, yet is there not too much Reason to apprehend from it, great Injuries, & that the Community will be endangered, thereby? & may not this be prevented by giving to the Governor a negative only so far as the proceedings of the Legislature may affect the powers of the Executive? Indeed I have but little Time to attend to such Matters, and well knowing your Sentiments to have been on all Occasions against arbitrary & dangerous powers, I am not much concerned about the Event. One Maxim however, in Matters of Government I think to be just, that the Officers are generally best, whose powers are least subject to Abuse. I remain sir with the warmest Sentiments of Friendship & Esteem, your very humble sert,   E. Gerry

[P.S.] The Salary of a Minister is fixed at £2500 sterling & of his Secretary at £1000.

Your Appointment I think ought not to be divulged at present, but find that is generally known, & as generally approved.

RC (MHi: Adams Papers).
    [1] For further information on Adams' accounts, see James Lovell to Adams, August 20, 1779, note 4. For the recent arrival of John Lowell in Philadelphia, see John Fell's Diary, October 9, 1779, note.
    [2] This provision enlarging the powers of secretaries to missions abroad had been incorporated into the form of commissions adopted by Congress on October 9. *JCC,* 15:1159–60.

Samuel Holten's Diary

[October 12–13, 1779]
12. Tuesday. I wrote to General Count Pulaski, & to Mrs. Holten (No. 79).[1] The weather is warm & showrs. this eveng.

13. Wednesday. I met a Committee this evening on Genl Arnold's Accounts.[2]

MS (MDaAr).
[1] Neither of these letters has been found. Pulaski had been mortally wounded on October 9 during a cavalry charge against the British defenses at Savannah, Ga.
[2] Holten had been appointed on October 1 to a committee to examine the accounts of Gen. Benedict Arnold for his nine months' service as commandant of Philadelphia in 1778–79. See *JCC*, 15:1126, 1134; and John Fell's Diary, October 1, 1779.

Samuel Huntington to Philip Schuyler

Sir,   Philada. Octr 12th 1779
    I am directed by Congress to lay before the Commissioners for indian Affairs in the northern district of which you have the honour to be Chairman copies of General Sullivan's letter of the 2d instant, his Speech to the Oneidas &c and their Answer which you will receive herewith enclos'd.[1]
    I have the honour to be, with Sentiments of esteem & regard, your humble Servt,   S. H. President

LB (DNA: PCC, item 14).
[1] See *JCC*, 15:1161. In his October 2 letter to Congress, John Sullivan had expressed optimism that the measures he had recently taken would bring about the repentance of hostile Iroquois warriors and reassure the friendly Oneidas, who had long been favorably disposed to the United States. In his speech to the Oneidas, he had asserted that Congress would "totally extirpate the other five nations except those who have joined you & continued friends to the United States & such others as may think proper to come in & enter into a firm league to join our friends the Oneidas." Sullivan's letter to Congress, with his enclosed speech to the Oneidas and their response, are in Sullivan, *Letters* (Hammond), 3:137–41. The MSS of the first two documents are in PCC, item 160, fols. 328–33, but the last has not been found.

Woodbury Langdon to Meshech Weare

Sr.   Philadelphia Octobr the 12 1779
    The reasons why I have not done myself the honor of writing to you before are these. Soon after my arrival I was taken very ill of a Fever which confined me to my Bed a considerable time and since my recovery General Whipple has gone home who from his long residence and experience at Congress will be able to give you a more perfect Account of the transactions here than can be expected from me.
    Since my recovery I have attended Congress with the closest application and shall endeavour to exert myself if my health continues to the utmost of my abilites while here. You will have received sundry Resolutions relative to Vermont from the President of Congress a

Copy of the last of which I herein inclose, the others of the 24th September were pass'd while I was confined and I cannot say are altogether to my mind. This Business in my opinion is of the greatest consiquence to New Hampshire and requires her most serious attention for many very weighty Reasons among which give me leave to mention the following. That as the thirteen united States have declared themselves independent which they will beyond all doubt support and at the same time have reserved to each State its particular seperate independence and sovereignty and as New Hampshire without Vermont will be very small and weak compared with her neighbouring States and it cannot be expected in the nature of things *but* that some day or other differences will arise between that State and her neighbours in which case she will be under great disadvantages on Account of her weakness, it therefore is her indispensable duty in the first seting out to endeavour by all proper means to be as much on a footing with her neighbours as possible, of the truth of this I am more & more convinced every day, it will also give her greater weight in the grand Councils of America and be an amazing saving of Tax—both which are objects well worthy consideration. The same reasons will apply to Vermont against her being a seperate State and in favour of her being connected with New Hampshire, indeed there does not appear to me the least probability that Vermont will be allowed to be a seperate State and every step that has been or may be taken by New Hampshire to countenance it weakens her claim far beyond what many Gentlemen of New Hampshire have any conception of, and will be so construed in disiding the dispute, therefore I wish most heartily that New Hampshire and the Inhabitants of what is called the Grants or Vermont would for the interest of both lay aside every thought of making the latter a seperate State and unite in their endeavours to be one State in which case in my opinon they will succeed, but if Vermont persists in endeavoring to be a seperate State and New Hampshire appears to acquiese they will very likely both be disappointed and in all probability Vermont will be adjudged to New York. I confess I am anxiously concerned for the settlement of this Matter and when I declare that I have no private Interest in the Tract of Country called Vermont and never expect to have it will I flatter myself be admitted that I can have no view seperate from the true Interest of New Hampshire when I endeavour to prevent the Grants from being loped off from New Hampshire of which without vigorous exertions there appears to be danger.

The Delegates of New York, Massachusetts Bay and New Hampshire have most of them thought it best to recommend to their several States a particular form of an Act to answer the end of the Resolutions referred to above, in order that there might be a similiarity in the Acts, the Delegates from the two former States have accordingly sent a form of an Act to their respective States, a Copy of which I have thought it my duty to inclose herein;[1] and the General Court will adopt it or not as they may think proper. If it should be adopted it may be very necessary to add a Clause makeing it of force provided New York and Massachusetts Bay pass similar Acts otherwise not, as it is at present very uncertain what will be done by those States and I hope I shall be pardoned when I say that I hope that care will be taken in forming every part of the Act that no disadvantage or embarrasment may accrue to the State hereafter in consiquence of it.

Yesterday was forwarded to you by Express Sundry Resolutions of Congress respecting a Supply of the Treasury, the Letter accompanying them together with the inclosed of the 13th Septr.[2] past sufficiently point out the necessity of the measure without my ading anything on the Subject, it gives me much pain to find that there appears to be a necessity for calling on the States for such large Supplies and confess that I am not without my fears respecting the success of it, but you must see what will be the consiquence if it does not succeed. Your Delegates have been able to procure the Proportion of Tax for New Hampshire to be much lower than what it has hitherto been,[3] but it must be remembered that when hereafter the proportions of the Taxes of each State shall be finally fixed agreable to some former Resolutions of Congress if it shall then appear that New Hampshire or any other State has been dificient it will be then liable to make good such deficiency and on the other hand if any State has been overrated it will have credit for the same.

The peculiar situation of my family and other concerns renders it necessary for me to leave this place early in December in order to return home which I hope will not be taken amiss by the Court as they will remember it is agreable to my engagement with them, it will always be the height of my ambition to render the State every possible service in my power—dobtless care will be taken that such Persons are chosen to represent the State in Congress as are fully acquainted with the dispute relative to Vermont and to instruct them fully in that Business. I am with all due Respect, Your most obedient, Hble. Servt.   Woodbury Langdon

RC (Nh–Ar: Vermont Controversy Collection). *N.H. State Papers*, 10:355–58. RC damaged; missing words supplied from Tr.

[1] For this draft "Act," see Massachusetts Delegates to the Massachusetts Council, October 4, note 3; and John Jay to George Clinton, October 5, 1779. According to Jay, Langdon was a moderate on the issue of New Hampshire's territorial claims and had proposed making "the Ridge of mountains instead of Connecticut River, the Boundary between us," thereby dividing the disaffected Vermonters between New Hampshire and New York, and rendering "the Reduction of them to good order less difficult." See John Jay to George Clinton, October 7, 1779.

[2] Langdon subsequently discovered that he had failed to send Weare this circular letter "of the 13th Septr." from Congress to the states, and accordingly enclosed it with his next communication. See *JCC*, 15:1051–62; and Langdon to Weare, October 19, 1779.

[3] New Hampshire's share of the $15 million required of the states monthly from February to October 1780 was $400,000, a reduction of $100,000 from her quota for 1779. See *JCC*, 13:28, 15:1150.

Henry Laurens to Richard Henry Lee

My Dear sir.   Philadelphia 12th October 1779.

Since my last Letter to you under the 28th September I have not been honored with any of your favors, nor from a former intimation, could I have expected to hear from you.[1]

We remain without any addition to the first advises of Count d'Estaing's arrival near Georgia, this circumstance detains me in Philadelphia, which I cannot conveniently depart from, until I shall have seen & conversed with the Young Gentleman lately appointed Secretary to the Embassy at Versailles,[2] I mean to give him a faithful unbiasing account of Foreign & domestically-transacted-foreign affairs & leave him to judge & determine if he reads my heart he will return thanks & decline acceptance.

You will receive with this a Copy of the Journal containing the Yeas & Nays formerly spoken of, the different principles alluded to by a Note in the Margin were—J—— thought 10 or 15 by far too little. L—— was of opinion that *anything* would be too much.[3] The Report for which a certain Monday was *"set apart"* remains unconsidered & probably will remain so to the day of Judgement. Yesterday I received Packets & Letters ten in number directed to yourself & Colo. F. L. Lee from France which I have delivered to Mr. Lovel who has shewn me Copies of two which will be read this Morning in Congress, I shall move to have them printed, if refused, & I can obtain Copies, they shall be printed—Mr. Lovel will enlarge on these points.[4] The P.S. to my Letter above recited informs you that I had paused upon the propriety of transmitting a Paper which had been inclosed,[5] upon mature reflection & considering circumstances which have since happened I see nothing improper in it, therefore I shall inclose it with this in its original state, probably it may at this distance of time convey no information. The Salaries to Ministers Plenipo: £2500 Sterling per Annum, to their Secretaries £1000—in full of all expences &c. passages excepted. I moved for £2000 & £700 & was uniformly no! against everything higher & my motives & reasonings I trust will meet the approbation of my thinking fellow Citizens—we have made the appointments where are the funds? Mr. Carmichael had no competitor, but I refused my Vote;[6] upon proper reflection I am persuaded he himself will applaud my candor & I will take the liberty of adding, my judgement.

He who had repeatedly acknowledged that he had called an American Minister in Office a Rascal & did not deny that he had called him Villain too & said he would display his Villainy to Congress, must have been either right or wrong. I need not deduce the logical conclusion, I think I have acted as if I understood it.

The two Legs are made Ult. but yesterday there was a proposition for reconsidering & expunging the Southernmost, I opposed it, after an hours debate, adjourned—we shall hear more of it today.[7] I told the advocate for expunction, I had long since heard every word he had offered in support of his motion—*out of doors*.

The Confederacy is still at Chester her Passengers will embark in the course of this Week.

God bless you my Dear Sir, have patience & all things will work together in support of honesty & truth.

I am with sincere Esteem & regard, Your obedient & most humble Servt,   Henry Laurens.

[*P.S.*] I have heard some people impudently talk of meanness in a —— but I have not in my life seen more marks of sordid meanness than has been for some Days past displayed by a monosyllable.[8]

RC (PPAmP: Lee Papers).

[1] The "former intimation" has not been identified, but the circumstance alluded to probably involves Lee's experience with post riders, which he also discussed in an October 15 letter to Laurens. Lee, *Letters* (Ballagh), 2:159.

[2] Laurens is referring to his son John.

[3] The subject is the congressional debate of August 26 concerning compensation for Silas Deane's expenses. John Jay and James Lovell are undoubtedly the delegates referred to here.

[4] See James Lovell to Richard Henry Lee, October 13, 1779.

[5] The enclosed "Paper" has not been found, and the incident to which it pertained has not been identified. Laurens had prepared this enclosure for his "last letter" to Richard Henry, but before transmitting it he had a mysterious meeting with the person involved in the episode and decided at the last moment not to send it, because to do so, he explained, would be "inconsistent with my honor." See Laurens to Richard Henry Lee, September 28, 1779, note 6.

[6] Laurens had refused to support William Carmichael's election as secretary to the minister to Spain because of Carmichael's refusal in September 1778 to testify against Silas Deane although he had previously intimated that Deane had misappropriated public funds. See these *Letters*, 10:653n.3, 661, 707–9, 717–20, 11:114, 309–10.

[7] The "two Legs" made ultimata were the fisheries and navigation of the Mississippi River. For the maneuvers involved in attempting to expunge "the southernmost, " see Gouverneur Morris' Draft Motion, October 13? 1779.

[8] Laurens may be referring here to John Jay.

Francis Lewis to George Clinton

Dear Sir,   Philada. 12th Octobr. 1779

I have the honor to enclose Mr. Charles Phelps's receipt for three hundred Dollars, upon his applycation to the Delegates of our State, for which the State is accountable to Congress, and Phelps to the Treasurer.

I am also requested by the New Jersey Delegates to transmit you the inclosed Publication,[1] the Post going off immediately will not permit me the time to peruse it, but as I am informed it is intended for public Utillity, should be glad to receive your Sentiments thereon.

We are anxious for the arrival of the Count de Estaing at the Delaware Capes; where there is Pilots stationed, and every other necessary for the accommodation of his fleet, but we are under some concern at not hearing officialy from him since his of the 8 Ulto from Georgia; the moment we receive any authentick advices Shall inform you. I have the honor to be with great sincerity, Your Excellency's very Humble Servant.   Fra Lewis

RC (PHi: Conarroe Collection).
[1] The "inclosed Publication" was the public form of a New Jersey proposal to limit prices, which had been read in Congress on October 11. See John Fell's Diary, October 11; Henry Marchant to William Greene, October 12; and Samuel Huntington to the States, November 22, 1779.

James Lovell to Benjamin Franklin

                                                             Oct 12. 1779
Mr Girard having been particularly applyed to relative to the affairs of Mr Du Coudray by the Heirs, has the original Certificate of which is a (2 plicate or triplicate) but Doctor Franklin will mark out for himself a line of conduct referring properly to the Civility due to Mr Gerard, and the Interest of Mr Du Coudrays Heirs.[1]
                                          Signed James Lovell

FC (DNA: PCC, item 79).
[1] On September 9 Congress had referred "the claims of the heirs of the late Monsr. du Coudray, against the United States" to the Board of Treasury. Congress did not settle the claim until September 25, 1781. See *JCC*, 15:1041, 21:1014.

Henry Marchant to William Greene

Sir,   Philadelphia Octr. 12th 1779
Mr. Collins sat out last Tuesday for Providence, meaning however to take the Camp in his Tour; and proposed to wait there a few Days for Count De Staing's Arrival, and to put himself on Board if possible. Before the Receipt of this your Excellency will have recd. the Address of Congress, and the late subsequent Resolutions calling upon the States for all future Supplies. Your Excellency will perceive that from an Arbitrary and unreasonable Depretiation of the Currency, no Ways proportioned to the Emissions, the amasing high Prices have caused the-monthly Expenditures for the Support of the Army & the Common Cause to be very enormous. It cannot be doubted,

but that the very Assessment of those Taxes, at least the first & second monthly Collections must have an Effect upon Prices and appretiate the Currency, as soon as this shall be happily effected; I should presume that Congress will be able proportionably to relax in the future Taxes. As the State I have the Honor to represent has hitherto taken more than its Proportion of Taxes, and its Situation from the Invasion of the Enemy, and the Consequent scattering of a great Part of its Inhabitants, and other Considerations have most severely distressed the State—I was so happy as to prevail in reducing Our Proportion of the Taxes for the Year 1780 One third less than heretofore.[1] Should the Enemy at Rhode Island either be taken, or find themselves constrained to evacuate it—the State will have an Opportunity, if they shall see proper so to enlarge their Taxes as in some Measure to lighten their own internal Debt. For while on the one Hand we feel the Weight of the present Taxes it will be plainly seen that, Monies will never be raised with more ease than when the Currency is in its greatest depreciated State. That Time I must presume is now, For I must please myself with the Reflection that the Virtue, Generosity & Patriotism of my Countrymen will strike a most decisive Stroke to the last Hopes of Our Enemies, which are alone built on the Destruction of Our Currency, and will by the most vigorous Measures, and by almost any temporal Sacrifice regain a Confidence in the Currency, which shall confound Our Enemies, and speedily establish Peace, Liberty and Independance to the United States. The first Sacrifice is allways the cheapest—And the Way to preserve our Property & thereby enrich Ourselves is to make a great present Sacrifice of partial Interest.

The State of New Jersey have addressed Congress in the strongest Terms upon the Subject of regulating Prices and pray that Congress will take it into serious Consideration, and recommend a Plan for that Purpose to all the States. Indeed New-Jersey never repealed their Former Act, but suspended it only till as they say the Wisdom of the other States should perceive as they do the absolute Expediency of the Measure. Congress have committed the Address of New-Jersey to a Committee of one Member from each State. The Legislature of New-Jersey have sent forward to the Delegates of all the States in Congress, an Address to every State, requesting that those Addresses may be forwarded by the Delegates of their Respective States, And I have accordingly enclosed One to your Excellency.[2] Should such a Measure take Place; the Expenditures would be diminished, and Taxes I presume proportionably lessened. I should be glad of the Sense of my Constituents upon so important a Subject. Should I not receive any—I shall endeavour to act from such Principles, as I conceive were the Inducements in their late Transactions in Convention.

We are in momentary Expectations of hearing of the Count De Staing near these Shores. We have no late official Accounts. Report says that an Attack had been made upon the Garrison at Beaufort, that after an Action of three Hours & a Quarter, it was carried, Nine hundred of the Enemy made Prisoners—All their Baggage & Stores taken, & their Shiping there destroyed—That the Count had ordered his Ships up the Savannah to cooperate with Genl. Lincoln. A few Days must give us full Information. Our Affairs Abroad are in the most prosperous Train. Most of the European Powers wish us well, and if all of them do not, we know of no Enemy but Britain— And we know not that they have a Friend in Heaven or Earth. It behoves us however to be our Own Friend—so may we expect the further Blessing of Heaven & the Completion—a happy Completion to the glorious struggle and I trust Heaven is ready to hand it out to Us as soon as we shall be fully disposed to receive it. That so glorious is the sincere prayer of Your Excellencys most obedient & very humble Servt.   Hy. Marchant

P.S. I enclose your Excellency the Weekly Journals of Congress in Course down to the 28th of August.

RC (R–Ar: Letters to Governors).
[1] Rhode Island's new assessment was $200,000 of the $15 million required from the states monthly for 1780 compared to $300,000 of the $15 million required for 1779. *JCC*, 13:28, 15:1150.
[2] For New Jersey's "Address," see John Fell's Diary, October 11, 1779.

Marine Committee to the Eastern Navy Board

Gentlemen   October 12th. 1779
We wrote you the 6th instant by Captain James Nicholson whom we have appointed to Command the Trumbull, since which we are favoured with yours of the 23rd ultimo.[1] We have now to inform you that we have named the New ship Building at Middleton the Bourbon and have given the command of her to Captain Thomas Read who will go from hence in a few days to superintend the fitting and manning of her—respecting which you will give him the necessary Orders and use your endeavours in getting ready that Ship as soon as possible.
We enclose you a Resolve of Congress of the 17th Ultimo appointing Colonel Silas Talbot a Captain in the Navy of the United States, and we have determined that should you purchase the Thorne he shall command her;[2] we expect to hear shortly if you have purchased that vessel. The Ship Confederacy being destined for france and other opportunitys from this place affording sufficient conveyances for the Public despatches, the Packets now at your port which have been kept for that purpose need not be longer detained but may be employed in importing Articles for the use of our Navy. You will please therefore to load them with Tobacco or such Other Articles as can be procured that will be suitable at the Bilbao Market and

dispatch them for that Port, ordering back the returns in Rigging, Sail Cloth, Powder, Lead & such other articles as are most wanted for your Department. Should it be necessary to provide Prison ships at Boston or Portsmouth in New Hampshire you are Authorized to do so, and to furnish the Commissary General of Prisoners or his Deputy with Cartel vessels when they are wanted.

We are Gentn, Your Hble Servts

LB (DNA: PCC Miscellaneous Papers, Marine Committee Letter Book).
[1] The board's September 23 letter to the committee is in the Eastern Navy Board Letterbook, NN.
[2] JCC, 15:1075-76. For a discussion of Talbot's achievements and the failure of these efforts to secure him a suitable ship as a reward for his exploits as commander of the *Argo*, see Henry Marchant to Silas Talbot, August 9, 1779, note 2.

Virginia Delegates to Benjamin Harrison

Sir   October 12th [1779]

The good Intentions of a neighboring state having committed to our charge the conveyance of the enclosed paper,[1] we do ourselves the honor to hand it to the Virginia assembly under your address. We have only to add that in consequence of a representation from the same state addressed and received by Congress the business is so far began as to be committed to a member from each state.

We have the honor to be, Sir, your most obedient humble Servants,

C Griffin

Js. Mercer

William Fitzhugh

Tr (DLC: Edmund C. Burnett Collection). Endorsed: "Copied from the original, then in the possession of Mr. Stan V. Henkels."
[1] For the enclosed New Jersey representation on price limitations, see John Fell's Diary, October 11, 1779.

Committee for Foreign Affairs to Arthur Lee

Sir   Octr. 13. 1779.

This is officially to convey to you the Knowledge of the Appointment of a Minister plenipotentiary in lieu of a Commissioner at the Court of Spain; and also a Resolve of Congress of this Day[1] upon the Reading of your Letter of the 31st of May.[2] Mr. Jay will probably be in a short Time in Europe to execute his Commission.

I am, Sir, your most humble Servant,

James Lovell, for the Comtee. of forgn. Affairs

RC (ViU: Lee Family Papers). Written and signed by Lovell.

[1] Congress had resolved "that Mr. A. Lee be informed of Mr. Jay's appointment, and that, agreeably to his request, he is at liberty to return to America." *JCC*, 15:1165–66. Lovell had made this motion because he feared that Lee would be embarrassed by being informed of his replacement through the newspapers, which had printed extracts of Congress' resolves appointing John Jay a minister to Spain. See Lovell to John Adams, October 5, note 1, and to William Whipple, October 5, 1779, note 1.

[2] Lee's May 31, 1779, letter offering to resign his commission is in PCC, item 83, 2:268–71; and Wharton, *Diplomatic Correspondence*, 3:196. See also James Lovell to Richard Henry Lee, this date, note 2.

Committee of Commerce to the Pennsylvania Council

Commercial Committee of Congress. Phila. 13 Oct. 1779.

The Commercial Committee being directed by Congress to ship off provisions for supplying his Most Christian Majesty's fleets & Troops in the West Indies, procured the Continental Packet boat Eagle, Capt. Ashmead, to be laden with two hundred bbls of salted Pork, and fifty bbls. of Bread, since which, the pressing demand for powder & woolens for the Army, has induced Congress to direct the sending said Vessell & Cargoe to St. Eustatius, where the above articles can be procured, provided the Honble Councils permission be obtained for clearing said Vessell at the Naval Office. Per Order-

Fra. Lewis

RC (PHi: Gratz Collection). Written and signed by Francis Lewis. Addressed: "To His Excellency the President in Council." Endorsed by Timothy Matlack: "Read in Council & granted Octob. 14th. 1779. TM Secy."

Committee of Congress to Jeremiah Wadsworth

Sir,   Philadelphia Octr 13th 1779

We wrote you in our last that 800 barrels of flour would be obtained from this State & forwarded directly. We are Sorry to inform you that on Examination only 47 barrels are on hand. The Compliment of 500 barrels will be furnished as fast as it comes in—& one hundred barrels in the hands of the Commercial Commtee. will be ordered on. This information we judged necessary to prevent a dissappointment. Have nothing new—respecting the Count, our expectations are very Sanguine. Your obedt. humble Servt.

Jesse Root Chairn. of
Commttee. on your Deptm.[1]

RC (CtHi: Wadsworth Papers). Written and signed by Root.

[1] That is, the committee for superintending the commissary and quartermaster departments. The committee's work at this time also involved procurement of wagons for the transportation of provisions collected for Wadsworth, and accordingly Root and fellow committeeman Daniel of St. Thomas Jenifer met with the Pennsylvania Council on both October 15 and 16 to discuss "the Pay of Waggons now to be called into the service of the United States." Wagon hire was regulated in Pennsylvania, and runaway inflation had made it impossible to procure wagons at the rates currently established. For the council's meetings with Root and Jenifer, and an October 15 letter to them on this subject from Joseph Reed, see *Pa. Council Minutes*, 12:131–32; and *Pa. Archives*, 1st ser. 7:750.

John Fell's Diary

Wednesday Octr 13 [1779].

Coml Committee. Congress. Dispatches, Letters & Memorials were Read, Also Reports from the Board of Treasury. Dr Weatherspoon moved for the Ultimatom in the Instructions to the Minister of Spain,[1] instead of insisting on the Free Navigation of the Missisipi to have a free Port only 6 ayes, 4 Noes, 1 devided.[2]

MS (DLC).

[1] See Gouverneur Morris' Draft Motion, this date.

[2] Fell undoubtedly reversed the vote on Witherspoon's motion which had, according to the journals, "passed in the negative," four yes, six no, and one divided.

Samuel Huntington to Jonathan Trumbull, Sr.

Sir   Philadelphia 13th Octor 1779

I do my Self the Honour to acquaint your Excellency that the papers you Transmitted to Col. Laurens are referd to a Committee appointed to Consider the subject matter of their Contents.[1]

Have also taken the Liberty to enclose an extract of a letter from Mr. Diricks lately receivd in Congress.[2]

It gives me pleasure to find your Excellencies Correspondence with Baron Van der Capellen is likely to prove of public utility.

I congratulate your Excellency on the Success of the western Army under Genl. Sullivan, & with pleasure add; we have this day received Intelligence from Fort Pitt that the Success of Col. Broadhead against the more western Tribes in destroying their Town & Settlements is allmost equal to that of Genl. Sullivan's & without loss on our part.

I am with Sentiments of Esteem & Regard, your Excys. humble Servt.   Samel. Huntington

RC (Ct: Trumbull Papers).

[1] See Henry Laurens to Trumbull, September 26, note 1, and October 19, 1779, note 1.

[2] Jacob Gerhard Diriks' July 10 report to Congress on prospects for a Dutch loan and on his delivery of letters from Trumbull and William Livingston to Baron van der

Capellen, which was referred to committee this day, is in PCC, item 78, 8:327–30. *JCC*, 15:1167

James Lovell to Richard Henry Lee

Dear Sir   [October 13, 1779][1]

I believe I made some mistake in putting up the Papers for you by last post, as I find a Letter of the Kind which I intended to have sent. Direction on the Cover—

His Excellency The President of Congress

Paris June 5th. 1779

I beg the favor of your Excellency, to lay my Respect before Congress; with a Repetition of my most earnest request to be recalled. I should most willingly continue to sacrifice as I have hitherto done, my private Interests to the public good. But I am satisfied that the dissentions raised concerning me, will be continued by a continuance of my Commission, and will be of more injury to the public than I can be of Service. And as the public good was the sole motive of my accepting the Commission, the same reason now induces me to desire most earnestly to resign it.

I have the honor to be, with the greatest respect, Your Excellencys most obedient humble Servant.

Tho' dated June 5th it is the exact Copy of May 31st. which was this day read in Congress and produced the inclosed Resolve.[2] I imagined such an Entry on the Journals would be a sort of decency beyond total silence and therefore moved it. The Letter was listened to with Gravity and some Remarks I made were approved & confirmed by each one who spoke and by no one more than Mercer who acknowledged that this Letter gave him *new* & pleasing Ideas of Mr Lee. I was sure yr. Brother would so Conduct if he found his *Ability* to serve these States to be *impaired* by the malignant Arts of his avowed Enemies strengthened by the unbecoming Tameness of those who ought to be the Patrons of his Honor on the meer ground of official Relation, to say nothing of his proved Capacity for acknowledged Integrity and his unwearied Zeal.

I did not mention to put into the Presidents Letter, as a copy *now* sent, one of the old Letters of March 1st[3] for had I been interogated as to its arrival I should not have been in the State that *honest* Davus wished to be in regard to the placing of the Infant, *ut liquido faciam* says he, if I am called upon to deny it. There would be a meaness in putting in *now* what I intend readily to own, when there is occasion, that I aided to Suppress.

I have by me a Letter from Capt. Fowler to a Friend of his here Col. Semple,[4] in which, upon Sight of Rowlands Peice of Augst. 10th,[5] he was induced to insert the strongest Testimony of the Stock jobbing Schemes of Wharton, Bancroft &c. wishing however to have his own name concealed. He writes from Ohio Sepr. 22

RC (ViU: Lee Family Papers). In Lovell's hand, though not signed.

[1] Although undated by Lovell, this letter can be dated by Lovell's statement below that Arthur Lee's May 31, 1779, letter was "this day read in Congress," which was October 13. *JCC*, 15:1165–66.

[2] See Committee for Foreign Affairs to Arthur Lee, this date.

[3] No March 1, 1779, letter from Arthur Lee has been found, but it also may have dealt with his resignation.

The suppression of Arthur's resignation, which Lovell had managed since mid-July (see Lovell to Samuel Adams, July 16, 1779, note 6), was also a subject of the following letter from Richard Henry to Arthur written on October 12, 1779.

"Your |enemies| have triumphed at last," he wrote in explanation of Congress' September 27 selection of John Jay as minister to Spain, " |wicked| persevering and under no kind of |restraint| they have fairly |worried| out the |friends| of |virtue| and their |country|. By various manoeuvers and after repeated and frustrated attempts to recall, one was fallen upon that succeeded and Jay of |Congress| is to go |plenipotentiary| to |Spain|. Mr John |Adams| is to |negotiate| the |peace| with G.B. when that comes on. I sent your |resignation| long since to philadelphia to be submitted, as to presentation, to Americas best friends, and it was determined to |withhold| it until it was seen how |Congress| would act in |Deane's| affair. In the mean time, the above manoeuvers took place—I believe it will not be presented. Your best friends are of the opinion that you should come immediately over and before |Congress| demand a full hearing and complete vindication—If it is |refused| the |public| will, on an |appeal| do right to the injured. In your Letter to Loudoun of May 28 Last, you deliver a sentiment that is perfectly just, that in a free country like ours their is no disgracing a man who is shielded by innocence and evidence—far less can a wicked faction do any such thing. Bad men may impose for a time, but cannot stand against the truth fairly displaied and properly enforced. Our |frigate|, [*Confederacy*], will carry |Gérard| (and perhaps |Deane|) home, by her |return| you and Ludwell may |return| here. These two men have been most intimate here, and tho constantly declaring for many months past that they must depart in a few days yet they never stirred until their |point| was |gained| and now I suppose, as a certain gentleman says, they are glutted (even to statiety with revenge) they will realy go. Wisdom and perseverance are excellent qualities, to secure success and to vanquish finally all wicked combination. If you can, I would advise you to land at Portsmouth in Newhampshire where I am assured you will be well received, at that place and at Boston you will have an opportunity of seeing General Whipple and Samuel Adams Esqurs. with other wise and virtuous friends of America, who loving their Country, esteem and honor its able and virtuous Citizens. You will thus have an opportunity of seeing a valuable part of this union which you have not yet been personally acquainted with. Mr. John Adams, since his arrival here and before he came has in his Letters (for he has not been at Congress) done great justice to your character. The above business was determined in Congress before the arrival of the Chavalier de la Luzerne. He has since arrived at Philadelphia. The Virginia Delegates in Congress are James Mercer! Wm. Fitzhugh of Chatham! Flemming! Cyrus Griffen! Mery Smith[!] I wish that Mr. Wm. Lee and Mr. Izard would come with you. Farewell,
|First Survivor Brother|.
"|Congress| neglected for very obvious reasons to publish your |Vindication|, but I expect to get it done immediately leaving out such parts as might be improper on account of |foreign powers|. An honorable Member of Congress says he doubts not but that your Country will yet do you honor. I think so too. A temperate, firm, and wise conduct is only necessary." Lee Papers, MH–H; and Burnett, *Letters*, 4:481–82. Words printed in braces were written by Lee in cipher, for which see these *Letters*, 9:654n.2.

[4] Alexander Fowler, auditor of the army in the western district, and William Semple.

[5] Richard Henry had written a number of essays defending Arthur Lee that were printed in the *Pennsylvania Packet* during August over the pseudonym "Rowland." See Lovell to Richard Henry Lee, August 17, 1779, note 3.

Gouverneur Morris' Draft Motion

[October 13, 1779][1]

That the Minister of these States to his Catholick Majesty be privately instructed to recede from the Claim of a free Navigation of the River Mississippi mentd. in his Instructions below the 31st Degree of North Latitude on Condition of the Grant of a free Port therein also Mentd. if the obtaining such Navigation shall be found an inseperable Bar to the proposed Treaties of Amity & Commerce between these States & his Catholic Majesty. Provided always that if the Power herein contained be confined to the said Minister & not in Case of his Death or Absence to be exercised by any other Person.[2]

MS (DLC: Force Collection). In the hand of Gouverneur Morris.

[1] This document, which agrees verbatim with the "motion . . . made by Mr Witherspoon, seconded by Mr Morris" and recorded in the secret journal for October 13, was the copy given to Secretary Thomson, as the vote of the delegates on this motion is recorded on the verso in Thomson's hand. The handwriting on the motion was misidentified by Worthington C. Ford as that of John Witherspoon in the published journal, which for this entry was reconstructed from Thomson's secret journal. See PCC, item 1, 23:36–38, item 5, 1:352–53; and *JCC*, 15:1168n.2.

[2] This motion reflects the concern of some delegates that Congress had pressed too far in demanding "free navigation of the river Mississippi into and from the sea" in its September 17 resolution on the negotiation of a Spanish treaty. The delegates, however, stood by the resolution as originally adopted by a vote of six to four. For the formulation of the instructions to the minister to Spain, see Henry Laurens' Notes on a Treaty, September 9–17, note 1; and Samuel Huntington to John Jay, October 16, 1779.

Nicholas Van Dyke to Thomas Bradford

Sir,[1]   13 Octo. 1779.

The inclosed Bill of Cost you'l perceive is made out by the Goaler of New Castle County, to whom the Prisoner's therein named were Committed, when taken from on Board the small French Schooner lately brought into Philada, being retaken by the Mate, she was bound from Baltimore on a Cruise to Caegin with Plank & Tarr. The Reason of the Prisoner's being landed here was, the Mate was fearful he was not safe in keeping them on Board, as he looked on himself alone except the Hands put on Board by the Privateer who took him—after which as soon as he procured Hands to assist him to go to Philada. he proceeded without calling for the Prisoners. You'l be pleased to allow what is usual in such Cases, & pay the same to

Mr. George Garland the Bearer whose Receipt will be sufficient for the same.

I am Sir, yr. Most obdt.   Nichs. Van Dyke

RC (PHi: Society Collection).
[1] Bradford, who published the *Pennsylvania Journal and Weekly Advertiser* in Philadelphia, had been appointed deputy commissary general of prisoners in January 1778. See *DAB*; and Washington, *Writings* (Fitzpatrick), 10:310.

Committee for Foreign Affairs to Benjamin Franklin

Sir   Octr. 14th. 1779, Philada.

By a letter of July 16th the Superscription of Letters to "Our great faithful beloved Friend & Ally" was submitted to your Judgement.[1] You ought however to be told Mr. Gerard has one to deliver directed in the same manner, the double of which you herewith receive, to be kept for him, to serve in case he may have been forced to sink his Papers. The Opportunity by him from this Port being so good I only now send a few of the latest Prints and Journals, large Packages being on board the Confederacy.

Your most humble Servant,
James Lovell
for the Comtee of forgn. Affrs.

RC (PHi: Franklin Papers). Written and signed by Lovell.
[1] See Committee for Foreign Affairs to Franklin, July 16, 1779, notes 3 and 4.

John Fell's Diary

Thursday 14th Octr [1779]

Coml Committee. Congress. Long debates about the title to be given the President of Congress whether Excellency or Honor[1] and the filling up the Secretary Commission. Dr Wetherspoon not in Congress, State not Represented.[2]

P. M. Marine Committee.

MS (DLC).
[1] Although the journals contain no mention of these "long debates," the president of Congress continued to be addressed "Excellency."
[2] Fell's observation indicates that William Churchill Houston and Nathaniel Scudder were also absent at this time, as New Jersey required the presence of "any two" delegates for a quorum. Scudder had last voted on September 17, Houston on October 6. *JCC*, 15:1074, 1148.

Samuel Holten's Diary

[October 14–15, 1779]

14. Thursday. Congress agreed to recommend to the states the 2d Thursday of Decr. next, for a day of thanksgiving.

15. Friday. I wrote to the Council of Massa Bay.[1] I attendd. the tryal of the Spanish vessels.[2]

MS (MDaAr).

[1] See Holten to the Massachusetts Council, October 15, 1779.

[2] Holten is undoubtedly referring to the appeals in the cases of the Spanish ships *Valenciano* and *Holy Martyrs* from the Massachusetts Admiralty Court to Congress, which had been referred to the Committee on Appeals on October 9. For further information on these cases, see John Jay to Conrad Alexandre Gérard, April 25 and May 24; and Committee on Appeals Decree, November 1 and 6, 1779.

Samuel Huntington to John Sullivan

Sir   Philada October 14th 1779

Your letter of the 2d &   instant to the President of Congress have been duly received.[1]

I have the Pleasure to communicate an Act of Congress of this day herewith enclos'd, expressing their thanks to yourself & the other brave Officers & Soldiers under your Command for effectually executing the important expediton against such of the indian Nations as encouraged by the Councils & conducted by the Officers of his Brittanic Majesty had perfidiously waged an unprovoked & cruel war against these United States.

I am Sir with Esteem & regard, yours &c.   S.H. President

LB (DNA: PCC, item 14).

[1] The letter whose date Huntington left blank was undoubtedly Sullivan's long September 28 letter to Washington written from the frontier post Chemung, "giving an account of his successful expedition against the hostile Indians," which Washington had enclosed in his letter to Congress of October 9, received this day. It was this letter that inspired the resolution Huntington enclosed to Sullivan expressing Congress' thanks for his recent expedition against the Indians. See *JCC*, 15:1169–70; and PCC, item 152, 8:81–102. For Sullivan's letter of October 2, see Huntington to Philip Schuyler, October 12, 1779, note.

It should be noted, however, that Sullivan had also written directly to Congress on September 30, and that that letter had been received on October 5. See *JCC*, 15:1146; PCC, item 160, fols. 302–17; and Sullivan, *Letters* (Hammond), 3:123–37.

Samuel Huntington to George Washington

Sir,   Philadelphia Octor 14th. 1779

I am honoured with your Excellency's favours of the 7th & 9th Instant with their Several enclosures.[1]

By the Act of Congress of this day herewith enclosd you will receive their Thanks for directing the important Expedition which hath been so Effectually executed by General Sullivan & the Brave Officers & Soldiers under his Command.

Be assured Sir it is with pleasure I have the honour of Communicating to your Excellency the continued approbation & Thanks of Congress on account of your eminent & unremitting Services in the Cause of your Country, And that I am with the highest Sentiments of Esteem and regard your humble Servt,

Saml. Huntington President

RC (DLC: Washington Papers).

[1] For Washington's October 9 letter to Congress, enclosing several documents concerning John Sullivan's expedition against the Indians, see *JCC*, 15:1169; PCC, item 152, 8:81–116; and Washington, *Writings* (Fitzpatrick), 16:440–41. But no letter of the seventh from Washington to Congress or to Huntington has been found. He did write a brief October 7 letter to the Marine Committee (a draft of which is in the Washington Papers, DLC), introducing a pilot "intimately acquainted with the passage of Hell Gate," who might be of use to the comte d'Estaing, and Huntington may have passed this on the to committee, although no mention of it is found in the journals.

John Jay to James Duane

Dear Sir   Pha. 14 Octr 1779

Your obliging Favor by Mr. Phelps has remained thus long unanswered because till very lately I promised myself the Pleasure of seeing you, but that has now become very improbable as we expect to sail in a few Days.

Your Reelection and Consent to Return to Congress are Circumstances which I consider as fortunate ⟨in the present Situation of our State⟩. Your intimate acquaintance with our Controversies respecting Jurisdiction will not only enable you but your Colleagues to render the State very important Services. I hope the Train in which I shall leave these Matters meets with your Approbation, and I assure you it will give me very sensible Pleasure to hear of their being drawn to a Conclusion satisfactory to New York. The sooner you take your Seat, in my opinion the better various Considerations, which will readily occur to you point out the Propriety of this Measure. The State will be unrepresented after Tomorrow. Mr. Scot I am told will soon be here. I hope you will bring Floyd & L Homedieu with you. Morris it seems is not in the Delegation & I regret it. He would have been useful and particularly in the Vermont Business with Respect to which you are so circumstanced,[1] as to be less serviceable on the Floor than on other occasions.

If there be any Services in my Power to render you abroad, be pleased to command them. A Line for you will accompany all my public Letters, and you will oblige me by a constant Correspondence.

With the best wishes for your Health & Happiness, I am Dear Sir, your most obt Servt.

[*P. S.*] My Respects to Mrs. Duane & all the Family.[2]

FC (NNC: Jay Papers). In the hand of John Jay.

[1] Jay may have been referring to Duane's substantial landholdings in Vermont, which like other New York claims in that region, were jeopardized by Vermont's assertion of independence. See Edward P. Alexander, *A Revolutionary Conservative: James Duane of New York* (New York: Columbia University Press, 1938), pp. 120–21.

[2] Jay also wrote a brief letter this day to George Washington, acknowledging Washington's letter of October 7 and paying his respects before going abroad. Jay Papers, NNC.

James Lovell to John Adams

Dear Sir   Octr. 14 –79

I inclose to you a Peice of Intelligence perhaps altogether new. The uti possidetis offered by Spain will appear alarming perhaps to some but we are told She acted upon full Knowledge that King George the 3d of England had *sworn* in his Cabinet that he would not acknowledge our Independence. Spain at least knew that we would never enter into any commercial Treaty without a total relinquishment of the 13 States by Britain. I am glad her offer was rejected. I own I do not like such Experiments.

I do not see how you and the others lately elected to Missions from hence will get immediate Supply but by the Way of Doctr. F——[1] to whom a Promise will be made of speedy Repayment and also of the Establishment of Funds directly for the Purpose of supporting all Embassies from the United States. I will give you an Account of the Decision upon a Report to be made Tomorrow morning.[2]

Yrs. affectionately   J.L.

RC (MHi: Adams Papers).

[1] On October 15 Congress resolved to instruct Benjamin Franklin "to take the most effectual means for supplying the Ministers appointed to treat with his Catholic Majesty and with his Britannic Majesty and their Secretaries with two thousand Louis d'ores to be distributed in proportion to their respective salaries, and giving the strongest assurances . . . that Congress will immediately take measures for replacing the said sum, as well as for establishing a fund in Europe for the future support of all the Embassies from these States." *JCC*, 15:1179–80.

[2] See Lovell to Adams, October 19, 1779.

James Lovell to Arthur Lee

Dear Sir   *private*   Oct 14th. 1779

Mr. Bonfield on the 30th of June & 22d of July wrote to us[1] and forwarded many Letters from you one only of which was new.[2] A Letter of May 31 which was read in Congress Oct 13th and produced an Entry somewhat paliative in regard to the Doings of Sept. 27.[3] I know not whether you was in France at the Time Mr. Bonfield wrote. I had been hoping that you would finish yr. Commission in Spain before Mr. Jay's Voyage could be compleated. The late Conduct of the Court of Madrid seemed to give a fair opening for it. I lament the Length of Time between the Dates & Receipt of yr. Letters. I was sure that if you found your Ability to serve us to be in fact impaired by the malignant Proceeding of Deane & the unbecoming Tameness of those who ought to have shewn themselves the Patrons & Guardians of yr. Honor, you would tell us so, and make way for a Successor. Your Letter of May 31st was listened to with gravity, and commented upon with Approbation as well by former Cons as by constant Pros. Mercer owned he conceived *new* Ideas of you, and he looked Repentance. He has a curious Correspondent, a Brother[4] of the same name in France who is very ready wth his Opinions on Our Affairs there. I would have you know his real Business. It has been hinted to me that he is in Pay as a Spy upon our Agents at Court.[5]

I cannot but hope to find you very speedily in America & think it highly interesting to yr. Suit that you should be on the Spot.

The Circumstance of yr having only 3 Months allowed after yr. Recall may prevent you from waiting the Arrival of the Confederacy with Mr. Gerard &c. I have therefore covered to Mr. Bondfield & Mr. Schweighauser what is for you of Importance by that Opportunity which is expected to sail in a very few Days. I really cannot send Copies of the many Sheets put up to go by her.

Doctr. Shippens Family are in Health. Your Friends in Virginia were so Sepr. 25th.

Your affectionate humble Servant,   J. L.

RC (MH–H: Lee Papers).

[1] John Bondfield's June 30 and July 22 letters were read in Congress on October 11, 1779. See *JCC*, 15:1161; and PCC, item 92, fols. 429–35.

[2] According to the journals, letters from Lee of April 22 and 26, May 21, and June 21 to the Committee for Foreign Affairs were also read in Congress on October 11. PCC, item 83, 2:172–75, 224–27, 260–67, 272–75; and Wharton, *Diplomatic Correspondence*, 3:131, 138, 171–74, 229. Lee's June 21 letter was actually directed to President Jay rather than to the committee.

[3] See Committee for Foreign Affairs to Arthur Lee, October 13, 1779, note.

[4] That is, George Mercer, brother of James and former Stamp Act distributor in Virginia. Louis W. Potts, *Arthur Lee: A Virtuous Revolutionary* (Baton Rouge: Louisiana State University Press, 1981), pp. 40–41, 81.

[5] Lovell also sent a second copy of this letter to Arthur, which is marked "Duplicate AL" on the cover. The first two paragraphs, which he significantly revised when copying it, contain additional information and read as follows.

"By Letters from Mr. Bonfield of the 30th of June and 22d of July I do not discover that you were gone to Spain as has been reported, nor do I know by them that you were yet in France. A Copy of yr. Letter to the Presidt. of Congress to which the inclosed Resolve refers, has come to hand dated June 5th from Paris. I had been hoping that the late Turn in the affairs of Spain would have been embraced by you so far as that you would gain an Acknowledgement of us openly if not conclude a Treaty, before Mr. Jay could perform his Voyage.

"Many Things have concurred to give force to the Schemes of yr. inveterate Foe. But I lament most of all the Length of Time between the Dates and Receipt of yr. Letters. The principle on which you asked to be recalled May 31st governed the Votes of some good men in the Business of appointing a *Minister Plenipotentiary* in Lieu of a Commissioner, and in their consequent Ballot, while others went on *fas aut nefas.* Some of the Delegates of Virginia have conceived as they say *new* Ideas of you from yr. Letter, particularly Mr. Mercer who has a curious Correspondent *near* our *Plenipo* at Paris. I Pray you to get and bring with you accurate accounts of the *real* Business of that Correspondent at this Time in France. He is Brother of the Delegate of the Same Name. I am told he is a Spy on our affairs." bMS Am 811.5, MH–H.

John Armstrong, Sr., to George Washington

Dear General　　　　　　　　　　　　　Philada. 15th Octobr. 1779.

The Counts expected approach to these Shores begins to be thought tedious, but the lodgment of the Enemy to the South being in two places considerably distant from each other, I'm persuaded no time has yet elapsed wherein we cou'd reasonably look for an Official account of that event. A letter from Hampdon of the 9th Inst. asserts the certainty of a compleat Capture of Provosts [Prevost's] Army & various Vessels &c. which however doubted by many I'm inclined to think favourably of as our late Southerly winds might give a quick passage to that intelligence.

You know Sir that the present moment however premature will create military Speculation—Some that a great Post or two will fall, Others that it's impossible otherwise than by Starving, or at least that the Sacrifice must be too great—Again—the attack must be general and uniform by Land & Water &c &c. I dare not with so imperfect knowledge of the situation &c. form an Idea of either a general or particular Rule in a great effort, but pray god to form & determine for you, but confess the Idea of piece-male work Strikes me as naturally as any other, that is the Operation of the Fleet upon that of the Enemies—first removing out of the way Such batteries as may be practicable & by which the inbound passage of the Shiping may be much Obstructed. So much for guess work. A Sufficient Supply of Provisions and ammunition are important points, the former very clearly and Seasonably pointed out by your Excellency which from the distance and Small Stock on hand requires faithfull attention. I am much pleased that Governor Ried will command his Own Militia.[1]

It has not been in my power with any degree of facility, yet to get on the farther *Subsistance* for the General Officers of the Army, but a good foundation is laid for it, and a Short time will bring it on I hope to their Satisfaction without the necessity of a memorial.[2] A farther provision for the Surgeons of the Hospital, has been already committed and will probably soon be reported. Mr. Gerard & Mr. Jay sets out in two or three days—preparations for foreign Courts & the revision of Some points formerly determined, has of late much engrossed the attention of Congress, in which I cannot but apprehend that rather hard measure has fallen to the Lot of Dr Lee. The Late appointment of Mr. John Adams may Serve as a Spunge to wipe of the Stain of culpable neglect—a tryal this Sufficient in my Opinion to all that gentlemans gravity and plain brown hair.

22. Permit me to recommend to the honor of yr. Excellencies acquaintance my good hibernian friend Doctor Shiell, and thro' your farther polite offices to the General Officers of the Pennsylvania Line, to whom at present I cannot write. The Doctor is a Young Gentleman of liberal Sentiments & education possessed of a handsome fortune, a warm Whigg & a man of Sense. I am now leaving Congress having exerted the last dregs of any remaining talent I had under various impediments.[3] Finance, (for which I never had any talent) is the only present ghost that Stares every honest man in the face. Taxation, altho' the radical means of appreciation as well as of the payment of publick debt, is a remedy too remote for our Support. The disease has ran too long to be overtaken by any common cure. A general regulation of prices by Law is said to be impracticable. I have therefore wished to throw out some higher inducement to money holders on lone than any yet offered rather than the Ship Shou'd get aground, but a large majority thought the present offers sufficient to procure all we shou'd want untill supplyed by Tax. The expectation is futile & without political foundation. I presume however that some new push will be made for a foreign Loan. Retrenchment of expences is in it's place highly necessary & Sooner or later a great Share of the burthen of such a plan is likely to fall upon you, which rather ought to be done by others. I shall take the liberty of amusing you a moment in reading the inclosed,[4] only because it is the clearest account of the occasions of the late misfortune at Penobscot that has yet reached this place, and as likely to be true. Major Armstrong on that occasion has been indulging young ambition in following that Army, I suppose with Jacksons Regimt. and probably without the approbation of Genl. Gates, until the wiser winds corrected the error.

I am with perfect respect & every wish for your Safety & Success— Your Excellency's Most Obedient humbl. Servt.

John Armstrong

[*P.S.*] I had the pleasure of your Obligeing letter, and perfectly Satisfied with you Say on the Subject in Berkley.[5]

RC (DLC: Washington Papers).

[1] In response to Washington's call in August for turning out the militia, in anticipation of d'Estaing's arrival and joint Franco-American operations in the middle states, Pres. Joseph Reed had turned over the chair of the Pennsylvania Council to Vice-President William Moore and assumed personal command of the state's militia then rendezvousing at Trenton, N.J.

[2] Congress had received numerous complaints from Continental officers concerning erosion of their finances by the devastating depreciation of the Continental dollar, and on August 18 had increased monthly subsistence rates for most of the Continental Army. See John Jay to Washington, August 20, 1779, note 1. Because no adjustment had been made for generals and some staff officers, however, a committee was appointed on October 19 "to take into consideration what allowance ought to be made to the officers . . . to whom the provision . . . of the 18th of August last doth not extend," and almost as Armstrong was writing this letter to Washington a petition for the relief of general officers was in preparation. This document was eventually signed by 27 Continental generals and was referred on November 18 to the same committee, then consisting of Gouverneur Morris, Jesse Root, and Philip Schuyler (who had replaced Samuel J. Atlee, resigned). See *JCC*, 15:1188, 1274, 1286; PCC, item 21, fols. 217–18; and Philip Schuyler to Washington, November 18, 1779, note 3.

[3] Armstrong left Philadelphia at about this time for his home in Carlisle and did not return to his seat in Congress until the following May. His accounts with the state of Pennsylvania, dated October 4 and 14, 1779, indicate that he claimed compensation for service in Congress during 1779 from February 18 through October 20, including travel time to and from Philadelphia. Gratz Collection, PHi.

During the next several months, Armstrong continued to write of congressional affairs to Washington and other correspondents, and extracts from six of these letters were printed by Edmund C. Burnett in his edition of delegate correspondence. The first of these, printed here in its entirety, is dated "Carlisle 30th October. 1779," and is addressed to Gen. William Irvine, an old friend and Carlisle resident.

"Dear General, A Cold joined to a late hour disenables me to say more at present than that I reached home about a Week ago—And found Mrs. Irvine & Children, with my own Family also in usual health—and that I beg you will favour me with a line on the prospects of an investiture of New York, which by the way I consider through the unexpected Stay of the Count & many other circumstances, as abortive for this Season.

"Before this time I hope farther provision is made for the Subsistance of the General Officers of the Army, which at leaving Congress I impressed on the minds of Some members who promised Suddenly to have it on the Carpit, and to which I think there wou'd be no Oppossion. If any uneasiness shou'd arise to you, my advice Still is that you write either to Congress directing to the President, or to the Board of War—mentioning only the facts & your confidence that justice will be done you. My Compliments to Coll Hay. I am dear General Sincerely Yours, John Armstrong.

"Wheat £15 per Bushel—Indian Corn 9 pounds &c.

"I suppose Doctor Shiell, lately from Dublin will Visit the Camp, give me leave to recommend him to your particular notice. He is a Gentleman—A Genuine Whigg & a Man of very good Sense & breeding." Irvine Papers, PHi.

Abstracts of other "nondelegate" letters from Armstrong during this interval at home will be printed below under the dates December 15, 1779, January 12 and 24, February 16, and March 15, 1780.

Another such letter, to Joseph Reed, dated November 27, 1779, in which Armstrong, hoping to retire, expressed disappointment that he had not been left off the new slate of delegates to Congress selected by the Pennsylvania Assembly on November 12, is in *Pa. Archives*, 1st ser. 8:31–32.

[4] A copy of an August 30 letter from his son, Maj. John Armstrong, Jr., an aide to Gen. Horatio Gates. Young Armstrong had accompanied the Massachusetts expedition to Penobscot, but contrary winds had prevented his ship from reaching its destination until after the expedition had been dispersed by the British, affording him an

opportunity to query the retreating American forces and assessing the causes of their failure.

[5] For the meaning of this allusion to Armstrong's interest in acquiring a tract of land in Berkeley County, Va., see Armstrong to Washington, June 29, 1779, note.

John Fell's Diary

Friday 15th Octor. [1779]

Coml Committee. Congress. Mr Jay requested leave for Lt Coll Livingston to goe with him to Spain, a furloe was granted for 12 Months.[1]

Marine Committee.

MS (DLC).

[1] See Jay to Samuel Huntington, this date.

Samuel Holten to the Massachusetts Council

Sir.   Philadelphia Octr. 15th. 1779.

The inclosed address, from the Legislative-Council & General Assembly of the State of New-Jersey, came to hand a few days since;[1] which I do myself the honor to transmit; the representation made to Congress therein mentioned, respecting the Utility (&c) of the measure is now under consideration of a Committee of twelve, being a member from each State.

The late application from the honble. Board to Congress, respecting the Penobscot affair, is referred to a committee.

Yesterday Congress agreed to recommend to the several states to set apart the 2d Thursday in Decr. next, for a day of public thanksgiving throughout the united states.[2]

Congress have received no intelligence (to be depended upon) from the Southern Army, or the Count De Estaign, since my last, but are daily expecting news of importance from that quarter.

I have the Honor to be with the greatest respect, Sir, your most obedient servant,   S. Holten

RC (M–Ar: Revolutionary War Letters). Addressed: "The Honorable, The President of the Council of Massa. Bay."

[1] See John Fell's Diary, October 11, 1779.

[2] See Samuel Huntington to the States, October 20, 1779.

John Jay to Samuel Huntington

Sir   Philadelphia 15 Octr. 1779
    Governor Livingston having consented that his Son whom Congress have honored with the Commission of Lt. Colonel, should go with me to Spain, I join with him in requesting the Favor of Congress to grant him their Permission.[1]
    I have the Honor to be with great Respect & Esteem, Your Excellencys most obedt Servt.   John Jay[2]

RC (DNA: PCC, item 78).
    [1] Congress immediately complied with Jay's request, granting his brother-in-law Henry Brockholst Livingston a twelve-month leave of absence from the Continental Army to continue his employment as Jay's secretary. *JCC*, 15:1173. President Huntington's October 15 letter to Livingston enclosing this resolve is in PCC, item 14, fol. 208.
    [2] This is the last Jay letter printed in this edition of delegate correspondence. For two letters touching on congressional affairs, which he wrote on board the *Confederacy* just before weighing anchor for his voyage to Spain, see his letters of October 25 to George Clinton and to Robert R. Livingston in Jay, *Papers* (Morris), pp. 659–66. To Governor Clinton, he recommended that New York more vigorously press its claims to Indian lands, and to Livingston he sent a cipher, which is discussed at length by the editors of Jay's papers, to facilitate their correspondence while he was abroad.

John Fell's Diary

                                    Saturday. October 16th [1779].
    Coml Committee. Congress. After the dispatches &c were read, Congress went in to a Committee of the whole on a Report for obtaining a Loan for 5 Million of Dollars and having the same sold in Bills of Exchange or laid out in the Purchase of Goods to be disposed of by order of Congress, with a long train of Commissioners &c.[1] After debate adjournd.

MS (DLC).
    [1] The ways and means committee's October 15 report, which recommended that "a credit" be obtained "at the Courts of Versailles and Madrid" for the purchase of $5 million of merchandise for resale in the United States by commissioners appointed by Congress, was rejected by the committee of the whole on October 19. See *JCC*, 15:1174–77, 1181, 1186–87; and Fell's Diary, October 18 and 19, 1779.

Samuel Holten's Diary

                                                    Octr. 16. 1779
    Saturday. We have a report that the enemy in Georgia are all made prisoners.

MS (MDaAr).

Samuel Huntington to John Adams

Sir,   [October 16, 1779]
You will herewith receive a commission giving you full power to negotiate a treaty of peace with Great Britain,[1] in doing which you will conform to the following information & instructions.[2]

First. The United states are sincerely desirous of peace and wish by every means consistent with their dignity and safety to spare the further effusion of blood. They have therefore by your commission and these instructions laboured to remove the obstacles to that event before the enemy have evidenced their disposition for it. But as the great object of the present defensive war on the part of the allies is to establish the independence of the united states, and as any treaty, whereby this end cannot be obtained, must be only ostensible and illusory, you are therefore to make it a preliminary article to any negotiation, That Great Britain shall agree to treat with the united states as Sovereign, free and independent.

Secondly. You Shall take especial care also, that the independence of the said States be effectually assured and confirmed by the treaty or treaties of peace, according to the form and effect of the treaty of alliance with his most Christian Majesty; & you shall not agree to such treaty or treaties, unless the same be thereby so assured and confirmed.

Thirdly. The boundaries of these states are as follows viz, These States are bounded, North, by a line to be drawn from the North-west angle of Nova Scotia along the highlands, which divide those rivers which empty themselves into the river St. Lawrence from those which fall into the Atlantic Ocean, to the northwestermost head of Connecticut river, thence down along the middle of that river to the forty fifth degree of North latitude, thence due west in the latitude forty five degrees north from the equator to the Northwestermost side of the river St. Lawrence or Cadaraqui, thence straight to the south end of lake Nipissing, and thence straight to the source of the river Mississippi; *West,* by a line to be drawn along the middle of the river Mississippi from its source to where the said line shall intersect the thirty first degree of North latitude: *South,* by a line to be drawn due east from the termination of the line last mentioned in the latitude of thirty one degrees north from the equator to the middle of the river Appalachicola or Catahouchi, thence along the middle thereof to its junction with the Flint river, thence straight to the head of St Mary's river and thence down along the middle of St. Mary's river to the Atlantic Ocean: and *East,* by a line to be drawn along the middle of St. John's river from its source to its mouth in the bay of Fundy; comprehending all islands within twenty leagues of any part of the shores of the United states and lying between lines to be drawn due east from the points where the aforesaid boundaries between Nova Scotia on the one part and East Florida on the other part shall respectively touch the bay of Fundy and Atlantic Ocean. You are therefore strongly to contend that the whole of the said countries and islands lying within the boundaries aforesaid and every citadel, fort, post, place, harbour and road to them belonging be absolutely evacuated by the land and sea forces of his Britannic Majesty and yielded to the powers of the states to which they respectively belong, in such situation as they may be, at the termination of the war. But notwithstanding the clear right of these states and the importance of the object, yet they are so much influenced by the dictates of religion and humanity and so desirous of complying with the earnest requests of their allies, that if the line to be drawn from the *mouth* of the lake Nipissing to the head of the Mississippi cannot be obtained without continuing the war for that purpose, you are hereby empowered to agree to some other line between that point and the river Mississippi, provided the same shall in no part thereof be to the southward of latitude forty five degrees north: And in like manner, if the eastern boundary above described cannot be obtained, you are hereby empowered to agree, that the same shall be afterwards adjusted by commissioners to be duly appointed for that purpose according to such line as shall be by them settled and agreed on as the boundary between that part of the State of Massachusetts bay formerly called the province of Maine and the colony of Nova Scotia agreeably to their respective rights: And you may also consent that the enemy shall destroy such fortifications as they may have erected.

Fourthly. Although it is of the utmost importance to the peace and commerce of the united states, that Canada and Nova Scotia should be ceded and more particularly that their equal common right to the fisheries should be guarantied to them, yet a desire of terminating the war hath induced us not to make the acquisition of these objects an ultimatum on the present occasion.

Fifthly. You are empowered to agree to a cessation of hostilities during the negotiation, provided our ally shall consent to the same, and provided it shall be stipulated that all the forces of the enemy shall be immediately withdrawn from the United States.

Sixthly. In all other matters not abovementioned you are to govern yourself by the alliance between his most Christian Majesty and these states; by the advice of our allies; by your knowledge of our interests, and by your own discretion, in which we repose the fullest confidence.

Done at Philadelphia this sixteenth day of October in the year of our Lord one thousand seven hundred and seventy nine and in the fourth year of our Independence. By the Congress of the united states of America,   Saml. Huntington President
Attest, Chas Thomson secy.

RC (MHi: Adams Papers). Written and attested by Charles Thomson, and signed by Huntington. Addressed: "The honble John Adams esq minister plenipotentiary appointed to negotiate a treaty of peace."

[1] Adams had been named "minister plenipotentiary for negotiating a treaty of peace and a treaty of commerce with Great Britain" on September 27. *JCC*, 15:1113. For his commissions and the related documents that were transmitted to him a few days later, see Huntington to Adams, October 20, 1779.

[2] For the origin of these instructions, which were drafted before August 14 by Gouverneur Morris as chairman of a committee appointed to formulate a response to Spain's offer to mediate a peace with Britain, see *JCC*, 14:955–60; and PCC, item 25, 1:147–49. See also the following entry.

Samuel Huntington to John Adams

Sir,   [October 16, 1779]

You will herewith receive a commission giving you full power to negotiate a treaty of Commerce with Great Britain,[1] in doing which you will consider yourself bound by the following information and instructions.[2]

First. You will govern yourself principally by the treaty of Commerce with his most Christian Majesty; and as on the one hand, you shall grant no privilege to Great Britain not granted by that treaty to France, so on the other, you shall not consent to any peculiar restrictions or limitations whatever in favour of Great Britain.

Secondly. In Order that you may be the better able to act with propriety on this occasion, it is necessary for you to know that we have determined. 1st. That the common right of fishing shall in no case be given up. 2. That it is essential to the welfare of all these United States, that the inhabitants thereof, at the expiration of the war should continue to enjoy the free and undisturbed exercise of their common right to fish on the bank of Newfoundland and the other fishing banks and seas of North America preserving inviolate the treaties between France and the said States. 3. That application shall be made to his most Christian Majesty to agree to some article or articles for the better securing to these States a share in the said fisheries. 4. That if after a treaty of peace with Great Britain, she shall molest the citizens or inhabitants of any of the united States in taking fish on the banks and places herein after described, such molestation, being in our Opinion a direct violation and breach of the peace, shall be a common cause of the said states and the force of the union be exerted to obtain redress for the parties injured. And 5. That our faith be pledged to the several states, that without their unanimous consent no treaty of commerce shall be entered into, nor any trade or commerce whatever carried on with Great Britain without the explicit stipulation herein after mentioned. You are therefore not to consent to any treaty of commerce with Great Britain without an explicit stipulation on her part not to molest or disturb the inhabitants of the united states of America in taking fish on the banks of Newfoundland and other fisheries in the American seas anywhere, excepting within the distance of three leagues of the shores of the territories remaining to Great Britain at the close of the war, if a nearer distance cannot be obtained by negotiation: And in the negotiation you are to exert your most strenuous endeavours to obtain a nearer distance in the gulf of St Lawrence and particularly along the shores of Nova Scotia, as to which latter, we are desirous that even the shores may be occasionally used for the purpose of carrying on the fisheries by the inhabitants of these states.

Thirdly. In all other matters you are to govern yourself by your own discretion as shall be most for the interest of these States, taking care that the said treaty be founded on principles of equality and reciprocity so as to conduce to the mutual advantage of both nations, but not to the exclusion of others.

Done at Philadelphia this sixteenth day of Octr. in the year of our Lord one thousand seven hundred and seventy nine and in the fourth year of our Independence. By the Congress of the united states of America,   Saml. Huntington President
Attest, Chas Thomson secy.

RC (MHi: Adams Papers). Written and attested by Charles Thomson, and signed by Huntington. Addressed: "The honble John Adams esqr minister plenipotentiary appointed to negotiate a treaty of Commerce with Great Britain."

¹ Adams had been named "minister plenipotentiary for negotiating a treaty of peace and a treaty of commerce with Great Britain" on September 27. *JCC,* 15:1113. For his commissions and the related documents that were transmitted to him a few days later, see Huntington to Adams, October 20, 1779.

² For the origin of these instructions, which were drafted by Gouverneur Morris as chairman of a committee appointed to formulate a response to Spain's offer to mediate a peace with Britain, see *JCC,* 14:955–56, 960–62; and PCC, item 25, 1:149–51. See also the preceding entry.

Samuel Huntington to Benjamin Franklin

Sir,   Philadelphia Octr. 16. 1779.¹

Congress have appointed the honble. John Jay esq minister plenipotentiary for negotiating a treaty of amity and commerce and of alliance between his Catholic Majesty and the united states of America. And the honble. John Adams esqr. Minister plenipotentiary for negotiating a treaty of peace and a treaty of commerce with Great Britain.

The honble. William Carmichael esqr. is appointed secretary to the first and the honble Francis Dana esqr secretary to the last mentioned embassy.

Mr Jay and Mr Carmichael will embark on board the Confederacy, continental ship of war now in the Delaware ready to sail for France. Mr Adams and Mr Dana will probably take their passage on board Le Sensible, one of his most Christian Majesty's frigates in the harbour of Boston.

The salaries annexed to these appointments respectively are two thousand five hundred pounds Sterling per annum to the ministers and one thousand pounds sterling to the secretaries. As in order to enable th[ese] gentlemen to enter without embarrassment upon the duties of their several functions, I am authorized by an Act of Congress of the 15 instant, a certified copy of which will accompany this, to request you Sir, to take the most effectual means for supplying them with two thousand Louis d'ors in distributions proportioned to their respective salaries and to assure you on the faith of Congress that speedy and proper measures will be adopted both for repaying that sum and for establishing a fund for the future support of all the embassies of these united states in Europe.[2]

You will likewise find enclosed a certified copy of an act of Congress of the 4th instant,[3] by which you will be informed that your Salary is also to be two thousand five hundred pounds sterling per annum, and that John Laurens esqr. a member of the house of representatives for the state of South Carolina and lieut col. in the army of the United states is appointed by Congress to be secretary to the minister plenipotentiary at the court of France.[4]

I have the honour to be, Sr., Your obedient humble Servt,

Saml Huntington President

RC (DLC: Franklin Papers). In the hand of Charles Thomson and signed by Huntington.

[1] For the preparation of this letter, which was drafted by Henry Laurens as chairman of a committee originally appointed on October 13 to prepare instructions for John Jay, minister plenipotentiary for negotiating with Spain, see PCC, item 25, 1:163–66; and *JCC*, 15:1167–68, 1178–83.

[2] See *JCC*, 15:1179–83.

[3] *JCC*, 15:1143–46. The extract from the journals of this resolve which Charles Thomson actually enclosed for Franklin was misdated October 5, 1779. Franklin Papers, DLC.

[4] See Huntington to John Laurens, October 2, 1779.

Samuel Huntington to John Jay

Sir,   [October 16, 1779][1]

By the treaties subsisting between his most Christian Majesty and the united states of America, a power is reserved to his Catholic Majesty to accede to the said treaties & to participate in their stipulations at such time as he shall judge proper, it being well understood nevertheless, that if any of the stipulations of the said treaties are not agreeable to the king of Spain, his Catholic Majesty may propose other conditions analogous to the principal aim of the alliance and conformable to the rules of equality, reciprocity and friendship. Congress is sensible of the friendly regard to these states manifested by his Most Christian Majesty in reserving a power to his Catholic

Majesty of acceding to the alliance entered into between his Most Christian Majesty and these united states; And therefore that nothing may be wanting on their part to facilitate the views of his Most Christian Majesty and to obtain a treaty of alliance and of amity and commerce with his catholic Majesty, have thought proper to anticipate any propositions which his Catholic Majesty might make on that subject by yielding up to him those objects which they conclude he may have principally in view, and for that purpose have come to the following resolution,

"That if his Catholic Majesty shall accede to the said treaties and in concurrence with France and the united states of America continue the present war with Great Britain for the purpose expressed in the treaties aforesaid, he shall not thereby be precluded from securing to himself the Floridas; on the contrary if he shall obtain the Floridas from great Britain, these united states will guaranty the same to his catholic Majesty; provided always that the united states shall enjoy the free navigation of the river Mississippi into and from the sea."

You are therefore to communicate to his most Christian Majesty the desire of Congress to enter into a treaty of alliance and of Amity and commerce with his Catholic Majesty and to request his favourable interposition for that purpose; At the same time you are to make such proposals to his Catholic Majesty as in your judgment, from circumstances will be proper for obtaining for the united states of America equal advantages with those, which are secured to them by the treaties with his most Christian Majesty, observing always the resolution aforesaid as the ultimatum of these united states. You are particularly to endeavour to obtain some convenient port or ports below the 31st degree of north latitude on the river Mississippi free for all merchant vessels, goods, wares and merchandizes belonging to the inhabitants of these states.

The distressed state of our finances & the great depreciation of our paper money incline Congress to hope that his Catholic Majesty, if he shall conclude a treaty with these states, will be induced to lend them money; You are therefore to represent to him the great distress of these states on that account, and to solicit a loan of five million of dollars upon the best terms in your power not exceeding six per centum per annum, effectually to enable them to co-operate with the allies against the common enemy. But before you make any propositions to his Catholic Majesty for a loan, you are to endeavour to obtain a subsidy in consideration of the guaranty aforesaid.

You are to use your utmost endeavours for obtaining permission for the citizens and inhabitants of these States to lade and take on board their vessels Salt at the island of Salt Tortuga; and also to cut, load and bring away Logwood and Mohogony in and from the bay of Hondurus and its rivers and to build on the shores storehouses and Magazines for the woodcutters and their families in the extent ceded to his Britannic Majesty by the seventeenth Article of the definitive treaty concluded at Paris the tenth day of February 1763 or in as great extent as can be obtained.[2]

Given at Philadelphia this sixteenth day of October in the year of our Lord one thousand seven hundred and seventy nine and in the fourth year of our Independence, by the Congress of the united States of America.   Saml Huntington President[3]
Attest, Chas Thomson secy.

RC (Privately owned original, 1974). Written and attested by Charles Thomson, and signed by Huntington. Addressed: "The honble John Jay minister plenipotentiary appointed to negotiate a treaty of Amity and Commerce and of alliance with his Catholic Majesty." Endorsed by Jay: "Instructions to John Jay, 16 Octr. 1779."

[1] These instructions for negotiating with Spain, prepared by a committee consisting of Elbridge Gerry, John Mathews, and Meriwether Smith appointed on September 17, had already been developed in substance during a number of debates on foreign affairs the preceding six weeks. For the background of these debates see Henry Laurens' Notes on a Treaty, September 9–17, 1779, note 1. The first four paragraphs of instructions were apparently "agreed to" by Congress on September 28 (although Meriwether Smith's draft of them was endorsed by Charles Thomson "Instruction relative to Spain. Agreed to Sept. 20. 1779"), and the final paragraph was adopted on October 15.

The documentary record pertaining to congressional policy toward Spain during this period is difficult to interpret, not only because Secretary Thomson maintained a record of congressional proceedings on foreign affairs only in his secret journals, but also because the modern printed edition of them is a composite of documents sometimes linked capriciously or even erroneously. In addition, Congress addressed the subject so sporadically from February to October that continuity in the debates is difficult to perceive, and few of the principal delegates involved in developing that policy were continuously in attendance the entire period of its formulation. Thanks to the survival of this text, however, there can be no doubt of the final instructions Jay actually received. For the origin and evolution of them, see *JCC*, 14:924–26, 937–38, 15:1041–43, 1046–48, 1080–85, 1118–20, 1140–41, 1168, 1179; and PCC, item 25, 1:325–28. See also the related instructions drafted by Meriwether Smith and endorsed by Thomson "Report of the comee. on Instructions to Minister plenipo. relative to Alliance with Spain. postponed," in PCC, item 25, 1:329–32; and *JCC*, 15:1120.

[2] For the addition of this paragraph to Jay's instructions on October 15, see *JCC*, 15:1140–41, 1168, 1179.

[3] For Jay's commission, "agreed to" on September 28, and the letter of credence, adopted on October 15, which were probably delivered with these instructions, see *JCC*, 15:1121, 1178–79; and PCC, item 25, 1:333–34.

James Lovell to Horatio Gates

Dear General   Oct. 16. 79.

I beg you to send on to the navy Board at Boston by the first Express or good private hand going that Way, the 4 Pacquets which will be delivered to you by Mr. Richmond. Two Boats are going from thence, immediately to France. Arthur Lee is at Liberty *agreably to the Request of his Letter* May 31st to return to America.[1]

If the Disappointments in southern News had not been what you well know they have, I would now tell you that a North Carolina Colonel heard one of Govr. Caswell's Councellors 10 Days ago read a Letter from Govr. Rutledge informg. that all the Vessels in Beauport Harbour surrendered without Opposition to the Count Destaing, the Fort made a Resistance of an Hour & 50 Minutes but was then carried. The Count then proceeded to Savannah where, without any Resistance the Enemy surrendered at discretion. Your Lincoln was in such Positions that the Letter concluded not even a single Tory would escape, with all his Knowledge of the Passes.

This same Coll. was told that the Spaniards had certainly taken St. Augustine.

Perhaps I shall get the Bearer to convey to you a Journal of 1777.

Your affectionate, humble Servant,   James Lovell

[*P.S.*] I had the Pleasure of knowing of yr. Health by Mr. Guild some Days ago & by Mr. McCullogh yesterday.

RC (NHi: Gates Papers).
[1] See Committee for Foreign Affairs to Arthur Lee, October 13, and Lovell to Arthur Lee, October 14, 1779.

Samuel Huntington to George Washington

Sir   Philadelphia Octor 17th 1779
You will herewith receive enclosd a Memorial from two Officers Stediford & Bicker which Congress have referd to the Commander in Chief.[1]

I am Sir with the greatest Respect your Excys. humble Servant,
                                         Saml Huntington President

RC (DLC: Washington Papers).
[1] Captains Garret Stediford and Henry Bicker, Jr., had been, respectively, regimental quartermaster and adjutant of the Third Pennsylvania Battalion when captured at the fall of Fort Washington in November 1776, and they had been unable to find suitable vacancies since their exchange in 1778. For Washington's disposition of their case, which he referred to Gen. Arthur St. Clair in a letter of December 21, suggesting that they be introduced "into the 4th. Pennsylvania Regt. under the Resolve of Congress of the 24th. Novemr. 1778," see Washington, *Writings* (Fitzpatrick), 17:82, 299.

Marine Committee to Seth Harding

Sir   October 17th 1779
In addition to our Instructions of the 17th Ultimo which has been delivered to you, we now direct that you will receive on Board the Confederacy His Excellency John Jay Esquire, his Secretary, and

family, whom you are to treat with all the respect due to his Character and on your passage you are to consult with him and Mr. Gerard and be governed by their Orders with respect to any occurrences which may happen and the port to which you are to proceed. We are sir,   Your Hble Servants

LB (DNA: PCC Miscellaneous Papers, Marine Committee Letter Book).
[1] This day the Marine Committee also sent the following brief letter to the Eastern Navy Board over the signature of chairman John Mathews. "We desire you will Consult with the Honble John Adams Esqr. respecting the Stores which are necessary for himself & his family on their passage to France which you are to provide and also such Accomodations as may be wanting on board the Frigate in which he is to embark." Adams Papers, MHi; and Paullin, *Marine Committee Letters,* 2:122–23.

Committee for Foreign Affairs to William Carmichael

Sir   Philadelphia 18 Oct 1779
    I enclose to you Copies of Some resolves respecting the examination of Accounts in Europe by Mr Johnston.[1] It appears to me to be a very undefined Sort of business, as it has been managed, both in respect to that Gentlemans attestation and recompence. Such as it is, I beg you would Communicate one of the copies to Dr Franklin, and one to Mr Johnston. Ask the Doctor to let certified Copies he sent to all who he knows ought to have them, as I shall only forward by other Opportunities a Number Sufficient to Secure arrival at his hands in case you Should be unfortunately obliged to throw your papers overboard. Deus Meliora.
    Your humble Servant,   Signed James Lovell
                                   for the Com. for F. Affairs[2]

FC (DNA: PCC, item 79). In a clerical hand.
[1] Congress had appointed Joshua Johnson on September 29 "to examine the accounts of the several commissioners, commercial agents and others in Europe, entrusted with the public money of these United States." *JCC,* 15:1114–15, 1126.
[2] Carmichael's October 25 reply to this letter, which is mistakenly identified as directed to the president of Congress, is in PCC, item 88, fol. 35–36; and Wharton, *Diplomatic Correspondence,* 3:393.

Committee of Commerce to John Ashmead

                                   Commercial Committee of Congress
Sir[1]   Philadelphia 18th October 1779
    You will proceed in the Eagle Packet with the utmost expedition to the Island of St. Eustatia, and there address yourself to Messrs. Curson and Gouverneur Agents for the United States, to whom you

will deliver the Packets and letters directed to them,[2] together with the Cargo now on board.

You will be careful before you leave the Delaware to have your Packets and Letters prepared for sinking, in case of imminent danger of their falling into the hands of the Enemy, which you are by no means to suffer.

We have directed Messrs. Curson and Gouverneur to procure a Cargo for the Eagle on her return; as the principal article will be Gunpowder, we must recommend to your peculiar care to see it securely stowed.

As the Winter Season is advancing you will make all possible dispatch so as to be here again before the severe weather setts in, but should it so happen that you are obliged to put into any other Port on this Continent, you are to advise this Committee thereof by Express.

We recommend to you frugality during the course of this voyage, and wishing it may be a prosperous one, We are, Sir, Your friends & humble Servants,

Fra. Lewis

James Searle

John Fell

RC (Joseph G. Deering, Saco, Me., 1974). In the hand of Moses Young, and signed by Fell, Lewis, and Searle.

[1] John Ashmead (1738–1818), a Philadelphia mariner, commanded the packet *Eagle*, which was owned by James Searle, a member of the Committee of Commerce and a signer of this letter. For the details of Ashmead's long career, including the loss of the *Eagle* on this voyage, see William Bell Clark, "The John Ashmead Story, 1738–1818," *PMHB*, 82 (January 1958): 3–54.

[2] Not found.

John Fell's Diary

Monday the 18th Octr. [1779]

Coml Committee. Congress. After the dispatches, went in to a Committee of the whole when the Loan was agreed to & some Persons Put in nomination, for Negotiating the Loan and a long debate about Importing the Goods.

MS (DLC).

Samuel Huntington to Thomas Jefferson

Sir,   Philada Octr 18th 1779

In answer to your letter of the 25th Septr last I have the honour of inclosing you an Act of Congress of this day.

The board of War to whom your letter was referr'd apprehend great inconvenience from removing or separating the Convention troops and damage to the public in supplying them with wheat flour in the manner pointed out in your letter. As indian Flour is equally wholesome they must be contented with that unless the Commander in chief of the British Forces will supply them with Wheat flour in the Manner prescrib'd by Congress.[1]

I am Sir, your Obedient hble Servant,   S.H. President

LB (DNA: PCC, item 14).

[1] In his September 25 letter to Pres. John Jay, Governor Jefferson had explained that because of "various calamities" Virginia was experiencing a wheat shortage and would be unable to furnish the Convention troops at Charlottesville a normal allotment of flour "for the ensuing year." He therefore suggested that the Continental commissary general should plan to have the year's supply—estimated at ten thousand barrels—shipped down the Chesapeake to Richmond. PCC, item 71, fols. 271–74; and Jefferson, *Papers* (Boyd), 2:93–94. For the Board of War's report on Jefferson's letter and the resolves Congress adopted this day in response, see PCC, item 147, 2:531–33; and *JCC*, 15:1185.

Henry Laurens to James Laurens

My Dear Brother.[1]   Philadelphia 18th October 1779.

I have reason to believe that few, if any, of your Letters to me within a Year & half last past have miscarried, I have received originals or Copies a great many during my residence in this State. You have been long & anxiously conjecturing upon the cause of silence on my side, I will tell you in a few words—my close attachment to the service of America has shut out every other consideration, I am as ignorant of the state of my private affairs in South Carolina as you are. You know as well as I do, that our worthy friends Mr. Manigault & Mr. Gervais act as my Attornies, & you also know as well as I do, what have been the products of my Estates, at what prices such products have sold, what Monies have been paid or received on my Account. I have not received a single Account in the course of near 2 1/2 Years. Another cause of my silence I believe has been a dread of having my Letters intercepted & published in all the News Papers of England & New York, a practice which was early adopted by both parties of the present contention—but neither public avocations nor any other consideration shall hinder me from embracing this favorable opportunity of paying my respects to you, chiefly to inform you that I am now on the point of returning to my own Country, where, if I continue to enjoy good health I will reassume the charge of your affairs & from whence you shall hear from me by every proper conveyance.

Your Nephew Colonel Laurens, was well on the 7th Sepr & was then going towards Savanna to take a command. I expect every hour to hear from or of him, the intermediate moments will not pass altogether free from anxiety.

I might, if it were proper, give you a long detail of American public affairs, but omission, appears to me to be best & safest at present, in general they wear an aspect which the most sanguine had no foresight or conception of in 1774. An aspect, which if Great Britain were truly informed of would induce her for her own sake & for the sake of humanity, to withdraw her forces & to spare the lives of her own subjects. Sound Policy would dictate, That it is high time, having a view to her own Interest only, to effect with the United States of America, a reconciliation according to the fashion of Independent Nations.

Present me in the most affectionate terms to my Dear Sister & to my daughters, be assured that to bear the cruel seperation which I have experienced, requires all the fortitude I am possessed of, to bear it with perfect equanimity requires a degree of Stoicism which I am not possessed of. I am sometimes tempted, at all hazards, to make a Voyage to France & tis' far from impossible, I may carry this wish into effect before June next.

My Dear Brother I pray God to bless & protect you, & I remain with the most sincere affection Your faithful freind & obedient servant.   Henry Laurens

RC (CSmH: HM 39005). Addressed: "Mr. James Laurens, at Nismes in France."

[1] Laurens' brother James (1728–84), a retired Charleston, S.C., merchant, had moved to England in 1775 for the recovery of his health. Although this is the only surviving letter to James written by Laurens during his career as a delegate to Congress, their voluminous correspondence in earlier years can be followed in Henry Laurens, *The Papers of Henry Laurens*, ed. Philip M. Hamer et al. (Columbia: University of South Carolina Press, 1968–).

Nathaniel Peabody to Josiah Bartlett

Dear Sir   No. 12.[1]   Philada. 18th Octobr. 1779.

I have been honr'd with your kind favour of the 2d instant.[2] The information you have given me of the Enigmatical Conversation, & Conduct of the incomprehensible old Mr. D—p—t,[3] and the Diabolical Designs of the *Hanoverian* myrmidons, gives me Some uneasiness, however Can't Suspect that the old man is aiming by his ambiguity & Versatility to Circumvent those who are Justly intitled to every degree of Respect from him Short of Adoration. And as to the *Faction* I have nothing to fear from them, but the want of proper Courts Established, So that Law & Justice might be duly adminished in the County of Grafton. Mr. Lowell from Boston is now here upon Some meratime Causes and Gives it fully as his opinion that the first Grant must inevitably hold the Lands against all Subsequent Claims. I Should write you particularly respecting the Vermont affair but

Suppose Genl. Whipple who is fully possesd of that affair, will personally give you every Necessary information upon that head. No
official News here from Count D'Estaing Since the first account of
his Comming on the Coast of S. Carolina tho, reports about Town
are that he has wholly extirpated the British Troops & Tories in that
Quarter of the world. I hope Soon to have this report Confirmed,
that the way may be open for future Success. Monsrs Gerard, and
Mr. Jay with their attendance this day left Philada. for Europe. I
forget whether I have inform'd you that Mr. J. Adams of Boston was
Elected Minister Plenipo. to Negociate Treaties of *Peace* & Commerce with G. B———n & Mr. Danna for his Secretary—Mr. Jay minister Plenipo. for the Court of Madrid, & Carmichael his Secretary &
Col. John Laurence Secty to the Court of Versailles—the particulars
of which I have forwarded to Genl. Whipple. These things are mostly
upon the Secret Journals but if I had a Sure Conveyance would
Transmit you many matters that might be agreable, & yet Safe when
in your hands Tho you, as well as others, are not wholly exempted
from Companions who if I am not mistaken are of Such a kind,
benevolent and Religious Temper & Disposition, as to Embrace every
opportunity, in giving friendly advise & intelligence, even to our
Enemies!! Youll please to observe, I dont Say you have a *Man* in your
Secret Councils that is of Such a Religious Turn of mind. Some
suspicions you & I formerly had of Certain Persons I think were not
ill founded. Congress have Call'd for a Tax of 15 million dollars per
month for nine months Commincing on the first of Feby Next &
Ending in Ocr. in the apportioning of which among the Several
States, by a Committee of which I had the honr. of being a member,
with much difficulty the Quota of New-Hampr. was Reduced one
hundred thousand dollars per Month below its former proportion. I
am uncertain how much advantage it will be to the State—as what we
overpay will be placed to our Credit on interest, on the Contrary
Shall be Charged the interest of any Sum we may finally be found in
arrears. Congress have recommen[d]ed the 2d Thursday in Decr.
next to be observed as a day of Thanks giving throughout these
States. I have the honor to inclose you the Copy of a Letter from Mr.
J. A.[4] which will give the fullest acct. of the real Situation of Europe—
last Spring or rather in the Summer. I think the letter was dated in
July or Augt. 79—which I find is omitted in the Copy. Genl. Whipple has Carried a Copy with him So that it is very probable you may
have read it before this reaches you, however as it Contains So many
useful observations hope tho, late it will not be disagreable to you.
My Knowledge of your prudence forbids the necessity of hinting
that the aforementiond Letter is Transmitted in Confidence, & not
to be made Public. I am Dear Sir, most Sincerely your obedt. Humle.
Servt.   Nath Peabody

P.S. My best Complements to the Hond Committee & others.
N.B. Pray excuse blunders as I have not time [*to*] read it much less to Copy.

RC (NhD: Bartlett Papers).
    [1] Peabody's "No. 11" letter to Bartlett consists of the following brief note of October 12, 1779. "I recd. yours of the 25 ulto. [*not found*] late last eveng—have not time to answer it by giving any intelligence, nor have I matter worth Communicating. I inclose Some News papers & Journals which may be sent you instead of a Sensible Letter." Bartlett Papers, NhD.
    [2] Not found.
    [3] Perhaps Joseph Davenport, who had earlier asked for the New Hampshire government's help in settling a land grant dispute in "the Towns of Landaff &c." *N.H. State Papers*, 8:609.
    [4] Peabody enclosed a copy of John Adams' lengthy August 4, 1779, letter to Congress, on which he wrote the following covering note to Bartlett:
    "This Copy of a Letter which was writen to C—g—s by the Same Mr. J. A. which wrote the Letter, from which I inclosed Some Extracts in my letter of the 7th ulto. to Col. Bartlett—is now humbly Transmitted to the Hone. M. Weare & J. Bartlett, (to be Communicated to Such only as they may Judge Expedient) by their Most obedt. Humble Servt. Nathl. Peabody.
    "N.B. I will not answer for the Correctness of this Copy as it was Copied by a boy & I have not fully Examined it.
    "Genl. Whipple has Carried forward a Copy &c." Bartlett Papers, NhD.
    See also Peabody to Bartlett, September 7, 1779, note 3.

John Fell's Diary

Tuesday 19th [October 1779].
    Coml Committee. Congress. After the dispatches, went in to a Committee of the whole, when the Question was put abt Importing the Goods carried in the Negative Per a great Majority.[1] Afterwards a Printed Report of another Committee was read, (full of complexd Idieas)[2] Committe Rose and had leave to sett again. After some motions made in Congress Adjournd; Mr Huston came today.[3]
    PM Marine Committee.

MS (DLC).
    [1] See Fell's Diary, October 16, note.
    [2] Fell is doubtless referring to the report of the committee on departments, which had originally been read on July 23 but was not taken up by the committee of the whole until October 18. Sixty copies of the intricate report had been printed for the use of Congress. See *JCC*, 14:872–80, 15:1186–87; PCC, item 39, 2:62; and Evans, *Am. Bibliography*, no. 16,632. For the May 28 appointment and subsequent work of the committee that drafted the report, see John Dickinson's Committee Notes, June 7, note 1; Dickinson's Proposed Resolutions, ante July 9; and Dickinson's Notes, ante July 23, 1779.
    This day Congress reached "no resolution" on departmental reform and postponed consideration until December 4 when it passed the plan to a new committee. Finally, on January 20, 1780, Congress assigned the whole matter to three commissioners, one of whom was to be a member of Congress, with instructions to cooperate

with Washington and the heads of the departments in seeking retrenchments and making recommendations to Congress. *JCC*, 15:1343, 1349, 16:75–77.

[3] William Churchill Houston, who had been absent since at least October 14, for which see Fell's Diary of that date.

Woodbury Langdon to Meshech Weare

Sr.   Philadelphia Octobr. the 19th. 1779
   The circular Letter refered to in my last[1] I neglected to send at that time but have herein inclosed it, tho' you must have received one long ago from the President of Congress. Inclosed is also a Paper from the State of New Jersey which I am desired by the Delegates from that State to forward,[2] the Subject therein recommended is now before Congress but what will be the result of their deliberations thereon is very uncertain but I think it must be clear to every man for obvious reasons and late and repeated experience that it is very impolitic for any particular State to regulate Prices unless it becomes general throughout the united States and in determining *that* Question I hope that Wisdom & Prudence will direct. I have also inclosed the Journall of August and shall continue to forward them to you monthly for the future while I remain here, I shall send you the Journals from the date of those sent by General Whipple to the present time when they are ready and there is an oppertunity (they are not yet printed for part of the year 1777 & the whole of the year 1778). We have various favorable Accounts from the Southward of the French Fleet, but they do not yet come in such a way as to authorise me to give you the particulars, but hope to be able to do it in my next. The Fleet is dayly expected off New York and great preparations are made to joyn the Count de Estaing in such opperations as may be thought advisable to attempt. I have the honour to be with the utmost Respect, Your most obedient Humble Servt.   Woodbury Langdon

RC (Nh–Ar: Weare Papers).
   [1] See Langdon to Weare, October 12, 1779.
   [2] See John Fell's Diary, October 11, note; and Samuel Huntington to the States, November 22, 1779, note.

Henry Laurens to Jonathan Trumbull, Sr.

Dear Sir,   Philadelphia 19th October 1779.
   Since the date of my last of the 26th September I have not been honoured with any of Your Excellency's favors. After repeated tenders to Congress of the Letters which Your Excellency desired should be presented to the House I obtained, about a week ago, a Commit-

ment of them without reading. Yesterday I put them into the hands of Mr. President Huntington when they were read & again Committed,[1] therefore they are now out of my reach, otherwise they should have accompanied this, the translation of the Dutch Book goes on slowly. Mr. Muhlenburg who was so obliging as to undertake to get that work performed says the translator is nevertheless not Idle.

I should have explained on the first abovementioned Commitment by saying the Committee had made a favorable Report on the Letters & then returned them into my hands. I was desirous because you seem to have been so, & because the Letters deserved attention, to have them read in full Congress. This was done yesterday & thence came the second Commitment.

When I said to Your Excellency in my last *"were he my Son I should dissuade him,"* I had no Idea that *my* Son would indeed be made without his knowledge, a Candidate for the very place, your Son wished for. My declaration was very sincere & my subsequent conduct consistent therewith. I do not beleive Colo. Laurens will accept the appointment which Congress have elected him to.[2] I have written to him desiring he will not determine until he shall have given me an opportunity of conferring with him & communicating a faithful & accurate state of our affairs foreign & domestic. If it shall please God to favor me with such an interview, & that my Son can read my heart he will return thanks to Congress & decline accepting the intended honor. At the same time I must confess that as far as I know him he does not want qualifications for filling the Office of Secretary to a foreign embassy with Credit, but a Man tender of his reputation will well consider the times before he accepts of *a place.*

Your Excellency's Packet addressed to the Baron Van der Capellen is committed to the protection of Monsr. Gerard with a particular request to convey it in such manner as to avoid a heavy expence of Postage; Mr. Gerard is now on board the Confederacy at Chester & will sail with the first fair Wind, probably this day.

If the intelligence which we have received through various Channels of the Count d'Estaing's success at South Carolina & Georgia shall prove true, those States will enjoy a temporary tranquility & the Enemy will feel the weight of a heavy loss & severe mortification; according to those accounts, we have ground for expecting to hear of the Admiral's arrival at Sandyhook or Rhode Island to day or to morrow. All this looks very fair—but alas! alas! We are threatned with an empty Treasury before the lst day of December—vigoros & virtuos exertions of the Citizens of these States, immediately put into action, must so far heal the wound given by rash bad policy as to save us from a violent convulsion. Your Excellency has before this day seen the Plan of ways & means, the medicine is rather rude, but if it be taken in time & in chearful spirits it may produce much relief, but cannot perform a radical cure. How is that possible when the expenditures continue to increase beyond the stretch of the amazing expected returns of 15 Mil. per Month—it will however afford us a little time for breathing & recollection, & will stimulate the States to look a little more narrowly into things which concern their temporal Salvation.

I am with the utmost Esteem & Regard, Sir, Your Excellency's Obedient & most humble, servant,   Henry Laurens.

RC (Ct: Trumbull Papers).
[1] For the letters Trumbull had "desired should be presented to the House," see Laurens to Trumbull, September 26, 1779, in which Laurens had explained some of the delays that had prevented him from obtaining prompt congressional consideration of them. Laurens probably obtained the "Commitment of them without reading" on October 13, the day he was appointed to a committee concerning John Jay's mission abroad. To that committee a number of documents from Jacob Gerhard Diriks pertaining to a Dutch loan were also committed, and on October 15 Congress adopted the committee's recommendation for appointing "a proper person" to negotiate a loan in Holland. Three days later Congress proceeded to the nomination of a commissioner to conduct these negotiations, and it was apparently at that time, when a committee was appointed to prepare the commissioner's instructions, that Laurens obtained the second commitment of the documents Trumbull had sent. There is no explicit mention in the journals of either "commitment," but for the proceedings in Congress summarized here, see *JCC*, 15:1167, 1179–81, 1186.

It was against this background of involvement in the study of prospects for a Dutch loan that Laurens himself was appointed the commissioner for this mission on October 21, the general purpose of which was spelled out in a number of congressional resolves adopted on the 26th. *JCC*, 15:1196–98, 1210–11. See also Samuel Huntington to Laurens, October 30, 1779.
[2] See Laurens to Trumbull, September 26, note 3; and the letters of Samuel Huntington and Henry Laurens to John Laurens, October 2, 1779.

James Lovell to John Adams

Dear Sir,   Octr. 19th. 1779

I begin to be very impatient at not hearing from you; and this not barely from the Number of days elapsed since my Information of Sepr. 28 &c. &c but from the Opinion dropped by Mr Lowell that we should not be able to obtain your Consent again to trust *us here*. It is the Desire of many that you shod. execute an intermediate Negociation with Holland, and you are named but others think it would be proper to make a distinct Appointment. This will be attended to on Thursday.[1]

Mr. Gerard went on Board the Confederacy Yesterday with Mr. J. J., *his Wife* & other Passengers. I fear that the Gentleman who carries such Comfort with him will find Embarrassment the Consequence 2500 per Annum will not support Introductions to the Queen of Spain if I am rightly informed.

By the Way, There is a Circumstance which you ought to know. Such is the State of our Finances that Doctr. F—— is desired to furnish 2000 Louis dors immediately to the 2 Ministers & their Secretaries or rather 3 Secries. to be divided, & his is promised *immediate* Replacement by the commercial Committee as well an Investment of Funds for the whole Support of the Embassies.[2] I think from what I have seen of commercial Punctuality here, that I would not trust myself without Letters of Credit from private Persons to serve on an Emergency rising from public Negligence or Disappointment.

I have meditated myself into a sort of Capability of Chagrin at not having a Chance of voyaging *with you*. For you are to observe I will not consent to conclude *you* will not venture once more.

Your affectionate humble Servant,   J.L.

[*P.S.*] Seal & send to the Navy Board the enclosed to go by two Opportunities.

RC (MHi: Adams Papers).
    [1] The post of commissioner "to negotiate a loan in Holland" went to Henry Laurens. *JCC*, 15:1198.
    [2] See Lovell to Adams, October 14, 1779, note 1.

Gouverneur Morris to Robert R. Livingston

Dr Robert   Phila. 19th Octr. 1779.
    That I have not untill this Moment written to you I beseech you to impute to my Situation which hath been and is much occupied. When I arrived the World (or at least such Parts of it as I warmly love) was on the Wing. Old Systems are at once deranged and new ones to be adopted consistent with the old. I should say *were* &ca. for by what I learn from your Quarter I am no longer to be that wretched Creature a Statesman. The Instant I came into the House I was placed upon an important Committee[1] & that succeeded by a Variety of others so that I am already again distracted with Attention to different Things. Can you give me as good Reasons for your Taciturnity? I fear not. Remember that domestic ones cannot be received for that I shall *set off* like domestic Cares. Our Politics and our News are now alike public. The mighty Questions which have agitated us & torne the People of America settle down to a Calm. We hope much, expect much and are Certain of this only That every Thing in this World is uncertain. There is from thence a strong Argument for acting inconclusively and so inconclusive an Animal is Man that it is kind to have found the Argumts. for him. Adieu my dear Friend. Beleive me with Sincerity, yours,

                                                        Gouv Morris[2]

RC (NHi: Robert R. Livingston Papers).
    [1] Morris had returned to Congress on October 6, and he was appointed the same day to a committee to apportion the "sums to be paid into the continental treasury by the respective states." *JCC*, 15:1148–49.

[2] Morris also wrote the following brief letter to an unidentified friend this day. "Permit me to catch a Moment in Order to simply ask how you do. I will enclose you this Day's Paper because it will as effectually give you the *News* as I can do. As for *Intelligence* I can give you none nor indeed would I by the uncertain Conveyance of a Post. Yesterday I parted with my Friend Jay who departed this City to embark at Chester on Board the Confederacy. What may be, and what may be the Effects of, the Count's Movements it is for Time to discover. What will be the Success of the Enemy's Defensive Operations the same Mother of Events must declare." bMS Am 1649.8, MH–H.

George Partridge to Joseph Ward

Sir   Philadelphia Octr. 19th. 1779
I receivd yours of the 9th current in Answer to which I can only say that Mr Laurens alone remains in Town of the Commee who were appointed on that Business, he informs me that he will immediately apply for an addition to the Commee & proceed to the Business. Your Expectations are Reasonable & I believe that the matter will be soon determind. I shall not be wanting to contribute my Mite to this Business—every man who is concerned with publick Business Needs Patience, I hope yours will not be worn out.[1]
We have various Accounts of our Successes Southward tho nothing Official. Tis said that the Enemy in that Quarter are totally subdued. This no Doubt will soon be the case tho I think that our Advice wants confirmation, which I expect very soon.
I am Sir with great esteem your most Obedient, Humble Servt.
                                              Geo. Partridge

P.S. Be so kind as to forward the inclosed as directed. G.P.

RC (ICHi: Joseph Ward Papers). Addressed: "Col. Joseph Ward, Muster Master Genl., Head Quarters North River."
[1] For a discussion of the reform of the mustermaster general's department that ended in its abolition, see Joseph Spencer to Ward, August 23, note; and Partridge to Ward, November 31? 1779.

John Fell's Diary

                                        Wednesday Oct 20th [1779].
Coml Committee. Congress.
A number of dispatches, Reports from Committees &c. A Report for the form of the Prayer to be used on Thursday the   day of Decr.[1] was read and agreed too. (Mr. Huston gone home having had an Acct of the death of his Child).

MS (DLC).
[1] That is, December 9, the date set for "a day of general thanksgiving." *JCC*, 15:1191.

Samuel Holten's Diary

[October 20–21, 1779]

20. Wednesday. I met the Committee & we prepaired a Proclamation for a day of General Thanksgiving.[1]

21. Thursday. I attended the committee on general Arnolds affairs.

MS (MDaAr).
[1] See Samuel Huntington to the States, this date.

Samuel Huntington to John Adams

Sir   Philadelphia Octor. 20th 1779

I have the honour to transmit you herewith enclosd Two Commissions wherein you are Authorized and appointed Minister Plenipotentiary from these United States to Negotiate Treaties of *Peace* & *Commerce* with Great Brittain; Accompanied with instructions in each Case, for your government in the Execution of those Several Commissions.[1]

For your further Information and benefit, are enclosd Copies of the Instructions to the honble. Ben. Franklin & John Jay Esqrs our Ministers Plenipotentiary at the Courts of Versailes & Madrid.[2]

Also two Acts of Congress of the 4th & 15th Instant Ascertaining your Salary & making provision for your Subsistance on your Arrival in France.[3]

The nature & Importance of the Trust committed to your charge, will, I perswade myself engage your Immediate Attention & induce you to undertake the Service, and Embark for France without loss of time.

Wishing you a prosperous Voyage and Success in your Embassy,

I have the honour to be, with Sentiments of the highest Esteem & Regard, Your humble Servant,   Saml. Huntington President

P.S. The honble Francis Dana Esqr is appointed your Secretary.

RC (MHi: Adams Papers).
[1] Adams' two commissions, signed by Huntington, attested by Charles Thomson, and dated September 29, 1779, are in the Adams Papers, MHi. For their origins, see John Dickinson's Draft Commission, August 4, 1779; and *JCC*, 15:1116–17. For his "instructions in each Case," see Huntington's letters to Adams of October 16, 1779.
[2] See Huntington to Franklin and to Jay, October 16, 1779.
[3] *JCC*, 15:1143–46, 1179–83.

Samuel Huntington to Francis Dana

Sir   Philadelphia Octor 20th. 1779
    You will herewith receive enclosd, a Commission as Secretary to
the honorable John Adams Esqr, Minister plenipotentiary from the
United States of America for Negotiating Treaties, both of Peace &
Comerce with Great Brittain.
    I have also enclosd two Acts of Congress of the 4th & 15th Instant
Ascertaining your Salary and making provision for your Subsistance
on your Arrival in France.
    I have the honour to be with Sentiments of Esteem, your humble
Servt,   Saml. Huntington President

RC (MHi: Dana Papers).

Samuel Huntington to the States

Sir,   Circular   Philadelphia Octr 20th 1779
    You will receive inclos'd herewith an Act of Congress of this day
recommending to the several States that Thursday the ninth of
December next be appointed a day of public thanksgiving.[1]
    I have the honour to be, with Sentiments of esteem & regard, your
Excy's hble Servt,   S. H. President

LB (DNA: PCC, item 14).
[1] For the work of the committee appointed to prepare the enclosed Thanksgiving
Day proclamation, and the draft of it written by committee chairman Jesse Root, see
JCC, 15:1170–71, 1191–93; PCC, item 24 fols. 447–48; and Burnett, *Continental
Congress*, pp. 421–23.

John Dickinson to Caesar Rodney

Sir,   Philadelphia, October 21st. 1779
    The inclosed[1] being put into my Hands on my Arrival in Town, I
thought it proper immediately to transmit it to You, as our Assembly
is now sitting.
    I am, Sir, your very hble Servt.   John Dickinson

[P. S.] I shall be much oblig'd to You, if You will have the inclosed
Letter delivered to Thomas Smith by some very careful Hand, as
soon as possible.

RC (NN: Rodney Letters).
[1] The "inclosed" given to Dickinson on his return to Philadelphia, possibly from the
"Trip to Kent" mentioned in his September 25 letter to Rodney, was probably the
New Jersey memorial on price regulation that had been read in Congress on October

11 and assigned to a committee composed of a member from each state. See John
Fell's Diary, October 11, 1779. Delaware's delegate on the committee, Nicholas Van
Dyke, was apparently not attending Congress at this time, having last voted on October 6. Since the state was unrepresented until Dickinson's return, it became impera-
tive that Dickinson forward the memorial, "as our Assembly is now sitting." Rodney
laid the "inclosed printed paper" before the assembly "Immediately" upon receipt of
Dickinson's letter. See *JCC*, 15:1148, 1162; and Rodney, *Letters* (Ryden), p. 324. For
Congress' resolves on price regulation, see Samuel Huntington to the States, November 22, 1779.

John Fell's Diary

Thursday Octr. 21st [1779].
Coml Committee. Congress. Some dispatches and several Reports
from Committees, Order of the day for Balloting for a Person to be
sent to Europe to Negotiate a Loan. Mr Laurens was appointed. Mr
Laurens 8 Votes, Mr Adams 3.[1] NB. Mr Scudder.[2]

MS (DLC).
[1] The balloting on this election is not recorded in the journals. *JCC*, 15:1198.
[2] That is, Nathaniel Scudder had returned to Congress.

Marine Committee to Thomas Read

Sir   October 21. 1779
As you have been appointed to command the Continental frigate
Bourbon now at Middleton in the State of Connecticut we desire you
will immediately proceed to that place and take the command of the
said frigate which you are to use your best endeavours to have fitted
for the Sea with all expedition. When you arrive at Middleton you
are to inspect the State of the Bourbon and give an account thereof
to the Commissioners of the Navy Board at Boston who will order
every thing necessary for equipping her and you are occasionally to
inform that Board of your proceedings and be governed by their
orders in all matters relating to your Ship.
We are Sir, Your Hble Servants

LB (DNA: PCC Miscellaneous Papers, Marine Committee Letter Book).

Gouverneur Morris to George Washington

Dr General.   Philaa. 21st Octr. 1779
Two Days ago I was placed on a Committee to report the neces-
sary Provision to be made for Officers not heretofore provided for.[1]
I recollect at present the general Officers & Erskine's Corps (The

Surgeons are already reported & the Report set down for this Day when as the Devil will have it I cannot attend) but as it would produce many Inconveniences to make this Provision which Congress intend to be general in any Respects partial I am sure you will pardon me the Liberty of requesting your thoughts as to the two Points. 1st. Who further shall be provided for, & 2ly. What Provision all things considered is properly consistent with the last Step taken by Congress relative to the Line.[2] Most sincerly I am, Dr Sir, yours,   Gouv Morris

P.S. I recollect that it is long since I received a Letter from you recommending Union in Congress.[3] I could not answer it then as I wished for I would *truly* say it existed or was like to exist. I would not go into a Detail of the Reasons, it would have involved too much Egotism and of Consequence could not have been quite impartial. At length let me congratulate your *virtuous Moderation* (I do not compliment) that we are united as much as is safe for the Public.

RC (DLC: Washington Papers).
[1] See John Armstrong to Washington, October 15, 1779, note 2.
[2] Washington's November 6 reply is in Washington, *Writings* (Fitzpatrick), 17:79–80.
[3] In his May 8, 1779, letter, Washington had urged Morris to "pacify party differences." *Ibid.*, 15:26.

John Fell's Diary

[October 22–23, 1779]
Friday October 22d 1779. Coml Committee. Congress. Memorials, Letter, Treasury Reports &c.
Saturday 23d. Com Committee. Congress. After the dispatches the order of the day on the Report for the Sallerys of the Treasury Bd. agreed as follows, That the Commissioners and other Officers have their Places during Pleasure (Resolve past some time since that the Election should be annual).[1]

Sallerys Per Annum

Treasurer	15,000 Dolls.
Commissioners of the Board of Treasury . . .	14,000
Auditor General	12,000
Commissioners of Chamber of Accounts	12,000
Assistant Auditor General	10,000
Secretary to the Board of Treasurey	10,000
Clerks in the above Offices	7,000

MS (DLC).

[1] The ordinance establishing the Board of Treasury and providing for annual elections had been adopted July 30. On September 4 Congress assigned that part of the report pertaining to annual elections and salaries of officers to a committee of three, which reported October 20. See *JCC*, 14:903–8, 15:1027, 1190, 1204–6.

Samuel Holten's Diary

[October 22–23, 1779]

22. Friday. I met the committee on the Post-office,[1] & the Come. of 12[2] & the come. on Genl. Arnolds Accounts.

23. Saturday. Congress settled the Salary's of the new board of Treasury. I attended the Come. on the Post-Office. Warm weather.

MS (MDaAr).

[1] The post office committee was apparently preparing the report that it submitted to Congress on October 25. *JCC*, 15:1203–4.

[2] That is, the committee appointed on October 11 to consider New Jersey's price control proposal. *JCC*, 15:1162.

Marine Committee to Seth Harding

Marine Committee

Sir   Philadelphia October 22d, 1779

This Committee having received information that you have lately Impressed on board the Confederacy several seamen Citizens of this state who have left families in this City in a distressed Situation. If this should be true you are hereby Ordered immediately to discharge them.[1]

We are Sir, &c

FC (DNA: PCC Miscellaneous Papers). In the hand of John Brown.

[1] The Marine Committee wrote this letter in response to Congress' directive to "take order . . . and report to Congress" on Pennsylvania President Joseph Reed's complaint against Captain Harding's impressment of Pennsylvanians. See *JCC*, 15:1201, 1204; *Pa. Archives*, lst ser. 7:761–62; and the following entry.

Samuel Huntington to Joseph Reed

Sir   Philada. Octr. 23d 1779

Your letter of the 21st instant was immediately laid before Congress. Enclos'd is their Act of yesterday informing the Proceedings which have been adopted in Consequence thereof.[1]

I am with great respect, your Excellency's hble Servt.

S.H. President[2]

LB (DNA: PCC, item 14).

[1] See the preceding entry.

[2] This day Huntington also wrote a brief letter to Major Noirmont de La Neuville, transmitting an October 22 resolve adopted as testimonial to his "personal merit and military character" to allay the "uneasiness" he had expressed to the Board of War over failure to obtain a promotion to lieutenant colonel. See PCC, item 14, fol. 212; and JCC, 15:1201.

Henry Laurens to George Washington

Dear sir.　　　　　　　　　Philadelphia 24th October 1779.

I had the honor of addressing you in a Letter under the 7th & 9th Inst. which went forward by a Messenger from the Dep. Qu. Master's office.[1]

Yesterday I received from Charles Town in South Carolina by a Letter & News Papers, intelligence in brief, of the operations of the combined arms in & near Georgia to the 2d Inst.

Colo. Maitland with so many of his Troops as were inclined & able had made his escape from Beaufort & joined General Prevost at Savanna leaving behind him, his whole Hospital, Artillery, Baggage & Stores. I know the swamps which the Colonel must have penetrated; a detail of his line of March, if he really went that way, would excite a mixture of compassion & laughter.

The Enemy were strongly fortified by lines & redoubts in the Town of Savanna, where the soil is sand & sandy clay—their number about 3000, exclusive of Negroes & other rubbage.

Count d'Estaing had landed 5000 Troops & formed a junction with General Lincoln who must have had under his command about 4000. Count Pulaski & General McKintosh had been detached southerly, probably to secure the Town of Sunbury about 40 Miles distant from Savanna & to intercept retreating parties by land & inland navigation, which in that country may be attempted with great prospect of success.

The allies finding General Prevost so strongly intrenched had determind after a fruitless summon[s] to make regular approaches in preference to assault, Colo. Lomoy chief Engineer had announced that his works would be complete on the 1st October & it was expected, the Batteries consisting of 38 pieces of heavy Cannon & 8 Mortars would open in the same instant on the 2d or 3d.

Sorties in two attempts had been made by the beseiged on the working parties, in both instances the assailants were beat back & suffered greatly in killed & wounded. A flag had passed from Gen. Prevost to Count d'Estaing with a request from the General for a Passport in favor of Madame Prevost, her plate & effects. The Count had replied that his politeness so far as respected the Lady could not be questioned, but that he understood the Plate &ca. had been acquired in such a way from the Allies of his Master as induced him to believe the General could not in honor & conscience expect to enjoy it—or something like this.

The Sagitaire had taken the Experiment commanded by Sir James Wallace after a brave resistance, it is said that on board the Experiment were General Vaughan & about 20 other Officers, & Cash for paying the British Troops in Georgia, that dispatches had been found on board intimating an embarkation of 4000 Men at New York intended for So Carolina in consequence of which ten Ships of the line had been detached for convoying them in—this may account for the fleet which lately appeared at the mouth of Chesepeak.

The Ariel, Fowey, & a sloop of 18 Guns, British Men of War, a large Ship with 2200 Barrels of Bread & flour, a large quantity of Beef & Pork, 4000 suits of Clothing &c. &c.—all the Enemy's Store & Transport Ships had fallen into the French Admiral's hands, besides many others Captured at Sea.

Mr. Alexander Cameron formerly British Deputy, now, Superintendent of Indian affairs in the Southern district had prevailed on a part of the Cherokees to break faith with South Carolina, these had been severely chastised by General Williamson, their Towns & provisions totally destroyed & Cameron driven out of the Nation—the General had returned & would join General Lincoln with about 1000 Men on the 29th or 30th September.

The Camps of the Allies in perfect health & harmony & every body in full prospect of repossessing Savanna & of having the British General, his Troops & the wrong Governor Sir James Wright prisoners of War within a week.

Your Excellency well knows how to make proper abatements from such jumbled accounts—the bulk I believe to be true & there are no doubt many favorable truths untold.

"I have not heard (says my friend) from Colo. Laurens since he went to Georgia he commands the Light Infantry, but by Letters to others I learn he was well the 27th Septem. after the reduction of Savanna he intends to return to his General." This is all I have received concerning Your Excellency's Aid de Camp, my friend adds that deserters from the Enemy came in daily.

On Thursday last Congress were pleased to appoint me to go to the United States of Holland, when I am informed of the nature & extent of commands to be laid on me,[2] I shall be better qualified to determine on the propriety of accepting the Charge, be this as it may, I mean to begin my journey towards South Carolina on the 29th Inst.[3] There & in every other place where God pleases to lead me I shall continue to bear a grateful remembrance of Your Excellency's paternal care of my Country & shall count every opportunity of testifying my Love & Esteem for you an happy event. Under these professions I take my leave & with great sincerity subscribe, Sir, Your much obliged & obedient servant,   Henry Laurens.

RC (NHi: Vail Collection).

[1] See Laurens to Washington, October 7, 1779.

[2] For the "commands" laid on Laurens for negotiating a Dutch loan, see Samuel Huntington's second letter to Laurens of October 30, 1779.

[3] Although Jesse Root wrote to Gov. Jonathan Trumbull on November 12 that Laurens left Philadelphia "last Saturday," i.e., November 6, there are explicit references to Laurens' departure on November 9 in the November 10 issue of the *Pennsylvania Gazette*, in the November 11 issue of the *Pennsylvania Packet*, and in Nathaniel Peabody to William Whipple, November 9, 1779. The matter is significant because Secretary Charles Thomson recorded a Laurens' motion in the journals on November 8, which, on the basis of Root's statement, Edmund C. Burnett conjectured was in error. Cf. *JCC*, 15:1250, and Burnett, *Letters*, 4:lxiii.

James Mercer to the Treasurer of Virginia

Sir,   Philadelphia. Oct 24th 1779.

Please to pay Capt. Alexander Dick two thousand Dollars which please to place to my attendance as a Delegate to Congress, not having drawn any money here on that account, this & a former draft for 500 Dollars in favour of my Brother Majr Mercer, amount to less than the state of Virginia owes me on that Account.[1] I am Sir, Yr. very humble Servant,   Js. Mercer

RC (Vi: Continental Congress Papers).

[1] After he returned home, Mercer wrote another brief note to the Virginia treasurer on November 22 requesting an additional "£61.2.0 Virga.," which he appended to an account claiming expenses for his attendance in Congress ("from 9th Sept to 31 Oct. inclusive, 53 days 40 Dollrs. £696.") and travel to and from Philadelphia. The latter expenses he listed as follows (in "Virginia Currency"): "To allowance for travelling to Philadelphia Per way of Baltimore, 231 Miles @ 6s. Feriages, Colchester 12s, Potowmack 42s, Patuxent 12s, So River 18s, Patapsco 50s, Susquehana 50s, Shullkill 4s.4." "To travelling from Philadelphia by Kent Island, 201 miles 6s. Feriages at Schullkill, 10s, Christeen 8s, Kent Island narrows 40s, across the Bay £28, So. River 30s, Patuxent 12s, Potowmack 36 & at Colchester 12s." This document is in the James S. Copley Library, La Jolla, Calif.

His account with the state of Virginia submitted March 24, 1780, lists additional expenses of £1085.18.4 for the period September 3 to November 19, 1779. This document is in the Continental Congress Papers, Vi, and was printed in Burnett, *Letters*, 4:505.

William Sharpe to Richard Caswell

Sir,   Philadelphia Oct. 24th 1779[1]

I have the honor of informing your Excellency that by Genl. Washington's letter dated the 21st Inst.[2] we learn that the Enemy have demolished and evacuated their posts of Stoney and Verplanks point, and retreated to New York. By intelligence of the 15th from Genl. Gates we learn there was reason to believe that the Enemy were about to evacuate Rhode Island and repair to New York where it appears the Enemy are centering all their force in order to make the greatest possible defence against Count de Estaing and Genl. Washington. The Enemy have sunk several hulks of vessels in the channel at the narrows & have made strong works on Long Island, Staten & Governors Island. Inasmuch as the season is far advanced, we have no reason to be very sanguine about possessing ourselves of New York. If the Count comes to the Northward, I doubt not but vigorous attempts will be made. The commander in chief had called for 2000 militia from Massachusetts Bay, 3000 from Connecticut, 2000 from New York, 2000 from New Jersey, 1500 from Pennsylvania.[3] Congress has received no authentic accounts from the combined Fleets in Europe. We have flattering hopes of good news from Georgia.

Congress has lately appointed the Hon. Wm. Laurens[4] to negociate a Loan in Holland.

I have the honor to be with great esteem your Excellys Mo. ob. huml. Servt,   Wm. Sharpe

P.S. Three days since Mr Gerard & Mr Jay saild for France.

Tr (Nc–Ar: Governor's Letter Books).

[1] Sharpe may actually have written this letter on the 28th. The information from Washington discussed by Sharpe was dispatched from West Point the evening of the 21st but was not read in Congress until the 25th. Moreover, Sharpe noted in his postscript that Gérard and Jay, who sailed aboard the *Confederacy* on October 25, had departed "three days since." Errors of transcription in this letterbook are not uncommon.

[2] For Washington's two letters of October 21 informing Congress of the imminent evacuation of the British posts on the Hudson and then confirming that the enemy had indeed "retreated to New York," see Washington, *Writings* (Fitzpatrick), 17:1–2, 7.

[3] For Washington's preparations for an attack upon New York should d'Estaing's fleet arrive before winter, see Freeman, *Washington*, 5:136–38.

[4] Sharpe probably wrote "Mr. Laurens," which was misread by the transcriber.

Thomas Burke to the North Carolina Assembly

[October 25? 1779][1]

Among the variety of Business which came before Congress from the begining of January '79 to the midle of August, the following Objects Seemed to your Delegates to be of highest Importance to the united States in general. The Army, Finances, and foreign affairs. The Votes and transactions relative to the two first are to be found in the Journals, Copies of which are transmitted to the Governor for the use of the State. I[2] presume therefore that your Delegates are not required to give any particular Information relative to them unless Some passages require Explanation, or their own particular Votes Stand in need of Justification. If Such be the Case, I hope and request that they may be Questioned on Such Votes and passages specially, praying leave to Suggest that any other mode would be tedious, difficult and unsatisfactory and Protesting that I am at all times ready and willing to give all the Satisfaction in my power to the Assembly in any mode which shall to that honorable Body Seem Most eligeable.

I am aware that Some obvious remarks which will Occur on perusing the Journals require Answers and will Endeavour to give Such as appear to me true, and hope they will prove Satisfactory. Tis obvious that much time is Spent on unimportant Subjects, that many Questions of Order are debated and some of them perhaps decided in a manner that may appear extraordinary to Legislative Assemblies.

The latter is Occasioned by the Nature of Congress which is a deliberating Executive assembly, to whose proceedings the rules of order Established for deliberating Legislative assemblies will not always apply without manifest Inconvenience and as utility is the principle which gives rise to all rules of order, So whatever rule appears to a Majority to be Contrary to utility must Necessarily be rejected as not order.

It must be Confessed, and ought to be lamented that those Circumstances make the rules of order in that assembly very arbitrary and uncertain—hence frequent disputes arise thereon, much time and debate are wasted, and the decisions at length depend upon the Integrity of a Majority. Thus rules of Order Cease to be, what they ought, Common Checks upon Excesses; and, being always in the power of a Majority, if that Should be factious or Vitious will be unavailing against them, but always powerful Instruments in their hands. This Inconvenience Can only be remedied by fundamental alterations in the Constitution of Congress, which ought to be beyond their own power to alter except by unanimous Consent—but the present times afford not leisure for Such Improvements, and tis to be hoped that the Virtue of the present race will prevent any great degree of Injury, before a Season of Tranquility Shall arrive.

The former arises also from the Imperfect Constitution Of Congress which cannot reject any Business, addressed to them by way of despatch through the President, before it has undergon Some Consideration. When Such applications respect the Interests of Individuals it too often happens that Some Member patronises the application, and a Debate Necessarily Ensues which consumes much time, for it must be Confessed that particular Interests are too frequently very Strenuously Contested and the very Effort to get rid of Such applications in order to make way for more Important Business takes up a great part of that time which ought to be Sacred to great and general Concerns. Your Delegates with great pleasure assisted in passing a resolution to Correct this Evil in Some Measure Vizt that on a motion for postponing no member Should Speak more than Once,[3] and they have had the Satisfaction of observing very good Effects from it, the House being thereby enabled to come to a resolution for dismissing improper business, with much less Debate, and waste of time than heretofore. As the most Effectual remedy for this Evil, it is much to be wished that the Delegates in Congress were free from the Solicitations of Interested Individuals, or immoveably firm against them, either, tho much to be wished for, yet, Considering the frailty of human Nature, Can Scarcely be expected, and the remedy for this Evil like many others must be referred to Seasons of Sufficient Tranquility for fundamental Amendments.

In general with respect to the army your Delegates relied on the approved Experience, Abilities and Virtue of its Illustrious Commander for all Military Enterprises and Operations. In what related to arrangements and appointments, they always favored whatever tended to make their Condition more Comfortable and Satisfactory, whatever tended to hold out prospects of future glory and Competence to the gallant and faithful Soldier. But they were careful to admit no Ideas of Power in the Military Order repugnant to, or interefering with the Civil Authority, nor Insolence to the Civil Magistrate of any State to pass with impunity,[4] and they always Opposed every attempt to exercise Arbitrary Acts of Power over any military person, always Stedfastly maintaining that a Soldier does not forego the rights of a free Citizen by taking arms in defence of his Country. That the rules of his Conduct, mode of his trial, and measure of his punishments aught to be found in the promulgated Civil and military Codes, to the former of which he has given the general Consent of a Citizen, and to the latter by Subscribing the articles the particular Consent of a Soldier.

Your Delegates are happy in the Conviction that in all that relates to this important object they maintained principles, and observed a Conduct Consonant to the Ideas of their Constituents, of which they Consider as Cogent proofs the Several acts of assembly made in favor of that Useful, Virtuous and Meritorious part of our fellow Citizens who are Chearfully undergoing all the Dangers and distresses of Military Service for their Country and they beg leave to express their Concern that those acts are not in all things Executed so as to give the full Effect to the liberality of the assembly.

With respect to finance your Delegates were of Opinion that the public Credit ought to be maintained by very Copious Taxation, well knowing that the ability to pay Taxes must always increase in proportion to the Increase of money, and much wishing that Taxes might have the Salutary Effect, of diverting much of that time which is now wasted every where in America in blameable Idleness, or frivolous Amusements, to Industrious Exertions for Increasing the resources of our Country. They also wished to Correct the abuses in the Expenditure of public Money, but I am Sorry today that such abuses are So Inveterate that they admit of no adequate Cure but from

Vigorous Exertions of the States to furnish the Necessary Supplies in kind according to their respective abilities.

All the Efforts of Congress have been directed to the lessening of Expenditures, to the procuring of Supplies of money by Loans and Taxes, and by Such means to prevent further Emissions. But all their Efforts must prove Ineffectual, if Not powerfully aided by Similar Efforts of the States for Carrying their resolutions into Execution.

Many States are availing themselves of the present plenty of money for the raising as much as possible by Taxes. The advantage of Such policy and the Injury of delaying Taxation until the Money becomes more difficult to be obtained, your Delegates presume are obvious, and cannot escape the Sagacity of the General Assembly.

What relates to foreign affairs being preserved in the Secret Journals of Congress will require a more particular detail, and I will here give as full a relation as the Injunctions of Secrecy which [I] am under will permit. Premising, that tho I hold myself not at liberty to declare any thing which I have been enjoined to keep Secret, unless I perceive its tendency to be Injurious to my Constituents; or, unless I am particularly required by the Assembly to lay such matters before them without reserve, Yet in Such Cases I Consider the obligation I am under to my Constituents, Superior to any which can be laid on me by Congress.[5] But in the Conduct of Wars, and foreign Negotiations many things will Occur which if divulged might lose every beneficial Effect, and produce Consequences very Injurious to the general Welfare. Such it is to be presumed no one State would require to be divulged, unless their own peculiar Safety made it Necessary, and I am too well Convinced of the Wisdom, discretion and public Spirit of my Constituents, to doubt their permitting Silence on all affairs of Such Nature. The foreign affairs have been Considered in Congress under two general Heads—the State and dispositions of foreign Courts; the Conduct and Character of our foreign Ministers—and each afforded very Interesting objects, and produced long protracted Questions and debates.

With respect to the Conduct of our foreign Ministers It was So Indiscreet that dissentions and Animosities had arisen amongst them which produced reciprocal Suspicions and Accustations. Nor had they the prudence to Suppress or Conceal them, on the Contrary, they Suffered them to break out into heats and altercations disgraceful to the Country in whose Service they were. The Consequence was, that they ⟨lost the Confidence of the Court at which they resided and⟩ became almost useless.

Doctr F. & Mr Dean who principally conducted our affairs at the Court of Versails Seemed to act in perfect Harmony, and to be fully possessed of the Confidence of the Court. Doctor Lee who was Joint Commissioner with them, accused them both of peculation, and Criminal waste and misapplication of public money. Mr. Dean Accused

Doctor Lee of being Froward, proud, Supercilious, Malevolent, Suspicious to So unreasonable a degree as to take unfounded Conjectures for facts, and to draw from them uncandid and disengenuous Conclusions—with all, to be of a temper Sordid and disgusting—and by his Correspondence and Connexitions with British Subjects and Emissaries to have become Suspected by the French Court of Infidelity—and Doctor Franklin Considered the same Gentleman as laboring under a Disorder of his Understanding.

The appointments of the other Gentlemen were found to have been Useless and their part in the Enquiries, and proceedings of Congress, being inconsiderable it Seems enough to Inform the Assembly that they were discontinued in office.

The Congress made a very Minute and painful Enquiry Concerning all the allegations of the different accusers and accused, but So deficient were they in Matterials for affording Testimony that no Satisfaction Could be obtained with respect to the guilt or Innocence of any.[6]

Mr Dean alledged that his accounts would very fully refute the charge of Mr. Lee, but that not knowing that he was recalled for any other purpose than to give Congress Information of the Political State of Europe as it affected the united States, and being desirous of giving them Satisfaction without delay, and of hastning the Departure of Count DeEstaing for America with the fleet under his Command, he did not take time to Settle them before he left France.[7] The accusations against him were founded upon Conjectures, Surmises and Inuendoes, and the Settlement of his accounts would Certainly prove either his guilt or Innocence, but they were in france, and all farther proceeding became impossible So that the Sense of Congress on the indisputable Merit of Mr Dean as our Assiduous, able, faithful, and Successful Minister Could not with propriety be given while he lay under So heavy a Charge as that of peculation. Doctor Franklin was involved with Mr Dean.

The Charges against Doctor Lee were no better Supported, and he himself was not present to answer. Upon the whole it appear'd to your Delegates, and in their Opinion to a great Majority of Congress, that the Charges on all hands were much more the result of personal Ill will and resentment than of Calm dispassionate Observation and Enquiry. The Indiscrition of the Ministers and their Consequent Inutility were to your Delegates and many others perfectly Evident. They also thought that when Ministers of such high trust were accused of Such Enormities nothing less than a full and clear Investigation by putting the parties personally on their defence before their Country, and obtaining all possible light concerning their Transactions, ought to Satisfy the public. This was impossible unless the Ministers were present, and therefore your Delegates were of Opinion that they ought all to be recalled. Agreeably to this principle they Voted for the recal of Doctor Franklin,[8] but, they Confess, it was with great reluctance. They had a high Opinion of his Merit and Services, and gave little or no Credit to the Charges against him—but they did not presume to think their Opinion of his Innocence to be Sufficient to Satisfy the public without a Trial. They are glad of this Opportunity of Explaining their Vote with respect to that able and faithful Minister, and venerable Patriot, and also to testify the pleasure they afterwards had when the Minister of France Informed Congress from the King that the appointing him Sole Plenipotentiary to his Court gave him the highest Satisfaction, and would engage his utmost Confidence.[9]

But the Sentiments of your Delegates, and of many others in Congress were very different as to Doctor Lee. From his Letters, and from the concurring Testimony of many who were personally acquainted with him they Conceived him to labor under that Imperfection of Capacity which gives to trifles too much Importance, and to be of a temper So Suspicious and unconciliating as to embarass all public Business in which he might be engaged. They had also indubitable proof that he was not only denied the Confidence of the Court of Versails, but deeply suspected by them: and the Connection and participation of Councils and Sentiments, between that Court and the Court of Madrid were so well known to your Delegates that they Could not doubt of his Standing in the Same Predicament with both—and Consequently to be, not only, useless, but injurious at either. The proofs referred to are the following.

In Debate on the Subject a Gentleman from Massachusetts Bay (Mr S. Adams) declared that he had it from the highest Authority, that Mr. Lee was not denied the full Confidence of the Court of Versails. One of your Delegates (Mr Burke) remarking this declaration, and observing that it was directly opposite to the Concurring representations of all who came from Europe, and to the general opinion as he was informed, of France and America he requested the Gentleman to name the authority he alluded to that other gentlemen might have an equal Opportunity of obtaining Such good Information which might prevent their giving their Votes to the prejudice of a gentleman who possibly might be a man of great worth, tho misrepresented through prejudice and popular Error. The Gentleman declined naming the Authority, and Mr Burke in Company with General Nelson a delegate from Virginia paid the Minister of France a Visit, in which the Conversation being introduced, the Minister delivered himself to the purport which is contained in a paper hereto annexed. Mr Burke reduced it to writing, and Comparing it with Mr Nelson both agreed that the Substance of the Conversation and almost the words were recited.[10]

Other Delegates Impelled by the Same Motives made more direct application to the Minister and Mr Paca a Delegate from Maryland, and Mr Drayton a delegate from South Carolina, obtained from him an Extract of a letter from the Count de Vergens which Communicated Certain dispositions, and transactions in European Courts to be Committed in Confidince to Congress, of which our own Minister were entirely Ignorant, and which in the Extract referred to accounts for that Ignorance by declaring that he feared Mr Lee and those about him. These several Testimonies were laid before Congress,[11] but to the great Surprise of your Delegates and many others the votes were, for recalling Mr Lee 4—against it four—and four divided. By this Division he still Continued Plenipotentiary to the Court of Madrid.

Your Delegates are unable to account for this division on any other ground than that of a Secret Combination in his favor formed by his Brothers who had been Members of Congress for a long time preceding, but this, tho it obtruded itself on the observation and Conviction of your Delegates and many others in Congress, yet as it can only be the result of Conjecture, and from its Nature is incapable of direct proof it does not become your Delegates to Assert it as a fact, and therefore they only Suggest it as a Conjecture which forced itself on the Minds of many of the Delegates, and which obtained additional Force from many Circumstances that could not escape observation, particularly the following. It was observed that Several Gentlemen in debate threw out Suggestions that the House was divided into partizans of Mr Dean and Mr Lee, and that the Endeavour to recall the Latter was an attempt to Sacrafise him to the former. Your delegates heared those Suggestions with Indignation, and Considering all Individuals and their Interests as inconsiderable objects Compared to the public Service, and being firmly persuaded that Neither of those Gentlemen could any longer be useful, they wished to See both removed. A Motion was made by one of your Delegates (Mr Burke) for detaining the one and recalling The other for the purpose of Investigating more fully their allegations of Mr. Lee against Mr. Dean. This motion was lost by an equal division, the members voting against it who favored or made the foregoing Suggestions.[12]

Upon the whole, your Delegates could find no Sufficient Cause proved for degrading any of the foreign Ministers tho they Saw plainly that none Except Doctor Franklin Could be any longer useful and even him they thought it right to recall in Order to give Satisfaction to the public by a trial, and that all of them, not excepting Doctr Lee, had some Merit, particularly unwearied attention and Industry.

With respect to the State and disposition of foreign Courts Early last February the Minister of France in a private Audience informed Congress[13] by the special Command of his King That England had failed in her application to the Court of Russia for Succors—that peace had taken place between that and the Ottoman power under the mediation of his Master, that Austria and Prussia had also Submitted their differences to his Mediation, in which at his own request he was Joined by Russia—That from all the Arrangements in Europe it appeared Certain that Britain could Obtain no alliance among the Northern powers nor had our Confederacy any thing to apprehend from thence. That the King of Spain had offerred his Mediation between Great Britain and France, declaring that if it should be refused or Evaded he would no longer Stand Neuter and See the Arms and power of France Injured and Insulted. That as a preliminary article the Indepen[den]ce of the united states of America must be Acknowledged. He in the name of his Master also recommended to the Congress to be prepared to take their place in a Negotiation for Peace which would probably take place, under such Mediation, and might be daily Expected, and to furnish their Ministers with an ultimatum, as moderate as possible; remembering always that the Events of War are uncertain, that peace is Exceedingly desireable as well to France as America—That nothing of Importance ought to be Committed to the former which could be obtained without, and That nothing ought to retard the latter which was not absolutely necessary to our Safety.

That in the Cabinet of Britain there was as early as October '78 a great party in the favor of acknowledging our Independance, and that it was prevented only by the Hopes which the Commissioners gave of disunion amongst us, to excite and Continue which they had employed and rewarded Several Individuals in America. He also recommended Secrecy and dispatch that Spain might be properly informed of our resolutions and enable to press Britain to a decisive declaration in time to take part in the War and to Commence her Opperations with the then Ensuing Campaign.

Also that as it was possible the Pride and Obstinacy of the British Monarch might still hinder the much wished for peace, we should be prepared to carry on the war against him with Successful Vigor, in order to which it was very adviseable to Come to a friendly understanding with Spain, and engaging her in alliance with us as well as with France, to obtain Effectual aid both of Force and Money from her, that in such Event we might obtain from her a Subsidy on very easy Terms which if prudently managed might restore the Credit of our Money—that the King his Master was prepared with all his force, which he would employ without reserve to force Britain into an acknowledgement of our Independence— That this was the only object which he proposed by the War, and when obtained he would chearfully lay down his Arms—But that he would assist with all his weight and Influence to obtain for us by Treaty any thing farther which we might require.

In Considering this Important Communication the Congress were necessarily led to take a view of all the objects which were Interesting to the States Individually or Collectively—to Insist on what were Essentially Necessary to the latter was unanimously agreed to. But great difficulties arose Concerning Such as might be deemed peculiarly important to Some, and remotely So to all. Almost every State could point out Such as were to her peculiarly Interesting, but the Importance of many of them to the whole depended on remote Contingencies, and the right to them was founded more on Casuistry, and Metaphisical reasoning, than on the received Laws and Customs of Nations.

Your Delegates Considered that the State of America in general made Peace too desireable to be delayed for the discussion of Such rights, or for the obtaining of such objects, and very early fixed their resolution to observe a profound Silence with respect to all Such objects, and insist only on such as were Indispensably Necessary for the Safety of the whole. Thus to leave to the more vigorous growth of future ages to assert disputed claims while they would Secure to the present what might be necessary for fixing Deep the roots, and cherishing the National Strength to a prolific Maturity. Pursuant to this resolution they declined insisting on Some objects which were undoubtedly of great Importance to this and many of the Neighboring States, the delegates of Such States Concurring with them. The Delegates from Some very respectable States did not Seem Impressed with an equal Sense of the great Expediency of peace and insisted very Strenuously and pertinaciously on Making a Certain object[14] part of our ultimatum which was peculiarly Interesting to the States they represented, and which is far from being indifferent or unimportant to the whole. Some part of this object, (and in the Opinion of your Delegates Sufficient for the purposes of America for many ages if not forever) appeared to be involved in the general Rights of Sovereignty and Independance and So far every one was willing to Insist at all Events. But these claims Extended So far as to Interfere with the rights which must by the Law of Nations belong to britain after the war, and Such rights as Britain is always Jealous of in so a high a degree that She would make war at any time to prevent encroachments on them. The Delegates alluded to attempted to Support their claim to the Extended object on the right of Occupancy. ⟨*It appeared to your Delegates and to many others That Such Occupancy could not be an Occupancy of the united States, because their political Existance would not admit of it.*⟩[15]

Your Delegates and many others who could not perceive the Justice or force of their arguments Concluded that insisting on such an object would be, in Effect, refusing to make peace, and might even expose us to be deserted by our ally who might not think himself engaged to Continue in a State of Hostilities with a powerful Nation for such an object for his ally, and not chusing to risque the Continuance of the Calamities of War on the Success of reasonings which appeared to them futile, and which they were well persuaded would be wholly disregarded by Statesmen, they vigorously opposed the making of the object in the Extent required, an ultimatum. But being extremely desirous to gratify as far as they Could the States who were peculiarly Interested, for whose People they have the highest respect, they Consented that it should be an ultimatum Provided our ally should be in Condition to Continue Hostilities for it in Conjunction with us. This passed the Congress by very general if not unanimous Consent but not being Satisfactory to the Delegates who contended for the object they moved to reconsider it and were Indulged. It was now the 24th of March, and every day for a Considerable time was expected to be the last which should delay this important Business. But tho' they and many others used their utmost Efforts to bring the affairs to a Conclusion yet it could not be Effected before the middle of August,[16] during all this time it was often postponed for Business which appeared to your delgates of far less importance, and they were Sometimes obliged to Concur for prudential reasons which the Sagacity of this Assembly makes unnecessary to mention.

The Struggle was very arduous and pertinacious on both Sides, The one Considering a peace as inadmissable without an absolute acknowledgement of the right they claimed, and a Security for the undisturbed Exercise thereof, The other Considering the claim to all that Exceeded what was involved in the general right of Sovereignty and Independance as Extravagant and Insupportable, all, So involved, as Necessarily Secured by a Peace acknowledging that Sovereignty and Independance, and too well Convinced of the Expediency of Peace to Consent to its being delayed for objects of ambition or rapacity. The former availing themselves of all their Ingenuity and address to obtain resolutions of Congress, which, tho not apparently, might by [. . .] in Consequence prevent a peace until their favorite object Should be Secured, the latter firmly persuaded that the Sense of the great Body of the People through all the united States was with them, because Such must arise from their Interests and Circumstances that it was their Indispensable duty to prevent every obstruction to peace but such as were unavoidable, and that the direct operation of every resolution which should be passed on So important a Subject Should be plain and unequivocal were ever watchful to pervade every proposition, and by proposing Amendments, to Strip it of every Artificial Coloring until it was brought to the Simple Question "Shall the War be Continued merely for that object?" As in this form it was impossible to obtain a Vote of Congress to the Affirmative, So when it was perceived that no Question Could be put but what must plainly come to this point those who Contended for making the object an ultimatum availed themselves of advantages which the rules of Debate and forms of proceeding in Congress gave them, and prevented the decision alltogether. Thus was much time wasted in Endeavouring to reconcile Opinions So Opposite on subjects of the highest Importance. At length it was rested on a resolve passed Early in the progress, that the object as far as it i supposed to be involved in the right of Independance Should in no Event be given up, but no other Stipulations relative to it in a Treaty of peace were permitted to be a part of the ultimatum. Some resolutions were entered into for the better Securing the undisturbed Exercise of the right as above [limited?] in which your Delegates did not Concur, not being [convinced?] or that their powers Extended to the entering into Such Engagements as were proposed.[17] But it would be premature and Improper to mention the particulars of Such Engagements at present. Your Delegates hope it is Sufficient to inform the assembly that their dissent will appear on the Journal, and the State may avail herself thereof Should it hereafter be deemed Expedient.

The Minister of France had a Second private Audience of Congress in July and then informed us of Some difficulties which prevented the Success of the Mediation of Spain which it required the Wisdom and Moderation of Congress to remove. The Congress resolved on the Measures which appeared to them the best for removing them, and if not too late, your Delegates have Strong hopes in their Success.[18]

No Conclusive resolutions were entered into relative to the proposed alliance with Spain, while any of your Delegates who have now the honor of informing the assembly remained at Congress.[19]

MS (Nc–Ar: Secretary of State Records). Written by Burke and endorsed by him: "rough of an Address to the People drawn when member of Congress in 1779."

[1] In mid-October the North Carolina assembly ordered its congressional delegates, Burke, Whitmell Hill, and John Penn, to appear before it and "give information with respect to Matters which have come under the deliberation of Congress since January last." *N.C. State Records*, 13:833, 922. While three of the four journal entries recording the adoption of the resolution specify that the delegates attend on "Friday next" (October 22), the message from the house to the senate reads "Monday next." Whatever the reason for the discrepancy, Burke and Hill clearly attended the assembly on Monday, October 25. Although there is no mention of the report in the journals, they received the thanks of the Senate and House of Commons to which they responded in kind. Their responses are in ibid., pp. 854, 945–47; and Legislative Papers, Nc–Ar. The report itself, which covers the period from "the beginning of January 79 to the midle of August" when Burke left Congress, was probably not drafted until a few days before its presentation to the assembly.

[2] Burke originally wrote this statement as if it were from the entire delegation ("Your Delegates presume therefore that they"), but later amended a considerable portion, although not all, of the text by changing the pronouns and verbs to make it appear to be a personal report. He also made other, minor alterations in phraseology.

[3] See *JCC*, 14:523.

[4] Burke may have been referring to the case of Maj. Matthew Clarkson, for which see John Jay to Joseph Reed, January 27, 1779, note 2.

[5] For the "Injunctions of Secrecy" under which the delegates labored, see, for example, James Lovell to Samuel Adams, July 10; North Carolina Delegates to Richard Caswell, July 15; and Lovell to Richard Henry Lee, July 17, 1779.

[6] For Congress' "Minute and painful Enquiry," see especially the Foreign Affairs Inquiry Committee Minutes, January 21, 1779.

[7] For Silas Deane's "narrative" of his mission to France, see these *Letters*, 11:285–87, 383–84, 393–94.

[8] See *JCC*, 13:499–500.

[9] See *JCC*, 14:830; and Committee for Foreign Affairs to Benjamin Franklin, July 16, 1779.

[10] See Thomas Burke's Statement Respecting Gérard's Views on Arthur Lee, April 16, 1779.

[11] See William Paca and William Henry Drayton to Congress, April 30, 1779.

[12] See *JCC*, 14:711–14; Henry Laurens' Notes on William Paca's Motion, April 26; and Laurens' Notes of Debates, April 30, May 6, June 10–11, and June 11, 1779.

[13] For Gérard's "private Audience" with Congress, see William Henry Drayton's Notes, February 15, 1779.

[14] Undoubtedly, the fisheries.

[15] Although Burke had written "dele" in the margin beside this passage, he did not cross it out.

[16] The delegates approved the ultimata for a treaty of peace on August 14, the last day that Burke is recorded as present. See *JCC*, 14:956–60.

[17] For these resolutions, see *JCC*, 14:749–52, 765–70, 790–93, 863–65, 884–86, 896–97, 920–22; Henry Laurens' Notes of Debates, June 19; John Dickinson's Draft Petition, July 22; and Dickinson's Draft Resolves, July 24, 1779.

[18] For Gérard's "private audience" with Congress on July 12, see James Lovell to Samuel Adams, July 10, note 5. For the "measures" that Congress considered to remove obstacles to negotiations with Spain, see Burke's Draft Report, August 5, 1779.

[19] Burke was reelected as a delegate to Congress on October 26. On the 28th the House of Commons drew up instructions for its delegation and authorized the governor to prepare commissions. See *JCC*, 15:1361; and *N.C. State Records*, 13:868–69, 948, 960, 962. Among these October 28 instructions to the North Carolina delegates was an assembly resolve declaring the state's willingness to join a confederation of fewer than thirteen states if unanimous ratification could not be obtained. North Carolina Journal of the House of Commons, October 18–November 10, 1779. DLC(ESR).

Burke, however, objected to the concept of a "partial Confederacy" and presented the following appeal to the assembly on October 31st: "To the Honorable the General Assembly of the State of North Carolina.

"Thomas Burke, one of the Delegates of the said State to the Congress of the United States, (his Colleagues being absent,) most respectfully represents:

"That, by the articles of Confederation, Nine States are required to consent to every affirmative vote for Peace, for War, and for borrowing and emitting money—and five States, consequently, have a Negative.

"That, being now in a state of War, this negative might prevent a peace, tho' offered on reasonable Terms.

"That even a smaller number would be invested with this dangerous power, should any one or more of the States be absent, which has happened with respect to Georgia for many months, and may also happen with respect to any which may be overrun by the enemy.

"That for every purpose of common defence and common Exertions in the progress of the present War and for the conclusion thereof, the States are unquestionably, united by former acts of the Several States, nor can this union derive strength from a partial Confederacy for the same or other purposes; on the contrary, such partial confederacy may lay the foundation of disunion, or, by seeming to do so, may have such Effect on the hopes of the British Ministry as to induce them to a longer Continuation of Hostilities. The present times are critical, and it seems prudent to decline every thing which may occasion, even an appearance of divided councils; a partial Confederacy must be followed by confusion, the states so confederated, and such as are now so Confederated, could no longer form one Common Council; and separately they could not form or Execute any Common resolutions; in a word, it would destroy the old union.

"It is Evident that the Confederacy, formed for thirteen, will not fit a smaller number, and that if a partial Confederacy be found Necessary, the articles thereof must be previously adjusted. The said Thomas Burke, for these reasons and many others, most respectfully submits to the Consideration of the honorable Assembly whether it be Expedient that the Delegates from this State *be peremptorily required* to recommend or enter into any partial Confederacy, pursuant to the instructions and resolutions of the 28th instant? or whether it be more Expedient to impower them to Act as Circumstances may require in a matter of so much Delicacy and Importance whose Consequences cannot now be actually foreseen." *N.C. State Records*, 14:349–51.

That Burke's appeal was successful is evident from the fact that the assembly ordered the resolve deleted from its manuscript journal. Cf. Journal of the House of Commons, October 28, 1779, DLC(ESR); and *N.C. State Records*, 13:957–60. The assembly doubtless intended that its delegates act, in Burke's words, "as Circumstances may require."

John Fell's Diary

Monday October the 25th. 1779

Coml Committee. Congress. Letter from Genl. Washington dated 21st advising that the Enemy had Evacuated Stoney and Ver Plancks Point, and Reported they were going to leave Rhode Island.[1] Report from the Committee with Instructions to Mr Laurens to Negotiate a Loan.

MS (DLC).
[1] See William Sharpe to Richard Caswell, October 24, 1779, note 2.

Daniel of St. Thomas Jenifer to Thomas Johnson

My dear Sir,   Phila. Octr. 25th. 1779.

I am favored with your Excellencys Letter of the 22d Inst.

Our situation is truly alarming from the depreciated State of our Money. Tho' for eight days past Gold has been falling in value dayly—from 35 for one it is now at 26—But Goods & produce rising. Flour is so essentially necessary at this time, that every expedient must be made use of to procure it.

Congress have applied for Loans in Europe & lately reinforced their applications, and there is now some prospect of Success. I have still hopes that the Back Lands, at least a considerable part of them, will come under the direction & disposal of Congress. It is thought by many that the Count D'staign would be in Possession of Savannah the 12th Inst. so that he may now be Hourly expected. The Enemy are making the greatest preparations to receive him. He has evacated Stony & Verplank points; first have'g Distroy'd & burnt everything in His power. The Cayuga's & some others of the Six nations are Sueing for peace.

No late intelligence from Europe.

I did intend to Set out for Annapolis as to day, but the business I mentioned in my last not being yet brought before Congress, owing to the Absence of Mr. Witherspoon I have determind to stay all the week rather than leave this business unreported.[1] I must therefore request the Senate (should I not be down in time) to chuse a President in my room. By Thursday the 4th of November if God spares me I shall be down, in the meantime I am with the greatest affection & esteem, Dr Sir Your friend & Servt,

Daniel of St Thos Jenifer

RC (MdAA: Red Books).

[1] Jenifer, who had applied for a leave of absence on October 23, was apparently waiting for chairman John Witherspoon's arrival to conclude the business of the committee appointed October 8 to consider the memorials of the Indiana and Vandalia land companies. Witherspoon returned to Congress on October 26 and the committee reported the following day, although its report was not considered until October 29–30. Jenifer apparently departed for Annapolis immediately thereafter. See *JCC*, 15:1155, 1202, 1213, 1224, 1226–30, 1232; and John Fell's Diary, October 26. For Congress' handling of the sensitive issue of its jurisdiction over western lands, see Samuel Huntington to the States, October 30, 1779.

John Fell's Diary

Tuesday 26th Octr. [1779]

Coml Committee. Congress. After some dispatches were Read the Report for Instructions to Mr Laurens was taken up and debated the whole day to no Purpose.

PM Marine Committee.

NB Dr Weatherspoon.[1] Confederacy and Eagle Packet Saild this day from the Capes.

MS (DLC).

[1] That is, John Witherspoon, who had been absent since October 14, had returned to Congress.

Samuel Huntington to Jean Holker

Sir   Philadelphia Octor 26th. 1779

Your favour of the 22d Instant I receivd last night.[1] Your kind offices in forwarding those Letters and giving me this early intelligence is very acceptable and Claims my Acknowledgements.

You will receive herewith enclosd a letter which came under cover directed to me from Captains Landolphe, Raux, and Patot who it Seems have put into New London in Connecticutt, in distress.[2]

I Suppose you will Judge it properly in your department to give them the necessary Assistance.

I Shall ever be happy to See any relief in our power readily granted to our good Allies, I have communicated the Letter to le Chevalier de la Luzerne.

The enclosd paper will furnish you with the latest Intelligence I have receivd from Georgia & the Count De Estaing. I am Informd by Genl. Washing[ton], the Enemy have evacuated both their posts at Kings ferry viz. Stoney, & Verplanks points burnt & destroyd their works; also by the last advice from Newport every thing apeard to Indicate a Speedy evacuation of that place, Say last Sunday.

I am Sir with Esteem and Regard your humble Servant,

Saml. Huntington

RC (DLC: Holker Papers).
[1] Holker's letter is not in PCC.
[2] See the following entry.

Samuel Huntington to Captains Landolphe, Patot, and Raux

Gentlemen,   Philada Octr 26th 1779

Your letter of the 13th instant I received last evening, have communicated the same to the Minister of France Le Chevalier de la Luzerne, & shall lay the same before Monsr. Holker the Consul of France at this Port & marine Agent, hope he will take the necessary Measures to relieve your present Distresses & procure you the necessary Supplies.[1]

You may be assured of receiving all proper assistance & relief that these United States can afford their good Allies.

I am with esteem & regard, your hble Servant,

S.H. President

LB (DNA: PCC, item 14).
[1] Jean Landolphe, P. Patot, and Th. Raux were captains of three French vessels that had sailed from Cape François in August in convoy with the comte d'Estaing, but which were heavily damaged in a storm encountered on September 16, after which they had made their way to New London, Conn., on October 12. Their letter of explanation to Huntington, which the president enclosed with the preceding entry, is in the Holker Papers, DLC.

Their plight is also discussed in another document in the Holker Papers, an October 14 letter to Holker from Thomas Mumford, Continental agent at New London. The three ships, Mumford wrote, "must be unloaded & have Large Repairs before they Can Leave this Port. I have informed them," he went on to explain, "I transact business for you here, & wou'd Render them any Service in my power. . . . Masts that they want I have by me, which are scarce here."

James Lovell to Richard Henry Lee

Dear Sir,   Oct. 26th. 1779

Your Favor of the 3d reached me early yesterday, & those of the 9th & 16th this morning by Col Loyaute. There are Letters of mine on the Road to you which will reach you with the Registers. By the by, I did not give the Printers, as I ought to have done, Extracts of those Books for Publication. I wish, for the Sake of a thorough Friend Col. Peabody that I could have in print or out that Passage where orders are given for *more rigorous Treatment* of us than formerly. I am so pressed now that I cannot give you Vouchers or Extracts but by Mr. Laurens I will aim to do it. I shall attend to what you say of the Post Office, And a Report is this Day in Train.[1] I hope the Office will have added to it all or most of the present Expenditures for Expresses; or rather, that the Office will be *enriched* with one twentieth Part of that *enormous Sum*. You must e'r this have heard of the *Secretaries*, and Joshua Johnson to examine accounts. But as Mr. Laurens is going to Holland I think he will be able, if directed to Scrutinize many Things in France also.

I hear nothing from Mr. Jno A—— & Fr—— D yet. But if the latter refuses I understand that Gov. M. & Sr. J J[2] are desirous of filling that Vacancy or the principal one if J A refuses. I would even strive, *therefore*, for the 2d place.

I hope I shall have more Leisure to write by next oppertunity. Yr, affectionate Friend & humb Sert,   J L

RC (ViU: Lee Family Papers).

[1] The report of the post office committee had been submitted to Congress on October 23, when further consideration was postponed to "Tuesday next," which was October 26. According to the journals, Congress did not resume consideration of the report this day, but returned to the report on December 1. See Samuel Huntington to Richard Bache, December 2, 1779.

[2] The persons referred to by Lovell are, respectively, John Adams, Francis Dana, Gouverneur Morris, and Sir James Jay.

Henry Marchant to William Greene

Sir,   Philadelphia Octr. 26th. 1779.

I was yesterday favoured with Your Excellency's Favour of the 12th Instant. I have with the greatest Pleasure communicated to Congress the spirited Measures which continue to be exerted by the Legislature, and by all Ranks and Degrees of the good People, of the State I have the Honor to represent. At the same Time I have not failed repeatedly to represent the Difficulties, grievous Expences, and peculiar Distresses, that State hath hitherto sustained. I shall make an Application for a further Supply of Monies on Account.

But as all Supplies are in future to be expected from the States, Your Excellency will readily suggest how difficult it may be to procure such an Order from Congress. My most strenuous Efforts shall not be wanting, and I am confident there will not be wanting a Disposition in Congress to comply with the Request of the State, Yet I dare not flatter myself or the State, with any great Success.[1]

I enclose your Excellency the Papers of the Weak. I congratulate You upon the prosperous Train of Affairs in Georgia.[2] The Count De Staing has however been detained longer than was hoped for, but We may expect in a few Days a happy Conclusion of Affairs there, and the Appearance of the Count, when if not before, I expect to hear that Newport is evacuated.[3] It will be a pleasing Circumstance that Wallace is at Length a Prisoner.

The Enemy have destroyed their Works at Stony & Verplanks Points, and are hiveing themselves in New-York. I hope a Sulphurious Vapor will soon arise there, to their utter Destruction.

I pray Your Excellency, present my Respects to the Honorable the Genl Assembly and assure that Respectable Body that I am Their & Your Excellency's most devoted, and obedient humble Servt,

                                                              Hy. Marchant

RC (R–Ar: Letters to Governors).
[1] On November 12 Congress authorized a $300,000 warrant for the Rhode Island legislature "payable out of their quota of the continental tax." *JCC*, 15:1260.
[2] Marchant is referring to the Franco-American siege of Savannah, which ultimately failed. For further information on this venture, see Alexander A. Lawrence, *Storm over Savannah; the Story of Count d'Estaing and the Siege of the Town in 1779* (Athens: University of Georgia Press, 1951).
[3] Although Congress had received notice from General Washington on October 25 that the British were preparing to evacuate Newport, Marchant was unaware that the evacuation of Rhode Island had actually been completed on the 25th. See John Fell's Diary, October 25 and November 5, 1779.

Marine Committee to John Beatty

Sir   October 26th 1779
     The enclosed Papers have been laid before this Committee by two Gentlemen[1] lately returned from captivity at the Island of Antigua whereby you will find that Americans are treated there with great severity. We request you will immediately apply to the British Commissary at New York on the subject of Exchanging our People who are Prisoners at that Island and use your utmost endeavors for Speedily Effecting the same.
     We [are] Sir,   Your Hble Servants

LB (DNA: PCC Miscellaneous Papers, Marine Committee Letter Book).
[1] Not identified.

Marine Committee to Elisha Hinman

Sir   October 26th 1779
   I am Ordered by the Honorable the Marine Committee to send
you the enclosed Extract from their Minutes approving of the sentence of the Court Martial held for your trial.[1]
   I am Sir Your Hble Servt,   John Brown Secy

LB (DNA: PCC Miscellaneous Papers, Marine Committee Letter Book).
   [1] Capt. Elisha Hinman had been cleared of all charges against him stemming from
the March 1778 surrender of the Continental ship *Alfred*. Morgan, *Captains to the
Northward, pp. 123–24, 154–55.*

Nathaniel Peabody to Meshech Weare

My Dear Sir   No. 7.   Philadelphia Octor. 26th. 1779
   I Shall for-bear, to attempt giving you a narration of proceedings
in Congress further than to mention that I fear the large, nominal,
Sums Calld. for, to defray the public expenditures, the ensuing year
will be more than the people of New Hampshire will be able to pay,
however as their Quota is one fifth less than heretofore, it may be a
Temporary Easment to them. Sir you will perhaps Think it Strange
when I assure you that if the States Should pay their Taxs. punctually
at the Times perfixed, unless Something Can Speedily be done to
reduce the prices of the Necessaries of life, regulate our finances,
and retrench expences, The Treasury will Scarce be Supplied. The
late Tragical Tumult in this City, was productive of Such Serious
Consequences. The Committes have Since ceased their exertions to
restrain the extortioner &c. whereby every article immediately doubled the price, which before was intolerable, to give you a Specimen,
mens ordinary Shoes here are from 70 to 90 Dollars the pair, a yard
of Cloth that formerly Cost from 13. to 15/0 Sterling per yd. is now
from a 115 to £150 Currency per yd—and other things in proportion. How long, how long, Shall, or Can these things be Suffered or
born with. These things, your prudence will forbid making Known,
as the monopolizers & Speculators with you would avail himself of
many advantages thereby. The last official News we have from
Count D'Estaing is that he, with our Troops, had *invested Savanah*
and were likely to be Successful &c—vid this days paper. The affair
of Vermont is a matter of Serious Consideration for if I can Judge
by present appearances, that District will finally be adjudged, either
to N. Hampr. or N. York, and not to be a seperate Jurisdiction. It
therefore becomes Necessary for the State of N. Hampr. to Exert
every Nerve to prevent a State by her vast Extent of Territory, and
Still Greater Claims, already Troublesome to her Neighbors and
Tyranical to the last degree over all Such as are the unhappy victims

of their resentment—from Extending Jurisdiction as to Circumvolve the State of New Hampr. However I rest assured that the wisdom of the General Assembly is Equal to the importance of the undertaking, and it might Justly be Stiled Arrogance in me to pretend to point out a mode of procedure for them. My worthy friend Genl Whipple is able to give the fullest account of the most material Circumstances, and I have no doubt but his opinion will be attended to. I imagine there is a Copy of a proposed act[1] respecting the Grants Sent forward to Some Gent in the State which I am far from thinking will Suit a N. Hampr Tast[e] if I can Judge of others by my own palate if Such a Draught Should appear. I beg leave Just to observe to you that it was *hatched* up by N.Y. and Consented to by Some who are better aquainted with N.Y. *Air* and Secret designs than I have the *honor* to boast of!! I Suppose the State of N. Hampr Competant without *my* particular *direction* to pass Acts, if agreable, per exactly to Comport with the Several resolutions of Congress relative to the Grants. The Situation of my private affairs is Such as makes it Exceeding difficult for me to Tarry here Longer than this fall; and by Some *Innuendos* lately dropt by ———[2] here have reason to imagine he has been inform'd from Some of his friends, that my return home is Soon *expected* by the *State*—however that may be give me leave to assure you with that Sincerity which becomes the Noblest works of the Deity, that I have not a Secret wish to be Continued here, a Single moment longer, and hope Some Gentleman will be appointed to Take my place whose abilities may be adequate to the arduous Tasks, Not that I Should ever be unwilling to Serve my Country at any future period if I Should be So happy as to obtain their approbation.

I am Dear Sir, your most obet. Humle Sevt,

N. Peabody

N.B. I will finish this Letter Next Time I have the Honr to write.

RC (MHi: Weare Papers).

[1] A copy of the "proposed act" drafted by John Jay had been enclosed in Woodbury Langdon's October 12, 1779, letter to Weare. See also Massachusetts Delegates to the Massachusetts Council, October 4; and Jay to George Clinton, October 5, 1779, note 1.

[2] Peabody is probably referring to Woodbury Langdon, the other delegate from New Hampshire then in Philadelphia, whose relationship with his fellow delegates is revealed in the following letter, which he wrote to Peabody from Portsmouth on December 5, 1779, soon after he returned to New Hampshire.

"Folsom setts off tomorrow for Congress." Langdon explained. "He goes in such a hurry I suppose least the new General Court who meet next Week might prevent him, as many Persons are very angry at the late scandelous management respecting you and myself and you may be assured that everyone of the Persons who I have frequently named to you in our conversations were principal Actors in that business and President Wear himself I am fully convinced was concerned in it notwithstanding his flattering Letters, also the Kingstown Gentleman [Josiah Bartlett] in particular, however our Friends have made such movements that I fancy those Gentlemen are very sick of the matter. I am very glad to find that all my Friends have exerted themselves as much for you as they have for me and we all desire that you will not think of leaving Congress untill next Spring and I wish that the situation of my Family had been such as to have permitted me to have remaind with you untill that time in which case I would have made Folsom appear in a very rediculous light as I dare say you will. You may expect now that you will have Letters from those Gentlemen who used to write you & from others in order to apologize for what is past and to desire you to take notice of Folsom & to introduce him &c that he may thereby be enabled to answer their designs in sending him, that he may be acquainted with what business has been done or may be doing &c in order to communicate it to them, but I trust that after such intollerable treatment & from those who you expected were your Friends that you will not pay any regard to any such recommendations nor take the least notice of Folsom in any respect whatsoever, but let him stand upon his own legs and be answerable for his own folly. I should be sorry even to hear that you both live in one House. As I have but just got home have not been able to procure the Votes you desired to send at this time but will take care to send them by next, notwithstanding the Letter which we received from Coll. Wear before I left you, he has ackowledged to me that it was the design of those Persons who promoted the Choice of Genl. Whipple & Folsom thereby to superceed you & myself. I have not time to go into any further particulars at present but shall endeavour to inform you of every thing worth notice by every oppertunity and shall take care that no injury happens to you that I can prevent. Let me desire that you would not fail to inform me of every thing that transpires by all means by every Post, especially of foreign affairs, if any offers for Peace and every thing else worth knowing. I hope you will always attend in the morning at reading the Dispatches and give me every material Intelligence. You may be assured that whatever you communicate to me in confidence will remain, which is what I shall expect from you." Miscellaneous Manuscripts, DLC.

For additional information on Langdon's relations with New Hampshire leaders, particularly "the Kingstown Gentleman," Josiah Bartlett, see also William Whipple to Bartlett, August 10, 1779, note 1.

Nathaniel Scudder to John Stevens

Dear Sir,[1]   Philadelphia Octobr. 26th 1779

Being informed that you are again elected in Council, and presuming you will again preside therein, and consequently in all Probability be reelected to the Chair of the Joint Meeting, I presume to write to you on a Subject, which I know requires the greatest Delicacy, however my peculiar Circumstances and Feelings impel me to it; and I will freely rely on *that Candor* for which you are so distinquished, and *that Friendship* which I flatter myself you entertain for me, in the Use you shall make of this Letter; only requesting, that if any Person shall nominate me at the ensuing Election & persist in it, you will read such Part of it in joint Meeting, as you think will prevent my being at all balloted for—for, my Dear Sir, I think it would be equally hard on an old faithfull Servant to be balloted for, and, on Account of his particular Friends kindly withholding their Votes, loose the Election; or, after his earnest Sollicitations, to be excused from further public Service, to be elected and from the Peculiarity of his Circumstances compelled to decline the honor. I will only further entreat you to be assured, that this Address is not from a Presumption that I should be again elected or even nominated; was it not for the partial & unmerited Attachment of some of my Friends; with whom I have conversed; more especially as I am daily more and more convinced of my great Unfitness in evey Respect (except in Point of Integrity and Application) for this arduous Task; and that there are many Men to be found in the State more equal to it. I now proceed to state my Circumstances freely to you, & I am not ashamed of them. I early entered into this Contest, firmly resolved never to retire from such Service as my Country should call me to, untill the Liberties of my Country (dearer to me than Fortune or Life) should be firmly established, or untill real Necessity should compel me to it. This Resolution was finally the only proponderating Circumstance in Favor of serving in Congress the last year, when I gave Way to the pressing Instances of many of the Members of our Legislature, and hardly was induced to Promise them that if I was again honored with the Delegation, I would devote as much of my Time to it as possible. This I *have done*, and beyond my Expectation shall be able nearly or quite to compleat my Quota of Attendance. This has added so much to the Reduction of the small remains of my private Fortune, to the Distresses & Uneasiness of my Family, to the Injury of my Childrens Education, that another Year's Attendance here would be ruinous. The following Declarations are made on the Veracity of an honest Man. First. I have during my public Service, for more than five years past, sunk much the greatest Part of my private Fortune, & do not repent it. 2dly. I have almost totally sacrificed a lucrative Business, by which and other Ways & Means I might have reputably made great Additions to it. 3dly. I have been under the Necessity ever since my Delegation to Congress and on Account of the Narrowness of my own Circumstances, to live in a Stile, in my own Opinion, really beneath the Dignity of a Representative of a free & independent State, and very very much below the Stile of the Delegates of most other States, having never been able to keep a Servant, and seldom a horse since I left Yorktown, and I believe the other Delegates of the State are in the same predicament. 4thly. All the Wages I ever have received, or am to receive since my first Election into the Council of the State have little if any more than half paid for my Food & Raiment with other small contingent Charges, and I am ready at any Time to submit my Frugality and Œconomy to the strictest Scrutiny. Indeed I must confess that I am much mortified when I reflect that the State has never to my knowlege given a public Dinner, nor have I myself in three Instances been able to invite half a Dozen of my most select Friends to a neat Family Dinner at my Lodgings notwithstanding innumerable Instances of Invitations from Members of Congress & other Gentlemen. I say not these things as the least Reflection on my Constituents, or under an Expectation of any further Compensation than my legal Wages for my past Services, but sincerely for the Benefit of the State, least *that same* Necessity, which now compels my Declination, may soon occasion other faithful Servants to retire from it's Service; when possibly their Places may be filled by ambitious designing Men or by others, who being Persons of like contracted Fortunes with myself may not perhaps so fully withstand those powerful lucrative *Temptations*, which *here* surround us, as I *firmly* boast *I have* done.

I am sorry I have it not in my Power to copy this Letter; such as it is it must go, please to preserve it carefully till I see you.

I am Dear Sir in greatest Haste, as Congress hour is arrived, but with great Respect & Esteem Your Friend & Hble Servant.

Nath. Scudder

RC (NjHi: Stevens Papers).

[1] Stevens is identified in these *Letters*, 1:331.

John Fell's Diary

Wednesday Octr. 27th [1779].

Coml Committee. Congress. Several Memorials, Letters & Reports from Board of War and Treasury. A Report from the Medical Committee for further Provission for the Director General, Surgeon, Phisicians &c in the Army for Subsistance, Cloathing &c.

MS (DLC).

Samuel Huntington to Louis Duportail and Alexander Hamilton

Gentlemen,   Philada Octr 27th 1779

I am favour'd with your letter of yesterday also one from Colo Hamilton of the 19th instant.[1]

I have not receiv'd any official or particular intelligence from the Count D'Estaing or the Southern Army since you left this City.

The enclos'd papers contain all the information I am able to give you either from the southern, northern or eastern Armies.

I am with esteem & regard your hble Servt.   S.H. Prest

LB (DNA: PCC, item 14).

[1] Neither of these letters is in PCC. Gen. Louis Le Bégue de Presle Duportail, commandant of the Continental corps of engineers, and Lieutenant Colonel Hamilton had been dispatched by Washington to Lewes, Del., to confer with the comte d'Estaing on the subject of combined Franco-American operations when the French fleet reached northern waters. Although Washington was disappointed in d'Estaing's failure to appear as anticipated, his correspondence with Congress, d'Estaing, and Duportail and Hamilton on this subject can be followed in Washington, *Writings*

(Fitzpatrick), 16:428, 441, 453–54, 483–84, 17:4–6, 28, 55–56, 93–94. See also Marine Committee to Henry Lee, October 29, 1779; and Freeman, *Washington*, 5:136–38.

Samuel Huntington to James Wilkinson

Sir   Philada. October 27th 1779

You will herewith receive enclos'd an act of Congress of this date, ordering that a warrant issue on the Commissioner of the continental loan Office in the State of New York in your favour for fifty thousand dollars and as it seems uncertain who may be the Person that shall discharge the warrant at the time of payment, you will observe you are to inform the board of treasury of the name of the person who may discharge the same.[1]

I am Sir your hble Servt.   S.H. President

LB (DNA: PCC, item 14).
[1] For Congress' order authorizing Clothier General Wilkinson to collect $50,000 from the Continental loan office in New York "for the use of the hide department," which Wilkinson had requested in a letter to Congress of October 16, see *JCC*, 15:1211.

John Fell's Diary

Thursday Octr. 28th. 1779

Coml Committee. Congress. After the dispatches, A Report from the Marine Committee was taken up to Establish a Board of Admiralty consisting of 3 not Members of Congress as Commissioners & two Members of Congress wth a Secretary. Sallery of the Commissioners 14000 Ds Per Annum and Secretary 10,000.[1]

MS (DLC).
[1] For the establishment of the Board of Admiralty, see John Dickinson's Notes, September ?, 1779, note 1; and Samuel Huntington to Thomas Waring, November 27, 1779.

Samuel Holten's Diary

[October 28–29, 1779]

28. Thursday, It is said the enemy have done sum damage in the Jersey's.

29. Friday. Congress spent part of the day considering the Indiana affairs.[1]

MS (MDaAr).
[1] For Congress' consideration of the "Indiana affairs," see John Fell's Diary, September 14, note 1; and Samuel Huntington to the States, October 30, 1779.

Samuel Huntington to John Rutledge

Sir,   Philada Octr 28th 1779
    You will receive herewith enclos'd an Act of Congress of this date
authorizing the board of War to purchase a quantity of leather in the
State of South Carolina & draw upon the Governor of that State for
such sum as may be necessary to pay for the same & requesting the
monies may be advanced out of the taxes raised on Continental
Account.[1]
    I have the honour to be with sentiments of Esteem your Excy's
hble Servt,   S.H. President

LB (DNA: PCC, item 14).
    [1] For this resolve and the report of the Board of War on the "scanty supply of
leather" available in the northern states, see *JCC*, 15:1215–16; and PCC, item 147,
2:547–50.

John Dickinson to Caesar Rodney

Sir,   Philadelphia, Octr. 29th, 1779
    I recd. yours of the 27th this Day, and have this Moment communi-
cated its Contents to Congress, who have referr'd an Extract to the
Treasury.[1]
    I have not yet been able to procure a Report from that Board, tho
I have sollicited them every Day, on the recruiting Business which
was referr'd to them some time ago, as I informed You.
    I have applied to the Delegates of Maryland &c for Information
concerning the Terms on which the Supply recommended by Congress should be obtained—but they can say Nothing on the Subject.
It is expected each State will manage the Business with a laudable
Competition for Frugality.
    I write this Letter in Congress. This Instant We receive Advice,
which seems to come in a very good private Way from the Fleet at
New York—that there has been a severe Engagement in Europe
between the combined Fleets of France & Spain & that of Britain, in
which the latter was defeated & oblig'd to retreat into Harbour—
That in this Battle the Ardent, Admiral Gambier, went to the Bottom with Colours flying. I am, Sir, your very hble Servt.
                                                        John Dickinson

[*P.S.*] I shall be obligd to You for sending the inclosed as directed.

RC (NN: Rodney Letters).
    [1] On October 9 Congress had requested that Delaware, Maryland, and South Caro-
lina purchase flour and rice for use of the army, for which see Delaware, Maryland,
and South Carolina Delegates to Thomas Johnson, October 9, 1779. In his letter of
October 27, Rodney informed Dickinson that "an account of the monies" in the

Delaware treasury made it unlikely that "the Quantity of Flour recommended by the Delegates" could be purchased "from that Quarter." By December 21, however, Congress ordered an express sent to Delaware requesting the state to procure "as much flour as can be obtained within their State, the necessities of the army calling for their immediate and most strenuous exertions." See *JCC*, 15:1151, 1157, 1219, 1399; and Rodney, *Letters* (Ryden), p. 324.

John Fell's Diary

[October 29–30, 1779]

Friday 29th. Coml Committee. Congress. After the dispatches &c were Read, the Committee to whom was Referrd the Memorials of Col Morgon and Coll Treat[1] Respecting Lands claimd Per Virginia brought in a Report, which Virginia objected to on which a long debate ensued. PM Marine Committee.

Saturday 30th. Coml Committee. Congress. Resolved to Reccomend to the State of Virginia not to dispose of any unlocated Lands &c.[2]

MS (DLC).
[1] That is, George Morgan and William Trent.
[2] See Samuel Huntington to the States, October 30, 1779.

Samuel Huntington to George Washington

Sir,   Philada October 29th 1779

I am honour'd with your favours of the 21st instant, and have the pleasure to transmit your Excellency the enclos'd Act of Congress of the 27th instant pass'd in consequence of the intelligence contain'd in your letter from Colo Broadhead.[1]

I have the honour to be, with the greatest respect, Your Excellencys hble servt,   S.H. President[2]

LB (DNA: PCC, item 14).
[1] Washington's October 21 letters to Congress are in PCC, item 152, 8:123–26, 131–32. For the extract from Col. Daniel Brodhead's September 16 report on his recent expedition from Pittsburgh against the Indians and Congress' vote of thanks to Brodhead and his men "for executing the important expedition against the Mingo and Muncey Indians, and that part of the Senecas on the Alleghany river," see ibid., fols. 135–37; and *JCC*, 15:1212–13. Huntington also transmitted this resolve in a brief letter of this date to Colonel Brodhead. PCC, item 14, fol. 216.

[2] Huntington also wrote the following letter this day to John Lawrence, Continental loan officer for Connecticut.

"You will herewith receive enclos'd an act of Congress of this day directing you to pay unto the Executors or administrators of John [Hotchkiss] deceas'd two hundred and seventy dollars in full for the Certificate by you given in his lifetime as mentioned in the Act of Congress and for the reasons therein assigned." See PCC, item 14, fol. 215; and *JCC*, 15:1219.

Marine Committee to Henry Lee

Sir   October 29th 1779

Captain Patrick Dennis being employed to wait the Arrival of the Count D Estaings fleet off the Hook and being a Gentleman in whom we have the greatest confidence.

We request that you will Afford him every Assistance in your power to enable him to make the necessary Observations before the Appearance of the fleet.[1]

We are Sir, Your Hble servants

LB (DNA: PCC Miscellaneous Papers, Marine Committee Letter Book).

[1] Maj. Henry Lee had been ordered by General Washington to take up post in Monmouth County, N.J., "as near the coast as you can," to await the arrival of the comte d'Estaing. Washington, *Writings* (Fitzpatrick), 16:278–80.

Samuel Huntington to Henry Laurens

Sir   Philadelphia, Octor 30th. 1779

You will herewith enclosd receive a Commission & Instructions of this date Authorizing & directing you as Agent for these United States to Negotiate a loan not Exceeding Ten Million dollars on the Terms therein Specified and directed.[1]

I have the Honour to be, with the highest Regard, your humble Servant,   Saml Huntington President

RC (PRO: C.O. 5, 43). This is one of a number of documents taken from Laurens when he was captured off Newfoundland en route to Europe, September 3, 1780.

[1] For Laurens' commission, see *JCC*, 15:1230, 1235–36. For his instructions, see the following entry.

Samuel Huntington to Henry Laurens

Instructions to the honorable Henry Laurens Esqr. Agent appointed to negotiate a loan for the United States of America.[1]

Sir   [October 30, 1779]

You will herewith receive a commission Appointing you agent for and in behalf of the United States of America, to negotiate a loan: And you are instructed to borrow a sum not exceeding ten million dollars at the lowest rate possible not exceeding six percentum per annum.

You are empowered to employ on the best terms in your power some proper mercantile or banking house in the City of Amsterdam or elsewhere in the United Provinces of the low countries to Assist in the procuring of loans, to receive and pay the money borrowed, to keep the accounts and pay the interest.

You are also empowered to pledge the faith of the United States by executing such Securities or obligations for the payment of the money as you may think proper, And also that the interest shall not be reduced, nor the principal paid during the term for which the same shall have been borrowed without the consent of the lenders or their representatives.

You are directed to give notice to Congress, of any loan made by you or under your authority, and to direct the house by you employed to accept and pay the bills of exchange which may be drawn under the authority of Congress.

Done in Congress this thirtieth day of October in the year of our Lord one thousand seven hundred and seventy nine, And in the fourth year of our Independence.

Saml Huntington President

RC (PRO: C.O. 5, 43). In the hand of George Bond, attested by Charles Thomson, and signed by Huntington. See also the preceding entry.

[1] For Laurens' appointment as "a proper person to negotiate a loan in Holland," and the drafting (by Gouverneur Morris), evolution, and adoption of these instructions, see *JCC*, 15:1186, 1196–98, 1210–11; and PCC, item 25, 1:169–72. For additional information on Laurens' interest in the negotiation of a Dutch loan, see also Laurens to Jonathan Trumbull, Sr., September 26 and October 19, 1779.

Samuel Huntington to the States

Sir   Philada October 30th 1779

You will receive herewith enclos'd an Act of Congress of this date earnestly recommending to the State of Virginia to reconsider their late Act of Assembly for opening their land Office. And to that and all other States similarly circumstanced to forbear settling or issuing warrants for unappropriated lands or granting the same during the continuance of the present war.[1]

I am with Sentiments of esteem & regard your Excys hble Servt,

S.H. President

LB (DNA: PCC, item 14). The RCs of this letter are designated "Circular."

[1] For this October 30 resolve, adopted in response to the protests of the proprietors of the Indiana and Vandalia land companies against Virginia's recent land office act, see *JCC*, 15: 1223–24, 1226–30; and John Fell's Diary, September, 14, 1779, note 1.

Virginia's decision to promote settlement of its unappropriated lands, in part a tactic to undermine Maryland's resistance to ratifying the Articles of Confederation, was viewed with concern by most of the delegates outside of Virginia and North Carolina as productive of "great mischiefs" and a threat to the unity of the states "against the common enemy." The origins of her 1779 land office act have been analyzed at length in Jefferson, *Papers* (Boyd), 2: 133–38; and Mason, *Papers* (Rutland), 1: 408–9. For Virginia's response to this appeal "to reconsider their late [land office] Act," see Virginia Delegates to Benjamin Harrison, November 2; and Mason, *Papers*

(Rutland), 2:549–50. For other aspects of Congress' concern over Virginia's western land claims and the expansion of settlers into the region, see also North Carolina Delegates to Richard Caswell, November 4; and Huntington to Thomas Jefferson, November 9, and December 30, 1779.

Committee of Congress to William Livingston

Sir   Philadelphia 1st Novemr. 1779
The Commissary General of purchases has Orders to contract for a Supply of Flour for the Current Year, not to exceed two hundred thousd. Barrels on the most reasonable terms—Of this quantity it is expected your State will furnish twenty thousand Barrels.[1]
The exhausted Condition of our Magazines and the pressing wants of the Army call for the vigourous Exertions of the powers of your State to aid & facilitate Col. Blaine Deputy Commissary General of Purchases (who will wait on your Excellency with this) in supplying the Necessities of the Army with Bread & preventing the most disagreeable Consequences.
Your knowledge of the public wants & your known Zeal in promoting the Common weal supercedes the necessity of mentioning any other Consideration to engage your attention & Influence.
I am in behalf of the Committee of Congress on the Commissary & Quarter Master Genls. Department, Your Exellencys Most Obedt. & most Hble Servt.   Jesse Root

RC (MHi: C.E. French Collection). In a clerical hand and signed by Root.
[1] Root wrote a nearly identical letter this day to Pennsylvania president Joseph Reed, with the notable variation that Pennsylvania's quota was "seventy thousand Barrels." *Pa. Archives*, 1st ser. 7:774.

Committee on Appeals Decree

November 1st 1779.
Stephen Cleavland Lib[ellan]t & App[ell]ee ⎱   Appeal from
vs. The Ship Valenciano her Cargo &c.   ⎰   the State of
Joachim Luca Claim[an]t & App[ellan]t   Massachusetts Bay[1]
We the Commissioners appointed by Congress to hear, try and determine all Appeals from the Courts of Admiralty of the several American States to Congress having heard and fully considered as well all and singular the several Matters and Things set forth and contained in the Record or Minutes of the Proceedings of the Superior Court of Judicature, Court of Assize and General Gaol Delivery began and held at Boston in and for the County of Suffolk on the last Tuesday of August Anno Domini 1779 in the above Cause as the Arguments of the Advocate of the respective parties to the above

Appeal do thereupon adjudge and decree that the Sentence of the
said Superior Court &c. passed and published in the said Cause be in
all its parts confirmed and established Save and except only as to the
Goods, Wares, Merchandizes, Matters and Things mentioned and
contained in the several Bills of Lading exhibited in the said Cause
and marked, numbered and containing as follows to wit: No. 1. 120
Pipes of Olive Oil; No. 3. two Barrels of Cochineal marked Ⱡ., no. 2
& 134; No. 5. two Barrels of Cochineal marked JTC; No. 6. five
Barrels of Cochineal marked JTC, no. 1012–1016; No. 9. 8 Barrels
of Cochineal marked MC, no. 1–8; No. 11. 12 Barrels containing
twelve Zurrons[2] of Cochineal marked MS, no. 1–12; No. 13. four
Barrels of Granilla marked JPL, no. 1–4; No. 15. nine Zurrons of
Indigo, one Case of Saffron, and one Packet containing Samples of
Indigo marked *,[3] no. 42–51; No. 22. five pipes of Sherry and seven
half pipes of Red Wine marked Δ, no. 1–7, 7 Medn.; and No. 27.
One half pipe and one quarter Cask of Sherry Wine marked LM. All
which said several Goods, Wares, Merchandizes, Articles and Things
mentioned and contained in the said Bills of Lading & in Rapallos
Invoice Marked *[3] and in the Schedule exhibited by the Boatswain of
the Ship particularly set forth and described by their several Marks
and Numbers We do adjudge and decree be forthwith restored and
redelivered unto Joachim Luca the Claimant and Appellant abovenamed his Agent or Attorney to and for the Use of himself and
others on whose behalf he claims and appeals And we do further
adjudge and decree that the party Appellee pay unto the party
Appellant eleven hundred Dollars for his Costs and Charges by him
expended in supporting and sustaining his said Appeal &c.

Hy. Marchant   Jas. Mercer
Jesse Root   Cyrus Griffin

MS (DNA: RG 267, case no. 58). In a clerical hand, and signed by Griffin, Marchant,
Mercer, and Root.

[1] A jury of the Massachusetts Court of Admiralty for the Middle District had awarded
the ship *St. Francisca de Paula,* alias *Valenciano,* and most of her cargo to Stephen
Cleveland, merchant, and Capt. Hugh Hill, commander of the privateer armed ship
Pilgrim.   On February 21, 1779, Captain Hill had captured the *Valenciano,* commanded by Peter White, on the high seas as the ship was bound to Cadiz from
London. Joachim Garcia de Luca, former captain and "owner" of the *Valenciano,*
argued that the ship had been sold to him on June 5, 1778, in Cadiz. Nevertheless, the
jury found on April 6, 1779, that the ship and most of her cargo were English but that
some of the goods were Spanish and therefore not subject to seizure. Cleveland and
Garcia de Luca both appealed to the Massachusetts Superior Court of Judicature,
where the lower court was upheld. Captain Garcia then appealed to Congress, where
the case was referred on October 9, 1779, to the Committee on Appeals.

The committee in this decree affirmed the decision of the state court, except for the
goods listed therein which were decreed to be Spanish property. See case file no. 58,
RG 267, DNA; and *JCC,* 15:1159.

For further information on congressional involvement in this case, see John Jay to
Conrad Alexandre Gérard, April 25 and May 24, 1779.

[2] That is, a small leather bag, or provision-bag.

John Fell's Diary

Monday November the 1st. 1779.
Coml Committee. Congress. The Instructions & Commission for Mr Laurens, his Sallery £1500 Sterlg. and a Secretary £300 Sterlg. Dr Wetherspoon gone home.

MS (DLC).

Samuel Huntington to John Connolly

Sir   Philada Novr 1st 1779
You will receive enclos'd an Act of Congress of this day: authorizing the Commissary General of Prisoners to exchange you for any Lieut. Colonel in the Army of the United States who is now a Prisoner to the enemy.[1]
I am Sir your hble Servt,   S. H. President

LB (DNA: PCC, item 14).
[1] For this resolution and the recommendation of the Board of War that Connolly be exchanged, see *JCC*, 15:1231; and PCC, item 147, 2:557–60. Although the proceedings of Congress contain no further mention of Connolly, whose case had long troubled prisoner-of-war negotiations, his exchange was still not effected until October 1780. Some of the principal developments in the case can readily be followed in the correspondence of the commander in chief. Washington, *Writings* (Fitzpatrick), 18:324–25, 328, 19:16, 69, 160–61, 436, 20:69, 136, 218.

James Lovell to John Adams

Dear Sir   Novr. 1st. [1779]
Your Favor of Octr. 17th came this day to hand by the Post and contains such flattering Sentiments in regard to my subserving Your Mission as almost to intoxicate me into a Wish that I had not spurned much personal Honor and family Emoluments in pursuing a comparitively evident public Interest. But, nearly drunken as you have made me, depend upon it I am sober enough to distinguish between the Champaign with which my Regale began and the adulterated Cup which you hold out to me while you pledge yourself, in Case of future Correspondence, not to be in *debt* more than by the Difference in the intrinsic Value of the Letters *will be unavoidable*. Let me ask where you learnt such Language. It is not roman, it is not even french, and I am sure it is not such english as *you* were accustomed to

talk before you travailed into *strange* Countries. Be that as it may, un peuégaré, you recover your whole Self again shortly after, in the Affair of Mr. Iz.[1] I shall pursue yr. Injunctions.

I sat about giving you some Idea of the Temper of Congress as to the Ultimata by extracting the Propositions & offered Amendments,[2] but I found myself soon bewildered. You may by a little Conversation with our Friend SA[3] know more than a great deal of my Fatigue in the Way mentioned would convey. In short the great Difference sprung from our varying Quantum of Obsequiousness to the Dictations of a Foreigner as they were retailed to us through the mouths of either Fear or Roguery, and not from our being wide of each other in Opinion of our Rights, *if* we were in Condition to assert them or *if* our Ally would consent to join in a determined Assertion. But this said some must be quite on *new Ground* and not on the subsisting Treaties, for the whole End of these is the *Assurance* of our Independence formally or *tacitly*. And France to be sure would never think, at least would never insist that a common Right in the Fishery was included in our *Independence in Matters of Commerce*. For if this should be done, the Principle established would let in other nations, which France & England would *both* chuse not to do. I am greatly pleased with the Confirmation by yr. travailed Experience to Sentiments springing from my own natural Temper—That the way to insure the lasting Regard of France is by showing independant Virility instead of colonial Effeminacy.

Novr. 2d. The Bearer unexpectedly calls me to seal. I see my Correspondence with Portia is all over. She cannot write because I should see the mark of the Tear on the Paper.

Heaven bless you both.   J.L.

[*P.S.*] I do not think it will be easy for me to send you the Vols. you wish by Way of Boston but if you can borrow a few Sets there I will be upon Honor to repay them as Oppy. serves and I will attend to chances from this River but I cannot promise 20 Setts.

ENCLOSURE

reported Feby. 23d. 1779
3d. That a Right of fishg. & curing Fish on the Banks & Coasts of the Island of Newfoundland equally wth. the Subjects of France & Gr. Br. be reserved, acknowledged and ratified to the Subjects of the United States.

Others agreed to in Lieu.

4th. That the Navigation of the River Miss. as low down as the southern boundy. of the U.S. be acknowledged & ratified absolutely free to the Subjects of the U.S.[4]

5. That free Commerce be allowed to the Subjects of the U.S. with some Port or Ports below the southern boundary of the said States

on the River Miss. except for such Articles as may be particularly enumerated, and

In Case the Allies of these U.S. will agree to support them in such claims by continuing hostilities, then to insist that Nova Scotia & its dependencies be ceded to the Und. Sts. or declared independent.[5]

March 22d.

3d. Article as amended by the comtee. of the whole. That a common right in these States to fish on the coasts, bays & banks of Nova Scotia, banks of Newfdld. & Gulph of St. Laurence, coast of Labradore & Straights of Belle Isle be acknowledged, and in case of refusal that the war be continued unless the circumstances of our Allies shall be such as to render them utterly unable to assist in the prosecution of the war, in which case as ample priviledges in the fishy. be insisted on as can possibly be obtained: That in case Gr. Br. shod not be prevailed on either to cede or declare N Scota. independent the Priviledge of curing Fish on the Shores and in the Harbours of N Scotia be required.

In Lieu of which a Substitute was moved by Mr. Morris as follows.

That an acknowledgmt. be made by Great Br. of a common right in these States to fish on the coasts, bays & banks of N. Scota. the banks of New foundld. & Gulph of St. Laurence, the Coasts of Labradore & Straights of Belle Isle, *& a Stipulation for the Right of curing fish on the shores of N Scota.* provided always that the Allies of these States shall be in circumstances to support them in carrying on the War for such acknowledgement *& stipulation*; but that in no Case by any Treaty of Peace the common right of fishing as above described be given up.

This Substitute being adopted, a Motion was made & carryed to strike out the markd Words.

Questions were put on the parts & carried in the Affirmative.

March 24th

3d. Article as amended & passed the 22d reconsidered a motion made by Burke to strike out all after "to fish," as far as "provided" and to insert "on all & singular the fishing banks to the eastward of the island of Cape Breton and of N Scotia which by the Treaties of Utricht & of Paris were ceded to the Kg of Gr. Br. in Exclusion of the Subjects of France."

A motion by R H Lee 2d by Col. Dyer as a Substitute.

That the Right of Fishing on the Coasts and Banks of North America be reserved to the United States as fully as they enjoyed the same when subject to the Kg of Gr. Br. excepting always what shall have been excepted by the Treaty of Paris between France & the U.Ss. the whole to be explained by the Treaties of Utrecht and of Paris with Gr. Br. And of Paris with the United States of America.

Carried in the affirmative as a Substitute, and in Lieu of the Article passed on the 22d and the Amendmt. proposed by Mr. Burke.

On the 24th of March a proviso was moved on the Mississippi Business by Burke, 2d by Drayton "provid that the Allies of these United States shall declare themselves in circumstances to afford effectual assistance for carrying on the War until the said acknowledgement & ratification shall be obtained."

Pased in the *Negative*.

Question on the main passd. in the *negve*.

Since which a free Navigation is insisted on, perhaps it will delay the proposed Treaty with Spain.

RC (MHi: Adams Papers). Enclosure (MHi: Adams Papers). In the hand of Lovell and endorsed by him: "Extracts respectg. Fishery." Endorsed by Adams: "Mr. Lovel. Novr. 2. recd on Board Le Sensible Novr. 17. 1779. Debates and Votes about the Fisheries and the Missisippi."

[1] That is, Ralph Izard.

[2] See enclosure.

[3] Samuel Adams.

[4] In the margin beside this paragraph Lovell had written: "Mar. 24. disagreed to, vid 3d page."

[5] In the margin beside this paragraph Lovell had written: "lost June 17."

Nathaniel Peabody to William Whipple

My Dear sir   No. 5.   Philadelphia 1st of Novr. 1779.

I have the Honr. to acknowledge the receipt of your agreable favour of the 18th ulto. which Just came to hand per Post.[1]

Tho your leaving Congress, was to me a very disagreable occurrence, and I exceedingly regret, being deprived of your Company, and assistance at this difficult and Critical Period, which, your Long Absence from home, and our Political Situation being so Circumstanced at that time, you Judged was a Necessary Event. Yet give me leave to assure you, the information of your Safe arival at Portsmouth has ministred no small degree of Solace to my mind, for I had been much Concerned lest the fatigues of the Journey, would have increased Some disorders you were Subject to. However as you give me no hint of that kind—expect the Tour might have the Contrary Effect—and hope you found Mrs. Whipple and all Connections in the most agreable Circumstances.

In my letter No. 3 dated the 12th ulto.[2] I inclosed a Sketch, of proceedings on foreign affairs, Containing the most material Circumstances and facts relative to Some Congressional determinations upon the Great and fundamental Doctrines of *Election* & *Reprobation*, At the bar of which Tribunal it was Solemnly adjudged that no Patriotic efforts in the Cause of the Country, No Acts of Political or Relegious Virtue, Could be Esteemed *Meritorious*—When to the utter distruction and Reprobation of an honest man,[3] a faithful Servant, of the Public, One of the most perfidious of the Whole Tribe of Jesuits whose sole views had been to divide the Councils of America, Bannish a Spirit of Republicanisim from *her* Sons, to introduce and Establish a General Aristocracy, or perhaps the domination of a British Tyrant, And who had wholly Joined himself to Idols, (and ought to have been let alone) was Elected to a most important office, Taken into the Bosom of the Beautiful, once Chast, Virgin, *America* there like a Vulture to prey, without Controul, upon her Vitals. These transactions, My friend, however orthodox they may be, are Malancolly Consideration. Thus Stood our foreign affairs till about the 21 of Octr. when it was resolved according to a previous order of the day to proceed to the Election of a Proper Person to Negociate a Loan with Holland &c. The Gentlemen in nomination were the Hone. H. L——s and J. A——s.[4] The *Tall man* from N.Y.[5] who, in Your hearing, has often offered to Sell his Vote, upon the Decission of important Matters, for a Pinch of Snuff, from first, to last in this affair, took every method to make the Appointment, and mode of Conducting it, so far as it could respect those Gentemen indellicate and disgustful—and I imagine with intent to Get rid of them both, by their refusing to accept any Public appointment, in order to make room for himself. Upon taking the Ballots they stood thus, viz N.H, M.B, R.I, N.J, P——a, V——, N.C, & S.C, were for Mr. L——, and Ct, N.Y, & M.L. for Mr. A——!! So Mr. H. L——s was Elected agent to negoicate a Loan with the United Provinces in the Low Country &c for a Sum not exceeding 10 miln of Dollars, at a rate not to Exceed 6 per Cent per Anm. interest—Thus much for this time on that head. According to the order of the day Novr. 1st proceeded &c and Mr. H.L——s was unanimously Elected Commissr. to negociate a Treaty of Amity and Commerce with the United Provinces in the Lower Countrys.[6] After Long debates &c &c—*yeas* & *nays* &c. his Salary was fixed at 1,500 Stirling per anm. for Service & Expence—with liberty to appoint a Secretary with a Salary not to Exceed £300 Sterling per anm.

I hope youll excuse these Pedling Sort of letters when I inform you that in order to keep up the Correspondance which is so agreable to me I am obliged to write in this way for want of intelligence that might be more agreable to you. The Most of the lies of the day are in the papers. Adieu my dear Sir, and believe me to be most Sincerely your friend and very Humble Servt,   Nathl Peabody

NB. It is very late therefore youl please to over look blunders.

RC (Capt. J. G. M. Stone, Annapolis, Md., 1973).
    [1] In his October 18, 1779, letter to Peabody, Whipple had asked for details on the selection of foreign ministers. Roberts Collection, PHC.
    [2] Not found.
    [3] That is, Arthur Lee.
    [4] Henry Laurens and John Adams.

[5] That is, Gouverneur Morris. In a November 22 reply to this letter, Whipple made the following comments about Morris and "*swiveled Eyed*" James Duane, and their possible impact on the "Vermont business."

"The tall Boy will not be hereafter troublesome to you as I hear he has no longer a seat in a Room where he has at least shewn a disposition on some occasions to perplex business. I could wish another person whose heart in my opinion is much more mischeviously inclined had also been droped, their *swiveled Eyed* genious will give much trouble in the Vermont business. I Understand your Colleague intends soon to leave you, but you will not be long alone as Genl. Folsom will set out within a fortnight. I hope you will continue where you are till the Vermont business is compleated. Mr. Livermore is appointed to prosecute the Claim of N. H. but by what I can learn is not to have a seat in Congress." Roberts Collection PHC.

[6] Neither the nomination of John Adams nor the vote on Henry Laurens' election is recorded in the journals. See Samuel Huntington to Laurens, October 30, 1779.

Jesse Root to Oliver Ellsworth

Dr Sir   Philadelphia Novr. 1st. 1779.

I recd your favours of the 13 & 17th ult. with one Inclosed to Mr Wilson which I delivered. This day recd yours of 25th, with the inclosed paper & thank you for the Communication. Our delegation is out this day & we are not Informed of any New appointment. Conclude the State dont mean to be without a delegation in Congress,[1] Shall be glad to be at liberty to return home however at any rate shall leave Congress the latter end of this Month & depend you will releive me as I conclude you will be reappointed altho, you have Modestly omitted your own name in the Votes for Nomination. . . .[2]

From your Obedt. humble Servt.   Jesse Root.

P.S. Mr. Laurence is appointed to go to Holland to negociate a loan & settle a treaty of amity & Commerce.

This letter I opened after it was sealed.

Tr (DLC: Burnett Collection). Extract made for Edmund C. Burnett from William B. Sprague Collection, Congregational Library, London. Addressed: "To Oliver Ellsworth Esqr., at Hartford In Connecticut. per Mr. Cushman."

[1] The expiration of the Connecticut delegates' credentials left Congress without its president, Samuel Huntington, and also deprived Connecticut of its vote in Congress. Unable to do business on November 2 and 3, Congress resumed work on November 4 with Secretary Thomson substituting for Huntington. Connecticut delegates did not vote and Huntington did not return to the president's chair until November 10 when, according to Root, "By several letters recd. we were able to satisfy Congress of our right to sit in Congress." Root to Jonathan Trumbull, November 12, 1779. The credentials of the Connecticut delegates, extending their authority to March 1, 1780, were read in Congress on November 24. See *JCC*, 15:1236, 1254, 1301; John Fell's Diary, November 2–3, 4, and 10; and Samuel Holten's Diary, November 2–3, 1779.

[2] The transcriber here omitted an unknown number of words.

John Fell's Diary

[November 2–3, 1779]
Tuesday Novr 2d. Coml Committee. This day a doubt ariseing whether the Connecticut Delegates could set after the first Monday in this month, and not being Members sufficient without them no Business was done.[1]

Wednesday 3d. Coml Committee.[2] This day no Business done for the reasons mentiond Yesterday.

MS (DLC).
[1] See the preceding entry, note 1.
[2] This day the committee forwarded a second copy of an earlier letter to Oliver Pollock to which they attached a second postscript explaining that they had just paid $1,500 to Joseph Conand in accordance with "your Bill on the Committee." See the Committee of Commerce to Pollock, July 19, 1779.

Elbridge Gerry to Francis Dana

Dear sir   Philadelphia Novr 2d 1779
The President of Congress having sent on your Commission & Letter of Credence, as Secretary to the Embassy, & Charge d'Affairs, has rendered it in some Degree unnecessary to communicate the particulars mentioned in your Favors of Octr 21st, but lest his Information should be insufficient, give me Leave to inform You that there is no Difference in the Forms of the powers or Credentials of the several Secretaries, that they are appointed to the Embassies, &c &c to receive One thousand pounds sterling per annum, respectively, & that their pay is to commence at the Time of their leaving their places of Abode, to continue three Months after Notice of their Recall, & to be in full for their Services & Expences. The Appointment is so honorable that many Members of Congress will readily accept it, & some are making Interest for it in Case of your Refusal. I am informed that Mr. G —— M—— of N—— Y——[1] is desirous of it, Sr. J——J——[2] requested my Interest in his Favour, & a Gentleman in this City is urging the propriety & Advantage of giving it to D——r B——t.[3] Mr. L——[4] likewise stands ready, & if You decline the office, there is reason to expect much manoeuvreing to obtain it.

I remain sir with much Esteem your Friend & very humble Ser
E. Gerry

P.S. The Salary of the Minister is £2500 sterg per Annum but considering the Difference of the Expenses of the two offices, the Secretary will probably realize as much as the Minister. Mr Laurens is to negotiate a Loan in Holland & will take Care to suppy the sums required in addition to what is already orderd.

RC (CSmH: Townsend Collection).
  [1] That is, Gouverneur Morris.
  [2] Sir James Jay.
  [3] Perhaps Dr. John Berkenhout.
  [4] James Lovell.

Elbridge Gerry to Joseph Ward

Sir   Philadelphia Novr 2d 1779
    I have attended to the Subject of your Favr of the 25th of Octr
last, & am clearly of Opinion, that further provision should be made
for the officers acting in your Department. A Committee has been
lately appointed to extend the provission made for Officers of the
Line to those of the Staff,[1] whose Allowances are inadequate, to their
Services, & I have communicated Your Letter to Colo Root the
Chairman of that Committee, who has promised to confer with his
other Brethren Mr Morris & Colo Attlee on the Subject, without
Delay. I Would recommend your writing a Line to them, shewing
the Necessity of their coming to a Conclusion on this Business, &
remain sir with Esteem your very humble serv.   E. Gerry[2]

RC (ICHi: Joseph Ward Papers). Addressed: "Joseph Ward Esqr., Muster Master
General, at or near Head Quarters."
  [1] See *JCC*, 15:1188; and John Armstrong to George Washington, October 15, 1779,
note 2.
  [2] Gerry also wrote the following brief letter this day to his brother Samuel R. Gerry,
a merchant in Marblehead, Mass.
  "Messrs. S & R Purviances having by yesterdays Post inclosed to me a Bill on their
Brother, for the Ballance of your Account, amounting to 134 1/3 Dollars, or £50.7.6
Maryland Currency, I now transmit You the same, presuming that the order will be
paid without Hesitation. When Oppertunity offers, You may inform me of the receipt
of the Money, & the Circumstances of our Family affairs, of which I have received but
little Information for three years past." S. R. Gerry Papers, MHi.

Cyrus Griffin to Thomas Jefferson

Sir,   Philadelphia, Nov. 2nd. [1779][1]
    My Colleague Mr. Mercer has charged himself with the naval
Commissions mentioned a post ago in a letter from your excellency.[2]
    We have a report from the Eastward that a bloody Engagement
has happened in English Channel, and that the admiral of his
Britanic Majesty was sunk with sails and Colours flying; but we do
not give the utmost credit to the Intelligence.
    I have the honor to be, Sir, Your excellency's most obedient and
humble Servant,   C. Griffin

RC (DLC: Jefferson Papers). Jefferson, *Papers* (Boyd), 3:152.
  [1] The year is undoubtedly 1779 since James Mercer only attended Congress from September 9 to October 30, 1779, and was returning to Virginia at this time.
  [2] For Jefferson's October 16 letter to Samuel Huntington requesting "blank letters of marque for use in this state," see Jefferson, *Papers* (Boyd), 3:107.

Cornelius Harnett to Richard Caswell

Dear Sir   Philadelphia November 2d. 1779
  This part of the Continent, has been for many weeks past, anxiously Expecting the Count DeEstang on their Coast. I hope the business will be Compleatly ended to the Southward *in the first place.* It is believed by some that the Enemy have Evacuated R Island; Appearances seem to indicate this; but no Authentic Accounts have as yet been recieved by Congress.

  I take the Liberty to inclose the last papers which Contain very little News; A Packet or two are hourly expected from Europe, which very probably may inform us of the Opperations in that Quarter of the World. It is feared, the Season *is,* or will be too far advanced, by the time the Count Compleats his Opperations to the Southward for him to proceed Northward; but he has Still Eight weeks before him.

  A Resolution of Congress passed Yesterday[1] will be transmitted to Your Excellency to be laid before Our General Assembly, to put a Stop to the further granting of Vacant Lands until the Conclusion of the war. The reason held forth for the adopting this measure, is the very great Emigration of people which will naturally follow the Measure, which I must acknowledge has some weight. But it is a well known fact that the Ostensible reason is, that the States at the end of the war, may Appropriate such vacant lands to the benefit of All the States in the union, to enable them to pay the Public debt. Virginia & No. Carolina Opposed this measure, and it is left to the wisdom of the Legislatures of the States similarly Circumstanced with Virginia, to agree, or not, with this Proposal. I have to request that Your Excellency will be pleased to send forward the Delegates to relieve us, it is impossible for *you* Sir, to conjecture how *disagreeable* it must be to the State to pay the extravagant expences we are at here; and how much more *disagreeable* it will be for us to require it. I have Called out of the Treasury more than the half of my Sallery & shall be obliged to Call for more to enable me to return to my family, where I hope I shall have the happiness to spend the remainder of my days in retirement; my time of life requires it. Genl. Washington is advancing by degrees towards New-York, to be ready to lend his aid to the Count D Estaing should he come thus far. Mr. Laurence our former President, will call on your Excellency in his way to So. Carolina; from thence he proceeds to Holland on Public business. To him, I beg leave to refer you for News. And am certain you will proffit much by his acquaintance.

I have the honor to be with the greatest respect—Your Excellencys, Most Obed & very hul Servt.   Cornl. Harnett

[*P.S.*] Your Excey. will percieve this Letter is not intended, for the Perusal of the Public, as I have not Copied it fair.

RC (MH–H: bMS Am 1649.5).
[1] Actually, on October 30, for which see Samuel Huntington to the States, October 30, 1779.

Samuel Holten's Diary

[November 2–3, 1779]

Novr. 2. 1779. Tuesday. I wrote to the Inhabitants of Danvers, to Mr. Needham, to Mr. Warner, to Colo. Hutchinson, to Mr. Avery, to Mrs. Holten (No. 82) and to my daughter Sally.[1]

3. Wednesday. Congress have done no business this two days past on Acct. of the state of Connecticut not being represented; The Prest. being from that state.[2]

I dined with the Honl. Mr. Griffin.

MS (MDaAr).
[1] None of these letters has been found.
[2] See Jesse Root to Oliver Ellsworth, November 1, 1779, note 1.

James Lovell to John Adams

[November 2, 1779][1]
Oct. 15. 1777 [i.e., 1779]

Resolved:[2] That a Letter be written to the Minister plenipo. of these States at the Court of France desiring him to take the most effectual means for supplying the Ministers appointd. to treat with his Catholic Majesty and wth. his Britannic Majesty, & their Secretaries wth. two thousand Louis dores to be distributed in proportion to their respective salaries, & giving the strongest Assurances to the said minister that Congress, will immediately take Measures for replacing the said Sum as well as for establishing a fund in Europe for the future Support of all the Embassies from these States.

The Comtee on the Letter of J.G. Dericks & other Papers having reported that it appears to them that a Loan may be obtained in Holland.

Resolvd. That a proper Person be authorized & instructed to negotiate that Business on behalf of these States.

The same Comtee. to bring in an Draught of a Letter to the Ministr. plenipo in France.

Octr. 16.

They report & Congress accept.

Sir.

Congress have appointed the Honble. John Jay Esqr. Minister Plenipotentiary for negociating a Treaty of Amity & Commerce & of Alliance between his Catholic Majesty & the United States of America. And the Hon. John Adams Esqr. Minister Plenipotentiary for negociating a treaty of Peace & a treaty of Commerce with Grt. Britain; The Hon. Wm. Carmichael Esqr. is appointed Secretary to the first & the hon. Francis Esqr.[3] is appointed Secretary to the last mentioned Embassy.

Mr. Jay & Mr. Carmichael will embark on Board the Confederacy continental Ship of War now in the Delaware ready to sail for France. Mr. Adams & Mr. Dana will probably take their Passages on Board La Sensible one of his Most Christian Majesty's Frigates in the Harbour of Boston.

The Salaries annexed to their appointments respectively are two thousand five hundred pounds Sterling per anm. to the ministr. & one thousand pounds Sterling to the Secretaries, And in order to enable these Gentlemen to enter wth.out Embarrassmt. upon the Duties of their several functions, I am authorized by an Act of Congress of the 15th Instant a certified Copy of which will accompany this, to request you, Sir, to take the most effectual means for supplying them with two thousand Louis dors in distributions proportioned to their respective Salaries & to assure you on the faith of Congress that Speedy & proper measures will be adopted both for repaying that Sum & for establishing a fund for the future support of all the Embassies of these United States in Europe. You will likewise find enclosed a certified copy of an act of Congress of the 4th instant by which you will be informed that your Salary is also to be two thousand & five hundred pounds sterling per annum, and that John Laurens Esqr. a Member of the house of representatives for the State of South Carolina & Lt. Colonel in the army of the United States is appointed by Congress to be Secretary to the Minister Plenipotentiary at the Court of France.

I have the Honor to be

Oct 18

Congress proceeded to the nomination of a proper person to negociate a Loan in Holland when Mr. John Adams was put in nomination by Mr. G. Morris.

Mr. H. Laurens by Mr. Mathews

Mr. Woodbury Langdon by Mr. Sharp

On Motion of Mr. Morris, 2d. by Mr. Mathews, Resolved that a Comtee. of three be appointed to prepare Instructions to the person who may be empowered to negotiate a foreign Loan.

Mr. Morris, Mr. Mathews, Mr. Gerry.

I presume the President has sent you a Copy of the Letter to Doctr. Franklin. I will enquire this day.   Nov. 2d

RC (MHi: Adams Papers). In the hand of Lovell, though not signed, and endorsed by him: "Extracts from the sect Journals."

[1] This date is taken from the last paragraph below.

[2] Although Lovell had enclosed substantial extracts from the secret journals of February and March 1779 concerning the peace ultimata with his letter to Adams of November 1, he subsequently proceeded to copy the following extracts from the secret journals of October 1779, appending a brief concluding paragraph concerning Dr. Franklin and adding the date "Nov. 2d."

[3] That is, Francis Dana.

Virginia Delegates to the Virginia House of Delegates

Sir,   Philadelphia. Novr. 2d. 1779.

Our Collegue Mr Smith[1] having charged himself with the Copies of the Petitions of the Indiana & Vandalia Companies then before Congress, to lay before the House of Delegates of Virginia, It falls to our Lot to hand the enclosed[2] to you for the further & full Information of your House as to the progress of that business A Business which we conceive may in Consequences greatly affect the Interest of Virginia in the first place—& ultimately injure the Rights of all the States in the Union.

Your Honble. House may be assured that no pains were spared by the Virginia Delegates to defend the Rights of the State & to prevent Congress from establishing a Precedent so dangerous to the common Rights of the United States—but to how little purpose may be readily discovered, when you are informed that tho' the Committee determined this Case privately & without notice to any of the Virginia Delegates—and tho' their Report was so expressly counter to the Instruction of Congress—Yet 8 States to 3 were against recommitting the Report.

We must however observe that we understood on that Occasion that some of the voters agt. the recommitment were agt. the Jurisdiction of Congress, upon Information of the facts laid before the Committee which were read in Congress & not denied. But we are sorry we are obliged to say that Congress were so determined to proceed upon this business agt the Rights of Virga. that on the next day, tho' the business of Indiana & Vandalia was an order of the Day, & we had no Doubts the Said Petitions wou'd be rejected—we discovered the Members for this business had changed their Ground & not only declined proceeding on the Resolution of the Committee, thereby meaning to retain that pretence for interferring in this Business—But were also pleased to pass the Resolution of the 30th a Copy of which is now subjoined to the other Proceedings.

Youll please observe that the ostenseable motives for this Resolution expressed in the preamble by the words *much Mischiefs* were understood to be the Clamours of Maryland & the discontented States of Jersey & Delaware—and the general Inconvenience of weakening the United States by encouraging Emigrations to parts remote from the defence agt. the common Enemy—the later assertion being thought improper for the public knowledge, was avoided & thought to be sufficiently expressed in the words before alluded to.

We have been thus particular in the detail of this business, that your House being fully informed may consider this business on its true Principles without regard to the misconduct of Congress—and adopt such Resolutions thereupon as they may think consistant with the Interest of Virginia & the United States.

We have the Honour to be, Sir, Yr. most obedt. & very huble Servts.   C. Griffin

Js. Mercer

Wm. Fitzhugh[3]

P.S. I beg the House to be informed that I was directed by the Comee. on my first Conference with them—to commit my objections to writing, & forbid to mention any thing of *Charters or prior Treaties with Indians* which Rule I adopted to prevent their having any pretence for going into the Merits of the Treaty of Fort Stanwix on which the Indiana Company founded their Claim.   Js. Mercer

RC (IU–HS). Written by Mercer and signed by Mercer, Fitzhugh, and Griffin. Addressed: "The Honble. The Speaker of the House of Delegates of Virginia."

[1] Meriwether Smith, who had obtained a leave of absence on September 28, for which see James Mercer to the Virginia House of Delegates, October 1, 1779, note 2.

[2] The "enclosed" has not been identified, but for the resolve Congress adopted in response to Virginia's determination to begin the sale of "unlocated" western lands, see Samuel Huntington to the States, October 30, 1779.

[3] Although Mercer and Fitzhugh signed this letter, the terms to which they had been specially elected in June had expired on November 1 and neither attended Congress after Saturday, October 30. Mercer, in fact, had resigned his position in the new delegation a month before, for which see Mercer to the Virginia House of Delegates, October 1, 1779.

John Fell's Diary

Thursday 4th [November 1779].

Coml Committee. The Secretary did Business to day in the absence of the President. PM Marine Committee.

MS (DLC).

Samuel Holten's Diary

[November 4–5, 1779]
4. Thursday. We had the intelligence of the enemies leaving R. Island.[1]
5. Friday. I attended the medl. come.[2] & the marine board. It is cold.

MS (MDaAr).
[1] Official news of the October 25 British evacuation of Newport arrived in an October 27 letter from Gen. Horatio Gates, which was read in Congress on November 5. *JCC*, 15:1241.
[2] The Medical Committee undoubtedly met this day to carry out Congress' November 4 order directing the committee to "transmit to the Commander in Chief the memorial of Thadeus Benedict and others, against Dr. Forster, and such other papers as they may have respecting the matter." They may also have considered Dr. Isaac Foster's request for a court of inquiry, which was read in Congress on the fifth. *JCC*, 15:1237, 1240. For the committee's investigation of Dr. Foster as director of hospitals in the Eastern Department, see Medical Committee to George Washington, November 15, 1779.

North Carolina Delegates to Richard Caswell

Sir   Philadelphia Novr. 4th 1779
We have the honor of sending inclosed to your Excellency a copy of sundry Acts of Congress, in which we concieve the State over which you preside and that we have the honor to represent in Congress is both directly and indirectly interested; and on which we beg leave to make a few remarks.

The principle on which the Indiana company found their Memorial *is*,[1] that the Territory which they claim is not within, nor subject to the Jurisdiction of either of the States; but to the whole United States in Congress Assembled. A principle which we humbly conceive, by no means admissable, it being against one of the principles of the general union. This controversy is not between two States; but between one State and individuals; therefore we are of opinion that Congress, more especially in an unconfederated state, has not jurisdiction and if Congress has no jurisdiction, consequently it was an improper subject for their deliberation, which was the foundation of the objection against committing it to a special Committee; nevertheless you may see *that* was overruled by a majority on the 14th of Septr. last. Two or three States objecting to balot for a Committee was the reason why that subject lay dormant until the 8th of Octr. at which time a Committee was appointed with an instruction to report first on the question respecting the jurisdiction of Congress; it being thought by some as a proper and necessary preliminary. You will please to observe how cautiously that matter was evaded in the

Committee's report, which brought on the question for recommitt-
ment in order that the Committee should pursue the direction of
Congress. We need only refer you to the Journal of that day Viz the
29th of Octr. for the farther explanation of the report of the
Committee.

On the next day you may observe that to cut the matter short a sett
of propositions were moved instead of the report, and were found to
be in Order as appears by the Journal.

On the whole it appears to us that there are great jealousies particularly respecting Virginia's extensive claim of Territory and generally of the other States under similar circumstances. We are induced
to believe that with many the question respecting the justice or injustice of the claims of the Indiana and Vandalia companies is not so
much in View as that of laying down some principle or pursuing
such a line of conduct as may be most likely to obtain the main
object, namely, that Congress shall have the disposal of all the
unapropriated lands on the western frontiers of these States and
that such lands may become the common property of the whole. We
believe that at present the representatives of some States do not wish
Maryland to confederate, hoping that by some means or other those
States who Claim the back Lands may be prevailed on to surrender
them.

According to present appearances, Newhampshire, Massachusetts
bay and Connecticut who formerly insisted strenuously on their claim
to Lands Westerly, are indifferent about them.

The Legislature of Maryland at their last Session advised their
Constituents to give them explicit instructions on the subject of
confederation, against the Session which is now setting. What effect
that measure will produce is not yet known to us.

These things we think our indespensible duty to communicate
through your Excellency to the Legislature of Our State, as a subject
worthy their serious attention; and we beg leave to reiterate our
wishes that their Delegates in Congress may be seconded by being
furnished with explicit instructions on that subject; as we apprehend
it is very probable it may yet be a subject of serious debate in Congress.

In the mean time we shall oppose to the utmost of our power
every measure which appears calculated to injure our claim or vio-
late the Charter in which our State has pointed out our Territorial
Rights, and over which we have declared the right of our Citizens in
Sovereignty.

The good sense of our Legislature will give due weight to many
reasons which they will concieve induced Congress to recommend it
to Virginia to reconsider their late Act of Assembly for opening their
Land Office. In our last[2] we inclosed a copy of the debit of Our State
in the Auditor generals Office in which there was sundry errors. We
have now the honor of inclosing another copy together with a Letter
from Mr. Nourse to Mr. Sharpe explanatory of that matter.[3]

We have the pleasure to congratulate Your Excellency on the evacuation of Rhode Island by the enemy on Monday the 25th Ulto.

With the highest esteem & consideration, We have the honor to be, Your Excellencies Most Obt Humble Servants,

Cornl. Harnett

Wm. Sharpe

P.S. Mr. Hewes has been confined to bed with sickness five days past and his situation not very promising.[4]

RC (In). Written by Harnett and signed by Harnett and Sharpe.

[1] For Congress' response to the memorial of the Indiana Company, see Samuel Huntington to the States, October 30, 1779.

[2] Not found.

[3] Not found. However, a report of Assistant Auditor General Joseph Nourse to the Board of Treasury concerning the North Carolina accounts is in PCC, item 36, 3:379–80.

[4] Joseph Hewes, who last attended Congress October 29, died November 10.

John Fell's Diary

Friday 5 [November 1779]

Coml Committee. Congress. Letter from Genl Gates acquainting that he took Possession of Rhode Island the 26th Octr the Enemy having left it the day before.[1]

PM Marine Committee.

MS (DLC).

[1] See Samuel Huntington to Horatio Gates, November 7, 1779.

Samuel Huntington to John Jay

Dear Sir,   Duplicate   Philadelphia 5 November 1779

I have been honored with your Favours of the 19th & 20th Ultimo,[1] but had not an Opportunity to return any Answer before you sailed.

I have now the Pleasure to inform you the Enemy evacuated Newport on the Night of the 25th October. They made no wanton Destruction on their Departure, left about fourteen Hundred Tons of Hay, four hundred fifty Cords of Firewood, a large Quantity of Peet & Straw in their Magazines. General Gates with his Troops took Possession of the Town next Day.

The Express which brings me this Intelligence, says, there are in Newport large Quantities of Salt & Dry Goods in [town].

I presume you got Intelligence the Enemy had evacuated Stoney & Verplanks Points before you sailed.

It is conjectured that most, if not all the Enemy which left Newport are come to New York.

Please to make my Complements acceptable to your Lady, and believe me to be, with the most sincere Esteem & respect, Sir, your most obedt & hbble servant.   Sam. Huntington

RC (NNC: Jay Papers). In a clerical hand and signed by Huntington.
[1] Not found.

Marine Committee to John Beatty

Sir   November 5th 1779
We have received your letter of the 26th ultimo and hereby authorize you to take such Order on the Subject thereof as you may think proper. The Postscript which relates to the Spanish Prisoners at New York we shall lay before Congress for their determination which we shall inform you of.[1]   We are Sir, Your Hble servants

LB (DNA: PCC Miscellaneous Papers, Marine Committee Letter Book).
[1] Beatty's October 26 letter has not been found, but for an extract from it concerning "the Spanish Prisoners," and Congress' response to his query about provisioning them, see *JCC*, 15:1273; Samuel Huntington to Beatty, November 18; and Marine Committee to Beatty, November 20, 1779.

Marine Committee to William Smith

Sir   November 5th 1779
Congress having by their Resolution of the 29th ulto Ordered that the Marine Committee to provide the Bearer hereof Major Weddersheim with a passage to Europe by the first Opportunity,[1] and as no such Offers in this Port we therefore request that you would procure for this Gentleman a passage in any Vessel from Baltimore bound to France or Holland (in the Ship Buckskin if possible) if this can be effected you will furnish Major Weddersheim with a few necessary Stores for his Voyage and transmit the Cost to this Board who will immediately reimburse you.
                          We are Sir, Your Hble servants

LB (DNA: PCC Miscellaneous Papers, Marine Committee Letter Book).
[1] Ernest Ludwig de Widdersheim, "major in his majesty, the King of Denmark's service," had unsuccessfully petitioned Congress for an appointment in the Continental Army. See these *Letters*, 13:504.

Nathaniel Scudder to Richard Henry Lee

Dear Sir.   Philadelphia Novr. 5th. 1779.

I doubt not you have long e'er this received a short Letter from me[1] acknowleging the Receipt of yours of the 19th Septr. which I wrote in Jersey. I have been some Time here again, but have not had the Pleasure of hearing from you since my Arrival.

On my Return I enquired, and found Mr. Lovel had transmitted you Copies or Duplicates of the Papers which you wished me to send you,[2] therefore thought it unnecessary to repeat them.

This Letter will be also a *short* one, as I have the Satisfaction of sending it by the Honble Mr. Laurens, who will call on you in his Journey to Charles Town and consequently be able to give you a more general and accurate Detail of Business and News than I could possibly do in the Compass of a Letter.

I will only congratulate you on the Evacuation of Rhode Island, and on the Birth of your *Cassius*; the first on public, the second on private Account. I sincerely wish *him* to live, and to shine with distinguished Lustre on the public Theatre of that great Republic, in founding which his Father has labored with Such assiduity & Applause.

Commend my warmest Expressions of Esteem and Respect to your amiable Consort, and permit me to add, that I am most affectionately & sincerely Your Friend & Obedt. Servt.

                                             Nath. Scudder

RC (ViU: Lee Family Papers).

[1] Not found.

[2] Scudder had been absent from September 18 to October 20; he may be referring to "Copies or Duplicates" transmitted in James Lovell's letters to Lee of September 27 or October 13.

Committee on Appeals Decree

                                             November 6th. 1779.

Samuel Cabot & al Lib[ellan]ts & App[ellan]ts ⎫   Appeal from
vs. The Ship Neustra Seniora de Merced &c. ⎬   the State of
Matthias Segarra Claim[an]t & App[ell]t ⎭ Massachusetts Bay[1]

We the Commissioners appointed by Congress to hear, try and determine all Appeals from the several Courts of Admiralty of the American States to Congress having heard and fully considered as well all and singular the Matters and Things mentioned and contained in the Record or Minutes of the Proceedings of the Maritime Court of the Middle District of Massachusetts Bay in the above Cause as the Arguments of the Advocates of the respective parties to the above Appeal do thereupon adjudge and Decree the several Goods,

Wares, Merchandizes, Articles and Things mentioned and contained in the several Bills of Lading exhibited in the said Cause and marked and numbered as follows to wit: No. 19 & 20. One half pipe of Wine marked EW; No. 23 & 24. four Barrels of Cochineal marked *,[2] no. 1–4; No. 25 & 26. Two Barrels of Cochineal marked MR, no. 1 & 2; No. 27. four Barrels of Cochineal marked PA, no. 1–4; No. 28. seven Barrels of Cochineal marked JL, no. 1–7; No. 29 & 30. Two Barrels of Cochineal marked *,[2] no. 1 & 2; No. 31, Two Zurrons[3] of Indigo marked ICB, no. 28, 29—to be lawful Prize if appearing unto Us from the Evidence produced in the Cause that the same were British Property And We do order that the same be sold for the Benefit of the Party Libellants in the said Cause according to the prayer of their Bill, they paying the customary freight for said goods, And We do further adjudge and decree that the said Ship or Vessel called the Neustra Seniora de Merced, her Tackle, Apparel, Furniture and all the Rest, Residue and Remainder of the Goods, Wares and Merchandizes laden and found on board her at the Time of her Capture be forthwith restored and redelivered unto the abovenamed Matthias Segarra the Claimant in the said Cause his Agent or Attorney to and for the Use of himself and others on whose behalf he claims and appeals it appearing to Us from the Testimony exhibited in the said Cause that the said Vessel & that part of her Cargo were the property of the Subjects of his most Catholic Majesty the King of Spain And We do further order and decree that the Party Libellant pay unto the party Claimant one thousand and fifty six Dollars for his Costs and Charges by him expended in supporting the Appeal aforesaid in this Court &c.   Tho. M: Kean

                                                    J Root
                                                    C. Griffin

MS (DNA: RG 267, case no. 57). In a clerical hand, and signed by Griffin, McKean, and Root.

[1] The Massachusetts Court of Admiralty for the Middle District had declared on September 17, 1779, that the brigantine *Neustra Senora de Merced* and part of her cargo were Spanish property and therefore not lawful prizes, but that most of her cargo was British and therefore was awarded to Samuel Cabot and Stephen Cleveland, merchants and agents of Capt. Hugh Hill, commander of the privateer *Pilgrim*.

The *Pilgrim* had captured the *Neustra Senora de Merced* on the high seas as it was carrying a cargo from London to an unidentified port. The captain of the Spanish brigantine, Matthias Sagarra, claimed she was a neutral ship, but a jury in the Massachusetts Court of Admiralty awarded the bulk of the cargo to Hill and his agents. Both sides then appealed to Congress where on October 9, 1779, the appeal was referred to the Committee on Appeals. In this decree the committee upheld the decision of the state court. See case file no. 57, RG 267, DNA; and *JCC*, 15:1159.

[2] Asterisk substituted editorially for the intricate symbol drawn by the committee's clerk at this point in the MS.

[3] That is, a small leather bag, or provision-bag.

Committee on Appeals Decree

November 6th. 1779

Nathaniel Tracy &al Lib[ellan]ts & App[ellan]ts ⎱   Appeal[1] from
vs The Brigantine Holy Martyrs her Cargo &c. ⎰   the State of
Joseph De Lano Claim[an]t & App[ell]ee   ⎰ Massachusetts Bay

We the commissioners appointed by Congress to hear, try and determine all appeals from the Courts of Admiralty of the several American States to Congress having heard and fully considered as well all and singular the several Matters and Things mentioned and contained in the Record or Minutes of the Proceedings of the Superior Court of Judicature of Massachusetts Bay held at Concord on the second Tuesday in April last &c. in the above Cause as the Arguments of the Advocates of the respective parties to the above Appeal do thereupon adjudge and decree that the Bill of the said Nathaniel Tracy and others exhibited and the Appeal by them demanded and filed in the above Cause be dismissed with Costs And that the said Brigantine or Vessel called the Holy Martyrs, her tackle, Apparel and Furniture and all and singular the Goods, Wares and Merchandizes laden and found on board her at the Time of her Capture as mentioned in the said Bill be forthwith restored and redelivered and the said Joseph De Lano the Claimant in the said Cause his Agent or Attorney to and for the Use of himself and all others on whose Behalf he claims and appeals And We do further order and decree that the party Appellant pay unto the party Appellee one thousand and fifty six Dollars for his Costs and Charges by him expended in defending the said Appeal in this Court &c.

Tho M:Kean

J. Root

C. Griffin

MS (DNA: RG 267, case no. 60). In a clerical hand, and signed by Griffin, McKean, and Root.

[1] A jury of the Massachusetts Court of Admiralty for the Middle District declared on April 6, 1779, that the brigantine *Santander y los Santos Martires [Holy Martyrs]* was Spanish property but that her cargo was British. The court therefore awarded the cargo to Nathaniel Tracy and John C. Jones, merchants and owners of the armed schooner *Success*, commanded by Philip Trask, which had captured the *Holy Martyrs* on December 30, 1778. Both parties appealed to the Massachusetts Superior Court of Judicature, which upheld the maritime court. Tracy and Jones then appealed to Congress, where the case was assigned on October 9, 1779, to the Committee on Appeals.

The committee in this decree affirmed the decision of the state court. See case file no. 60, RG 267, DNA; and *JCC*, 15:1149.

For further information on congressional involvement in this case, see John Jay to Conrad Alexandre Gérard, April 25 and May 24, 1779.

John Fell's Diary

Saturday Novr. 6th. 1779.
Commercial Committee. Congress. After the dispatches &c a
Report of the Committee to answer the Speech intended to be made
Per the Chevalier Lusern was Read.[1]

MS (DLC).
[1] On November 4 the French minister presented to Congress his letter
of appointment from Louis XVI and a copy of the speech he intended to make at his
public audience, both of which were referred to a committee composed of John
Dickinson, William Churchill Houston, and Gouverneur Morris. The committee's
report, read this day, was "debated by paragraphs" and approved on November 8.
For some reason, however, La Luzerne transmitted "another copy" of his speech to
Congress on November 12. The same committee, chaired by Morris, thereupon drafted
a second reply which was debated and approved the following day, when the delegates
set aside November 17 for La Luzerne's "public audience" and "an entertainment to
be given by Congress." See *JCC*, 15:1238, 1247, 1251–52, 1262, 1266–67; and Fell's
Diary, November 8 and 17. For the chevalier's "letter of credence," his speech, and
the president's response, see *JCC*, 15:1278–84.

Samuel Holten's Diary

[November 6, 1779]
6. Saturday. The medical committee met in my chamber. Mr.
Lowell paid me a visit this evening.

MS (MDaAr).

Samuel Huntington to the Massachusetts Council

Sir   Philadelphia Novemr 6th. 1779
    Congress having directed that the enclosd Copy of a Letter from
Mr J. Bradford to the Honble. Francis Lewis Esq one of the Commercial Committee Should be sent to the Council of the State of Massachusetts Bay;[1] I do my self the Honour to Transmit the same to you
to be laid before that Honorable Body.
    I am with great Respect, your Honours most Obedient humble
Servant,   Saml. Huntington President[2]

RC (M–Ar: Revolutionary War Letters). Addressed: "The Honbl President of the
Council of the State of Massachusetts Bay."
[1] John Bradford's October 21 letter to Francis Lewis, in which he expressed fear for
the safety of the sugar and rum he was holding in storage in Boston, is in PCC, item
78, 3:367–70. For Congress' terse November 4 order on the subject ("that a copy
thereof be transmitted" to the Massachusetts Council, apparently simply to secure the
state's protection for Bradford's warehouses), see *JCC*, 15:1238.

[2] This day Huntington also wrote the following brief letter to Capt. Lt. John Van Dyke of the Second Continental Artillery, whose request for leave had been forwarded on October 17 to Congress by Washington with a recommendation by Dr. John Cochran. See *JCC*, 15:1246–47; PCC, item 152, 8:117–22; and Washington, *Writings* (Fitzpatrick), 16:473.

"You will receive herewith enclos'd an act of Congress of this day granting you leave of absence for eight Months, that you may take a Voyage to Sea, this being judged necessary for the recovery of your Health." PCC, item 14, fol. 219.

Marine Committee to John Barry

Sir   November 6th 1779

As you have been appointed to Command a new Continental Ship[1] that is now on the Stocks at Portsmouth in New Hampshire you are hereby directed to repair to that place and hasten as much as may be in your power the compleating of that Ship which we are desirous to have done with all dispatch. We have now communicated our desire on that head to the Honble the Navy Board at Boston, on whom you will please to call in your way and receive such orders as they may think proper to give you.[2]

Should Mr. Langdon & you Agree that any alteration can be made in this Ship that will render her more suitable than the present design, you will please to communicate your plan and a state of the ship which we shall consider.

We are sir, Your Hble Servants

LB (DNA: PCC Miscellaneous Papers, Marine Committee Letter Book).

[1] The 74-gun ship-of-the-line *America*. For Barry's appointment to this command, see William B. Clark, *Gallant John Barry, 1745–1803* (New York: Macmillan Co., 1938), pp. 184–86.

[2] In keeping with which, the committee wrote the following brief letter this day to the Eastern Navy Board.

"Captain John Barry will deliver you this in his way to Portsmouth in New Hampshire where he goes to hasten the building and fitting of the New Ship on the Stocks at that place which we have appointed him to command & which we request you will push forward with all possible expedition." Paullin, *Marine Committee Letters, 2:127*.

Samuel Huntington to Horatio Gates

Sir   Philadelphia Novemr 7th. 1779

I have the pleasure to Acknowledge the receipt of your favour of the 27 Ulto. by Majr Armstrong which was Immediately laid before Congress. Please to accept of my Congratulations on your obtaining possession of the Town & Island of Newport.[1]

I was happy in having an Opportunity of transmitting to France the agreable Intelligence you gave me; Immediately after the receipt of your letter.

We have no Authentic Intelligence from Georgia later than the 4th of Octor; the Capture of the Brittish forces was not then Effected, though the appearances were favourable, but there Seems an unaccountable delay of Intelligence from that quarter.

By recent Accounts and Information from New York (on which I place Some dependence) it is Said the 57th Regiment, Raudans [Rawdons] Corps and a detachment of Artillery were to sail for Hallifax on the 29th Ulto. and they were to be Accompanied by all the heavy Ships except the Europa. The Daphne Frigate was to Sail for England at the Same time. That a packet had arrivd the 23rd Ulto. The accounts brought by her seemed very Alarming to Friends of Government. That it was *Reported* the Ardent of 64 guns was taken (which is since confirmed) [. . .] the Brittish fleet Chased into Portsmouth by the Combined fleet of France & Spain which remaind of that port Several days.

I have the Honour to be with great Respect, your most humb Servt,   Saml. Huntington

Novr 11. P.S. Since writing the foregoing we have receivd the disagreable accounts of the defeat of the Expedition against Savannah of which the Bearer can inform.   S.H.

RC (NHi: Gates Papers).
[1] Gates' October 27 letter to Congress, in which he reported that he had just occupied Newport, as "this Island was Evacuated by The Enemys Troops on the Night of the 25th Instant," is in PCC, item 154, 2:194–97.

Committee on Appeals Decree

November 8th. 1779

John Bradford Lib[ellan]t & App[ell]ee   ⎫   Appeal from
vs The Ship Viper her Cargo &c.   ⎬   the State of
Martin Brimmer Claim[an]t & App[ellan]t ⎭ Massachusetts Bay[1]

We the Commissioners appointed by Congress to hear, try and determine all Appeals from the Courts of Admiralty of the several American States to Congress having heard and fully considered as well all and singular the several Matters and Things mentioned and contained in the Record or Minutes of the proceedings of the Maritime Court of the Middle District of Massachusetts Bay in the above Cause as the Arguments of the Advocates of the respective parties to the said Appeal do thereupon adjudge and decree that the Appeal of the said Martin Brimmer demanded and filed in the said Cause be & the same is dismissed hence with Costs And that the Judgment or Sentence of the said Maritime Court pronounced and published in the said Cause be and the same hereby is in all its' parts confirmed and established And We do assess the said Costs at one thousand

and fifty six Dollars which Sum We do order and adjudge that the
party Appellant shall pay unto the party Appellee for his Costs and
Charges by him expended in defending the said Appeal in this
Court &c.   Tho M:Kean   J Root.

                                 Hy. Marchant   C. Griffin

MS (DNA: RG 267, case no. 54). In a clerical hand, and signed by Griffin, Marchant,
and Root.
  [1] The Massachusetts Court of Admiralty for the Middle District had awarded the
armed ship of war *Viper* and her cargo both to Continental agent John Bradford and
to Samuel Nicholson, commander of the Continental frigate *Deane*.
  Capt. Nicholson had captured the *Viper* on January 24, 1779, off the Massachusetts
coast and Bradford had libeled the ship and cargo on behalf of Nicholson and the
Continent, claiming that the ship, cargo, and "appurtances" should be distributed to
"the captors and others concerned therein." Martin Brimmer, a Boston merchant,
filed a second libel on behalf of Nicholson and his crew, however, claiming that the
ship, cargo, and "appurtances" should be distributed "among the captors only." In
their libels both Bradford and Brimmer cited unspecified congressional resolves.
Under a congressional resolve of October 30, 1776, concerning the division of prizes,
the captain and crew of Continental armed vessels were entitled to the entire value of
"all ships and vessels" in case of the capture of armed vessels of war, rather than the
customary one-half for merchantmen or other unarmed-vessels. The resolve did not
mention the cargo and "appurtances," however. When the Massachusetts court awarded
the ship and cargo to Bradford on June 28, 1779, to be divided between the captors
and "others concerned therein," i.e., the Continental government, Brimmer appealed
on behalf of captain and crew to Congress, where on July 24, 1779, the case was
referred to the Committee on Appeals.
  In this decree the committee upheld the Massachusetts court decision. See case file
no. 54, RG 267, DNA; and JCC, 6:913, 14:883, 1188–89.

John Fell's Diary

Monday Novr. 8th. [1779]
  Coml Committee. Congress. The Report of the answer to the
Ministers Speech was agreed to.[1]

MS (DLC).
  [1] See Fell's Diary, November 6, 1779, note.

James Lovell to John Hancock

Sir   Novr. 8th. 1779.
  I hope never to have *invincible* arguments delivered to me by the
Lips of consequential Sufferers to lead me to repent of having preferred the Public Good to my private Emolument on very singular
Occasions. But *strong* Arguments I must expect to hear, for my own
mind suggests them; and my Wants which prompt that Suggestion
are trifling compared to what others connected in my private For-

tune must experience. My Wants, too, may be easily removed by your Assistance, and that is secure on simple Demand. Know then, Sir, that it is totally impossible for me to keep myself decently clad by any purchases here without totally taking all my Income from my Family. Shoes are 85 Dollars, a Hat more that $200, Buff Breeches 200 and the making of every Thing boundless. I am not in absolute Want except of what the Girls call, Men's *Small Cloaths* & Stockings and Hatt. If Capt. Bradford or Messers. Otis & Henly have such Things and you will interest yourself to get them for me, I shall make a great saving in the difference of Exchange between Boston & this City of Sodom, by Procuring something of a Surplus in the Articles I may make a part turn out very Reasonable. For Instance in Knit Patterns or other Stuff for 3 pr. I may make 2 Cheap or get one for nothing. So in Hose 6 pr. would make 3 & 4 cheap.

I have not ventured to say a Word of Linnen but have it I must and it would really be better to buy it in Boston than here even if dearer in the first cost, because my Wife or some of my former Schollars would save the making which here would be an *Estate nominal*. Mr. W. Greenleaf did me great Favor in the Shoe & Hose Way when I was there, it is not impossible that He may have good Opportunity now. I send an odd Shoe, as my Size is out of the common Road, that in case of a Chance I may be fitted. I will repay to yr. Order by any Express or private Gentleman. I say repay. I chuse to repeat it, because I know your common Doings. The public ought to maintain *me*, and it will. It is quite enough for you and one or two more that you take almost the whole, Care of Wives & Children whom other men have chosen & manufactured. As your Kindnesses to *mine* have an obligatory Weight double of what they would have directed to *me*, be satisfied with having put me already into an insolvent State in their Score; and make me not yr Debtor on my own further than by yr. obliging Prompts to the Gentlemen whom I named in the Beginning.

As Mr. Lowell & Mr. Hitchburne will converse with you it is needless for me to write any Thing about Count D'Estaing or other unpleasing Circumstances; especially is it needless that I should add any Thing to what I have already scratched about our Money.

The Gout apart, I may venture to hope Your Health better than my own and wish the Continuance of it.

I am, Sir, your obliged Friend, and humb. Servant,

James Lovell

RC (MiU–C: Miscellaneous Manuscripts). Addressed: "Honble. John Hancock Esqr., Boston."

Thomas McKean to John Adams

My dear Sir,   Philadelphia. Novemr. 8th. 1779.
  On my return from the circuit a few days ago I was honoured with
your letter of the 20th Septemr. last, and proud to find that I was
not forgotten by one I so much esteem. You must have had your
difficulties in these times, I know, I too have had my full share of the
anxieties, cares & troubles attending the present war.[1] For sometime
I was obliged to act as President of the Delaware State and as Chief
Justice of this; General Howe had just landed at the head of Elk
River, when I undertook to discharge those two great trusts. The
consequence was to be hunted like a fox by the enemy and envied by
those who ought to have been my friends. I was obliged to remove
my family five times in a few months, and at last fixed them in a little
Log house on the banks of the Susquehanna above an hundred
miles from this; but safety was not to be found there, for they were
soon obliged to remove again, occasioned by the incursions of the
Indians. In Decemr. 1777 I went again into Congress, where for
some months the United States had but nine voices and thirteen
members, sometime only Eleven, and their affairs almost desperate.
When the war is over we shall talk of these matters more at large—
Cur jubes me renovare dolorem.[2]
  Since the date of your letter I suppose you have been fully informed
of what has passed in Congress respecting our foreign Ministers,
and particularly yourself. You might have been Minister to Spain,
which would have been a more permanent Appointment than that
of Minister Plenepotentiary to negotiate a peace, but your friends
had a greater regard to the interest of their Country than to your's;
however I rest assured you will have peace (if to be obtained at all)
on such terms, as will intitle you to the gratitude of that Country,
and to secure such a proof of it as to render the present employment
not only more honorable but more beneficial than the other.
  You have escaped the obliquy but not the jealousy of one of the
parties in Congress, tho' the latter is almost done away. I have not
been able to find that any of your Colleagues have censured you;
they have been rather silent respecting you, tho' Doctor Arthur Lee
considers you as an honest man and as his friend. In short he seems
willing to submit his conduct abroad to your decision. Upon the
whole I really think he has been not well treated either by Messrs.
Franklin or Dean, or by Congress. His fate almost renders it dangerous to serve in a public character abroad.
  Do not my friend be discouraged by what I have said; difficulties,
public and secret attacks, will eternally attend public Characters and
high Stations. The man who discharges his Trust with fidelity &
according to the best of his abilities will always have the consolation
of his own mind (a consolation the world cannot give) and he may be

happy in the approbation of his country, but will never be miserable in the want of it—he will always also find a distinguishing, a worthy few, to support and applaud him.

Doctor Franklin, I really believe, would have been recalled last April only for myself. The intention in some Gentlemen in Congress appeared to me to be the removal of all our foreign Ministers in order to make way for themselves. My fears were, that a change of men, at that critical period, would imply both in Europe and America a change of measures, and I was reluctant to give up old servants for new men, whom I could not so well confide in.

Doctor Franklin still continues Minister Plenepotentiary at the court of Versailles, Colo. Laurens (the son of the late President of Congress) is appointed his Secretary. Mr. Jay is appointed Minister to the court of Madrid and Mr. Carmichael his Secretary. Mr. Laurens was appointed last Monday Commissioner to the United Provinces for the purpose of negotiating a treaty of Amity and Commerce, but particularly a Loan of money, and he has the nominating his own Secretary. Your's is the Post of danger and of honor; Our friend Mr. Dana is appointed your Secretary. Nothing more is yet done, but some Consuls must be appointed.

You percieve the freedom with which I write to you. I correspond with none, except officially, but in this way, tho' I am induced to be more free with you, because, notwithstanding I hereby compliment myself, I am certain we have had the same views throughout this whole contest, the good of our country and the happiness of mankind; we have also acted openly and without guile. It will give me great pleasure to hear from you often, and when you are on t'other side of the Atlantic I will as frequently communicate what passes here.

Count D'Estaing has not been heard from since the 4th of October, nor have we had a line from General Lincoln, but we flatter ourselves all is well.

I am, dear Sir, with sincere esteem, Your most obedient humble servant,   Tho. M:Kean

FC (PHi: McKean Papers). In the hand of Thomas McKean and endorsed by him: "Rough draft of a Lre. to the Honoble. John Adams Esq; Novr. 8th. 1779."
    [1] A measure of "the anxieties, cares & troubles" McKean faced in performing his multiple duties is reflected in an open letter to his Newcastle County constituents published in the *Pennsylvania Packet* of September 7, 1779, in which he resigned his seat in the Delaware assembly. "Gentlemen," he explained, "Near seventeen years have expired since you first chose me to represent you in General Assembly. The continuation of that choice, especially during the last five years (when I resided out of your State) exhibits the strongest proofs of your approbation of my political conduct, and must manifest to the world, that the sentiments of the representative and the represented, particularly respecting the great and important contest with Great-Britain, and the measures adopted to obtain peace, liberty and safety, were the same. Your affairs now wear the most promising aspect both at home and abroad; and, as I find it to be absolutely impracticable for me to discharge my duty to you as I wish in my present station, I must reiterate my request, that at the ensuing annual election you

will be pleased to choose some other person to occupy the seat I have the honor to fill in your Legislature."

  [2] An allusion to Dido's command to Aeneas to recount the painful story of the overthrow of Troy. Virgil *Aeneid* 2.3.

Marine Committee to Henry Laurens

Sir,   Marine Committee Novr. 8. 1779.

    This Committee having no proper person in South Carolina to execute the above Order,[1] Request that Collo. Laurens would undertake the necessary provision himself. And draw on this Committee for the amount.

    We are Sir, with great respect, Yr. most Obedt. Servts,

                                   Jno. Mathews Chairman

RC (NN: Emmet Collection). Written and signed by John Mathews.

  [1] "The above Order," which was written on the page above this letter, was an extract from the secret journal of November 1 directing the Marine Committee "to make the like provision for the passage of Mr. Laurens to Europe as was directed to be made for Messrs. Jay & Adams."

William Sharpe to Richard Caswell

Sir   Philadelphia Novr. 8th. 1779

    I have the pleasure of sending you inclosed an Extract of a Letter from Genl Gates informing of the evacuation of Rhode Island and an extract of a Letter from Genl. Washington which you will observe ought not to be exposed to public view.[1] We have no better accounts from Europe than it contains.

    We are not a little surprized at the silence in the Southern States, Congress has received no Authentic accounts from that quarter since the Count arived on the Coast, altho private Letters and other scraps of intelligence gives us flattering hopes.

    Mr. Laurens is appointed to negociate a Loan in Holland. A small fund in Europe might be applied so as to have a happy effect on our Finances, by disposing of Bills of Exchange and otherwise.

    The astonishing prices of the necessary supplies for the Army and the low State of our funds are very alarming and does require the most vigorous exertions of all the States.

    I am under an almost absolute necessity of being home before the hard of winter. I hope to see Mr. Penn and some other gentleman here soon. If none have set out, be so obliging as to interest yourself in that matter. Our State as much as the others ought by no means to be one day unrepresented. I have the mortification to inform you that Mr. Hewes is in so low a state of health that his recovery is much dispaired of—his complaints are Bileous & consumptive.

With the highest esteem and regard, I am. Sir, Your Most Obt.
Servt.   Wm. Sharpe.

RC (MH–H: bMS Am 1649.5).
[1] Washington's November 2 letter, which was read in Congress this day, contained
intelligence concerning the redeployment of British regiments at New York and
British naval reverses in the English Channel. See *JCC*, 15:1249; PCC, item 152,
8:155–58; and Washington, *Writings* (Fitzpatrick), 17:64–65.

Committee of Congress to Thomas Sim Lee

Sir   Philadelphia Novr. 9th 1779
When Count de Estaing, Some time past, was hourly Expected
from the Southward in want of provisions, our Magazines being
then low, and the Commissary of purchases unable At Once to furnish the Supply that would be probably wanted for our own Army
and the Count, Mr Holkers Agents, in Concurrence with the Governor of Maryland took Measures to procure 8,000 Barrels of flour in
your State of which the Commttee of Congress was informed & did
approve as being necessary at that time, but being Since told that
there is great reason to Suspect that Certain persons being actually
or pretendedly Agents for Mr Holker have Made large purchases of
flour beyond the quantity aforesd and by creating a Competition &
outbiding our Commissaries, have greatly inhanced the price of flour,
and retarded those Supplies which are necessary for the Subsistance
of our Army, we request your Excellency's attention to this affair,
and that proper enquiry be made and that all the flour purchased by
any person whatever except the Complement of Eight thousand
barrels aforesd. & of 4,000 before in Mr Smiths hands for Mr. Holker
be turned over to the Commissary Genl. of purchases, as the only
Channel through which Supplies for our army & our allys can in
futur be regularly obtained and delivrd that hereafter no purchases
of flour on publc account be allowed in your State but by the Commissary General & his Deputies and we refer you to Col. Blain for
more particular Information on this head.
Per order of the Comttee of Congress on the Comsy. & Qur Mstr
Generals departments, your Excellencys most obedt humble Servant,
                                        Jesse Root Chairman

P.S. The flour purchased to Carry to Virginia agreable to the resolve of Congress for that purpose, is not to be affected by any thing
in the above letter.

RC (MdAA: Executive Papers). Written and signed by Root. Addressed: "His Excellency The Governor of Maryland. Favd per Col. Blain." Thomas Sim Lee had just
been elected on November 8 to succeed Gov. Thomas Johnson. *Md. Archives*, 43:10.

John Fell's Diary

Tuesday the 9th [November 1779]
Coml Committee. Congress. Agreeable to the order of the Day
Balloted for Commissioners of Treasury Board. vizt. Appointed
            Forman   Turnbull ⟨*John Gibson*⟩ Auditor of Accts.
Millegen—Deputy Auditor General.[1]

MS (DLC).
[1] For a more complete and accurate record of the elections held this day for staffing the newly reorganized Board of Treasury, see *JCC*, 15:1251–52. See also James Lovell to William Whipple, this date, note 2; and Samuel Huntington to Jonathan Trumbull, Jr., November 12, 1779.

Cyrus Griffin to the Virginia House of Delegates

Sir,   Novem. 9th. [1779.]
I beg you will do me the honor to lay this letter before the house.

I am at present alone in this important delegation;[1] perhaps abundantly more important than my Constituents suppose. A majority of states in Congress shew a manifest inclination to lessen the weight of Virginia in the general scale of the union; and the Continental Credit is already upon the very brink of ruin. At such a period the assembly are satisfied that my abilities and Influence are greatly inadequate to represent so vast a Country as Virginia, even upon the supposition I had the power of voting in Congress. I feel exceedingly for the rights of my Country, and the Welfare of America, and I hope to be excused when I express some degree of astonishment that at least three members are not sent forward to Philadelphia, and members too of the first abilities and character.

After a great deal of heat and debate Congress have thought proper to pass a resolution relative to the Land office, which resolution and other proceedings were transmitted by the last post.[2] I am sorry to observe that so important a measure as that should have taken its origin from the Memorial of two private Companies claiming a large extent of Lands within the Bounds of Virginia to their own use and benefit, and offering a recompense to Congress of ten thousand pounds sterling for a confirmation thereof; and however as a member of the Virginia assembly I might be induced to make *some* compensation to the *Indiana* Claimants which they are very desirous to accept, and wish to acknowledge the Jurisdiction of Virginia and to defend the state against all opposition whatever, yet I think Congress have no business to interfere with such matters at the expence of our chartered rights, and the rights of an independant Legislature. When Virginia instructed her delegates in Congress to sign the declaration of Independency what did she mean by reserv-

ing the sovereignty and internal Government of the state? No deception could be intended of any latent claim to extended Boundary;
for Virginia ceded to Pennsylvania and Maryland and the two Carolinas all the Countries within their respective charters which might
be supposed a part of her chartered territory and then adds "the
western and northern extent of Virginia shall in all respects stand as
fixed by the Charter of King James the first in the year 1709 [1609],
and the public Treaty of Peace between Great Britain and France in
1763."

Yesterday a letter was read in Congress from Colonel Brodhead
with a late date at Pittsburg giving Information that some Inhabitants from the Counties of Yoghagania and Ohio had committed
Trespasses upon the Lands of the Indians on the farther side of the
Ohio River, which produced the enclosed Resolution.[3] With my affections to the assembly, I have the honor to be with great esteem
&c.   C. Griffin

RC (Vi: Executive Papers).
[1] For attrition in the Virginia delegation, see also the letters of James Mercer, the
Virginia Delegates, and Meriwether Smith to the Virginia House of Delegates, of
October 1 and November 2 and 25, respectively.
[2] See Samuel Huntington to the States, October 30, 1779.
[3] See the next entry.

Samuel Huntington to Thomas Jefferson

Sir,   Philadelphia Novr. 9th 1779.
Your Excellency will receive herewith enclosed an Act of Congress
of the 8th Instant together with the copy of a letter from Colonel
Broadhead of the 26th Ulto.[1]

In pursuance of the orders Contained in the Act of Congress
enclosed I am to request your Excellency's endeavour to prevent a
repetition of the trespasses mentioned in the letter from Col.
Broadhead. The Evil tendency of such practices are too obvious to
leave room For a doubt that proper exertions will be used on the
part of Virginia to prevent the like in future.

I have the honor to be, with great respect, Your Excellency's Humble Servant,   Saml. Huntington President

Tr (DLC: Burnett Papers). Endorsed: "Copied from the original, then in the possession of Mr. Stan V. Henkels ."
[1] Col. Daniel Brodhead, commander of the western department at Fort Pitt, had
complained that Virginia settlers had recently crossed the Ohio River and trespassed
upon Delaware Indian lands. He had, he explained, destroyed their "Hutts" and
chased them from the area. To prevent a retaliatory raid, he attempted to reassure
the Delawares that this isolated incident posed no threat to their security but he
urged Congress to enjoin Virginia officials to intervene "to prevent a future trespass
& the Murder of many innocent Families on the Frontier." Upon reading Brodhead's

account of this incident, Congress immediately adopted the enclosed resolve to implement his recommendation. *JCC*, 15:1249. His letter to Congress is in PCC, item 78, 3:383–86. For other documents reflecting similar concerns over Virginia expansionism and western land claims at this time, see also Huntington to Jefferson, October 30 and December 30, 1779.

Samuel Huntington to William Livingston

Sir,   Philada. 9th Novem. 1779
I am honour'd with your Excellency's favour of the 29th Ultimo and have the Pleasure to transmit you enclos'd an Act of Congress of the 4th instant expressing their Satisfaction in your Conduct for carrying into effect their resolutions of the 9th. July last.[1]
    Agreable to your Excellency's request have also enclos'd the acts of Congress of the 6th & 7th ulto for raising the necessary supplies &c.[2]
    I have the honour to be, with great respect, your Excy's hble Servt,
                                                    S.H. President

LB (DNA: PCC, item 14).
    [1] *JCC*, 15:1237. In his letter of October 29, Livingston explained that he had discharged Mr. Thomas Stockton as purchasing commissary for the hospital at Princeton, pursuant to the powers vested in the states by Congress' resolves of July 9, for which see John Jay to the States, July 14, 1779, note 1.
    [2] Livingston had asked for additional copies of these acts because during a recent British foray he had been forced to abandon his house at Raritan and after his return had been unable to locate the papers Huntington had enclosed in his letter concerning the states' quotas. See Huntington to the States, October 9, 1779; and PCC, item 68, fols. 475–78.

James Lovell to William Whipple

                                                    Novr 9th. 1779
    Two of yr. Letters are before me: And I should be doubly unjust if I took Advantage of yr, kind Hint about late Hours & meat Suppers, so far as not to notice yr. Epistles while I drive as hard as ever in writing to others. The Dates of yr. 2 Favors are Oct 11th and 26th. I find that at the latter period you was not well informed as to Mr. JA's Commission. He is *minister plenipoteny* for the special Purpose known to you. Mr. D. is Secy to *the Embassy* not to *JA*;[1] but it is not yet quite certain whether he will proceed. Should he not, I think the Person you hint at would not fail of obtaining what he would be very well pleased with. Your Conjectures about D Estaing from the Beginning, get every day fresh Proofs of their Judiciousness.
    I feel the cloudy Weather confoundedly this moment. I seem to see a naked starving Army in Opposition to a vigorous well fed irritated compact one now at New York. I wish this was the Weather only on my Spirits.

Mr. Hewes is probably within 10 or 12 Hours of his long long long
Home. We are balloting our Pens Ink and Paper out about the
Treasury. A Mr. Ezekiel Foreman & Mr. Jonathan Trumbull are
chosen Commissrs.[2] But the Post will go if I do not close without
telling more Tales. You will Probably soon see Mr. Lowell who will
tell you all about us.

Affectionately,   J.L.

RC (MH–H: bMS Am 1832).
[1] That is, Francis Dana and John Adams.
[2] Ezekiel Forman and Jonathan Trumbull, Jr., were elected two of the three permanent members of the Board of Treasury, which under the treasury ordinance of July
30, 1779, was to consist of three permanent members and two members of Congress,
who were to be appointed for six-month terms. John Gibson, the former auditor
general, was elected as the third permanent member on November 25, and when
Trumbull declined the post, William Denning was selected in his place.
    After the board assumed office on November 30, 1779, it took over most of the
routine business of requisitions and the preparation of reports.
    For an account of the appointment and operation of the reorganized Board of
Treasury, see Edward F. Robinson, "Continental Treasury Administration, 1775–1781:
A Study in the Financial History of the American Revolution." (Ph.D. diss., University
of Wisconsin, 1969), pp. 200–57.

Henry Marchant to William Greene

Dear Sir,   Philadelphia Novr. 9th. 1779.
    I most heartily congratulate your Excellency, the State, and
America; upon the Evacuation of Newport by that motly Savage
Host that hath so long infested Our Country. It is a happy Event—
and I hope will soon be followed with the entire Extirpation of the
British Forces out of America. I could have wished for your Excel-
lency's own Communication to me of so important an Event.
    Your Excellency & the other Branches of the Legislature, amidst
all the joy, will have an immediate Occasion of important Considera-
tions. The future Safety of the Town of Newport & the State in
General: The proper Line to be adopted as to the internal Enemies—
which permit me to suggest, it is expected, will be wise, just and
Firm. Not only the present Peace, but, the future Welfare of the
State, if not of America will attend much upon this.
    The next and perhaps no less important Consideration, will be the
Defence necessary against the more open Foe. How far the Town of
Newport is capable of a full Defense? The Difficulty & Expence on
the One Hand—the Advantages as to the State & the Common
Cause on the other. How far the State of Herself is capable of mak-
ing & supporting a Defense in present & future—and how far the
United States are interested therein now, or may be hereafter—and
how far they ought to be called upon. The best of Military and political wisdom ought to be consulted upon this Occasion.

I am but capable of suggesting broken Hints. However such as they are, I find myself constrained to make Them from the Love I bear to the true Interest & Happiness of the State I have the Honor to represent, and the Glory, Happiness and Independence of America. I am with great Truth Your Excellency's most obedient and very humble Servt.   Hy. Marchant

P.S. I inclose your Excellency two of the Weekly Journals of Congress down to Sept. 11. 1779—& the Weekly Papers.

RC (R–Ar: Letters to Governors).

Nathaniel Peabody to Josiah Bartlett

My Dear sir,   No. 14 Philada. 9th Novr 1779[1]
    Your favours of the 9th & 20th ulto have Come to hand.[2] I am extreamly obliged by the Continuance of your Letters, and Should have done my self the Honr. of writing more particularly if I had Certainly known where to have directed my letters to be left in order that they might find a Safe Conveyance, without the danger of their being intercepted. However I have wrote Genl. Whipple Some anecdotes respecting the management of foreign Ambassys—with the names of Persons Elected for that Purpose &ca,[3] which as you are acquainted with many Characters here might be Somewhat amusing. There Seems a little Prospect of obtaining a foreign Loan, in Some of the Low Countrys—our Freind Mr. H. L——ns[4] is to negociate that business. No official Accounts from Count D'Estaing, Since that of his having besieged the Savannah—Nor of the movements of the Enemy worth Notice Since their Evacuating R. Island. In Dunlaps Paper of last Saturday you will See a very Curious Manifesto[5] which may be relied upon as authentic altho not officially Recd. I must beg of you to Seal the Cover directed to Mrs. Peabody, inclosing its Contents & forward it, after having read the News papers, I take this method as being less expensive, and may Serve for the purpose of Communicating the News to you, & my friends in Atkinson without much inconvenience. I have heard that our friend S. H——t[6] of Exeter is Taxed with being Guilty of Evil Communication &c. I most Sincerely wish you Success in deleating those Secret Vulturs who cease not day & night to prey upon the vitals of America. When the Truth Comes to light it will be found there is more than one or two—in the Conspiracy. By this days Paper you may observe the Treatment that Such People meet with in this State.[7]
    I am my Dear Sir, with Sentiments of Esteem your most obedt. & very Huml Servt,   Nathl Peabody

P.S. My Compliments to friends.

RC (NhD: Bartlett Papers).

¹ This letter is misdated "5th Novr." in Burnett, *Letters*, 4:508–9.

² Bartlett's October 20 letter to Peabody is in Bartlett, *Papers* (Mevers), p. 271.

³ See Peabody to William Whipple, November 1, 1779.

⁴ Henry Laurens.

⁵ A "Manifesto, on the Motives of the Conduct of the King of France relative to Great-Britain," was printed in the *Pennsylvania Packet*, November 6, 1779.

⁶ That is, Samuel Hobart, a member of the New Hampshire House of Representatives and Committee of Safety in 1779. Bartlett, *Papers* (Mevers), p. 273n.4.

⁷ Peabody added this note in the margin to explain the "treatment" of loyalists in Pennsylvania: "9 have been Convicted & are to Suffer death for being Concernd in Counterfeit money & other Treasonable practices—but find I am mistaken as to its being in the paper."

Nathaniel Peabody to William Whipple

My Dear Sir,   No. 6   Philada. Novr 9. 1779

I have the Honr. to acknowledge the Rect of Your kind favour, of the 26th Ulto—And am much obliged to you for its Contents.[1]

Mr Garards visit to Camp most Certainly was for the purpose of Concerting measures for Military Operations. And Mr Holkr & others have been in the Jersies ever since his return from Camp Expecting to See The Count Destaing—but alas there is No official accts. from him Since that of his having beseiged the Savannah. I will endeavour to forward the Journals regularly as they Shall be published, which you well know will give but a faint Idea of our proceedings. As to the books belonging to the Square box I shall extract from time to time, & forward Such parts thereof, as I think worth your reading. Mr. L——ns[2] Sets off from hence, this morng for So Carolina in order to Embark &c. Congress have allowd. him to Appoint a Secry with a Salary not Exceeding £500 Sterlg in Stead of the £300 first voted.

No official Accts. here of the Enemies movements, worth Notice, Since their Evacuating R. Island. You will find by the public papers that Genl. Sullivan having Accomplished the design of his *Mission* has returned with *Eclat*.

I am not Surprized that a Certain Gentleman at Exeter begins to Show his *foot*, and is under arest,[3] but think it unPolite for him to Stand alone, and leave his *friends* unnoticed.

Since you left this, there has been Nine Capital Convictions in this State Chiefly for being Concern'd in Counterfeit money—it is thought not more than three of them will be Pardoned, the Rest are to be Executed. Finances remain much at one in Congress But out of Doors the Devil himself Riegns Triumphant, to Speak in a Clinical Stile, for almost every article of Support is from two to four times the Price they were when you left this place. The New appointmts of Delegates in the State of N. York for the ensuing Year are Genl. Schuyler, Mr. Duane, Genl. Scot, Mr Floyd, & Mr. L'Hommedieu—

And The Chanceller Mr Livingston is Appointed Special Delegate for the Vermont business—but none of them have as Yet Come on. The assembly of that State have Set a Trap for the N. Hampr. Grants, by adjourning, to meet next at *Albany*. In Dunlaps Paper of the 6th youll find a Curious Manifesto, that I think may be relied upon as authentic tho not officially Recd.—but that I be not further Tedious beg leave only to Subscribe, Yours most Sincerely,

Nathl Peabody

NB. Compliments &c.

RC (Capt. J. G. M. Stone, Annapolis, Md., 1973).
[1] Whipple's October 26, 1779, letter to Peabody is in John Farmer and Jacob B. Moore, eds., *Collections, Historical and Miscellaneous, and Monthly Literary Journal*, 3 vols. (Concord, N.H.: Hill & Moore, 1822–24), 2:343; and Miscellaneous Folders, NN.
[2] That is, Henry Laurens.
[3] That is, Samuel Hobart, whose "arrest, or something like it, for evil communications." had been reported by Whipple in his October 26 letter. See also the preceding entry, note 6.

John Fell's Diary

Wednesday Novr. 10th. 1779

Coml Committee. Congress. President Huntington in the Chair.[1] This day Receivd from Genl Lincoln the disagreeable Acct of Count DeEstaing Raising the Seige of Savanna in Georgia. Mr Hewes Died this day.[2]

MS (DLC).
[1] Fell is doubtlessly referring to the return of the Connecticut delegates, who had not been attending Congress because their credentials to attend after November 1 had not been received. See Jesse Root to Oliver Ellsworth, November 1, 1779, note 1.
[2] Congress had resolved this day to attend Joseph Hewes' funeral, which was held the following day, "in a body" and to "continue in mourning for the space of one month." See *JCC*, 15:1252.

Samuel Holten's Diary

[November 10–11, 1779]

10. Wednesday. We had the disagreeable news from Genl. Lincoln, that our army have not succeeded against Savannah. The Honl. Mr. Hughes one of the delegates from N. Carolina deceased this morning.

11. Thursday. I wrote to the President of the Council of Massachusetts Bay.[1] I attended the Funeral of Mr. Hughes.

MS (MDaAr).
[1] See Holten to the Massachusetts Council, November 11, 1779.

Samuel Huntington to George Washington

Sir,   Philadelphia Novembr. 10th. 1779.
I have the honour to transmit your Excellency copies of two letters from Genl. Lincoln of the 22d Ulto.[1] which will give you the disagreeable intelligence of the failure of the expedition against Savannah with the Causes and Circumstances attending the Expedition and failure.

As Major Clarkson who came Express with this intelligence had an Opportunity from his situation of remarking many particulars not mentioned in the letters; it was thought expedient to send him forward with these dispatches, that he might give your Excellency personally all the information in his power upon the subject.

Congress have given orders for three of the Frigates now at Boston to sail for Charlestown South Carolina with all possible dispatch; and also appointed a Committee to consider and report what farther measures may be expedient for the security and defence of the southern department, as soon as may be.

I have the honor to be, with the greatest respect, Your Excellency's Humble Servt.   Saml. Huntington President

RC (DLC: Washington Papers). In the hand of George Bond and signed by Huntington.
[1] These letters, which were addressed to President Huntington and to Henry Laurens and the congressional committee appointed to correspond with the commander of the southern department, are in the Washington Papers, DLC.

Marine Committee to the Eastern Navy Board

Gentlemen   November 10th. 1779
You are hereby directed to use the most indefatigable endeavours to send to Sea immediately the three frigates formerly directed by this Committee to proceed for Charles Town in South Carolina. You are to give them the same Orders that was at that time directed to be given.[1] The Salvation of that State in a great measure depends on these Vessels Arriving there before the enemy can send any reinforcements. Under these circumstances we trust no time will be lost on your part in executing this business.[2] We are Gentn,
                              Your Hble servants

P.S. You are to give the following further Orders to the Commanding Officer—that if he should find the Port of Charles Town blocked up on his Arrival there he is to return Again to Boston with the Vessels under his command.

LB (DNA: PCC Miscellaneous Papers, Marine Committee Letter Book).
[1] For the committee's previous correspondence ordering the Continental frigates

Boston, Deane, and *Queen of France* to South Carolina, see Marine Committee to the Eastern Navy Board, September 22 and 28, 1779. The present directive was adopted by Congress this day pursuant to a motion of John Mathews, a delegate from South Carolina who was chairman of both the Marine Committee and the committee appointed expressly for corresponding with the commander of the southern department. *JCC,* 15:1253–54.

² Committee chairman John Mathews also sent a brief letter this day to General Washington informing him that the three frigates were being ordered "immediately to proceed" to South Carolina. Washington Papers, DLC; and Paullin, *Marine Committee Letters,* 2:127.

John Fell's Diary

Thursday 11th. [November 1779]
Coml Committee. This day chiefly spent in debate about the sending some Troops and Stores to So Carolina.
PM Attended the funeral of Mr Hewes.

MS (DLC).

Samuel Holten to the Massachusetts Council

Sir   Philadelphia Nov. 11th, 1779.
Yesterday Majr. Clarkson arrived here with dispaches from Genl. Lincoln,[1] by which, Congress are informed, that, on the 9th ulto. an attempt was made, to storm the lines of the enemy at Savannah, which fail'd of success, and that the Count Estaing could not tarry any longer, so that the Seige was raised; The General not having been able to ascertain a regular return of our loss, when the express came away, but is supposed to be about 170, among which is the Brave Count Pulaski; The Count Estaing having received a slight wound in the attack.

The committee have not reported upon the application of the Honble. Court, respecting staying part of the Continental taxes 'till the accounts can be liquidated respecting the Penobscot expedition, but I do not expect much from their report; altho' I have been heard before them, & given it as my opinion, that, it will not be in the power of the State to comply with the Resolutions of Congress, respecting paying in their taxes unless something is done; I shall carefully attend to the same when it comes before Congress.[2]

The proceedings of the Commissioners at Hartford, have been received by Congress, and committed to the committee of twelve, and said committee, have agreed to report to Congress a number of resolutions, for recommending to the several states a general regulation of prices.[3]

The application from the Honorable Board to Congress, respecting the removal of Colo. Heazels [Hazen's] Regiment from some part of our frontiers, or New Hampshire, have been refered to General Washington, with directions for him to take order thereon.[4]

The sum of money that Congress are at liberty to emit, will be all expended in a very short time, and they will then depend upon the several States to supply the Continental treasury; and if they should fail; I must leave it to the Honble Court to consider what will be the consequences; I think it is a matter of such importance, that it requires the first attention.

I have the Honor to be, with the highest sentiment of respect, Sir, your most obedient servant;   S. Holten

P.S. Yesterday the Honble. Mr. Hughes, one of the Delegates from North Carolina, deceas'd.

RC (M–Ar: Revolutionary War Letters). Addressed: "The Honorable, The President of the Council of Massa. Bay."

[1] See Samuel Huntington to George Washington, November 10, 1779.

[2] On November 16, Congress rejected Massachusetts' request to retain $6 Million of their tax quota. *JCC*, 15:1273. For a similar request from Connecticut, see Jesse Root to Jonathan Trumbull, Sr., November 12, 1779, note 1. For the eventual reimbursement of Massachusetts by Congress for this expedition, see James Lovell to Samuel Adams, February 28, 1780, note 7.

[3] The "proceedings of a convention of committees from the five eastern states, met at Hartford for the regulation of prices" was read in Congress on November 10 and assigned to a committee already studying similar recommendations from the New Jersey legislature. See *Public Records of Connecticut*, 2:562–71. For Congress' response to these appeals for action to promote the regulation of prices in all the states, see Samuel Huntington to the States, November 22, 1779.

[4] See Samuel Huntington to George Washington, this date, note 2.

Samuel Huntington to Richard Caswell

Sir,   Philada. Novemr. 11th 1779

Your Excellency will receive herewith enclos'd an Act of Congress of this date requesting that the Governors of Virginia & North Carolina use their utmost exertions to have the whole of the Troops order'd from their respective States sent forward to join Genl Lincoln's Army without loss of time &c. I perswade myself that the pressing exigency of the Case leaves no room to doubt that all the despatch in your Excellency's Power will be given in compliance with this request of Congress.

I have the honour to be, with great respect, your Excy's hble Servt.   S.H. President

LB (DNA: PCC, item 14).

Samuel Huntington to John Hancock

Sir,   Philada Novem. 11th 1779
 I do myself the Honour to transmit the enclos'd Act of Congress
of the 8th instant desiring the late & former Presidents to lodge as
soon as they conveniently can in the Secretaries Office copies of all
public Letters by them respectively written during their President-
Ships.[1]
 I have the honour to be, with great respect, your most humble
Servt.   S.H. President

LB (DNA: PCC, item 14).
 [1] See *JCC*, 15:1249–50. Since Hancock's presidential letterbooks remained in his
possession at his death, and subsequently became part of the regular collections of the
Massachusetts Historical Society and then of the Library of Congress before being
added to the "Papers of the Continental Congress" now at the National Archives,
Hancock apparently failed to respond to this request. No other body of Hancock's
presidential letters is known to exist.
 For Huntington's repetition of this request, see also Huntington to Hancock, February 27, 1781, note 2.

Samuel Huntington to Benjamin Lincoln

Sir,   Philadelphia 11th Novr. 1779.
 I am favour'd with your letter of the 22d Ulto. by Major Clarkson,
containing an Account of the failure of the Expedition in Georgia.[1]
 You will herewith receive enclosed an Act of Congress of this day;[2]
Also an Act of the 10th Inst.[3] and a Copy of an Act of the 27th July
last and the letter accompanying the last mentioned Act, Ordering
General Scott to forward the troops under his Command to Charlestown as expeditiously as possible.[4] By these several enclosures You
will be informed of the measures Congress have taken from time to
time, and are still taking to reinforce the army under your command
And aid the States of South Carolina and Georgia; also that you are
to cause a court of enquiry to be held on Brigadier General Scott for
disobedience of the Orders above mentioned.[5]
 It was thought expedient that Major Clarkson should proceed
with Copies of your dispatches, to the Commander in Cheif, and
give his personal information to his Excellency General Washington
on the subject.
 I am with great respect, Your humble servt,
                                                Saml. Huntington President

RC (MHi: Lincoln Papers). In the hand of George Bond and signed by Huntington.
 [1] Lincoln's October 22 letter to Congress is in PCC, item 158, fols. 279–84.

[2] This "Act" consisted of a number of emergency measures Congress was ordering for the relief of South Carolina. See *JCC*, 15:1255–56.

[3] Undoubtedly Congress' resolution ordering three frigates at Boston to sail immediately for South Carolina. *JCC*, 15:1253.

[4] See John Jay to Charles Scott, July 29, 1779.

[5] *JCC*, 15:1256.

Samuel Huntington to John Rutledge

Sir,   Philada Novemr 11th 1779

Your Excellency will receive herewith enclos'd several Acts of Congress viz of the 10th & 11th inst[1] also of the 9th & 29th of March last by which you will be inform'd of the Measures adopted by Congress to reinforce the Army under Genl Lincoln & aid the States of South Carolina & Georgia.[2] It is to be hoped that the vigorous & speedy exertions of the several States of Virginia & North Carolina in aid of South Carolina will give them timely Assistance in their expos'd situation since the failure of the expedition against Savannah.

I have the honour to be, with great respect, your Excy's hble Servt,   S.H. President

LB (DNA: PCC, item 14).

[1] See the preceding entry.

[2] For the measures Congress had taken in March for bolstering the army and defending South Carolina and Georgia, see *JCC*, 13:298–99, 385–88; and these *Letters*, 12:242–44, 246–48.

Samuel Huntington to George Washington

Sir.   Philadelphia Novr. 11th. 1779.

Since my letter of the 29th Ulto. I am favour'd with your Excellency's letters of Octor 30th & Octor 17th.[1]

I had the honor of addressing you in my letter of yesterday enclosing dispatches from General Lincoln by Major Clarkson.

Your Excellency will receive herewith enclosed an Act of Congress of this date among other provisions for the southern department, containing a resolve that the North Carolina troops and such others as may be conveniently spared from the main army, reinforce General Lincoln without delay; Your Excellency must be the best Judge what troops can *Conveniently* be spared.

I have also enclosed an Act of Congress of the 6th Instant granting leave of Absence for eight months to Capt. Lieut. Van Dyke of the Artillery; Also the Copy of a letter from the President of the Council of Massachusetts Bay of the 22d Ulto. accompanied with an Act of the 8th Instant directing Commander in Cheif to take order.[2]

I have the honor to be, with great respect, Your Excellency's Humble servant,   Saml. Huntington President

RC (DLC: Washington Papers). In the hand of George Bond and signed by Huntington.

[1] Washington's letter of October 30 and two letters of the 17th are in PCC, item 152, 8:117, 127–30, 139–40; and Washington, *Writings* (Fitzpatrick), 16:473–74, 17:42–43.

[2] See *JCC*, 15:1249. In its October 22 letter to Congress, the Massachusetts Council had complained that Col. Moses Hazen's regiment, which had recently completed cutting a road "from Newbury to within thirty Miles of Canada," was being reassigned and would therefore leave the area defenseless. It therefore appealed for an order to keep Hazen's Regiment, or "other suitable force," on the state's frontier. PCC, item 65, 2:13–16. For Washington's November 20 letter explaining why he could not spare any troops "for the defence of the Frontiers of New Hampshire and Massachusetts bay," see Washington, *Writings* (Fitzpatrick), 17:150–53.

James Lovell to Horatio Gates

Dear General   Philada. Novr. 11th 1779

Your Favor by Mr. Guild & that by Capt Bowen appear not endorsed as heretofore acknowledged. Ill Health and an unconscionable Load of Business flowing from Arrangements or rather Derangments of foreign Affairs must be my Excuse. As to Canada Matters, if they were not properly attended to in a favorable Season last Summer they will be now probably altogether neglected.[1] Perhaps we shall Scarcely again think of operations in Concert of Land & Sea Commands. Fame will have prepared you for a Detail which I am about to give you from the Letters of our amiable tho unfortunate Friend Lincoln.[2]

He writes from Charlestown Octr. 22d mentioning his former Information of the 5th of Septr. that Count DEstaing was arrived off Savannah. Orders were immediately given for assembling the Troops. They reached Zubly's Ferry on the 11th, on the 12th & 13th crossed with their Baggage under many disadvantages from Want of Boats & from the badness of the Roads, destroyed Bridges &c. &c. &c. encamped on the Heights of Ebenezer 23 miles from Savannah & were joined by the Troops from Augusta under Genl. McIntosh. 14th, remained there not know where the Count was, 15th, heared the Count wd. that night take post nine miles from Savannah, moved and encamped at Cherokee Hill 9 miles from the Town. 18th formed a Junction before Savannah. Reconnoitred and determin'd to make approaches to try the Effect of Artillery. From 18th to 23d landed the heavy Ordnance and Stores with difficulty for want of travailling Carriages. On the Evening of the 23d broke Ground: On the 5th of Octr Batteries of 33 Cannon & nine Mortars were opened & continued till the 8th—without the wished for Effect. The Period having long elapsed which the Count had assigned & the Engineers informg. that much more must be spent in *regular approaches*—and his longer

Stay being impossible, matters were reduced to the alternative of raising the Seige immediately or reducing the Garrison by Assault— the latter was agreed on and in the morning of the 9th the attack was made—it proved unsuccessful. We were repulsed with some Loss. Soon after the Count communicated his Intentions of raising the Seige, he could not be diverted from it as his Departure was become *indispensible*. The Ordnance & Stores were reimbarked on the 18th, the American Troops marching that Eveng. reached Zubly's next morning crossed & encamped that night in Carolina. The french troops encamped on the Eveng. of the 18th about 2 miles from Savannah. The[y] were after twenty four hours to embark at Kincaids Landing. "Our Disappointment is great and what adds much to the Poignancy of our Grief is the Loss of a Number of brave officers & Men, among them the late intrepid Count Pulaski." "Count D Estaing has undoubtedly the Interest of America much at heart. This he has evidenced by coming to our Assistance—by his constant Attention during the Seige—his Undertaking to reduce the Enemy by Assault when he despaired of effecting it otherwise— and by bravely putting himself at the Head of his Troops and leading them to the Attack. In our Service he has freely bled. I feel much for him—for while he is suffering the distresses of painful wounds, he has to combat the Torments of Chagrin. I hope he will be consoled by an Assurance that, although he has not succeeded according to his Wishes & those of America, we regard with high Approbation his Intentions to Serve us, and that his Want of Success will not lessen our Ideas of his merit."

No Returns—the Adjt. Genl not being arrived—from Memory, the killed & wounded amount in the whole to 170.

There is another Letter from the Genl. to the correspondg. Comtee such as you will conjecture. The State of Sth. Cara. have *thought* we neglected them, we *know* they neglected themselves. They will not *draught* to fill up their Battalions, they will not raise *black Regiments*, they will not put their militia when in Camp under continental Rules. However, we must exert ourselves for them in every Way. They have not been neglected by *us here* but their Neighbours have not regarded our Recommedations.

I wish I had stopped to mend me Pen just now—it is not at present worthwhile.

You must not give this to Printer. We shall do it here shortly.

I shall be watchful on the Score of yr. Recommendations & the Bearer's Merit.

I send you Journals as far as I can. I shall soon see you or you me, which is the same Thing in amount. In sight or out I am most affectionately Your humble Servant,   James Lovell

RC (NHi: Gates Papers).
[1] Love l, a longtime critic of General Washington, was at this time particularly piqued hat the commander in chief had recently reassigned Col. Moses Hazen's

regiment from a project to cut a road into Canada, leaving Massachusetts more vulnerable on its northern frontier. See the preceding entry, note 2. As this decision nearly coincided with a general redeployment of Continental resources to South Carolina (Massachusetts particularly resisted the reassignment of the Continental frigates at Boston), the Massachusetts delegates were pessimistic that vigorous measures against Canada could be revived in the foreseeable future.

[2] See Samuel Huntington to Washington, November 10, and to Benjamin Lincoln, this date.

Committee of Congress to Benjamin Lincoln

Sir,   Philadelphia Novr. 12th. 1779
We received your letter of the 23d of October, the 10th Inst.

We are extreamly sorry the expedition to Georgia (on which we had formed the most sanguine expectations of success) has ended so unfortunately.

It therefore now behoves us to be doubly industrious, in indeavouring to prepare against the worst that may happen in consequence thereof.

It is unnecessary for us to inclose you Copies of the Acts of Congress on this subject, as they will be now forwarded to you by the President.[1]

The succours from hence we are sensible will be in no capacity to render you any service for a length of time, & we place no dependence in their being able to reach you, so soon as the reinforcements to the enemy from New York, will them. However as we are induced to believe Virginia & North Carolina will, at the present alarming Crisis, strenuously exert themselves to afford you *substantial* Aid, we flatter ourselves, we shall not be again disappointed in our expectations from that quarter, in consequence of which, you will be enabled to make a tolerable stand, untill the troops from hence can come up.

We have little doubt, but what the expedition now forming at New York, is directed against the Southern States. Apprehending this to be the case, Congress have ordered three of the Continental Frigates, to proceed immediately for Chs. Town, to be under your Command, and which we think, will be of essential service to you in the defence of the Harbour.[2] Whatever else can be from time to time thought of, for the better defence, & Security of your Command, will be properly attended to.

We hope you will be more frequent in your communicating to us, as we think it is necessary to be informed as often as can be done, of your situation, & what might be further necessary for promoting the service of your department.

We congratulate you on the happy event of the evacuation of Rhode Island caused we conceive from an expectation of a visit from Count D'Estaing.

We are Sir, with much Esteem & regard, yr. most Obedt. Servts.

Jno. Mathews Chairman

RC (MeHi: Fogg Collection). Written and signed by John Mathews. Endorsed: "Jno. Mathews, Chairman Committee of Correspondence, Novr. 11. 1779."
[1] See Samuel Huntington to Lincoln, November 11, 1779.
[2] See Marine Committee to the Eastern Navy Board, November 10, 1779.

John Fell's Diary

Friday 12th [November 1779]

Coml Committee. Congress. Reports from the Board of War and Treasury. Balloted for a Commissioner of Treasury Board.[1]

	1st	2d	3d	4h
Wm Denning	5 Votes	6.	5.	4
John Gibson	6.	5.	5.	6
John Milligen[2]	1.	1.	. . . .
Marine Committee.				

MS (DLC).
[1] The journals do not mention this ballot, but John Gibson was elected the third commissioner of the Board of Treasury on November 25. See Samuel Huntington to Jonathan Trumbull, Jr., this date, note 3.
[2] Undoubtedly James Milligan, who had recently been elected auditor general. *JCC*, 15:1251.

William Churchill Houston to Caleb Camp

Sir,   Philada. 12 Novr. 1779.

In my last[1] I was under a Misconception relative to the Embargo Law of the State of Pennsylvania. I find that by a transient attention to it, I accidentally mistook for an Act, a Bill printed in the Pennsylvania-Packet for publick Consideration, and which did not pass. The Embargo now in operation here is not conditional, but absolute as ours. It is my Duty to notice the mistake lest it should be instrumental in giving Impressions unfavourable and unjust.

Every Day brings me fresh Uneasiness respecting the Supply of the general Treasury. The Expectation of Count D'Estaing's visiting our Coasts, in this Quarter, has created a Flood of Expense, and the Means of defraying it are narrowing fast. If the Taxes for the present year are not fully and punctually paid in, every Thing, but Hope, holds up discouraging Prospects. All the States must see the Necessity of Exertion, and I dare believe New-Jersey will not be behind the foremost. The Close of this Campaign is set down for the Era of Reformation in the Percentage—departments, to say no more, and especially if we are so fortunate as to carry through a Limitation of Prices. Afterwards, it is to be confided, Expenditures will be much less.

As to the Payment of the Taxes for 1780, I mentioned in my last that it was hardly to be imagined any monthly assessment or Collection could be made in our State, though if it were practicable it has it's advantages. It is rather to be supposed the Legislature will lay the Amount in two or three Payments, and collect the Taxes for Support of Government along with one or all of them. I have before mentioned the Case of two Payments. If three are preferred, being one Million twelve Thousand five Hundred Pounds each Payment, they come, at equal Intervals, the first of February, May and August. The Legislature may also probably consider whether Taxes are not more easily paid in the Spring than in the Summer, and lay more at that Season. There would also be another Advantage in this Policy, the Money will probably be more wanted at the Time these Taxes are calculated to begin, than towards the Middle or latter End of the Year.

There is one clear and obvious Principle on which all Taxation ought to be rested, and if it could be laid as the Groundwork and extend through our Tax-laws, Payment would not only be practicable but light and easy; it is "That every Man be called upon to pay in exact Proportion to his Ability, all Things considered." The Practice of this Principle, I confess, can never be attained precisely, but it is a Point of Perfection to which Laws may be directed, and to which they may continually more and more verge. The nearer an Assessment approximates to this, the more just it is. Why is it not proper to estimate every Part of the whole aggregate Estate, be the Kind of Property what it may, according as it is of use and Emolument to the Ower or Possessour, and all Acquisitions currently arising from Advantages and Opportunities? This Maxim is practised upon in some of the States, and comprehended in the short Description of "Taxing a Man according to his Faculty." The whole Debt of the Union does not amount to one Hundred Dollars a head, and if set off on Scale of strict Justice, would not perhaps to the Poor be more than the Price of three or four Days Work on a Taxable. Our State, it would seem, has always been in the Custom of taxing Lands too deeply, and there are many Kinds of Property, and Sources of Wealth and Income which have never paid any Thing.

I enclose for the Perusal of such as are curious, and have not seen it "The Case of the Sloop Active,"[2] which has produced a Dispute between Congress and the State of Pennsylvania. The Nature of this Case will be plainly collected from the printed Proceedings of the Court of Admiralty before which it was tried. I mention what further is necessary to give an adequate Idea of the Cause of Difference. In the Court of Admiralty the Jury gave one fourth to the Insurgents and three fourths to the Libellant and another Cruiser in Sight at the Time of the Capture. From the Decision, which is said to be wholly on Matter of Fact, the Insurgents appealed. The Court of Appeals decreed the whole to them, and directed the Judge of Admiralty of the State of Pennsylvania to see their Sentence executed. The Judge refused, as the Law by which the Maritime Court is established in that State, allows an Appeal on Matter of Law only, and does not permit the Facts found by a Jury to be re-examined. Much Law-Ammunition has been spent on the Occasion, and the Difference is not yet adjusted. Certain it is that the Resolutions of Congress of 1775, on Admiralty jurisdiction, say, the Facts shall be established by a Jury. Lawyers say there is this Distinction between Trials by Jury and Trials by Witnesses, that in the former Case the Facts found are not re-examined, in the latter they are. Our Law for erecting a Court of Admiralty allows an Appeal in all Cases whatsoever, but it must be acknowledged that an Appeal on Matter of Fact from the Verdict of a Jury has not a good Sound. And yet Juries are too often worse qualified to decide in maritime Causes than any other.

You have also a report of the Commissioners appointed by General Washington in April last, to settle a Cartel for the Exchange of Prisoners with the Commissioners of General Clinton. It has been already published in the News-papers.[3]

It is with Pleasure I also send an Extract from the General Orders of the Commander in Chief of 29 July last. The Virtues of this aimiable Man as a Citizen are no less conspicuous, than his Spirit and Perseverance as a Soldier.

Tomorrow will be published, by Order of Congress, the News from the Southward.[4] You will hear it with Concern. The raising of the Siege of Savanna is not so much to be regretted in itself, as the consequent Exposure of a large Extent of Country, the Inhabitants of which must unavoidably suffer before Succour can arrive to them. Let us however remember what has so often happened, that Confidence is the Road to Disappointment, and where our Prospects are least promising, from thence Success often comes. Nusquam desperandum est de Republica.[5]

I am, Sir, with due Regard, your obedt hble Servt,

William Ch. Houston

RC (Nj: State Papers).

[1] Not found.

[2] *The Case of the Sloop Active, &c* (Philadelphia: Hall and Sellers, 1779). Evans, *Am. Bibliography*, no. 16,220. For the "Dispute" produced by this case, see also Samuel Huntington to Jesse Root, October 1, 1779, note.

[3] For the May 10 report of Cols. William Davies and Robert H. Harrison, see John Jay to Washington, June 4, 1779, note 2.

[4] That is, Gen. Benjamin Lincoln's letter of October 22 to Pres. Samuel Huntington reporting the failure of the allied assault on Savannah, which appeared in the November 13 issue of the *Pennsylvania Packet*, and the November 17 issue of the *Pennsylvania Gazette*.

[5] That is, we need never despair of the Republic.

Samuel Huntington to John Sullivan

Sir,   Philada 12th Novemr 1779
    I am honour'd with your favour of the 9th instant. I much lament
the ill State of your health & especially as you seem to be Perswaded
it is such as renders it necessary you should retire from the Service
on that account. It is very unhappy that brave & experienced Officers should be under a Necessity of leaving the Service for want of
Health. Your letter will be laid before Congress as soon as they meet
tomorrow & due attention will no doubt be paid thereto.[1]
    I have the honour to be, with great respect, your humble Servt.
                                            S.H. President

LB (DNA: PCC, item 14).
    [1] Sullivan's November 9 letter to Congress, which was referred to committee after a
motion to refuse his resignation was offered by Elbridge Gerry, is in PCC, item 160,
fols. 340–43. The committee's recommendation to accept the general's resignation
was subsequently adopted by Congress on November 30, and Huntington transmitted the decision to Sullivan in a letter of December 2. See *JCC*, 15:1263–64, 1333; and
PCC, item 14, fols. 238–39.

Samuel Huntington to Jonathan Trumbull, Sr.

Sir   Philadelphia Novemr. 12. 1779.
    I am honourd with your Excellencys favour of the 1st Instant.[1]
Capt Nicholson was appointed before I arrived at Congress being
made acquainted with it I foretold as I foresaw the difficulty that
would ensue.[2]
    Col. Laurens had left this place before your Excellencys Letter to
him Arrivd & as he is bound to Holland with all possible dispatch
(inter nos) I thot. it uncertain whether the Letter if forwarded would
reach him in America.[3] Mr. Brown Informd me your former directions in his Letters had been if he was gone the Connecticutt Delegates Should open them.
    Under these circumstances I took the liberty to open his Letter &
finding your request to have Baron Van der Cappellens Letter Translated I presume you Intended it should be returnd, accordingly
have ordered a fair Translation to be made & shall return all the
papers as Soon as may be with the Translations.
    If I have erred it was with a good Intention & through mistake &
hope for pardon on that Account.
    I have the honour to be, with the greatest Respect, your Excellen-
cys humbl Servt.   Saml. Huntington

P.S. Haste obliges me to refer your Exy to Col. Roots Letter for
other Intelligence.   S.H.

RC (Ct: Trumbull Papers).

[1] No letter from Trumbull of November 1 is in PCC. As his November 2 letter to Huntington (PCC, item 66, 2:33–36) concerns a topic very different from any mentioned here, it seems clear that the former was directed to Huntington in his capacity as a Connecticut delegate rather than as president of Congress.

[2] For Nicholson's appointment to command the Continental frigate *Trumbull* at New London, see the Marine Committee's letters to the Eastern Navy Board and to James Nicholson, October 6, 1779.

[3] See Henry Laurens to Trumbull, October 19, 1779.

Samuel Huntington to Jonathan Trumbull, Jr.

Sir   Philadelphia Novr. 12th. 1779.

You will receive herewith enclosed three Acts of Congress of the 30th July, 23d of October, and 9th Instant by which you will be informed of your Appointment as one of the Commissioners of the Treasury; what the present salary is; and what the arrangements & regulations are.[1]

Shall be happy in receiving an Answer of your Acceptance as soon as may be.[2]

Congress have not yet appointed the third Commissioner.[3]

I am Sir, with esteem, and regard your Humble servt.

Saml. Huntington President

RC (CtHi: Jonathan Trumbull, Jr. Papers). In the hand of George Bond and signed by Huntington.

[1] See *JCC*, 14:903–8, 15:1204–6, 1251–52. Huntington also sent these "three Acts of Congress" in a letter of this date to Nathaniel Mumford, who with William Geddes, William Govett, Eleazer McComb, John D. Mercier, and Resolve Smith had been appointed "one of the Commissioners of the chamber of accounts ." PCC, item 14, fol. 226.

[2] Trumbull ultimately declined the appointment on March 10, 1780. See *JCC*, 16:275; and PCC, item 78, 22:665–68.

[3] Ezekiel Forman had been named a treasury commissioner with Trumbull on November 9. John Gibson was elected to this remaining position on November 25, a decision communicated to him by Huntington in a letter of November 26. See *JCC*, 15:1307; and PCC, item 14, fol. 234.

Henry Marchant to Nathanael Greene

Dear Sir,   Philadelphia Novr 12th. 1779

I recd. you Favour of the 2d Instant; and be assured that nothing could afford more Satisfaction than the open candid and confidential Sentiments you have expressed yourself in. They are such as I ever wished to live in the Enjoyment & free Communication of. I do indeed most heartily congratulate with you, Our Rhode Island Friends and Our Country in general upon the happy & important Event of the Evacuation of Newport & the Deliverance of the State of Rhode Island &c. I wish they were in no Danger of any future Invasion. What Effect the Disaster at Georgia will have upon the future movements of the Enemy I am at a Loss to conjecture. Yet I have great Consolation in this as in the Failure against Rhode Island, in a full Belief that it will eventually be for the best. Call it Accident, Fortune or what you will—I presume there will be found to have been the Wise Hand of divine Providence strikingly so—in these two Events.

You will before this Reaches you have Major Clarkson, & Copies of the Dispatches which have been recd. from Genl. Lincoln. The Minister of France has had no Letters from Count De Staing. It is presumed he has sent Dispatches by Water. Col. Laurens I suppose is on his Passage by Water.[1] The length of Time since he must have sailed makes me doubtfull of his Safety.

Our Attention is now drawn to the important Consideration of the necessary Steps for the Defense of South Carolina. I doubt not Genl. Washington's Thoughts are employed upon the same Object. In the mean Time, I hope the future Safety of Rhode Island will not be forgot, or entirely unassayed.

I have had my Mind struck much in the same Manner as Yours has. I know a full Defence of that Town & Island must be attended with great Expence and much beyond the Abilities of that State to cope with. And how far The United States are at present competent to it I am unable to Judge—or how far the Importance of that Port to Us—& the Disadvantage it may be of to the Enemy should it be kept out of their Hand, may or ought, to induce a Continental Exertion is a Subject of great Importance, and which I could wish might be early discussed in the Cabinet and in the Councills of the Field with mutual Communications. Genl. Gates has now an Opportunity of forming his own Judgment & furnishing Materials for others to form theirs upon. I have one Wish, and that is that the most able Engineer might be sent there as soon as Possible to take a thorough View. For the present I would hope that a Defense agt. Ships, or a small Body of Land Force might be attempted. I believe from what I have seen done there, that might be effected with a little Expense comparative to the Importance of the Object to that State in particular, To the States in General—And to Our allies—whose largest Ships may there have a Safe & good Port. I hope the Contl. Force there may not be withdrawn without the most urgent Necessity.

I have wrote the Governor[2] and some other Friends[3] my poor broken Sentiments upon This Subject and also upon a Line of Conduct That I believe ought to be adopted towards the Disaffected. I will venture one Thought to you upon that Subject. I know you will be able to make greater Improvements upon it than I can and to give greater Weight to Decisions that may be made in that State or Elsewhere. Those who have withstood every Act of Favour & Grace that have been tendered to Them thro' this Conflict, and have obstinately persevered in their Attachments to the Common Enemy, whether by actually entering into Their Service—or by basely preferring their Protection and their Cause; will never be Our Friends whatever Appearances they may put on under pressing & necessitous circumstances. At least They will ever be ready to enter into Parties and Intrigues destructive of the Interest & Happiness of the United States. They will promote every Measure that shall tend to sow the Seed of Disunion amongst Us. They will—which is the Point I mostly aim at—when a Peace shall suceed to this War—Fall into a British Party, stir up Jealousies against the French, and distract the Minds of good People as much as possible. They will merge the Destination of Whig and Tory, into that of Gallican, and antigallican— and possibly in future Time raise their own Popularity upon the Ruin of the true honest Whig, whose gratitude will be lasting to the French Nation and whose Resentment Against Briton may not easily be assuaged.

A line of prudence and Firmness ought to be adopted & if possible very similar throughout the States.

A word more as to the present Intentions of the Enemy. It is thought most generally they will send a large Detachment to Carolina—may they not first attempt Virginia—and Maryland? While I was writing this, I was honored with yours of the 7th Instant by Coll Webb. I doubt not but Congress will early pay Attention to the Application which may be made. My Inclination will lead me in every Instance to gratify the wishes of brave and unfortunate Gentlemen when it may not be inconsistant with their greater Interest & the Honor and Safety of the States. My closest attention to the Subject when it comes on, I hope will lead me to a proper Determination as far as it respects myself, and I shall be happy that it may coincide with Your Wishes and the Feelings of those worthy & brave officers who conceive themselves so much interested in the Question. Should I find myself constrained to an opinion contradictory to those wishes I shall feel a sensible Reluctance in the Complyance with such a Duty.

I am very sorry that any Dispositions made with respect to seperate Commands—or your appointment in the Staff should have deprived you of an Opportunity of doing Justice to your own Character in the Line. I was ever sorry you came into the Line—had I been present when it was done, as I have before told You, I should have opposed it. From what I knew of it, I was confident of the Difficulties in some Measure that would arise, I was doubtful whether in the Event it would be to your Interest, I knew however it would generally be conceived you had made an ample Fortune. I knew then there was not much of Character to be given—tho' much at Stake—and that You ran the Risk of sinking the Military Character into the Staff. My Friendship to You, & the Duty I owe the Publick will lead me—so far as may be in my Power—to assist in restoring you entirely again to this Military Character. And to Such a Situation as you may be able to do Justice to Yourself and the greatest possible Good to your Country. But this I fear cannot speedily be done, at least not untill another year shall open upon us—And which I could wish may open with Peace, Liberty and Independence to these States. Our next authentick Intelligence from Europe may satisfy us upon this Subject.

I am sorry Genl. Lincoln is not altogether so happy a Man, as you viewed him when you last Wrote. That Reflection in your Mind, I presume, as is natural, caused some of those Reflections as to your own Situation. May we not learn this Useful Lesson—That in whatever situation we are in, let us strive therewith to be content. Religion & true Philosophy teaches us so to be. I wish I could conform myself to it. Forgive this moral Digression, if so it may be thought. I expect Mr. Ellery Our very good Friend is now upon the Road for Congress to relieve me. I propose to set out by the 25th of this Month, and in Company with Mr. Wm. Redwood who goes to see how his Interests stand at Newport &c. If Head Quarters shall not be too far out of our Rout, I will endeavour to see you. However that may be, be assured I am yr. sincere Friend & humble Servt.

Hy. Marchant

P.S. You will excuse this Scrawl—I cannot submit to make a Copy of it.

RC (RNHi: Letters of Henry Marchant).
[1] Lt. Col. John Laurens had been in Charleston and was en route with news for Washington and Congress from the comte d'Estaing.
[2] See Marchant to William Greene, November 9, 1779.
[3] Marchant's letters to "some other Friends" have not been found.

Jesse Root to Jonathan Trumbull, Sr.

Please your Excellency   Philadelphia Novr. 12th 1779
    Providence by another Striking Instance has reproved our Confidence in an arm of flesh and taught us the vanity of humane power, however great, to insure Success, has defeated our flattering prospects to the Southward & tumbled our Towring Expectations to the ground. By dispatches from Genl. Lincoln In Congress the Combined armies of America & France under Genl Lincoln & the Count de Estaing laid Seige to Savanna, Opened their batteries on the 5th of Octr. & Continued the Seige with little intermission untill the 8th of Octr. without bringing the Enimy to Surrender, and the time being elapsed which the Count had liberty to Stay, no alternative was left but to raise the Seige or attempt to Carry the Town by Storm—the latter was Concluded upon, the necessary preparations were made and in the morning of the 9th ulto. they attempted to Storm the place and were unfortunately repulsed with Considerable loss. Pre-

cise returns are not transmitted but Genl Lincoln Says in his letter he had about 174 killed & wounded. Count de Estaing is wounded in two places, he behaved with great Spirit on the Occasion & appeared greatly Chagrined at the misfortune. Count Poulaski is killed & the loss of the French is said to be between three & four hundred killed & wounded. The French Troops have reimbarked on board their Ships & Genl Lincoln has retired to South Carolina & left the Enemy in possession of Georgia. The French army Consisted of three thousand, the troops under Genl Lincoln between one & two thousand. The Enemy, after Col Maitland Joined them, were about 3000 Strong. The Lord Reigneth, who will make us to know that the glory of our Salvation he will not divide with another. I beleive Such disappointments are necessary & that which now appears to be a Misfortune will prove the means of our final Safety.

Your Excellency's letter respecting the monthly requisitions of the State of Connecticut has been laid before Congress & is Committed,[1] how Successful it will be am unable to determine, as almost every reason Suggested therein were urged by the Delegates in Congress against so large a Sum, at the time of making the requisition—however Shall do every thing in my power to have the Sum reduced. By Several letters recd. we were able to Satisfy Congress of our right to Set in Congress & now hold our Seats their althoug we have received no official Information.[2] Mr Sherman is returning home. I expect to leave Congress about the 25th Inst. before which time I Expect to be releieved. Mr. Laurence left this last Saturday[3] to go to Charlestown from whence he is to go to Holland to negociate a treaty of amity & Commerce with those Provinces & to obtain a loan. He was gone before Mr Brown arrived. The President took your letters directed to Mr. Laurence. Since writing this letter Genl Lincoln letter is published in the paper to which I refer your Excellency for a particular Acct. and am Most respectfully, your Excellency's, most obedt humble Servant   Jesse Root

P.S. Colo Jonth Trumbull is appointed a Commissioner on the Board of Treasury during the pleasure of Congress with a Salary of 14,000 dollars per annum.[4]

RC (Ct: Trumbull Papers).

[1] Gov. Trumbull's November 2 letter to Congress requesting permission to retain a part of Connecticut's 1780 quota for defraying "the Extraordinary expences" incurred defending the state against the British raids at New Haven and Fairfield the previous summer, was read and referred to committee on November 10. Although its report was submitted on December 7, Congress did not adopt the committee's recommendation to reject the state's appeal until December 28. See *JCC*, 15:1254, 1357, 1415–17; PCC, item 66, 2:33–36; Roger Sherman to Trumbull, December 20; and Samuel Huntington to Trumbull, December 29, 1779.

[2] "Official Information" of the Connecticut delegates' credentials was not presented to Congress until November 24. *JCC*, 15:1301. See also Root to Oliver Ellsworth, November 1, 1779, note 1.

[3] Root was mistaken. For Henry Laurens' departure from Philadelphia, see Laurens to George Washington, October 24, 1779, note 3.
[4] See Samuel Huntington to Jonathan Trumbull, Jr., this date.

William Sharpe to Richard Caswell

Sir,   Philadelphia Novr. 12th. 1779.

Our great disappointment in Georgia is very disagreeable as well as the dangerous situation Charles Town is now in—the loss of which would sensibly be felt by No. Carolina particularly & all the states generally.

The reasons why the former order; for the march of the North Carolina Brigade, was countermanded is so obvious to your Excellency that it needs no explanation.[1] To march Troops so far and with the necessary expedition must be extremely fatiguing, and yet I have no doubt *that* virtuous body of men will undertake and execute the orders with all the patience and fortitude of the Soldier. In case the Enemy send immediately a considerable reinforcement from New York to Prevost, the consequences may be very disagreeable. The Enemy at New York recieved despatches from their court, the 23d Ulto. the Contents of which has not yet transpired. Some suppose they have recieved orders to embark the greatest part of their Troops either to the West Indies or to Britain. It is true that there was a considerable appearance of an embarkation before they could have heard of the siege being raised in Georgia, a part of which is said to be homed for Halifax, particulars we have not heard. If wisdom was applicable to their Councils, we might have good reason to conclude they would repair immediately either to Europe or the West Indies and endeavour to hold something substantial and quit pursuing the shadow of conquering these States. A few days more will probably develope these things.

I have the honor to send you inclosed an Extract of the Journal of Congress, a part of which will be sent officially by the President; I thought it best to give you a full view of what passed on that very interesting occasion, altho a degree of secrecy was judged necessary, and to which I take the liberty to add that three Continental Frigates will be immediately forwarded from Boston for the farther defence of Charles Town—If they arrive in time.[2]

I have to give you the disagreeable news of the death of Mr. Hewes, whose remains was interred last evening.

With the highest esteem & respect, I have the honor to be, Your Excellency's, Most Obt. Humble Servt,   Wm. Sharpe

Tr (Nc–Ar: Governor's Letterbook). Tr (DLC: Edmund C. Burnett Collection). Endorsed: "Copied from the original, then in possession of Mr. Stan V. Henkels."
[1] For the orders sending two North Carolina regiments to the southern department, see Samuel Huntington to Washington, October 5, note 2; and November 11, 1779.

[2] For the measures recently taken to reinforce the southern department, see Samuel Huntington to Benjamin Lincoln, November 11, 1779.

Committee on Appeals Decree

November 13th. 1779.

Francis Gurney &c Lib[ellan]t & App[ell]ee ⎫   Appeal from
vs. The Schooner Good Intent Cargo   ⎬   the State of
Tam Ploy Claim[an]t & App[ellan]t   ⎭   Pennsylvania[1]

We the Commissioners appointed by Congress to hear, try and determine all Appeals from the Courts of Admiralty of the several American States to Congress having heard and fully considered as well all and singular the Matters and Things mentioned and contained in the Record or Minutes of the Proceedings of the Court of Admiralty of the State of Pennsylvania in the Above Cause as the Arguments of the Advocates of the respective Parties to the above Appeal do thereupon adjudge and decree that the Appeal of the aforesaid Tam Ploy demanded and filed in the above Cause be and the same is hereby dismissed with Costs And that the Judgment or Sentence of the said Court of Admiralty passed and published in the said Cause be and the same hereby is in all it's parts confirmed and established And we do assess the Costs in this Cause at one thousand an sixty Dollars and hereby order and adjudge that the party Appellant pay unto the party Appellee the said Sum for his Costs and Charges by him expended in defending the said Appeal in this Court &c.   Tho M:Kean   Hy. Marchant

C. Griffin   J Root

MS (DNA: RG 267, case no. 44). In a clerical hand, and signed by Griffin, Marchant, McKean, and Root.

[1] The Pennsylvania Court of Admirality had awarded the schooner *Good Intent* and her cargo to Lt. Col. Francis Gurney and his troops of the 11th Pennsylvania Regiment who had captured the schooner on January 10, 1777, when it foundered on the New Jersey shore while sailing to New York from Jamaica.

The ship was not formally libeled by Gurney until two years later, however, when the owner, Tam Ploy, appeared in the United States. After the Pennsylvania court decision on January 9, 1779, Ploy appealed to Congress, where the case was referred to the Committee on Appeals on February 8, 1779. Ploy argued that the schooner was really *La Puella*, bound for Philadelphia with a consignment for one of the firms of Robert Morris.

The Committee on Appeals rejected the appeal in this decree and confirmed the state court's decision. See case file no. 44, RG 267, DNA; and *JCC*, 13:152.

John Fell's Diary

Saturday November 13th. 1779.
Coml Committee. Congress. A Letter from Genl Sulevan to Resign.
Referrd to a Committee, Letter from Coll Webb for leave for Genl
Philips & Genl Redsell to go to New York. Majr Gen Green Quarter
Mastr General Reced from April 6th 1778 to Octr 20th 1779
62,583,511. 30/90.[1]

MS (DLC).
[1] Fell may have noted these figures in connection with an application made the
previous day for a warrant for an additional $3 Million for the quartermaster general's
department. *JCC*, 15:1261.

Samuel Huntington to George Washington

Sir,   Philadelphia 13th Novr. 1779.
Since my letter of the 11th Instant I am honored with your
Excellency's favors of the 3d & 5th Instant with the enclosures.[1]
You will herewith receive enclos'd an Act of Congress of the 12th
Instant respecting regimental Paymasters not being of the rank of
Captains, Quarter-masters and Adjutants; And also the eleven Com-
panies of Artificers rais'd by the quarter master general.[2]
I have the honor to be with the greatest respect your Excellency's
most humble servt.   Saml. Huntington President[3]

RC (DLC: Washington Papers). In the hand of George Bond and signed by
Huntington.
[1] For Washington's letters to Congress of November 3 and 5, see PCC, item 152,
8:159–66; and Washington, *Writings* (Fitzpatrick), 17:68–69, 78–79.
[2] For these two November 12 resolves concerning the subsistence of certain Continental officers and a delegation of authority to the commander in chief to "arrange"
the artificer companies of the quartermaster corps as he "shall deem proper," see
JCC, 15:1261–62. Huntington also sent these two resolves to Quartermaster General
Nathanael Greene with a brief letter of this date. PCC, item 14, fol. 227.
[3] This day Huntington also sent the following personal letter to Jeremiah Wadsworth.
"As I am constraind to tarry in Congress I have Sent Mr. Brown the post rider with
a Carriage to wait upon Mrs. Huntington to this Place.
"Am to desire the favour of you to give him such Aid & Assistance as you think
proper to facilitate & Accomodate her Journey, your kind Assistance in the matter
Shall be gratefully Acknowledged by your Esteemd, and humble Servt,   Saml
Huntington
"[*P.S.*] You will hear before this comes to hand of the failure of the Expedition in
Georgia. S.H." Emmet Collection, NN.

Thomas McKean to William A. Atlee

Dear Sir,   Philadea Novr. 13th. 1779.

Having so good an opportunity by Mr. Sheriff Johnston of Cumberland I now sit down to answer your favor of the 4th instant.

Mr. Johnston will deliver you the printed Votes of the last Assembly, by which you will find that you have a right to draw for £4500 beside the former £1500, for the year ending the 3d Septemr. last: I believe the present Assembly will put the officers of Government on a more respectable footing than they have been since the Revolution.

We must take Bail from the villains, who have uttered counterfeit emissions of our paper money since the 25th May 1778, but as the sum is discretionary, it ought to be very high. I have full proof that Thomas Bulla, whom we bailed at Lancaster, is deeply concerned, there being many charges against him.

Mr. Laurens had engaged a Secretary before your Letters came to hand; a young Gentleman, who has lived with him these two years past, is now gone with him in that quality.[1] It would have given me great pleasure to have been able to have accomplished the wishes of your friend, but it was impracticable.

Our disappointment in Georgia has somewhat deranged us, but Count D'Estaign's Efforts upon the whole have proved very beneficial; he was streightened in point of time, but before he was obliged to return to the West-Indies he agreed with General Lincoln to assault the Savannah on the 9th of October in the morning, which was done; but from a variety of untoward circumstances not uncommon on such occasions, we were repulsed, with a loss of 172 in killed, and wounded belonging to the American army; how many of the French we cannot learn, but Count Pulaski is killed and Count D'Estaign had two balls thro' him, that is flesh-wounds not dangerous.

There are likely to be considerable changes in Congress, Governeur Morris & Francis Lewis Esquires are left out in New-York, your brother[2] and Mr. Wynkoop in our State, & some other Gentlemen in the other States. It seems the General Assemblies resent the treatment of Doctor Arthur Lee by Congress. Colo. Atlee tells me this was the cause in Pennsylvania. I think [every] member of Congress has a right to exercise his own judgment in cases wherein he has no instructions from his State.

My family are well. Mrs. McKean joins me in presenting our best compliments to Mrs. Atlee and your fireside. Adieu, Dear Sir, Your friend & most obedient servant,   Tho. M:Kean

RC (DLC: Peter Force Collection).
[1] That is, Moses Young.
[2] Pennsylvania delegate Samuel J. Atlee.

Henry Marchant to William Greene

Sir,   Philadelphia Novr. 14, 1779.

Your Excellency having heretofore informed me that a Warrant upon the State Treasurer would be acceptable for a Sum of Money to be paid out of the Taxes as they might be collected, and having since repeated to me the Necessities of the State especially as they were now called upon to provide Cloathing for Their own Troops—I have been unremitted and incessant in my Applications under but small Hopes of Success—merely from the State of the Contl. Treasury, and the Supplies of Money which must very soon be derived only from the States. But happily and beyond my Fears and Expectations I have obtained a Report of the Treasury, & a Resolution of Congress thereon in Favour of the State for three hundred Thousand Dollars, to be paid out of the Taxes as they are or may be collected. I enclose Your Excellency the Resolution;[1] as you may be informed without Delay, the Warrant will be forwarded.

I wish I could have congratulated your Excellency & the State upon Success in Georgia. The Event has been unfortunate, Tho' many Advantages have been derived from the Count De Staings Appearance there, and his Conduct has been a Proof of his highest Attachment to Our Cause and Interest, and an Ernest of the Future Support we may expect not only from Him but his Nation.

The Proceedings of the Convention at Hartford have been recd. & Are under Consideration; I am confident they are well approved of.[2] For indeed previous to them, a Comee of each State by Order of Congress had under Consideration a Plan for a general Limitation of Prices &c and the Report is now ready to be made.

The Minister, Chevalier De Luzerne is to make his publick Entrance next Wednesday.

I expect Mr. Ellery in a few Days; and propose to set out by the 25th of this Month at furthest. I hope to meet your Excellency in Health & the State invigorated by their late Deliverance. I am with great Truth yr. Excellency's & the States most obed't and very humble Serv't,   Hy. Marchant

[P.S.] I enclose yr. Excely. two of the weekly Papers.

RC (RHi: R.I.H.S.M.)
  [1] See *JCC*, 15:1260; and Marchant to Greene, October 26 and November 16, 1779.
  [2] See Samuel Holten to the Massachusetts Council, November 11, 1779, note 3.

Samuel J. Atlee to John Bayard

Sir[1]   Novr. 15th. 1779

Upon looking into a late Act of Assembly of this State intitled "An Act for the more effectual Supply and *Honorable reward* of the Penn-

sylvania Troops in the service of the United States of North America"
I find to my very great astonishment that myself with many others
early Adventurers and in the Time of the greatest dangers are totally
neglected.[2]

It may be well remembered Sir that so early as the 21st March
1776 by Resolve of the House of Assembly I was appointed to the
Command of the State Regt. of Musquetry, which Regt. was raisd,
Cloath'd, Arm'd, dessiplen'd and in the Actual service of the United
States before some others previously ordered to be raized in this and
other of the States for the Continental Line.

What Services were performed by this Regt. during the Time I
had the Honor to Command it, particularly on the fatal 27th of
Augt. 76 You, Sir, as well as the House will find in the inclosed
extract from my Journal.[3]

Their Actions subsequent to the 16th of Novr. are more particularly within your own Knowledge.

The three Pennsylvania Battalions were shortly after thrown into
one Regiment, the Seeds of that dissipline they have in the Course of
the war so often display'd, I flatter myself I had the Honor of
planting. And was very happy in the Accounts given me by Col.
Miles on his return to New York in January 1777 of my Countrys
not having forgot me but that the Command wou'd be reserved for
me, promising myself to have reaped at their Head, the Honors I
flattered myself I was intitled to. A Regiment I am bold to say deservd
as well the notice and consideration of those by whom they were
appointed as any other in the Service. A Regiment by whose efforts
in a great Degree was preserved our retreating Troops on the 27 of
August.

Least I should have been thought Vain I have hitherto suppressed
any account of this days proceedings nor mentioned my many
Dangers, losses, labours and sacrafisis of domestic Tranquillity in
the service of my Country, a Recital of which I always viewed as a
disagreeable Task, and inconsistent with the fine feelings of a Soldier.

After my Release from Captivity—a long Captivity of 26 Months—
No Vacancy then in the Army—I thought myself highly Honored by
my Country when I cou'd not partake the Dangers of the Field, to be
called to the Labours of the Civil Cabinet, in the great Councill of
the Nation.

Alas! How deceitfull are appearances. Instead of meeting, (as I
flattered myself I meritted) the Applause of my Country, I have
been cruelly disgraced and that in such a manner as adds insult to
the injury, by the Grand Inquest of the State; without knowing my
Crime or having publickly an opportunity of Vindicating my injured
Honor.[4]

I am now, Sir, to return to the *Sweets of Domestic Life* with a Con-
sciousness of having to the utmost of my Abillities done my duty to
my Country, whether in the Civil or the Military Line.[5]

I am Sir, with due Regard, Your most Obt., Hble Servt.
Saml. J. Atlee

RC (PHarH: Records of the Executive Council).

[1] This letter was undoubtedly directed to Bayard in his capacity as speaker of the Pennsylvania Assembly.

[2] The object of Atlee's complaint was not actually "a late Act of Assembly," but only a proposed bill, a draft of which had been reported out of committee on November 9. The minutes of the proceedings of the assembly indicate that this letter from Atlee was received on November 16 and "ordered to lie on the table," but no other mention of his protest is recorded. The effect seems nevertheless to have been to delay the progress of the bill, for not until March 1, 1780, during the following session of the assembly, was it finally enacted into law, although its coverage still failed to include some disbanded army units such as Atlee's former musket battalion. *Minutes of the [First and Second Sessions, 1779–80] . . . of the Fourth General Assembly of the Commonwealth of Pennsylvania,* DLC(ESR).

[3] This extract from Atlee's "Journal" is in *Pa. Archives,* 2d ser. 1:512–16. Atlee, appointed commander of the Pennsylvania State Battalion of Musketry in March 1776, was captured on August 27, 1776, during the battle of Long Island and had been a prisoner of war until October 1, 1778. See John B. B. Trussell, Jr., *The Pennsylvania Line: Regimental Organization and Operations, 1776–1783* (Harrisburg: Pennsylvania Historical and Museum Commission, 1977), pp. 167, 177–80.

[4] The Pennsylvania Assembly had just elected delegates to Congress on November 12, reducing the delegation from seven to five members and omitting Atlee from the new slate. He was, however, reelected to Congress in 1780 and 1781 and attended intermittently during 1780–82. For the credentials of the Pennsylvania delegates elected in November 1779—John Armstrong, James McLene, Frederick A. Muhlenberg, James Searle, and William Shippen, Sr.—see *JCC,* 15:1263.

The other Pennsylvania delegate omitted from the new slate was Henry Wynkoop, for whom no "delegate" letters have been found, but he later claimed compensation for "attendance in Congress from April the sixth 1779 until October [i.e., November] the twelfth, 222 days at £9 per day, £1998." Henry Wynkoop Accounts, March 25, 1780, Emmet Collection, NN; and *Pa. Council Minutes,* 12:288.

[5] The difficulties experienced by prisoners of war such as Atlee are also reflected in the following letter written two weeks later to treasury commissioner John Gibson, whose assistance he sought in the settlement of his claim for subsistence while a prisoner.

"After my Dismission," Atlee wrote on November 27, "I wrote Congress a Line [*not found*] requesting an allowance in Specie of my pay and Subsistance whilst a prisoner, to reimburse the Cash procured for my Subsistance by my Family. Congress not having it in their power to provide for the Prisoners at that early period, I was happy to hear from Mr. Mughlenberg that not a member in the House objected to it, and that it was referred to the Board, at which I presume you will preside. I must therefore beg your early Notice of me (as I am daily called upon by those of whom the Money was obtained, but have it not in my Power to Answer their Demands untill I can procure it from those in whose Service it was expended) and Report a Warrant on the Treasurer, in my favour for the Amount of my pay and Subsistance as a Colonel from the 27th Augt. 1776 the Time I was captured until the 1st Octr 1778 the Time of my Release, deducting the Sum mentioned [in the] Letter to Congress referred to your Board. I think I ought in Justice Receive Interest at least from the Time of my Release. I have been paying since it was Borrowed for my Use, a great deal of it immediately after I was taken.

"As I seek but for Justice, I can with the more boldness warmly press this Matter upon you, and doubt not your utmost Assistance." PWcHi.

For the ultimate settlement of his claim in April 1780, see *JCC,* 16:215, 335–37, 365–66.

John Fell's Diary

Monday Novr. 15. [1779]
Coml Committee. Sundry Letters &c. Motion from Mr Gerry that
no member of Congress, should hold any Office or be chose while a
Member or for 6 Mo after.[1] Nominated Gentlemen for the Admiralty Board.[2]

MS (DLC).
[1] For Elbridge Gerry's previous attempt to pass a similar motion, see Henry Laurens'
Notes, September 24, 1779.
[2] For the election of the board's commissioners, see Samuel Huntington to Thomas
Waring, November 27, 1779.

Medical Committee to George Washington

Sir,   Philadelphia Novr. 15th. 1779.
In Pursuance of a Resolution of Congress of the 4th instant (a
Copy of which is enclosed) I am directed by the medical Committee
to transmit to your Excellency some Papers relative to a Complaint
filed by the Inhabitants of the Town of Danbury against the Deputy
director general of the eastern Department.
The Papers are marked from No. 1 to No. 4 inclusive, and will
with this, be handed you by Doctor Foster, who proposes to wait on
your Excellency in his Way to the eastward to receive your Commands.[1]
I have the Honor to be with the highest Esteem And most perfect
Respect, your Excellency's most Obedient And very Humble Servant,
Nath. Scudder[2] Chairman

RC (DLC: Washington Papers). Written and signed by Nathaniel Scudder.
[1] Dr. Isaac Foster's conduct as deputy director of the Eastern Department had long
been before Congress, the present charges stemming from a December 14, 1778,
memorial of "the Inhabitants of the Town of Danbury," for which see Samuel Holten's
Diary, June 4–5, 1779, note 1. Because Congress and the medical committee had
failed to take action on the town's charges, however, the author of the memorial,
Thaddeus Benedict, had renewed the attack on Foster in a letter to Congress of
October 26 citing recent denunciations of Foster in the *Pennsylvania Packet* and offering
to furnish depositions in support of the original charges. Thus on November 4
Congress ordered an investigation and directed the medical committee to send
Benedict's memorial to Washington along with "such other papers as they may have
respecting the matter." The following day Congress also received a letter from Foster
requesting an inquiry into his public conduct. See *JCC*, 15:1237, 1240. In addition to
Congress' November 4 resolution, the committee sent Washington "Papers . . . marked
from No. 1 to No. 4," which were undoubtedly a May 28 letter by Foster to the
medical committee, a May 27 certification by Dr. William Burnet in support of Foster,
and Benedict's and Foster's October 26 and November 4 letters. All are in the Washington Papers, DLC, with the latter two clearly marked "No.3" and "No.4."
On December 4 Washington replied that "whenever the trials that have been previously directed are finished, I shall pay the earliest attention to the enquiry ordered."

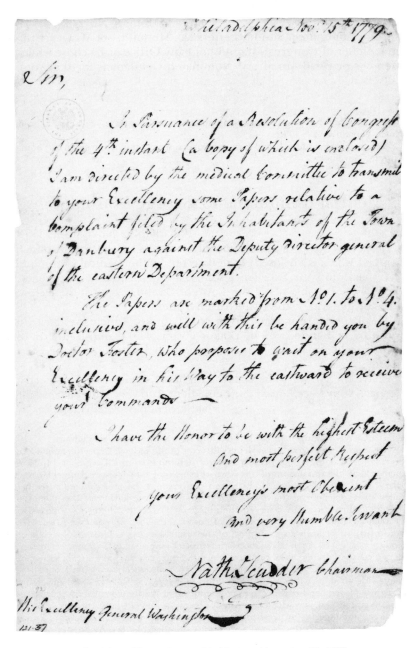

Philadelphia Nov. 15th 1779

& Sir,

In Pursuance of a Resolution of Congress of the 4th instant (a Copy of which is enclosed) I am directed by the medical Committee to transmit to your Excellency some Papers relative to a Complaint filed by the Inhabitants of the Town of Danbury against the Deputy Director general of the eastern Department.

The Papers are marked from No. 1. to No. 4. inclusive, and will with this be handed you by Doctor Foster, who proposes to wait on your Excellency in his Way to the eastward to receive your Commands —

I have the Honor to be with the highest Esteem And most perfect Respect your Excellency's most Obedient And very Humble Servant

Nathl Scudder Chairman

His Excellency General Washington

121-37

Nathaniel Scudder to George Washington, November 15, 1779

Washington, *Writings* (Fitzpatrick), 17:217. Whether or not the court of enquiry was ever held, Foster was not included in the new arrangement of the hospital department in October 1780 and he wrote a bitter letter to the medical committee on November 29 complaining of being "turned off at the eve of a severe Winter to starve with a large family." See PCC, item 78, 9:491–92.

[2] Scudder, whose term expired on December 1 and who had apparently withdrawn from Congress on November 25, wrote to Nathaniel Peabody on December 6 asking whether " a *private* Citizen" could inquire about "*public* Business," especially "how you proceed in the Affairs respecting the medical Staff. I wish it may be possible to get that Business finished before the first of January, as that is the Time on which the whole Hospital Corps had determined to resign. I conclude Doctor Foster left their last Memorial with you, and I think it will be best, to present it to Congress before the Resolutions for granting them Quota of Lands & half pay are given in, as it may induce the House to take them up immediately." Roberts Collection, PHC.

Isaac Foster and officers of the hospital department had presented memorials and petitions to Congress on April 15, May 28, and December 10, 1779, in which they apparently requested clothing and subsistence allowances, half pay for seven years, and land bounties, all of which Congress had previously granted officers of the Continental line. Congress had been considering the report of the medical committee since October 27 and finally approved a schedule of clothing and subsistence allowances for medical officers on November 20. While the committee recommended that half-pay and land bounties be granted, Congress rejected both proposals on January 3, 1780. See *JCC*, 13:455, 14:661, 15:1213–14, 1216, 1277, 1293–97, 1366, 1423, 16:10–12.

Pennsylvania Delegates
to the Pennsylvania Assembly

Sir   Monday Nov. 15th, 1779.
    The Delegates of this State have the Honour to transmit the inclosed Resolution of Congress,[1] & beg You will be pleased to lay the same before the Honble. the Genl. Assembly.[2] We have the Honour to be with perfect Respect, Sir, Your most obedient, & very humble Servant,   James Searle

                                      Fredk. Muhlenberg

                                        Wm Shippen

RC (PHC: Roberts Collection). Endorsed: "Letter from Delegates of Penna. in Congress, informing that the Minister of France will have an Audience of Congress on Wednesday next." Addressed: "The Honble. John Bayard, Speaker of the Genl. Assembly of the State of Pensilvania."

[1] For this November 13 resolve concerning La Luzerne's reception by Congress on the 17th, see *JCC*, 15:1266.

[2] The Pennsylvania delegates this day also sent a nearly identical letter to Pres. Joseph Reed and the Pennsylvania Council. *Pa. Archives*, 1st ser. 8:9. For the council's attendance at that audience, see *Pa. Council Minutes*, 12:170, 173.

John Fell's Diary

Tuesday Novr 16 [1779].
Coml Committee. Letter from Commisary Baety relating to
Citizens, Prisoners &c Referrd to a Committee.[1]
Dr Wetherspoon.[2]

MS (DLC).
[1] Although the Marine Committee did communicate to Congress this day a paragraph of a letter from John Beatty, commissary general of prisoners, relating to
Spanish captives held on British prison ships in New York, Fell is undoubtedly referring here to Beatty's November 4 letter to Congress concerning his responsibility for
supplying money and clothing to private citizens of the United States captured by the
enemy. Beatty's letter had been read in Congress the previous day and referred to a
committee chaired by Fell. Although Fell's committee reported favorably on November 25 that such captives should be supplied "in the same manner as Captive Officers
and Soldiers of the Continental Army," Congress rejected the motion on December 1.
See *JCC*, 15:1268, 1273, 1310, 1337–38. Beatty's November 4 letter with enclosure is
in PCC, item 78, 3:393–402. Fell's committee report is in PCC, item 28, fols. 59–60.
[2] That is, John Witherspoon had returned to Congress. Cf. Fell's Diary, November
1, 1779.

Elbridge Gerry to John Clark

Dear sir,   Philadelphia Novr 16 1779
When your Memorial was read in Congress,[1] I stated briefly your
Exertions, Services, & Sufferings, & explained some Matters con-
tained in your Letter to me, & not mentioned in your Memorial; In
Consequence of which, it was committed to the Board of Treasury &
will undoubtedly be duly considered.
I have not attended the Board since the appointment of the new
Commissioners; & should the Memorial remain long unnoticed I
would advise You to write them a Line on the Subject, being sir, with
Esteem your Friend & hum serv,   E. Gerry

RC (DNA: PCC, item 41).
[1] In a November 1 letter, Maj. John Clark, "one of the auditors of Accounts in the
main Army," had requested "leave, on account of his weak state of health, to resign."
This request Congress accepted on November 4, and referred his letter to the Board of
Treasury. Clark then submitted a second "memorial" of November 10, which was
referred by Congress to the Board of Treasury together with a draft resolve in
Gerry's hand to allow Clark "the sum of   Dollars" for "Losses . . . and other
Considerations." See *JCC*, 15:1237, 1255; and PCC, item 41, 2:258–59, 280. See also
Gerry to Clark, February 17, 1780.

Cyrus Griffin to the Virginia House Delegates

Sir,[1]   Philadelphia Novem. 16th [1779]

On yesterday I had the honor to receive a resolution of the General assembly relative to the free navigation of the River Mississippi, the right of mooring vessels to the shores of the said River, the free navigation of the Gulph of Florida, a free port or ports in the Island of New-orleans, and the privilege of a consul to reside there.[2] In answer I am bound to let my Constituents understand that the honorable John Jay Esq. our Minister Plenipotentiary to the Court of Spain has already Sailed for that Country with positive Instructions in what manner this important business is to be conducted.[3] A part of the ultimatum stands thus—"That if his Catholic Majesty shall accede to the said Treaties and in concurrence with France and the united states of America continue the present war with Great Britain for the purpose expressed in the Treaties aforesaid: he shall not thereby be precluded from securing to himself the Floridas; on the contrary if he shall obtain the Floridas from Great Britain these united states will guaranty the same to his Catholic Majesty; provided always that the united states shall enjoy the free navigation of the River Mississippi into and from the Sea." Thus much for this part of the ultimatum, and most certainly it ought not to be generally known. "You must endeavor to obtain some convenient port or ports below the 31st Degree of south latitude on the said River free for all Merchant vessels, goods, wares and merchandise belonging to the Inhabitants of these states, also a loan of five million sterling, and an subsidy in consideration of the guaranty aforsaid." But if the assembly are of opinion something is still wanting for the welfare and safety of these states, in that case the other propositions can be made to Congress by way of additional Instructions to the said Minister, tho to my Judgment in our present circumstances and the absolute necessity of a foreign loan, there can be little proba[bi]lity of succeeding in such propositions.   C. Griffin

RC (NHi: John Jay Ide Collection).

[1] Undoubtedly the speaker of the House of Delegates, Benjamin Harrison.

[2] For the Virginia assembly's November 5 "Resolution instructing delegates in Congress, in treaty with Spain to stipulate for free commerce of Mississippi," see William W. Hening, *The Statutes at Large: Being a Collection of All the Laws of Virginia*, 13 vols. (Richmond: J. & G. Cochran, 1809–23), 10:537–38.

[3] For Jay's instructions, see Samuel Huntington to Jay, October 16, 1779.

James Lovell to John Adams

Dear Sir   Novr. 16. 1779

Not a Line by yesterday's Post from either you or Mr. Dana; nor indeed from any Person whatever in Massachusetts.

The Principles of Equality in the Treaty between France and us being held up *as a Model for future Treaties* may betray negotiators into an Error; because tho' the Equality in regard to France & America is conspicuous, yet Partiality to France compared with other Powers has been established; particularly in the *XIX* Art. of our *incorrect* copy. "On the contrary no Shelter or Refuge" &ca.[1]

In the *XIII* article, same Copy, French and Americans shall enjoy reciprocal Rights in the respective Dominions.[2] The banished Americans cannot be allowed this under the Title of the Subjects of the King of Gr. Br. The respective States of our Union who have passed Laws in their sovereign, independent Capacity, will not consent to repeal them, for the Sake of readmitting into their Bosoms capital Villainy.

This was hinted yesterday by Sth. Carolina and will produce an Instruction if you or we find it necessary.

If I do not accomplish to send you by Palfrey or Foster the Orders & Credit you mentioned in yr. last I will most assuredly see that you shall not be without them. There is no trusting to *Expedition* in the Remittances of Funds by our Committees, nor indeed to Expeditiousness of any Kind *here* though we are reduced to a few now; the *Gen'men* for the most part taking themselves home to *warm Lodgings,* while the Drudges alas must sleep but *few hours* under *slight Coverings & Alone.*

I will if I have Time say more respecting the Subject of yr. past Letters. Affectionately,   J.L.

RC (MHi: Adams Papers).

[1] This sentence in the treaty reads as follows: "On the contrary, no shelter or refuge shall be given in their ports to such as shall have made prize of the subject, people or property of either of the parties; but if such shall come in, being forced by stress of weather, or the danger of the sea, all proper means shall be vigorously used, that they go out and retire from thence as soon as possible." *JCC,* 11:434.

[2] See *JCC,* 11:429–30.

Henry Marchant to William Greene

Sir,   Philadelphia Novr. 16th. 1779

In my last[1] I enclosed Your Excellency a Resolution of Congress granting a Warrant in Favour of the State of Rhode-Island upon the Genl. Treasurer thereof for three hundred thousand Dollars, to be paid out of their Quota of Taxes. I now enclose your Excely. the Warrant. In a late appointment of Commissioners for the Chambers of Accounts I nominated Mr. N. Mumford and he was elected of which I have given him Notice.[2] How far it may be to his Interest I know not, or whether he may be more Serviceable within the State, or in this Appointment I am uncertain. I could wish that whenever

Our publick Accounts come to be settled there may be some Person near to explain any Difficulties that may arise. He will not, and by no means ought he to, be one of the Commrs. to settle & adjust them, as he audited them for the State by order of the Genl. Assembly; but, being present he may give much Light to those to whom the Accounts may be submitted for Settlement. However I had the publick Good in View in the Recommendation, as I looked upon him a complete Accomptant. At the same Time I conceived it would not be dis-agreable to the State, If they can dispense with his Service where he is.

I was yesterday honored with yr. Excely's Letter of the 5th Instant;[3] and for the several Articles of Information therein I am much obliged. As to Capt. Tyler's Affair, I wrote Your Excellency before,[4] it was committed. No Report is yet made—And I am well persuaded that nothing will be reported in the least to the Discredit of the Doings of the Genl. Assembly. Too much Caution however I think cannot be used upon every great political Question.

I have nothing to communicate of News but what may be in the enclosed publick Print—But I have still to assure your Excely. that I am Yours & the States most obedient & Very humble Servt.

Hy. Marchant

RC (R–Ar: Letters to Governors).
[1] See Marchant to Greene, November 14, 1779.
[2] Marchant's letter to Nathaniel Mumford has not been found, but see Samuel Huntington to Jonathan Trumbull, Jr., November 12, 1779, note 1.
[3] Greene's November 5 letter to Marchant is in Staples, *Rhode Island*, pp. 255–56.
[4] Marchant's letter to Greene has not been found, but in a November 9 reply to it, Greene stated that he had received "your letter of the 19th ultimo, respecting the affair of Isaac Tyler's petition to Congress." Greene's letter contained a long, official explanation of the Tyler case.
   Capt. Isaac Tyler of Providence had commanded the Rhode Island privateer sloop *Dolphin*, which had seized the schooner *Betsey* and additional property owned by residents of Yarmouth, Nova Scotia, who were known to be friendly toward America. When Tyler brought the ship, cargo, and other goods to Rhode Island, the state assembly ordered that they be restored to the owners. Tyler then appealed to Congress to reverse the legislature's decision, but Congress dismissed his petition on December 2, 1779. See *JCC*, 15:1184, 1341–42; Staples, *Rhode Island*, pp. 256–61; and Rhode Island Delegates to Greene, November 30, 1779.

Massachusetts Delegates to the Massachusetts Council

Sir   Philadelphia Novr 16th 1779
   We have the Honor of transmitting You by the earliest Opper-tunity, a Copy of the Resolution of Congress, upon the Application of the State of Massachusetts Bay of the 21st of September last, for retaining Six Million Dollars (which the State were to raise as a

continental Tax), to defray the Expences of the penobscot Expedition.[1] We perceive by some observations that were thrown out in Debate, that a Question will arise on the propriety of considering this as a continental Expence, notwithstanding it was evidently incurred to repel an Invasion of the Enemy in that State; & We are of opinion that as soon as the Necessary papers can be prepared & sent to Congress, it will be expedient to obtain their Sense on this important Subject. We wait the Directions of the honorable Assembly for conducting this Business, & remain sir With the greatest Respect for them & yourself your most obedt & very humble servts.

E. Gerry   James Lovell

S Holten   Geo Partridge

RC (M–Ar: Revolutionary War Letters). Written by Gerry, and signed by Gerry, Holten, Lovell, and Partridge. Addressed: "Hona. Jeremiah Powell Esqur. president of the Council of the State of Massachusetts Bay."

[1] This November 16 resolve denied Massachusetts' "request to retain the 6,000,000 of dollars mentioned in their letter of the 21st of September." See *JCC*, 15:1273–74 and Samuel Holten to the Massachusetts Council, November 11, 1779. President Huntington did not officially transmit this resolve to the Massachusetts Council until November 22. PCC, item 14, fol. 232.

Nathaniel Peabody to Meshech Weare

Sir,   Philada. Novr. 16th. 1779.

I have the Honr. to acknowledge your agreable favour of the 25th ulto which I most Cordially Embraced with as much *energical* affectian as a Zealous young *Convert*, in the *bloom* of life, and *Vigour* of health, *Passionately* touched with *Philanthropy*, ever *realized* the *absorbing* pleasures of her accelerated imagination, or *delightful* Dreams.

No Circumstance Could interupt the Satisfaction I feel upon this, and every like, occasion, Equal to a Consideration of the Trouble it has given to a paternal friend, I have So much reason to Esteem. I am much obliged by the Several Communications in your letter— But have nothing worth notice to give in return, except what is Contained in the papers herewith inclosed where you will find the disagreable News from Georgia except a few Circumstances attending the Seige & assault of Savannah Not worth Publishing. Altho this Southern Campaign has gained us Considerable advantages, by Causing the Enemy to Evacuate Some of their important Posts, leave others in a Defenseless Situation, And in many instances diverted their Attention from the pursuit of Objects, that would have distressed many of our fellow Citizens—And the Loss we Sustained, all things Considered, is not Great, Yet the disappointment has materially Deranged our Plans for future military Operations. I wish to make Some observations respecting my *Situation* but must omit them for the Present, as I hope Soon to be releived by Some person Comming on to take my Place agreable to the request in my letter to you by last Post.

Mr. Langdon Sets off for home in two or three days,[1] And Nothing Could induce me to Tarry *longer*, but the disagreable Prospect of leaving the State unrepresented, at a time So Critical & important as the present day, when it woud be difficult if not impossible to make Congress to Transact business, if another State Should be left unrepresented.

I am Sir in Great hast, Your most obedt and very Humle Servt,
                                                                Nath Peabody

RC (MHi: Weare Papers).
[1] In preparation for his return to New Hampshire, Woodbury Langdon successfully applied to the Pennsylvania Council on November 18 for an embargo exemption to permit him to leave Philadelphia with "Twelve Barrells of Flour for his own family use." *Pa. Council Minutes*, 12:173.

Philip Schuyler to George Washington

Dear Sir   Philadelphia Nov. 16th 1779
    I arrived here last evening and learnt from some Members of Congress that the necessity of writing to Colo. Hamilton was superceeded by a letter of Message which had been sent him from hence Intimating that his Stay on the Sea Coast was rendered unnecessary.

I shall take my seat in Congress this Morning and when the house adjourns shall Communicate your Excellency such Information on a Certain Subject as I may be Able to Obtain.[1] The sad reverse of fortune we have experienced In Georgia does not Seem to make an Impression here in any degree adequate to the extent of the Evils with which It will probably be attended.

Be so Good as to Intreat the Gentlemen of Your family to Accept of my best wishes and be assured My Dear Sir that I am with the most sincere Affection & Esteem Your Excellencys Most Obedient Humb Servant,   Ph. Schuyler

RC (Nh-Ar: Revolutionary Papers, 1773–1789).
[1] See Schuyler to Washington, November 18, 1779.

Nathaniel Scudder to Richard Henry Lee

Dear Sir,   Philadelphia Novr. 16th. 1779.
    Our Life is a strange Kind of checquered Work, one Day we rejoice, on another we lament; in one Letter we congratulate, in the

succeeding one we condole. Alas! for the southern Disappointment! Indeed the same Day often exhibits a Medley of Mourning and Festivity, of Joy & Lamentation; witness the 11th instant, the Day after we received the melancholly Confirmation of the Repulse of the allied Armies at Savannah. On that Day the President of this State was elected and proclaimed, and on that Day the Funeral of our Friend & fellow laborer Mr. Hewes of North Carolina was attended with the usual mournfull Formalities. About 12 o'Clock the President of the State, *Mr. Reed,* was proclaimed from the Court House Steps, and a *Feu de Joy* fired on the Occasion; after which there was a Procession *to* & Collation *at* the City Tavern, the Bells chyming joyously &c. &c. About 4 o'Clock the funeral Procession of the Honble Mr. Hewes began, the Same Bells ringing muffled; and as we proceeded down Market-Street we had a fine View of the continental Colours displayed on Market Street Wharf in Honor to the President. When we arrived at Christ's Church we were entertained with the usual Service, and a very solemn funeral Anthem, after which the Body was interred. Scarce had the Attendants reached their Homes, before the Bells again unmuffled resumed their festive Sounds, with firings as usual, and the Evening closed with a grand Serenade at the governor's Door. *Sic eminet; & sic transit gloria Mundi.*

I observe by the last Boston Paper that Mr. Samuel Stockton, who has for a considerable Time acted as Secretary to Mr. William Lee in various parts of Europe,[1] is arrived in that City from Amsterdam; I daily expect him here, and hope for much usefull Information from him, as from our former Intimacy I expect to find him unreservedly communicative. I doubt not he will be very able to unravle some of our foreign Mysteries.

Congress is at present very thin, rarely more than 10 States represented, often but 9. Many important Businesses on Progress much as usual. What can the Neglect of your State be attributed to? only one Member here for many Weeks.[2] Mr. Duane is again in the Delegation from New York—Goverr. Morris left out. Mr. Floyd in again, Mr. Lewis out—General Schuyler, Mr. Scot, Mr. Livingston & a Mr. Lommedeau added. Our old worthy Friend Mr. Sherman left out by Connecticut, this I think not a little ominous, as he is one of the *Originals.* In short, what with the Effect of Manœuvre on the one hand, and of Necessity on the other, I fear, *entre nous,* both *that* State and New Jersey will next year appear in different Colours from what they have heretofore done. As for myself, sheer Necessity compels me to retire, and I have therefore so ordered it with my Friends as that I expect not even to be balloted for. My Time expires on the first of December, so that I shall be here only one Week after this.[3] I wish I may be happy enough to hear from you before I leave Philadelphia.

To morrow at 12 o'Clock is fixed for the public Audience of the New Minister of France. There will be a public Dinner.

The Enemy received the first Account of our Defeat in Georgia from Philadelphia. They had a great *Feu de Joy* on Saturday last. We can learn Nothing of their intended Movements, tho' there is undoubtedly a capital Embarkation on Foot; I fear for Savannah, Charles Town or your Neighbourhood. I wish soon to hear you are returned to Congress.

Make my most respectfull Compliments acceptable to your Lady and believe me to be with great Affection & Sincerity, your Friend & very Hble Servt. Nath. Scudder

P.S. I am this Morning told Mr. Deane is going to Virginia to take his passage on Board a 50 gun Ship belonging to Beaumarchais now in your Bay. It is said he has discovered, that his Bail cannot be made accountable unless some person will swear that Doctor Lee has actually sustained Damages to the Amount. N. S.

RC (ViHi: Lee–Ludwell Papers).
[1] Samuel W. Stockton (1751–95), younger brother of former New Jersey delegate Richard Stockton, had been secretary to the commissioner at the Courts of Vienna and Berlin. See Milton Rubincam, "Samuel Witham Stockton, of New Jersey, and the Secret Treaty with Amsterdam in 1778," *Proceedings of the New Jersey Historical Society* 60 (April 1942): 98–116.
[2] For the attrition in the Virginia delegation, see James Mercer to the Virginia House of Delegates, October 1, 1779, note 2.
[3] Scudder apparently withdrew from Congress on November 25 or 26.

John Fell's Diary

Wednesday Novr 17th. [1779]
Coml Committee. This day at 12 oClock The Chevalier DeLaLuserne the Minister Plenoptentiary from France had his Audience of Congress.[1]

MS (DLC).
[1] These congressional proceedings were made public, substantially as they appear on the journals (*JCC*, 15:1279–84), in the *Pennsylvania Packet* on November 20 and in the *Pennsylvania Gazette* on November 24. They were printed with the following introductory statement. "Last Wednesday an entertainment was given by Congress to the Minister Plenipotentiary of France, at which were present by invitation several Foreigners of distinction, and gentlemen of public character."

Samuel Holten's Diary

[November 17–18, 1779]
Nov. 17. 1779. Wednesday. Chevalier de la Luzerne was admitted to a public audience with Congress; & dined with congress.

Anne-César, Chevalier de La Luzerne

18. Thursday. The Cevalier paid us a visit, by leaving a card & Mr. Marbo[is].

MS (MDaAr).

Marine Committee to John Bradford

Sir   November 17th 1779
   Your letter of the 25th ultimo addressed to the President of Congress having been referred to this Committee, we think proper to direct that you adhere strictly to the Orders already given you respecting the Sugar to be delivered to the State of New York.[1]
   We are sir,   Your Hble Servants

LB (DNA: PCC Miscellaneous Papers Marine Committee Letter Book).
[1] For Congress' directive to Bradford to deliver sugar and rum to New York, see Samuel Huntington to George Clinton, October 1, 1779, note.

Marine Committee to the Eastern Navy Board

Gentn.   November 17th 1779
   It is become unnecessary any longer to retain the Pilots that you were directed to provide for the Count D'Estaings fleet, therefore on receipt of this we desire they may be discharged. We are
Gentlemen,   Your Hble Servts

LB (DNA: PCC Miscellaneous Papers, Marine Committee Letter Book).

John Fell's Diary

Thursday Nov 18th [1779].
Com[mercial] Com[mittee]. Congress. Sundry Letters, Memorials and Reports, One from the Committee of 12 in order to Regulate Prices was Read & debated.

MS (DLC).

Samuel Huntington to John Beatty

Sir,   Philada Novem 18th 1779
   You will herewith receive enclos'd an act of Congress of the 16th instant,[1] By which you are directed until the further Order of Con-

gress to make the same provision for the spanish prisoners in New York as is made for the prisoners of the United States keeping a separate Account thereof.

I am Sir with respect, your hble Servt,   S. H. President

LB (DNA: PCC, item 14).
[1] For this resolve and Beatty's original query concerning the needs of "some Spaniards on board the prison-ship at New York," see *JCC*, 15:1273; and Marine Committee to Beatty, November 5, 1779.

Samuel Huntington to the States

Sir   Circular   Philada Novem. 18th 1779
You will receive herewith enclos'd two acts of Congress of the 12th & 16th instant for reforming the eleven Companies of Artificers raised by the Quartermaster General, making provision for, & granting certain benefits to that Corps in particular that they be consider'd as part of the quotas of the eighty Battallions apportion'd on the several States to which they respectively belong.[1] Also another Act of Congress of the 16th instant requesting the aid of the several States for obtaining witnesses & depositions in the trial of cases before Courts martial.[2]

I have the honour to be &c,   S.H. President.

LB (DNA: PCC, item 14).
[1] See *JCC*, 15:1261–62, 1276.
[2] For this resolve, which was adopted to enable Dr. John Morgan to collect evidence to support charges he had brought against the director general of hospitals, Dr. William Shippen, Jr., see *JCC*, 15:1277–78.

Huntington also sent a copy of this resolve to Judge Advocate John Laurance with a brief cover letter the following day. PCC, item 14, fol. 230–31.

Samuel Huntington to Jeremiah Wadsworth

Sir,   Philadelphia Novem. 18th 1779
You will herewith receive enclos'd Copy of an Act of Congress of the 15th Instant by which you will be inform'd That two Million of Dollars are advanced to Col. Blaine for the use of the Commissaries Department & for which the Commissary General is to be accountable.[1]

I am Sir with much Respect your humble Servt.
                          Saml. Huntington President

RC (CtHi: Wadsworth Papers). In a clerical hand and signed by Huntington.
[1] *JCC*, 15:1269.

Samuel Huntington to George Washington

Sir.   Philadelphia Novr. 18th. 1779.

By the act of Congress of this day herewith enclosed, you will perceive I am directed to inform your Excellency that they approve of your sentiments and Opinion as expressed in your letter of the 14th Instant, and leave the future measures on that subject to your direction as shall be thought proper upon the Intelligence you may have received.[1]

It is presumed your Excellency must have received before this Copies of the dispatches from Genl. Lincoln by Major Clarkson enclosed in my letter of the 10th Inst.

I have the honor to be with the greatest respect, Your Excellency's humble servant.   Saml Huntington President

RC (DLC: Washington Papers). In the hand of George Bond and signed by Huntington.

[1] In his letter of the 14th, Washington had suggested that both the lateness of the season and the poor condition of the Continental Army militated against undertaking significant operations yet this year, hinting that the time had arrived to abandon preparations for the joint Franco-American operations he had been hoping for some time to undertake. See PCC, item 152, 8:171–74; Washington, *Writings* (Fitzpatrick), 17:104–7; and *JCC*, 15:1286.

Philip Schuyler to George Washington

Dear Sir,   Philadelphia Nov. 18th. 1779

This morning Your Excellencys letter of the 14th Instant was read In Congress. The necessity of being explicit on the Subject and ordering a Suspension of the preparations for the Intended Co-operation with Count d'Estaing was earnestly urged and a motion made for a resolution Conformable to these Ideas, but prevented by a Prior motion which was Carried and which I suppose you will receive by this Express.[1]

Our Finances are so exceedingly deranged, the depreciation proceeding with the most Alarming rapidity, Every department so deeply In debt and no plan adopted which gives the least prospect of remedy to these Evils that I very seriously apprehend the most disagreable Consequences.

It is said that Count De Grass with eight Ships of the line and Some frigates are In Cheasepeak. What his Object is we know not, Should he return to the West Indies, It is proposed to send the troops ordered to Georgia under his protection as Convoy.

Nothing has Yet been done In the Intended new arrangment of the Quarter Master General & Commissary General department. I fear the time which the latter[2] has limitted for retiring from the business will Expire before another is appointed unless Congress is pushed to It both here and from Your Quarter.

A Memorial of the Gen. Officers[3] was Yesterday[4] read and Committed, to Mr. Root, Mr. Morris & Mr. Schuyler. I shall urge a Speedy report, but Entre nous, people here are not So Attentive to business as the vast variety and Importance of what is on hand seems to require.

I am Dear Sir with the most Ardent wishes for Your Happiness, Respectfully & faithfully Your Excellency's most Obedient hum Servant,   Ph. Schuyler

RC (DLC: Washington Papers).
   [1] See the preceding entry.
   [2] That is, Jeremiah Wadsworth. See Samuel Huntington to Wadsworth, December 4, 1779.
   [3] A November 15, 1779, memorial of general officers was read in Congress on November 18 and referred to "the committee appointed to consider what allowance ought to be made to the officers in the different departments of the army, to whom the provision of 18 August last doth not extend." Schuyler had been appointed on November 16 to replace Samuel Atlee on that committee. The committee's report, which is in the hand of Schuyler, was read in Congress on December 1, but apparently no action was taken. See *JCC*, 15:1274, 1286, 1335–37; and PCC, item 41, 7:259–66. See also Samuel Huntington to Alexander McDougall, August 13, 1780.
   Schuyler's work on the memorial of the general officers is also reflected in the following letter to him from Maj. Gen. Benedict Arnold. "Since I saw you this morning," Arnold wrote on November 24, "I made the Inclosed minutes [*not found*] by which you will see that Six Rations, & Sixteen hundred & Fifty Dollars Subsistance money, is by no means equal to the Rations which the General Officers have allways received. I don't believe it is the wish of the General Officers to have any Addition [to t]heir Rations. Their pay made good and [a new?] Establishment after the War I believe will [co]ntent them. I have shown the minutes to Mr. Root who is of opinion that it will not be best to make any Alterations in the Rations." Schuyler Papers, NN.
   [4] Schuyler may have completed this letter on November 19. The memorial of the general officers was read in Congress on November 18; and this paragraph is slightly separated from the preceding at the bottom of the page.

John Fell's Diary

                                              Friday Novr 19th [1779]
   Com[mercial] Com[mittee]. Congress. Report for regulating Prices @ 20 for 1 agreed to for all home Manufactories &c and all imported articles to bear a Proportion to the above.[1]

MS (DLC).
   [1] Samuel Holten also noted in his diary of this date that "Congress passed several resolutions for regulating prices." MDaAr. For these resolves, see Samuel Huntington to the States, November 22, 1779.

Samuel Huntington to Nathanael Greene

Sir,   Philadelphia Novemr 19th 1779
You will receive herewith enclos'd three Acts of Congress viz on[e]
of the 12th & two of the 16th Instant for reforming & incorporating
the eleven Companies of Artificers raised by the Quarter master
General & making further provision for them as specified in the
several Acts.[1]
Capt Pendleton hath been very faithful & persevering in this
Business, & had the Misfortune to be confin'd with Sickness consider-
able Time in this City.
I am Sir with Sentiments of Esteem & Regard, your humble Servt,
Saml Huntington President

RC (PPAmP: Greene Papers). In a clerical hand and signed by Huntington.
[1] *JCC*, 15:1261–62. These resolves for reforming the artificer companies had been
adopted at the urging of Quartermaster General Greene. For his August 30 letter to
Congress explaining his recommendations, the Board of War's endorsement of those
recommendations, and a September 18 letter of Capt. Daniel Pendleton whom Greene
had sent to Congress with a petition from the officers of the artificers companies, see
PCC, item 78, 18:247–50, item 147, 2:577–80, item 155, 1:159–62.

Samuel Huntington to George Washington

Sir   Philadelphia Novr. 19th. 1779.
Your Excellency will receive herewith enclosed five Acts of
Congress, Viz one of 12th and four of the 16th Instant; respecting
the eleven Companies of Artificers raised by the Quarter master
general;[1] The procuring of Witnesses and depositions in trials before
Courts martial;[2] and the constituting a sub cloathier for the Artillery,
Cavalry, Artificers and Corps composed of troops from different
States.[3]
I have the honor to be, with the greatest respect, Your Excellency's
humble servt.   Saml. Huntington President

RC (DLC: Washington Papers). In the hand of George Bond and signed by
Huntington.
[1] See Huntington to the States, November 18, 1779.
[2] Ibid., note 2.
[3] For this November 16 resolve, which had been recommended by Washington and
endorsed by the Board of War, see *JCC*, 15:1276; PCC, item 147, 2:581–84; and
Washington, *Writings* (Fitzpatrick), 16:438–40. Huntington also enclosed this resolve
with a brief letter of this date to Clothier General James Wilkinson, PCC, item 14, fol.
231.

Massachusetts Delegates
to Samuel Adams and John Hancock

Gentlemen   Philadelphia Novr. 19. 1779

We beg Leave to inclose You a Copy of a Subscription, originated in this City for the benevolent Purpose of Supporting & educating the Children of our late worthy Friend Major General Warren,[1] by which it will appear that the Name of the General Assembly & also of the Council of Massachusetts Bay is inadvertently used in a Manner which may not be approved by them; for this, & *other* Reasons, We have tho't it our Duty to suggest the Impropriety of the Measure, to the Gentlemen who promoted it; *for*, should the Subscription be more successful than We expect, yet, it is not probable that a Sum will be raised adequate to the purpose, & it may also be hurtful to the Feelings of the Children, to reflect hereafter on the Mode proposed for affording them Relief. Notwithstanding, We shall chearfully contribute in our private Capacity, We are still of Opinion, that considering the Merit of General Warren, the Services which he rendered to his Country, & the distressed Circumstances of these Orphans, some Provission should be made by the publick, more advantageous to the former & consistent with the Honor due to the Memory of our deceased Friend, than what is proposed by the Subscription, & We shall move that a Committee appointed by Congress some Time past to consider this Matter, may be directed to report.

How far it will be proper to communicate the Matter to the General Assembly & to urge their Beneficence, We submit to your Consideration, & shall acquiesce in your Opinion relative to the same.

We remain Gentlemen with Respect, your very huml Servants,

E Gerry

James Lovell

RC (NN: Emmet Collection). Written by Gerry and signed by Gerry and Lovell.

[1] For further information on the private subscription for the children of the late Gen. Joseph Warren, which was promoted by Gen. Benedict Arnold but opposed by the Massachusetts delegates because they sought public support for Warren's dependents, see these *Letters*, 12:111–12. A copy of the subscription notice is printed in Adams, *Writings* (Cushing), 4:171–73.

On July 1, 1780, Congress resolved to pay for the "maintenance and education" of Warren's children "to the amount of the half-pay of a major-general, to commence at the time of his death, and continue until the youngest of the said children shall be of age." *JCC*, 17:581.

John Fell's Diary

Saturday Novr 20th [1779]
Coml Committee. Congress. The Resolution brought in to Reccomend to the States the Altering the Law for obliging Cred[itor]s to take the money for Debts, long debated and Postponed.[1]
Report of the Medical Committee. Rain.

MS (DLC).
[1] According to the journals, this resolution, which formed the final paragraph of the report of the committee on the limitation of prices, was considered on November 19 and postponed. There is no mention of any debate on the committee's report in the journals for November 20. See *JCC*, 15:1292–96. See also Samuel Huntington to the States, November 22, 1779, note.

Marine Committee to John Beatty

Sir   November 20th 1779
The enclosed Resolve of Congress was passed in consequence of your last letter to the Marine Committee whereby you are directed to supply the Spaniards on board the Prison ship at New York with Provisions keeping a Seperate Account thereof.[1] I am ordered by the Committee to request that you will propose to exchange Mr. Thomas Bryer late Purser of the Hope Sloop of war in the Kings Service a prisoner here, for Mr Nathaniel Galt of this City who has been a long time in Captivity at New York, and whose family on that account are in distressed circumstances. The Committee from motives of humanity are anxious for his Exchange and have desired me to request that you will use your most speedy endeavours to effect it.
I am Sir, Your Hble servant,   John Brown Secy.

LB (DNA: PCC Miscellaneous Papers, Marine Committee Letter Book).
[1] See *JCC*, 15:1273; Marine Committee to Beatty, November 5; and Samuel Huntington to Beatty, November 18, 1779.

Marine Committee to the Eastern Navy Board

Gentlemen   November 20th 1779
Congress having authorized this Committee to appoint Advocates for the Continent within the respective States,[1] in consequence thereof we have appointed John Lowell Esquire Continental Advocate for Massachusetts Bay, and John Pickering Esquire for the State of New Hampshire who are to be employed in all Cases in which the Continent is concerned, with which you will please to acquaint the Continental Agents in those States and direct them to Act Accordingly.

We have appointed Captain George Jerry Osborne to command the
Marines on board the New ship building at Portsmouth, conceiving
that he may be useful in doing many matters relative to that Ship
before there is Occasion for raising his men—of this please to
Acquaint him and also Captain Barry that he may be employed
Occasionally.[2] We have directed Mr. Bradford[3] the Agent to reserve
30 hhds Rum & 10 hhds Sugar for the use of the Navy which you
will please to receive into your care.

We are sirs,   yr Hbl serts[4]

LB (DNA: PCC Miscellaneous Papers, Marine Committee Letter Book).

[1] On November 16 Congress had authorized the Marine Committee "to appoint
advocates for the purpose of taking care of and managing the maritime causes, in
which the United States are or may be concerned." *JCC*, 15:1278.

[2] For this purpose the committee also wrote the following letter to Capt. John Barry
this day. "Agreeable to your desire we have appointed Captain George Jerry Osborne
to command the Marines on board your ship [*America*], but as it will be a considerable
time before there is occasion to raise his men, we have been so early in his appointment on the principle of his being useful in doing matters relative to the Ship until
that time, which you will please to Observe and employ him occasionally in such
business as you may think proper." Paullin, *Marine Committee Letters*, 2:131.

[3] Thus the committee wrote the following letter to John Bradford this day. "We
desire you will deliver to the Order of the Committee of Congress for Superintending
the Quarter Master & Commissarys Departments All the Rum & Sugar in your care
belonging to the Continent, except 30 hhds Rum & 10 hhds Sugar which are reserved
for the use of the Navy and which you are to deliver to the Honble the Commissioners
of the Navy Board." Ibid., pp. 131–32.

[4] The four letters written by the Marine Committee this day are the last to be found
in the committee's letterbook and the last that will appear in this edition of delegate
correspondence. The committee continued to function for nearly two weeks after
commissioners to the new Board of Admiralty were first appointed on November 26,
until the new chairman Francis Lewis assumed practical control of naval administration,
but no committee letters from that period have been found. For the surviving correspondence of the Board of Admiralty, which commences December 10, 1779, see
Paullin, *Marine Committee Letters*, 2:135–272.

Charles Thomson to the States

Sir,   (Circular)   Secretary's Office Novr. 20th 1779.

I take the liberty of transmitting you a duplicate of an Act of
Congress passed the 16th of March 1778,[1] the Utility of which is
apparent: And as it may be proper & necessary that you should be
informed of the several Acts & proceedings of Congress I have
herewith sent you a copy of their Journal from the 1st of Jan. last
& shall continue to send you from time to time their weekly publications.[2] On the other hand as a communication of your Acts may
be advantageous, and lodging them in this office, for the information of the Delegates of the other States beneficial to the Union,
& tend to facilitate the transmitting to posterity the rise & progress
of these infant States, I take the liberty of requesting you to transmit

to this Office a copy of the constitution or form of Government adopted by your State upon the declaration of Independence & of all the public acts passed by your legislature since that period. If you can add any Pamphlets or documents relative to the controversy & revolution they shall be carefully deposited & preserved & thereby you may do an Acceptable service to posterity and oblige Sir your humble servt.   C. T.

LB (DNA: PCC, item 18).
[1] For this "act," requesting copies of all state legislation passed "in pursuance of recommendations of Congress," see these *Letters,* 9:313n.2.
[2] In keeping with this promise, Thomson next sent journals to the states with the following cover letter of December 17. "Referring to my letter of the 20th of November last, I have the honor of transmitting you the journals of Congress published since that time and shall henceforward send them Monthly." Red Books, MdAA.
For bibliographic notes on the manner in which Congress made its journals available to the states after March 31, 1779, see *JCC,* 15:1459–62.

Committee on Appeals Decree

November 22d. 1779.

Yelverton Taylor qui tam &c.	Appeal from
vs. The Sloop Polly her Cargo &c.	the State of
John Bunch Claimant	Pennsylvania[1]

We the Commissioners appointed by Congress to hear, try and determine all Appeals from the Courts of Admiralty of the several American States to Congress having heard and fully considered as well all and singular the Matters and Things mentioned and contained in the Record or Minutes of the Proceedings of the Court of Admiralty of the State of Pennsylvania in the above Cause as the Arguments of the Advocates of the respective parties to the above Appeal do thereupon adjudge and decree that the Appeal of the said John Bunch demanded and filed in the above Cause be and the same hereby is dismissed with Costs And that the Judgment or Sentence of the said Court passed, pronounced and published in the said Cause be and the same hereby is in all its' parts confirmed and established And We do further order and adjudge that the party Appellant pay unto the party Appellee in the said Cause one thousand and sixty Dollars for his Costs and Charges by him expended in defending the said Appeals in this Court &c. Tho. M:Kean

Hy. Marchant

C. Griffin

MS (DNA: RG 267, case no. 33). In a clerical hand, and signed by Griffin, Marchant, and McKean.
[1] The Pennsylvania Court of Admiralty had awarded the sloop *Polly* and her cargo to Yelverton Taylor, commander of the privateer *Comet.* Taylor had captured the

Polly, commanded by Charles Rowland, on the high seas on July 1, 1778, while it was carrying supplies to the British forces in New York. After the Pennsylvania court's decision on September 6, 1778, John Bunch of New Providence, the owner of the *Polly*, claimed that his ship was heading for Halifax to obtain supplies for New Providence and was therefore exempt from seizure by Congress and he appealed to Congress where the case was referred to the Committee on Appeals on October 20, 1778. The committee in this decree dismissed Bunch's claim and reaffirmed the state court's decision. See case file no. 33, RG 267, DNA; and *JCC*, 12:1024.

John Fell's Diary

Monday the 22d. [November 1779]
Com[mercial] Com[mittee]. Congress. After the dispatches, Committee on ways and means brought in a Report, to draw Bills on Mr Laurens and Mr Jay for £100000 Sterlg Each. After long debate agreed to go in a Committee of the whole house to morrow: Mr Griffin and Mr Harnet were appointed to the Commercial Committee.

MS (DLC).

Samuel Huntington to the States

Sir,   (Circular)   Philada Novem. 22d 1779
You will receive herewith enclos'd an Act of Congress of the 19th instant earnestly recommending to the several States forthwith to enact Laws for establishing & carrying into execution a general limitation of prices throughout their respective Jurisdictions, to commence in their operations from the first day of February next.[1]
I have the honour to be &c.   S.H. President

LB (DNA: PCC, item 14).
[1] An October 7 "representation" from New Jersey seeking "a general regulation of prices," with a view to "restoring and rendering permanent the public credit," had been read in Congress on Octcber 11 and referred to a committee of 13. A month later, the October 20–28 proceedings of the Hartford convention on price regulation were also referred to the same committee, which submitted a report that was read, debated, amended, and adopted on November 15, 18, and 19.
  In addition to seeking passage of state laws for regulating prices and wages, the enclosed resolves also provided guidelines for state price limitations ("not to exceed twenty fold of the prices current through . . . 1774"), specified exemption ("salt and military stores"), recommended "strict laws against engrossing," and enjoined all Continental purchasing officers and agents "to conform strictly to all regulations . . . established in the several states." A decision on the committee's more controversial recommendation for revision of state legal tender laws was postponed, and Congress did not address itself to the Hartford convention's call for a follow-up convention to be held in Philadelphia early in January, which had been sent directly to all the states from New Hampshire to Virginia. See *JCC*, 15:1162, 1254, 1272, 1287, 1289–93; PCC, item 26, fols. 39–44, item 33, fols. 369–90, item 67, 2:218–25, item 68, fols. 467–74; John Fell's Diary, October 11, 1779; and the following entry.

New Jersey Delegates to Caleb Camp

Sir,   Philada 22 Novr 1779.

Enclosed you have the result of the Deliberations of Congress on the representation of the 7th ulto respecting a general Limitation of Prices.[1] We beg Leave to say that with Attention to the Interests of the Union in general and the State in particular, and also to the Convenience of the Legislature, we have left no Means untried to give Success and Dispatch to the Business. The Legislature, we flatter ourselves, will be disposed to overlook any Defects in the Plan recommended by Congress compared with the Scope and Tenour of their representation, when they reflect that different States as well as Individuals, however they may coincide in the main Substance of a Measure, vary often in their Ideas on particular Parts, and also when they are informed that what we have now the Pleasure to transmit has passed with a great Degree of Unanimity. For the Sake of this and greater Expedition, Policy dictated to concede a little. From Appearances we think ourselves justified to say that the measure recommended will, in all probability, be universally adopted throughout the Union. The Date of Commencement is more distant than could have been wished, but when the remoteness of some of the States is considered, as also that many of the Legislatures are not sitting, and that the Limitations ought to take Place at the same Time every where, it could not well be gainsayed. Other Arguments also have been urged tending to shew that this will give fuller Efficacy to the Measure by giving People, an Opportunity to provide against Losses and Disappointments to their essential Prejudice. The ratio of the Prices to those current formerly, though by many thought too large, is set at a Limit which we hope will produce an easy Turn to the Tide of Depreciation, and make a further reduction in due Time more natural and practicable.

We have the Honour to be, with all respect, your obedt hble Servants,   Jno Witherspoon   Nath. Scudder

      John Fell   William Ch. Houston

RC (Nj: State Papers). Written by Houston and signed by Houston, Fell, Scudder, and Witherspoon. Addressed: "Honorable Caleb Camp, Esquire, Speaker of the House of Assembly of New-Jersey, Mount-Holly."

[1] See the preceding entry.

Nathaniel Scudder to Henry Laurens

My Dear Sir,   Philadelphia Novr. 22d. 1779

I was yesterday, by the Hand of Colonel Laurens honored with your agreeable Favor of the [16th] and 17th instant, and I most sincerely thank you for [them.]

The Account we have received since your Departure of our Repulse & Disappointment at Savannah compelled me to adopt the Adage contained in the fi[rst] Line of your Letter, and I think upon the Whole I [can] say "Aye"—altho' I must confess I cannot fairly see how.

Our worthy & amiable Friend Colo. Laurens is gone to Head-Quarters, where I hope he will be determined to quit his military Engagements, and to accept his Appointment to Paris—may I venture to say I [can] hardly forgive his Father for not having used his Influence to prevail on him to do so—however being fully acquainted with the Prudence & Delicacy of the Gentleman, who sustains that happy Relation to him, I freely acquiesce.

We did not elect a New President on Monday [nor] have we since, but after Several Days absence Mr. Huntington resumed the Chair by general Co[nsent] and Business has proceeded as usual. Congress h[as been?] very thin, rarely more than ten States represented, and frequently no more than nine. Genl. Schuyler and Mr. Robert R. Livingston are now here from New-York. Neither the Doctor[1] nor myself are elected for the ensuing year. The Members elected by New Jersey are [Mr. Fell,] Mr. Houston and Colo. Henderson, who, if he accepts, w[ill be a very? goo]d Man. Congress is doing every Thing possible for the Assistance of the southern States, and we hope to be able to embark the North-Carolina Brigade, and any other Troops General Washington can spare on Board Count De Gras's Squadron in Chesapeak, which if effected will afford a speedy Reinforcement to your City, and save immense Expence and fatigue. I rejoice to hear some french Frigates are [yet] at Charles Town for it's present Defence; and I am of Opinion the Embarkation from New York will not take Place while the french Line-of-Battle Ships continue hovering on our Coast. We have indeed some Accounts from thence which say they have debarked a great Number of Troops, which they had put on Board.

I am now, my Dear Friend, retiring to a private Life, this being my last Week in Congress;[2] but believe me I have no Idea of shrinking from any further Share in this important Contest—No Sir—I will continue to exert myself on all Occasions for the public Good, both by a spirited Opposition to all peculators & public Defaulters, and, if necessary, by again taking up the Sword, and even in the Ranks with those (over whom I lately held a high Command) exposing my *Life*, which with my *Honor* are almost all I have left *to expose* out of that List of Valueables, which when I early signed the General Association I solemnly devoted to the good of my injured Country. I know *you* pity me for the unequal Sacrifices I have made—I thank you for it. But *I* know that I have done nothing more than every honest man ought to have done; and I appeal to Heaven [. . .]nk *Necessity* alone which compels me [. . . ac]cept public Station. Congress has at Length adopted a set of Resolves whereby they recommend to the States a general Limitation of Prices, so that no Labor or Country Produce shall exceed 20 Prices of the Year 1774. What the Effect will be Time only can demonstrate.

We were yesterday, and shall be this Day [laying] a Plan for drawing upon yourself and Mr. Jay for 100,000 Sterling at 6 months sight—whether we venture a Leap in the Dark I know not; I rather [think] we shall—how would you like to meet with a Number of these Bills on your Arrival at Amsterdam. Desperate Diseases require desperate Rimedies.

Mr. John Adams & Mr. Francis Dana accept the Appointment & will sail in a few Days.

I thank you for your kind Expressions in Favor of myself and Family, and were it not that I fear to offend your generous Delicacy, I would in the most emphatical Language paint my Gratitude to you for that unmerited Attention you have paid me in Person and for the numerous Favors you have conferrd upon me and my Son—but I will not give you Par[ticulars.] I only wish to continue to share the Honor of [your] Friendship, and that my Son,[3] whom you have been [. . .] so kindly to patronise, may render himself worthy of your goodness and future Attention. He and [his] Sister join in presenting you their most respectfull Complements, and in wishing you a safe & prosperous Voyage. You have my most ardent Prayers for this and every other Success and Blessing [tempora]l & spiritual to which your most sanguine W[. . . as]pire. I shall esteem it a peculiar happiness to hear from you immediately after your safe Arrival in Europe, and as often afterwards as your important Business there will permit. I shall hold my Son attendant on your Commands at least untill the Beginning of the Summer; [In the] mean Time shall urge him to make every Improvement in his Power.

If it be agreable to you, you will please to place your Letters to me under cover to the President of Congress, who can conveniently hand them to my Son—mine to you will come through the same Conveyance.

And now, my Dear Sir, permit me to repeat my anxious Wishes for your future Wellfare, and to subscribe myself with the highest Regard, Your sincerely affectionate Friend, & most obliged Humble Servant,   Nathl Scudder

[*P.S.* Nothing?] in this Day's Paper worth enclosing.

RC (PHi: Jenkins Collection). RC damaged, but many missing words conjectured in an unidentified hand. Alternate readings have been supplied where necessary.

[1] That is, John Witherspoon.

[2] Scudder's term was to expire December 1; he apparently last attended Congress on November 25 or 26.

[3] Probably Joseph Scudder, who was a clerk for the Board of War.

John Fell's Diary

Tuesday 23d [November 1779]

Com. Committee. Congress. This day Resolved to draw Bills on Mr Jay and Mr Lawrence for £200000 Sterlg at 6 Mo. sight.[1] I was against the measure.

MS (DLC).

[1] For the action taken by Congress on the bills of exchange to be drawn on John Jay and Henry Laurens, see *JCC*, 15:1297, 1299–1300, 1315–16, 1326–27; and Fell's Diary, November 29, 1779.

James Forbes to Thomas Sim Lee?

My Dear sir,[1]   Philadelphia Novr 23d 1779

I have the pleasure of yours of the 19th Currt. The Inclosed papers gives you all our publick news. Our Army are moving into Winter Quarters, no accounts from N York that are to be depended on, respecting the movements of the Enemy.

Congress have recommended to the States a limitation of prices not to exceed twenty for one, to what they were in 1774, should this & the raising Taxes be complyd with a stop may be put to the amazing Depreciation of our money. I hope shall soon have the pleasure of seeing you, as I flatter my self some of our new Delegates will soon appear in Congress. I ever am with perfect Esteam & regard, your affe Friend & Servt,   James Forbes[2]

RC (NN: Emmet Collection).

[1] Probably Thomas Sim Lee, with whom Forbes corresponded regularly in similar terms. In this letter Forbes also expressed his expectation of being left off the slate of Maryland delegates that were soon to be elected, and in his December 30 letter to Lee he reported his great disappointment that he was included in the new delegation elected December 22.

[2] This day also the following brief letter was written by Pennsylvania delegate Frederick A. Muhlenberg to the Board of War.

"There is a certain Captn. Brightman now a Prisoner in the new Jail, who was taken on his Passage from the West Indies to New York in an unarmed Vessel. I should be extreamly happy if Your Honourable Board would admit him on his Parole, & I will be answerable for his good Behaviour & strict Adherence to it." Society Collection, PHi. The object of Muhlenberg's solicitation may have been James Brightman, captain of the *William*, who had been captured by a Pennsylvania privateer and was lodged at a Mr. "Boyles" in January 1780. See *Pa. Archives*, 1st ser. 8:93.

Cyrus Griffin to Benjamin Harrison

Sir.   Philadelphia Novem. 23d. 1779.

I do myself the honor to inclose two Acts of Congress which the assembly may perhaps consider as containing matters of some importance.

The demands for money upon the Continental Treasury are great indeed. The different States must supply those demands, or the period will shortly arrive when the whole Continent may totter to its foundation, at least I fear a general stagnation must be the consequence.

A Captain this moment from the West Indies confirms the account of a Boston paper, that a bloody engagement has taken place between the Combined Fleets and that of great Britain; the latter were severely beaten from superiority of numbers; two considerable ships destroyed, and three of the largest taken. The French lost one of their best which went to the bottom during the heat of Battle. From circumstances We give some credit to this account; and particulary as it does not come from the Southward.

It is well ascertained that the great object of the Enemy in the present stage of the Contest is to get possession of Charles Town, and of consequence to secure the two southern states. To *my* Judgement the assembly ought to give the utmost assistance to prevent so great a misfortune *even* to the common Cause; but in particular as most assuredly the subsequent movements of the Enemy would tend to the state of Virginia—for the purpose of commanding the Chesapeak.

I have the honor to be, with great respect, Sir, Your most obedient and humble servant.   C. Griffin

RC (NjMoHP: Lloyd W. Smith Collection).

James Lovell to Abigail Adams

Dear Ma'am   Novr. 23. 1779

Instead of sending the inclosed[1] to the Navy Board I shall from Time to Time direct them as now, that after you have had the Amusement (such as it is) of reading them you may forward them to the Friend for whom they are designed, through the Care of the Navy Board at Boston. If you are quite indifferent as to this method, I will lodge them in future where those for Mr. Dana are lodged by my Direction. Yrs. affectionately,   J L

[*P.S.*] Col. Langdon Yesterday carried some Papers from me directed to Mr. A or in his Absence to the Navy Board. They were only of the *Kind* now sent—but *former Numbers.*

RC (MHi: Adams Papers). Adams, *Family Correspondence* (Butterfield), 3:239.
[1] Lovell was enclosing the weekly printed journals of Congress. See Lovell to Abigail Adams, November 27, 1779.

Henry Marchant to William Greene

Sir,   Philadelphia Novr. 23d. 1779.

I have nothing of Moment to communicate to your Excellency since my last, save that seven or Eight Ships of the Line & several Frigates of Count De Staings Fleet are in Chessepeak Bay. The Count himself with the other Part of his Fleet were in Georgia when We last heard from Him. What will be his next Opperations is not yet known. Mr. Ellery is not yet arrived, altho' from his last Letter I was led to expect him by the 20th of this Month.[1] I must at all Events set out in a few Days—The Circumstances of my Family will absolutely require it; As well as some other Considerations.

I enclose Your Excellency four of the Weekly Journals of Congress bringing them down in Course to the 29th of Octor—as also several News Papers. I am with the highest Esteem and Respect yr. Excellency's most obedt. and very humble Servt.

Hy. Marchant

RC (R–Ar: Letters to Governors).
[1] Ellery did not attend Congress until November 30, the day Marchant obtained a leave of absence from Congress. *JCC*, 15:1330, 1334.

John Fell's Diary

[November 24–25, 1779]

Wednesday 24th. Com[mercial] Com[mittee]. Congress.

Sundry Letters, Reports &c.

Mr Gibson was Elected to the Treasury Bo'd.

Gibson[1]	Millen [Milligan]	Denning
5	6	
6	5	
6	2	2
8		2

Thursday Novr 25. 1779. C[ommercial Committee]. Congress. Several dispatches, Report[s of] Committees, Board of War, Treasury &c. (Snow)

MS (DLC).
[1] John Gibson was actually elected on November 25. *JCC*, 15:1307. This entry of Fell's diary (which was copied by him in its present form sometime after the date of his concluding entry), appears at the bottom of a left-hand page; the balloting recorded here was written on the opposite page and linked to the November 24 entry with a brace. The entry for November 25 is at the top of the right-hand page.

Elbridge Gerry to Abigail Adams

My dear Madam: Philadelphia, Nov. 24, 1779.

Agreeable to Mr. Adams' request in his favour of the 8th instant I have enquired the price of silver in this city and it is sold at the rate of 37 and 40 for 1. The pamphlets which he sent here for the minister and Secretary of France, are delivered and were very acceptable.[1]

I presume Mr. Adams is by this time embarked for France, and sincerely wish him health and happiness and success in the discharge of his important trust. At the same time give me leave to assure you Madam that I am much concerned at the unavoidable interruption of your happiness on the present occasion, but flatter myself that a prospect of his future services to his country and consequent honor to himself will reconcile you to a temporary loss of his company and finally terminate in the completion of our warmest expectations. Should it be in my power to promote the welfare of yourself and family I shall be much obliged to you for information thereof and am with every sentiment of friendship and esteem, Your most humble servant,   E. Gerry

MS not found; reprinted from *The Collector* 23 (September 1909): 110.

[1] In his November 8 letter, John Adams had asked Gerry to "deliver the Essex result to the Chevalier, who is curious to collect things of this kind." *Ibid.*, p. 110; and Adams Letterbook, MHi. "The Essex result" was a pamphlet strongly opposing the Massachusetts constitution proposed in 1778, and according to one student of the period it was "the first systematic statement of the eastern moderate position" on the state government. Stephen E. Patterson, *Political Parties in Revolutionary Massachusetts* (Madison: University of Wisconsin Press, 1973), pp. 191–92.

Samuel Huntington to John Beatty

Sir,   Philada Novemr 24th 1779

You will receive herewith enclos'd a petition to Congress from John Burrows with two letters from Elias Boudinot late Commissary of Prisoners.

The subject matter of this petition & papers which accompany the same are relative to the wanton destruction of Mr Burrows's Mill & store with a Quantity of flour; by the British Troops. Congress have this day order'd that these papers be transmitted to the Commissary General of Prisoners.[1]

I am Sir with due regards, your humble Servant,
                                        S.H. President

LB (DNA: PCC, item 14).

[1] *JCC*, 15:1302. In his December 20 response to this letter, Beatty asked whether it was the desire of Congress that he simply file the enclosed papers "until a general

liquidation of accounts should take place, . . . [or] make a requisition of payment from the present Commandant of New York." PCC, item 78, 3:425–28; and *JCC*, 15:1410. No evidence of Congress' response to this query has been found.

Samuel Huntington to Joseph Reed

Sir,   Philada November 25th 1779
    Your Excellency will receive herewith enclos'd a petition from John Palfrey which you will please to observe by the indorsement is refer'd to the President & Supreme Executive Council of this State to take order thereon.[1]
    I have the honour to be, with great respect, your Excy's hble Servt,   S.H.President

LB (DNA: PCC, item 14).
[1] John Palfrey, a prisoner on parole who had been captured by the militia of New Jersey, had submitted a petition to Congress on November 20 which was simply referred to the Massachusetts Council because he had formerly been a citizen of that state. *JCC*, 15:1296. Upon learning of this action, Palfrey had submitted a second petition, explaining that he had not lived in Massachusetts for many years and had no money to undertake a trip to Boston, and asked that his case be referred to the authorities of Pennsylvania, "where the real situation of his case is much better known and understood." For the Pennsylvania Council's disposition of Palfrey's appeal, which it referred to the state of New Jersey with the opinion that it would be "a bad precedent to admit Prisoners of War to take the oaths and release them from Captivity, while we have so many officers in that condition with the Enemy," see *Pa. Council Minutes*, 12:194.
    The documentation of this case is somewhat confused by the fact that Huntington's letter to the Massachusetts Council enclosing Palfrey's petition of the 20th and Congress' resolution of the 22d, is dated November 19, 1779 (PCC, item 14, fol. 229); and according to the journals Congress referred his case to Pennsylvania on the 24th although his petition requesting this action is dated the 25th (cf. *JCC*, 15:1302 and PCC, item 42, 6:232–35).

Meriwether Smith to the Virginia House of Delegates

Sir,   Wm.burg. 25t Nov. 1779
    Under the present Act of the Genl. Assembly, I consider myself still in the Delegation to Congress; And as I have yet some Matters which I conceive may be of Importance if communicated to the Genl. Assembly; I think it my duty to request a further audience, as soon as it may be convenient to both Houses.[1] I have the Honor to be Sir, your most obedt. & Hble Servt.   Meriwether Smith

RC (MeHi: Fogg Collection).
[1] Smith had been reelected to Congress on June 18, 1779, for one year beginning November 1. Because his position in Congress had been eroded by the passage of

antimerchant legislation by the House of Delegates, however, he had resolved to give "a Satisfactory Account of my Conduct, at their next Meeting," for which see Smith to Thomas Jefferson, July 6, 1779.

Smith obtained a leave of absence from Congress on September 28 and returned to Virginia, where he was examined by the combined House and Senate on October 28–29 "respecting the state of public affairs in Congress" and was subsequently voted the thanks of the House for his "independent and upright conduct" and for "the faithful discharge of his duty." In this letter, however, Smith requested "a further audience" before the assembly, which was held on December 3. Shortly thereafter, he submitted a letter of resignation from Congress which the House accepted on December 13. See *JCC*, 15:1115; and the *Journal of the House of Delegates of the Commonwealth of Virginia* [October 4–December 24, 1779] (Richmond: Printed by T. White, 1827), pp. 27–30, 34–45, 72, 78, 87–88.

Smith was reelected to Congress the following June. It is clear from an affidavit submitted with his account for attendance in 1778–79, which was taken up by the House of Delegates in March 1781, that he made an effort to disengage himself from trade during the fall of 1780 in order to qualify for attendance in Congress at that time. Executive Communications, Vi. Smith returned to Philadelphia in February 1781, for which see Smith to the Virginia House of Delegates, February 25, 1781.

Committee of Congress to Jeremiah Wadsworth

Sir   Philadelphia Novr. 26th 1779

Inclosed you have a resolution of Congress of the 16th Inst ordering all the rum & Sugar belonging to the public to be delivered to this Committee Except so much as will be Sufficient for the Navy— also an order from the Marine Committee to Mr. Bradford to deliver the same accordingly Except 30 Hhds of rum & ten of Sugar—also an order from this Committee to Mr Bradford to deliver the rum to you or your order Except as above.[1] Likewise you have another resolution of Congress of the 25th Inst puting the departments of the Staff under the direction of the board of war[2] So that in future your applications will be made to the board of war. The board wish to be informed how you Could dispose of the Sugars in the best manner to serve the public. Congress have not yet appointed a new Commissary Genl.

I am now returning home. Mrs. House expects you here this Winter. Col Blain is gone to Maryland hope he will be Successful in procuring flour. In haste dear Sir—your Friend & humble Servant,

> Jesse Root, Chairman for the last time
> of the Commttee of Congress for
> Superintending the staff departments

RC (CtHi: Wadsworth Papers). Written and signed by Root.

[1] See Samuel Huntington to John Bradford, October 1; Marine Committee to Bradford, November 17; and Marine Committee to the Eastern Navy Board, November 20, 1779, note 3.

[2] Root had seconded the motion made by Henry Marchant, to dissolve this committee and transfer oversight of the commisary and quartermaster departments to the Board of War. *JCC*, 15:1312.

John Fell's Diary

[November 26–27, 1779]

Friday Novr 26. Commercial Comm[ittee]. Congress.[1]
Letter from General Washington with the State of the Army &c.
Sundry Letters &c. Elected two Members for the Admiralty Board
viz. Mr Warring and Mr Whiple.[2]
Saturday Novr. 27th. Com Com. Congress. Several Reports Read
and debated.
NB Dined with Mr Griffin.

MS (DLC).
[1] This day Congress considered the report of the committee appointed July 22 to respond to the memorial of Pierre Eugène Du Simitière, who sought congressional support to compile and write his proposed "Memoirs and observations on the origin and present state of North America," based on his extensive collection of books, pamphlets, manuscripts, and maps. Although Congress at first responded favorably to the committee's report, Du Simitière's plan was ultimately rejected in July 1780. See *JCC*, 14:861, 15:1316–18, 1410, 17:606, 613, 648. For an analysis of Du Simitière's career and his collections, see Paul G. Sifton's "Pierre Eugène Du Simitière (1737–1784): Collector in Revolutionary America" (Ph.D. diss., University of Pennsylvania, 1960), especially pp. 1–40.
   Consideration of Du Simitière's memorial also may have stimulated an interesting motion by Elbridge Gerry aimed at establishing a sound basis for American Revolutionary historiography. Evidence for the motion, which is not in the journals or PCC, comes from a letter of John Adams to Gerry written 30 years after the close of the war. "Had your motion in Congress been adopted, and a Man of Sense and Letters appointed in each State to collect Memorials of the Rise Progress and Termination of the Revolution: We should now Possess a Monument of more inestimable Value than all the Histories and Orations that have been written. . . . That Mr. Jay, the President of Congress when your motion was made, admired it, is no Surprize to me. His head could conceive and his heart feel the importance of it." See the *Warren-Adams Letters*, 2:380–81. If such a motion was made during Jay's presidency, it would undoubtedly have been between July 22 and September 28, 1779.
[2] See Samuel Huntington to Thomas Waring, November 27, 1779.

Samuel Huntington to Oliver Wolcott

Sir   Philadelphia Novemr 26th. 1779
   I am agreably favord with your Letter of the 18th Instant, and had fortune favoured you with black Eyes it seems I might have still been more happy in being favourd with your personal conversation & company, however it seems the matter is not yet so fully desided but that I may have some hopes that good grey eyes will possibly do.
   The Request you make in behalf of Mr Murdoch shall be attended to and if I can obtain any usefull Information on the Subject it shall be communicated to you or Mr Murdoch.
   Before this comes to hand you will be Informd Congress have *again* recommended a limitation of prices Consequent upon the Result

of the late convention at Hartford, you well know that every Individual in Congress is not So wise as allways to Judge conformable to their resolves and this in particular is a Subject on which Time and Experience only, & the latter repeated will bring all men to agree in Judgment.

I have little if any news of Importance which you have not receivd. A part of Count D. Estaings Squadron tis said about Eight Ships of the line and Some Frigates are arrivd in the Chesapeake but their future destination is yet unknown perhaps to refresh & victual & return to the west Indies but this is bare conjecture.

I have the pleasure to inform you that as great harmony & concord Subsists in Congress as ever I knew or can be expected in Such a body, however by a refind practice we use a little too much Scripture language for my taste i e our language is too too much ay & no, but tis a Custom Some are fond of as being usefull in their Opinion. I hope the Wisdom of Congress and of the Several States will lead to such Measures the ensuing winter that we may be prepared for peace or war as events may be but I most Sincerely wish the former.

I am with Compliments to your Lady & Sincere Esteem & regard for yourself [I am] your humble Servant,   Saml Huntington

RC (CtHi: Oliver Wolcott Papers).

William Churchill Houston to Robert Morris

Dear Sir   Philada. 27 Novr 1779
Yours of 3 instant[1] I received a few Days after Date, and beg you will accept my Acknowledgments for it.

The Question relative to the Crown-lands which you mention,[2] is never out of Sight; and I am more and more convinced must, for the Peace of the Union, be settled upon some different Principles. I am as fully convinced of the Weakness of the Claims as before I came to Congress, and not less doubtful whether they will ever tend even to the pecuniary Interest of those who set them up. Certain I am they will never promote, but will probably ruin their political Interest. It is not however the less just that we should have our Share of the Proceeds of those Lands; and here arises a Question which I recommend to your Consideration. Whether had we better contend for this on *United or Confederated Grounds.* [Mary]land says, as we are; others are of a different Opinion. I would be happy to hear your Sentiments on so interesting a Question, as I am far from being clear that the Charters of some States, or any Muniments by which they can justify a Claim, extend as has been too credulously supposed.

It gives me much Pleasure to hear of the Success of the Loan in your County, and am persuaded if Gentlemen of Influence would equally exert themselves in other Places the Effect would be the same. But many rather set idle and wish that Things may go right, than put their Exertions to work to forward them. The Progress of Loans for a while in the present Exigency, is a desirable Object, but this pressing Crisis over, they had better be discontinued in future as being a disadvantageous way of raising Money.

You speak of the Eligibility of foreign Loans to a moderate Amount; and I am fortunate to find you agree with my Ideas on this Matter. You know already, or will ere long that this is not a Subject dormant or untouched. But you hold with me I trust that it would not be best to go so far as to make one Tittle of Exertion at Home, and in our own Power, unnecessary. A domestick is preferable before a foreign Debt, unless the latter is contracted at considerable Advantage above the former. The Idea of interesting European Powers in our Favour, is worthy of the Attention of Statsemen.

I hear little from my Friends at Mount Holly but am contented to be neglected, if the high Concerns of the State engross their whole Attention. Can you steal Half an Hour to inform me what is done and doing?

The Army, the General writes us, is moving to Quarters, principally in New-Jersey. I hope this will be some Relief to our Militia. No News of much Importance, but a Report from the West-Indies that the English Fleet are worsted in the Channel. We wait for a Confirmation, as it has no Mark of Authenticity yet.

If you spare Time to look into this [tent?] of Hurry, Squabbling and Noise, beg you will not pass by.

Your sincere Friend and hble Servant,

William Ch Houston

RC (NjR: Robert Morris Papers).
[1] Morris' draft of his November 3 letter to Houston is in the Morris Papers, NjR.
[2] Houston had discussed Virginia's opposition to the claims of the Vandalia and Indiana companies in his letter to Morris of October 2, and Morris had returned to the subject in his November 3 response. "The new Argument you mention," Morris noted, "when inquired into I am perswaded will prove ill founded like the others. If the Crown was not intitled [i.e., to grant vacant lands] who was? & in whose name were the Grants made. The denying the right of the Crown, destroys the title to the past Locations & militates against themselves. But suppose the right contravested. This possession was confessedly in the Crown. Let that possession be transferred to Congress & I trust they too will have force to retain it & do the Union justice, at least I'll stake my life on the Contest." Ibid. For their continued discussion of the western land issue, see Houston to Morris, March 6, 1780. For the views of a New York delegate, see Philip Schuyler to George Clinton, November 29, 1779.

Samuel Huntington to Thomas Waring

Sir,   Philada Novemr 27th 1779
    You will receive herewith enclos'd an Act of Congress of the 28th ulto establishing a board of Admiralty to superintend the naval & marine Affairs of these United States.[1]

Also another Act of Congress of the 26th instant by which you are appointed one of the Commissioners of that board, The other Gentleman William Whipple Esqr belongs to Portsmouth in New Hampshire, the third Commissioner is not yet elected, but will probably be a Gentleman from some one of the more central States,[2] it being thot beneficial to the whole to take the Commissioners from diferrent parts of the United States.

I am Sir with esteem & respect, your hble Servant,
S.H. President.[3]

LB (DNA: PCC, item 14).

[1] *JCC*, 15:1216–18. Although adoption of this October 28 resolve for establishing a Board of Admiralty brought a long period of indecision to an end, many weeks elapsed before the new administrative system was in operation. The resolve specified that the new board would "consist of three commissioners not members of Congress, and two members of Congress," but all three nonmembers originally appointed—Waring, William Whipple, and George Bryan—declined their posts. Thus not until Francis Lewis accepted one of these positions on December 8, joining delegates William Ellery and James Forbes, was the new board organized, the day Congress also resolved to transmit to it "all matters heretofore referred to the marine committee." For discussion of this administrative reform and the difficulties Congress experienced in staffing the board, which consequently consisted essentially of Lewis and Ellery during most of its life, see Charles O. Paullin, *The Navy of the American Revolution: Its Administration, Its Policy, and Its Achievements* (Chicago: Republican Printing Co., 1906), pp. 184–94, 216–19. See also John Dickinson's Notes, September ? 1779.

[2] Waring, about whom very little is known, was from Charleston, S.C. For the names of those who were put in nomination for commissioners ("not members of Congress") of the Board of Admiralty on November 15 and 16, and the election of Waring and Whipple on November 26, see *JCC*, 15:1271, 1277, 1318. For those nominated on November 30 and December 1, and the election of George Bryan of Pennsylvania on December 3 for the third post, see *JCC*, 15:1330, 1339, 1344.

[3] Huntington also wrote a similar letter this day to William Whipple. PCC, item 14, fol. 235. The replies to Huntington from Whipple, Waring, and George Bryan declining these appointments, as well as Francis Lewis' letter of acceptance, are in PCC, item 78, 3:411–14, 14:295–98, 24:163–66, 171–74.

Samuel Huntington to George Washington

Sir,   Philadelphia Novemr 27th 1779

Since the receipt of your Excellency's favours of the 3d & 5th instant acknowledg'd in my letter of the 11th I am honour'd with yours of the 14th, 18th, & 20th instant.[1]

Your Excellency will receive herewith enclos'd a Letter from Doctr J Morgan of the 22d instant together with an Act of Congress of the 24th instant ordering the aforementioned Letter from Doctor Morgan to be transmitted to the Commander in Chief.[2]

I have the honour to be, with the greatest respect, your Excy's hmble Servt,   Saml Huntington President

RC (DLC: Washington Papers). In a clerical hand and signed by Huntington.

[1] Actually, Huntington had acknowledged the general's letters of November 3 and 5 in his letter to Washington of November 13, since which he had also acknowledged Washington's November 14 letter on November 18. Washington's letters of November 18 and 20 are in PCC, item 152, 8:175–84; and Washington, *Writings* (Fitzpatrick), 17:125–32, 150–53.

[2] *JCC*, 15:1302–3. In his November 22 letter to Huntington, Morgan had complained that although he had impeached Dr. William Shippen, Jr., "of Malpractices and Misconduct in Office," Shippen remained free and had since made attempts "to bribe and corrupt Witnesses, to put it out of my power to appear against him." And in order to impress Congress with the urgency of the case and to secure Shippen's immediate arrest, Morgan specified additional charges. Morgan's letter, "herewith enclos'd," is in the Washington Papers, DLC. A copy of it is in PCC, item 63, fols. 143–50.

In his December 4 reply to Huntington, Washington explained that "the moment circumstances will admit of it, Doctor Shippen shall be put in arrest, and his trial will be proceeded on immediately after the Trials of General Arnold and Colo [Robert Lettis] Hooper are finished." Washington, *Writings* (Fitzpatrick), 17:216. For Morgan's pursuit of Shippen, see also Whitfield J. Bell, *John Morgan, Continental Doctor* (Philadelphia: University of Pennsylvania Press, 1965), pp. 220–36.

This day Huntington also sent a copy of Morgan's letter and Congress' November 24 resolve to Dr. William Shippen, Jr. PCC, item 14, fol. 236.

James Lovell to Abigail Adams

My dear Lady   27th of Novr. [1779]

I cannot recollect whether I sent No. 31[1] before. I promised yr Husband to continue to forward the Journals: But my Wish is not to break the Numbers so as to spoil a Set for any body else. If therefore I at any Time repeat a Number you will be so good as to return it; and if I omit one you will demand it. I suppose Mr. A did not leave the 1st, 2d or 3d Vol.[2] in his Library. If he did I will send you a Set of 1779 to keep at home; and forward myself directly to the Navy Board what I design for him. But you must not keep any of the Pages of 1778, because I shall have but one Course of them.

Yours, with affectionate Respect,   James Lovell

RC (MHi: Adams Papers). Adams, *Family Correspondence* (Butterfield), 3:239–40.
[1] That is, number 31 of the weekly printed journals of Congress. See Lovell to Adams, November 23, 1779.
[2] That is, the journals of Congress in volume format for 1774–75, 1776, and 1777.

Nathaniel Peabody to Meshech Weare

Sir   No.10   Philadelphia Novr. 27th. 1779.

I have the Honr. to acknowledge the Receipt of your favour of the 6th instant, which with the inclosed Copy of my reappointment came to hand the 22d; Just as Mr. Langdon was Seting off for home.[1]

And Give me leave to Assure you that I intertain a *due* Sense of the repeated Honrs done me by the free Suffrages of my fellow Citizens,

And Although my private interest is dayly injured by My Absence from home, And vehemently urges my immediate Attention, Yet as it is of the utmost importance that the State Should be represented at this Critical Conjuncture and as I enjoy a tolerable State of health Shall Esteam it an indispensable duty to endeavour with fidellity to discharge the trust reposed in me by this appointment till the State Shall be otherwise represented in Congress, unless Sooner *recalld*, during which I Shall assiduously aim that the State may not have Occasion to regret their Appointment.

It would be a happy Circumstance in my favour if I Could Set off from hence So as to arrive home before winter Sets in, for it will be very disagreable taking So long a Journey at that Season of the year—however Shall not leave the State unrepresented in Congress without giving at least one months previous Notice, unless Necessitated by Some unforeseen Occurrence.[2]

I have the Honr to be Sir, with the highest Considerations of Esteem Your Hons most obliged obedt And very Humble Servt,

Nath Peabody

RC (MHi: Weare Papers).

[1] Peabody's "reappointment" was in reality an extension of his and Woodbury Langdon's authority as delegates "until further order of the General Assembly." Nathaniel Folsom and William Whipple had been appointed New Hampshire's delegates "from the first day of November next and until relieved or recalled by order of the General Assembly." Peabody continued as a delegate until mid-1780, but Langdon did not return to Congress, and Folsom arrived at Congress on December 30, 1779. *N.H. State Papers*, 8:833; *JCC*, 15:1301, 1423.

For another example of a New Hampshire delegate's confusion over his authority "to tarry" at Congress, see William Whipple to Josiah Bartlett, August 10, 1779, note 1.

[2] One of Peabody's assignments at this time concerned the examination of Gen. Benedict Arnold's accounts by a committee to which he had been appointed on October 1, 1779. It was probably in connection with this business that Peabody wrote the following brief note to Arnold on November 25. "Sir, Your favour of this morning I have Just Recd. and shall embrace the Earliest opportunity to Comply with your Reasonable Request." Peabody Papers, NhHi.

John Fell's Diary

[Mon]day November 29. 1779.

Coml Comm. Committee Reported respecting the Bills [to b]e drawn and after several amendments the Yeas & Noes were calld carried in the Affirmitive. I was No.[1]

MS (DLC).

[1] For the origin of the measures authorizing bills of exchange to be drawn on Henry Laurens and John Jay, see Fell's Diary, November 22 and 23, 1779.

In his diary for this day Samuel Holten noted that "being unwell I did not attd. Congress." MDaAr.

Samuel Huntington to Philip Schuyler

Sir,   Philada Novemr 29th 1779
   Notwithstanding the many injuries committed by the Savages Congress are disposed to peace.[1] The Conditions on which they insist are, First, That it shall be supplicated on the part of the Enemy, Secondly That they shall surrender all the Americans in their Hands, Thirdly, That they shall expell all British Agents and emissaries, Fourthly, That they shall covenant to deliver up such as shall hereafter go among them. Fifthly, That they shall covenant not to take up the Hatchet again under penalty of being driven from their Country, and sixthly That they shall give Hostages for their strict Adherence to the promises to be by them made.
   I am Sir with esteem & regard, your humble Servant.
                                        S.H. President.

LB (DNA: PCC, item 14).
[1] In a letter of October 17, which had been referred to a committee consisting of James Forbes, Gouverneur Morris, and William Sharpe on October 22, Schuyler had requested instructions from Congress for treating with the Six Nations in the aftermath of Gen. John Sullivan's devastating expedition against them. With it he had also enclosed copies of his recent correspondence on the subject with General Washington, Lt. Col. Cornelius Van Dyke, and Indian agent James Deane. The committee's report, written by Morris and debated on November 27, consisted of a draft of the present truculent letter plus the following paragraph that was apparently deleted during debate.
   "Congress further Wish that they shall make considerable Offers of Territory to stand recorded against them and serve as the most pointed marks of their Contrition but they mean that the Commissioners should decline an Acceptance of the Offer to convince them of the superior Generosity of America compared with their Experience of others. At the same Time as many of the Inhabitants have just claims for Damages done Congress do not wish to preclude them, on the Contrary it is their Desire that it should be expressly left open in the Treaty so as to be afterwards settled in a fair & equitable Manner by Commissioners from the Whites & Indians." See JCC, 15:1201, 1237, 1320–23; and PCC, item 19, 5:311–12, item 153, 3:462–78. See also Schuyler to George Clinton, this date; and James F. and Jean H. Vivian, "Congressional Indian Policy during the War for Independence: The Northern Department," Maryland Historical Magazine 63 (September 1968): 269–71. As Schuyler had also been appointed in October by New York "to represent this State in any treaty of pacification" with the Six Nations, his role in subsequent Indian negotiations was both state and Continental. See Clinton, Papers (Hastings), 5:334–36.

Philip Schuyler to George Clinton

Dear Sir.   Philadelphia Nov. 29th 1779
   I arrived here on the 15th at night, on the next day I took my seat In Congress where I have constantly attended Every day since. The Journals copy which I have the honor to Inclose Your Excellency will Shew what matters have Claimed the Attention of Congress—a

vast variety of the most Important affairs ought to Claim their Immediate notice and Speedy decission. Our Finances are deranged to a most alarming degree, heavy demands constantly made on the Treasury which is empty, Our Army In want of Flour and that Article already arisen to Sixty pounds per hundred and will probably in ten days more rise to one hundred pounds. I wish I could say that There was one member of Congress adequate to the Important business of Finance.

Congress has not yet decided wether peace Shall be granted to the Indians, I have repeatedly urged to have the business brought on, as soon as It is Compleated I propose Setting out for Albany, to try and bring about a reconciliation with the Savages.[1] In my way up I shall do myself the honor to Call on Your Excellency If Hudsons river should be passable. The disaster In Georgia has afforded matter for fresh distress, troops are ordered from the main Army to that Quarter, we are In hopes they will Embark on board of some of the French men of war which are arrived In Cheasapeak and whose destination It is Imagined will be to the West Indies as soon as they have taken In a Stock of provision.

A report prevails that preparations for a Capital embarkation are making at NYork. They however come In such a way as to render the Intelligence far from Certain.

Pray make my Complements to Mrs. Clinton. I am Dear Sir with real affection and Sincere Esteem Your Excellency's Most Obedient Humble Servant.   Ph Schuyler

RC (NjMoHP: Lloyd W. Smith Collection).

[1] For Congress' instructions for treating with the Six Nations, see the preceding entry.

Although Schuyler left Philadelphia almost immediately (via Washington's headquarters to carry out a committee assignment), he subsequently wrote at length on the congressional debate over these instructions, explaining his role in securing them and speculating on the impact on New York of any Indian land cession "for the Benefit of the United States in general and grantable by Congress." This report, dated "Albany January 29th 1780" and directed to the New York legislature, is generally heavy reading, but it sheds considerable light on the ramifications of congressional Indian policy and the land claims of individual states.

"Deeply impressed with a Sense of the extensive Advantages which would probably result to the United States in general, and this in particular, from a perfect and permanent Reconciliation with an Enemy so formidable to a weak and extensive Frontier as fatal Experience has evinced the Indians to be, to whom Distance of Situation seems no great Obstacle to prevent or retard their Incursions; reflecting, with the most anxious Concern, on the Desolation and Variety of Distress incident on a Savage War; apprehensive that they would consider themselves without any Alternative but that of recommencing Hostilities; dreading the Effects of a consequent Desperation on their part; firmly believing that the greatly deranged State of the public Finances would render it exceedingly difficult to procure the necessary Supplies for that Army only which must keep the Enemy's Force on the Sea Board in Check; doubtful whether Detachments of sufficient Force to protect the Frontiers could be spared from our Army whilst the British retained their present position; aware of the Distresses and Expence incident on calling forth the Militia for the purpose; convinced that an Obstacle of very interesting Importance would be removed if Events should happily arise which would permit us to turn our Attention to the Reduction of Canada or the Enemies Fortresses in the interior parts of the Country; persuaded that no farther offensive Operations could be prosecuted against the Savages with any probable prospect of adequate Advantage I embraced the earliest Opportunity to advise Congress of the Overtures made by the Cayugas, and took the Liberty strongly to point at the Necessity of an Accommodation with all the Savages; but not being honored with an Answer as early as the Importance of the Object seemed to require, and wishing to improve the Advantage which the first Impulse occasioned by the Disaster the Indians had experienced would probably afford us, I hastened to Congress to sollicit their Determination which was obtained on the   November last, Copy whereof I have the Honor to enclose.

"Whilst the Report of the Committee in the Business I have alluded to was under Consideration a Member [Henry Marchant] moved in Substance 'That the Commissioners for Indian Affairs in the Northern Department should require from the Indians of the six Nations, as a preliminary Article, a Cession of part of their Country, and that the Territory so to be ceded should be for the Benefit of the United States in general and grantable by Congress.' A Measure so evidently injurious to this State exceedingly alarmed and chagrined those whose Duty it was to attend to its Interests. They animadverted with Severity on the unjustifiable principle held up in the Motion; the pernicious Consequence of divesting a State of its undoubted property in such an extrajudicial Manner was forcibly urged: the Apprehensions with which it would fill and affect the Minds of a people who had been as firm in the present glorious Contest; who had made more strenuous and efficacious Exertions to support it; had suffered more and still suffered as much as any were strongly painted. The Improbability that the Indians would acceed to a Reconciliation when such a preliminary was insisted upon was observed by many Members and urged on a Variety of Considerations. The Gentlemen in Favor of the Motion attempted to support it on the general Ground that what was acquired or conquered at the common Expence ought to enure to the common Benefit; that the Lands in Question, altho' they might be comprehended within the Limits of the State of New York (which however was not acknowledged) was not the property of the State; that being either in the Natives or by Right of Conquest in the United States. The Motion was nevertheless after some farther desultory Debate rejected: but from what drop'd in the Debate we had Reason to apprehend that several who were opposed to the Motion founded their Opposition on the Necessity of a Reconciliation with the Indians, against which, they imagined the Spirit of the Motion would militate. And we had a few Days after a convincing proof that an Idea prevailed that this and some other States ought to be divested of part of their Territory for the Benefit of the United States, when a Member afforded us the perusal of a Resolution for which he intended to move the House purporting 'that all the Lands within the Limits of any of the United States, heretofore grantable by the King of Great Britian whilst these states (then Colonies) were in the Dominion of that prince, and which had not been granted to Individuals should be considered as the joint property of the United States and disposed of by Congress for the Benefit of the whole Confederacy.' The Necessity and propriety of such an Arrangement was strenuously insisted upon, in private Conversation, and even supported by Gentlemen who represented States in Circumstances seemingly similar to our's with Respect to the Object of the intended Resolution. It was observed that if such States whose Bounds were either indefinite or were pretended to extend to the South Seas would consent to a reasonable Western Limitation that it would supercede the Necessity of any Intervention by Congress other than that of permanently establishing the Bounds of each State: prevent Controversy and remove the Obtacle which prevented the Completion of the Confederation. As this State would be eminently affected by such a Measure it was deemed of Importance as fully to investigate their Intentions as could be done consistent with that Delicacy and prudence to be observed on so interesting an Occasion and a Wish was accordingly expressed, as arising from mere Curiosity, to know their Idea of a reasonable Western Limitation. This they gave by exhibiting a

Map of the Country, on which they drew a Line from the North west Corner of Pennsylvania (which in that Map was laid down as in Lake Erie) thro' the Strait that leads to Ontario and thro' that Lake and down the St. Lawrence to the forty fifth Degree of Latitude for the Bounds of this State in that Quarter. Virginia, the two Carolinas and Georgia they proposed to restrict by the Allighany Mountains, or at farthest by the Ohio to where that River enters the Missisippi and by the latter River to the South Bounds of Georgia. That all the Territory to the West of those Limits should become the property of the Confederacy. We found this Matter had been in Contemplation some Time; the Delegates from North Carolina having then already requested Instructions from their Constituents on the Subjects, and my Colleagues were in Sentiment with me that it should be humbly submitted to the Legislature, if it would not be proper to communicate their pleasure in the premises by Way of Instruction to their Servants in Congress." Burnett, *Letters*, 5:20–22.

William Ellery to William Greene

Sir,   Philadelphia Novr. 30th. 1779
Mr. Marchant who will hand this to your Excellency will give you such information as we have to communicate.[1]

It was my intention to have waited upon the Genl. Assembly at their Session in South-Kingston, and to have presented my account; but the evacuation of Rhode Island prevented it. Thither I was called to see whether there were any remains of the property I was once possessed of in that Island; and to provide some articles for my family in my absence.

All the destructible property I had there was utterly destroyed. The warm attachment I had always shown to the rights of my country asked better treatment from men who had boasted of their regard to justice and humanity. If I should hereafter return to Newport I will hope that the General Assembly will assist [me in] procuring some Tory habitation until better times shall enable me to provide for myself.

There is a considerable ballance due to me, and your excellency & the General Assembly are sensible that in the depretiated state of our money it requires a very large Sum to give a family but a slender support. I shall be much obliged to the Assembly if they will order the General Treasurer to advance to me One thousand dollars, myself to be accountable.

I hope to be informed seasonably of the doings of the Genl. Assembly, at their respective Sessions until my return; of the State of our Taxes, Loans &c and of every matter of a public nature; that I may be able to give every necessary information to Congress from time to time. On my side nothing shall be wanting to promote the interest of the State I have the honor to represent, and the interest of the United States of America.

I am with every Sentiment of Respect, Your Excellency's most obedt humble Servt.   Wm Ellery

William Ellery

RC (R–Ar: Letters to Governors).
[1] Henry Marchant obtained leave of absence from Congress this day, after Ellery began attending Congress earlier in the day. *JCC*, 15:1330, 1334.

John Fell's Diary

Tuesday the 30th [November] 1779
Com[mercial] Com[mittee]. Congress. Some dispatches were Read, after moved for finishing the appointment of an other Commissioner for the Admiralty Board which cause a long debate and nothing done.[1] General Sulevans Resignation was accepted. Commercial Committee gave in a Report [to] Put that in Commission Per the Style of the Board of Trade.[2]

MS (DLC).
[1] For the structure of the new Board of Admiralty, see Samuel Huntington to Thomas Waring, November 29, note 1.
[2] This report of the Committee of Commerce, in the hand of Francis Lewis, contains two endorsements: "Delivd. Novr. 29, 1779," and "Aug 24, 1781, Not to be acted upon ." PCC, item 29, fols. 307–14. It is printed in *JCC*, 15:1327–29. As a member of the committee, Fell is probably correct concerning the date of delivery.

The report itself languished in Congress for nearly two years. On May 9, 1780, a committee appointed to assign priorities to "the reports on file" listed this report as the fourth of seven that required consideration. This priority committee never completed its work, however, and on August 24, 1781, Congress decided its recommendations were "Not to be acted upon." In the meantime, another committee instructed to "revise the several reports now before Congress which have not been acted upon or finished," also recommended, on August 23, 1781, that the Committee of Commerce report "Ought not to be acted upon." See *JCC*, 16:414, 17:416, 21:788, 900, 908–9; and PCC, item 23, fols. 55–57, 69–74.

Samuel Huntington
to the Massachusetts Legislature

Gentlemen,   Philada Novemr 30th 1779
I am directed by Congress to transmit you the enclosed papers from Mr Bingham. They contain an account of his proceedings relative to a vessel said to be danish property captured by the Sloop Pilgrim and carried into Martinique about which as he says a suit is now commenced against him in your superior Court. Upon a full examination of the papers you will judge of the Measures which ought to be adopted to prevent on the one hand injustice to individuals and on the other the embarrassment of Agents who are obliged to conform to the will of the ruling powers at the place of their residence. As Courts are now instituted at Martinique for the trial of such Causes Congress submit it to you whether it would not be

adviseable to stop the suit already commenced till Judgement is obtained upon the principal question after which it will be in Mr Bingham's power to discharge himself by delivering to the true owners the property placed in his Hands for their Use. If you should be of a contrary opinion they request you to furnish Mr Bingham's Agent with the enclosed papers.[1]

LB (DNA: PCC, item 14). Addressed: "To the Legislature of the State of Mass. Bay."
[1] William Bingham's October 6, 1779, letter to the Committee for Foreign Affairs explaining this case was received and referred on November 24 to a committee consisting of Robert R. Livingston, Henry Marchant, and Roger Sherman. The committee's report, which Congress adopted on November 29, simply recommended that the president transmit Bingham's letter and enclosed documents to the Massachusetts legislature with this letter of explanation, which was drafted by Livingston. See *JCC*, 15:1302, 1332; and PCC, item 19, 1:345–46, item 90, fols. 180–205. The following extract from the proceedings of the Massachusetts Council and House of January 4, 1780, pertaining to this case is also filed with these papers in PCC, item 90, fol. 206.
"That as in the usual course of Law the two Actions [commenced against Bingham] will be continued to April Court in the County of Suffolk and there is a probability in the mean time of an Accomodation of the Matter in dispute, that the further Consideration thereof be refer'd to the next Session of this Court."

Robert R. Livingston to George Clinton

Dear Sir,   Philadelphia 30th Nov'r 1779.
I did myself the honor to write to you last week,[1] but missing the post you will receive that letter by this conveyance, since which nothing material has hapned here, except that I find a violent inclination in most of the States to appropriate all the western Lands to the use of the United States, & in proportion, as they feel the weight of taxes, that inclination will increase, till I fear it will at last overpower us, unless we contrive to make a sacrafice of part to secure the remainder. This I think we may do to advantage now, while they treat our title with some respect. I would, therefore, submit it to your Excellency whether it would not be prudent for our Legislature to empower us to agree to make a north line, extended from the northwest corner of Pensilvania to the lake Ontario our western boundary, & from thence along the northwest shore of lake Ontario & the river St. Lawrence to the bounds of Canada, & from thence along those boundaries to the State of New Hampshire. This will secure Niagara to us, and the navigation of Lake Ontario. It will put our claim out of dispute, enable Congress & us to apply our Lands to counter secure our money. In every view this matter appears important to me. I wish our Legislature may see it in the same light.[2] We have already had one attack which we very fortunately warded, tho Virginia is unrepresented. The attempt convinces me of the risk we run by being too insatiable in our demands.[3]

We have not a word of foreign news except vague reports from the West Indies of a battle in the Channel, but nothing that can be depended upon. You may believe that we are very impatient for the Issue of so important a conflict.

I am sorry to tell you that money has fallen below any thing that you can suppose. I need give you no other proof of it than by telling you that I this day paid £537 this money for a plain suit of cloaths, £21 for plain buttons to a servant's coat & putting them on, & 26 dollars for sawing a cord of wood; grain & country produce have even risen beyond foreign articles.[4] But still I do not despair of retrieving it if my plan sh'd be adopted & be well seconded by the Legislatures. I shall do myself the honor to transmit it to you when it is properly digested. I am, Sir, with great respect y'r Excellency's most obt. Hum. Serv't   Robt. R. Livingston.

Reprinted from Clinton, *Papers* (Hastings), 5:382–83.

[1] Not found.

[2] In his January 7, 1780, letter to Livingston, Governor Clinton responded: "I agree with you, that it may be to our interest to give up a part of our western lands; if by this we may be able to enjoy the Remainder free from every claim. On this condition I would for my own Part be contented with the Boundary described in your letter." Clinton, *Papers* (Hastings), 5:445–46. For a discussion of Livingston's views on New York's land claims, see George Dangerfield, *Chancellor Robert R. Livingston of New York, 1746–1813* (New York: Harcourt, Brace & Co., 1960), pp. 118–19.

[3] See John Jay to Clinton, October 7, 1779.

[4] Livingston's accounts for his service as a delegate contain additional evidence of the impact of inflation during 1779–80. In claiming pay "from the 19 November 1779 to the 27 September 1780 [less 20 'Absent days']," Livingston listed the specie value of the dollars he had received at the Continental Treasury from January to September 1780, and for these transactions he recorded exchange rates of 40 for 1, 60 for 1, 72 for 1, and 75 for 1 successively. Miscellaneous Manuscripts, N.

George Partridge to Samuel Freeman

Dear Sir   Philadelphia Novr. 30th 1779

I have receivd yours of the 17th Instant & shall order your Paper to be superscribd, according to your Request. Mr. Gill told me that he would send me a paper weekly.[1] Be so kind as to give my Complts to him, & inform him that I have not receivd one from him since I have been here. You inform me that the House have voted a tax of 5,800,000. I feel for many honest people on whom this Tax must fall very heavy; but I as sensibly feel the necessity of the punctual payment of the money. You mention a Commee to Settle with the Army. I am at a Loss what kind of Settlement you mean, & should be pleasd to be informed. Congress have increasd. the subsistance of a Colo. to 500 Dollars per Month & others in proportion;[2] this mode of relieving them was preferred to increasing their pay, as half pay for 7 years had been previously granted. A Petition of the Genl Officers

[is] now before Congress which will soon be acted upon. I wish I had taken with me the number of Inhabitants in our State above the Age of sixteen & desire you would send it to me.

I should also be glad to be furnished with the number of Militia which have at sundry times been called into service since the Enemy Left Boston & the Service and term of time for which the Drafts were orderd. Perhaps this may be done by the Comme for Stating Accts &c without much Trouble. For news refer you to the inclosed papers only ading that some french ships of War are in Chesapeake Bay—Destination unknown. I am Sr. with Respect yr. most Humbl Servt,   G. Partridge

[*P.S.*] Yesterday a Resolve passed ordering Officers to be chargd. no more than 50 per Cent for Clothing above the former prices.[3]

RC (MiU–C: Loammi Baldwin Papers). Addressed: "Saml Freeman Esqr, Clerk to the House of Representatives, Boston."

[1] John Gill, the publisher of the *Continental Journal and Weekly Advertiser* (Boston).

[2] Congress had taken this action on August 18, 1779. See *JCC*, 14:978; and John Jay to George Washington, August 20, 1779, note 1.

[3] Congress actually took this action on November 25 as part of a comprehensive plan to clothe the army and help Continental officers cope with inflation. *JCC*, 15:1304–6. For a discussion of the background of this problem, see Erna Risch, *Supplying Washington's Army* (Washington: U.S. Government Printing Office, 1981), pp. 296–98.

Nathaniel Peabody to Josiah Bartlett

Dear Sir   No. 16   Philada Novr. 30th. 1779

Your favour of the 4th instant has been duly Recd.[1] And am extreamly Obliged to you for the information therein Contained— have nothing worth Your Notice to Communicate only that Genl Whipple is appointed a Commissr of the board of high Admiralty for these United States.[2] I earnestly wish your influence with him, to Accept the appointment, as it is a matter of the highest importance, Especially to the Eastern States, for that board to Consist of members whose Knowledge in those matters is Equal to the important Trust that will be reposed in them.

C——ss have agreed to Draw Bills of Exc—— on Mr J—y to the amount of £100,000 Sterg and the like Sum on Mr L——ns payable at 6 mo. Sight which are to be Sold at the Current Rate of Exchange for the Supply the Treasury.[3] What Effect this will have Cant Say and time only will make Known. I am Sir in hast Your most Obedt. and very huml Servt,   Nathl Peabody

[P.S.] As I Recd. no letters from your Quarter this Post, Suspect they were intercepted by the *way*.

RC (NhD: Bartlett Papers).
[1] Bartlett's November 4, 1779, letter to Peabody is in Bartlett, *Papers* (Mevers), pp. 272–73.
[2] See Samuel Huntington to Thomas Waring, November 27, 1779.
[3] On November 23 Congress had resolved to draw £200,000 sterling in bills of exchange on John Jay and Henry Laurens in Europe, and on November 29 a specific plan for drawing the bills was adopted. *JCC*, 15:1299–1300, 1326–27.

Rhode Island Delegates to William Greene

Sir,   In Congress. Philadelphia Novr. 30th, 1779
    Mr. Ellery arrived Yesterday and this Day took his Seat in Congress. By Yesterdays Post we were honored with your Excellencys Letter of the 19th Instant enclosing a State of the Proceedings of the Genl. Assembly respecting Capt. Tyler.[1] We have laid that State before Congress who have referred it to the Comee to whom the Petition of Capt. Tyler was referred. We conceive it will give full Satisfaction to Congress as it certainly throws the Matter in a very different Light from the Suggestions made in Capt. Tylers Petition.
    Your Excellency must before this have recd. Mr. Marchant's Letter wherein he enclosed a Warrant in Favour of the State for three hundred thousand Dollars, upon Our State Treasurer.[2]
    This We conceive superceeds the Necessity of any Application in the mode Your Excellency has pointed out—That Sum most certainly is the last the State may expect out of the Treasury of the United States or from any of their publick Funds—For all Monies must now come from the States for every Purpose. We are therefore well assurd the State will be deeply impressed with the Necessity of strict œconomy and every possible Exertion. We enclose Your Excellency the Weekly News Papers & beg Leave to subscribe Ourselves Your most obedient and very humble Servts.   William Ellery

                                                    Hy. Marchant

P.S. Mr. Marchant proposes to set out tomorrow.

RC (R–Ar: Letters to Governors). Written by Marchant, and signed by Marchant and Ellery.
[1] Governor Greene's November 19 letter to the Rhode Island delegates is in Staples, *Rhode Island*, pp. 264–65. For a discussion of the case of Capt. Isaac Tyler, see Henry Marchant to Greene, November 16, 1779, note 4.
[2] See Marchant to Greene, November 16, 1779.

George Partridge to Joseph Ward

Dear Sir   Philadelphia Novr. 31st. 1779[1]
    Yours of the 18th instant is come to hand. I am very sorry that the Busin ss to which you refer has not been acted upon before this

time, as a state of suspense is very disagreeable & perhaps injurious, there are two Reasons which have occasioned the Delay, the one is the variety of publick Matters which in our present fluctuating State arrests the Attention of Congress; the other is, the Oppinion of Some Gentlemen in Congress that the Department is an unnecessary Expence, and that the Business would be done as well by the Inspectors of the Army. This oppinion has prevailed with the Commee. on your memorial who have made a Report accordingly. I am not well enough acquainted with the Numbers or the Duty of the Inspectors to determine whither the Business can be done to Advantage by them, or what is the Number or Expence of the Officers under you. I wish you would inform me of these Facts as the Report may lay for sometime.[2] I Am convincd. of your Integrity and Patriotism & am sure that you would not wish that the Publick should incure an Expence without receiving a Solid Advantage even if you were the Gainer.

The Sentiments containd in your Letter relative to other matters I read with Pleasure but have not Leisure just now to Answer. I am Sr. with great Esteem your most obedt. Humbl Servt,

Geo. Partridge

P.S. The oppinion of Gentlemen to discontinue the Department of Musters does not in the least arise from want of confidence in the Integrity and Ability of the Officers on the Contrary I think of no Department in the Army, except yours, against which I have not heard many Complaints.

N.B. You are not [to] determine from what I have said of the Report of a Commee that a new arrangment will take place, that is very uncertain.   GP

RC (ICHi: Joseph Ward Papers). Addressed: "Coll. Joseph Ward, Commissary Genl of Musters, Camp West Point."

[1] Although clearly dated "Novr. 31st" by Partridge, the letter is obviously misdated. Since he wrote another letter (to Samuel Freeman) on November 30, it seems likely that Partridge actually wrote this one on December 1.

[2] The report of the committee, which recommended the abolition of the "Mustering Department" and its replacement by "the Inspectors of the Army," is in the hand of Partridge, who had been added to the committee on November 16. *JCC*, 15:1274. It is endorsed: "Report of Comee on Petition of Azariah Horton in behalf of Officers in Muster Master dept. Delivd. Novr. 29, 1779." "Acted upon Jany 12th. 1780." See PCC, item 19, 3:187–89; and *JCC*, 15:1329–30.

For the ultimate dissolution of the "Mustering Department," see Joseph Spencer to Ward, August 23, 1779, note.

Samuel Holten's Diary

[December 1–2, 1779]

Dec. 1. Wednesday. Congress dined with the Minisr. of France; the diner was grand & elegant. My health is better.

2. Thursday. A very Stormy day, the rain has been very heavy. I returned from Congress unwell, before they adjourned.[1]

MS (MDaAr).
[1] This day Holten also wrote the following brief letter to the Board of Treasury, which immediately complied with his request. *JCC*, 15:1344.
"Gentlemen, I shall consider myself under obligations, if you'l report to Congress a resolution in my favor for five thousand dollars, for which sum, the state I've the Honor to represent, will be Accountable." Holten Papers, DLC.

Samuel Huntington to Richard Bache

Sir,   Philada Decem 2d 1779
    You will receive herewith enclos'd an Act of Congress of the first instant refering the Accounts of the Postmaster General to the board of Treasury to be adjusted and liquidated and also augmenting the salaries of the Postmaster General & the Comptrolers to commence on the first Day of September last.[1]
    I am, Sir, with great respect, your humble Servt,
                                                    S.H. President

LB (DNA: PCC, item 14).
[1] This December 1 resolve was a belated response to Bache's October 5 letter to Huntington reminding Congress of the insufficiency of Post Office department salaries and of his continued inability to pay post riders punctually because payments on the department's accounts were chronically in arrears. See *JCC*, 15:1149, 1203–4, 1338–39; and PCC, item 61, fols. 43–46, 459–62.
    Congress had long been aware of deficiencies in the Post Office, but seemed incapable of offering more than piecemeal reforms, as it adopted recommendations of the Post Office Committee on four occasions between October 1779 and January 1780 in response to Bache's complaints. See Huntington to Bache, December 29, 1779, and January 8, 1780; *JCC*, 15:1411–12, 1415, 16:19, 21–22; and Jennings B. Sanders, *Evolution of the Executive Departments of the Continental Congress, 1774–1789* (Chapel Hill: University of North Carolina Press, 1935), pp. 155–57.

Samuel Huntington to John Rutledge

Sir,   Philada Decem 2d 1779
    You will receive herewith two Letters directed to the Governor or President of Georgia, they contain Acts of Congress the same as those address'd to your Excellency which accompany this.[1]
    As we are ignorant whether there be any Governor or Civil Government at present existing in Georgia *under the revolution* I am to desire your Excellency to forward those letters to the Governor or Supreme executive power in Georgia if any such there be otherwise to retain them until such powers exist in Georgia.[2]
    I have the honour to be with great respect, your Excy's hble Servt,
                                                    S.H. President

LB (DNA: PCC, item 14).
 [1] The identity of Huntington's enclosures can only be conjectured, but they may have consisted of all the resolutions for the relief of South Carolina and Georgia Congress had adopted since November 10 when Lincoln's report on the failure of the siege of Savannah was received. See *JCC*, 15:1255–57, 1296, 1313–15. If this surmise is accurate, Huntington was sending the first group of these resolves to Rutledge a second time, for he had already transmitted them to the governor the day they were adopted. See Huntington to Rutledge, November 11, 1779. Finally, Huntington may even have enclosed Congress' December 4 resolve endorsing Washington's decision to march the Virginia troops under his command to South Carolina, since this letter appears in the presidential letterbook after other letters dated December 4 and may be misdated. See PCC, item 14, fols. 240–42; and Huntington to Washington, December 4, 1779. See also John Mathews to Benjamin Lincoln, December 9, and Huntington to Lincoln, December 18, 1779.
 [2] For discussion of conditions in Georgia during this period and her inability to maintain representation in Congress, see Edward Langworthy to John Houstoun, April 5, 1779, note 2.

Samuel Huntington to James Wilkinson

Sir,   Philada Decem 2d 1779
   You will receive herewith enclos'd two printed Acts of Congress of the 25th & 26th ulto for your Government on the subject to which they relate in the clothing department.[1]
   I am Sir, your hble Servant,   S.H. President

LB (DNA: PCC, item 14).
 [1] For these "printed Acts" concerning the issuance of clothing for the Continental Army, see *JCC*, 15:1304–6, 1313–14; and Evans, *American Bibliography*, no. 16,583.

John Fell to Robert Morris

Dear Sir,   Philada. Decemr 3d. 1779
   I hope my not answering your oblidging favour of the 7th ulto.[1] will not be imputed to neglect, but to other reasons. Agreeable to your kind invitation I had thought of Paying you a Visit at Mount Holly, but these [fears?] of delicasey prevented as it was just about the time of Election for Delegates, another reason just when I Received your Letter Mrs. Fell and Son Peter came to pay me a visit, and you know I could not well leave them. They have been gone 10 Days and very unlickely for me about that time, Dr Weatherspoon and Dr Scudder, left Congress and I cannot leave Mr. Houston without leaving the State unrepresented. As yet we hear nothing of our new Collegue, and I have been informd he will not come,[2] neither have I heard what is like to be done for us. I wait impatiently for the determination of your Honorable House regarding our allowance as on that must depend my continuing or not in this disagreeable situation.

There is now a Motion before Congress to Remove to Hartford, it was deliverd in but has not yet been debated. Yesterday Coll. Blaine was appointed Commissary General of Purchases and to have a Sallery of 20000 Ds. is Proposed, but no Commission, and I hope no more Commissions will ever be allowed to any Officer in future either in the Staff or Civil departments. The Treasury Board is put in to Commission, the Members are Mr. Ez. Forman, Mr. Turnbull of Connecticut, and Mr. Gibson late Auditor General. The Marine Committee, now the Board of Admiralty, is also just now finish'd being Put in Commission, the Members chose are a Mr. Warring for S Carolina, Mr Whipple from New Hampshire and Mr. Bryant late Vice President and now a Member of Assembly of this State (Pennsylvania). (Much against my opinion). The Sallery of the Commissioners is to be 14000 Dolls Per annum for Each Board. The Commercial Committee have Reported, to have that Put in Commission, by the Style of the Board of Trade.[3] I am Confident if this Board had been Put in Commission with good Men, Millions would have been saved, (from the Experiance I have made). This moment Congress have determin'd to leave Philadelphia (past 1 oClock) now debating about the time, next will be the Place. I do not imagine the Debates will be finishd this Day. (The time is fixt to Remove on the last Saturday in April; The Places in Nomination are Hartford, Albany & Fredericksburgh. The question to appoint the Place to remove to, is Postponed to the first Monday in January, in order to accomodate the Southern and Eastern Gentlemen, I mention'd Burlington for their Consideration;)[4] I am Dear sir, With great Respect Your Real friend & Humble Servt,   John Fell

RC (NjR: Robert Morris Papers).

[1] The draft of Morris' November 7 letter to Fell is in the Morris Papers, NjR.

[2] Dr. Thomas Henderson (1743–1824), who had been elected November 17 to serve with Fell and Houston for the ensuing year, declined the appointment, serving instead in the New Jersey assembly, 1780–84. Abraham Clark, who was elected December 25 to take Henderson's place, took his seat in Congress on January 25, 1780. *JCC*, 15:1323–24, 16:84–85; *DAB*.

[3] For the fate of this report, see Fell's Diary, November 30, 1779, note 2.

[4] William Ellery's December 1 motion seeking "Congress's removal from the city of Philadelphia" was debated on December 3 when Congress resolved that it would "adjourn from the city of Philadelphia" at the termination of its meeting "the last Saturday of April next." Consideration of the site was postponed first to January 3, then to February 28, and finally to March 13, when it was delayed indefinitely. Two weeks later, however, Ellery proposed that Congress adjourn to Hartford at the end of April. This motion, as well as a similar one in favor of Trenton, was rejected. Congress also voted against a suggestion that it repeal its December 3 resolution altogether. Nonetheless, this flurry of activity ended the attempt to remove Congress from Philadelphia until 1783 when it became a central and divisive sectional issue. See *JCC*, 15:1339, 1344, 16:9–10, 211–12, 255, 291–93.

Samuel Holten's Diary

[December 3–4, 1779]
3. Friday. The President of Congress drank tea with us, No news this day.
4. Saturday. Congress Spent part of the day, considering the commissaries & Quarter masters departments.

MS (MDaAr).

Samuel Huntington to Juan de Miralles

Sir,   Philada Decemr 4th 1779
The bearer Mr Umberland is the Express who brought your Despatches from Mr Hall[1] at South Carolina.
I find upon enquiry he came express for that purpose and is not one of our stated Expresses.
Congress are content you should pay this Express for his service if you please.
I am Sir with great respect, your hble Servt,
                                            S.H. President

LB (DNA: PCC, item 14).
[1] George Abbot Hall, who had forwarded a sealed pouch of papers to Miralles from the governor general of Cuba, Diego José Navarro, for which he charged 4,000 pesos. Miralles' December 31, 1779, letter to Navarro explaining the circumstances of the delivery of this packet and its great expense, is in Papeles Procedentes de Cuba, Legajo 1281, Archivo General de Indias, Seville (Aileen Moore Topping translation, Manuscript Division, DLC).

Samuel Huntington to Jeremiah Wadsworth

Sir,   Philadelphia Decemr 4th 1779
You will receive herewith enclos'd two Acts of Congress; one of this day and one of the 29th Ulto by which you will be inform'd that your resignation is accepted & Colo Blaine appointed to succeed you in the Commissaries Department, at the same time you are desired with the Deputies under you to continue in the business until your Successor is in capacity to execute the Duties of the Office.[1]
I am Sir, with great respect, your hble Servant,
                                        Sam. Huntington President

RC (CtHi: Wadsworth Papers). In a clerical hand and signed by Huntington.
[1] Congress had resolved on November 29 that Commissary General Wadsworth "have leave to resign his office on the first day of January next," but added on December 4 that Wadsworth should "continue in the business of supplying the army"

until his successor, Ephraim Blaine, took up the duties of the office. *JCC*, 15:1326, 1349.

Huntington had informed Blaine of his election as commissary general of purchases on December 2, in a brief letter of the third. *JCC*, 15:1343; and Blaine Papers, DLC. In his December 7 reply, however, Blaine indicated that before he could assume the new office he must first confer with Wadsworth and General Washington, and not until January 5 did he signify that he was ready "to enter upon the business of my Department" as soon as Congress made explicit provision of compensating him and his deputies, which it did almost immediately. See PCC, item 165, fols. 307–13; and *JCC*, 16:18, 20–21.

Samuel Huntington to George Washington

Sir,   Philadelphia Decemr 4th 1779
I am honour'd with your several favours of 23d, 24th, 27th & 29th Ulto.[1]
By the enclos'd Act of Congress of this Day your Excellency will be inform'd it is their desire that the Troops of the Virginia line be immediately put in Motion agreable to what is mentioned in your letter of the 29th of November.[2]
I have the honour to be, with the greatest respect, your Excy's hble Servt,   Sam Huntington President

RC (DLC: Washington Papers). In a clerical hand and signed by Washington.
[1] Washington's letters to Congress of November 24, 27, and 29 are in PCC, item 152, 8:185–98; and Washington, *Writings* (Fitzpatrick), 14:177–80, 202, 206–8. The letter of the "23d" is probably Washington's letter of that date to Lt. Col. Morgan Connor, who enclosed it with a December 2 letter to Congress requesting leave of absence, which Washington had endorsed and Congress immediately granted. This decision Huntington reported to Connor in a brief letter of the following day. See *JCC*, 15:1340; and PCC, item 14, fol. 240, item 78, 5:429–36.
[2] *JCC*, 15:1347.

North Carolina Delegates to Charles Stewart

Philadelphia Decr. 4th. 1779.
We beg leave to recommend Mr John Cheesborough to you[1] for the appointment of D. Commissary Genl. of Issues in the southern department. This gentleman has served long in the Army, and has behaved with ability, assiduity and integrity, and has the fullest confidence and approbation of the officers of the North Carolina Brigade.
With due esteem we are, Sir, Your Most Obt. Humble Servts,
                              Cornl Harnett

                              Wm. Sharpe

RC (MH–H: bMS Am 1243). Written by Harnett and signed by Harnett and Sharpe.
[1] Colonel Stewart was commissary general of issues.

William Sharpe to Richard Caswell

Sir,   Philadelphia Decr. 5th. 1779
    The North Carolina Brigade is at this place on their way to join
Genl. Lincoln.[1] Their number is about seven hundred rank & file. It
is not altogether certain whether they will go by land or water, I
rather think, the former. Genl. Washington holds the Virginia Troops
in readiness to march there also; yesterday Congress sent advice for
them to move on immediately.[2] Their number cannot be reckoned
at more than 13 or 1400 as a large number of that line will have
served out their time for which they were enlisted, in March next.
Three or four weeks ago the enemy at New York had embarked
8000 Troops, but were countermanded, supposed to be in consequence of Count de Grass being in or near Chessepeak. Genl. Washington is of opinion that they are preparing to embark again; but
cannot learn their distination. They have lately received dispatches
from their Count, the contents of which has not transpired.
    We have repeated accounts of an engagement in the English Chan-
nel on the 4th of Septr., and that the combined Fleet was victorious;
but not authenticated agreeable to our wishes. Our Army is busy
Cantoning—one Divission on the east side Hudsons river—the Cavalry near Danbury in the border of Connecticut—the main body
near the Scots plains on this side the river. It is supposed head
quarters will be at Morris Town.
    It would be improper to mention to you on paper the number of
Our Army—much might be said of their Virtue, good order &
discipline.
    The collected force of the enemy in New York & it's
vicinity is supposed to be upward of sixteen thousand. If they were
enterprizing the consequences might be serious.
    Our Treasury is nearly exhausted—we have great dependance on
the several States for its restoration. We are about to negociate, to
the amount of £200,000 stirling in Bills of exchange on our Minister
at Madrid & our Commissioner who is gone to Holland, from which
we hope for some relief.
    I momently look for Messrs. Burke, Penn & Jones to deliver Mr.
Harnett & myself from this House of bondage.[3]
    I intreat your Excellency to do me the honor to address a few lines
to me in Rowan which is a place destitute of good intelligence.
    With the utmost esteem & respect I am, Sir Your Most Obt
humble Servt.   Wm. Sharpe

P.S. I this moment recollected my having taken an extract of Genl.
Washingtons Letter of the 20th Ulto, which I enclose you—that to
which it refers is of a secret nature.[4]   Wm. Sharpe

RC (PHi: North Carolina Manuscripts).

[1] For the movement of the North Carolina troops, see Samuel Huntington to Washington, October 5 and November 11, 1779.

[2] See Huntington to Washington, December 4, 1779.

[3] In fact, Harnett was granted a leave of absence on December 7 and received $5,000 from the Continental treasury on December 11 for the use of the North Carolina delegates. Sharpe, who last voted on December 4, received $3,500 from the treasury on December 6. *JCC*, 15:1348, 1353, 1360, 1371. In his expense account submitted to the North Carolina Assembly on February 8, 1780, Sharpe claimed payment of $19,264 for travel expenses and expenses while attending Congress from April 12 to December 14, 1779. Miscellaneous Manuscript Collection, DLC; and Burnett, *Letters*, 5:30–31n.

[4] Washington's letter of November 20, expressing concern over the vulnerability of the southern states, was read in Congress on November 26 and assigned to a committee which reported the following day and again on November 30, when Congress appointed a committee of two—Philip Schuyler and Henry Marchant—to confer with Washington at headquarters. See *JCC*, 15:1312, 1323, 1331–32; Washington, *Writings* (Fitzpatrick), 17:150–51; and the following entry.

Committee at Headquarters to Congress

Head Quarters, Morris Town, Decr. 7th 1779

The Committee appointed to repair to Head Quarters for the purposes mentioned In the resolutions of Congress of the 30th ult. beg leave to report.[1]

That having laid before the Commander In Chief the resolutions of Congress they were charged with and the papers referred to In the same, His Excellency was pleased to furnish your Committee with Copy of a letter he had the honor to address Congress on the 29th ult.,[2] that they perfectly agree with his Excellency on the propriety of detatching the Virginia line to reinforce the Forces under the Command of Major General Lincoln, That the reasons given by his Excellency in the letter referred to for Conveying them thither by water appear to Your Committee Conclusive. They therefore Intreat permission to Recommend that the Commander of The French fleet now In Cheasapeek Bay Should be pressed to afford Sufficient Convoy and the necessity of It urged on the principles Stated In the General's letter, and on the recommendation of the Minister of france "that the Attention of Congress should be Given to the Overtures made by Don Juan de Miralles."[3]

Your Committee beg leave further to Observe that so Capital a detatchment from this Army, Considering the Extensive posts to be maintained & the Enemys position and force, may Induce them to an offensive operation against It, which In the decreased Strength of the Army, when the Virginia troops Shall be detatched, would they Conceive be attended with at least very disagreable If not ruinous Consequences: they therefore humbly recommend that Immediate and decisive measures should be adopted To draw from the Several States In the Union their respective Quotas to Compleat the battalions now on the Establishment as they humbly Conceive that the

Militia which the Commander In Chief is Impowered by the seventh resolution to Call Into the field is a resource too precarious to be depended upon In the present Situation of Affairs.

Your Committee beg leave further to report that having conferred with the Commander In Chief on the Subject Matter of the papers transmitted to Congress by the Minister of France & Don Juan De Mirallis,[4] they find his Excellency's Sentiments perfectly coinciding with theirs on the Subject, to wit, that It would be highly Imprudent to Enter on any Offensive Operation against any of the Enemys fortifications Or forces South of Georgia, previous to the reduction or expulsion of the British Force from that State. It is therefore humbly Submitted that It Should be proposed to their most Christian & Catholic Majestys Ambassadors, Agents, Governors or Commanders, that a fleet In Such force of both or either of said powers as would in all probability Insure a Superiority on the Coasts South of South Carolina over any british naval force which may reasonably be Expected In that Quarter, should be sent as Early as possible to Charles Town together with five thousand land forces to Operate In Conjuction with what American force may be In that quarter against the British in Georgia, that after having reduced or expelled the Enemy from that State, the Combined force should proceed to the reduction of the british Garrisons In East or West Florida as should be deemed most Expedient by the Contracting parties, And that having Accomplished this or faild In the operations the American troops Should be reconvoyed to Such of the united States as may be agreed upon.

Your Committee beg leave to Observe on that part of the paper delivered by Don Juan de Miralles which regards a Supply of provisions for the Inhabitants of the City of Havanna and Isle of Cuba, That It would be Improper to Make a pointed promise to furnish Such Supply In part or the whole until It is put beyond all doubt, that there will be a Surplus after the Army and Navy of the united States, and the fleet of our Ally are amply provided, That nevertheless, as an Inducement to procure a Spanish force to Cooperate with our troops In Georgia, If they cannot do It without an aid in point of provision, some risk Should be run and a dependance put on Extraordinary exertions to procure provisions In this Quarter for our own Army.

All which Is humbly Submitted,   Ph. Schuyler

                                                  Hy. Marchant

RC (DNA: PCC, item 33). Written by Schuyler and signed by Schuyler and Marchant.
    [1] On November 30, after considering General Washington's November 20 letter on "the state of matters in the Southern Quarter," Congress appointed Henry Marchant and Philip Schuyler a committee "to repair to head quarters and confer with the Commander in Chief, on the state of the southern department." They were also instructed to confer on "the subject of the papers transmitted to Congress by the

Minister Plenipotentiary of his most Christian majesty and Don Juan de Mirailles."
JCC, 15:1331–32.

This report of the committee was read in Congress on December 11, when it was
referred to Robert R. Livingston, John Mathews, and Roger Sherman, whose recommendations were read and adopted on December 16. These included the draft of a
letter for the chevalier de La Luzerne to be sent over the signature of President
Huntington and instructions to Gen. Benjamin Lincoln "to correspond and concert
with the Governor of Havanna . . . to insure the reduction of the enemy's force" in
Georgia and East Florida. See *JCC*, 15: 1368–70, 1386–88; and Samuel Huntington to
La Luzerne, December 17, and to Lincoln, December 18, 1779.

[2] In his November 29 letter to Huntington, Washington again discussed the southern theater in light of new reports "that the Enemy are making or preparing a pretty
considerable embarkation of troops from New York." Washington, *Writings* (Fitzpatrick), 17:206–8.

[3] This is a translated extract from the chevalier de La Luzerne's November 26 letter
to Congress urging support for a memorial from Don Juan de Miralles. See Samuel
Huntington to La Luzerne, December 17, 1779.

[4] See ibid., note 2.

Samuel Holten to William Gordon

Revd. & dear Sir.   Phila. Decr. 7th. 1779.
Your favor of the 22d of Apl. last came safe to hand; And I
Should have done myself the pleasure of noticeing it before, had it
not been for the length of time between your letters & an expression
in your last which induced me to believe that it wou'd be most agreeable to you, to drop a correspondence,[1] which, I always considered
must be burthensome on your part; and tho I have ever considered
myself under obligation for your letters, yet I knew I was not wantg
in point of numbers before this; But fearing you might think I had
treated your last with some neglect is the reason of this address,
which, I expect will be the last as I hope soon to have the pleasure of
seeing you in Boston.

I believe I should have attempted, to have given you my Sentiments of the state of affairs in Europe respecting America; but
considering you have lately had (no doubt) the best intelligence on
this head from the Hon. J. Adams; I shall ownly mention that if the
combined fleets should get the better of the english fleet, I expect
that an negotiation may even take place, otherwise not.

I recollect, that some time since a letter was read in Congress
from T.P. inclosing part of a letter from a correspondence of his (as
I understood it) mentioning some words that had been expressed by
a late member from New-york;[2] I had reason to think I knew the
hand, and I believe some others did, but (I think) no order of Congress was taken thereon.

The disordered state of our Finances are truly distressing; and the
greatest exertions of the several states are become absolutely necessary to supply the Continental treasury with money sufficient to pay
the current expences.

I am happy to inform you that there is great union in Congress, & things here are going on as well as can be expected, under our present circumstances, respecting our money. I am Sir with great respect your most obedient Servant.

FC (DLC: Holten Papers). In the hand of Samuel Holten.

[1] No prior letters from Holten to Gordon have been found.

[2] Holten was apparently referring to Thomas Paine, who had enclosed with his April 23, 1779, letter to Congress an accusation directed at Gouverneur Morris. Paine's enclosure was an extract of a letter from an unidentified person containing an "advertisement" signed "An Impartial American," which included the following damaging quotation attributed to a delegate from New York. "Thank God, we of this State [*i.e., New York*] hold the *keys* of the thirteen States in our own hands, & it is in our power, to give them up to the king of Great Britain, if they won't secure to us those lands, that we so justly claim." On the authority of a friend, Paine's informant identified the offending New York delegate as Gouverneur Morris, who was reported to have made the statement "before he was chosen a delegate." See *JCC*, 14:501; and PCC, item 55, fols. 55–61.

Samuel Huntington to George Washington

Sir,   Philadelphia 7th Decemr 1779

I am honour'd with your Excys favours of the 2d & 4th instant.[1]

You will receive herewith enclos'd two Acts of Congress of the 6th instant. By the one your Excellency will observe that Congress approve of Colo Baylor's Regiment of Dragoons being sent to South Carolina, and have directed the board of War to give the necessary orders for that purpose.

The other is designed to regulate the proceedings with respect to Officers absent beyond the term of their furloughs, or without leave & such as shall neglect or refuse to join their respective Corps or appear before a Court Martial when properly notified as the nature of the Case may require.[2]

I have the Honour to be, with the greatest respect, your Excys hble Servt.   Sam. Huntington President

RC (DLC: Washington Papers). In a clerical hand and signed by Huntington.

[1] Washington's letters are in PCC, item 152, 8:199–206; and Washington, *Writings* (Fitzpatrick), 17:212–13, 216–17.

[2] This resolve was adopted pursuant to a Board of War recommendation, which had already had Washington's approval. See *JCC*, 15:1351–52; and PCC, item 147, 2:631–34.

Philip Schuyler to Robert R. Livingston

Dear Sir   Morris town Tuesday Decr. 7 1779

I arrived early on Sunday morning. Mr Marchant didn't Join me until Yesterday at noon.[1] The General has Confidentially Communicated to me his apprehensions from the distressed State of our public affairs, his army is scantily fed from hand to mouth and Such a Scarcity of Forrage prevails that he has been under the necessity of permitting a very large number of horses to go to such a distance from Camp that a Sudden push of the Enemies unless he Could maintain his Ground would expose him to the Mortification of losing his Stores. The public officers are without money and Incredibly In debt In that Every Specie of distress is Experienced In this Quarter and Confident I am It will Increase to such a degree as will bring on a Seperation of the Army, or the necessity of living on free quarter, unless the most Speedy & Strenous exertions are gone Into to Supply provisions & Cash, For Gods Sake urge that Something be done with the Money, that is to Establish It at some rate of depreciation, that only can and will relieve us.

Pray let no time be lost In Calling on the States to Compleat their Quotas of troops, but do not ask It as supplicants. Alarm them by a true State of your Situation and Call on them In a tone of authority.

Gen. Greene wished my opinion on the time & manner of making his resignation with the least Injury to the public. I have urged the necessity of his continuing, advised for his own sake that he should Continue to Serve on any Salary Congress should offer wether he Should Conceive It adequate or not, and that he should Strongly recommend to his deputys not to quit the Service. I recommended that he should send Congress his Opinion on the proper Salarys for his Deputys. I believe he will do It, and have hopes that he will Continue to Serve.

If Mr. Blaine does not Accept of the Commissariate pray offer It to Mr. Royal Flint who will be Supported In the duty of office by Wadsworth. G. Greene Informs me that Flint is a man of Business & resource.

Pray favor me with a line from time to time. If Congress adjourns to Albany I wish to know It without delay.

If the board of war should be organized On Your plan and the appointment be offered as You wish It will be necessary to give more Ample powers than the board at present possesses. I shall leave this In ten minutes.

Adieu My Dear Sir, I am affectionately & Sincerely Your &c &c

P Schuyler

RC (NHi: Robert R. Livingston Papers).

[1] Schuyler and Henry Marchant had been appointed on November 30 "to repair to head quarters and confer with the Commander in Chief on the state of the southern department." See Committee at Headquarters to Congress, this date.

Samuel Huntington to
the Chevalier de La Luzerne

Sir,   Philadelphia Decemr 8th 1779

I am favour'd with your friendly intelligence of the 6th instant respecting the capture of the Greyhound by eight American Sailors and the proceedings of the Judges of the admiralty at Port au Paix consequent thereon.

I have the honour to transmit you two Acts of Congress of the 14th of October 1777, and the 6th instant, by the latter you will please to observe it is the pleasure of Congress that the money arising from the Sale of the Capture be paid to the Captors agreeable to the Act of Congress of the 14th of October above mentioned, which entitles them to receive the same, so that the monies arising from the Sale of the Capture will remain with the Secretary of the Court of Admiralty at Port au Paix and await the order of the Captors their Agents or Attornies to receive the same.[1]

I have the honour to be, with great respect, your hble Servt

LB (DNA: PCC, item 14).

[1] For the two resolves Huntington enclosed, see *JCC*, 9:802, 15:1356. In his letter of December 6, the French minister had simply sought advice on disposing of the proceeds from the sale of the *Greyhound*, a British vessel captured by eight American sailors and condemned at Port au Paix, St. Domingue. PCC, item 95, 1:37–42. In his December 11 reply to this response from Congress, La Luzerne went on to suggest that Congress make explicit provision for having the money in question paid to the captors or their agents and initiate a search for the seamen in Massachusetts and Rhode Island, their last known residences. Ibid., 1:17–20. For Congress' response to the minister's second letter, see Huntington to La Luzerne, December 11, 1779.

Samuel Huntington to William Shippen, Jr.

Sir,   Philada Decemr 8th 1779

You will receive herewith enclos'd the Copy of a report from the Chamber of Accounts on the Memorial of Lewis Weiss, together with an Act of Congress ordering that the Copy be transmitted to you with directions to report especially thereon.[1]

It may be proper to observe the memorial was exhibited to Congress by Mr Weiss as Attorney to John Brown [Bonn], Warden of the single brethren at Bethlehem. The Account of their demand has been refer'd to the board of Treasury & liquidated by the Chamber of Accounts as per copy of their report inclos'd, the expence being incurr'd in the medical department Congress have thought proper it should be transmitted to you with directions to report especially thereon as by their act enclos'd I have before mentioned.[2]

I am Sir with esteem & respect, your hble Servant,
S.H. President[3]

LB (DNA: PCC, item 14).

[1] For the enclosed December 4 "Act of Congress" and "report from the chamber of Accounts," see *JCC*, 15:1349; and PCC, item 136, 3:873–74. For the memorial of Lewis Weiss, seeking compensation for the use of Moravian buildings in Bethlehem, Pa., by the hospital department in 1777–78, and supporting accounts and vouchers signed by John Bonn, "Warden of the Single Brethren of Bethlehem," see *JCC*, 15:1209, 1269; and PCC, item 41, 10:399–422.

[2] The commissioners of the chamber of accounts, Eleazar McComb and Resolve Smith, had recommended payment of $3,077 to John Bonn on this claim, and in his December 13 response to Huntington's letter, Dr. Shippen endorsed the commissioners recommendation. See *JCC*, 15:1373; and PCC, item 19, 6:513–14.

[3] President Huntington also wrote brief letters this day to John Brown (longtime secretary to the Committee of Commerce and the Marine Committee) and to William Grayson, notifying the former that he had been appointed secretary to the new Admiralty Board and the latter that he had been elected commissioner to the Board of War. See PCC, item 14, fols. 243–44; and *JCC*, 15:1344, 1360.

John Mathews to Benjamin Lincoln

Dear Sir,   Philadelphia Decr 9th 1779

Major Clarkson called on me late last evening to inform me of his intention of setting off this morning for Chs. Town this being the day appointed for Thanksgiving renders it impracticable to collect the Committee,[1] but as I think it is necessary you should be acquainted with what is done respecting your Department I shall take the liberty of communicating the same to you individually.

After much altercation I have at last, prevailed on Congress to consent to the Virginia troops proceeding to join you. The great impediment that has hitherto been in the way, was the long & difficult march & the hopes of procuring the aid of the French fleet as a Convoy, has suspended the determination for some time but convinced myself of the urgent necessity of an immediate reinforcement, & seeing no prospect of the so much to be wished for aid, I yesterday moved Congress to permit the troops to proceed by land, which after long, & warm debate was consented to. The Genl. was directed by a Resolve of the 4th Inst to put the Virginia line in motion for this place,[2] their being previously ready, I suppose they are so by this day. & in consequence of the Resolve yesterday, they will now continue their march with all possible expedition. The No Carolina Brigade left this City the 5th. In addition to the Virginia & No Carolina Infantry, I have procured the whole of Bayler's horse who will march from hence (where they now are) on the 4th Inst. The State of the troops are as follows. 1066 Virginians, 409 No Carolina, for the War. 775 V., 71 N.C. engaged untill 31 March. 58 V., 160 N.C. till last of April. 128 V., 64 N.C. till last of June. 157 V., 24

N.C. till last of Septr. Total Infantry 2912. The times of Service of the horse, I don't exactly know, but their numbers are 125. Makes the whole force intended to join you 3037. I wish to God they were all safe with you. I would readily compound for your getting 2000. I should be obliged to you to communicate the contents of this to the Governor, not having time to write to him. Had I earlier notice should have wrote more fully to yourself.

I am Dr General, with the most sincere Esteem, Yr Obedt Servt,
Jno. Mathews[3]

MS not found; reprinted from Frederic R. Kirkland, ed., *Letters on the American Revolution in the Library at "Karolfred,"* 2 vols. (Philadelphia: Privately printed, 1941–52), 2:66–67.

[1] On November 10 Mathews had replaced Henry Laurens on the committee appointed "to correspond with the commanding officer in the southern department." *JCC*, 15:1253.

[2] See Samuel Huntington to Washington, December 4, 1779. For the consequences of this decision, see also Committee at Camp to Congress, December 7, 1779.

[3] Mathews also wrote a letter to Lincoln on December 15, from which only the following extract survives: "Col. Washington informs me, that about 50 of his men are mounted on heavy waggon horses, totally unfit for the service they are appropriated to, and the State of the Continental Treasury at present, will not admit of purchases to replace such as are unfit . . . . as a body of good horse are capable of rendering essential Service in that Country, and considering the imminent danger that now threatens it, I should imagine Gentle'n who had horses fit for the purpose would not scruple to devote them to the immediate, and necessary defence of their Country. From the death of Pulaski, I imagine that Legion will soon dwindle into nothing. I therefore intend applying to Congress to have them reduced, and incorporated into the other Corps. . . ." *C. F. Libbie Catalog* (November 15 and 16, 1889), item 583.

Samuel Holten's Diary

[December 10–11, 1779]

Decr. 10. Friday. I spent part of this day with the come. on Genl. Arnold's Accounts.

11. Saturday. We have had no new intelligence this day. Congress sit late. My health is much better.

MS (MDaAr).

William Churchill Houston to John Stevens

Dear Sir   Philada. 10 Decr. 1779.

I have heard from several Quarters that the Legislature do not approve the Delegates drawing Money on Account from the Continental Treasury. Indeed I am a good Deal in the same Sentiment, And therefore have never done it. On this Footing I hope they will take the same Precaution. They did last year which was to entitle the

Treasurer of the State to pay on aproved Account, without having it laid before the Houses for Approbation. The prodigious Exorbitancy of this City has brought me experimentally to know the Want of Money, and I must be under the Necessity of drawing in the recess.

I can scarcely recollect so great a Dearth of News as at present. Every thing stagnant both at home and abroad. Our Dispatches in Congress are quite as barren as the Papers I have the Honour to enclose.

I used to think that attending the Legislature was laborious Business, but should be glad of a little of it now as relaxation. Excuse this Trouble.

I am, with much regard, your obedt Servant,

William C. Houston

RC (NjHi: Stevens Papers).

Samuel Huntington to Thomas Jefferson

Sir,   Philada Decemr 10th 1779

By the act of Congress of this day herewith enclos'd your Excellency will be inform'd, That Congress approve of the Measures taken by the Executive of the State of Virginia in providing Guards to the Convention Troops at Charlotteville, that those Guards all be considered in Continental Service & receive Continental pay & rations while doing duty at the Convention Barracks.

That the party of Colo Bland's light Dragoons now at Charlotte Ville are to proceed to South Carolina and the Commander in Chief is directed to appoint a Successor to Colo Bland resign'd.[1]

I have the honour to be with the highest respect, your Excy's hble Servt,   S.H. President

LB (DNA: PCC, item 14).
[1] For this resolve, one of a number of measures taken early in December to provide reinforcements for the southern department, see *JCC*, 15:1366–67; PCC, item 147, 2:643–46; and the following entry. For the background of this decision, which is discussed in Governor Jefferson's November 16 letter to Huntington, see PCC, item 71, 1:287–90; and Jefferson, *Papers* (Boyd), 3:191–92.

Samuel Huntington to George Washington

Sir,   Philadelphia Decemr 10th 1779

I am honour'd with your Excys favour of the 8th instant.[1]

By the act of Congress of this day herewith enclos'd your Excellency will be informed, The Party of Colonel Bland's Regiment of light Dragoons now at Charlotteville are to proceed forthwith to

South Carolina & Join the Regiment there, other guards for Barracks being provided from Virginia.[2]

That Colo Bland's resignation is accepted and it is the pleasure of Congress your Excellency should appoint a proper Officer to succeed him in the Command and immediately proceed to that post and take upon him the direction of affairs there.[3]

I have the honour to be, with the highest respect, your Excy's hble Servt,　　　　　　　　　　　　　　　Sam. Huntington President

RC (DLC: Washington Papers). In a clerical hand and signed by Huntington.

[1] According to the journals, this letter was read as the first order of business on December 11. See *JCC*, 15:1367; PCC, item 152, 8:215–18; and Washington, *Writings* (Fitzpatrick), 17:238–39.

[2] See the preceding entry.

[3] In response to this resolve, Washington appointed Col. James Wood on December 14 as Theodorick Bland's successor to command the detachment guarding the Convention Troops at Charlottesville. Washington, *Writings* (Fitzpatrick), 17:260–62.

In a brief letter of December 10, Huntington also sent Bland Congress' acceptance of his resignation. PCC, item 14, fol. 247.

Committee for Foreign Affairs to John Jay

Sir,　　　　　　　　　　　　　　　　　　Philada. Decr. 11th. 1779

By the inclosed Resolves of Congress[1] you will find that we are become more dependent upon your vigorous Exertions for the Amelioration of our Currency than you perhaps expected when you left Philadelphia. We think it of so much Importance that you should be early apprized of the Measures determined upon respecting Bills of Exchange that we do not chuse to omit this good Opportunity of communicating them, though unattended with a full Explanation of the Reasons which urge Congress to draw; more especially as you are so well enlightened by your late Presence in their Assembly.

We are with every Wish for your Prosperity, Sir your humble Servants,　　　　　　　　　　　　　　　⌈ James Lovell

　　　　　　　Comtee. of　　　　　⟨ Robt R Livingston

　　　　　　　foreign Affairs[2] ⌊ Wm Ch Houston

RC (NNC: John Jay Papers). Written by Lovell and signed by Lovell, Houston, and Livingston.

[1] The "inclosed Resolves," also in the hand of Lovell, were those of November 23, authorizing the drawing of bills of exchange "to the amount of one hundred thousand pounds sterling" on both Jay and Henry Laurens, and of November 29, approving a plan for the Board of Treasury to issue the bills and directing the Committee for Foreign Affairs to inform Jay and Laurens of the plan. *JCC*, 15:1299–1300, 1326–27; Jay Papers, NNC.

[2] The committee sent an identical letter of this date to Henry Laurens. Fogg Collection, MeHi

Samuel Huntington to
the Chevalier de La Luzerne

Sir,   Philada Decemr 11th 1779
  It is with peculiar pleasure that I notice the particular attention
which the Minister of France has been pleased to pay to the Case of
the eight American Seamen who captured the Greyhound.
  By the act of Congress of this day which I have the honour to
inclose[1] you will please to observe that it is the pleasure of Congress
the monies arising from the Sale of that Capture be paid to the eight
American Seamen the Captors or their Attornies in equal shares;
and that measures will be taken to convey intelligence to the said
Captors that they may apply for & receive the same.
  I have the honour to be, with the most perfect respect, your hble
Servant,   S.H. President

LB (DNA: PCC, item 14).
  [1] This "act of Congress" was adopted in response to a letter of this date from the
French minister, for which see Huntington to La Luzerne, December 8, 1779. For the
"measures" prescribed by this act and the steps taken to implement them, see *JCC*,
15:1372; and Massachusetts Delegates to the Massachusetts Council, December 15,
1779.

Samuel Huntington to William Livingston

Sir,   Philada Decemr 11th 1779
  You will receive herewith enclos'd two acts of Congress of this day
requesting the several States therein mentioned to furnish certain
quantities of flour & grain for the use of the army.[1]
  Your Excellency will observe the particular resolve which respects
the State of New Jersey requests that part of the eight thousand
Barrels of flour therein mentioned be furnished as soon as possible
to answer the immediate demands of the army.
  It is the sense of Congress that I should mention the pressing
necessity of a supply for the present wants of the army which admit
of no delay.
  The well known repeated exertions of the State of New Jersey
leaves no room to doubt that all possible despatch will be given to
procure a present supply of flour for the army. It is needless for me
to mention the fatal consequences that might ensue in this critical
conjuncture of affairs should the army now in that State be without
bread. The matter is of such importance that I am to request the
necessary information on the subject as soon as possible. I have only
to add that Congress have now under consideration the measures

proper to be adopted in order that Justice may be done to any State that shall furnish provisions at a lower price than others.

I am with the highest esteem, your Excy hble Sert,
S.H. President

P.S. I am honour'd with your Excy's favour of the 6th instant with the letter therein referr'd to enclos'd.[2]   S. H. Pt.

LB (DNA: PCC, item 14). Tr (DLC: Burnett Collection). Endorsed: "Copied from the original, then in possession of Mr. Stan V. Henkels."

[1] These resolves, recommended by "the committee for procuring supplies for the army," specified the quantities of flour and Indian corn requested from Virginia, Maryland, and Pennsylvania "on or before the first day of April," and from Delaware, New Jersey, and Connecticut "as soon as possible." *JCC*, 15:1371–72. Huntington transmitted these resolves to Pennsylvania in a letter of the 13th, but he did not write to the other four states until December 14, the day Congress adopted an additional resolve concerning state quotas. See Huntington to Joseph Reed, December 13, and to Thomas Johnson, December 14, 1779, note 3.

[2] Livingston's December 6 letter and the enclosed one of July 16, 1779, from Baron van der Capellen, are in PCC, item 68, fols. 487–502.

Samuel Huntington to John Beatty

Sir,   Philada Decemr 13th 1779

You will receive herewith enclos'd a Petition from Mary Keer, what the poor Woman means to petition for is that her Husband might be permitted to come home on parole. I understand he is a 2d Lieutenant, & now a prisoner on Long Island, Congress have refer'd this petition to you. If it be in your power to get the Man releas'd on parole or by Exchange I wish it may be done.[1]

I am Sir with respect & esteem your hble Servt,
S.H. President[2]

LB (DNA: PCC, item 14).

[1] *JCC*, 15:1373. The journals record only that the petition of Mary Kerr "be referred to the commissary general of prisoners"; it is not in PCC.

[2] President Huntington also wrote a brief letter this day to Lt. Col. Charles Pope of the Delaware Regiment informing him that Congress had accepted his resignation. See *JCC*, 15:1373; and PCC, item 14, fol. 251, item 78, 18:263–66.

Samuel Huntington to Joseph Reed

Sir   Philadelphia Decemr 13th 1779

Your Excellency will receive herewith enclos'd two Acts of Congress of the 11th instant requesting the several States therein named to furnish certain Quantities of flour & grain for the use of the Army.[1]

You will please to observe by the same Act which requests a supply from this State, a Committee are appointed[2] to confer with your Excellency & Council upon the Subject and it is hoped very beneficial Consequences may result therefrom.

I have the honour to be, with the highest respect, your Excys hble Servt.   S.H. President[3]

LB (DNA: PCC, item 14).

[1] See Huntington to William Livingston, December 11, 1779, note 1.

[2] That is, "the committee for procuring supplies," consisting of William Ellery, Robert R. Livingston, and Roger Sherman, which had recommended adoption of the resolves Huntington enclosed with this letter. See *JCC*, 15:1343, 1372; and *Pa. Council Minutes*, 12:197–98.

[3] Huntington also wrote the following letter to Reed on December 14.

"I have the honour to transmit your Excellency the enclos'd act of Congress of this Day, though it may have been allready communicated by the Committee from Congress appointed to confer with your Excellency & Council on the same subject to which it relates.

"Please to accept my acknowledgements for the agreeable intelligence you have honoured me with respecting the success of Capt [John Paul] Jones &c." PCC, item 14, fol. 253.

George Partridge to Caleb Davis

Dear Sir[1]   Philadelphia Decr. 13th. 1779

There is a very old Proverb which says that Charity begins at Home. Perhaps it is from a like principle that I feel myself anxious to know the Complexion of publick Affairs in *our* State & the present Disposion of the People, especially as many interesting Events have taken place since I left it, such as the pressing Call of Congress for large sums of money—the Penobscott affair, a Regulating Act adopted & (as I am told) broke over—a new form of Government sent out &c &c.

I tho't it rather strange that our Assembly should move for another Convention at Connecticut when our Regulations were crumbling to pieces. However at the Request of that Convention and the State of New Jersey, Congress have taken up the Matters and passed Resolves which you have doubtless seen. I wish to know your Oppinion whither a *Genl.* Regulating Law can now be carried into effect in our State after our late attempt, I own that I am doubtfull about the Matter, tho at the same time I think that at all events we must not flinch & leave our Sister States in the Lurch, as we were accusd. of doing in a similar case heretofore, and which is seriously remembered to this Day. It will not do to play the same game over again when the Convention Originated in our Court. I have not heard Whither the Assembly have taken any Measures to recruit our Regiments. It is an arduous Business in our present circumstances & I think ought to be early attended to; & also measures for clothing them. The North

Carolina & Virginia Troops are ordered to the Southward which (by the bye) I believe I should not have mentioned. The Report this morning is, that a Detachment of six or 8000 men are imbarking at N York their object is said to be either Virginia & the french ships there, or South Carolina. Another Report is that a Ship arrivd in the Deleware from France last night with Advice that the British & the combined Fleets are gone into their several ports, that the latter carried in with them the Duke, & British 90 gun ship, that no general Action had taken place.

I hope you have appointed some Person to Represent the State in my Room. I have been expecting Mr Hancock ever since the 20th of Sept. which was the time he mentioned, but find myself disappointed.[2] Would it not be best for the state to order only three Gentlemen to attend here at a time, especially as expences are so enormous at this Place—but as long Letters are tedious I will add nothing more than that I am, with the greatest Regard yr. most obedient humble Servt,   Geo Partridge

RC (MHi: Davis Papers).
   [1] Caleb Davis, a Boston merchant, has been identified in these *Letters*, 11:288n.1.
   [2] John Hancock did not attend Congress in 1779.

Committee of Commerce to Samuel Curson

Sir[1]   Philadelphia 14th Decr. 1779

We have this moment recd your favour of the 11th Inst.[2] informing us of the unlucky accident that has happend to the Eagle Packet which gives us very great Concern as the Supply of Powder we expected by that Vessel is of very great consequence to the united States. We have this moment procurd from Congress an order for Bills on Holland at Six Months Sight for Four thousand pounds Sterling which we mean imediately to forward either to you or to your House as you may direct.[3] We have therefore to desire you will instantly Give orders to your House in St. Eustatia to provide Fifty Tons of powder & Coarse woollens Sufficient for Five thousand pair of Overalls for the Soldiers without delay. This However is understood to mean That the Bills we remitted by the Eagle for One hundred thousand livres Turnois are distroyd which we apprehend is the Case. In which Case the above sum is meant to replace those Bills if distroyd. We write this in great haste that no time may be lost & shall write imediately to your House to this Effect & also more fully to you on the Subject in a few days. We are, sir, Your most Obedt. Servants.   James Searle

John Fell

Cyrus Griffin

RC (MeHi: Fogg Collection). Written by Searle and signed by Searle, Fell, and Griffin.
[1] Curson is identified in these *Letters*, 11:179n.
[2] Not in PCC.
[3] For Congress' resolve this day directing the Board of Treasury to supply "bills of exchange on Holland, to the amount of four thousand pounds sterling," for the Committee of Commerce to procure gunpowder and clothing, see *JCC*, 15:1381.

William Ellery to William Greene

Sir,   Philadelphia Decr. 14th. 1779
    Since Mr. Marchant left us nothing new hath turned up.
    Congress are employed in devising ways for supplying the Army at the least expence; for preserving the credit of our money; and defending the Southern States. The States I believe will be soon called upon to furnish such provisions, and other necessary articles for the war as they can supply with the greatest convenience, to be credited therefor in the quotas of monies to be raised by them respectively:[1] The Officers in the great civil departments of the Army, it is proposed, should hereafter instead of receiving commissions be paid by fixed Salaries &c &c.[2] The North Carolina Brigade are gone on for So. Carolina, and will be followed by the Virginia Troops.
    Our Intelligence from N. York is, that eight or ten thousand troops are about to embark. Their destination uncertain. I presume R. Island is not their object. The force is too great; and if so great a force should be employed in any other quarter there will not be troops enough to spare to attempt the repossession of that Island; so that I think our State will not be molested by the enemy this winter.
    We have late letterr from Mr. Bingham continental agent at Martinico;[3] but not a word of news. No letterr from our Plenipotentiary for some months past.
    The inclosed News-Paper will give you all the news we have. The Articles from Alicant I believe came to the French Consul here.[4] I wish they may be true. The destruction or capture of four of the enemy's capital ships would be a heavy blow indeed.
    All their dependence is upon the depretiation of our money. It is the great duty of every state to avert that mighty evil. The radical cure for depretiation is Taxation. I don't doubt but that our State will apply the remedy as far as it is in their power and do every thing within their exertions to produce a speedy and an honorable Peace.
    I am in great haste and as great respect, Yr Excellency's most obedt and most humble Servant,   Wm. Ellery

P.S. I hope your Excellency will excuse both the paper & writing. The former is the best the Secry's office affords, and the latter as good as the time will allow.

RC (R–Ar: Letters to Governors).
[1] See Samuel Huntington to Certain States, this date.

[2] Ellery, Robert R. Livingston, and Roger Sherman were appointed a committee on December 2 "relative to the commissary general of purchases." On December 4 they were also assigned consideration of "the report of the committee for regulating departments." After intermittent consideration of the reports of Ellery's committee, Congress adopted a series of resolutions on December 31, 1779, and January 1, 1780, fixing commission rates and salaries for the commissary and quartermaster general's departments and establishing accounting procedures for the departments. *JCC*, 15:1343, 1349, 1370, 1421, 1423, 1426–27, 16:5–7.

[3] William Bingham's November 3, 1779, letter to the Committee for Foreign Affairs was endorsed by Charles Thomson—"Wm. Bingham, recd. Decr. 10"—but its receipt is not mentioned in the journals. PCC, item 90, fols. 209–13.

[4] A "letter from a Gentleman . . . dated at Alicant, Sept. 21, 1779," reporting that a French fleet and army were poised to invade England and that the Spanish siege of Gibraltar was succeeding, appeared in the *Pennsylvania Packet*, December 14, 1779.

William Floyd to George Clinton

S'r,   Philadelphia 24 (?) December 1779.[1]

Inclosed is a bond for the Delivery of Peter Fraer to the Commissioners at Poughkeepsie and also a Resolve of Congress which will Lay a foundation for the Doing of Justice to Such States as may by their attention to the publick Good, furnish the army with necessaries at Reasonable Rates.[2]

Congress are very Sensible of the Exertions, I may Say the Extraordinary Exertions of our State, and they will and the members do Say, many Clever things of our State; But When we talk of Compensation for the Sacrifices that has been made by the [state] already, then they Incline to be Silent, So that tho' it is Just a Compensation Should be made, yet I am fearful whether we Shall be Ever able to obtain it. From the present temper and disposition of the members in general towards New York, I think it will be a very favourable time to bring on the Business of Vermont; from what I can discover they will be Inclined to do us Justice.

I must Refer you to the papers herein Enclosed for the news, which I believe Contain all of any Consequence that is passing here. From, S'r, your most obed't humble Serv't,

                                                        Wm. Floyd.

P.S. By the postscript to one of the newspapers,[3] you will See that Paul Jones is fighting them on the Coast of England as by their own papers.

Reprinted from Clinton, *Papers* (Hastings), 5:407–8.

[1] Although this letter was dated in the Clinton *Papers* "24 (?) December," Floyd probably wrote it on December 14 and 16. With it he enclosed a December 14 resolve of Congress and a December 16 "Postscript" of the *Pennsylvania Packet* that he mentioned in his own postscript to this letter. And the "bond for the Delivery of Peter Fraer" that is the subject of Floyd's opening paragraph is also mentioned by him in his letter to Clinton of December 21, printed below.

[2] Floyd enclosed Congress' December 14 resolve pledging that despite the difficulties of converting state contributions of provisions to a monetary scale, "to suit the convenience of the several states," "accounts shall be finally compared and adjusted so as to do equity to all the states." *JCC*, 15:1377.

[3] The December 16 "postscript" of the *Pennsylvania Packet* reprinted letters from a September 27 London newspaper describing recent actions of John Paul Jones and his fleet off the British coast, including the capture of the *Serapis* by the *Bonhomme Richard*.

Samuel Holten's Diary

[December 14–15, 1779]

14. Tuesday. The post came in & brought me a certificate of my being appointd. to represent the state for the year 1780.[1] I wrote to Joseph Hall Junr. & to Mrs. Holten (no. 89).[2] No news. A very cold day.

15. Wednesday. Congress sit late. We have nothing new this day. A cold day.

MS (MDaAr).

[1] The credentials of the Massachusetts delegates for 1780 were read in Congress on January 1, 1780. *JCC*, 16:2.

[2] Neither letter has been found.

Samuel Huntington to Certain States

Sir,   Philada. Decemr 14th 1779

You will herewith receive enclos'd an Act of Congress of this day, by which you will observe they have determin'd to call upon the several States to furnish their quotas of such supplies as may from time to time be necessary for carrying on the war; and that care shall be taken to suit the conveniencies of the several States and Justice done to all in the final settlement of the accounts.[1]

I have the honour to be &c.   S.H. President

LB (DNA: PCC, item 14). Addressed: "Circular to the States of N. Hampshire, M. Bay, N. York, Rhode island, N. Carolina, S. Carolina, Georgia."

[1] For the enclosed resolve, which was drafted by Roger Sherman of the "committee on supplies," see *JCC*, 15:1377–78; and PCC, item 21, fols. 189–90.

Samuel Huntington to Thomas Johnson

Sir,   Philadelphia Decemr 14th. 1779

Your Excellency will receive herewith enclos'd two acts of Congress of the 11th instant[1] and one other Act of this day;[2] by which you will be inform'd that Congress have determin'd to call upon the several States to furnish their Quotas of such supplies as may from time to time be wanted for carrying on the war taking due care to suit the conveniencies of the several States and the articles by them respect-ively furnished shall be credited towards their quotas of the monies they are called upon to raise for the United States at equal prices for articles of the same kind & quality and for others in due proportion, and the accounts finally adjusted so as to do equity to all the States.

By the separate act of the 11th inst. you will observe the Quantity at present requested from the State of Maryland is five thousand barrels of flour & five thousand barrels of indian Corn, in addition to the fifteen thousand barrels of flour heretofore required. It is the desire of Congress that each State should use all possible œconomy & dispatch in procuring the Articles requested of them.

So soon as Congress are inform'd that the several States can & will furnish the provisions necessary for the army the many persons heretofore employed in the purchasing Commissaries department for that purpose may be dismiss'd.

I have the honour to be, with the highest respect, your Excy's most obt Servt,   Sam. Huntington President[3]

RC (MdAA: Red Books). In a clerical hand and signed by Huntington. Although addressed "His Excellency Governor Johnson," the letter was actually received by Maryland's recently elected Gov. Thomas Sim Lee.

[1] For these "two acts," see Huntington to William Livingston, December 11, 1779, note 1.

[2] See the preceding entry.

[3] Huntington also wrote similar letters this day to Governors Thomas Jefferson, Caesar Rodney, and Jonathan Trumbull, transmitting the resolves mentioned herein to Virginia, Delaware, and Connecticut, who were called upon to supply 20,000 barrels of Indian corn, 10,000 barrels of flour, and 8,000 barrels of flour respectively. See PCC, item 14, fols. 250–57.

Samuel Huntington to William Livingston

Sir,   Philadelphia Decemr 14th 1779

In my letter of the 11th instant I had the honour of transmitting your Excellency two acts of Congress of that Date.

The Act ——— of this day herewith enclos'd[1] is intended in addition to those in order to facilitate the same design, by which you will be inform'd that Congress determin'd to call upon all the States to furnish their quotas of such supplies as may from time to time be wanted for carrying on the war and in making the requisition due care will be taken to suit the conveniency of the several States and the articles by them respectively furnished will be credited towards their quotas of the monies they are called upon to raise for the United States at equal prices for Articles of the same kind & quallity and for others in due proportion and the accounts finally compared & adjusted so as to do equity to all the States.

It is the desire & Expectation of Congress that each State may procure the articles of them requested with the utmost œconomy & dispatch; if the necessary provisions can be obtained in this mode the many persons heretofore employed in the purchasing Commissaries department for that purpose may be dismiss'd.

I have the honour to be, with the highest respect, your Excy's hble Servt,   Sam. Huntington President

RC (Nj: Revolutionary War Documents). In a clerical hand and signed by Huntington.
[1] See Huntington to Certain States, this date.

John Armstrong, Sr., to James Searle

Carlisle 15th Decemr. 1779. "Your Absence with Mrs. Searle which prevented me the pleasure of Seeing you when I left Congress, joined to the indispossion under which you laboured about that time, naturally excites my earnest desire to hear from you, particularly respecting the recovery of your health." Hopes to hear soon from Searle about various current topics. "Amongst these I cou'd wish to know, How the publick funds hold out, and whether there is any prospect of appreciation? Cannot Mr. Wharton, Brother to the late President, be introduced to the Board of Admiralty or Naval Department? What are the particular reinforcements intended for S. Carolina? I have heard of the North Carolina Troops & Bailers [Baylor's] Horse—and a loose acct. or Surmise of Sending G[eneral] Wane & the light infantry—this last in my Opinion ought not to be done, without *a certainty* of the Enemy having first sent a Strong reinforcement to Georgia, which I much query except they had a greater Naval force. I apprehend *a Secret* somewhere, respecting the Count and his Fleet. How like you the New Minister? What new members are there in Congress?

"Prices are enormous here & daily rising, so that it is doubtfull how our Army can be Supported. The money I hear is in effect refused in various places & a kind of little Barter taking place. A regulation by Law Ought Suddenly to take place when every refined notion in finance has thus failed 'tis high time to leave these fantastick bye paths & attempt the highway of publick Authority, to which also Shou'd be joined another means—that of every farmer laying in at Some appointed place some Quantity of Grain & perhaps meat at such a Settled rate, in part or whole of his Tax. This I presume will be found a wise & Salutary measure, not only productive of certainty but of Economy, nor is there One moment to be lost in Congress's recommending it to the States.

"I have just heard that Mr. Wadsworths resignation is accepted & much pleased that Congress have appointed Coll Blain in his room, who no doubt will do as much as can be expected from an individual in these times but have great apprehensions of his difficulty on account of the lowness of the Money & perhaps Scarcity of Grain too, which in this part of the State yeilds but little indeed, yet are the Stills it's said going on at top Speed.

"In a Newspaper of the 9th of November a Gentleman at this place Shewed me Genl. Gates's letter to Congress on the Evacuation of the Enemy at New Port—a few days after, I saw that same letter published on the 10th with an *additional paragraph* in favour of Major Armstrong, both published by Order of Congress. Why this last parag[raph] was omited on the 9th & published on the 10th I cannot conceive, the Printer Mr. Bradford having made no appology on his part. My Son wrote me when in town but of this said not a word, nor has any other friend explained the paradox! This being of a private or personal nature is comparatively Small, but as a publication of Congress it is a different thing. As a body I'm confident the House never ordered the paragraph to be Suppressed, and if by mistake of an individuel it is easily pardoned, but if thro' *envy* whether pointed agst. the young man or the General, is it [not] of the lowest kind— and if by any Officer or Servant of Congress is it not [a ma]licious insult of that body, and gross violation of publick trust? He that is not faithful in a little is not to be trusted with much. But I hope some friendly answer will explain the matter."

RC (PHi: Conarroe Collection). Addressed: "The Honorable James Searle Esqr. In Congress, Philadelphia. Or in his absence To Mr. Jas. McClane. Favoured by Coll. John Davis ."

Samuel Huntington to the States

Sir,   Circular   Philadelphia Decemr 15th 1779
    Your Excellency will receive herewith enclos'd an Act of Congress of this day recommending to the several States to continue embargoes where already laid, & when not, to lay embargoes: to prohibit the exportation of the several articles mentioned & described in the resolution of Congress of the 21st of August last.[1]

    The necessity of this Measure is so obvious it is the desire & full expectation of Congress that every State in the Union yield a ready & punctual compliance with the recommendation without loss of time.

    I have the honour to be &c.   S.H. President

LB (DNA: PCC, item 14).
    [1] *JCC*, 15:1383. For Congress' previous recommendation to the states to extend

their embargoes on provisions from September 1 to the end of the year, see John Jay to Caesar Rodney, August 30, and to the States, September 14, 1779.

James Lovell to Henry Laurens

Dear Sir   Decr. 15. 1779

Fearing yr. Son will suddenly leave this City, I am induced to take up my Pen to communicate an *undecided* Peice of Business, that perplexes my mind greatly. Was you here I should not feel that Perplexity an hour longer; as my Respect for your Judgement would of course give deciding Weight to whatever Opinion my critical Situation might draw from your Friendship, which I am sure is prompt to serve me in every honorable Way.

Your Son having declined going to France, it was determined that Tomorrow a Secry. shall be chosen—no Nomination is yet made but Govr. Morris will be the man unless others are named to be in Competition.[1] I know yr. Opinion of him. I think I may say you would not *rejoice* at his Election; nay you woud have Fears from the measure. Honestly I had rather have suffered many Pains & Penalties than to have this new Occasion to chuse, and a double number of them than to be chosen. Yet I am not absolutely decided against the latter. And my Reasons I mean now to explain. The 1st & greatest is of the preventive Kind, the 2d is a certain Conviction that I shall have every friendly Aid from you advisory & pecuniary, and the 3d is that you will probably succeed the Doctr.[2] in Case of that Event which makes it necessary to have a faithful Hand now near him at his advanced Age.

If I am obliged to leave this City I will not do it without writing to you again on this Subject. I wish you to cover any Line you may think fit to favor me with to Mr. Peabody. Your affectionately attached humble Servant,   James Lovell

RC (ScHi: Laurens Papers, no. 23).

[1] For Lovell's explanation of the intricate maneuvering that became involved in this "Competition," which he was not reluctant to enter personally in order to forestall the selection of Gouverneur Morris, see Lovell to Laurens, December 17; and Lovell to Richard Henry Lee, December 18, 1779. See also Nathaniel Peabody to Laurens, December 17; and Robert R. Livingston to John Jay, December 22, 1779.

[2] That is, Benjamin Franklin.

Massachusetts Delegates
to the Massachusetts Council

Sir   Philada. Decr. 15th. 1779

The inclosed Extracts[1] will show the present State of a Business interesting to some brave Men of Massachusetts Bay & Rhode Island who probably are returned from Cape françois and stand in need of an authentic Advertizement of the mode in which they may obtain the Property adjudged to them at Port de Paix.

It is not unlikely that *Boston* is used for Massachusetts Bay in more Instances than that of Cyren Peek; and it appears as if some of the Names are falsely spelt: One is omitted; but the Seven can tell who the Eighth was.

With much Respect, We are, Sir, Your most humble Servants,

E. Gerry   James Lovell

Geo. Partridge   S. Holten

RC (M–Ar: Revolutionary War Letters). Written by Lovell and signed by Lovell, Gerry, Holten, and Partridge. Addressed: "The Honorable, The President of the Council of Massachusetts Bay. By Mr. McLane."

[1] The "Extracts" were from "the Proceedings at Port de Paix relating to the Capture of an English Vessel by Eight American Sailors" in July 1779 and December 6 and 11 resolves of Congress related to the case.

According to the proceedings, the eight Americans had sailed from Boston in April 1779 bound for Cape François but were captured and taken to Jamaica. There they enlisted as sailors on board the British-owned *Greyhound*, which they in turn took control of on July 12 and carried into Môle St. Nicholas, Haiti.

The French Admiralty officials at Port-de-Paix awarded the ship to the Americans but withheld payment until they "might take proper Steps to authorize them to receive the proceeds." Nearly one-half of the prize money was advanced to the Americans, but the remainder stayed in French hands. On December 6, the French minister, La Luzerne, brought the case to the attention of Congress, and on December 11 Congress approved the payment of the money in "equal shares" and directed that the letters and documents be given to the delegates from Massachusetts and Rhode Island, the sailors' states of residence.

Consequently, the Massachusetts delegates forwarded the information to the Massachusetts Council with this letter. According to the council clerk's endorsement, the council ordered that the extracts "be Published in Two Boston News Papers in order that the Captors of the Greyhound may be properly advised of the way in which they may Obtain the Property adjudged to them at Port de Paix." The extracts, which are also in Lovell's hand, are in the Revolutionary War Letters, M–Ar. See *JCC*, 15:1356, 1372; and Samuel Huntington to La Luzerne, December 8 and 11, 1779. See also Huntington to George Wattson, March 25, 1780.

Philip Schuyler to James Duane

Saratoga, December 16th 1779. Has just returned home from Philadelphia.

"When I arrived at Congress [*i.e., ca. November 16*] I pressed for the sense of the house whether we should give peace to the Indians or not, and on what terms. The Committee who had been appointed on a letter of mine on that Subject were ordered to report, which was done, and Inclosed you have Copy of the resolutions as agreed to by the house.[1] An additional one was moved 'That the Indians should be required to cede part of their Country for the benefit and behoof of the united States In General to be disposed of by Congress.' This produced an Animated debate, but was after Some management rejected, happily for us not a Member In the house in favor of the resolution recollected, or seemed to recollect, the Act passed by our legislature In their last Session, for making a Simalar demand In favor of this State; I verily believe had It Occured that the resolution would have been carried, and we should at least have had much trouble In a future day; The sentiment however is not given up for before I left Congress I saw A motion In Mr. Shermans hand which he Intended to Introduce, purporting 'that all lands heretofore Grantable by the King of Great Britain whilst Soveraign of this Country, In whatever State they might lay and of which Grants had not Already been made, Should be Considered as the property of the united States and Grantable by Congress.' He Insisted Strenously on the Equity of the Measure as did the Gentlemen from Maryland and Some others the Interest of whose Constituents lay or appeared to lay the other way, but they added If New York and such other States whose western bounds were Indefinite or were pretended to Extend to the South seas would be Contented with a reasonable western extent, It would Afford Satisfaction, prevent disputes and Complete the union, I answered that out of mere Curiosity I would wish to know their Ideas of 'a reasonable western extent, as they might widely differ from others, I was then Carried to the map and Mr. Sherman explained himself by drawing a line from the Northwest Corner of Pensylvania which is in lake Erie as laid down In the map thro the Strait which leads to Ontario and thro that lake and down the St Lawrence to the 45th degree of Lattitude for the bounds of New York In that Quarter. Virginia, the two Carolinas and Georgia he proposed be bound by the Alleghehany Mountains or at farthest by the Ohio to where It Enters the Missisippi and by that river below the Junction and he proposed that all the territory beyond the bounds I have mentioned and within the united States, should become the Joint property of the united States and to be in the disposal of Congress. The Gentlemen from North Carolina I found had Already requested Instructions from their Constituents on the Subject, permit Me to Intreat your Attention to this Matter against the meeting of the legislature, when I hope For the pleasure of seeing you, and when I shall Strive to Convince you that It would be Impolitic & Injurious to the State In the present Conjuncture to Insist on a Cession of territory by the Indians.[2]

"The derrangment of our Finances and the Ill-policied System under which the Civil departments of the Army are Conducted are a fruitful Source of distress, I have ventured to hand over the outlines of a plan to remedy the evils occasioned by the depreciating state of our Currency. If It meets your approbation I shall Judge It feasible. New arrangements are to take place In the Civil departments. I was much pressed to take the direction of one or both, and from the

Attention which was paid me I have Every reason to believe they would have restored me to my rank In the Army If I had Acceeded to their proposals, but as the civil Offices are deemed lucrative I declined Accepting, I hope you will Judge I decided with propriety.[3]

"Some Gentlemen have proposed to me the Office of Secretary at war, as the Objection I had against the other did not hold here, I desired time for Consideration, and have concluded to Accept of It, If offered and If restored to my rank In the Army, after what I have experienced In public life you will be Surprized at this determination, but the Considerations which Induced me I trust you will approve of. I defer giving them until I have the pleasure of a Tete-a-tete with You.

RC (NHi: Duane Papers).

[1] Schuyler is discussing Congress' adoption on November 27 of instructions to him for conducting negotiations with the Six Nations, for which see Samuel Huntington to Schuyler, November 29; and Schuyler to George Clinton, November 29, 1779, note.

[2] Schuyler's description of the debate over congressional Indian policy and western land cessions is not recorded in the journals, but for a similar concessionary statement on New York's western land claims by a fellow New York delegate, see Robert R. Livingston to Clinton, November 30, 1779.

[3] For Schuyler's ultimate refusal to accept appointment either in the "Civil departments" or as "Secretary at war," see Livingston to Schuyler, December 20, 1779, note 3, and January 27, 1780.

Samuel Huntington to
the Chevalier de La Luzerne

Sir   Philadelphia Decemr 17th. 1779[1]

I am directed to inform you that Congress in order to testify their attention to the interest of his Catholic Majesty, appointed a Committee to Confer with General Washington on the subject of your letter accompanying the representation of Don Juan de Miralles;[2] And though from the result of their conference they have reason to believe that our grand Army Cannot be weakened, while the enemy retain their present force at New York, without considerable danger; Yet they have Upon Mature deliberation determined rather to incur that danger than not comply as far as is consistent with our Circumstances, with the views of his Catholic Majesty to whom they feel themselves bound by that Union of interest which a common enemy creates; by the favorable disposition manifested by his Catholic Majesty to these United States, and by those pleasing ties which connect the house of Bourbon with the happiness of mankind. Under these impressions they have ordered a Considerable detachment from the grand Army to join the troops in Carolina; which together with the forces already there or on the way will amount to about four thousand men, exclusive of the militia of the southern States whom

Congress have called for upon this Occasion. Congress have also Ordered three of their Frigates to Charlestown to be put under the direction of the Commanding Officer in that department. This force they conceive will make so powerful a diversion in favour of his Catholic Majesty's arms as to afford probable hopes of their being crowned with success. You will perceive, Sir, that any other co-operation with the troops of Spain is impossible while Savanna Opposes a barrier to a junction of our force. This from its present strength will not be easy for us to remove, till a more decided superiority in this quarter enables us to transfer a greater proportion of our Army thither, unless in the mean time the Governor of the Havannah shall think proper to furnish such aid, as when joined to the forces of the United States in that quarter will be sufficient to effect the purposes before mentioned. But as Congress are desirous of extending their Views still further, and Conceiving the Conquest of East Florida to be an Object of great importance as well to his Catholic Majesty as to these States, they have therefore directed me to inform you, and through you Don Juan de Miralles by whom the intentions of his Catholic Majesty are communicated, that they have given full power to their general Commanding in the southern department to correspond and concert with the Governor of the Havannah or any other person or persons Authorised by his Catholic Majesty for that purpose, such plan as can be agreed upon between them for carrying our Views into execution.[3]

I am, Sir, directed further to inform You that though Congress cannot promise any Considerable quantity of provisions until the Army of the United States are supplied, yet as soon as this can be done every means will be used to furnish provisions for his Catholic Majesty's Islands and fleet. But in the mean time they Conceive that a large supply of rice may be Afforded by the State of South Carolina which Congress will readily aid the Agents of Spain in procuring.

I am Sir with great Respect, your humble Servant,
Copy   Sam. Huntington President

FC (DLC: Continental Congress Miscellany). In the hand of George Bond, with dateline, close, and signature by Huntington.

[1] The translations of this letter located in the French and Spanish archives (cited in note 2) are dated December 16, 1779, the day Congress adopted the committee report recommending that Huntington communicate this letter to the French minister.

[2] Miralles' November 24 "representation" to Congress had contained an announcement that Spain had declared war on Great Britain and a request that the United States revive plans for the conquest of St. Augustine in cooperation with the Spanish which had been abandoned the preceding year. He also broached the subject of securing American provisions for the relief of Spanish troops and the inhabitants of Cuba. Advised by the delegates to consult the French minister on this proposal, however, Miralles also wrote the following day to La Luzerne, who on November 26 wrote to Congress to confirm French interest in an expedition against East Florida and to assure the delegates that the French fleet would be duly alerted to opportunities for supporting the undertaking should the operation prove feasible. See *JCC*,

15:1301–2, 1318; PCC, item 95, 1:13–16, 21–31; and Wharton, *Diplomatic Correspondence*, 3:412–16.

The work of the committee to whom these letters were referred was subsequently merged with a proposal for sending a committee to headquarters to confer with Washington, who was consequently consulted on the feasibility of Miralles' request and on prospects for a significant diversion of American forces to the southern department. That committee's findings were then referred to yet a third committee, which drafted the present letter to explain the response of Washington and Congress to Miralles' queries. See *JCC*, 15:1386–88; PCC, item 25,1:283–88; and Committee at Headquarters to Congress, December 7, 1779.

La Luzerne reported this result to the comte de Vergennes in a December 17 dispatch ("No. 18") in which he enclosed a ciphered translation of this letter from Huntington. Archives du ministère des affaires étrangères: Correspondance politique, États-Unis, 10:115, 118. Miralles reported his communication with Congress and his consultation with Philip Schuyler on behalf of the committee to which his representation had been referred, in dispatches to José de Gálvez, minister of the Indies, of December 12 and 17, and to Diego José Navarro, governor general of Cuba, of December 18, 1779. Audiencia de Santo Domingo, Legajo 2598, and Papeles Procedentes de Cuba, Legajo 1281, Archivo General de Indias, Seville. See also William E. O'Donnell, *The Chevalier de La Luzerne: French Minister to the United States, 1779–1784* (Bruges: Desclee de Brouwer, 1938), pp. 96–98.

[3] See Huntington to Benjamin Lincoln, December 18, 1779.

James Lovell to Henry Laurens

Dear Sir   Philadelphia Decr. 17. 1779.

I hope the Numbers of the Journals which your amiable Son has to deliver to you will prove duly consequent to those which you took with you from hence.

I have already hinted to you the Risque into which the Secretaryship of the Embassy to France was thrown by Col. L's Nonacceptance.[1] Yesterday had been appointed for a new Choice, but passed without even a nomination, so that I hoped there would be some lucky offer of a Character in which Congress would see fit to unite for a Ballot. This morning, however, Mr. Mathews named G Morris, Mr. Ellery instantly named me, I named Col. Hamilton & Mr. Plater named Col. Steuart of Maryland.

Having once intreated to have my Name taken back as you may remember, I was under a Necessity of remarking now that neither my own Opinion nor the Practice of Congress since that Period supported the Motives upon which I then proceeded—that I consented to let my name stand to Serve in Case in Necessity thro the Indetermination of Congress in regard to others. The mission is by no means my Wish. I find it will be painful to consent to accept it if it should be offered. One Thing, needless to mention, would be more painful. My predominating motives are of the preventive Kind.

The members present are
N.H. Peabody
Mass. Gerry, Lovell, Holten, Partridge.
R Is. Ellery

Con. Huntington, Sherman, Ellsworth.
N Yk RR Livingston, Floyd, L'Hommedeau
N Jy. Fell, Houston
Pens. Searle, Mulenbergh, McLane, Shippen
Maryld. Plater, Forbes
Virginia, Griffin
N. Car. Penn, Burke, Genl. Jones
S Car. Mathews
The Treasury Bd. & Admiralty are in action. The latter Mr. Lewis
and two Members of Congress Forbes & Ellery. It is very doubtful to
me whither Mr. Whipple will accept.[2]

We are upon Measures to fill the Army & save Money. "High
Time" you may justly say. Genl. Green is desirous of relinquishing
the Quartermastership but at a Time when there is no Forrage
provided so that a Change would be dangerously critical at this day.
The States must be called upon for Produce essential to the Army
instead of Paper.

I say nothing of News. Your Son will give you all that is passing.

I must at this Hour of Midnight put a Fit of the Cholic into Bed.

Heaven protect & prosper you by Land & Sea.

Respectfully & affectionately Your Friend,

James Lovell

RC (ScHi: Laurens Papers, no. 23).
[1] See Lovell to Laurens, December 15, 1779.
[2] William Whipple had been elected to the Admiralty Board on November 26, but
as Lovell surmised, he declined the appointment.

Nathaniel Peabody to Henry Laurens

Hond. and Dear Sir   Philada. Decr 17th. 1779

The polite and favourable Notice you was pleased to take of me
during the Short tho. agreable acquaintance I had the Honr. of
having with you, while together at Congress, has Necessarily Impressed my mind with Indelible Sentiments of Gratitude; And I
Should do Violence to my feelings in Suppressing an acknowledgement thereof by this opportunity.

I have the pleasure of informing you that the truly *Patriotic* and
Heroic Colo. Laurens has this evening favoured me with a Short but
an agreable visit which has if possible heighten'd him in my Esteem—
And tho. I have a passionate regard for him yet you will give me
leave to Say, that his resignation of the appointment of Secretary, to
the Court of Versailles, at [such a] Critical Juncture of our public
affairs notwithstanding I am fully Convinced it was done upon the
most Noble and pure principals, has fill'd me with very Great Anxiety.

The Gentlemen Now in nomination to fill that important office are Mr *Lovel* by Mr Elery, Mr G. Morris by Mr. Mathews, a Lt Col Hamilton by Mr Lovel, and a Lt Col Stewart by Mr. Plater—but who will be Elected I cannot Take upon me to Determine, as I See a Storm Gathering, and the *Cloven foot* appears again as heretofore. Mr Lovel will Transmit the Journals of Congress published Since your departure, and Some News papers, however will Just observe, that Mr. Gibson, Mr. Trumbul, & a Mr. Foreman are appointed Commissrs at the board of Treasury. And Genl Whipple & a Mr. Wearing, of S. Carolina, and old Daddy Lewis Commissrs to the board of Adm[iralty]. A Col. Greyson a Commissr [to the] board of War.

It would be needless for me to attempt mentioning anything Concerning the Army, as Col Laurens who has so lately Come from H. Quarters will be able to give you the most Authentic Account upon that Head.

A Line from you at any time I Should Esteem an Honr done me and would place it among my Choicest Treasures.

I most ardently wish you Success equal to the *rectitude* of your Intentions.

I am Honr. Sir, with the highest Consideration of Esteem Your most obedt and very Humble Servt,   Nath Peabody

RC (Mr. Sol Feinstone, Washington Crossing, Pa., 1979). Endorsed by Laurens: "17th Decr. 1779. Rec'd 11th Janry. Answd. 24th."

Elbridge Gerry to Benjamin Lincoln

My dear sir   Philadelphia the 18th Decr 1779

Since Your Departure from this place, I have been so involved in Business, & thereby so reduced in my Health, as to have been under the disagreable Necessity of giving up the pleasure of corresponding with those whom I most esteem, but I flatter myself that You will never entertain any Doubts of my warmest Friendship.

By Colo Laurens, who will inform You particularly of the State of our affairs in this Quarter, I beg Leave to inclose You the latest Papers, containing some agreable Intelligence.

I am now liberated from the Burthen of a Member of the Treasury; & hope my Engagements will be so far lessened as to admit a Communication of such Occurrences, as may be interesting or agreable to You, & not officially transmitted from the Offices of Congress. I remain sir with every Sentiment of Friendship & Esteem, your most obedt. & very hum sert.   E. Gerry

RC (MH–H: Autograph File).

Samuel Holten to Benjamin Lincoln

Dear Sir.   Philadelphia Decr. 18th. 1779.
   Colo. Laurens informs me he sits out this day to the southward, and my personal respect for you, induces me to embrace so favorable an oppertunity of writing you; tho' we have nothing in particular here that deserves your attention, but what will be delivered you in a formal manner, or communicated by the bearer.
   The disordered state of our Finances, under our present circumstances is truly distressing, & calls for the greatest exertions of the good people, in paying in their Taxes and loaning their money, so that the public treasury may be supplied.
   I have nothing late from Boston, owing (as I suppose) to the roads being much block'd with snow.
   The Hon. J. Adams, & F. Dana Esqrs. sailed from Boston about four weeks since for France, being charged with important affairs from Congress, which I suppose you are acquainted with.
   The Chevalier de la Luzerne the new Minister, & Mr. Marbois his secy., are very agreeable Gentlemen, and appear desirous of strengthening the alliance between the two Countries, and assisting us against the common enemy.
   I inclose you the last public prints.
   I am, Sir, with great respect, your most obedient servant,
                                                            S. Holten

RC (MB: MS 448).

Samuel Huntington to Benjamin Lincoln

Sir,   Philadelphia Decemr 18th 1779
   You will receive herewith inclos'd a Copy of my letter of the 17th Instant to the Chevalier De la Luzerne Minister of France, and also an Act of Congress of the same date.[1]
   By these papers you will be informd not only of the measures Congress have taken for the defence of Charles Town and to reinforce the Army under your command, but also the designs of his Catholic Majesty against the Floridas and the inclinations of Congress in Case that Spain by the instrumentallity of the Governor of the Havannah or other ways will assist the American Arms with a Naval Force & Troops sufficient so as to regain the possession of Georgia, to cooperate with them in the reduction of East Florida.
   For this purpose Congress have been pleased to authorize you or the Commanding Officer for the time being to correspond & concert with the Governor of the Havannah &c such plans as shall in your opinion be best calculated to ensure the reduction of the Enemies

force in the State of Georgia, and for the Conquest of East Florida; and the State of South Carolina is also requested to afford every Assistance in their power for carrying the same into effect.

These Matters will by the first conveyance be communicated to his Excellency Governor Rutledge,[2] and the greatest Secrecy the nature of the Case admits is enjoined. You will probably receive other intelligence on this Subject as soon as time will admit from the Governor of the Havannah or some other person on the part of his Catholic Majesty if the propos'd plan should take Effect.

I am Sir, with much Esteem, your humble Servt.

                                        Sam. Huntington President

RC (MHi: Lincoln Papers). In a clerical hand and signed by Huntington.

[1] See Huntington to the chevalier de La Luzerne, December 17, 1779. Actually the "Act of Congress of the same date" is one of December 16 not 17.

[2] This day Huntington wrote a similar letter to South Carolina Governor John Rutledge, which contained the following additional paragraph.

"You will also observe it is the Desire of Congress that the State of South Carolina may afford a supply of Rice if practicable to his Catholic Majesty's Islands and Fleet on their request." PCC, item 14, fols. 258–59.

James Lovell to Richard Henry Lee

Dear Sir   Decr. 18th 1779

Yr Favr. of Novr. 30th[1] reached me too late on Tuesday the 14th to permit a Line in Return. I now find what you asked for and some french Vouchers intended originally for You. I add some Letters recd. last Evening.

I am now to surprise you more than heretofore by telling that Thursday last being fixed upon for the Election of a Secretary to Doctr. Franklin or rather the Embassy which Lt. Col. Laurens had not accepted, the Day passed without even a Nomination. But Yesterday Mr. Mathews named G Morris who is making all Smooth to obtain it. I had intended to name Col. Hamilton. Ellery however was beforehand & put me up. I pursued my Intention & Mr. Plater named a Col Steuart of Maryland. I mentioned to Congress that I should not as some time ago desire my name to be withdrawn as I had not the Opinion of a Self denying Ordinance which I then had, and was fortified in my Change of Sentiments by the late Proceedings of Congress. I declared that my Wish was not implyd but my meer Consent if the Ballots should not happily be general for another. I am pained at my present Situation.[2]

You must be free in yr. Opinion upon this Conduct, let the Event be what it may.

Yrs. affectionately,   James Lovell

[P.S.] I shall attend very particularly to yr. Memoranda formerly sent if I should be under the necessity of leaving this City soon.

I have detained an open Address of Doctr. Lee dated July 12, 1779[3] supposing you have published what I sent before. It begins "in 1775" & ends "made them."
I will fix a Cypher with you.

RC (ViU: Lee Family Papers).
[1] Not found.
[2] For Lovell's "Situation" with regard to the selection of a secretary to the minister plenipotentiary to France, see Lovell to Henry Laurens, December 15 and 17, 1779.
[3] Not found.

Committee of Congress to Charles Pettit

Sir,   20th Decr. 1779.
The Committee are desirous of knowing the quantity of Forage now on hand in the Quarter–Master–General's Department—Where his Magazines are formed, and what further supplies will be wanted, and at what Magazines, during the course of this Winter—what number of Teams will be necessary, and what sums of Money defraying their expence during the same season.
The Committee do not desire very accurate returns or Estimates, but wish to have such information as will direct their judgments in recommending measures for obtaining the requisite supplies.[1]
Your answer is requested as soon as possible.
I am, Your very obedient servant.   Thos. Burke

RC (PSC: Biddle Manuscripts). Written and signed by Thomas Burke.
[1] Thomas Burke, who had returned to Congress December 8, had been appointed to a committee of five on December 17 with instructions to obtain "estimates" of provisions and supplies required for the Continental Army in 1780 and "the quantities and kinds which each State ought to furnish as its quota thereof." Congress also resolved that if any state undertook to procure its quota of the articles required, all purchases of such articles by Continental commissaries and quartermasters in that state would be discontinued. See *JCC*, 15:1360–61, 1391. The reply from assistant quartermaster general Pettit is not in PCC. For Burke's direct appeal to the president of Pennsylvania for emergency assistance while his committee was assembling information needed to set the states' 1780 quotas, see Burke to Joseph Reed, December 22, 1779.
The complexity of the system to be worked out eventually entailed the appointment of a larger committee consisting of a member of each state, which did not finally issue a detailed report until February 25, 1780. See *JCC*, 16:68, 196–201; and Samuel Huntington to the States, February 26, 1780.

Samuel Holten's Diary

[December 20–21, 1779]
20. Monday. A very cold day, no post in. Genl. Washington informed Congress that the army is in great want of Supplies.[1] No new intelligence.

21. Tuesday. I dined with the minister of France. I wrote to Mrs. Holten, no. 90.[2]

MS (MDaAr).
[1] For the immediate response of the delegates to the "deplorable distress" described by Washington in his December 15 letter to Congress, see *JCC*, 15:1396, 1399; Samuel Huntington to Caesar Rodney, December 21; Thomas Burke to Joseph Reed, December 22; and Robert R. Livingston to La Luzerne, December 22, 1779.
[2] Not found.

William Churchill Houston
to William Livingston and Caleb Camp

Sir   Philada. 20 Decr. 1779
    It is with reluctance I trouble you once and again on the critical Situation of Affairs at this Time. To cast round and examine the risques and Difficulties which stack up every where has a Tendency to send the Mind in every Direction for Succour. A Treasury without Money and an Army without Bread, is really alarming. I have already observed that the Failure of Supplies in the Staff-departments is unexpectedly great; but so it is, and the Question now is, the most immediate Means of providing against the worst of Consequences. In a Prospect so embarrassed, there is still however Hope and Encouragement, because the Means are among us, and the Mode of producing and applying them to the Exigency is not impracticable: and when the well-being, not to say Existence, of our Cause depends upon it, Importunity will be forgiven and every Exertion made.
    The Commissary General is now here; I have conversed with him fully. I write on the Evidence of his positive Declarations, that his Supplies are exceedingly small, and what he has cannot possibly get to Camp in Season to prevent an absolute Want of Bread. That the Army is already at short Allowance every where; in many Places totally destitute. It is not worth while to stand discussing Causes when the Effect is taking Place and the Moment calls for Interposition. I do not therefore wait at present to trouble the Legislature with Explanations, but do earnestly entreat, that, long as they have been together, they will not rise till Measures are taken to secure an immediate competent Supply of Flour, as far as it can possibly be had, and till a Plan is adopted to draw forth all the State can spare afterwards. In the request which went from Congress some Days since,[1] I could not but be of Opinion the Quantity was rather large, though it was not disproportionate to what was assigned to some others: however the Legislature can pretty well determine this Point. It is to be expected that what has always happened on similar Occasions, will again be the Case, that many who can spare will not, some for one reason others for another. Impressment has therefore

become necessary, and in such Conjunctures, if in any, is justifiable. It is confessed to be an Evil, but the less of the two. If the Legislature cannot tarry to complete an adequate Plan, the Constitution of the Executive is such that, one would think, the best Citizen may feel himself perfectly secure in trusting it, even much farther, were it necessary, than an Extent like this which involves a little personal Property only. The Inconveniences which attend the Appointment of Agents in every County would seem to make four or five active intelligent Men preferable before the largest Number. Nor would this prevent the fullest Efforts of the disinterested and publick-spirited every where, or abstract from the Use of their Services. I am not capable to determine whether, at this Time, it would be best to put a Stop to the Continental Purchasers, though I suppose they are as numerous as ever, and do as little Good and receive as high Commissions. There is at the same Time a Danger from a Competition of Prices. The Allowance for the Flour till the first of February will probably be at the current, or however a generous Price, lest Complaint and Discouragement should take Place; and perhaps a Prospect of a falling Rate will induce a readier Supply. This representation has hitherto been confined to Flour, but I beg Leave to mention that Meat is not likely to be more plentiful, though there is a little Quantity more immediately within reach. Perhaps sufficient for some weeks without resorting to the salted, which is also dispersed and scanty. From the Commissary General I learn, that no considerable Purchases are making, his Deputies being out of Cash. I mention this as it may perhaps be thought adviseable to pay a little Attention to it also.

It is unnecessary to detain you further than to explain a little more in Detail why so much Dependence is unavoidably placed on New-Jersey, and their Interference more immediately requested. New-York is nearly drained, not to mention that large Detachments of the Army are in that State; the Assembly of Pennsylvania are not together, nor could they be convened much, if any, sooner, than the Time to which they stand adjourned, and the Executive are not vested with Power adequate to the Object; as to the Supplies bought up in the adjacent States, they cannot be transported so as to reach the Army in Season, still less so, the Navigation of the Delaware being already interrupted. In the Southern Quarter a Post will be wanted for the Troops marching that Way.

I enclose Resolutions of Congress of the 14 and 17 instant,[2] which have probably already reached His Excellency, the Governour from the President. Nearly all the radical Principles are adopted for a Change of those Systems which have so long been obnoxious to the People. I cannot but hope that the Alteration will be approved and useful.

I have only further to beg Indulgence for the Liberties I have taken, with a sincere Intention to do what I thought right.

Am, Sir, your obedt Servt,   Wm Ch Houston

RC (Nj: Stryker Collection). Addressed: "His Excelly The Governour and Speaker of the Assembly of New-Jersey."

¹ See Samuel Huntington to William Livingston, December 11, 1779.

² For these resolves concerning state quotas of provisions and supplies for the Continental Army, see *JCC*, 15:1377–78, 1391; and Samuel Huntington's letters to Certain States and to William Livingston, December 14, 1779.

Samuel Huntington to Jonathan Trumbull, Sr.

Sir   *Private*   Philadelphia Decemr 20th. 1779

I do myself the Honour of Transmitting your Excellency, Baron Vander Cappelan's Original Letter of the 6th of July together with the Translation which I have procured, and also your Excellency's letter Addressd to the Honorable Henry Laurens Esqr, their Seeming no prospect it could overtake him in America.¹

I have the pleasure to Congratulate your Excellency on the Success of Capt J. P. Jones with his little Squadron on the Brittish Coasts more especially in the port at Hull, the particulars of which I have deliverd to Capt Root the Bearer.

Mr Ellsworth is arrived in Congress to my great Satisfaction, and I could wish Connecticutt might continually have three Delegates in Congress.

I am distressd on account of Supplies for the Army, I fear they will not be fed thro' the winter without vigorous Exertions by the Several States, alltho' from the best Intelligence I can obtain their is a fullness in the Country, Individuals Seem to have laid aside all thoughts of danger, and are pursuing their private gains in Opposition to the public.

I am morrally certain that if proper measure could be adopted to keep up a Respectable Army this winter in readiness; & have them early in the field the next Spring, a Peace would ensue without another Campaign; our resources are Sufficient, but the Embarrassments of our finnances, & the Security of the Inhabitants or rather great inattention to public good & Safety may Still continue our Trouble & perhaps increase our danger. I have the Honour to be with the greatest Respect, your Excys & Obedient Servt,

Sam Huntington

RC (CtHi: Huntington Papers). Endorsed by Trumbull: "Sam Huntington, Private, enclosing my Letter to Mr Laurens, rcd. Dr. 1779."

¹ Baron van der Capellen's letter to Trumbull had been laid before Congress and referred to the committee of the whole on November 23, 1779, but no copy of it was retained in PCC. *JCC*, 15:1299. Trumbull's December 13 letter to Huntington, in which he discussed his correspondence with Laurens and van der Capellen, is in Trumbull, *Papers* (MHS Colls.), 2:458–60.

Robert R. Livingston to Philip Schuyler

Dear Sir   Philadelphia 20th Decr. 1779.

I was favored with yours from Camp[1] and shod have answered it earlier had not the bad wheather occasioned the failure of the next post. The picture you draw of the State of the great departments of the ———[2] is very alarming but we have seen it greatly hight[e]ned since, nor can we tell how to remedy it unless the States will be more punctual in their remittan[ces] of taxes. We have resolved to call for a certain [pro]portion of supplies in kind from each of the states [& ha]ve appointed a Committee to adjust them. I pro[mise] myself some advantage from this as it will [en]able us with the more facility to give the fixture of our money which you so strongly recommend but which it is impossible to do in the present embarrassed situation of our affairs, at least the experiment wd. be extreamly hazardous.

Green has offered his resignation which we have for the present refused, all eyes are fixed upon you, wd. to God you could be perswaded to take it with [y]our former rank, write to me on this subject as soon as possible.[3] The troops ordered to the [Sou]thard are stoped by the Ice so that they will be ob[li]ged to go by Land after every arrangemt. had been made to send them down the bay.

We have certain accounts of Lord Hows being at the head of the British navy so that I think it probable that a change in the administration has taken place tho of this we are ignorant yet. This may probably bring about a great change in the british Counsels which I more & more expe[ct] & hope will look to a general peace. We have received a considerable addition of members since [you] left us but still have more on hand tha[n] we can perform. I write in the committee cham[ber] & am called upon. If any thing worth your atten[tion] turns up you shall hear from me. I forgot to inform you that Congress had resolved to adjou[rn] in April from Philadelphia, but have not yet fixed the place to which they will go.[4] I am, Dear Sir, Your Most Obt Hum. Servt,   Robt R Livingston

RC (NN: Schuyler Papers).

[1] See Schuyler to Livingston, December 7, 1779.

[2] Perhaps, of the "commissary and quartermaster general," or the "army," whose problems were the subject of Schuyler's December 7 letter to Livingston.

[3] Schuyler immediately rejected the suggestion that he accept appointment as quartermaster general. "I find all my friends in Sentiment with me," he replied to Livingston on January 18, "that It would not only be Improper but extreamly Injurious to my reputation to Accept of the Quarter Master department. I hope therefore that I will not be put in the disagreable predicament which an offer of It would expose me to." Furthermore, Schuyler then went on to explain that he could not now even accept an offer of the office of "Secretary at war," which he had previously indicated he would accept in a December 18 letter to Livingston. Both of these letters from Schuyler are in the Robert R. Livingston Papers, NHi. See also Livingston to Schuyler, January 27, 1780.

[4] Congress had adopted this resolve on December 3, which was apparently the day Schuyler set off for his assignment as a member of the committee appointed to go to headquarters. According to Charles Thomson's corrected journal entry for December 1, Schuyler had seconded this motion when it was originally made by William Ellery, but action on the matter had been postponed at that time. See *JCC*, 15:1339, 1344.

Roger Sherman to Jonathan Trumbull, Sr.

Sir   Philadelphia Decr 20th. 1779

Your Excellency's Letter to Congress respecting the lessening the States Quota of the monthly Taxes, and retaining the money raised on the last continental Tax was referred to a Committee who report as to the first that it would be attended with great difficulty and inconvenience to alter the Quotas, of any of the States—and that the State of the continental Tresury will not admit of a compliance with the latter. They have reported to allow continental pay and rations to Militia raised for the defence of the State.

The report has not been acted on by Congress, tho' I have moved Several times to have it considered. I Supposed it will be accepted.[1] There are very great complaints of the want of money in every department, and Congress depends wholly on the Several States for Supplies except what comes in to the loan offices. Warrants will be drawn on the Several States for the Monies that will become due by the first of January, and unless they are punctually answered very disagreable consequences may be expected. I was not here when Congress resolved not to Emitt Bills of Credit beyond the amount of two hundred Million dollars, but what remains of that is not near Sufficient to discharge the debts contracted by the Commissaries & Quarter Masters. Some Warrants have been already drawn on the State Treasuries And if there is not a very vigorous exertion of the States to aid in procuring Supplies not only of money but provisions the Army cannot be kept together. Congress has resolved to call on the Several States for their Quotas of the Supplies in kind, that are Necessary for carrying on the war, and to Credit all articles of the Same kind & quality at the Same prices, and other at proportionate prices. The Estimates and quotas are now preparing and as Soon as any State agrees and is prepared to procure its quota all purchases by Commissaries and Quarter Masters in Such State is to be discontinued.

As to the quota of the monthly taxes, if Connecticut had not Suffered any by the Enemy its just Quota would not have exceeded 1,400,000 dollars, and North Carolinas ought to have been the Same whereas but 1,000,000 dollars per month is required of that State. I have heard of no complaint from any State except Connecticut as to the apportionment and Several of the States if not all have actually passed laws for raising the money—So that it would be difficult to alter the proportions; if the Honble Assembly of our State dont think proper to raise the whole I Should think it would be best to raise about 1,400,000 dollars per month and trust to Supplying the deficiency by Economy in expenditures, or Some other way.

Col. Wadsworths resignation of his Office of Commissary General is accepted—and Col. Blaine is appointed but has not given his answer, & Col. Wadsworth and his deputies are requested to continue until a New one is ready to transact the business.

General Green has requested leave to resign the Office of Quarter Master General, but it is not Yet granted. Jonathan Trumbull junr Esqr is Elected a Member of the Board of Treasury, the other members are present, transacting the Business and are very desirous to have him joyn them. I dont learn that he has yet given an Answer. I Suppose he has been duly notified of the appointment, I wish he may accept it. The Salary tho' it Sounds high is really low as prices are at present, but it is the intention of Congress that the Members of that Board Should have adequate Salaries. I hope we Shall before long return to our old Standard of Lawful money. A Committee consisting of a member from each State reported to recommend to the Several States to revise their laws making the paper currency a tender, and frame them So as to Prevent injustice to Debtors or Creditors, but it has not yet passed Congress.[2] For copying the resolutions recommending a general limitation of Prices the Secretary omitted that, approving the doings of the Hartford Convention, the whole are contained in the enclosed Paper—those resolutions passed *nem. con.* the good effect expected from them is to reduce the prices to a level in all the States, with expectation that by the operation of Taxes they may be kept So, and even reduced below the limitation.

We have had no official Accounts from Europe Since the Minister of France came from thence. The Enclosed papers contain our latest Accounts from London. The Secretary Says that he transmits the Journals of Congress monthly to each State. Mr. Ellsworth arrived here last Wednesday. Mr. Huntington and he are well. I want to return home. Wish Col. Dyer or another of the Delegates would come as Soon as possible—we ought to have three at least constantly attending.

The Assembly of Pennsylvania have passed a resolve to apply to the Assembly of Connecticut to Submit the Controversy respecting the disputed territory to be decided agreable to the Articles of Confederation.[3] I wish that controversy and every other of like kind were Settled right, but doubt whether this is a Suitable time to have it duly attended to.

I am with the greatest respect, Your Excellency's humble Servant.

Roger Sherman

RC (Ct: Trumbull Papers).

¹ Congress adopted this "report" on December 28. *JCC*, 15:1415–16. See also Jesse Root to Trumbull, November 12, note 1; and Samuel Huntington to Trumbull, December 29, 1779.

² A recommendation that the states be asked to revise their legal tender laws had been considered on November 19 as part of the report of the committee studying the New Jersey and Hartford Convention proposals on price controls, but it did not pass Congress until March 20, 1780. See *JCC*, 15:1289–93, 16:269; and Samuel Huntington to the States, March 20, 1780, note 2.

³ The Pennsylvania Assembly had voted on November 18, 1779, to refer its jurisdictional dispute with Connecticut over the Wyoming Valley to Congress "to be adjusted and determined in the manner directed in and by the Articles of Confederation."

The Connecticut Assembly, however, declared in early 1780 that it could "not at present agree to the proposal made by the State of Pennsylvania," although the state would "comply to a decision of the cause agreeable to the Articles of Confederation at some reasonable and convenient time hereafter to be agreed upon or fixed." *Public Records of Connecticut*, 2:463. See also Connecticut Delegates to Joseph Reed, February 18, 1780.

William Ellery to William Greene

Sir,   Philadelphia Dec. 21st. 1779

The inclosed extract & copies are sent forward to your Excellency that Intelligence may be given to the captors of the Grayhound of the determinations of Congress respecting the capture of that Vessel. The delegates from the Massachusetts-Bay do also transmit extracts to the President of their executive Council.[1]

Your excellency will observe that the names are not properly spelled, and that our Providence is called *new* Providence. These are mistakes of the French which the translator could not correct.

As the delegates of the Massachusetts-Bay have given information to their State perhaps it may not be necessary to publish an advertisement on this occasion. If it should be done all the concerned can be notified at the same time. But of this as well as the mode of giving intelligence to Mr. Wood and the other Seamen your excellency is a proper judge.

The Cry for money from every department is so vehement and peremptory, that unless the Treasury is very soon supplied the most alarming consequences will take place; therefore I hope that our and the other States will with all possible dispatch collect what may remain uncollected of their taxes. Congress are at their wits end. Unless taxation and loaning, expecially the first, goe on briskly, notwithstanding all our successful efforts, we may be undone. We are now at the very pinch of the game, if I may so express myself. If we can but supply our army a few months, without further emissions of money, the game is our own. We then can at our leisure, and as may be most just and convenient, appretiate our currency; and thereby force the enemy to make peace with us, whose whole dependence now is that our army will disband for want of supplies, and that we shall sink under the load of multiplied emissions of Paper

Bills. The motives to vigorous exertions are great & pressing, I hope that the exertions of the several States will be proportionate.

We have nothing new. I am with every sentiment of respect, Yr. Excellency's most obedt Servt. Wm Ellery

RC (R–Ar: Letters to Governors).
[1] For the capture of the *Greyhound* and the distribution of the prize money at stake, see Massachusetts Delegates to the Massachusetts Council, December 15, 1779, note.

William Floyd to George Clinton

Sir, Philadelphia, December 21st 1779

I have this Day Rec'd your favour of the 24th of last month and am very Sorry to hear that your Excelency's proclamation Intending to prevent the wicked practice of plundering, is not like to have the Desired Effect; yet I cannot but hope that your Second application to Governor Trumbull may answer Some valuable purpos.

Several applications has been made to us as Delegates by persons from our State, to assist them in getting their friends out of prison here, that they might Remove them to the State of New York, which by their Extraordinary Solicitations we have been Induced to do; tho with great Reluctance, as we did not know whether it would be agreeable to you or not.[1] They have given Bonds for the Delivery of those Prisoners to the Commissioners at Poughkeepsie, or Albany. I hope they will fulfill their obligations. As we are at a loss to know whether it is proper to have them Removed from this State or not, we would beg if Such a Step is improper you would be pleased to Signifie it by a line; lest there Should be Some other application of a Similar Nature, and we be Induced to assist them without knowing whether it would be agreeable to the State or not.

One obligation I enclosed to you a few Days Since by one Shearer it is against (Frear & Baker) the other is herewith Inclosed which I hope will Come Safe to hand.

Congress have Resolved to Remove from this place the 1st of May next But have not yet Determined on the place where they will Remove to.

You will not be surprized at their wish to Quit this City, when you are informed of the amazing Expense of Living here; Beef in the market Current at 3 Doll's pr. lb; pork four; wood 100lb pr. Cord; flour 100lb pr. hundred w't, and other things in proportion; it Seems as if the Devil was with all his Emmisaries let loose in this State to Ruin our money, and they, the authorities of this State are So Slow in the Collecting their taxes, that it will have but little Effect towards preventing it.

However Critical and Difficult our Situation may be, yet it Cannot be improper you Should know it. Long Since Congress Resolved to

Stop the father Emition of money; Relying on the Taxes to be Raised in the Several States for Money to Carry on the war, with the Small Sums which they Expected to get by loaning.

But alass what is our Situation! Our Treasury nearly Exhausted, Every Department out of Cash, no Magazines of provision laid up, our army Starving for want of Bread, on the Brink of a General Mutiny, and the prospect of a Spedy Supply is very Small. This is a meloncholly Situation and would give our Enemies great pleasure if they knew it.

Under these Circumstances the grand Difficulty is to know what can be done for Relief, And it appears to me that if the Several States does not take on themselves to draw forth the Supplies for the use of the army, by a tax on the necessary articles, or Some other mode that may be in their power, God only knows what will become of us next Campaign; our army Cannot be kept together. But I'll Conclude the disagreable tale & Subscribe my Self your most Obed't & humble Serv't,   Wm. Floyd

Reprinted from Clinton, *Papers* (Hastings), 5:424–26.

[1] In his January 6 reply to Floyd, Governor Clinton discouraged efforts to return captured New York Loyalists to the state. "Except in some particular Instances where Persons have been previously captured by the Enemy & constrained to enter into their Service," Clinton explained, "it will be most agreable that they Continue under the Direction of the Comm'y Genl. of Prisoners, for Exchange & treated in every Respect as the other Prisoners of War. From Experience, we find that those who have joined the Enemy & have deserted from them & returned to the Country, are by no means profitable Members of the Community & we have no Reason to expect that those who we have made Prisoners will prove better. Besides, it is an Indulgence they are by no means entitled to & may serve as an Encouragement to others to be guilty of the like Treasonable Practices." *Ibid.*, p. 443.

Samuel Huntington to Caesar Rodney

Sir,   Philadelphia Decr 21st 1779.

In pursuance of the enclosed resolution passed by Congress, I think it my duty to inform you that the accounts received from our Army call for the most immediate & strenuous exertions of your State to forward a Supply of provisions.[1]

The enormous prices to which the necessary supplies for the Army have been raised have drained the public treasury, and the sole dependance of Congress for the Support of an Army & defence of our Liberties must rest on the exertions of the several States. The present exigenci admits not of the least delay, it is therefore hoped that you will procure & forward with all possible expedition as much flour as can be obtained in your State which shall be passed to your Credit in part of its Quota lately called for and due care will be taken that Justice be done to the State.

I am Sir &c,   S.H. President[2]

LB (DNA: PCC, item 14).

[1] For this December 21 resolve urging Delaware to "strenuous exertions" to procure "as much flour as can be obtained" for the immediate use of the army, see *JCC*, 15:1399.

[2] Huntington also wrote the following brief letter to Paul Fooks, "interpreter to Congress in the French and Spanish languages," on December 22, enclosing a resolve of the same date in response to his recent request for an increase in his salary.

"By the enclosed act of Congress you will be informed they have been pleased to augment your Salary to the sum of two thousand & four hundred dollars per annum." See PCC, item 14, fol. 261; and *JCC*, 15:1384, 1402.

James Lovell to Samuel Adams

Dear Sir					Decr. 21 1779.

This day your Favors of Novr. 23d & Decr. 2d to me, and one of the latter Date to Mr. Gerry & me came to Hand.[1]

I am not a little pleased as well as honored by the Fullness of the Ballot which you mention. But you say nothing of a certain Resolve which is innuendoed in the following Letter.

Copy

Honble Delegates of Massachuts			Boston Decr. 2d. 1779
    Dear Sirs

Before this reaches you, I imagine you will have recd. from the Secretary the Appointmt. of Delegates for 1780 in Congress; and as the Assembly have determined that the Delegates shall attend in Rotation, I request the favor to know yr. determinatn. with respect to yr. future Attendance, as it will influence my Conduct; if I do not hear from you, I shall set out so as to be at Congress the first Week in Jany. and attend there 3 months & then return home, as that will be the proportion of Time allotted me.

I am now in the Assembly, Table covered with Papers & much Business, that I can only add, that my best wishes ever attend you for the perfect Enjoyment of health and Happiness, & am with real Esteem, Dear Sirs, yr very humble Servant,			J.H.[2]

As to myself I cannot comprehend how the rotatory Form of 3 months is calculated, nor is it essential to know, because the Probability is great that I may be on the Road when he himself is. For you must know that upon finding Goveur.[3] was named and was solicitous to be with Doctr F[4] in the Place of Laurens who declines, I did not insist upon my Name being struck off the List on which Mr. Ellery had put it in Consequence of Mr. Mathews naming Gr.[3] I, however am so averse to going that I named Mr. Hamilton the Aid of Gl. Washington and Mr. Plater named a Col. Stewart. The House may do as they please I shall be satisfied allways but one. I declared my Unwillingness to go if the House appeared to be unembarrassed about another. This is a Situation quite ineligible to me, but I have not been chusing. I have been submitting to Situations for several years back.

If I do not go abroad, I cannot tarry here unless the State allow in some Proportion nearly resembling the Rise of Expences to me. You will be as much astonished when you come this Way as if you had not known Philadelphia last spring. The Example of 65 dollars for a pr. of Gloves that were high in Boston, at one, formerly, though Deerskins are plentier here than there may serve for a Clue to other Things. 10 & 12 Dollars for Butter is a Pretence for ruining Board. Murmur & Discontent must be the Consequence of the Taxation, for there certainly is not Currency enough circulating, for such Ratios of Demand. I will not say any Thing of the Wants of the Army at this severe Season, The Letter is bad enough already. Yr affectionate,

J.L.

[*P.S.*] Affairs of the nature of Capt. McNeilles have multiplied. Thompson & Saltonstall have made Applications,[5] but painful as the Condition of Individuals may be we have mightier Claims in too great number before us now to admit even of a prophesy *when* the former will be considered. We want immediately, four times more than all in the Treasury. We are dependent on the most strenuous Exertions of the States. I suspect Combinations of the speculating Kind against all our Expedients especially against that of our drawing Bills of Exchange. As to the Point of starving the army New York alone will prevent it, if only She can be certain that the Accounts of the Supplies from different States will be put on a just Ratio. But how can she give out her Produce at 12 or 15 or even 26 prices if this and other States have 50, 60, & 70, to be liquidated by Taxes hereafter imposed in the Citizens of New York in full Quota. I yesterday presented yr. Compliments at the Minister's. You have a Return in Kind.

In the present Stage of Uncertainty you will be cautious of writing to me what may go into wrong hands.   J.L.

RC (NN: Adams Papers).

[1] Samuel Adams' November 23 and December 2 letters to Lovell have not been found. His December 2 letter to Lovell and Elbridge Gerry is printed under a "Decr" dateline in Adams, *Writings* (Cushing), 4:167–68.

[2] That is, John Hancock.

[3] That is, Gouverneur Morris.

[4] Benjamin Franklin.

[5] Former Continental Navy captains Thomas Thompson and Dudley Saltonstall, like Hector McNeill, had recently appealed their court-martial dismissals from the navy. See *JCC*, 15:1193, 1334.

Thomas Burke to Joseph Reed

Sir   Philadelphia Decr. 22d. 1779.

The difficulties under which our affairs are now laboring cannot have escaped the attention of General Reed, A Gentleman So eminently trusted and respected by his Country, and whose Vigilence and abilities in her Service are so universally acknowledged and admired. Nor is it possible, but that his mind must have often been employed in Search of remedies for Evils So pressing and alarming. The Ideas of Such a mind may well be presumed to be important and a wish to call them out for public advantage will not, I hope, be deemed reprehensible. I wish for their assistance on an affair which now, officially employs my attention,[1] and I shall venture to request them without further apology.

The Quarter masters and Commissaries tell us that our Army will be in great distress for forage and provisions—and at the Same time Say that enough is within reach, if Money could be had to pay for them. Under our present mode of Expenditure it is not possible to say, how much money will be Sufficient for this or any other public purpose, and no Expedient can be fallen upon for obtaining a present Supply without Committing, or degrading the public Credit. Congress have, at length resolved to call on the States for Specific quotas as well as quotas of money, but Some time must elapse before this, I hope, radical remedy can be applied with full Effect. To make provision for that Interval is extremely Necessary and highly Important. Our Immediate Supplies of Forage and provisions must come from the States of Pennsylvania and Jersey, and perhaps Delewar, New York and Connecticut. I am persuaded Some Efforts might be made by the Magistrates of those States which might Extricate us from our present difficulties, and give time for the general Contributions to Come in for our future and more regular relief. If such be practicable I doubt not it will be undertaken with alacrity, and Congress ought, and I doubt not will enter into the most liberal engagements to give Indemnification, and to make the burthen be equally born by the whole union. I request you Sir to Communicate to me your Ideas as well with respect to Such Efforts as can be Immediately made by the other States in the Vicinage of the Army as that over which you preside, and also as to the Engagements Congress ought to Enter into in return. My request is, as from an Individual to a Gentleman, in his private Character, but one whose Station and abilities enable him to give Satisfactory, and important Advice and Effectual aid towards Executing Measures which may be adopted in Consequence thereof.

I am Sir, with unfeined Esteem and respect, your obdt. Sevt.

Thos Burke

RC (NHi Reed Papers).

[1] Although Burke explicitly states below that this request for information should be regarded "as from an Individual to a Gentleman, in his private Character," he was undoubtedly prompted to write this letter as a result of his recent appointment to a committee charged with ascertaining the provision and supply needs of the Continental Army for 1780 and recommending "the quantities and kinds each State ought to furnish," for which see Committee of Congress to Charles Pettit, December 20, 1779, note 1.

Robert R. Livingston to John Jay

Dear John   Philadelphia 22d Decr 1779
    I am told there will be an opportunity of sendg. this to you, I wish therefore to embrace it tho as I know not how safe the conveyance may be, I shall only deal in general. You who know the share that you have in a heart too susceptible of tender emotion will easily believe the pain it gave me to find no token of your friendship, no farewell line at this place, where I hastened immediately after my election[1] with the pleasing, tho distant prospect of seeing you here. I discovered that a Letter that I had entrusted to Duer's care did not reach you till after your embarkation, & took up another Letter which I had given to the Govr. to forward to you, written immediately after the recd. of your's, which by a strange blunder of your brother, & the negligence of Benson was not till delivered in a week after it came to Kingston tho' I was there everyday.[2] By this time I flatter myself that in conformity to the wishes of your friends, you & yours are arrived, settled, & recovered from the fatigues of your voyage. A new world is opened to you, & how gay & pleasing so ever the prospects may be which it affords, you will meet with no mercy if you do not look back upon the friends you left in this, they have participated in the pains & dangers of your voyage, it is but just that they shd. share your pleasures.
    Things here remain much in the state in which they were when you left us. The campaign has ended without any thing decisive, & our Army is at present in a better state as to numbers & discipline than it has been at any period during the war, And upon the whole the ballance has been greatly in our favor, if we except the unfortunate attempt upon Savannah of which I dare say you have particular accts. by the brave, but unfortunate, Count De Estaing who has arrived before this time if his evil genious has not continued to persecute him.
    The Enemy seem desirous of availing themselves of their success, & as we are informed, are about detaching from 8, to 10,000 troops which are already embarked as is supposed for that quarter. They have not yet sailed owing to their ignorance of the Station of Count De Grass, who was said to be in Chesapeak bay tho' he has, as the Chevalier informs me, arrived at Dominique, & the rest of his squadron at Martinique, some what injured by a storm. We have a report

in town that Pencola is taken by the Spanish troops,[3] I have not had leisure to inquire in to the truth of it tho from circumstances with which you are acquainted I give some credit to it. This is a wandring letter but I wish to crowd every thing in it which I can trust to paper that may serve to amuse you.

Coll. Lawrance has resigned his secretaryship & tomorrow we are to have a new election, tho as I beleive none of the persons in nomination will be elected, at least not yet. They are Lovel—Morris— *Coll. Steward* put in nomination by *Mr Plater* & Coll Hamilton. Floyd has very improperly namd me, agt. my express declarations, both in publick & private that I wd. not accept it, & has obstinately refused to withdraw his nomination.[4] I mention this that you may not be surprized if you see me stand upon the list without a vote (for I think I shall be able to carry the State against myself) nor argue from it, that I wish to have the place, or that I want interest to obtain it—one of which I know, & the other believe to be untrue. Duer is likewise a candidate tho he has not yet been named[5]—nor will he venture upon it till he sees whether Morris fails which I believe he will. I shall endeavour to support him, but at present, Lovels interest is the best, tho', I imagine not sufficient to bring him thro'. My plan wd. be considering all things & the character of the two Ministers to send Mr. Carmichael to France & Morris to you, who best know his trim, how far this will succeed I know not. I could wish to settle a cipher with you that I might for the future write with more freedom than I can now dare to do. For want of which I must close after desiring you to remember me most affectionately to Mrs. Jay, the Coll, & Mr. Carmichael. I write nothing about your friends, as Caty will tell you by this conveyance that they are all well. I wd. copy this but for two reasons—1st Because I am too Lazy—2d Because finding me unchanged in my negligence, you may argue from thence that I am equally unchanged, in the sentiments of affection, with which I always have, & hope ever to continue to subscribe myself, Dear John, Your friend,   Robt R. Livingston

RC (NNC: Jay Papers).

[1] In a special election to replace John Jay upon his appointment as minister to Spain, the New York legislature on October 18 had appointed Livingston a delegate to Congress "until the first day of April next." *JCC* , 15:1293–94.

[2] Only Livingston's October 6, 1779, letter to Jay has been found for this period. Jay, *Papers* (Morris), 1:617n.2.

Jay's October 25, 1779, letter to Livingston clearly reached New York after Livingston's departure, because "Clearmont" was crossed out in the address and Philadelphia substituted. Livingston did not receive it until February 1780. Livingston Papers, NHi. See also Jay to Livingston, September 16, 1779; and Livingston to Jay, February 10, 1780.

[3] This report proved to be false; Pensacola was not captured by the Spanish until May 9, 1781.

[4] In Secretary Thomson's journal entry for December 22, the following sentence is nevertheless lined out. "Mr. R.R. Livingston was put in nomination for that office

['secretary to Doctor Franklin'] by Mr. Floyd." See *JCC*, 15:1403; and PCC, item 1, 25:61. For later discussion of Livingston's candidacy for this position, see also Livingston to Jay, February 10; and James Lovell to Samuel Adams, February 16, 1780.

[5] William Duer's candidacy remained unofficial, and there is no evidence in the journals that Duer was ever formally nominated.

Robert R. Livingston to the Chevalier de La Luzerne

Sir.   Philadelphia 22d Decr 1779.

I did myself the honour to wait upon your Excellency this morning in order the more fully to explain to you the difficulties which obliged Congress to apply to Mr. Holker on the subject of supplies— But was so unfortunate as not to find you at home. Your Letter with which I was this day honoured affords me an opportunity to resume the subject & to assure you that nothing but the most urgent necessity & the express request of Genl. Washington could have induced Congress to make the application.[1] At least if I may judge of the general sentiment by that which I feel on this occasion—for tho thro' the perfect confidence I repose in yr. Excellency I could overcome that reluctance which we have to discover our weakness more especially if it can be traced back to causes which it was in our power to forsee & guard against, Yet I could not so easily bring myself to make a demand which may have the most remote tendency to embarrass the affairs of those whom we have so many reasons to wish to serve. Your Excellencys Letter has greatly added to my difficulties not only by shewing the need that his majesty may have for these supplies but by the very polite & friendly manner in which you consent to sacrafice yr interest to our necessities. Under the influence of these sentiments I have requested the Comy. to exhaust every resourse rather than make any demand for the provisions shiped by Mr Holker, But to consider them as a deposit which nothing short of the ruin of our army shd. reduce us to apply to any other use than that for which they were originaly intended.

Shd. we however find ourselves compelled to make the request your excellency will do me the justice to believe (as far as I am personally concerned in it) that it will be with a reluctance which nothing could conquer but my firm perswation that our interests are too nearly connected to be indifferent to our great Ally. There can be no doubt that the demands of the merchants to whom the ships belong will be satisfied by Congress. I flatter myself that am too well known to your Excellency to leave you the least room to doubt of my using my most strenuous endeavours with Congress to replace what your regard to our necessities may induce you lend from your stores. I have the honour to be with the sincerest profession of respect & esteem your &c.

FC (NHi: Robert R. Livingston Papers). In the hand of Robert R. Livingston.
[1] In a December 22 letter to Livingston, La Luzerne had objected to the Continental Army's use of flour collected for the French navy unless Congress gave strict assurances that it would be replaced. Livingston Papers, NHi.

The issue developed from General Washington's December 15 letter to Congress, detailing the army's dire need for provisions and suggesting that "the only temporary resource we seem to have left, 'till more effectual measures can be adopted, is this: to solicit a loan of four or five thousand barrels out of the quantity provided for the use of the french fleet and army. I am informed upwards of twenty thousand were collected in Maryland, all of which it is probable has not yet been exported." Washington's letter was read in Congress on December 20 and referred to a committee of James Forbes, Livingston, and Roger Sherman. It is clear from La Luzerne's letter that the committee first consulted the French naval agent, Jean Holker, and then La Luzerne about Washington's proposition. *JCC*, 15:1396; PCC, item 152, 8:247–50; and Washington, *Writings* (Fitzpatrick), 17:272.

Despite reservations, La Luzerne approved the release of several hundred barrels of flour collected for the French navy and loaded on three ships in Philadelphia harbor, on the condition that it be replaced and the French government indemnified, an arrangement he explained in a report to the comte de Vergennes of December 26, 1779. Archives du Ministère des affaires étrangères: correspondance politique, États-Unis, 10:125.

For a discussion of Maryland's seizure during the winter of 1779–80 of flour that had been purchased in the state by agents for the French navy, see Kathryn Sullivan, *Maryland and France, 1774–1789* (Philadelphia: Univeristy of Pennsylvania Press, 1936), pp. 70–76.

For a meeting of Livingston's committee with the Pennsylvania Council on December 20 in a related effort to obtain provisions from "sundry merchants" of Philadelphia during this emergency, see *Pa. Council Minutes*, 12:203.

James Lovell to Abigail Adams

Madam   Decr. 22d. 1779
Your sentimental Plaints and the Effusions of yr. estimable Friendship under Date of Nov. 20th yesterday only came to hand. I find a Sort of Novelty in my Passions at this moment my Head & Heart are brimful of respectful Affection for you and yet both admit a large measure of Pity upon the Sketch of yr. Situation under my Eye from your own Hand.

The Chances are great that I shall see yr. Friend & yr. Sons before you;[1] but I shall first see you. I am sure you will compassionate Mrs. L on the Occasion, and you will approve, notwithstanding, the preventive motives on which I act. Gr. M——s[2] was nominated.

Adieu,   J.L.

RC (MHi: Adams Papers).
[1] Lovell was referring to his chances of going to France as secretary to the minister plenipotentiary to France.
[2] That is, Gouverneur Morris.

George Partridge to Caleb Davis

Dear Sir   Philadelphia Decr. 22d. 1779

I very lately had the pleasure of addressing a Letter to you[1] which you will receive by Post & as I know that you will make the best use of every information relating to the public, I will take the Liberty to add That when our money was depreciating with an increased rapidity & would not purchase supplies except from those who were under an immediate necessity of Selling (which were very few here among Farmers) & the general cry of the people of all Ranks here was to stop the Press, Congress viewing viewed this as the only Alternative to preserve the credit or rather the circulation of the money, according adopted the measure when they had forty Millions of Dollars in their Power, which might reasonably be thot sufficient to purchase the remaining supplies for the Winter, & Salted provisions for the insewing Campaign, but alas the Depreciation did not Stop there, it was then said that the more than forty millions were yet to be issued & everything was raised 50 or 100 per cent, in a few weeks & flour is now here at £100 this Currency per C[wt] or more.

The Dependence for money & most of the Supplies is now on the Several States & Drafts are now making on our State Treasurer with others for Large sums which I know we must be illy able to discharge after our Penobscot Loss &c however every exertion is necessary to maintain our Army and to Convince the Enemy that we do not depend for emitting money to it. Requisitions have been made on States for a present supply of Flour which I trust will be complyd with but have not heard what is done.

The Inlistments of two thousand of the Massts. Troops will expire by the first of April next, & others at various Periods in the Spring & Summer as only about 15 or 16 hundred of our Quota were ingaged for the War, I mean of noncommissioned Officers & privates. Some other States have a Larger proportion for the war.

There is some Danger in writing particulars least the Letter should fall into bad hands, but I think it necessary to give some information to those whom I know are disposd to exert themselves, to remove every Difficulty & to improve every information to the public Advantage.

I design to be with you some time this Winter as I trust is expected from what passed before I left Boston. We are daily expecting Genl Hancock as he informd us that we might about this time.[2]

RC (MHi: Davis Papers). In the hand of George Partridge. Addressed: "To Caleb Davis Esqr., Member of Genl Assembly, Boston."

[1] See Partridge to Davis, December 13, 1779.

[2] Remainder of MS missing.

Samuel Holten's Diary

[December 23–24, 1779]
23. Thursday. I met the medical Come. Congress met early in the day.

24. Friday. Congress adjourned 'till monday next, being Christmass tomorrow.[1] No new intelligence.

MS (MDaAr).
[1] The following day Holten recorded these activities in his diary: "Christmass-day. I attended meeting, at the Roman Catho. Ch[urc]h in the forenoon, & at the Episcopal Church in the after-noon, I heard a good Sermon in the afternoon; But I do not know what I heard in the forenoon." Ibid.

Allen Jones to Richard Caswell

Sir,   Philadelphia, Decr. 23d. 1779

I take this opportunity of shewing you that I am not unmindful of my promise, but that rather than be worse than my word I write tho' I have nothing worth communicating. When I came here[1] I found our money depreciated beyond bounds and Congress taken up in finding out ways and means to remedy the evil. Before my arrival they had adopted the plan of recommending a limitation of prices to the different States, a place from which I do not promise myself much relief as I am apprehensive it will not be generally adopted. In the mean time they are busy in forming other Schemes of Finance, the foundation of which are loans both foreign and domestic. From these schemes likewise I fear nothing advantageous will arise. We have found it dangerous from experience to tamper with our money. Every step hitherto taken to appreciate it, having had the contrary effect. If we could check the expense in the departments of the Commissary and Quarter Master, I believe it would be a radical cure and until we do this, I shall think all other schemes useless. In order to do this, Congress seem determined to call on all the states for a certain part, of their Annual Quota of Continental Taxes, in kind, to be deposited in proper Magazines by such officers and at such places as the different States may think proper to direct. Upon the success of this plan, our salvation seems to me to depend, as by these means we should be able to do without a set of men who have taken care to amass most princely fortunes, at the same time that they have loaded us with debt and difficulties. I could descend to particulars on this subject, but it would carry me beyond the bounds of a letter. Thus Sir, I have endeavoured to give you an Idea of the present views of Congress, from which you will see that our situation is critical—as much depends on the measures we adopt.

This letter is not designed for the public Eye, but merely to shew you how sensible I am of your friendship, and in return to request the favor of a line whenever leisure and opportunity permits. I am with the most sincere esteem, Dr Sir, yours,   Allen Jones

Tr (Nc–Ar: Governors' Letterbooks).
[1] Jones, who had been elected October 26 for the ensuing year, first attended Congress on December 8, 1779. *JCC*, 15:1360–61.

James Lovell to Abigail Adams

Madam   Decr. 23, 1779

I inclose No. 36 of the Journals and a few News Papers in Course. I wrote you a few Lines by the Post two days ago,[1] but hope they will not reach you before these, because I wish to caution you against dropping a single Hint of what I then suggested of seing my worthy Friend abroad. A Gentleman of excellent Character is since nominated[2] so that my wishes to withdraw my Name get new Strength; in such an Event any Prior Talk of going would tend to make me appear either too changeable or defeated.

Madam, your affectionate, respectful Friend,   James Lovell

RC (MHi: Adams Papers).
[1] Actually Lovell's brief letter to Abigail of December 22.
[2] Robert R. Livingston, who had been nominated as secretary to the minister plenipotentiary to France on December 22. See Livingston to John Jay, December 22, 1779, note 4. For Lovell's view of Livingston's as opposed to Gouverneur Morris' candidacy for this post, see also Lovell to Samuel Adams, February 16, 1780.

William Churchill Houston to Robert Morris

Dear Sir,   Philadelphia 24 Decr 1779.

Yesterday I received yours of the 19th inst, and am sorry to be under the Necessity of postponing a reply to it for sheer Want of Time. Shall take the first Leisure Hour if you will please to inform me where to direct, for I suppose this is the last I shall be able to address to you at Mount Holly, the Stage not going again till next Wednesday, and your Adjournment am told is near.

It gives me inexpressible Pleasure to hear that the Legislature are upon the Subject of furnishing Supplies to the Army. The Exigency is alarmingly pressing. A Plan for ascertaining the Amount, and mode of procuring, the State Supplies will contain some further Arrangements than have been transmitted as yet,[1] but am in Hopes they will not be waited for. One probably will be that the Articles be delivered at certain Places most convenient for Transportation to the Army, under the Direction of the Executive of the State and

Comissary General of Purchases, an Officer [. . .] will still be necessary to [. . .] and regulate the [. .] of the Supplies purchased. It will
doubtless be the Case that if the Proportion of Taxes in any State, is
not equivalent to the Supplies to be furnished by them, they will be
paid the Balance by Monies raised in other States who do not furnish
so largely. Believe me, your obedt hble Servt,

William Ch Houston

RC (NjR: Robert Morris Papers).
  [1] For the work of the committee "ascertaining the Amount, and mode of procuring,
the State Supplies," see Committee of Congress to Charles Pettit, December 20, 1779,
note.

Samuel Huntington to John Laurance

Sir,   Philada. Decr 24th 1779
    You will receive herewith enclos'd an Act of Congress of the 21st
instant granting Subsistance to the Judge Advocate the same as the
present Subsistance of a Colonel, & to a Deputy Judge Advocate the
same Subsistance as a Lieutenant Colonel.[1]
    Also another Act of this day making further provision for procur-
ing Depositions & witnesses in trials not Capital before Courts
Martial.[2]
    I am Sir &c.   S.H. President

LB (DNA: PCC, item 14). Addressed: "John Lawrence Esqr Judge Advocate."
  [1] JCC, 15:1397.
  [2] JCC, 15:1409-10.

Samuel Huntington to George Washington

Sir,   Philadelphia Decr 24th 1779.
    I am honoured with your Excellency's favours of the 7th, 8th,
11th, & 15th instant, some of which have much engaged the attention of Congress.[1] I should have been happy to have had it in my
power before this time to communicate to your Excellency the proper
decisions of Congress on the important Matters contain'd in several
of those Letters.
    At present I have the honour to transmit your Excellency two Acts
of Congress of the 23d & 24th instant; The former ascertaining the
subsistance to be allowed to the Officers in the department of the
field Commissary of Military Stores;[2] and the latter making further
provision for the obtaining Depositions & witnesses in trials not
Capital before Courts Martial.
    I have the honour to be, with perfect respect, your Excy's hble
Servt,   Sam Huntington President

RC (DLC: Washington Papers). In a clerical hand and signed by Huntington. LB (DNA: PCC, item 14).

[1] In the LB this passage reads "7th, 8th, 10th, 11th, & 15th Instant." Furthermore, according to the journals Congress had recently received letters from Washington of December 7, 8, 10–11, 13, 14, 15, and 17 on December 11, 14, 17, 20, and 21 respectively, for which see *JCC*, 15:1367–68, 1374, 1389, 1396–97; PCC, item 152, 8:207–49; and Washington, *Writings* (Fitzpatrick), 17:230–32, 238–39, 241–44, 258, 262–63, 272–73.

[2] Huntington also enclosed a copy of this resolve this day with a brief letter to the field commissary of military stores, Samuel Hodgdon. See PCC, item 14, fol. 261; and *JCC*, 15:1403–4.

Nathaniel Peabody to Josiah Bartlett

My Dear sir,   No. 18.   Philada. 24th Decr. 1779

I have the pleasure of acknowledging your agreable favour of the 13th ulto.[1] which Came to hand the 15th instant and Should have acknowledged it at an Earlier period but the Irregularity of the Post Riders of late has been Such as that there was little dependence to be made upon them &c.

I am not disappointed at the Circumstance you mention, of the time of the Genl Assembly being Employed in matters that are not of the utmost Consequence. I hope Taxation, and every other probable means, for Supporting our Currency will be adopted & vigorously Prosecuted by the State. The Trial of *Rowell* is some what Alarming, And I Cannot Conceive what excuse Can be Given for that infamous Pattles being on the Jury, Since the affair of Thornton must have made Some disagreable impressions on the Minds of many true friends to the Country.

I wish to hear who are in the Genl. Assembly after the New Election, Tho I Suppose there will be Little, or no alteration in the Council but there may be in the House, I Should be peculiarly Gratified by being informed of the different movements of Electors in genl. but more particularly of those in Plaiston & Atkinson who Sets up &c. &c. The Expence of living here is intolerable, beyound Conception, and almost insupportable. Our Finances are in Such a Situation, that policy forbids me to entertain you upon a Subject of So delicate and interesting a Nature unless I was Sure of a *Safe* Conveyance. I Shall make those Extracts and Collections that whenever I return home and Should once more have the happiness of Seeing my friends face to face, Shall be Able to give a Tolerable account of proceedings &c. I have not missd attending Congress but part of one day Since I came hither and what makes it very Difficult a Number of us gener-ally attend from one to two hours in the morning before we Can make a Congress, And then are obliged to *Set* till Near *Sunset* before we adjourn—And by the time we have dined and done a Little Committee business it is near honnest bed time—which prevents my giving you Some hints that I otherwise Should—which possibly might be done without much hazzard under Types figures &c. Pray Send me all the Laws that have passed Since I Came *Out* from among you.

Adieu for this time, and believe me to be most Sincerely your friend & very Humle Serv,   Nath Peabody

[*P. S.*] If this is perfect nonsence pray excuse me upon the presumption that it is not a "*Natural production*." I never wrote in more hast and have not read what I have wrote.

RC (NhD: Bartlett Papers).
[1] Not found.

Committee of Congress to Benjamin Lincoln

Sir,   Philadelphia Decr. 27. 1779
We have within a few hours received certain information of the sailing of the fleet from New York.[1] Said to consist of 163 Sail. What number of troops are on board we do not learn. We thought it necessary to give you this information without a moments loss of time, & hope it will be able to reach you before the arrival of the fleet.

We are sir, with much Esteem, yr. most Obedt servt.
                                             Jno. Mathews Chairman

[*P. S.*] We must request of you sir not to detain the express longer than is absolutely necessary, & by him to give us a particular account of your situation, force &c,   J.M.

RC (NN: Emmet Collection). Written and signed by John Mathews.
[1] See the following entry, note.

Elbridge Gerry to Benjamin Lincoln

Dear sir,   Philadelphia Decr 27. 1779
I embrace the Oppertunity by Major Rice of transmitting You the Journals of Congress of 1777, & of 1779 as far as the 20th of Novr last. Those of 1778 & the Residue of the present Year are not yet printed.

Having wrote to You by Lt. Colo. Laurens who left the City last Week for Charlestown, I have only to inform You that by Letter from General Wayne to General Washington of the 23d Instant,[1] Copies of wch are transmitted to Congress, it appears "that 137 Sail of shipping lay at Sandy Hook at 8 o Clock" in the Morning of that Day; that soon after, 102 had weighed anchor & gone to sea amongst which was a large Man of War, supposed to be Admiral Arbuthnot; *that* the Remainder of the Fleet being 35 Sail, (And 28 Ships which sailed in the afternoon of the same Day) steered eastward. General Wayne further says "the probability is, that the 102 Sail mentioned, formed the first Division under Admiral Arbuthnot, & that the 28 with the 35 sail of Ships at the Hook, which may probably be joined by some more, from the second Division (or the Cork fleet) under Sir George Collier. I have no Account of what Troops are on board, but expect every Hour to be informed. Two prisoners report that 10,000 Men have sailed."

I salute You with the Compliments of the Season & remain sir your Friend & very hum Serv,   E. Gerry

RC (PPRF).
[1] Gen. Anthony Wayne's December 23 letter to General Washington was enclosed with Washington's December 24 letter to Congress. Both letters were read in Congress this day, and are in PCC, item 152, 8:261–62, 267–68. *JCC*, 15:1410.

Samuel Huntington to the Chevalier de La Luzerne

Sir,   Philada Decr 27th 1779
I have the honour to present you with an Act of Congress of the 16th Novemr 1779 together with a Copy of my letter of the 18th of Novemr last, enclosing the same Act of Congress, to Colo John Beatty Commissary General of Prisoners; and an Extract of his letter of the 20th instant in answer to mine, by which you will be informed of the Care taken and provision made by Congress for the Spanish prisoners at New York.[1]

I have the honour to be &c,   S.H. President

LB (DNA: PCC, item 14).
[1] For the enclosed "Act of Congress," see Huntington to John Beatty, November 18, 1779. Beatty's December 20 "answer" to Huntington is in PCC, item 78, 3:425–28.

James McLene to Joseph Reed

Sir   Pa. Decr. 27th 1779
Being informed this morning that in the Townships Near Carlisle in Cumberland County No Collecter has Demanded the fifteen million tax (& the State Being much Reflected on for Being Dilatory) I Submit it to your Excy whether it would Not be proper for you to write or Direct Mr. Ritenhouse[1] to write to the treasurer of Cumberland on the Subject &c.[2] I Remain Your Excys most obedient Hble Sevt.   Jas. McLene

RC (PHC: Roberts Collection). Addressed: "His Excy Joseph Reed President."

[1] David Rittenhouse, the Treasurer of Pennsylvania.
[2] Two other matters involving Continental affairs were also brought before the Pennsylvania Council this day. Delegate James Searle attended to present Congress' December 27 resolve concerning the disputed Pennsylvania–Virginia boundary, which elicited a proclamation from President Reed the following day. And the council adopted a report complaining of the neglect of the Philadelphia barracks since they had been turned over to Continental authorities, which the Pennsylvania delegates submitted to Congress on January 7, 1780. See *Pa. Council Minutes*, 12:208–11; *Pa. Archives*, 1st ser. 8:61–62; *JCC*, 16:21; and PCC, item 43, fols. 239–42.

Roger Sherman to Jonathan Trumbull, Sr.

Sir   Philadelphia Decr. 28th. 1779

Nothing remarkable has occurred here Since My last,[1] except the enclosed resolution of Congress for regulating the Post Office, and discharging all express riders, which establishment had envolved the public in a very enormous expence. It is Supposed that the Posts as Now ordered to be regulated will Answer for communicating Intelligence without employing expresses except on Some extraordinary Occasions.[2] I have likewise enclosed the Several resolutions respecting, the States furnishing Supplies.[3]

The Assembly's of New Jersy & Maryland have passed laws for regulating prices Agreable to the recommendation of Congress of the 19th of Novr last. Congress was led to this measure by an application from the Legislature of New Jersey, and the proceedings of the Convention of the five eastern States held at Hartford. It was the general Understanding that Wheat was one dollar Per Bushel in 1774 & other grain in proportion.

I am with the greatest respect, Your Excellency's humble Servant.

Roger Sherman

[P.S.] The enclosed Copies are true tho not attested. I Suppose have been or will be transmitted by the President.

RC (Ct: Trumbull Papers).
[1] Sherman to Trumbull, December 20, 1779.
[2] See Samuel Huntington to Richard Bache, December 29, 1779.
[3] *JCC*, 15:1377–78, 1391.

Elbridge Gerry to Joseph Ward

Sir   Philadelphia Decr 29. 1779

I have received by the post your Letter of the 23d Instant, & can give You no agreable Information relative to the Affairs of your Department. The Attention of Congress has been called from them, however important; to other Matters of Moment, which are still the Subjects of their Deliberation; I shall nevertheless take the first

Oppertunity to communicate the Substance of your Letter, to Congress, & to urge the Decision therein requested.[1]

I perceive by the Seal of your Letter, that It was opened before I received it, probably for the purpose of adding the postscript; but if it has otherwise happened, I wish the Matter may be traced, & inclose the Seal for your Inspection.

I remain sir with much Esteem, your Friend & huml Serv,

E. Gerry

RC (ICHi: Joseph Ward Papers).
[1] See Joseph Spencer to Ward, August 23, 1779, note.

Samuel Huntington to Richard Bache

Sir   Philada Decr 29th 1779

You will receive herewith enclos'd several acts of Congress of the 27th & 28th instant for regulating the Post Office &c.[1]

You will readily perceive the importance and necessity of carrying into execution these regulations with all possible despatch, the nature of the case admits.

I am Sir &c. &c.,   S.H. President

LB (DNA: PCC, item 14).
[1] For these resolves concerning Post Office expenses, postage rates, and the abolition of express rider service, see *JCC*, 15:1411–12, 1415; PCC, item 61, fols. 453–54, 463–64; and Huntington to Bache, December 2, 1779, note.

Samuel Huntington to Jacob Gerhard Diriks

Sir,   Philada Decemr 29th. 1779

By the act of Congress of this day herewith enclos'd, you will be inform'd that in consideration of the peculiar Circumstances attending your Case, they have been pleased to order that you be allow'd the pay & subsistance of a Lieut. Col. in the army of the United States from the Date of your brevet until the further order of Congress.[1]

I am Sir your &c,   S.H. Pt.

LB (DNA: PCC, item 14).
[1] In a December 15 letter to Congress, Diriks had reviewed his contributions to the United States since his plan for promoting a Dutch loan through Baron van der Capellen had been adopted in November 1778, and he had accordingly asked compensation commensurate to his expenses and services. Upon recommendation of the Board of War, to which Diriks' memorial had been referred, Congress immediately adopted the enclosed resolve paraphrased here by Huntington. See *JCC*, 15:1382, 1417; PCC, item 78, 7:269–72, item 147, 2:689; and these *Letters*, 10:419n.2.

Samuel Huntington to William Galvan

Sir,   Philada Decr 29th 1779
    In conversation with you this morning I misremembered the pro-
ceedings of Congress on your Letter of yesterday: enclos'd you will
receive their answer.[1]
    I am Sir your hble Servt.   S.H. President.

LB (DNA: PCC, item 14).
    [1] Huntington's enclosure was Congress' curt, December 28 resolve, adopted in
response to Galvan's solicitation of a lieutenant colonelcy in the Continental Army,
ordering that he "be informed his request cannot be complied with." See *JCC*, 15:1414.
Galvan's "request" is in PCC, item 78, 10:191–98.
    Galvan had, however, submitted his case to Congress on November 30, since which
time it had been under consideration by the Board of War, whose December 27
report on the matter was read in Congress, probably not coincidentally, this same day.
According to Charles Thomson's endorsement on the report, the board's recommendation that Galvan be commissioned a major in the Inspector General's Department
was almost unanimously opposed by the delegates, although no indication that the
recommendation was formally acted upon at this time appears in Thomson's journals.
Nevertheless, when consideration of the report was resumed two weeks later, Congress adopted the board's recommendation, ordering that Galvan receive the commission of major and "be employed in the inspectorship, as the Commander in Chief
shall direct." *JCC*, 15:1419–21; 16:44; and PCC, item 78, 10:183–86, item 147,
3:619–22. See also these *Letters*, 10:525–26, 12:208–9.

Samuel Huntington to Jonathan Trumbull, Sr.

Sir,   Philadelphia Decr 29th 1779
    Your Excellency will receive herewith enclos'd several Acts of Con-
gress of the 2d & 6th of June 1778 & the 28th instant.
    By the latter in answer to your Excellency's letter of the 2d of
Novemr last you will be informed that Congress cannot alter the
quotas assign'd to the several States by their resolution of the 7th of
Octobr last, nor in the present critical posture of affairs assent to the
retaining of any part of the taxes raised for general use.[1]
    That Continental pay and rations agreeable to the resolutions of
June 2d & 6th 1778 (which are enclosd) be allow'd for the service of
the militia which shall appear to have been necessarily employed for
the defence of the said State (Connecticut) between the first day of
April & first of Novemr last.
    I have the honour to be, with sincere Esteem & respect, your
Excys hble Servt,   Sam. Huntington President

RC (Ct: Trumbull Papers). In a clerical hand and signed by Huntington.
    [1] For Trumbull's November 2 letter to Congress requesting permission to retain a
portion of Connecticut's 1780 quota to defray expenses incurred in defending the
state against British attacks the previous summer, see Jesse Root to Trumbull, November 12, 1779, note 1. Although Congress delayed confronting the state's request for

several weeks, the delegates finally rejected its appeal on December 28, but added in compensation that the Connecticut militia mobilized against the British invasion of the state would draw Continental pay and rations during the crisis. See *JCC*, 15:1415–17; and PCC, item 20, 1:285–86.

For the rejection of a request from Massachusetts for a similar exemption, to defray expenses related to the ill–fated Penobscot expedition, see Samuel Holten to the Massachusetts Council, November 11, 1779, note 2.

Samuel Huntington to George Washington

Sir,　　　　　　　　　　　　　　　　Philadelphia 29th Decr 1779.

Your Excellency will receive herewith enclos'd two Acts of Congress of the 27th & 28th instant, for regulating the Post Office & discharging all Express riders retain'd in Constant pay at public Expence.[1]

It is expected this regulation of the Post Office punctually executed will supercede the necessity of keeping Express riders in Constant pay, & in a great Measure save the Expence of private Expresses, tho' from Necessity they must some times be employed on particular Occasions.[2]

I have the honour to be, with perfect respect, your Excy's hble Servt.　　　　　　　　　　　　　　Sam. Huntington President

RC (DLC: Washington Papers). In a clerical hand and signed by Huntington.

[1] See Huntington to Richard Bache, this date.

[2] Huntington also sent copies of the resolve of the 27th concerning the expense of expresses to Quartermaster General Nathanael Greene, this day, and to Assistant Quartermaster General Charles Pettit on December 30. See PCC, item 14, fols. 264–65, 268–69.

Congress' decision to discharge "all express riders in the pay of the United States," adopted in what has been characterized as "a fit of irritation" over the expense and unreliability of the express rider system, was quickly reversed. In his January 5 response to this letter, Washington simply declared that "the exigency and good of the service will not admit of a general discharge of the Express Riders," and that consequently he was suspending the operation of the resolve "till farther directions of Congress." "Circumstances very interesting frequently arise that demand an instant communication," he patiently explained, "and to places intirely out of the tract of the post. Nor does it appear to me that it would answer to rely on getting of occasional Expresses at the moment they are wanted, both on account of the delay that would often happen and the risk of employing improper characters. The preciousness of moments in military arrangements will often make the delay of an hour extremely injurious; nor am I clear how far this plan may be conducive to œconomy; for persons so engaged on an emergency will not fail to exact enormous reward . . . . If one half the present Expresses were dismissed, I should imagine this would be carrying the experiment as far as would be safe in the first instance, and we shall be better able to judge hereafter whether it may with propriety be extended any farther."

As a result, Congress resolved on January 14 "That the Commander in Chief be authorised to order so many expresses to be retained in the public service as he may judge necessary for the immediate purposes of the army," and subsequently left the supervision of the express service to Washington and the Board of War. Nevertheless, its intervention at this time resulted in the striking reduction in the number of expresses from 112 to 17, and the unauthorized use of them by staff and civilian officers significantly diminished. See *JCC*, 15:1412, 16:41, 56; Washington, *Writings* (Fitzpatrick), 17:355–56; and John C. Fitzpatrick,"The Continental Express Rider," *Daughters of the American Revolution Magazine* 57 (1923): 656–58.

Maryland Delegates to Thomas Sim Lee

Sir,   Philadelphia Decr. 29th 1779
   We received the inclosed from Major Lee the other Day, & beg Leave to forward it for the Consideration of your Excellency & the Council—being well assured that you will do all in your Power to relieve the Necessities of those valuable Men who are in Majr Lee's Corps. We have applied to the Board of War, & find nothing can be done here.[1] On the 23d inst an Embarkation took Place at New York, & from the Number of Vessels (one hundred sixty ships) we apprehend it to be very considerable—their Destination not certainly known, but from Circumstances we fear they are intended, in Part or the whole, to reinforce their Troops in the southern Quarter. We are with the highest Sentiments of Respect, Yr. Excellency's most obt. hble. Servts.   Geo. Plater

                                            James Forbes

RC (MdAA: Red Books). Written by Plater and signed by Plater and Forbes.
   [1] Gen. William Smallwood, the ranking Maryland officer, had denied Maj. Henry Lee's request for money and clothing for the Maryland officers incorporated into his Virginia partisan corps. Lee considered the decision "very injurious, especially when a late resolution of Congress declares the additional battalions to be on the same footing, as the troops from the State or States, to which they may respectively belong." The letters of Smallwood and Lee, dated December 21 and 23 respectively, are in the Red Books, MdAA. For Congress' resolution of July 1, 1779, giving the officers of the additional and state battalions equal preference, see *JCC*, 14:790. In an undated letter of late December or early January, Lee appealed to the Maryland delegates to hasten aid for the Maryland officers because "the season of the year is rigerous, the gentlemen destitute of cloathing & their brother officers from Virginia comfortably supplied." On May 24, 1780, the Maryland Council ordered that allowances be paid to captains George Handy and John and Michael Rudolph of "Major Lees Corps." See *Md. Archives*, 43:180, 399. See also Maryland Delegates to Thomas Sim Lee, January 5, 1780.
   In his letter of December 23 to the Maryland delegates, Major Lee also requested that Congress permit Capt. Allen McLane, of Delaware, "to draw the full allowance due the Maryland gentlemen." McLane's company of infantry had been incorporated into Lee's corps the previous July, for which see Delaware Delegates to McLane, July 5, 1779.

James Forbes to Thomas Sim Lee

My Dear Sir,   Philadelphia Decr 30th 79
   I have yours of the 21st Currt covering £6 Jersey Curry which shall endeavour to get exchanged, allso yours of the 25 Currt. I am

gratly disappointed in being continued in the Delegation to Congress, as I had desired Mr Jenifer in case I was put in the nomination to let them know, that I wisht to be left oute, And now shall be under the necessaty of resigning. I have wrote the Legislature on the occation and hope they will order one of the new Delegates up, in order to keep up the representation as I shall leave Congress, as soon as this event takes place.

Your request respecting the purchase of the Horses & Charriot shall be attended to, but am affraid he would not be able to make it but on the most extravagent terms. The Chariot you never mentioned before, Griffen will not take the 8000 Dollars for the Mairs, nor will he agree to waite your answer as to the 10,000 he says he is now out of the mind of selling. I am pleased with the liberallity of your sallery. Inclosed you have the papers. Make my most respectfull Compliments to your Lady & the Family at Millwood with that of the Season & be asshured that I ever am, Yours Affecty,

James Forbes

[P.S.] A Lettr from Genl Washington just cum to hand,[2] advises of a very large Embarcation from N Y being Sailed with Genl Clinton & a number of Horse he thinks their destination is Chesepeake Bay.

RC (MdHi: Middendorf Deposit, 1972).
[1] Despite his intention to resign, Forbes continued to sit in Congress under the terms of his December 22 reelection until ill health prevented his attendance in early March 1780. Forbes died March 25. See *JCC*, 16:273, 277, 285–86, 17:509.
[2] See Samuel Huntington to Thomas Sim Lee and Richard Caswell, this date, note.

Samuel Huntington to Joseph Baldesqui

Sir,   Philada Decr 30th 1779
    You will receive herewith inclos'd several acts of Congress of the 28th & 29th Instant, by which you will be inform'd that in the opinion of the Auditors of the Army you have discharged your duty as Paymaster to General Pulaski's Legion with strict Integrity & honour, and that Congress have been pleased to accept your Resignation.[1]
    I am Sir, your hble Servt,   S. H. Pt.

LB (DNA: PCC, item 14).
[1] In his December 11 memorial Capt. Joseph Baldesqui had sought relief from a May 17, 1779, resolve of Congress concerning his accounts as paymaster to Casimir Pulaski's legion, which he believed impugned his integrity in charging "want of regularity in keeping those accounts." This Congress granted on December 28, at the recommendation of the Board of Treasury, which concluded upon investigation that Baldesqui had "discharged his duty with strict integrity and honor."
    Baldesqui's memorial also contained a request to resign his position as paymaster, which he assumed could be dispensed with, since in the aftermath of Pulaski's recent death the legion would probably be dissolved. This request Congress approved on December 29, at the recommendation of the Board of War, to which that part of the

captain's memorial had been referred. See *JCC*, 14:598, 895, 15:1368, 1414, 1417–18; and PCC, item 41, 1:266–72, item 147, 2:691–92.

At the recommendation of the Board of War, Congress also simultaneously authorized the reorganization of Pulaski's legion, and accordingly empowered Gen. Benjamin Lincoln, commander of the southern department, "to incorporate such of the men as remain, into such of the regiments of horse and infantry under his command, as he shall think proper." This resolve Huntington had already transmitted to Lincoln with a brief cover letter of December 29. See *JCC*, 15:1418; PCC, item 14, fol. 266; and Wright, *The Continental Army*, pp. 134, 347–49.

Samuel Huntington to Thomas Jefferson

Sir,   Philada Decr 30th 1779
    Your Excellency will receive herewith enclos'd the copy of a letter from Thomas Scott to the President of Pennsylvania of the 29th of Novemr last with a copy of the proceedings of the President & Council of Pennsylvania of the 15th of Decemr, as also an act of Congress of the 27th Instant[1] consequent thereon recommending to the contending Parties not to grant any part of the disputed lands or to disturb the possession of any persons living thereon & to avoid every appearance of force until the dispute can be amicably settled by both States or brought to a Just decision by the intervention of Congress, That possession forcibly taken be restored to the original possessor and things in the situation they were at the Commencement of the war, without prejudice to the Claims of either party.
    I have the honour to be &c.   S.H. Pt.

LB (DNA: PCC, item 14). Jefferson, *Papers* (Boyd), 3:248–49.
[1] Thomas Scott's November 29 letter to Joseph Reed is in PCC, item 69, 2:165–67, and Jefferson, *Papers* (Boyd), 3:206–8. Reed's December 15 letter to the Pennsylvania delegates in Congress is in PCC, item 69, 2:157–64; and *Pa. Archives*, lst ser. 8:46–47. These had been referred on December 16 to a committee consisting of James Forbes, Robert R. Livingston, and Roger Sherman, whose report was read and adopted by Congress on the 27th. See *JCC*, 15:1384, 1411; and PCC, item 20, 2:63–64.
    Pennsylvania had been alarmed by the activities of Virginia officials and settlers in Westmoreland County in the aftermath of the state's adoption of a new land office act in June 1779, which had already led Congress to appeal to all the states "to forbear settling . . . unappropriated lands or granting the same during the continuance of the present war." See Huntington to the States, October 30, 1779. For Jefferson's response to Huntington and additional documents concerning the efforts of Virginia and Pennsylvania to settle their boundary dispute, see also Jefferson, *Papers* (Boyd), 3:77–78, 200, 216, 286–89.

Samuel Huntington to
Thomas Sim Lee and Richard Caswell

Sir   In Congress Decr. 30. 1779
    By order of Congress I have the honor of forwarding to you the enclosed important intelligence which is just come to hand.[1]

I am, Sr, Your obedient humble servt.

Sam. Huntington President

RC (MdAA: Red Books). In the hand of Charles Thomson and signed by Huntington. Addressed: "His Excellency Thomas Sim Lee Esqr., Governor of Maryland." LB (Nc-Ar: Governor's Letterbooks). Addressed: "Gov. Caswell."

[1] Huntington's enclosures consisted of copies of two December 27 letters, from Maj. Henry Lee to James Searle and from Washington to Huntington, and an extract of Gen. Anthony Wayne's December 26 letter to Washington, all on the subject of the sailing of a second British fleet from Sandy Hook on December 26. Lee's letter is in PCC, item 78, 14:303–4. Washington's letter and the extract from Wayne's that he sent to Huntington are in PCC, item 152, 8:271–76; the original of Wayne's letter is in the Washington Papers, DLC.

According to the journals, the "order of Congress" (of December 31) for forwarding the enclosed intelligence directed that it be sent "to the governors of Maryland and Virginia," but no mention was made of North Carolina. *JCC*, 15:1424. Huntington failed to enclose this intelligence with his letter to Governor Jefferson of Virginia this day, but did so with a brief letter to him of January 3, 1780, which is in the Dreer Signers Collection, PHi.

Huntington apparently sent these enclosures to the chevalier de La Luzerne also, as his presidential letterbook contains the following letter of this date to "The French Minister." "Sir, I do myself the honour to lay before you the important intelligence contain'd in the inclos'd papers." PCC, item 14, fol. 267.

Samuel Huntington to Baron de Miklaszewicz

Sir,   Philada Decr 30th 1779

By the act of Congress of the 23d instant herewith enclos'd you will be inform'd that there is no vacancy in the Marine Service at this time that you cannot be employ'd as there are a number of Officers in that line now out of employ.[1]

I am Sir, &c   S.H. President

LB (DNA: PCC, item 14).

[1] In a letter of December 15, Miklaszewicz had described himself as a captain experienced in the service of Poland and petitioned Congress for a commission as captain of marines. His petition was referred to the Board of Admiralty, whose recommendation against it was adopted by Congress on the 23d. *JCC*, 15:1400, 1406; and PCC, item 41, 6:164.

Before this decision was transmitted to him, however, he had submitted a second letter to Congress—seeking compensation for his expenses in coming to America and the loss of his baggage—which was not acted upon until January 21. Congress' resolve rejecting this second appeal was sent to him by Huntington in a brief letter of transmittal the same day. See *JCC*, 15:1410, 16:41, 78; and PCC, item 14, fol. 281, item 78, 15:615–18, item 147, 4:79–80.

Cyrus Griffin to Ephraim Blaine

Wednesday [December, 1779][1]

C. Griffin's Compliments to Colonel Blaine—would be exceedingly obliged to him to order one Barrel of Beef and one of pork to be made up in the best manner for the table use of C.G.—he did not intend to have troubled the public officers in this way, and finding it impossible to maintain his house at the market prices without absolute destruction, solicited to return home, but the state not granting his request, he is obliged to have recourse to some few Articles from the Continent. C. Griffin has also recd. from time to time a few Barrels of Flour, but so unlucky as never to get but one that was *good*, and which was intended for another Member of Congress—therefore if Colonel Blain will also order one Barrel of the best flour and a few bushells of rye meal, he would take it a particular favor.

C. Griffin's Direction is third street, near Lombard street.

C.G. is obliged to pay all market expenses out of his own pocket, but whatever the Continent furnish, the State of Virginia will reimburse, which makes a very great difference in so ruinous a place as Philadelphia. However C.G. does not mean to encroach at all upon the Provisions allotted to the real subsistance of the army, but would sooner spend every shilling of his own Fortune.

RC (DLC: Blaine Papers). Addressed: "Colo Blaine, Com. Gen. Purchases."
[1] Although dated only "Wednesday" by Griffin, this note is endorsed by Blaine "December 1779."

Cyrus Griffin to
the Virginia Board of Trade

Gentlemen,   Philadelphia, January 3rd. 1780.

In consequence of your letter to the Delegates of Congress in August last to procure from the Continent a sum of money adequate to purchases for the officers and soldiers in the Virginia line, I have this day with great difficulty negotiated 120,000 dollars with the board of Treasury which according to the determination of Congress must be instantly paid to the quarter-master general. Mr Moss upon an accurate settlement of his affairs in this City will fall in debt about that sum—and principally from the purchase of some light cloathing designed for the troops who are marching to the Southward.[1] It appears to me the purchase above mentioned was extremely judicious—to my Judgment things of that sort will be abundantly more expensive in the course of a few months, and perhaps not to be gotten at all. You will observe the order upon your board is drawn to the amount of 130,000 dollars; 120,000 being sufficient to answer the purposes of Mr Moss. I shall retain the remaining 10,000 dollars as so much of what the assembly are pleased to allow their delegates in Congress and the Treasurer will accordingly give your Board credit for that Sum and make it a charge agt. myself. I have the honor to be with great respect, Gentlemen, your most obedient and very humble servant,   C. Griffin

[*P.S.*] I suppose you have heard that Maryland has seized all the *flour* in that state designed for *Virginia*, and for the French fleet.[2]

RC (Vi: Executive Papers).
  [1] This day Congress ordered two $130,000 warrants issued, one on the treasurer in favor of Virginia agent John Moss who had purchased "certain supplies of cloathing, and other necessaries" for the use of Virginia's Continental troops and the other on the Virginia Board of Trade in favor of the quartermaster department "to reimburse the like sum this day lent to the said State." *JCC*, 16:8–9.
  [2] See Robert R. Livingston to La Luzerne, December 22, 1779, note 1.

Samuel Huntington to Jonathan Trumbull, Jr.

Sir   *Private*   Philadelphia January 3rd. 1779
    I am honourd with your two Letters of the 10th Ulto. Give me leave to hope that on serious Consideration you have determind to Accept your appointment, or at farthest will soon come to that determination.[1]
    Your Assistance, believe me, is much wished for & wanted in that Important department. The other two members Messers Foreman & Gibson have accepted, & entered upon the duties of their Office some time since. Alltho, the present nominal salary is of uncertain value, there is no doubt a decent Support will be allowd the members of the Treasury board.
    You Justly mention difficulties & Embarrassments, but my dear Sir let me Ask are there any difficulties Existing *equal* to what you & I expected when this Mighty Controversy began. I hope Sir Soon to hear of your Acceptance & wish for the pleasure to hear it from your own mouth.
    I have long been in the Sentiments you express, of the necessity of fixing a *Standard* for the currency, and am confident were it once fix'd it would remove many difficulties, but a free people must *feel* before they will unite in the necessary measures.
    I have ever been of one Opinion with regard to a regulating Act & now find my Sentiments coincide with yours on that Subject, but I find one Consolation very necessary in public life, that is to believe or at least act as if I did fully believe there are many wise men who can Judge better than myself on Important Subjects, & I have the happiness generally to unite in promoting their determinations, as

far as duty requires in any Sphere I am called to act in I am Sir with great Respect, your Obedient humb servt,

Sam. Huntington

RC (CtHi: Jonathan Trumbull, Jr., Papers).
[1] For Trumbull's appointment as a treasury commissioner and ultimate decision to decline the post, see Huntington to Jonathan Trumbull, Jr., November 12, 1779, note 2.

George Partridge to Joseph Ward

Dear Sir   Philadelphia Jany 3d 1780

Yours of the 7th ultimo was duely receivd, but I did not design to have answered it till I could have informed you of the Determination of Congress on your repeated application, but least you should misconstrue such Delay, I would inform you that I am almost weary of making fruitless motions on that Matter,[1] no wonder then you'll say that your Patience is nearly exhausted—true—but when you consider the State of our currency, the State of our finances, and the consequent Difficulty of supplying a suffering Army, the Necessity of recruiting the Regts. & a variety of other Matters which your own Ingenuity will suggest, you will not perhaps think it *so* strange that it should be difficult to draw the attention of Congress to any Matter which they do not think of the greatest importance immediately to attend to, and which will take them sometime [*to*] adjust. However I make no doubt but that your Officers will have their Subsistance made good to them equally as Officers of the Line, and to commence from the same time. I shall not be inattentive to the Matter, but you are sensible that I have but one voice, & that a feeble one.

It is my sincere wish that you may have ample Justice done you & speedily, & that you may continue to serve your Country in publick character being convinced that your abilities & Disposition are happily united to render it important Services.

I am with great Regard, your most obedt. Humbe Servt,

Geo. Partridge

P.S. My Colleagues tell me that they will join with me in pushing this Matter immediately.

RC (ICHi: Joseph Ward Papers). Addressed: "To Colo. Joseph Ward, Commissary Genl. of Musters, Morris Town."
[1] For the final resolution of "that Matter," which resulted in the abolition of Joseph Ward's mustering department, see Samuel Huntington to Ward, January 14, 1780.

William Ellery to William Greene

Sir,   Philadelphia Jany. 4th. 1780.

Since I last had the honour of writing to your excellency[1] nothing material hath occurred: But as I may be thought negligent unless I write now & then to the Assembly I therefore now resume my pen.

We have not received any foreign intelligence for a long time; and nothing domestick but the sailing of the long—talk'd—of embarkation from New York. They sailed in two divisions. The first, which consisted of more than an hundred sail, and which Genl. Washington says "it is generally imagined consisted of returning transports and private vessels bound to Europe," sailed on the 23d ultmo. The last division consisting of 110 sail, principally large ships, put to Sea the 26th.

A large number of troops were in this fleet; but how great the number, by whom commanded, and where destined is uncertain. It is generally thought that a part of them, at least, is bound to the Southward, and it is reported that Genl. Clinton in person commands the expedition. Genl. Parsons, who commands a body of troops advanced towards the sound, wrote Genl. Washington "that a number of southern refugees are said to be on board the fleet, among them Governor Martin."[2]

Last Tuesday we had a very heavy storm. I hope we may have the pleasure of adopting Queen Elizabeth's motto afflavit Deus et dissipantur. It is said that the Spaniard hath taken Pensacola. If this should prove true, and they should procede and capture St. Augustine, it would make a fine diversion in favor of Charlestown, provided the expedition from N. York should be intended against South–Carolina. A considerable body of troops are on their march to join Genl Lincoln; but will arrive there too late to succour Charlestown against the supposed intended attack.

We are busily employed in financing and procuring supplies for the army. Bills of exchange are falling; and some people begin to be apprehensive of evils from appretiation. These are favorable symptoms. As we have put a stop to further emissions, if tax procedes, it is improbable that the money should further depretiate. A letter from the Genl. Treasurer of our State to the continental Treasury board gave them and me great pleasure.[3] It seems by that letter that a great part of our quota of the Tax was collected, and that the whole would be [in] the treasury by the first instant.

Since I wrote the foregoing I have seen a gentleman from Maryland who informed me that Bills of exchange and every article were falling in that State when he left it, which was but a few days before.

I have also since that time seen a letter from Genl Lincoln; but it contained nothing new. Congress have order'd the Treasury board to prepare bills of exchange; to be sold at the rate of twenty five dollars for four & six pence Sterling, The purchaser when he receives his bill to deposit in the loan office, an equal Sum of contl. money to be estimated at that rate, for which he is to receive yearly six per Cent. I think I have expressed the Idea clearly; but the resolution will soon be published. The incessant and large demands of the Army, and the slowness with which taxes come in have made this measure necessary.

This is indeed a very critical period. If we can however but get along for two or three months I hope we shall proceed with more ease and satisfaction in future. A considerable body of men have inlisted for the war. This well recruited will make a very respectable army. The only difficulty is to furnish it with supplies. If we can but give steadiness to our currency, and the several States will exert themselves, and obtain the quotas of supplies which will soon be assigned and recommended to them all our difficulties will be removed. Wishing success to every measure calculated for the public benefit, prosperity to the State of Rhode–Island and Providence-Plantations, and health & happiness, with many New Years, to your excellency, I continue to be with great respect, Yr Excellency's most obedt. hble Servt.   Wm. Ellery

Please to turn over.
P.S.[4] Since writing the foregoing, Congress has received a letter from Gen. Washington, dated Dec. 30th, 1779,[5] in which he mentions that, by the last accounts he can get of the British troops, which left New York the 26th ultimo, they consist of six British regiments: The grenadier and light infantry of the army, Rawlins' corps, the legion, the queen's rangers and the Hessian grenadiers, which will make about five thousand effectives.   William Ellery.

RC (R–Ar: Letters to Governors); Staples, *Rhode Island*, pp. 270–72.

[1] See Ellery to Greene, December 21, 1779.

[2] This extract from Gen. Samuel Parsons' December 26 letter to General Washington was conveyed to Congress in Washington's December 27 letter to President Huntington, which was read in Congress on December 31. *JCC*, 15:1424. Washington's letter is in PCC, item 152, 8:271–73, and Washington, *Writings* (Fitzpatrick), 17:327. Parsons' letter is in the Washington Papers, DLC.

[3] The receipt of Rhode Island treasurer Joseph Clarke's letter to the Board of Treasury is not recorded in the journals, and the letter is not in PCC.

[4] This postscript is reprinted from Staples, *Rhode Island*, p. 272.

[5] Washington's December 30 letter to Huntington was read in Congress this day. *JCC*, 16:12. It is in PCC, item 152, 8:279–81, and Washington, *Writings* (Fitzpatrick), 17:333–34.

Samuel Holten's Diary

[January 4–5, 1780]
Jany. 4. Tuesday, no post this day. The Virginia troops marched thro' this city to S. Carolina. Cold.

5 Wednesday. No post come in yet. It is said some of the enemies vessels are ashore in the Jersey's.

MS (MDaAr).

Samuel Holten to Samuel Adams

Sir   Philadelphia Jany 4th. 1780
I was favor'd with yours of the 13th ulto, last eveng, with the inclosures, & please to accept my thanks for the same.[1]
I am sensible it is much easier to find fault with a Constitution of Government than to propose good amendments; I shall take notice of ownly one part of your proposed plan at present, which strikes me very disagreeably, that is, giving the first magistrate, "a negative upon all the laws"; the reasons assigned for it are (in my opinion) by no means sufficient, and I can't think of any that can be given to make it adviseable; neither can I see any necessity for it; if it should take place, I fear the good people will have cause to repent it when it is too late.
The situation of our affairs here are truly distressing, owing to the disordered state of our money & finances; An army in want of one days supply; and demands upon the treasury daily for millions, & little or no money there; Is the honl. court really sensible of our distressed state; I must suppose they be, for what can congress say more than they have done; But don't, my worthy friend, think, I dispaire of the common cause, no, not if the army should be all disbanded; which some think will be the case.
I am, my dear Sir, with great respect, your most obedient servant;
                                                                    S. Holten

RC (NN: Adams Papers).
[1] Not found; but from the contents of this letter, Adams' letter and enclosures concerned the newly formulated Massachusetts constitution.

Committee on Appeals Decree

                                                    January 5th. 1780.
Elisha Elderkin Lib[ellan]t & App[ell]ee ⎫   Appeal from
ad[versu]s   ⎬   the State of
Pierpont Edwards &c. Claim[ant]s &   ⎭   Connecticut[1]
App[ellan]ts
We the Commissioners appointed by Congress to hear, try and determine all Appeals from the Courts of Admiralty of the several American States to Congress having heard and fully considered as well all and singular the Matters and Things contained and set forth

in the Record or Minute of the Proceedings of the Court of Admiralty of the State of Connecticut in the above Cause as the Argument of the Advocate on the part of the Appellant in the said Cause and no persons appearing on the part of the Appellee (altho' sufficient Notice appeared to have been given) do thereupon adjudge and determine that the Judgment or Sentence of the said Court of Admiralty be in all it's parts revoked, reversed and annulled And that the Sloop or Vessel of forty five Tons burthen libelled against the said Cause together with the Tackle, Apparel & Furniture thereof be restored and redelivered to the said Pierpont Edwards, his Agent or Attorney to and for the Use of himself and all others on whose Behalf he claims and appeals he or they paying unto the abovenamed Elisha Elderkin his Agent or Attorney to and for the Use of himself and those on whose behalf the libels &c. the one full and equal Moiety or half part of the true Value of the said Sloop, her Tackle, Apparel and Furniture in Lieu of Salvage And We do further adjudge and decree that the party Appellee pay unto the party Appellant in this Cause one thousand and sixty Dollars for his Costs and Charges by him expended in supporting the Appeal aforesaid in this Court &c.

Tho M:Kean

William Ellery

Ezra L'Hommedieu

MS (DNA: RG 267, case no. 46). In a clerical hand, and signed by Ellery, L'Hommedieu, and McKean.

[1] A jury in the county court in New Haven, Conn., had awarded an unidentified British sloop and her cargo to Elisha Elderkin, captain of the privateer "armed boat" *True Blue*, which had captured the sloop in Oyster Bay, Long Island, on February 18, 1779. Pierpont Edwards of New Haven claimed one-half of the ship and cargo on the grounds that the sloop was really his sloop, the *Charming Nancy*, which had been captured by the British on November 18, 1778, and therefore Elderkin was entitled under the prize rules of recapture to only one-half the value of the ship and cargo and he was entitled to one-half. After the state court's decision was returned on April 7, 1779, Edwards appealed to Congress, where his appeal was referred to the Committee on Appeals on October 23.

The Committee on Appeals in this decree ordered the sloop and cargo returned to Edwards upon his payment of one-half the value to Elderkin. See case file no. 46, RG 267, DNA; and *JCC*, 15:1202.

Maryland Delegates to Thomas Sim Lee

Sir,   Phila. January 5th 1780

Since our last addressed to your Excellency we are favor'd with the inclosed from Major Lee which we take the Liberty to forward by General Smallwood,[1] who will give every Information relative to the

Subject—to him therefore we beg Leave to refer & are with the
highest Sence of Regard, Yr Excellencys most obt. & very hble Servts,

Geo Plater

James Forbes

[*P.S.*] The Troops sailed from N York by the last Intelligence[2] are
six british Regiments, the Grenadiers & light Infantry of the Army,
Rawdon's Corps—the Legion—the Queens Rangers, & Hessian
Grenadiers—making about five thousand effectives.

RC (MdAA: Red Books). Written by Plater and signed by Plater and Forbes.
[1] Maj. Henry Lee's undated letter is in *Md. Archives*, 43:399.
[2] For this "last Intelligence," see William Ellery to William Greene, January 4, 1780.

John Mathews to Thomas Bee

Dear sir,   Philadelphia Jany. [5?] 1780.[1]
I received yours of October 18 (intended by Mr. Rutledge) on the
30th Ulto. by Major Lucas, to whom Rutledge entrusted all his dispatches for this place, having at last given over all thoughts of being
able to reach the place of his destination. The account Majr. Lucas
gives me of him, is truely melancholy. I hope in God his disorder
may take some favourable turn, so as he may be preserved to us, for
I think his loss would be a heavy one to his Country, his family, & his
friends.

The present is not the time, further to discuss the matter of
taxation, as I expect 'ere this reaches you, you will be warmly engaged
in a business of a far different kind.

It is destressing beyond expression, to hear the accounts I do from
all quarters, of the disaffection, (I can call their late conduct nothing
less) of our back country people. Good God! is their nothing to be
done, that will tend either to perswaid, or coerce them to do their
duty? Indeed My Dear Friend, the day is not to come, it does not
depend on our Militia's not turning out to repel your *present* danger,
which may subject us to the imputation of a want of vigour, the
brand is already fixed on us. In passing through No. Carolina, &
Virginia, whenever I urged the necessity of their sending men to our
aid, the constant reply was "how can South Carolina expect we will
send our men to their support, when they will do nothing for
themselves. Our men go there, sacrifice their health, their lives, &
the So. Carolina Militia are snug at their own homes. It is too much
for them to expect us to fight their battles for them." Hints of the
same kind, have been thrown out in Congress. Where I have principally appologized for our men in the first instance, in the second, I
have treated such insolence, with the keeness [keenest] severity, for

let us be censured by whomever may, Congress are the last class of
men on earth, who ought to presume to do so. Before I had received
a Copy of Rutleges instructions, I had done everything that they
required, except sending some part of the Stores, & it is too late now
to be done. The three frigates are I hope safe with you as is likewise
the Vessel with Military Stores.

The Virginia & No. Carolina lines consisted of 3000 men, but on
examining into their times of serving, such as would expire before
they could reach you have been detained, which reduces them to
about 2300 very fine men. If they were with you, I should be under
very little apprehension about the loss of the town, but as they are at
this day some 500 & the rest 600 miles from you, I almost despair.
The great difficulty was in getting the men on their march, for
want of necessaries, particularly Shoes, without which it was impossible for them to encounter the inclemencies of the season. Indeed
some of the men suffered very severely in coming from camp here,
for want of shoes, but now that they are marched, I am confident
from the disposition of the Officers, not a moments time will be
lost, and if the No. Carolina Militia can but support you, so as to hold
the town, you need be under no apprehension about the expiration
of their times of service, for before that happens these troops will
certainly be with you. Blands & Baylors two Regiments of horse, I
am in hopes will not be long after Master Clinton. Had Congress
done their *duty* on the 10 of Novr. when I applyed to them for the
troops,[2] they might have been the best part of their way through No.
Carolina by this, but they first refused, then hesitated, untill the
rivers were shut up by the ice, so that the men must now march the
whole way by land. Which misfortunes are principally owing to a
want of proper spirit in them at first. I can with a safe conscience say,
I have done my duty to my Country, for there is nothing which I
thought could be beneficial to it, but what I have applyed for, & by
unremitted Sollicitations, as far as continental circumstances would
admit of, have in the end procured. If it is too late, the fault is not
imputable to me, & I flatter myself my Country will do me the justice
to think so, & acquit me of any want of attention to their interest.
You say, you wish to hear often from me. At any other time, such a
request would have afforded me infinite pleasure, which I always
have felt in communicated [communicating] my thoughts to so
esteemed a friend. But I am too much with you, & my whole facul-
ties are at present so much engroced by your destresses, that there is
no space left in my mind to turn to anything that passes here. I must
therefore reverse the proposition, & intreat of you to give me an
account of everything that passes with you, as often as you can find
leisure, & opportunity. I sent of an Express in two hours after we got
the account of the sailing of the fleet from New York, & I strictly
charged him to be there in sixteen days, which if he is, will give you
information of it, before they can reach you. God send you success &

as he has already twice preserved us from eminent danger, I hope he will yet once more guard over & protect us, from this greatest of all the tryals we have hitherto had to struggle with. And believe me to be, My Dr. Sir, with the most sincere regard, yr. most Obedt. Servt.

[*P.S.*] You know who I am without a name, which for various reasons had better be omitted.

RC (ScC: Bee Papers). In Mathews' hand, though not signed.

[1] Although there is nothing explicit in Mathews' letter indicating that it was written on January 5, his reference to "the sailing of the fleet from New York"—intelligence read in Congress January 4—suggests that Mathews penned this letter soon thereafter. See William Ellery to William Greene, January 4, 1780.

[2] Although Mathews had successfully moved Congress to order three Continental frigates to Charleston on November 10, 1779, his report on behalf of the committee on the southern department, recommending that troops be sent "to reinforce General Lincoln without," was submitted on November 11. See *JCC*, 15:1253–57; and John Fell's Diary, November 11, 1779.

Elbridge Gerry to William Hunt

Dear Sir,[1]   Philadelphia Jany 6th 1780.

Mr Cranch delivered me your Favour of the 14th Decr. & I had an Oppertunity last evening of further conferring with Colo. Pickering on that Part of your former Letter which relates to the Expence of Waggons &c in the issuing Departmt.; he appears to be in Favour of a new Regulation, & will perhaps be more convinced of the Necessity thereof, by your stating particularly to the Board of War, the proposed Alteration, the Abuses which it is intended to correct, & an Estimate of the Sums to be saved thereby.

With Respect to the Ballance due to You from the late Commissary Trumbull, I am unable to determine whether it will be possible or not, to obtain the payment thereof in Loan office Certificates bearing the Date of the Time at which the Money was advanced. Frequent Applications have been made to Congress to adopt that Mode of paying Debts, contracted by the Staff Departments for Articles supplied the Army, & all have been rejected; but there is a manifest Difference between Ballances due for Supplies on which the Creditor has charged his profit, & Cash Advanced by an officer to support the Credit & promote the Business of his Department, the latter of which as You have stated it, is precisely your Case. I am therefore of Opinion, that it will be best to profer a Memorial to Congress, & direct it to the president thereof, representing the Facts mentioned in your Letter, & in Support thereof, to transmit Mr Trumbulls Certificate.[2]

Mr Cranch informs me that he saw most of your Family & that they were well, which gives me pleasure, pray give my best Respects to them & to Miss Katy, who I am informed also lives with You, but was then absent. I remain Sir with Esteem, Your Friend & very hum Sert.   E. Gerry

RC (NjP: DeCoppet Collection). Addressed: "William Hunt Esqr. at Watertown."
[1] William Hunt (1749–1804), Watertown, Mass., lawyer and local official, conducted a business supplying the army during the war. Shipton, *Harvard Graduates*, 17:46–48.
[2] No memorial from Hunt pertaining to his accounts with former Commissary General Joseph Trumbull has been found in PCC.

Samuel Huntington to Jonathan Trumbull, Sr.

Sir,   Philadelphia Jany 6th 1780
    I am honoured with your Excellency's two letters of the 13th ulto with the papers to which they refer.[1]
    Agreable to your Excellency's request I have caused one of the lists of the Bonds transmitted to be endorsed which is herewith enclosed.
    I have the honour to forward by Brown two dozen blank Commissions with Instructions and Bonds.
    By late letters I have received from Amsterdam it is abundantly evident that your Excellency's Correspondence as also that of Governor Livingston with Baron V.D. Capelen hath enlighten'd & undeceived many people in Holland, & produced many Friends & favourable sentiments with respect to the cause in which we are engaged.[2] I hope Congress will take some honourary Notice of the Baron.
    I am told N. Jersey have Just passed a law appointing proper persons to purchase all articles of provision & forage for the army which that State can supply. I was in hopes to procure the act & send it forward by Brown. I believe a regulation of that kind will be generally adopted & cannot but hope it may be attended with beneficial consequences to the public. I have directed Mr Brown if he can obtain the above mentioned act in the Jersey's to take it with him.[3]
    I am favour'd with intelligence on which we place dependance that the late embarkation from N. York on the 23d & 26th ulto had Troops on board to the amount of 5,000 Effective Men their destination unknown & no intelligence has been received of them since they sailed.
    I have the honour to be, with the greatest respect, your Excy's hble & Servt,   Sam. Huntington

P.S. The papers formerly Sent to Mr Laurens were deliverd to a Committee of which he was one;[4] I called on him for them before his departure, he deliverd me some of them; The whole I have not been able to Collect, but Shall continue my Search, & if I can recover them will do my Self the honour to forward them immediately to your Excellency. Mr Laurens told me he met with great difficulty to get them Translated: few persons here understand the low Dutch, your last Letter from the Baron, I procured a Dutch Clergeman about Eight miles from this City to Translate. He appears perfect master of the Dutch language but does not write English Elegantly tho, I believe gives the litteral Sense with exactness.

I am ut Supra.   S.H.

RC (Ct: Trumbull Papers).

[1] One of these letters—endorsed "No 12. 13th December, 1779. To President Huntington, *de* my letters to Mr Laurens and general limitation of prices,"—is in Trumbull, *Papers* (MHS Colls.), 2:458–60.

[2] For Trumbull's correspondence with baron Joan Derk van der Capellen, see these *Letters*, 13:561n.1.

[3] Apparently the act he sent with his letter to Trumbull of January 17.

[4] For the "papers formerly Sent to Mr Laurens," see Henry Laurens to Trumbull, October 19, 1779, note 1.

James Lovell to Abigail Adams

Jan. 6. 1780.

You will see, lovely Woman, by the Papers which I have sent that we shall have more post-Advantages of Communication than we have had for some time back;[1] but I fear this Remark will tend to my Disadvantage, and if it was not for Œconomy I would throw by the present Sheet and take up another in which I would only tell you that I regard, esteem and respect you and will certainly write to you *as often as I possibly can.* But since I have hinted at increasing Opportunities of Conveyance, I must assure you that the days are too short for me at present by much to get pressing public Business off my Hands; and as to the Nights they are ten times more ruinous to my health than they were in Summer, I therefore hide myself from them within the Bed Curtains the Moment that *public* duty is discharged. In Truth, I am at length aiming to preserve some Remnant of a good Constitution for Situations into which you seem to think you would *chide* me if you was invested with those Rights of Chiding which a Church Parson's Certificate is presumed to have conveyed to another.

You may thus perceive that yr. Letter of Decr. 13 is before me. It was within two Minutes brought from the Office with Information that the Post sets out at 2 p.m. I ought now to be in Congress, but must scratch a Line or two for Boston.

Our Affairs are unpleasant in many Views, but not ruined. Every Patriot ought to be *allarmed* and then all will be safe. I think with Tristram about the Currency, now we have done with the Paper Mill and Press. It seems as if the Signature alone will not make Portia reject the Piece. *Yorick, Sterne and Tristram* are bearable but *Shandy* is a wicked Creature.[2]

Let me again mention to you to mind the pages of 1778 that if I have sent doubles you may return the 2d, or if I omit, you may demand a single Sheet of the Journals.

Thank Mr. Cranch for his kind Compliments left for me with Mrs. L. I wish him and his every Felicity.

I cannot consent so to stint my heartwarm extensive Vows for you— as to pass the Compliments of the Season from my Pen, and thereby risk a Supposition that I had done all which my Affections suggest at the Instant of subscribing myself—your Friend & h. Servt.,

JL

RC (MHi: Adams Papers). Adams, *Family Correspondence* (Butterfield), 3:256–57.

[1] Congress had voted on December 27, 1779, to have two regular post deliveries each week from Boston to Philadelphia. *JCC*, 15:1411.

[2] For Abigail's February 13 response to these allusions to Laurence Sterne and his literary characters, see Adams, *Family Correspondence* (Butterfield), 3:273–74n.l.

Roger Sherman to Andrew Adams

Sir   Philadelphia January 7th. 1780

I Obtain'd last Evening an Account of the prices of the Several Articles, as Stated by the late law of the State of New Jersy which, is to be in force the first of Next month which I have Enclosed.[1] I am informed the law is Absolutely to take effect at the time fixed, without any proviso in case the other States do not make Similar Laws. The State of Maryland has likewise passed a Law for the regulation of prices. New York Assembly is called on purpose to consider of the Matter. The Commissioners from Several of the States that were present Met last Evening pursuant to the recommendation of the Hartford Convention, viz two from New Hamshire, two from Connecticut, one from New Jersy, And one for Pennsylvania. Mr. L Homedieu was also present from the State of New York but he Says their Assembly made no Special appointment for this convention, & Supposes he has no right to Act.[2]

I dont hear that any other States have appointed Members. I believe they expected that the resolution of Congress would Supersede the necessity of this convention. So that I dont think it will be of any advantage for the Assembly to wait, in expectation of having a report from this Convention for I believe there will be None.

Mr. Bryan informed us that a great majority of the Assembly of this State were in favour of a regulation of prices before they Adjourned. They meet again the 19th of this month. I Should think Since the Press is Stopt it would not be difficult to reduce prices as low as twenty for one, Some people are much afraid the Money will Soon Appreciate very rapidly, and be attended with more pernicious effects than the depreciation has been. It appears to me that it is of great importance to have its value fixed & Stable. We have no News here but what is contained in the public papers.

I am with Great Esteem & Regard Your humble Servant.

Roger Sherman

RC (Ct: Trumbull Papers). Addressed: "To the Honble. Andrew Adams Esqr., Speaker of the House of Assembly at Hartford."

[1] Sherman undoubtedly enclosed a copy of New Jersey's December 21, 1779, "Act for Limiting the Prices of Various Articles, and to Prevent the Withholding from Sale the Necessaries of Life", which was suspended on February 26, 1780, until the neighboring states passed similar laws. *Acts of the General Assembly of the State of New Jersey, From the Establishment of the Present Government . . . 1784* (Trenton: Isaac Collins, 1784), pp. 104–5, 118.

[2] Sherman is referring to the first effort to assemble a quorum for the convention to limit prices that had been called by the Hartford convention in October to convene in Philadelphia on January 5, 1780, for which see Samuel Holten to the Massachusetts Council, November 11, note 3; and Samuel Huntington to the States, November 22, 1779. The two "commissioners" to the convention from New Hampshire were the state's delegates to Congress, Nathaniel Folsom and Nathaniel Peabody. Connecticut's two commissioners were delegates Oliver Ellsworth and Roger Sherman. Pennsylvania had selected John Bayard, George Bryan, John Bull, William Henry, and John Jacobs to represent the state at the convention, but it is not known which commissioner actually attended at this time. The representative from New Jersey also has not been identified, but it seems probable that he was not the state's duly accredited commissioner and, like New York delegate Ezra L'Hommedieu, merely appeared at the meeting as a goodwill gesture to indicate his state' intention to participate in this Continental effort to regulate prices. Silas Condict and Thomas Fenimore had been elected on December 14 to represent New Jersey at the convention, but since they were later explicitly requested to come to Philadelphia, it seems unlikely that either of them were at the meeting of January 6. See the proceedings of the convention in *Public Records of Connecticut*, 2:572–79. For the results of this convention of the 10 states from Virginia northward, see William Ellery to William Greene, February 15, 1780. See also Oliver Ellsworth to Jonathan Trumbull, January 30; Nathaniel Peabody to Woodbury Langdon, February 7; Connecticut Delegates to Jonathan Trumbull, February 15; and Elbridge Gerry to Samuel Adams, February 15, 1780.

Samuel Huntington to Richard Bache

Sir,   Philada Jany. 8. 1780

You will receive herewith enclos'd an act of Congress of the 7th Instant allowing to the Surveyors of the post Office their reasonable Expences in travelling the roads, their accounts of Expences to be rendered to the post master General on oath every three months, and repealing the late act of Congress giving them forty Dollars a day[1]

I am Sir, your hble Servt,   S.H. Pt.

LB (DNA: PCC, item 14).

[1] For this resolve concerning Post Office expenses, see *JCC*, 16:19, 21–22; PCC, item 61, fols. 465–68; and Huntington to Bache, December 2 and 29, 1779.

Samuel Huntington to Benjamin Lincoln

Sir,   Philadelphia 8th Jany. 1780.

You will receive herewith enclos'd an Act of Congress of this Day allowing & directing payment to be made for horses killed in Battle belonging to Officers whose duty it is to be on Horse back in time of Action.[1]

As also empowering the Commanding Officer in the southern Department to reform the four Georgia Regiments, & arrange them on some equitable rule & retain no more in the service than are necessary for two Regiments in the Manner as expressed in the Act, the residue are to be considered as Supernumeraries, as also the Georgia Officers of the Gallies & light Dragoons, who are on Continental pay.[2]

I am Sir, with great respect, your hble Servt,

Sam. Huntington President

RC (Sol Feinstone, Washington Crossing, Pa., 1980).

[1] Huntington also sent copies of this resolve with brief letters of this date to Quartermaster General Nathanael Greene and Deputy Quartermaster John Mitchell. See JCC, 16:26; and PCC, item 14, fols. 272–73.

[2] See JCC, 16:26–27. An unspecified defect in this enclosed resolve prompted Huntington to write the following brief letter to Lincoln on January 29 to cover a corrected copy of the document. "You will receive enclos'd an Act of Congress of the 8th Instant," he explained, "together with a printed Act of the 24th Novemr 1778 to which the first mentioned refers. A Copy of the same Act of the 8th Instant enclos'd in my letter of that Date you will find to be Erroneous by comparing it with the Act of the same date enclosed." PCC, item 14, fol. 288.

Samuel Huntington to Peter Muhlenberg

Sir,   Philada Jany 8. 1780

By the act of Congress of the 29th ulto. herewith enclos'd you will be inform'd that the Arrangement of the General Officers in the Virginia line was founded upon principals not affecting the personal Characters or comparative merit of those Officers.[1]

I am Sir &c.   S.H. President

LB (DNA: PCC, item 14).

[1] Congress adopted this resolution in response to Muhlenberg's continued displeasure with the 1778 settlement of the seniority dispute between four Virginia brigadiers that had ranked William Woodford above Muhlenberg, Charles Scott, and George Weedon. He had voiced his complaint in an April 22, 1779, letter to the Virginia delegates in Congress, which was referred to the Board of War, and the board had recommended against altering the original settlement while suggesting that Congress reaffirm their "favourable opinion of the merit and characters" of all the gentlemen involved. For the background of this dispute and the Board of War's recommendations, see these Letters, 9:105–6, 197–98; JCC, 13:490, 15:1418–19; and PCC, item 163, fols. 510–13.

Samuel Huntington to Jonathan Trumbull, Sr.

Sir,   Philadelphia 8 Jany 1780.

By the act of Congress of the 7th Instant enclos'd, I am directed to address your Excellency and express their apprehension on account of the small supply of beef for the present necessities of the army & to request the immediate aid of the Legislature of Connecticut to the Commissary General or his Assistant in procuring & forwarding the Same.[1]

The present necessity of the Army is truly pressing & alarming & the matter of supplies seems to admit of no delay. The Army are it is said without meat.[2] The Commissary will forward a Sum of money immediately to Connecticut to purchase supplies; in the mean time it is most earnestly requested that the Legislature of Connecticut will lend the necessary Aid to the Commissary to forward a Quantity of Beef with all possible Despatch. Congress are using every endeavour to lessen the public Expence & the quantity of provision as much as possible consistant with the public safety, and if the supplies can be obtained for the present it is to be hoped from the measures that are adopted it may be less difficult to obtain Supplies in future.

I have the honour to be, with perfect respect, your Excy's hble Servt.   Sam. Huntington President

RC (Ct: Trumbull Papers).

[1] For this emergency appeal to Connecticut, see *JCC*, 16:20–21.

[2] This concern was echoed by Samuel Holten in his diary entry for this date: "We have accts. that the army is in great want of provision. Cold." MDaAr.

George Partridge to the Massachusetts Council

Sir   Philadelphia Jany 8th. 1780

I receivd a Letter in Decr. ultimo from the Deputy Secretary advising me, that I had the Honor of being reelected one of the Delegates to represent the State in Congress; for the ensuing Year; I wish that it was as much in my Power as it is in my Disposition to render the Publick such Services as the importance of the Station to which I am appointed requires; to that End however my best Endeavours shall not be wanting while I continue here; but as my Duty to the Publick in another Department,[1] together with my private Concerns make it necessary that I should be at home early in the Spring, I hope that some Gentleman will then be appointed to succeed me here.

I am Sir, with the greatest Respect, your most Obedient Humbl. Servt.   Geo. Partridge

RC (M–Ar: Revolutionary War Letters). Addressed: "Honle. President of Council, Massachusetts State."

[1] Partridge was undoubtedly referring to the office of sheriff of Plymouth County—a post to which he had been appointed in 1777 and held until 1811. According to a biographer, the Massachusetts Council had already "considered the question of the conflict of duties involved, and decided that it was 'content' with the Sheriff's going to Philadelphia." Shipton, *Harvard Graduates*, 15:283. He was reelected a delegate to Congress six consecutive terms and attended a portion of each year from 1779 to 1785.

Roger Sherman to Jonathan Trumbull, Jr.

Sir   Philadelphia Jan. 8th 1780
You have doubtless had Official information of your being appointed a commissioner of the Board of Treasury.[1] Congress and the other members of the Board are very desirous that you would accept the trust and enter on the business as Soon as may be. The Salary Sounds high but we are all sensible that in the present State of the currency it is inadequate, but you may rest assured, that as Soon as we can have a Stable medium adequate Salaries will be allowed to the members of that Board, and a Suitable compensation for their Services before that time. The Committee who reported the Salaries, gave as their opinion that they ought not to be less than 2000 dollars in Specie. That part of the report is postponed; but I believe that the pay will be made as good as 1500 hard dollars a year at least. I believe you can't give a greater Evidence of your Patriotism, or render your Country a more essential Service than by accepting the office. I am with great Regard your humble Servt.   R. Sherman

RC (Sol Feinstone, Washington Crossing, Pa., 1980).
[1] See Samuel Huntington to Jonathan Trumbull, Jr., November 12, 1779.

Elbridge Gerry to John Wendell

My dear sir,[1]   Philadelphia 10 Jany 1780
It is some Time since You have favoured me with a Line, & much longer, since I had the Oppertunity of writing to You,[2] but be assured, that as the first is not imputed to the Want of Friendship on your Side, so the latter has, on mine, served rather to increase than diminish it.

In your Favour of the 15th April 1778 You mentioned me inclosing a Letter to General Sullivan, which had been intercepted; I suspect that many of my Letters have miscarried in this Way, & shall embrace every Oppertunity of tracing such Conduct.

In May last, You desired my Sentiments "on the State of the continental Debt, & the Redemption of the Money" since which, two Addresses & sundry Resolutions of Congress on these Subjects have been published, & furnished the Information required: if any Thing further is necessary, You'll please to inform me of it.

No Officers are yet appointed or proposed for the 74 Gun Ship, & as Recommendation founded on personal Knowledge have the greatest Weight, an application to General Whipple, who is a Member of the Board of Admiralty, in Favour of your Son[3] will probably have a good Effect, & I shall chearfully give my Assistance for rewarding his Merit.

A plan for establishing a Court of Appeals is under the Consideration of Congress; & nearly compleated.

I hope for more Leisure to correspond with my Friends in future, & inclose You some Papers containing the current Intelligence.

Pray give my Compliments to your Lady & Miss Sally & believe me to be, with much Esteem your Friend & humble sert,

E. Gerry

RC (CSmH: Emmet Collection).

[1] Although the recipient of this letter is not identified, Gerry probably wrote it to John Wendell, a Portsmouth, N.H., merchant with whom he had corresponded regularly in 1776–77. This conclusion is largely based on the finding that Gerry had closed two previous letters to Wendell with felicitations to "Miss Sally," who is also mentioned in his closing to this letter. Cf. these *Letters*, 4:188, 5:472.

[2] Gerry's last extant letter to Wendell was dated June 27, 1777. Ibid., 7:257.

[3] It is not known to which of Wendell's 11 children Gerry is referring.

Committee of Congress to George Washington

Sir,   Philadelphia 11th Jany 1780

We beg Leave to inclose your Excellency sundry Propositions referred by Congress to our Consideration,[1] & to request your Opinion thereon, being with Respect sir, your most obedt & very humble servants,   E Gerry

Robt R. Livingston

Jno. Mathews

ENCLOSURE

1. Resolved That the Commander in chief be directed to dismiss all the Troops whose Times will expire by the 1st Day of April next, who shall be willing to receive their Discharge.

2. Resolved That the Number of Regiments be reduced to sixty, & the Soldiers of such regiments incorporated with those that remain upon the Establishment.

3. Resolved That the Board of War report a plan for such Reduction.

4. Resolved That the reduced officers be allowed full pay exclusive of rations & Subsistence Money, during the War, & such other

Allowance after the War as is made to those Officers who have served during the War.

5. Resolved That any Vacancy in the sixty Battalions be filled up by Officers from the reduced regiments having Respect to the State to which such regiments belong.

RC (DLC: Washington Papers). Written by Gerry and signed by Gerry, Livingston, and Mathews. Enclosure also in Gerry's hand.

[1] Consideration of these remarkable "Propositions" for the reduction of the army had been postponed when they were introduced by Robert R. Livingston on January 8, and their referral to this committee on the 10th upon the motion of Elbridge Gerry was undoubtedly a bid to gain time and guarantee their ultimate rejection. Gerry, who had been chairing a committee considering proposals for strengthening the army in response to Washington's November 18, 1779, appeal, had first proposed that a committee be appointed to consult with Washington on Livington's proposals and to report to Congress, but his motion was defeated. See *JCC*, 16:28, 36–38. Two days later he urged Washington to make "a fresh Application" for troops lest the lack of preparation for the coming campaign damage relations with France, for which see Gerry to Washington, January 12, 1780. Washington's tactful and patient January 23 reply to the committee is in Washington, *Writings* (Fitzpatrick), 17:431–36.

Before Congress harmonized these conflicting recommendations, however, the French minister submitted a memorial to Congress on January 25 recommending that the 1780 campaign be prosecuted with new vigor to match efforts planned by France and Spain, apparently dooming Livingston's call for reducing the Continental Army. In the meantime, work had proceeded on Washington's previous appeal for recruiting the army to its authorized strength, and in early February congressional debate focused on a number of Board of War recommendations for implementing new state quotas totaling 35,211 men. See Samuel Huntington's letters to La Luzerne, February 2, and to the States and to Washington, February 10, 1780.

William Floyd to Pierre Van Cortlandt

Dear Sir   Philadelphia January 11th. 1780

I am now happy in being able to Inform you that the Divisions and party Spirit, which prevailed in Congress, During the last winter and Spring are Entirely Done away, and as that Spirit originated from Certain Questions Relative to Mr Dean & Mr Lee, That cause no longer Existing, it is to be hoped that the Effect will not happen again. A harmonious Disposition, to Do Business, prevails, And our Greatest Difficulty is, to know what to Do, in this Critical Situation of our Affairs. (Our money, our Army)

The Recommendation of Congress for the Several States to provide Supplies for the Army by their own Exertions, I expect is before the Legislature, New Jersey whose Legislature was then Sitting has passed a Law for the purpose, and I understand it is now Executing much to the Satisfaction of the Inhabitants of the State. They have forbid all Deputy Commissarys Except those of their own appointment, and who act under their Direction, agreeable to Certain Rules Laid Down for them in the Said Law. And I am happy to hear that they are like to Suceed in Getting allmost all the Spare provisions and forage in that State for the use of the army. I hope Soon to have a Copy of their Law which I will Do my Self the pleasure to Send you.

It would be Disagreable for me to mention and I believe for you to hear, the particulars of our Circumstances (and perhaps Improper). But it is necessary that you Should know, and our whole Legislature; that the Supplies for the army from the Several States, must be procured by their own Exertions, and if the four States nearest the Army, Should fail of Doing this; the worst of Consequences is to be apprehended.

The General Regulation of prices as Recommended By Congress I Expect will take place, Maryland has passed a Law for the purpose, and New Jersey also, But the last mentioned State, I believe will be But Little affected with it, as their purchasers are much Engaged and I expect will either, Realy purchase, or Secure, all the Spare produce of the State by the time the Regulation is to take place; and that at the now going prices.

Our money in this State (and I am told it is not much better in the States below this) is at a very ebb, a Dollar in this Market is Reckoned very little more than a penny, and yet it Goes if possible More Current than Ever and there is a great Cry of its being Scarce here, No wonder it is So, when it Requires near one hundred times as much as formerly, to do any Business.

I do not expect the money is Depreciated in our State to the Degree it has here; But I do Imagine it has fell Sufficiently to Convince every one, of the propriety of our puting off the Sales of our forfieted Estates to the time we Did, for it appears very Evident now that if we had ordered an Immediate Sale we Should have lost nearly one half their value. I have Conversed with the Delegate from New Hampshire[1] Respecting the Vermont title, and the Claims which those people on the Lands have to Independence, and he Seems to be full with me in opinion that it will not Do to Suffer them to be so, But I think I can Discover in him a hope, or Rather a wish, that they might be annexed to New Hampshire; or at least that part which Lays to the Eastward of the Mountain. But at the Same time I think I Discovered—a faintness in his hope, and a Doubt whether his wishes would be accomplished. I have not as yet understood that Massachusetts Intend to put in any Claims to that Country.[2]

Yesterday Congress Resolved to Inform General Lee that they had no further Service for him.[3] This Dismission, (tho' I never did like Lee, I have always Considered him as a very Imprudent man, Yet there appeared to me a kind of hardship, or Rather Cruelty in it) which prevented its having my Consent.

As soon as the Vermont Business is over and the Roads will permit, I shall Return home leaving a full Representation here, But I fear it will hardly be possible to Cross the Country with a Carriage till

Spring. My Compliments to the Gentleman of Senate. I am with & & & &,   Wm Floyd

[*P.S.*] I must Begg leave to Refer you to the papers enclosed for News.

Tr (NN: Van Cortlandt–Van Wyck Papers).

[1] Two New Hampshire delegates, Nathaniel Folsom and Nathaniel Peabody, were then attending Congress.

[2] According to the transcriber of this letter, Floyd also wrote the following marginal note related to the Vermont issue before Congress. "By what I can understand old Phelps [*i.e., Charles Phelps, who was employed by both New York and Massachusetts*] played a Double Game while he was here. I hope the Legislature will take Care of him so as not to be taken in by him." See also John Jay to George Clinton, September 25, note 5, and October 7, 1779, note 1.

[3] Floyd and the other New York delegates voted against General Lee's dismissal. See *JCC*, 16:33–34; and President Huntington to Charles Lee, January 14, 1780.

James Forbes to Thomas Sim Lee

My Dear Sir,   Philadelphia Jany 11th 1780

As I had not the pleasure of a line from you in answer to my last[1] I suppose you were oute of Town, I am affraid shall not be able to execute your order in Purchasing the Charret & Horses. Mr. Todd has been oute of Town. When he returns, shall apply to him. Mr. Dickinson has a very ellegant Coach for Sale which has been very little used. He is allso oute of Town: therefore can not let you know his terms. If they are any way reasonable, I shoud think it a better purchase than any thing of the kind I have seen in this place. I have been asked £5,000 for a Charret half worn, Youl please to give me your instructions on this head [on the return] of the post.

I find the Assembly was up before my resignation got down, as I am determind not to accept under the new Delegation I must begg you woud use your endeavours to get some of the Gentn to cum up, as soon as possable, as I shall be under the necessity if they dont cum, of leaving the State unrepresented,[2] which I shoud be gratly concernd at, but my present business makes it absolutely necessary that I shoud be at home. I shoud be obliged if you woud send me the Bill for Confisscaation of British property. Inclosed you have the papers to which refer you for News, And am, Dear Sir, Yours affectionately,   James Forbes

RC (MdHi: Lee, Horsey, and Carroll Papers deposit, 1985).

[1] Forbes to Lee, December 30, 1779.

[2] See ibid., note 1.

Roger Sherman to Jonathan Trumbull, Sr.

Sir   Philadelphia Jany. 11th. 1780
   Enclosed is An Act of the Assembly of the State of New Jersy for procuring Supplies.[1]
   We are informed that the Army have lately been at very Short Allowance of both Bread and Meat.
   Their principal dependance is on Connecticut for Beef. I wish there might be the most vigorous exertion to furnish a present Supply. The Commissary General informs me that he Sent to Your Excellency 200,000 dollars for that purpose. He will be furnished with a further Sum and intends to come that way himself very soon. Stopping the press Occasions a Scarcity of money. The States I believe are now collecting their taxes—but if they dont keep the money collected for the continent Seperate from that collected for their own use there will be danger of a deficiency of Supplies to answer the warrants drawn by Congress, which may be attended with dangerous consequences. Commissioners are arrived from Maryland to attend the convention, to consider of a limitation of prices. I was informed Some weeks ago by one of the Delegates of that State, that the Assembly had passed a law for the limitation of prices & he Shewed me an abstract of the Act, but it proves to be a mistake. A Bill was prepared but not enacted into a Law—and the Assembly is adjourned till March next. We hear nothing from Virginia or Delaware respecting that measure—nor do I learn that any persons are appointed by Massachusetts bay or Rhode Island to meet in Convention. We have reports that a forty Gun Ship & Several others of the British fleet that lately Sailed from New York were cast away on the N. Jersey Shore, it was Said that one of them was the Roebuck, but that is contradicted today. We have no foreign News here.
   I am with great Regard, Your Excellency's Obedient humble Servant,   Roger Sherman

[P.S.] I wish to have another Delegate come, and relieve me, for I want very much to return home.   R.S.

RC (Ct: Trumbull Papers).
   [1] Sherman enclosed a copy of the December 25, 1779, "Act for Procuring Provisions for the Use of the Army," which was passed by the New Jersey legislature to comply with a December 14, 1779, resolve of Congress. See *Acts of the General Assembly of the State of New Jersey From the Establishment of the Present Government . . . 1784* (Trenton: Isaac Collins, 1784), pp. 114–15; and Samuel Huntington to William Livingston, December 14, 1779.

John Armstrong, Sr., to George Washington

Carlisle 12th January 1780. Laments the "present distressing Aspect of our publick affairs. . . . On the Subtile Subject of finance my pretentions are truly Small, but on the necessity of some different measures from any yet adopted what man can Shut his eyes? To say nothing of the various aireal Schemes that have been thrown out, one thing is clear, that even such as have been tryed from their Shew of more reason and Solidity, either from their being inadequate in their nature, or too late in their application have palpably failed of the effect. For Some time past we have resembled a Patient far gon[e] in disease, given up of his Physicians and left to the mere efforts of nature. Now whether we Shall proceed in the same natural or rather slothful and timid way, leaving our internal commerce to regulate itself, and take chance for the event, or attempt the plain highway of Law & publick Authority, in the regulation of Prices generally, appears to be the Question, and that without an alternative that can promise Success. The latter however degraded by Merchants or exploded by some politicians of more refined Sentiments if I have any Opinion at all, is the better if not the only fundamental means of our political recovery. I know there are powerful Objections to this doctrine of regulation of prices by law, or rather they are powerfully made, for at this time I must in truth declare I think their whole operation impertinent, inconclusive & lost in the Superior force of these arguments which inevitably result from the present circumstances of this country, whereby the great Law of Necessity is now clearly introduced for the tryal of a legal regulation of Prices, and must at least fully justify the experiment. I know the grand difficulties, as well as the nicities attending Such regulations must lie in the execution, and penalties of this Law—hard they may be but ought not to be supposed insurmountable. True the virtue of the populace is very low but not altogether extinct, the latent remains whereof must yet instrumentally Save us, if so, how are we to animate these remains, when the natural Springs thereof are so much relaxed—No other probable or perhaps possible way but by the Salutary Stimulace of publick authority, and the encouragement they may derive from a near prospect of Peace, or at least of retrenching the extra expences of the Civil Staff of the Army, which wou'd naturally lead to Some farther Observation, I mean such as arises on the remarks, Sentiments and temper of many people far out of your Sight and hearing. . . .

"[*P.S.*] I cou'd sincerely wish the policy of Virginia respecting their Land-Office and extent of territory were otherwise timed—and more disinterested."

RC (DLC: Washington Papers).

Elbridge Gerry to George Washington

Sir,   Philadelphia 12th Jany 1780
The Requisitions to the several States for Reinforcements to the Army, proposed in your Letter of the 18th Novr. last, are not yet adopted by Congress, & a fresh Application from your Excellency, appears to me necessary for promoting that important Business. A Report has been long since made on the Subject, & been several Times under the Consideration of Congress,[1] but an Opinion has been lately suggested, & I fear with too much Effect "that the Number of Men inlisted for the War is already sufficient, & that Reinforcements are not necessary for the Army in this Quarter."[2] Should this Sentiment prevail, or the Requisitions be much longer delayed, We shall probably lay the Foundation of an inactive Campaign, if not of greater Misfortunes; & renew the Uneasiness of the Court of France, who last year remonstrated in very friendly, but *expressive* Terms, against the Delays of our military preparations, for that Campaign. As the Measures of our good Ally for the Establishment of our Independence, as well as those of the common Enemy against it, are prosecuted with the greatest Vigor, it appears to me that We are urged by every principle of policy, Generosity, & Honor to be equally vigorous & decisive, & I have been thus induced to trouble your Excellency on the Subject. I hope that the Measures taken, & such as are under the Consideration of Congress for obtaining Supplies of Provision, will effectually releive the Wants of the Army, which I confess distress me Exceedingly.[3]
I remain Sir, with every Sentiment of Esteem & Respect your most obed. & very hum sevt,   E Gerry

RC (DLC: Washington Papers).
[1] Washington's November 18 letter, explaining the deficiencies of the Continental Army and the chronic inability of the states to meet and maintain their recruiting quotas, had been read in Congress on November 26, and referred to a committee of Gerry, William C. Houston, John Mathews, Philip Schuyler, and Roger Sherman. The committee's report, which is in the hand of Gerry, was first considered and partly adopted on December 7. A supplemental report, also in Gerry's hand, was considered on December 14, 16, and 18 and January 18 and 24. On the last day of these deliberations, several resolves regulating army size and state quotas were adopted and the remainder of Gerry's report was referred to the Board of War, which subsequently submitted a number of recommendations that formed the basis for the resolves adopted on February 9 for maintaining the army at a strength of 35,211. See *JCC*, 15:1312, 1357–59, 1376–77, 1381, 1385–86, 1393–96, 1421, 16:72, 80–83; and PCC, item 19, 6:257–59, 263–65. See also Committee of Congress to Washington, January 11; and Samuel Huntington to the States, February 10, 1780.
[2] See Committee of Congress to Washington, January 11, 1780.
[3] For Washington's January 29 reply to Gerry, see Washington, *Writings* (Fitzpatrick), 17:462–64.

Samuel Huntington to Certain States

Sir,   Philada. Jany 12. 1780

You will receive herewith enclos'd an Act of Congress of this day together with Extracts of three Letters to which the Act refers.[1] These I am directed to lay before the Legislature of Connecticut or in their Reccess before your Excellency in Council, as also the other States therein mentioned, and to urge in the most pressing manner that Immediate supplies of provision be by those several States sent to the army.

After the facts stated in the papers enclos'd perswasion & importunity seems unnecessary. The Army must soon disband unless supplied with provisions, That cannot be obtained [at the present Conjunction of Affairs][2] without the Aid of the several States now called upon. The Country abounds with the necessary Rescources, but private gain seems the only Object of too many Individuals without any Concern for the public safety.

Congress have taken proper Measures to have Justice done those States that shall aford present supplies. The Exertions of N. Jersey are already called forth on the occasion. Must it be said that our Army disbanded for want of provisions in the midst of plenty?

Since the resignation of Commissary Wadsworth the Aid of the States is absolutely necessary to afford Supplies until such time as Matters are put in a proper Train which I trust will not be long.[3]

I have the honour to be &c,   S.H. President

LB (PCC, item 14). Addressed: "His Excellency The Governor of Connecticut. N.B. The same to New York, Pennsylvania, & Delaware."

[1] For this resolve, and the three letters from Washington, Gen. William Irvine, and assistant commissary Royal Flint, see *JCC*, 16:46; PCC, item 152, 8:321–30; and Washington, *Writings* (Fitzpatrick), 17:355–58.

[2] Although this passage does not appear in the LB, it is found in the letters that Huntington actually sent. His letter to Gov. George Clinton of New York is in the Clinton Papers, N; his letter to Pres. Joseph Reed of Pennsylvania is at the Omaha Public Library.

[3] For the January 15 response of the Pennsylvania Council to this appeal, see *Pa. Archives*, 1st ser. 8:87; and *Pa. Council Minutes*, 12:227.

Samuel Huntington to George Washington

Sir   Philadelphia January 12, 1780

Your Excellency will receive herewith an Act of Congress of the 8th instant, making further provision for the paying for horses killed in Battle and for reforming the Georgia Battallions &c.[1]

Your Excellencys favour by Col. Magaw have this moment receivd & Shall call the Attention of Congress to the Subject to which it relates at their Meeting in the morning that a decision may be obtaind as soon as possible.[2]

I have the Honour to be, with the highest Respect, Your Excys humbe servt,   Sam Huntington President

RC (DLC: Washington Papers).
[1] See Huntington to Benjamin Lincoln, January 8, 1780.
[2] For Washington's January 4 "favour by Col. Magaw" concerning new British proposals for reopening prisoner-of-war exchange negotiations, see Huntington to Washington, January 14, 1780, note 2.

James Lovell to Abigail Adams

Madam   Jany. 13. 1780

I send you a Continuance of the Journals.

The Printer having lately made a mistake in the Course of sending me the Sheets of 1778, I was led to think he had done so before, as to that which I have written to you about already, called by him H; I therefore now put up one, as well as M,N, which I am certain were not before inclosed to you. I would have you send all forward to our Friend, unless you should have found that I really committed the Error of sending you before both Mr. A's H & my owne. For you are to know that only two Copies are taken out of the Printer's Hands; and as I could not find all my own Pages I was induced to think I had sent them to you. But as you see above I have altered the Conjecture.

How *do* you do, Lovely Portia, these very cold Days? Mistake me not willfully; I said *Days*. For my Part, I was hardly able to write legibly at the Distance of only 18 feet from two Fire Places in the Congress Room at 4 oClock this afternoon. There is no Probability that the Cold will be decreased in 7 hours from that Time. I will strive however to refrain from coveting my Neighbour's *Blankets*. I shall find *that* not difficult. But really I doubt whether I shall be able to keep myself void of *all* Coveteousness. I suspect I shall covet to be in the Arms of Portia's Friend & Admirer—the Wife of my Bosom, who would be a whole Coverlid bettered, as well as I, by such an Approximation.

Upon casting my Eye back thro' what I have written, I find it would have been more justly comprehensible if the Page had been either a little longer or somewhat shorter. There was not Room to write *Turn over*. I hope, however, that you did not stop long without doing so Madam; because a quick Turnover alone could save the 10th Commandment intire; and you must now see plainly that I had not the smallest SUSPICION of my being driven by my present Sufferings to make a frantic Breach there.

I hope Mr. Adams is long e'er now in France where he will not have at his very Fingers Ends such nipping Reasons as I have to regret his Separation from that sweet Comfort which is held up to our Hopes among other Bible-Felicities. Eccles: IV. 11.[1]

We are still without News from any of our Agents or Ministers abroad. I will not fail to communicate the first we get that can amuse you. Respectfully & affectionately Yrs.,   JL

RC (MHi: Adams Papers).
[1] The passage from Ecclesiates that Lovell is citing reads: "Again, if two lie together, then they have heat; but how can one be warm *alone?*"

James Lovell to William Palfrey

Dear Sir,   Jany. 13th. 1780
Your Letter of Decr. 11th said to be by Genl. Fulsom did not reach me till long after his Arrival here. I am sincerely sorry for the ill State of your Wife & Children as to Constitutions; but I hope a favorable Change has taken place since the date of your Letter.

As to what you mention about the Agency,[1] it is not at all a Question here at present. But on every occasion you may expect I will be mindful both of your Merits & your Views.

I am almost frozen, your humble Servant,   James Lovell

RC (MH–H: bMS Am 1704.3).
[1] It could not be determined to which "Agency" Lovell and Palfrey, the paymaster general, were referring.

Roger Sherman to Jonathan Trumbull, Sr.

Sir,   Philadelphia. Jany. 13th. 1780
Since Sealing my letter of the 11th we have been Informed that all the States from New Hamshire to Virginia inclusive have appointed Commissioners to Attend the Convention to consider of a regulation of prices, except Massachusetts from whom we have had no Account. It [*is*] not expected that the Convention will enter on the business until the Middle of Next Week. Enclosed is the resolutions on the Commissaries department.[1] Also a paper containing [. . .] Estimate ⟨*of*⟩ the Quotas of the Several States of the Common expence.[2]

I am with the highest Sentiments of respect Your Excellency's humble Servant,   Roger Sherman

RC (NjP: DeCoppet Collection).
[1] Sherman probably enclosed Congress' January 1 resolutions on "proper salaries for the purchasing commissaries, and for regulating the departments of the commissary and quarter master."*JCC*, 16:5–7.
[2] This may have been a copy of the report, read in Congress on January 12, of the "committee appointed to apportion the quota of supplies &c." *JCC*, 16:44–46.

Board of Treasury to Nathanael Greene

Treasury Office, Philadelphia

Sir   14 January 1780.

In the Month of June last a Gentleman belonging to the Chamber of Accounts at the Treasury was appointed and comissioned to repair to Albemarle in the State of Virginia in Order to liquidate and receive Payment of the Accounts of the United States against the Troops of the Convention of Saratoga, which are become very considerable.[1] He did not succeed in his Mission, Major General Phillips, seniour Officer of the said Troops, alledging that he was not in Cash, but that, if he were, he did not consider himself as invested with competent Authority to order the Payment either in Money or Articles in Kind. Among the Papers delivered in by the Commissioner on his return we find also a Number of Exceptions taken to the Mode of stating such Part of the Accounts as fall in the Line of the Quarter Master General's Department, because the Supplies for the Troops of Convention were blended with those of the Guards, and the Proportion struck according to the comparative Numbers.

On the report of the Commissioner, Congress have passed a Number of Resolutions a Copy of Part of which is enclosed; and in Consequence it becomes our Duty to take Measures for pursuing this interesting Object.[2] We shall therefore appoint and impower a suitable Person or Persons to complete this Business agreeably to the Intentions of the said Resolutions, and will be indebted to you for every Assistance you can give. This will be advantageous in more Views, but particularly in this that doubtless the Objections against the Accounts in the Quarter Master General's Department will be revived and urged.

We also take the Liberty of mentioning the Necessity of giving Orders for collecting the Accounts which still remain unprepared as mentioned in the last Resolution of Congress. The sooner these can be ready the better. Part of them lie to the Eastward of Hudson's River, the remainder at the Albemarle Barracks in Virginia.[3]

We are, Sir, your most obedt hble Servants,

William Ch Houston, By Order

RC (PPAmP: Greene Papers). Written and signed by Houston.

[1] On June 21, 1779, the Board of Treasury, in response to a June 7 order of Congress, had appointed commissioner of accounts James Milligan to "settle the accounts of the United States against the troops of the convention of Saratoga" for the provisions and supplies that had been furnished them since March 1778. See *JCC,* 16:38–39; and Board of Treasury to William Phillips, June 28, 1779.

[2] On January 11, the Board of Treasury reported on the failed negotiations between James Milligan and Maj. Gen. William Phillips, then on parole in New York. Congress thereupon passed several stringent resolutions "for facilitating the settlement of the accounts." Should Phillips continue to refuse payment, demands would then be made

directly upon Sir Henry Clinton. Should he not comply, the guards would be doubled "at the expence of the British government, and the said troops kept on half allowance for the space of one month; on one third allowance for the succeeding month; and thenceforward one fourth allowance, till further order shall be taken for the equitable adjustment of the premises." The board was directed to give the necessary orders for collecting the vouchers and preparing the accounts. See *JCC*, 16:38–40.

The problem of the convention troops' overdue accounts, however, merged at this time with the larger issue of the general exchange of prisoners, for which see Samuel Huntington to Washington this date, note 2.

[3] For the instructions that the board issued to the commander in chief, see the following entry. For Washington's reaction to the board's instructions, see Samuel Huntington to Washington, January 27, 1780, note 2.

Board of Treasury to George Washington

Sir,   Treasury-Office Philadelphia, 14 January 1780

By your Excellency's Letter to Congress of the 4th instant[1] we are happy to be made acquainted that Proposals for an Exchange of Prisoners, by the Commanders in Chief of the American and British Armies, are in the Way of being opened. How far the Subject on which we now trouble Your Excellency may be involved, or ought to be thought of previous to or in any Discussion of this Matter, we cannot precisely determine, but conceive it our Duty thus early to mention it. At the same Time declaring that Nothing would tempt us to throw an unnecessary Obstruction in the Course of so desireable an Event.

In the Month of June last a Gentleman of the Chamber of Accounts at this Office, was appointed and commissioned to repair to Albemarle, in the State of Virginia, with proper Instructions and Powers to Liquidate and receive Payment of the Accounts of the United States against the Troops of the Convention of Saratoga. After much Correspondence, Conference and Explanation with Major General Phillips, seniour Officer of the said Troops, he has returned without effecting any Thing, though from the Documents produced, we are convinced he has left no proper Means unessayed to compass the End of his Mission.

On considering his report Congress have passed certain Resolutions, a Copy of which your Excellency has enclosed.[2] It is now become our Duty to take Measures for carrying the Determinations they contain, so far as we are directed to take Order on them, into Effect. In this, as we shall need so we wish to have all the Countenance and Assistance your Excellency's Attention to other pressing and indispensible Business will allow you to give us. The Accounts amount to a very considerable Sum, as nearly as we can judge, if those not yet collected are added to these prepared, not less than two Hundred Thousand Pounds in Specie, and we look upon the Settlement and Discharge of them as an Object of such Magnitude and national Concern, that we are unwilling the British Government or their Officers, should be in a Situation to venture a peremptory Refusal. The Difficulty also with which we procure Specie, absolutely necessary to be obtained for some Uses, prompts us to avail ourselves of this Resource for at least the Balance due for what can not be repaid in Kind, and for the Whole, if the Enemy chuse to repay no Part in that Way. But above all the Payment is to be expected as a Piece of Justice demandible on the Part of the United States to whom the Money is, and has long been, due for value received.

The Accounts against these Troops, previous to the Departure of General Burgoyne for England, or as far as they were collected and prepared at that Time, were paid off. The subsequent are founded on no new Principles, and it is therefore to be hoped that no further Hesitations on the Part of the Enemy will take Place. Major General Phillips's Objections were principally that he was not in Cash, but that if he were his Authority was incompetent. Some less capital Objections were also made against the Mode of stating such of the Accounts as came in the Line of the Quarter Master General's Department. The Matter perhaps may now be accomodated, and we earnestly hope it will never be necessary to carry the Penalty of a Refusal in any Degree into Execution.

If the Accounts now prepared and ready for Settlement are accepted and discharged, it is to be supposed that those due and not yet collected would be admitted on the like Ground when ready. The Amount of these is not inconsiderable, and we are not advised how far a Stipulation to discharge them when collected and adjusted would be necessary previous to a Release of the Prisoners, were the Exchange to extend to a large Proportion of them.

We shall, with all convenient Dispatch commission and instruct a proper Person to go forward and transact this Business as an Accountant, to whom we should be happy if your Excellency would join some active and intelligent Assistant from the Army, acquainted with the Train of Business in the Commissary, Quarter Master and other Departments to which the Accounts belong, and capable of conducting such a Matter with suitable Influence and Address.

If your Excellency approves this Idea, we wish your early Notice, and the Name of the Gentleman you would appoint, that we may join him in the Commission and give him concurrent Authority with the Person appointed from hence.

Whatever Your Excellency may have Leisure to suggest will be of great use to us in the Conduct of this Affair.[3]

We have the Honour to be, your Excellency's most obedt, most hble Servt.   William Ch Houston, By Order

RC (DLC: Washington Papers). Written and signed by Houston.

[1] See Samuel Huntington to Washington, this date, note 2.

[2] See the preceding entry, notes 1 and 2.

Oliver Ellsworth to Jonathan Trumbull, Sr.

Sir   Philadelphia Jany. 14. 1780

Congress have no late intelligence from Europe, nor do they yet learn the destination of the troops lately embarked from New York.

Four american Colonels, Magau, Ely &c are out from New York on short parole, with propositions drawn up by them & General Philips of the Convention troops, for a general exchange of prisoners; which bids fair to take place on the plan now proposed. It is referred by Congress to Genl. Washington, with power to take measures thereon at his discretion.[1]

Much credit is due & given to Connecticut for the supply of Beef said to be coming on from thence to the Army, whose distress has been great & situation yet remains critical for want of provisions. Eight dollars have been given in its vicinity by the Soldiers for a quart of meal & half a dollar for an ear of Corn. Flour & Grain are procured sufficient it is said for some months & now forwarding as fast as may be—& every attention will in future be paid to furnish money for the beef department.

The failure of that great resource the press, gives as was expectable a violent Shock, but it is hoped will prove a salutary one. The System of taxation urged by necessity is now establishing itself fast. All the States in the Union, so far as I can be informed are now Levying & collecting pursuant to the requisitions of Congress—tho' in some of them their assemblies have not yet been together to consider of the Quotas last required. Maryland Assembly has indeed lately been together & adjourned without making provision therefor—owing to their not being able to obtain a vote in the Senate for the Sale of British & Tory property—but as they have called on their people at large to shew their sense on that question & are soon to meet again there is no doubt of that obstacle's being removed & that Maryland will chearfully & fully furnish her quota. She is now making every exertion to supply the army with bread.

Greater unanimity has at no time perhaps prevailed in Congress than at present or ever been more necessary.

I have the honor to be, Sir, with very great respect, your Excellency's most obedt. & most huml. Servt.   Oliv. Ellsworth[2]

RC (Ct: Trumbull Papers).

[1] See Samuel Huntington to Washington, this date.

[2] Ellsworth also wrote a letter this day to his wife, Abigail, reporting that "I am in perfect health," and that "Mrs. Huntington on her arrival took the small pox by innoculation." Ellsworth further noted that "The weather is colder here than has been known for many years. Wood is £150 per Cord & thousands in this City are ready

to perish for want of it—great [*distress*] has also of late been in the army for want of provision—8 dollars has been given by the Soldiers to the needy inhabitants around them for one pint of Indian meal—& half a dollar for an Ear of Corn, but they have now some supplies & more going on." Ellsworth Papers, CtHi.

Samuel Huntington to Nathanael Greene

Sir,   Philadelphia Jany. 14. 1780

You will receive herewith enclos'd an Act of Congress of the 11th instant by which you will be informed That the Quarter Master General is directed to take efectual Care that the accounts of all supplies which may be furnished in future by his Department for the Troops of the Convention of Saratoga be kept separate from the accounts of Supplies furnished for the Guards.[1]

I am Sir, with Esteem & respect, your hble Servt.

Sam. Huntington President

RC (PPAmP: Greene Papers). In a clerical hand and signed by Huntington.

[1] *JCC*, 16:40. For the circumstances that led Congress to adopt this resolve, see the letters from the Board of Treasury to Greene and to Washington, this date.

Samuel Huntington to Charles Lee

Sir,   Philada Jany 14. 1780

By the act of Congress of the 10 Instant herewith enclos'd, you will be inform'd that they have no further occasion for your Service in the Army of the Army[1] of the United States.[2]

I am Sir &c,   S.H. President

LB (DNA: PCC, item 14).

[1] Thus in manuscript.

[2] This conclusion to General Lee's career in the Continental Army had been triggered by the receipt of an insulting letter from him declaring that "Congress must know very little of me, if they suppose that I would accept of their money since the confirmation of the wicked and infamous sentence which was passed upon me." Lee had dashed off this feisty challenge upon learning that an effort to dismiss him had been made on December 4, on the eve of the expiration of his one-year suspension for his conduct at the battle of Monmouth, and although the move had been defeated he was too enraged to respond constructively. When he received this letter and enclosed resolve from Huntington, he had second thoughts about his initial reaction and offered an apology, but the damage had been done and Congress took no special notice of his contrition. See *JCC*, 15:1348–49, 16:33, 158–59; PCC, item 158, 1:143–50; these *Letters*, 10:227–29, 596, 11:352–53; and John R. Alden, *General Charles Lee: Traitor or Patriot?* (Baton Rouge: Louisiana State University Press, 1951), pp. 286–88.

Samuel Huntington to the Pennsylvania Council

Gentlemen.   In Congress, Jan'ry 14th, 1780.

Pay to Charles Petit, assistant Quarter Master General, or his Order, the sum of two hundred thousand dollars, being part of the Monies raised by the State of Pennsylvania, for the use of the United States, on account of Major Gen'l Green, Quarter Master Gen'l and for the use of his department, for which he is to be accountable.[1]

I am, Gentlemen, Your humble Serv't,
                                   Samuel Huntington, President

MS not found; reprinted from *Pa. Council Minutes*, 12:228–29.

[1] Huntington wrote this letter pursuant to an order of Congress of this date endorsing a recommendation of the Board of Treasury. *JCC*, 16:55. The council's response exposed Pennsylvania's inability to meet Continental requisitions at this time, but instead of frankly acknowledging its embarrassment it resorted to the device of issuing an order for the payment while directing that it be charged against the state's Continental account. Thus, upon ascertaining that the treasurer was unable to defray this request, the council simply ordered "That the Treasurer be directed to pay the aforesaid draft of Congress . . . in the following words. Pay to Charles Petit, esquire, Assistant quartermaster General, or his Order, the sum of two hundred thousand dollars, agreeable to the within draft, and charge the same to the United States of America." *Pa. Council Minutes*, 12:229. For other instances in which the council used this same delaying technique when called upon for similar payments on January 24, 26, 28, and February 8, see ibid., pp. 232, 236, 239, 248–49.

Samuel Huntington to Joseph Ward

Sir,   Philada. Jany 14. 1780

By the Act of Congress of the 12 instant herewith enclos'd you will be informed that the Mustering Department is discontinued & the Officers thereof discharged.[1]

And that the Commissary General of Musters and those Officers who have continued in that Department under him for eighteen months are entitled to receive a sum equal to their pay respectively for the Term of Twelve Months from the Date of the Act.

I am Sir your hble Servt,   S.H. President

LB (DNA: PCC, item 14). Addressed: "The Commissary Genl of Musters."
[1] See *JCC*, 16:47. For the background of this decision to abolish the mustering department, see these *Letters*, 13:402.

Samuel Huntington to George Washington

Sir,   Philadelphia Jany 14. 1780

Your Excellency will receive herewith enclos'd seven Acts of Congress of the 10th, 12th, 13th, & 14th instant.[1]

By the act of the 13th respecting the Exchange of Prisoners your Excellency is fully authorized to negotiate & conclude all matters & proceedings necessary for an Exchange of Prisoners agreeable to the Act of Congress of the 5th March 1779.[2]

The Compass of a letter would not suffice to recapitulate the Subject Matter of the several Acts enclos'd and should I give myself that trouble in the present Case it would perhaps give your Excellency unnecessary reading.

The Officers who deliver'd me your letter of the 4th Instant[3] are Impatient to return & will have the honour of delivering your Excy these dispatches and as I am unwilling to detain them must beg your Excuse for not acknowledging in particular the receipt of several of your letters which have come to hand but are not now before me.

I have the honour to be, with every Sentiment of respect, your Excy's hble Servt,   Sam. Huntington President

RC (DLC: Washington papers). In a clerical hand and signed by Huntington.

[1] Huntington's "Enclos'd seven Acts" were apparently the eight resolves now in the Washington Papers concerning the following subjects: the dismissal of Gen. Charles Lee from the Continental Army (10th); British refusal to settle accounts for provisioning the Convention Army (11th); the early discharge of certain Virginia troops (12th); promotion of William Galvan to a majority (12th); an emergency appeal to Connecticut, New York, Pennsylvania, and Delaware for provisions (12th); Washington's authority to conduct prisoner exchange negotiations (13th); continuation of the French engineers Duportail, Laumoy, and Gouvion in the Continental Army (14th); and the retention of express riders at the discretion of the commander in chief (14th). See *JCC*, 16:33, 39–40, 43–44, 46, 48–52, 55–56.

[2] This act "respecting the Exchange of Prisoners" was adopted in response to Washington's letter to Huntington of January 4 explaining that four American officers had just been "permitted to come out of New York on parole, with some new propositions for an exchange of prisoners, the result of a conference between major General Phillips and themselves." He then went on to discuss some of the ramifications of this initiative and appealed to Congress for guidance. Negotiations aimed at arranging a general exchange of prisoners of war had already failed twice, and in view of his experience with the aborted Perth Amboy negotiations of April 1779, Washington was not eager to resume such talks without additional authorization. This Congress supplied by renewing the powers granted to him prior to the previous negotiations. And to simplify Washington's task, Congress simultaneously decided to appeal to the states to send him comprehensive information on all prisoners of war in their jurisdictions, whether taken on land or at sea, and to forbear from attempting to make exchanges in the future except through the Continental commissary general of prisoners. See Washington, *Writings* (Fitzpatrick), 17:352–54; and *JCC*, 16:47–52.

However, as these January 13 resolves were adopted just two days after Congress had passed tough, new measures for compelling British settlement of overdue accounts for Convention Army provisions, Washington immediately found that it was unrealistic to expect to implement the two sets of recommendations simultaneously and soon sought additional instructions. For the delegates' response to Washington's subsequent request for clarification, which led to the immediate repeal of the resolves concerning the Convention Army, thus removing that issue as an obstacle to reopening the prisoner exchange negotiations offered at this time, see Huntington to Washington, January 27, 1780. For the issue of the Convention Army accounts, see the letters of the Board of Treasury to Washington and to Nathanael Greene, this date.

The general course of British-American prisoner negotiations has been treated by Larry G. Bowman, "The New Jersey Prisoner Exchange Conferences, 1778–1780," *New Jersey History* 97 (Autumn 1979): 149–58. As Lt. Col. Alexander Hamilton was one of the commissioners appointed by Washington to negotiate a cartel at Perth Amboy in March, many of the documents pertinent to the conduct of those negotiations can be found in Hamilton, *Papers* (Syrett), 2:271–85, 287–92, 295–301.

[3] That is, Cols. Robert Magaw, George Mathews, and John Ely and Lt. Col. Nathaniel Ramsey, the four officers paroled by the British to prod the Americans into reopening prisoner exchange negotiations.

Samuel Holten's Diary

[January 15, 1780]

15. Saturday. Congress agreed upon a number of resolutions for establishing a Court of appeals, of members out of Congress.[1] No new intelligence.

MS (MDaAr).

[1] After lengthy deliberations, Congress this day passed resolves establising a court "for the trial of all appeals from the courts of admiralty in these United States, in cases of capture, to consist of three judges, appointed and commissioned by Congress."

Congress had heard appeals from the state courts of admiralty through the standing Committee on Appeals, but the system had experienced difficulties with questions of jurisdiction and venue, and it made great demands on the time of the delegates to Congress who made up the committee. Congress therefore attempted to overcome these defects by transforming the committee into a circuit court authorized to hear "all appeals," appointing judges who were not members of Congress and urging the states to pass laws authorizing the new court to carry its final decrees "into full and speedy execution." *JCC*, 16:61–64.

For further information on the creation of the Court of Appeals, see these *Letters*, 10:624n; and Henry J. Bourguignon, *The First Federal Court: The Federal Appellate Prize Court of the American Revolution, 1775–1787*, Memoirs of the American Philosophical Society 122 (1977): 114–18.

Samuel Huntington to Jonathan Trumbull, Sr.

Sir   Philadelphia January 17th. 1780

I do my Self the honour to Transmit your Excellency an Act of the state of New Jersey for procuring provisions for the Use of the Army &c.[1]

I am under the disagreable necessity of Requesting that two thousand dollars may be advanced to me or my order out of the public Treasury for which I will be Accountable, the profits of my own Estate which under my care with my own Industry used to afford me all necessary Supplies, hath been so long Neglected by me that I am unable to discharge the necessary Expenses incured, and in my present Situation I am unwill[ing] to request any Advancement from the Continental Treasury, which would be rather out of Character.

Must therefore beg the favour of your Excellency to lay this my request before the Assembly (if necessary:) in order to have it granted.

I am with the Greatest Respect, Your Excellency's Obedient Servant, Sam. Huntington

RC (Ct: Trumbull Papers)

[1] See Roger Sherman to Trumbull, January 11, 1780, note.

Samuel Holten's Diary

[January 18-19, 1780]

18. Tuesday. I dined with the minisr.[1] I wrote to Mrs. Holten (no.94.)[2] Three year this day since the deceas of my honr. Father.

19. Wednesday. Yesterday Mr. Searle cained the secy. of Congress, & the secy returned the same salute.[3] Very cold weather.

MS (MDaAr).

[1] That is, the French minister, the chevalier de La Luzerne.

[2] Not found.

[3] No other delegate comments on this confrontation between Secretary Charles Thomson and Pennsylvania delegate James Searle have been found. However, the French minster La Luzerne later made the following observation to the comte de Vergennes that undoubtedly refers to the same incident: "On a vu, il y a quelques Semaines un Délégué et le Sécrètaire du Congrès s'assaillir à coups de Canne en plain Senat, se blesser au visage et lendemain reprendre paisiblement leur séance." See La Luzerne to Vergennes, March 16, 1780, Archives du ministère des affaires étrangères: Correspondance politique, États-Unis, 11:83.

For Thomson's bitter relations with another delegate, Henry Laurens, see Laurens to a Committee of Congress, September 1; and Thomson to a Committee of Congress, September 6, 1779.

Samuel Huntington to John Lawrence

Sir   Philadelphia 18th January 1780

I am under the disagreable necessity of Requesting Two thousand dollars to be advanced to me in Continental bills from the Treasury of Connecticut on account of my Services. Must request you to pay the same to the bearer Ebenr Devotion Esq & Charge it to me, I am Compelled to give you the Trouble to apply to the Committee of pay table to get an Order for that purpose if you find it necessary.

In my present Situation Connecticutt is at no expence for my Support, as they are for their other Delegates, and it is out of Character for me to ask for any monies out of the Continental Treasury; my wages whatever the State Shall think fit to allow me are all due; Decency and a regard for the Honour of the State I represent, Obliges me to more Expence than in any Other Situation would be necessary or desirable by me; as I am obliged to receive the Company of all Forreigners of Distinction Especially the Foreign Minister & must appear decent in dress &c which is at this time very dear: I am Compelled to request the advancement aforementioned, which I Desire may be granted.

I have no Intelligence of Consequence, and am with Esteem, your humbl Servt,　　　　　　　　　　　　　　Sam. Huntington[1]

NB I have mentiond this matter to Gov. Trumbull as I am under real necessity for the money.

RC (Ct: Revolutionary War Collection).
[1] This day Huntington also wrote a brief letter to the commissary general of purchases, Ephraim Blaine, transmitting a resolve of Congress of the 17th authorizing him to appoint two clerks for his department, "Their Salaries to be the same as a Clerk of the Board of Treasury." See PCC, item 14, fol. 279; and *JCC*, 16:66–67.

Samuel Huntington to the Chevalier de La Luzerne

Sir　　　　　　　　　　　　　　　　　　Philada Jany 18. 1780
I have the honour to lay before you an Act of Congress of the 17th Instant which was passed in Consequence of your representation of the 10th Inst. made to Congress respecting the flour purchased in Maryland by the Marine Agent of his most Christian Majesty and said to be seised &c.[1]

I flatter myself those proceedings of Congress will effectually prevent or remove all operations in the State of Maryland which might embarrass the Measures of the Agent of his most Christian Majesty's Marine or endanger the success of military plans & operations of our Illustrious Ally.

I have the honour to be &c,　　　　　　　　S. H. President

LB (DNA: PCC, item 14).
[1] *JCC*, 16:41, 67–68. Congress adopted this resolution in response to a letter from La Luzerne of January 10 expressing concern that a recent Maryland law authorizing commissioners to seize grain stored in the state would cripple efforts of the French agent of marine, Jean Holker, to collect and export provisions for the French fleet and garrisons in the West Indies. To substantiate the threat, La Luzerne had enclosed for Congress a letter to him from Holker, a letter to Holker from his agent William Smith in Baltimore, and a letter from the Maryland Council to Smith explaining the state's refusal to exempt him from the operation of the seizure law despite his protests that his purchases had been made as an agent of France. These documents are in PCC, item 95, 1:45–63; and Wharton, *Diplomatic Correspondence*, 3:453–57. See also the following entry.

Samuel Huntington to Thomas Sim Lee

Sir,   Philada Jany 18. 1780
  You will receive herewith inclos'd an act of Congress of the 17th
Instant together with the Copy of a Memorial from the Minister of
France and Copies of three other papers refer'd to in the Memorial.[1]
  The Wisdom & prudence which have been repeatedly manifest in
the proceedings of the Executive of Maryland leave no room to
doubt they will chearfully comply with the recommendation of Congress contain'd in the Act enclosd in such manner as on the one
hand not to embarrass the Measures of the Agent of the Marine of
France; but give satisfaction to the Servants of his most Christian
majesty our Ally; that his plans and expectations may not be
disappointed; and on the other hand that any collusive practices
under false pretext by any of the Inhabitants of these United States
to monopolize flour may be prevented.
  I have the honour to be &c,   S. H. President

LB (DNA: PCC, item 14).
  [1] In response to an appeal from the French Minister La Luzerne, Congress hereby
"recommended" that Maryland "refrain from seizing the provisions which have been
purchased by permission of the State of Maryland for the agent of the marine of his
most Christian Majesty; to replace them in case they have been already seized; and to
permit the exportation thereof." See *JCC*, 16:67–68; and the preceding entry. To this
appeal, Congress also added a mollifying resolution explaining "That Congress entertain a high sense of the exertions of the legislature and governor and council of the
State of Maryland to procure an immediate supply of flour and other provisions for
the army."
  Upon receiving Congress' "recommendation," the Maryland Council wrote to La
Luzerne on the 24th to explain that it could not interfere with the operation of the
state's seizure law, but the council assured him that the act was designed only to
prevent "abuses" by purchasers operating under the cloak of the French agent of the
marine, Jean Holker, and once this goal had been achieved all legitimate purchases
for the French forces could be shipped from Maryland without interference. For this
explanation by the Maryland Council, and letters subsequently adopted by the council
on February 17 in response to continued complaints by Holker and La Luzerne
concerning Maryland's reluctance to follow Congress' "recommendation" against
interfering with French flour purchases, see *Md. Archives*, 43:66–68, 88–90; and
Maryland Delegates to Thomas Sim Lee, March 7, 1780. For Holker's previous difficulties with Maryland officials, see also John Jay to Conrad Alexander Gérard, July 7,
1779.

Samuel Huntington to the States

Sir   Circular   Philada Jany 18. 1780
  Your Excellency will receive herewith enclos'd two Acts of Con-
gress of the 13 & 14 Instant.
  The former containing the regulations adopted relating to prison-
ers of War whether taken by Continental Troops or captured by the
Arms of any particular State, either by sea or Land.[1]

Many difficulties have frequently occurred for want of such a general regulation too numerous to be recited. It is proper to observe that the first paragraph of the Act recommending to the Executive of the several States to transmit with all possible Expedition to General Washington the names & rank of all Officers and the number of privates belonging to the Enemy held as prisoners of War in each State and the places they are at &c should be complied with as soon as possible by those States that have any number of prisoners.

The other Act of the 14th Instant recommending to the Legislature of the several United States to make provision where not already made, for conferring like privileges & Immunities on the Subjects of his most Christian Majesty as are granted to the Subjects and Inhabitants of these United States by the recited Article in the Treaty of Amity and Commerce will no doubt be chearfully complied with by each of the States.[2]

His most Christian Majesty as soon as the Treaty became known published an Edict conformable to that Article Exempting the Subjects and Inhabitants of these United States from the Droit d'Aubaine &c.

I have the honour to be &c,   S.H. Prest.

LB (DNA: PCC, item 14).

[1] *JCC*, 16:47–52. For the context of the adoption of these resolves to facilitate the reopening of prisoner exchange negotiations with the British, see Huntington to Washington, January 14, 1780, note 2.

[2] For the enclosed resolution concerning "the recited Article in the Treaty of Amity and Commerce," which Congress adopted on January 14 in response to a recommendation of the Committee for Foreign Affairs, see *JCC*, 16:56–57. The original Franco-American treaty of amity and commerce had envisioned the mutual enjoyment of certain legal exemptions by citizens of each nation when residing within the territory of the other, but the individual American states had not yet taken steps to protect such rights for French citizens within their jurisdiction, although the French minister in Philadelphia had petitioned Congress to guarantee "the immunity of the flag" to Frenchmen in the United States and the king of France had already issued an appropriate proclamation concerning American citizens in France. In recommending that the states be called upon "to make provision, where not already made, for conferring like privileges and immunities on the subjects of his most Christian Majesty," the Committee for Foreign Affairs was merely calling for the fulfillment of a diplomatic obligation long overdue. See *JCC*, 11:429–30, 14:760, 15:1041; PCC, item 94, fols. 263–70; and Wharton, *Diplomatic Correspondence*, 3:228–29. For the related issue of the negotiation of a consular convention between the United States and France, which also raised difficult problems concerning the sovereignty of the states, see also Massachusetts Delegates to the Massachusetts Council, April 1, note 2; and John Jay to Joseph Reed, June 29, 1779, note 2.

Samuel Huntington to
William Livingston and Jonathan Trumbull, Sr.

Sir   Philadelphia January 20th 1780
  Your Excellency will receive herewith enclos'd an Act of Congress
of this day together with an Extract of Intelligence, therein refer'd
to; which I am directed to lay before your Excellency in order that
the most effectual measures may be taken to prevent such nefarious
practices of supplying the Enemy with provisions.[1]
  I have the honour to be, with every sentiment of respect, your
Excy's hble Servt.   Sam. Huntington President

RC (NN: Livingston Papers; Ct: Trumbull Papers). In a clerical hand and signed by
Huntington.
  [1] *JCC*, 16:74. The enclosed "Extract of Intelligence" ("relative to supplies sent to the
enemy from New Jersey and Connecticut"), was taken from a recent report of
Washington's "confidential Correspondent in New York," which the general had sent
to Congress with a letter of January 18. See PCC, item 152, 8:343–46; and Washington,
Writings (Fitzpatrick), 17:406–7.

Samuel Huntington to
the Massachusetts Council

Sir,   Philadelphia Jany 20.1780
  You will receive herewith enclosd an Act of Congress of the 17
Instant with the Copy of a Letter from General Washington of the
17 of Decemr & report from the Board of War referr'd to in the Act:
By which you will be inform'd that the Case of Monsr la Motte
therein mentioned, The Expediency of continuing him in his pres-
ent employment is referr'd to the Honble Council of Massachusets
Bay who are requested to adjust & settle his Accounts at Continental
Expence and if they deem his continuance unnecessary to discharge
him from any further service.[1] You will also please to observe The
Board of War have advanced him three thousand dollars on Account
of his pay.
  I am Sir, with great respect, your hble Servt,
                                    Sam. Huntington President

RC (M–Ar: Revolutionary War Letters). In a clerical hand and signed by Huntington.
Addressed: "The President of the Council of the Massachusets Bay."
  [1] In his December 17 recommendation of the Rev. Hyacinthe de La Motte, Washington had suggested that because of his French background and missionary work among
the Indians of the eastern department, La Motte might be usefully employed to "gain
intelligence of the enemy," but cautioned that if he should be inclined to work for the
enemy (as Col. John Allan had charged), the effects of employing him might be
"mischievous." The recommendation had been referred to the Board of War, which
on December 31 advised against employing La Motte, but because any mission he

might undertake into Canada would be under the direction of Massachusetts and Col. Allan, Congress resolved to refer the matter to the Massachusetts Council for a final determination. See *JCC*, 15:1397, 16:66; PCC, item 147, 4:75–78, item 152, 8:251–54; Washington, *Writings* (Fitzpatrick), 17:283–84; and John Jay to James Avery, August 11, 1779.

George Plater to Edward Lloyd

My Dear Sir.[1]   Philadelphia January 20th 1780
 I am favor'd with yours of 8th inst. I believe you had not then recieved my last, in which I mentioned some Rooms which I cou'd get for your Accommodation here, the Owner wishes to know your Answer, which I cannot give untill I know your Determination—& tho' you say you have Doubts whether you will enter upon the arduous Task, yet I think that Point must have been long settled with you, or you wou'd have told the Legislature so before they rose, when they had it in their Power to fill up the Vacancy. Forbes declares, & says he has written so to the Governor, that he will stay no longer than the End of this Month,[2] if so it will be indispensably necessary for some of the new to come up, or the State will be unrepresented, how pleasing this may be to our Constituents I submit to your Judgment. Congress has resolved to leave Philadelphia in April next, but when is not yet determined, perhaps the Uncertainty of being properly, or so well, accommodated in any other Place, may be a Mean of their continuing here—but this I do not positively say—was it left to me, I shou'd, thinking it necessary, remove tomorrow, if practicable. Flour is now conveyed with much Facility on Slays, & some has arrived here from Maryland & gone on to Camp. The Depth of the Snow prevented Cattle from being driven, & reduced our poor brave Soldiers to an Hering & Gill of Rice per Day, this they bore without murmuring. The Exertion of the States (upon which we must now solely depend) & the Roads being opened now, afford a Prospect of Subsistance to the Army, & I hope a little Perseverance in this Line of Conduct will fill our Magazines against the ensuing Campaign. Your recommendations will ever have great Weight with me, because I know you wou'd not recommend a bad Man, & I shou'd be happy to prove it by my Endeavour to promote Mr. Grayson, whom I view as a good Officer & skillful Mariner. But I must inform you that we have more Captains than Ships, our Marine being but in its Infancy. Many of these Captains, deserving in the highest Degree, are now obliged to go in Merchantmen to get a living. It will never do to put a Man over their Heads. The Enemy certainly sailed from N York on 26th Decr. with five thousand Troops, & I have great Reason to think Clinton with them, where destined we know not, but 'tis most generally thought to Georgia & Charles Town. Since their sailing there have been two severe Storms, from

George Plater

the good Effects of which we have much to hope. Since my Arrival here I have received another Letter from Mr. Chamberlaine[3] concerning the Land, I wrote him[4] that I had applied to you for your Determination, & then wou'd give him my Answer, which I wish to be enabled to do in a Post or two, the Weather may possibly prevent your going to the eastern Shore for some Time, & my Delay may be deemed by him neither candid or polite—therefore shall be glad you will say whether you will purchase or not. The Disposal of the Land at Wye is what I have not thought of, the Right not being fully in me, but shou'd such a thing happen, you may be assured it wou'd give me more Pleasure to vest it in you than a Stranger, nor can the mention be by any Means deemed offensive, well knowing that you intended none. I find it is my Fate to be detained here this Winter, very disagreable to me, & inconvenient to my domestic Affairs—I presume Mr. Hall[5] cannot think of leaving the Vineyard & Bub 'till warm weather gives Motion to Butterflies &c. The Weather is cold, but all agree, who have travelled, that the Roads are very dry & good, perhaps better than you may find 'em in April. Therefore it wou'd give me Pleasure to see you here. Mrs. Plater joins me in Love & Affection, & I am with most perfect Regard & Esteem Dr Col., Yr aff. & obt Servt.   Geo. Plater

RC (Herbert E. Klingelhofer, Bethesda, Md., 1971).
  [1] Edward Lloyd (1744–96), of Talbot Co., a member of the Maryland assembly and executive council, was elected a delegate to Congress on December 22, 1779, but his attendance there was confined to a brief period in 1783–84. *DAB*.
  [2] See James Forbes to Thomas Sim Lee, January 11 and 22, 1780.
  [3] Probably James Lloyd Chamberlaine of Talbot Co., Md.
  [4] Not found.
  [5] Former delegate John Hall (1729–97), of "the Vineyard" near Annapolis, had also been elected to Congress by the Maryland assembly on December 22, 1779, but he never attended after 1775. *JCC*, 17:509; *Bio. Dir. Cong.*

Samuel Huntington to George Washington

Sir,   Philadelphia Jany. 21st 1780
    I am honour'd with your Excellency's despatches of the 23d, 24th, 25th, & 27th of Decemr, the 2d, 4th, 5th, & 18th Instant which have not been in particular before acknowledged.[1]
    By the act of Congress of this day herewith enclos'd together with the letter from the Board of War therein refer'd to; you will be informed of the request of Colo Armand for promotion to the rank of a Brigadier & his claim as stated in the letter from the Board of War; and that I am constrained to request the opinion of your Excellency thereon.[2]
    I am Sir, with every sentiment of Respect & Esteem your Excy's hble Servt,   Saml. Huntington President

RC (DLC: Washington Papers). In a clerical hand and signed by Huntington.
    [1] These letters are in PCC, item 152, 8:255–62, 271–72, 283–90, 312–13, 321–24, 339–46; and Washington, *Writings* (Fitzpatrick), 17:307–8, 312, 319, 327, 339–40, 352–54, 406–8.
    [2] For this congressional resolve and Washington's opposition to Armand's promotion, see Huntington to the marquis de La Rouërie, February 11, 1780.

Ezra L'Hommedieu to George Clinton

Sr   Philadelphia January 21, 1780
    As I understand one great object the Legislature of our State had in view, in meeting at so early a day, was to carry into Execution The Resolution of Congress recommending a general limitation of Prices in the different States, I think it necessary to inform you, that at present I see no probability of its being speedily adopted by the states in general. The States of New Hampshire, Connecticut, New Jersey, Pensylvania, Delaware & Maryland, have sent Agents or Commissioners to this place (many of whom are their Delegates in Congress) to meet the Agents from the other States, in pursuance of the Recommendation of the Convention that met at Hartford; they have adjoined [adjourned] from Time to Time, without doing any Business, and are waiting expecting to hear from Virginia, who they are informed has apointed Agents to meet; and from the Massachusetts, from whom no Accounts have been received respecting this Business; Should this State or any other of Consequence refuse to join in the general Regulation proposed, it would much discourage the other States. Connecticut will not pass the law, except Massachusetts does the same, Maryland & Pensylvania are so connected with Virginia, that they cannot inforce such Laws except she joins in Similar Measures. I do not expect the States in general will pass the necessary Laws for the Limitation of Prices except conditionally till they know the result of this Meeting. I do not know that it would answer any valuable purpose for New York to send or impower agents to meet this Convention, as they have no Doubt of the States adopting the Measure if it should be general. New Jersey have passed the Law without any Reserve, at the same Time, they empowered Agents to buy the produce in the state, who likely before the act takes place, will buy up most of their Produce at the present going Prices there. Wheat for Instance at 50 Dollars per Bushel. Their Assembly are adjoined to meet at an early Day after the Act shall take place, so that they run little or no risk in proceeding in the Manner they have done. I shall be informed of the Deliberations & proceedings of this Convention and shall give you information thereof.
    The Distresses of the Army for want of Provisions has been very alarming, Occasioned for the want of Money to purchase; the Necessary Consequence of the prices being stopped & the extraordinary

Depreciation of Money, so that the Treasury was almost exhausted, the purchasors greatly in debt and out of Credit, before any Money could be procured from the States for Taxes. Bills on Spain and Holland are now issued, some of which will be sent to our State. This will give a Temporary relief. Maryland & Delaware being called on have procured a considerable Quantity of Flower, but except the prices can by some means be reduced, or Our Money fixed at some certain Rate I fear it will be with the greatest Difficulty that Supplies for the Army can be procured for the next Campaign. It is under Consideration to call on the several States for to furnish equal Quotas of Produce & other Necessaries for the Army & support of the war at certain prices to be credited to each State & to be paid for by them out of their Taxes. I am informed that Mr Shearman & some other Eastern Delegates have received information from the New Hampshire Grants [that] they are determined not to submit to the Decision [of Con]gress, their Claim to Independance; but have [named] Agents to send to Congress, with offers to confederate with the United States, or such of them as are willing to confederate with Vermont.[1] I have great reason to believe that great pains will be taken by some of the States (perhaps not openly) to put of[f] the Tryal & prevent any Determination respecting those Lands at present. They are continually strengthening themselves in the Eastern States by selling Lands but I trust Congress will see the necessity of immediately hearing and determining a Controversy of so great Importance as well to the United States as to New York.

I am Sr with great Respect, Your Obed Servt,

Ezra L'Hommedieu

Tr (DLC: George and James Clinton Papers).

[1] For the arrival of "Agents" from the New Hampshire Grants and their reception in Philadelphia, see James Lovell to Samuel Adams, February 1, 1780, note.

James Lovell to Abigail Adams

My dear Madam,   Jany. 21st. 1780

We have Letters from France to the Middle of Sept. only—none from Doctr. Franklin—nor any Thing material in those that we have seen.

Mr. Dóbrée the Son in Law of Mr. Schweighauser having been traduced, I wrote to the old Gentleman that I should be attentive to produce Counterparts to any Insinuations here to the Prejudice of the Young Man;[1] finding now many private Letters from that Company without any one for me, I took the Freedom to open that directed to my worthy Friend yr Husband supposing there might be confidential Communications to him on that particular Subject. I was n istaken—but no Harm is the Consequence. I convey the Letter to you, with a News paper; and beg a Return of one hundredth Part of the Affection with which I constantly subscribe myself your Friend.

J L

RC (MHi: Adams Papers).
[1] Lovell's letter has not been found, but for further information on the charges against Peter F. Dobrée alluded to here, see these *Letters*, 13:369n.3.

James Lovell to Samuel Adams

Jan. 21.1779 [i.e., 1780]

We have nothing material from Europe. A Lee writes to me in great haste Sepr. 11th acknowledging mine of 16 & 17 July, and inclosing a Letter to Congress requesting Copies of the Paca-Drayton & Carmichael Informations.[1] We had not a Line from Doctr. Franklin. The Vessel bringing the Letters was sent, I suppose, by Gillon of Sth. Carolina, because almost all the Letters were for that State, tho the Leaden-Mass was directed to Congress.

I have before said that I am astonished not a Line comes from you respecting either Vermont or the regulating Convention now sitting here. It is not less surprizing that we have only a Certificate of Election without any Reference to former Instructions.[2] You know that in the Cases of Georgia & North Carolina it was Determined that the Appointment of several Delegates to represent a State, without any specified No. for a Vote supposed Each *one* competent. New York demands that Priviledge. Virginia is now represented by one. And I believe every State must œconomize, The Expence having become intollerable!

I was vexed at ours and made Enquiry of Col. Floyd who is at Mrs. House's but I was far from bettering myself. He is charged forty times 40s for himself & 40 times 20s for his Servant and finds himself with every Thing but Bread, Meat & Lodging. Wood alone is an Estate. The Minister of France is incessant in his Invitations to dine in short weekly periodical. We have never invited him but once for which I dare say we shall have pd. 1000—600 of it & more being for the bare Dinner. We must either totally refuse his Invitations or be seemingly his Table Pensioners—or go into at least monthly Expence. This on a public Score. But what is to become of me on a private? I have been drawn on from one Fright of Prices to another till total Shabiness has come upon me. Indeed it is a Wonder I hang together, having bought one Suit & one Hat in 3 years. This latter hessian le haut being gone beyond Decency I am asked 400 Dollars. 300 for a pr. of Leather Breeches—125 for Shoes—a Suit of Cloaths 1600—that is not 16 pr. of shoes but it is enough to stance my Children unless the State have raised the Allowance for Time & Service to some nearer Proportion to the Expences which they pay for my Subsistance here—or consider my decent Cloaths in the Line of my Charge of Expenditures.

Thus I have plagued you as[3]

RC (NN: Adams Papers). In Lovell's hand, though signature is missing.

[1] Arthur Lee's September 11, 1779, letter to Lovell has not been found, but his September 10 letter to Congress was read on January 19 and assigned to the Committee for Foreign Affairs "that they take order thereon." He had requested copies of the "intelligence & information concerning me" that "Mr. Paca, Mr. W.H. Drayton, and Mr. Carmichael have been permitted to lay before you." See *JCC*, 16:72; PCC, item 83, 2:284–87; Wharton, *Diplomatic Correspondence*, 3:313; and these *Letters*, 12:410–11.

[2] The Massachusetts delegates' certificate of election had been presented to Congress on January 1. *JCC*, 16:2.

[3] Remainder of RC is missing.

James Lovell to Samuel Adams

Dear Sir   21 Jany. 80

Please to deliver or order to be deliver'd the inclosed two Letters from France, and forward to Mrs. Adams mine with the news Paper. I have written to you this Day by post, and hope for an Answer somewhat particular to the Contents of it.

We have nothing material from France to Sepr. 25th. A Lee was at Paris the 10th of that month[1] and had got the Journals of Congress to the 12th of June with my private Letters to July 17th.

We are, as usual, mightily divided on Elections. The 3 Judges of Appeals are to come from 10 or 12 Nominations.[2] Schuyler and Pickering are chosen for the reforming Comtee., the first as *the* Member of Congress.[3] Mifflin, Bull & Bodinot divide us; the Reasons given for *not* chusing the first, with all his Knowledge & Spirit, are from Devotees to Fabius,[4] who every now & then, by their Behavior & Arguments appear to think him a most malignant & revengeful Genius.

Tace. Paca, Duane, Bodinot, Hosmer, McKean, Lowell, R T Payne, Sullivan, Wythe are in nomn. for Judges. Huntingdon, Gerrey & Livingston wd. have their Names withdrawn.[5] I would not risque Coll. R H Lee in the present Temper of the House, though I think him extremely well calculated.[6] But, in the Course of Speakg the day before yesterday on Arthur's Request to have Copies of certain Papers, I found a number of Virulentissimses still cocked & primed at the very Name of Lee. I suppose I have told you that the Genl. of that Name is informed we have no need of his Services.[7]

I have other Business than the Duties of Friendship to attend, therefore Adieu,   J.L.

RC (NN: Adams Papers).
[1] See preceding document, note 1.

[2] See Samuel Huntington to Titus Hosmer, William Paca, and George Wythe, February 2, 1780.

[3] For the appointment of the "reforming Comtee," see Samuel Huntington to Thomas Mifflin and to Philip Schuyler, January 24, 1780.

[4] That is, George Washington. For Mifflin's opposition to Washington's leadership, see these *Letters*, 8:314–15, 549.

[5] Lovell's information on the nomination of judges for the newly created Court of Appeals varies significantly from that recorded by Secretary Thomson. Thomson's journal does not contain the names of Sullivan, Huntington, and Livingston; and the names of Gerry and "J Lowel" were written by Thomson but lined out, as was that of "J. Dickinson," who is omitted here by Lovell. Finally, the name rendered "J Lowel" (i.e., John Lowell) by Thomson, was misread by Gaillard Hunt and was misprinted in his edition of the journal "J Lovell." See *JCC*, 16:77; and PCC, item 1, vol. 25.

[6] After Wythe declined the appointment, Richard Henry Lee was nominated by William Ellery for the post on April 3, but Cyrus Griffin was nominated and elected to the position on April 28, 1780. *JCC*, 16:326, 366, 397.

[7] That is, Charles Lee.

North Carolina Delegates to Richard Caswell

Sir,   Philadelphia Jany 21st. 1780

Enclosed is an Extract of Intelligence received through the most authentic channel, and may be relied on.[1] The peculiar interest which our Country has in some part of it determined us to give the earliest advice in our power to you her presiding Magistrate, relying on your vigilance for every thing that can possibly be done to frustrate the designs of the Enemy. We flatter ourselves that a strict attention even to the most minute movements of the disaffected, which we know you will cause to be kept up will prevent the advantages, which they hope for from that ill judging class of our Citizens, and from our Negroes—and should they attempt to invade or penetrate any part of our Country, we have no doubt of hearing, that the vigor and valor of our people, will be exerted against them with decisive success. But we can not help wishing that the scene of action may be forever removed from our own state—and that the Enemy may be met in their most distant approach by a force sufficient to give them an Effectual Check.

Our apprehensions on the Article of Arms made us enquire if any succours of that kind could be sent, from this place, but we can derive no hope from the result. Virginia has lately had an acquisition of five thousand stand and we doubt not she will assist us if we shall be eminently threatened.[2] It would give us great satisfaction to learn that the long expected supplies of this kind are arrived for we should have no fears from such a force as the enemy can employ against our particular state if the militia were completely armed.

The Virginia line which is on its march, to reinforce the southern army, will be, we hope at least time enough to come to the relief of Charlestown should it be invested, at all events to check them in their approach to our Country.

We are well informed that the German Princes have refused Troops to Great Britain, and even permission to recruit in their dominions.

We have no other matter of important intelligence to communicate at present, and for ordinary occurrences beg leave to refer you to the enclosed papers.

We have the honor to be your Excellcy. ob. Servts,

> John Penn
>
> Thos Burke
>
> Allen Jones

Tr (Nc–Ar: Governors' Letterbooks).
[1] This undated and unsigned "Extract of Intelligence, " which confirmed that the British convoy that sailed from New York December 28, 1779, was "positively going to Charlestown," is in *N.C. State Records*, 15:324.
[2] For information that the delegates received concerning the availability of arms in Virginia, see North Carolina Delegates to Caswell, January 22, 1780.

James Forbes to Thomas Sim Lee

Dear Sir,   Philadelphia Jany 22d 1780

The Bearer Doctr Brown waits on you for your Permission,[1] to go into New York, in order to get a Passage to Scotland, As I am satisfyed the Facts stated in his Memorial are true, I hope there will be no dificualty in granting his request.

I have sent by him the papers to which must beg leave to refer you for News, I am very anctious to hear wheather any of the Delegates are coming forward, at any rate I am determin'd to leave this, the first of next month & ever am My Dr Sir, Yours Sincearly,   James Forbes

RC (MdHi: Lee, Horsey, and Carroll Papers deposit, 1985).
[1] Apparently Dr. Gustavus Richard Brown of Port Tobacco, Md. On April 1, 1780, the Maryland Council recommended that Washington or the commanding officer at Elizabeth, N.J., grant a license to Dr. Gustavus Brown "to go into the City of New York for the Purpose of obtaining a Passage to great Britain" and to be permitted to return again to Maryland "under the Peculiar Circumstances of his Case." *Md. Archives*, 43:126.

James Lovell to Horatio Gates

Dear Sir   22d of Jany. 1780

Your Favors of Decr. 30th and Jany. 9 are before me, valuable Proofs of your friendly Confidence in my honest Zeal for the Public Good. The News Papers which Mr McAllaster will deliver you contain many Speculations upon the Subject of Currency; but, of all,

Peletiah Webster bears the Bell in last Thursdays Publication of 2 Letters.[1]

We are aiming at a Curtail of Expence by Inspectors to visit & break up unnecessary Posts in the Staff Departments, and reduce the Number of Officers; and also to lessen the number of Horses & Waggons in the Army. In short we are beginning to do many Things that ought to have been done a Year ago.

We have no Money *now* to Squander upon A, B, C, & all the Letters of the Alphabet under the Sole Restriction of "he to be accountable."

We have Letters from France to the End of Sept. but nothing material. A Lee was then at Paris. On the 10th a Vote was carried "That major Genl. Charles Lee be informed that Congress have no farther Occasion for his Services in the Army of the United States" 5 ayes 4 noes 3 divided.[2] It was upon reading the following Letter which, in my Opinion, is forged.[3]

Berkley County

Sir, I understand that it is in Contemplation of Congress, on the Principle of œconomy, to strike me out of their Service. Congress must know very little of me, if they suppose that I would accept of their money since the Confirmation of the wicked & infamous sentence which was passed upon me. I am Sir your most humble Servant Charles Lee. Excuse my not writing in my own hand as it is wounded.   Charles Lee.

Superscribed The honble President of Congress. Philada.

I shall have a better opportunity of writing by Col Bull, I hope. I mean that I shall be less in haste.

Present my affectionate Compliments to your Lady & Son, and be assured of my most hearty Regards to yourself,   James Lovell

[*P.S.*] You Should have mentioned the No. of the Journals which you carried with you. I suppose I have gone far enough back. By Col. Bull I will send what may then be farther printed.

1780 will be given out *monthly* with*out* yeas & nays.

RC (NHi: Gates Papers).

[1] Lovell's reference is apparently to the two "Letters on Appreciation" that appeared in the Thursday, January 20 issue of the *Pennsylvania Packet*. His attribution of their authorship to Pelatiah Webster, a Philadelphia merchant and frequent contributor of economic articles to the press, contrasts with that of Elbridge Gerry, who subsequently reported that they were the work of "a Gentleman in Maryland." See Gerry to James Warren, January 25, 1780, note 2.

[2] See Samuel Huntington to Charles Lee, January 14, 1780.

[3] According to the journals, "the following letter signed Charles Lee, but not in his handwriting," was read in Congress on January 10, and this event precipitated the vote against Lee. *JCC*, 16:33–34. The letter is in PCC, item 158, fol. 143. Although Lovell concluded that the letter was a forgery, Lee subsequently confirmed his authorship of the note, acknowledged its "impropriety," and refused to request a reinstatement to the army. See *JCC*, 16:157–59; and PCC, item 158, fols. 147–49.

North Carolina Delegates to Richard Caswell

Sir   Philadelphia Jany 22d. 1780
    After closing our Letter of yesterday we received Information that
Mr Carter Braxton of Virginia has for Sale a great Number of Stands
of Excellent Arms, two thousand some time ago on hand, and more
daily expected. We deem it right to give you this Information, and
we beg leave to offer our advice that you Cause them to be purchased on the account of the State, if there shall appear any danger
of an Actual Invasion of our Country.
    We know you will excuse our Sollicitude when affairs are So Seri-
ous and important.
    We have the honor to be With the highest respect and Esteem
your Excellency's Obet h Svts,   John Penn

                                                     Thos Burke

                                                     Allen Jones

RC (Joseph G. Deering, Saco, Maine, 1974). Written by Burke and signed by Burke,
Jones, and Penn.

Charles Thomson to Robert Treat Paine

Dear Sir,   Jany 22. 1780
    I have long expected to have had the pleasure of seeing you in
Congress: but I now begin to despair. Pray Have you wholly disen-
gaged yourself from public affairs? I cannot persuade myself you
have. I should therefore be glad to know whether you at times turn
your attention to the nursing of *Salt petre making*, a child of your
own, which cost you much pains at the birth. I fear through the
carelessness of the nurses it is in a dangerous way.
    To Drop Allegory, I wish to know whether people continue the
manufacture of that useful article. And shall be much obliged if you
will send me a paper written on that subject by (If I recollect) a
clergyman pointing out an easy & expeditious method of making it
by mixing lye of ashes with the lye extracted from earth.[1] Your
Compliance will much oblige, Sr, Your sincere friend & Most humble Servt,   Cha Thomson

RC (MHi: Paine Papers).
[1] Thomson is probably referring to the work of William Whiting, a physician of
Great Barrington, Mass., with whom Paine discussed the making of saltpetre in 1775–76
when Paine was chairman of the saltpetre committee of Congress. See these *Letters*,
2:310–12, 3:455–56, 486–87.

Massachusetts Delegates
to the Massachusetts Council

Sir,   Philadelphia 23d Jany 1780
    The Bearer Colo Ephraim Blaine is lately appointed Commissary
General of Purchases in the room of Colo Wadsworth, & is on a
Tour to Boston to make the necessary Arrangements of his Department. He informs Us that he has no Connections or Acquaintances
in that Quarter, & is desirous of establishing such as will best promote the Business of his office. We conceive it of the utmost Importance that this should be accomplished, & have taken the Liberty to
recommend him, thro You sir, to the hona Council of the State for
Advice & Assistance. We have lately had the most painful Prospects from the want of Provisions for the Army, but sincerely hope
that the Activity & Zeal of this officer, & the subsequent Exertions of
the several States will speedily furnish the Supplies required for the
ensuing Campaign. We remain sir with every Sentiment of Respect
your most obed & very hum servts,   E. Gerry

                                                James Lovell

RC (M–Ar: Revolutionary War Letters). Written by Gerry and signed by Gerry and
Lovell. Addressed: "Hona. The President of the Council of the State of Massachusetts."

John Armstrong, Sr., to Joseph Reed

Carlisle 24th Janry 1780. Discusses a new Pennsylvania militia act
and the merits of corporal and capital punishment. Apologizes for
his limited knowledge of "that Subtile Science of Finance," but
expresses unwillingness to leave "the *deplorable state of our publick
affairs.* . .to a mere course of nature—As a Vesel deserted of her
Crew, or a patient of his physicians. The means that in my Opinion
appear the most proper for our recovery and deliverance, are Simply these—1st. *a Regulation of Prices by Law.* 2d A Speedy reformation
of abuses, and retrenchment of Expences in the two great lines of
the Civil Staff, and some other appendages of the Army, more immediately under the direction of the Board of War. Whether this last
shou'd extend to the line Military, the General will best judge, but
unless there are officers supernumerary the line cannot be touched.
3d. the laying in of certain Quantitys of Grain into publick Magazines,
or particular Mills appointed for the purpose. The Millars for the
sake of the Tole, I presume wou'd readily find Granaries; this grain
to be laid in at the regulated price, either in part or whole of the
Owners Tax, allowing him a moderate Mileage for Carriage. The
first of these I call, *the basis of every thing Salutary*—the mode is at

once, regular virtuous & necessary, and at present perfectly consistant with the Spirit of good Government—diametrically opposite therefore must the temper of that man be, who wou'd resist or evade such a Law. However arduous the Execution of this regulating law may be found to be, I humbly presume the necessity and expedience of it, must to every candid Observer be as evident as the noonday Sun, and this necessity must at least justify the Experiment. To Say that such a law is at no time practicable, is paying an odious Compliment both to God & Man; to him who hath the hearts of all men in his hand, the Original institutor & approver of all lawfull means, in the use whereof he may be said to Superintend the generallity of human affairs—to our Countrymen and fellow Citizens, as tho' their love of Nominal or even a little real superfluous wealth shoud lead them headlong to political destruction or that they Shou'd be found incapable of Society and the blessings thereof, by a lawless and refractory disposision rending asunder it's most Salutary bonds! forbid this Almighty God, the author of Order, of human nature itself, and giver of every good & perfect gift. The Hacknied Maxim, that Trade Must alwais Regulate itself, Is in our Situation as impolitick as it is arrogant and absurd, and patience but scarcely restrains from bestowing upon it the severer epithets due to a possition so very ill-timed. Amongst the Aerial or more refined schemes of Finance which have been exhibited most whereof must be considered as so many phantoms, it's said there is one lately Suggested by a Mr. Usher from Maryland,[1] which with the embroidery of a Loan to the publick of fifty millions of Dollars & a considerable sum in specie, I confess puts on a glittering aspect—having had but a cursory & perhaps an imperfect relation of that Gentlemans Scheme, the least we can say is that it's well Ushered in & perhaps with a good designe—but as it contains an antidote only to One branch of our disease, *Speculation* or private monopoly, we must doubt the effect like its cause wou'd only be partial—And the articles of commerce limited to certain Companys however large & free, might one day produce as boisterous a noise on our shores as the rising tides whereby they are introduced. The plain high way of publick authority for America, Wise & just Regulations by Law—Loping off every excrecence and superfluous branch in our several departments—persevering, but moderate Taxation, Such as every taxable may obviously bear— Honest Loans, justly if not generously requesting the lender whether he lent sooner or later in this conflict, but expecially those who have advanced or shall advance their Money in the publicks extreamity. These Measures together with the plain lines of œconomy & good government, will by the divine blessing which on the American cause we can never doubt (if we exclude it not by inattention or wicked works) will recover our finances—replenish our Treasury, support our Army and ensure the establishment of American liberty."

Laments the recent degeneration of public virtue but concludes nevertheless that "our people at large will yeild to a wise & equal regulation of prices & labour by law, as the basis of every other improvement in our affairs & of our political safety." On the other hand, "taxation must be mitigated" because of the present severe weather. "The people will pay tax willingly as they can bear it, but must have time; and on this condition also, that a reformation of abuses & curtail[ment] of the publick expence as Suddenly take place as the nature of things will admit—which reformation farther than the Outlines cannot possibly be performed by the General & assistants but ultimately & minutely by the Several States, and in their respective Counties. . . . My good friend Mr. McLane [James McLene] writes me his doubts of the propriety of a regulation of prices, as among other considerations he doubts whether the people wou'd bear such regulation & their high Tax, at the Same time. The matter admits of no doubt, they wou'd not, nor will they bear taxation as at present projected whether a regulation take place or not, but if it shou'd there will not be the same necessity for a high Tax, and the lower it can with safety be made, will have a powerful tendancy to facilitate the Operation of the regulating Law. I cannot Say that a majority are in favour of this Law, nor do I know the contrary—the more candid who have fallen under my notice yeild their consent & some loudly express their wishes for it, on the whole if generally gone into & candidly framed I'm fully of Opinion that in Our State it will meet with no considerable Opposition: & beside it, I know no remedy so just, general & Seasonable to our disease and am Obliged to believe that none Such exists in nature, except a Sudden peace, on which we must not presume."

RC (NHi: Reed Papers).
[1] Apparently Thomas Usher, a Chesapeake merchant who had recently been prompted to undertake a trip to Philadelphia to offer Congress a plan he had concocted for improving the country's dismal financial affairs. This "Scheme," Usher explained in a January 11, 1780, letter to Horatio Gates, "if attended to by Congress will induce much to extricate us from our present Calamities." Gates papers, NHi.

Samuel Huntington to the Chevalier de La Luzerne

Sir,   Philada Jany 24. 1780
    I am honoured with your letter informing you have appointed Monsr Danmour Consul of France for the State of North Carolina & enclosing his Commission for that purpose.
    Congress have been pleased to approve the same and ordered the Commission to be registered and notice of the appointment given to the Governor of North Carolina in the usual manner, as you will see by the Act enclos'd together with the Commision herewith returned.[1]

I have the honour to be &c &c,   S.H. President

LB (DNA: PCC, item 14).
[1] La Luzerne's January 24 letter informing Congress of his appointment of Charles-François-Adrien Le Paulmier, chevalier d'Anmours (consul in Maryland and Virginia), as French consul in North Carolina is in PCC, item 95, 1:65; and Wharton, *Diplomatic Correspondence*, 3:468.
  Notice of d'Anmours appointment was sent to the governor of North Carolina by Huntington in a brief letter of January 28. See PCC, item 14, fol. 287; *JCC*, 16:79–80; and these *Letters*, 11:135n.

Samuel Huntington to Thomas Mifflin

Sir,   Philada Jany 24. 1780
    You will receive herewith enclos'd an Act of Congress of the 20th Instant together with two other Acts of the 14th & 17th of Decemr. last to which the former refers.
    By these you will be informed, that Genl. Schuyler, Colo Pickering, & yourself are appointed Commissioners for the important & necessary service mentioned in the Act of the 20th Instant.[1] I am to request your Acceptance of this appointment, and to desire your attendance at Philadelphia as soon as Circumstances will admit. General Schuyler will be notified to meet Colo. Pickering and yourself at Head Quarters as soon as may be; but his distant situation will require longer time.
    In the interim Colo Pickering & yourself may be Imployed in Service very usefull to the public, as you will observe any two of the Commissioners are empowered to transact much of the business.[2]
    As you have had much experience in some of those departments, and must be fully sensible of the vast importance of proper regulations and the difficulty of procuring Gentlemen; as few have ability & experience equal to the Task; to perform the services requested in the proper manner. I flatter myself you will [*lay aside*] lesser considerations and chearfully undertake the service and again afford your Country the benefits of your Aid & Assistance.
    I am Sir with great respect &c.   S. H. Pt.

LB (DNA: PCC, item 14).
[1] The "Act of the 20th Instant," appointing three commissioners "to enquire into the expences of the staff departments," had its origins in the May 28, 1779, appointment of a committee charged with recommending "retrenchments and reformations" in the departments, which submitted a report on July 23. See *JCC*, 16:75–77, 79; and John Dickinson's Committee Notes, June 7, 1779, note 1. This resolution also specified that one of the commissioners was to be a member of Congress (Philip Schuyler, although then absent), and that at least two of them would visit Washington's headquarters and other posts "where officers of the staff are stationed" to collect information, "discharge supernumerary and delinquent officers, . . . and stop all issues of rations and other supplies not indispensably necessary for the service." When Schuyler declined this appointment, Congress declared on March 10 that the remain-

ing commissioners should "proceed in the business committed to them," in consultation with a newly appointed congressional committee consisting of Schuyler, Allen
Jones, and Roger Sherman, but little was accomplished beyond the formulation of an
elaborate plan to reform the departments that was submitted to Congress on March
27. And not until new dire warnings were received from Washington and Quartermaster General Greene did the delegates overcome their reluctance to empower a
regular committee of Congress to undertake a mission to headquarters and deal
forcefully with the ills besetting the army. See *JCC*, 16:244, 293–311, 332–33, 354–57;
Huntington to Mifflin and Pickering, March 11; and Congress' Instructions to the
Committee at Headquarters, April 6–13, 1780.

   [2] President Huntington also sent Col. Timothy Pickering a copy of this letter to
Mifflin with the following note, dated January 25.

   "The Letter address'd to General Mifflin which you will receive with this, contains
the Acts of Congress the same as the enclos'd. I desire the letters may be sent to him
without delay. I have requested him to repair to Philadelphia as soon as may be to act
in Conjuntion with yourself. Have also wrote to Genl. Schuyler & enclosed to him
Copies of the same acts of Congress, & desired him to repair to Head Quarters
without loss of time, and in the Interim to give previous notice of the Time he will be
at Head Quarters that the other Commissioners may meet him there." PCC, item 14,
fols. 284–85.

Samuel Huntington to Philip Schuyler

Sir,   Philada Jany 24, 1780

   You will receive herewith enclos'd an act of Congress of the 20
Instant together with two other Acts of the 14 & 17 of Decemr. last
to which the former refers.

   By these you will be informed that yourself with Colo Pickering &
Genl Mifflin are appointed Commissioners for the important & necessary service mentioned in the Act of the 20th Instant.

   As a member of Congress you are appointed to this Service and I
am to request you to repair to Head Quarters with as much despatch
as Circumstances will possibly admit.[1] If you will please to inform me
by a letter previous to your setting out what time you expect to be at
Head Quarters the other Commissioners shall be duly notified so as
to meet you there.

   From a Consideration of the necessity & importance of the service
to which you are appointed the difficulty of finding suitable Gentlemen of Experience & ability to perform the same, and as a Member
of Congress you are called upon for that purpose. I flatter myself
you will lay aside every lesser Consideration and without hesitation
or delay afford your Country the Benefit of your Aid & Assistance
in the service requested.

   I have the honour to be &c &c,   S. H. Pt

LB (DNA: PCC, item 14).
   [1] It was precisely because he was a member of Congress that Schuyler ultimately
declined the appointment herewith offered. His reasons for doing so obviously left
him uncomfortable, however, for he felt compelled to explain himself several times to
Congress, to Washington, and to friends, and the fine distinctions he drew in the

process apparently seemed unconvincing to many delegates. Upon receiving Huntington's letter at Albany, he hinted on February 15 that he could not accept the post
but offered little in the way of outright explanation except to state that he would set
off at once for Philadelphia to explain in person. PCC, item 153, 3:511–13. On the
same day he also unburdened himself to his friend Robert R. Livingston, and in the
process probably penned the most direct statement he made on the subject when he
wrote that under this appointment he would be acting not "as a member of Congress
but as a Commissioner associated with other Commissioners, and Consequently as a
Servant of Congress." Robert R. Livingston Papers, NHi. For his formal explanation
to Congress soon after his arrival in Philadelphia, see Schuyler to Huntington, March
6, 1780. For evidence that he was never able to commit a complete explanation of the
matter to paper, see also his letters to Washington of March 7 and 13; and Schuyler to
Jacob Cuyler, March 11, 1780.

Oliver Ellsworth to Samuel Lyman

Dear Sir,[1]   Philada. Jany. 25. 1780.
   Congress have lately recd. a packet from France with dispatches
down to the 9th Septr—but they contain no very material Intelligence more than you will pick out from the enclosed papers.
   The Convention for a Limitation of prices being attended only
from N Hampshire, Connecticut, N Jersey, Pensylvania, Delaware &
Maryland did not think proper to proceed on buisness especially as
a resolution of Congress passd. since their being called recommending a Limitation of prices seemed to have decided on the Expediency & necessity of the measure. They accordingly adjourned without day.[2]
   Despair not however of the currency's receiving a fixedness &
Justice being done. In my next I will write you more particular on
this Subject.
   The Army are again comfortably supplied. I wish to hear what is
done or doing at our assembly—& any thing else you will please to
inform me of.
   And am Sr. yr. huml Sevt.   O Ellsworth

RC (PHi: Dreer Collection). Addressed: "Samuel Lyman Esquire, Hartford, Connecticut."
   [1] Lyman is identified in these *Letters*, 3:192n.l.
   [2] For the reconvening and proceedings of this convention, see Ellsworth to Jonathan Trumbull, Sr., January 30, and February 8, 1779.

Oliver Ellsworth to Thomas Mumford

Dear sir,   Philada. Jany. 25. 1780.
   I thank you for your Letter of the 1t of Instt. recd. yesterday—&
the order you have been pleased to give Mr Breed to deliver me a
Barrel of Sugar, which I shall avail my self of with proper sentiments

of your disposition to oblige me & wish you to direct the Post to call on Mrs. Ellsworth & receive such pay therefor as you shall name to do your self justice.

Congress have no very special intelligence from Europe of late; all things however on that side the water continue to look favourable & flattering to American Independance. It is doubtless in Europe a winter of negotiation & I shall be as happy as you should the result be an honorable peace to America in the Spring.

As to a foreign Loan Congress have good reason to expect that a small one at least will be negotiated in Holland if not in Spain by the persons they have appointed & authorised thereto. Which if obtained I think it more probable that the money will be funded there & bills drawn thereon rather than that much if any of it will be imported in specie—but this is my own conjecture. A few Bills are now offered by Congress for Sale at 25 dollrs. for 4/6 Sterlg. an equal sum to the purchase money to be at the same lent the Continent on loan office certificates. The Bills I have no doubt will be honored, tho' I confess I do not like the terms of sale. If you incline to purchase you may doubtless soon be supplied at the Treasury office in Hartford. French Bills here are at 30 for 1 in dollars—& hard money at 38.

Measures are in contemplation which may perhaps fix the medium. The general talk this way on the Subject within doors & without is "do ample justice to the holders of the Bills & certificates as far as the nature of the case will admit."

If hereafter it shall at any time be in my power to give you any useful or important information, duty & inclination will prompt me to it.

I have not yet had the pleasure of seing Capt. Saltonstal whome you are pleased to name to me; but had other motives sufficient if you had added none to interest me particulary in wishing him a fair & impartial enquiry & I doubt not of his having it.

The Convention that was proposed to be held at this Place on the subject of a Limitation of prices, being attended only from N. Hampshire, Connecticut, N Jersey, Pensylvania, Delaware & Maryland—they did not think proper to proceed to business. There is very little probability now I think of such a measures taking place & am led to hope that the strenuous exertions of the States in taxes which they seem well disposed to, in conjunction with other regulations that may take place will in a great measure superceed the necessity of it.

You will be pleased to know that greater Unanimity has at no time prevailed in Congress & that the embarrasments you will easily conceive must attend them, does but strenthen their reliance on the exertions of America, & that good providence that has conducted us thus far.

I am, with sentiments of much Esteem & respect, Dear sir, Your very obedt. & huml Servt,   Oliv Ellsworth

RC (Robert J. Sudderth, Jr., Lookout Mountain, Tenn., 1973).

Elbridge Gerry to James Warren

My dear sir,   Philadelphia Jany 25 1780
    It is a long Time since We have heard from our Friends eastward, & We impute it to the Severity of the Winter, but yesterday I received by the Post your agreable Favour of the 27th Decr., the Desire of which was increased by the Detention.
    I should have been glad to have seen your Remarks on the anonymous Letter, but Mr Lovell informs me, he has not yet received them.[1]
    The Policy of America will succeed or fail in my Opinion, in proportion to her Exertions for establishing a Navy. I well remember that You was the first to promote it, & altho it was disapproved by some in Point of Time, the Benefit derived from the Measure has clearly manifested the Wisdom of it. The State of our Finances will check it's present Growth, but I doubt not that it will soon flourish, & that Time will suggest Improvements in the Arrangements & Regulations of the Boards that are appointed to cherish & conduct it. I am very sensible that the officers of these Departments have been poorly rewarded, & was lately of a Committee who reported that their present Salaries should have a Retrospect to Novr. 1778, but the Subject is not yet considered by Congress. I think however that You have their fullest Confidence.
    Congress have not yet determined whether to remove eastward or southward; both are talked of, but your Remarks respecting the Navy are conclusive in my Mind, in Favour of the former.
    The great objects of Attention in Congress are Œconomy & Resources. Necessity dictates their Measures, & I hope will produce salutary Effects. The Departments of the Muster & Barrack Masters are abolished & the Business of the former annexed to the Office of Inspectors. Generals Schuyler & Mifflin & Colo Pickering are appointed a Committee with full Powers to inform themselves by Inspection or otherwise of the State of the Staff Departments, to call in any of the Officers thereof for Information, to discharge all persons therein that are supernumerary or delinquent, to break up unnecessary issuing Posts, & establish others were requisite, to stop all Issues of Rations not indispensibly necessary for the Service, & in Conjunction with General Washington to reduce the Number of Horses & Waggons in the Service & Expence of Transportation, & to adopt a general Reformation of the Departments. The States are to be also called on for their respective quotas of Supplies, & authorized to stop all purchases by continental officers, when Measures are adopted for complying with the Requisitions of Congress; & to induce the States to purchase cheap they are to be credited equal prices for

Articles of the same Kind & Quality, & in proportion for other Articles. I inclose You the News papers containing three sensible Letters by a Gentleman in Maryland on "Appreciation",[2] & can give You nothing new, excepting certain Information from the Court of France that by their Interposition the british Court have failed in their Applications for Recruits to the several Powers of Germany.

The Massachusetts Delegates are sitting in Congress by Virtue of a Certificate of their Appointment from the Deputy Secretary. They have never aspired to be *commissioned*, but wish not to loose their Rank as warrant officers.

I observe your Apprehensions relative to a new QMG but have no Reason to suppose them well founded, altho the Matter has been suggested in Congress.

I remain sir with every Sentiment of respect your Friend & humble ser,   E Gerry

RC (MHi: Mercy Warren Papers).

[1] For Warren's remarks on "the anonymous Letter," an attack on Warren and the eastern navy board that James Lovell had enclosed in a November 29, 1779, letter to Warren which has not been found, see *Warren-Adams Letters*, 2:121–22. For Lovell's receipt of Warren's "Remarks" just a few hours after Gerry wrote these words, see Lovell to Samuel Adams, January 28, 1780.

[2] Two "Letters on Appreciation" discussing solutions for the nation's financial problems appeared in the *Pennsylvania Packet* on January 20 and a third appeared in the issue of January 25. Concerning Gerry's attribution of their authorship to "a Gentleman in Maryland," compare James Lovell to Horatio Gates, January 22, 1780, note 1.

Samuel Holten's Diary

[January 25, 1780]

25. Tuesday. Saml. Osgood Esqr. arrived here from Boston, charged with business from the Court.[1] I wrote to the Hon. Mr. Palmer, to Mr. Kittell and to Mrs. Holten (no. 96).[2] Very cold.

I recd. a letter from Colo. Hutchinson.

MS (MDaAr).

[1] Samuel Osgood, who is identified in these *Letters*, 2:343n.1, had been appointed by the Massachusetts legislature to serve with Elbridge Gerry as a delegate to the Philadelphia convention to limit prices. Adams, *Writings* (Cushing), 4:168–69. For information on Osgood's role as secretary of the convention and on its proceedings, see William Ellery to William Greene, February 15, note 1; and Elbridge Gerry to Samuel Adams, February 15, 1780, note 1.

[2] None of these letters has been found.

Samuel Huntington to George Washington

Sir, Philadelphia January 25. 1780

Your Excellency will receive herewith enclos'd an Act of Congress of the 20th Instant together with two other Acts of the 14th & 17th of Decemr to which the former refers.[1]

These Acts are calculated with a Design to retrench Expences in the several staff Departments and promote as much as possible Œconomy therein.

From a variety of Accounts there seems but too much reason to believe that great & unnecessary Expences have incurred in those departments remote from Head Quarters, and out of the View or Knowledge of the Heads of the Departments.

The Gentlemen appointed Commissioners in the Act of the 20th Instant will be notified to wait on your Excellency at Head Quarters as soon as Circumstances will permit to consult & advise on the Subject matter of their Appointment.

I have the honour to be with the greatest respect, your Excy's hble Servant, Sam. Huntington President

RC (DLC: Washington Papers). In a clerical hand and signed by Huntington.
[1] See Huntington to Thomas Mifflin and to Philip Schuyler, January 24, 1780.

Connecticut Delegates to Jonathan Trumbull, Sr.

Sir, Philadelphia Jany. 26 1780

Colo. Blain who will deliver your Excellency this, is now making the necessary appointments & arranging the business of his department; and will be happy to avail himself of any information & aid your Excellency may please to furnish him in the eastern districts.

We need not suggest to your Excellency how important it is become to give every facility to supplies for the Army & to place them on the surest footing, both from the present state of our magazines, & the necessity that seems to be opening upon us to replenish them for another Campaign. Peace is but little relied on as the result of the present winters negociations by those who are in the best scituation to judge of them.

Congress have recent assurances that France & Spain on the one hand as well as Great Britain on the other are sparing no possible measures & preperation for the ensuing Season & by taking early advantage thereof to render it decisive on the great question of American independance. And that these States might not be unfurnished for the necessary exertions on their part, his most Christian Majesty has in addition to timely communications passed an order to his ministers amply to supply them with arms & amunition.[1]

We beg leave also to acquaint your Excellency that Pursuant to appointment a number of Commissioners met here on the subject of a limitation of prices but not being joined by deputations from Massachusetts, Rhode Island, New York or Virginia, they did not think it proper to proceed to business & after waiting some time, & some conference upon the subject, adjourned without day. None of the States have as we are informed yet adopted a limitation except New Jersey, & it is now become impracticable for several of them to do it by the time recommended by Congress, their assemblies Standing adjourned to a later day. It is with pleasure however we can add that there appears in the States generally a good forwerdness to furnish their quotas of taxes & other supplies, which aided by measures now under consideration, it is hoped may produce effects equally salutary, if tho' a limitation of prices as proposed should not take place.

We have the honor to be, Sir, with very great Esteem & Respect, your Excellency's most obedt. humbe Servts. Roger Sherman

Oliv Ellsworth

RC (Ct: Trumbull Papers). Written by Ellsworth and signed by Ellsworth and Sherman.

[1] This information was provided in the chevalier de La Luzerne's January 25 memorial to Congress, which was read the same day and entered in the secret journals of foreign affairs. See *JCC*, 16:87–89; PCC, item 5; and Samuel Huntington to La Luzerne, February 2, 1780.

William Ellery to Timothy Pickering

Phil. Jany. 27th. 1780

As Congress have established a court of appeals which it is suppos'd will meet soon, The Commissioners of Appeals which consisted of members of Congress think it not proper to procede in rehearing the Cause of the Sloop Hope, or in trying any other Cause without the further direction of Congress.[1] I am with great respect, Yrs,

W Ellery

RC (MHi: Pickering Papers).

[1] The case of the sloop-of-war *Hope*, which had been referred to the Committee on Appeals on November 30, 1779, was eventually settled out of court. See *JCC*, 15: 1330; and case file no. 62 (*Harridan* v. *Hope*), RG 267, DNA.

Samuel Huntington to George Washington

Sir,   Philadelphia January 27. 1780

Your letter of the 24th Instant[1] was duly received and laid before Congress.

After the most mature deliberation, Congress from a full conviction of your knowledge of the subject, and that the honour and interest of the United States in the matter of negotiating and settling a Cartel may safely be trusted in your hands, have passed the enclosed resolves, and committed the whole to your prudence & discretion.[2]

By the second resolution they have repealed the final part of the resolution of the 11th Instant, leaving the settlement of Accounts to negotiation and that the demand of the money at this Juncture by the Treasury might not embarrass you, they have ordered the Board of Treasury to suspend the requisition, until the proposed negotiation for exchange of prisoners is finished; so that you are left to act upon the common principles of equality, Justice, and propriety, as if that Act had never passed.

As our Treasury is empty of hard Money & Congress relied on the payment of the Debt due for the Convention Troops to defray the Expences & Debts of our Officers in Captivity, I trust that Circumstance will not escape your Excellencies Notice, though at the same time you will be satisfied it is the intention of Congress a demand of that debt should not be made an Ultimatum, or a preliminary to prevent a Cartel in other respects admissible.

As Congress have been pleased to refer this negotiation wholly to your Excellency without any Direction or expressing their sense on any particular Articles which you had requested, The Event of the proceedings on the Subject must meet with their approbation.

I have the honour to be, with great respect, your Excy's hble Servant, Sam Huntington President

RC (DLC: Washington Papers). In a clerical hand and signed by Huntington.
[1] The letter in question is actually Washington's letter to Congress of January 19. PCC, item 152, 8:355–57; and Washington, *Writings* (Fitzpatrick), 17:408–10.
[2] In his letter of the 19th, Washington had sought clarification of the January 14 instructions he had received from both the Board of Treasury and Huntington concerning the negotiation of a cartel. Although Congress had granted him broad powers on January 13 to negotiate a prisoner exchange it had also adopted harsh measures on the 11th to compel settlement of the accounts against the Convention Army for provisions and supplies furnished since March 1778. Washington was concerned that the instructions he had received from the Board of Treasury required him to postpone further prisoner negotiations until the Convention Army accounts had been paid. Thus Congress immediately repealed its resolution of the 11th to permit him to proceed with negotiations "as he may judge most expedient," although simultaneously stating that it was nevertheless their hope that he could obtain assurance that the Convention Army accounts would be paid. See *JCC*, 16:85, 89–91; and the January 14 letters to Washington from the Board of Treasury and from Huntington.

Robert R. Livingston to Philip Schuyler

Dear Sir   Philadelphia 27th Jany. 1780.
I have only leisure to acknowledge the rect. of your favor of the 18th[1] & to return you my sincere thanks [as a] person deeply inter-

ested in the event of this controversy for the readyness with which you offer to sacrifice yr. private feelings to the general interest. I have sounded many members about it. Some I find extreamly well disposed to the measure while others again receive it with more coolness rather on account of the novelty of the Institution than from any other motives tho' perhaps the dismissal of Gen Lee which makes the rank you claim the more important may have some influence on their minds. But this last consideration is so much less weighty than the first, that I am persuaded if you would accept Greens place[2] which he wishes to [qu]it that you may have it on your own terms.

What I would particularly mention to you is my [earn]est wish that you will comply with the request contained in the resolutions of Congress transmitted to you [by] the President,[3] they apply to you as a member of Congress who are capable of extricating your country from the ruin that threatens it. Should you suffer any personal considerations to interpose or prevent your affording the assistance they request when you act not as their servant but as one of their body, You will offer room to your enimies to alledge that private convenience more than publick reasons have influenced your past conduct. Your Friends will be disappointed & hurt, And a measure which they have so much at heart (to which [they] consider this as preparatory) be entirely defeated. Let me therefore intreat you not only to accept the commission but to do it immediately & without reluctance. The publick requires it of you. And shd. your endeavours be crowned with success which they can not fail in some sort to be you will acquire more reputation than you or any other person could possibly attain in any other station or upon any other occasion.

I can not enlarge (as I fear I have already missed the post) but just so far as to tell you that we have not yet determined where to move to, that question being put off to the 1st of February.[4] Our Affairs are as much deranged as ever, our finance far from being restored— and our army living from hand to mouth. When we shall get thro' these perplexities I know not. I shall however contribute my mite tho' not I fear [with] the fairest prospect of success.

The fleet which left New York last Month has not yet been heard of. The Cold continues so intense that the Chesapeak bay is froze over. We have a report that St. Augustine & Pensacola are taken by the Spaniards & that Genl. Prevost has left Savannah. It comes by letter from Virginia to Griffin, but as we have yet had no truth from that quarter I doubt the authenticity of this. My best respects attend Mrs. Schuyler and the young ladies. I am Dear Sir, With the greatest esteem, Your Most Obdt Hum. Servt,   Robt R Livingston

RC (NN: Philip Schuyler Papers).
 [1] Schuyler had written to Livingston on both December 18, 1779, and January 18, 1780, and both letters discussed issues alluded to by Livingston in this letter. They are in the Robert R. Livingston Papers, NN. See also Livingston to Schuyler, December 20, 1779, note 3.

[2] That is, as quartermaster general—an offer Schuyler refused in the January 18 letter to Livingston cited in the preceding note.

[3] See Samuel Huntington to Thomas Mifflin, January 24, note 1; and Huntington to Schuyler, January 24, 1780, note.

[4] Congress had actually postponed consideration of a change of location for Congress until "the last Monday in February." *JCC*, 16:9–10. For a report on the action taken at that time, see James Lovell to Samuel Adams, February 28, 1780, note 4.

Thomas McKean to Caesar Rodney

Sir,   Philadelphia. January 27th. 1780.

Your favor of the 20th instant was delivered me by Captain Learmonth,[1] who has received thirty six thousand dollars for the recruiting service in our State, which is to be paid into your hands and charged to the State. When this is expended, on your application more will be obtained. I hope every exertion will be made to fill our Battalion, as peace will in a great measure depend upon the numbers of our army and the time they take the field. Every State in the Union is sensible of this, and I rest assured we shall have in consequence the largest army the next campaign we ever yet had, and that this circumstance will determine our Enemy to peace or war, as our success or the contrary in this measure may prove.

Our Army has been almost starved and our Treasury empty; but both are again in a good way. Our resources are great if properly and timely called forth.

We have no news of Importance. Mrs. McKean joins me in presenting our best compliments to Your Excellency and Miss Wilson. Please to pay my respect to Mr. Dickinson and the Chief Justice when you see them.

I am, sir, with great regard, Your Excellency's most obedient humble servant,   Tho M:Kean

RC (De–Ar: Military Archives).

[1] Undoubtedly Capt. John Learmonth of the 2d Delaware Regiment.

Committee on Appeals Decree

Jany. 28th. 1780

Yelverton Taylor &c. Lib[ellan]ts & App[elle]es ⎫ Appeal from
vs. The Sloop Lark and her Cargo   ⎬ the State of
Richard Downing Jennings & al Claimants & ⎭ New Jersey[1]
Appellants

We the Commissioners appointed by Congress to hear, try and determine all Appeals from the Courts of Admiralty of the several American States to Congress having heard and fully considered as well all and singular the several Matters and Things contained and set forth in the Record or Minutes of the proceedings of the Court of Admiralty of the State of New Jersey in the above Cause as the Arguments of the Advocates of the respective parties to the above Appeal do thereupon adjudge and decree that the Appeal of the abovenamed Richard Downing Jennings and others demanded and filed in the above Cause be & the same hereby is dismissed hence with Costs and We do further adjudge and decree that the Judgment or Sentence of the Court of Admiralty of New Jersey passed and published in the said Cause be and the same hereby is in all its' parts confirmed and established and We do assess the Costs in this Cause at fourteen hundred Dollars which Sum We do hereby order and determine that the Parties Appellant shall pay unto the Parties Appellee in the said Cause for their Costs and Charges in supporting and sustaining the said Sentence in this Court &c.

Tho M:Kean

Olivr. Ellsworth

Ezra L'Hommedieu

MS (DNA: RG 267, case no. 36). In a clerical hand, and signed by Ellsworth, L'Hommedieu, and McKean.

[1] The New Jersey Court of Admiralty had awarded the sloop *Lark* and her cargo on September 3, 1778, to Yelverton Taylor, commander of the privateer *Comet*, and Timothy Shaler, commander of the privateer *Chance*. They had captured the *Lark*, commanded by John Laing, on the high seas bound to New York from St. Christopher. After New Jersey Judge John Imlay awarded the *Lark* and her cargo to Taylor and Shaler, the commander of the two privateers, the owners of the sloop, Richard D. Jennings and Robert Campbell of St. Eustatius, claimed that the *Lark* was bound from St. Eustatius to Egg Harbor, N.J., with supplies for the Americans and appealed to Congress, where the appeal was referred to the Committee on Appeals on October 26, 1778.

The Committee on Appeals in this decree dismissed Jennings' and Campbell's appeal and reaffirmed the decision of the New Jersey court. See case file no. 36, RG 267, DNA; and *JCC*, 12:1061.

William Floyd to George Clinton

Sir,   Philadelphia Jany. 28th. 1780.

I Recd. your favour of the 6th Instant, two Days Since, and am Sorry to Learn, that the part of our Army on the North River are under Such Distressed Circumstances.[1] I was in hopes that those Difficulties did not Extend further, in any Great Degree, than to the Troops in New Jersey.

I am however happy to Inform you that the Roads Since the Snow has fallen, is much Better than before, which has facilitated the Transportation of provision to the Army at head Quarters, in Such a Manner, that with the Great Exertions of the State of New Jersey they are amply Relived for the present; and if the Roads Should

Continue as they Now Are for a few Weeks, I hope they will Obtain a Considerable Supply.

The Embarkation of General Clintons troops at New York with himself, and it is Said Cornwallace, left the hook two Days before the violent Storm. But we have not heard of them Since; Though We hope providence has Disposed of them to our Advantage.

Congress has for More than A Year had under their Consideration A plan, for Establishing A Court of Appeals in all Cases of Capture and Much time has been Spent upon it. They have at last finished it and Appointed their Judges. The Gentlemen Appointed are, Mr. Wythe of Virginia, Mr. Paca, of Mariland, and Mr. Hosmer of Connecticut. They are to begin their Courts at this place and they have it in their power to Adjourn to any place between Williamsburgh and Hartford, having an Eye to the Number of Causes that are or may be brought up to them.

In order to Correct abuses and Retrench our Expences, Congress have appointed Commissioners with Ample and Sufficient powers, over the whole Staff Department of our Army. The Gentlemen Appointed are General Schuyler, General Mifflin, and Mr. Pickering, who is now a member of the Board of war. If those Gentlemen will undertake this Business (and I hope they will not Refuse) they may Save Some Millions to this Continent and Render their Country Most Essential Service.

In my Letter Some time Since to the President of the Senate,[2] I gave it as my Opinion that a Regulation of Prizes in the Several States from Virginia Northward would take place. I founded my Opinion on an Information of the Delagates from Maryland that their State had passed a Law for the purpose a Copy of which they had Recd. (But I now understand it was only a Bill under the Consideration of their Legislature And which Did not pass at their last Session). New Jersey had passed a Law for that purpose. These, with what I expected from the Convention which was to meet on that Business at this place were the Reasons for that Opinion, But as the matter Now appears I am very Doubtfull whether there will be a General Regulation or not. As the Meeting of that Convention was not General, No Deputies from Virginia And those from Massachusetts and Rhode Island did not Arrive untill the Members that were met had Adjourned without Comeing to any Resolutions; But Since the Arrival of the Eastern Members I understand they have formed their Convention again and are now Consulting what is proper for them to Do Without Virginia, or New York, Though I believe they have no great Doubt that our State would come into any Measures of that kind provided all the Other States Should Do it.

For five Weeks past we have had the Severest Cold here, that has been known for that Length of time (as the people of this City Say) Since the Year 40. Last week an Ox was Roasted on the river and I am told the Ice is Near 2 feet thick. To the papers Inclosed I must

Beg leave to Refer you for the News, and after offering my Compliments to the Gentlemen of the Legislature, Subscribe my Self with the Greatest Respect and Esteem, your Most Obedt. and humble Servt.   Wm. Floyd

RC (PPRF).

[1] In his January 6 letter, Governor Clinton had reported that three feet of snow combined with immobilized flour mills had rendered the troops' situation "more distressing than any Thing we have experienced since the commencement of the War." Clinton, *Papers* (Hastings), 5:443–45.

[2] See Floyd to Pierre Van Cortlandt, January 11, 1780.

Samuel Huntington to Charles Stewart

Sir,[1]   Philada. Jany. 28. 1780

You will receive herewith inclos'd an Act of Congress of the 27th Instant, directing that all Issues of rations in the Department of the Commissary General of Issues made in pursuance of a resolution of Congress of the 2d of October 1777 be discontinued.[2]

Also directing and regulating the manner in which rations or parts of rations in future are to be delivered to Hospital Commissaries and the form in which returns &c are to be made of which all Commissaries of Issues, their Deputies; and Hospital Commissaries are to take notice and govern themselves accordingly.

I am Sir your hble Servt,   S.H. President

LB (DNA: PCC, item 14).

[1] Although this letter was addressed to "The Deputy Commissary Genl of Issues," it seems probable that it was actually intended for the commissary general of issues, Charles Stewart, rather than one of his deputies.

[2] The flight of Congress to York, Pa., in the wake of the British capture of Philadelphia in September 1777, had imposed a hardship on the delegates and various Continental officials who had reestablished their offices in the Pennsylvania village. As a consequence, Congress had resolved on October 2, 1777, that delegates to Congress and various Continental officials and employees could purchase provisions from the commissary and quartermaster departments, "for the use of themselves, their servants and horses." This January 27 resolve hereby abolished this privilege, one of a number of steps taken during this period to retrench Continental expenses. See *JCC*, 8:760, 15:1389–90, 16:99–100.

On the other hand, this change did not bring an end to the delegates' practice of purchasing forage for their horses through Jacob Hiltzheimer, superintendent of the Continental stables at Philadelphia, pursuant to a resolve of October 13, 1779. That Hiltzheimer did indeed continue to provide for the delegates' horses after passage of the January 27 retrenchment resolve is clear from the following entry in his diary of February 24, 1780. "Went to the Treasury Board and applied for money to enable me to purchase forage for the horses belonging to the members of Congress, agreeable to resolve of Congress." The resolve to which he here referred was doubtless that of February 16. See *JCC*, 15:1167, 16:170, 209; and Jacob Hiltzheimer, *Extracts from the Diary of Jacob Hiltzheimer*, ed. Jacob Cox Parsons (Philadelphia: W.F. Fell, 1893).

James Lovell to Samuel Adams

Dear Sir   28th of Jany. 80
Major Osgood[1] arrived here on the Evening of my last Date to you
(the 25th) when I mentioned not having seen Genl. Warren's Letter
referred to in one which had reached Mr. Gerry. The Major delivered it safely; Nothing had been said or done on the scurrilous
Information that caused the Remarks. I think McNeille cannot be
suspected of the Baseness, though his Mind must be irritated greatly
at his Fortune.[2]
   I do not know but the regulating Convention may again get effectively together, but if they do, I suspect the Consequence will only be
to let US and THEMSELVES down easily.
   Perhaps I shall find today that I can pennize & draytonize[3] enough
to *tell* you more than just summarily that we must endeavor to *act
vigorously in concert* next campaign. You must not know even this
from *me*, tho' the Continent ought to *think it seasonably.* I shall consult
wth. my Colleagues upon the Subject. It is very delicate to say that
there is not any hearty Wish for Peace *yet* in two of the Parties, who
may nevertheless give into negotiating *Formalities* for a Time.
                                                                    J L

RC (NN: Adams Papers).
   [1] Samuel Osgood had been appointed as a Massachusetts delegate to the Philadelphia convention for limiting prices. See Samuel Holten's Diary, January 25, 1780.
   [2] For this allusion to Hector McNeill and the anonymous attack on the eastern navy
board that had been circulated in November, see also Elbridge Gerry to James Warren,
January 25, 1780, note 1. Adams replied on March 5, that "In the Hint I gave you in
one of my Letters I was far from intending you should think I meant Capt. McNeil. I
am sure he is a Man of too much Honor to write the Anonimous Letter the Committee receivd." Adams, *Writings* (Cushing), 4:181.
   [3] By referring to John Penn and William Henry Drayton in this manner, Lovell
indicated that he was, in modern idiom, leaking confidential information.

Oliver Ellsworth to Jonathan Trumbull, Sr.

Sir,   Philadelphia, Jany. 30th. 1780.
   Since the Letter Mr Sherman & myself did ourselves the honor of
addressing to your Excellency by the last post,[1] a commissioner has
arived from Massachusetts to attend the Convention for a limitation
of prices,[2] which had adjourned sine die—also a Commission from
Rhode Island to their Delegate in Congress to the same purpose.[3]
Upon which the Assembly of Pensylvania to whom their Commissioners had made report, have reappointed others, to meet again[4]—&
a meeting has been thereupon had from Commissioners of all the
States who attended before, except New Jersey, with the addition of
Massachusetts & Rhode Island, at which also the delegates in Con-

gress from N. York attended, tho' not specially authorised & gave assurance that their State would abide the measures that might be come into. The Convention having again formed now stands adjourned to Wednesday next, for N Jersey Commissioners who are sent to, to come in—the result of which meeting will perhaps be a further adjournment to a distant day to give Virginia, who has not yet done it, oppertunity to appoint & send commissioners. It does not appear indeed what more can well be done at this time as some of the Commissioners present are not authorised to do any thing unless the Convention should be attended from all the States first proposed.

In return for Lord Sterlings late Expedition to Staten Island, a party of the Enemy consisting of one hundred horse & four hundred foot, last week surprised the out guards at Elizabeth Town & Newark & made four officers & about Sixty men prisoners, & burned some publick buildings at both places.

The supplies & prospects of the Army are now comfortable. The General was reduced to the necessity of demanding from the Several Counties in N Jersey specifeck supplies, which with much spirit they complyed with even beyond the requisition. Maryland is said also to have fully complyed with the requisition of Congress to that State for 15,000 barrels of Flour. Delaware has also exerted herself much, in the same way. The Assembly of this State are now together & seem disposed to furnish the 50,000 barrels of Flour requested of them as also to go into such further specifick supplies as may be necessary.[5]

South Carolina, justly apprehensive of her danger, is arming three Regiments of blacks. It is highly probable, unless the Embarkation from New York should have blown to the West Indies or suffered much in the Storm, that we shall soon hear of an Attack on Charlestown—tho' I trust there will be a defence sufficient at least to render it a serious one. The Town scituated on a Neck less than one mile across & not commanded by heights is defensible & well fortified on the land side—the entrance of the Harbour being very narrow is secured by a number of Frigates, which are the largest Ships that can come over the bar without taking out their Guns. Continental troops and Militia are now marching southward but may not arive in season for the Enemy's first attempts. That policy which has long since directed the Enemy to carry their operations & efforts southward seems now to be attending to & there is much reason to expect that the active part of the next campaign will be in that quarter.

I take the liberty to mention to your Excellency that the Scituation of my affairs renders it necessary for me to return home by the begining of March, & to express my wishes that some of the Gentlemen on the new election may find it convenient to take their Seats in Congress by that time.

I am, Sir, with the highest respect & Esteem, your Excellency's most obed Servt   Oliver Ellsworth

RC (Ct: Trumbull Papers).
[1] See Connecticut Delegates to Trumbull, January 26, 1780.
[2] The Massachusetts commissioner referred to here was Samuel Osgood, who had just arrived in Philadelphia on January 25. His credentials indicate that he was elected jointly with Massachusetts delegate Elbridge Gerry on December 18 to represent the state at the Philadelphia convention. See Samuel Holten's Diary, January 25, 1780; and *Conn. State Records*, 2:573.
[3] For the appointment of Rhode Island delegate William Ellery as a commissioner to the Philadelphia convention, see ibid., p. 574; and Staples, *Rhode Island*, p. 269.
[4] Although the Philadelphia convention had initially been unable to assemble a quorum, the Pennsylvania commissioners had reported to their assembly on January 28 that the convention might yet convene and conduct proceedings. Thereupon John Bull, William Henry, and William Moore were named to attend the convention in place of the five commissioners who had been elected in November—John Bayard, George Bryan, John Bull, William Henry, and John Jacobs. *Journal of the House of Representatives of the Commonwealth of Pennsylvania* [November 28, 1781], 2 vols. (Philadelphia: John Dunlap, 1782), 1:398, 401, 410, 412–13, 422.
[5] Congress had received notice on January 28 that the Pennsylvania Assembly had appointed a committee to confer with Congress and the state council on the problems of supplying flour and other provisions. *JCC*, 16:100.

Samuel Huntington to William Livingston

Sir,   Philadelphia Feby 1. 1780
    I have the pleasure to transmit your Excellency the enclosed Act of Congress of the 31 ulto[1] expressing the high sense they entertain of the attachment & Zeal of the Magistrates and Inhabitants of the State of New Jersey in the Common Cause and of their ready & effectual exertions in providing and furnishing the Army under his Excellency the Commander in Chief with provisions at a time when the difficulty of transportation rendered such Exertions absolutely necessary.
    May the laudable Example of New Jersey be immitated by the other States. A people possess'd of such generous Sentiments & who can call them into Action as necessity requires are not to be subjugated by any Tyrannical power.
    I have the honour to be &c,   S. H. Pt.

LB (DNA: PCC, item 14).
[1] Congress adopted this resolution in response to a January 27 letter from Washington in which the general had explained the recent easing of the army's provisions crisis because of the efforts of the magistrates and inhabitants of New Jersey. "They more than complied with the requisitions in many instances," he explained, "and owing to their exertions, the Army in a great measure has been kept together." See *JCC*, 16:111; PCC, item 152, 8:379–81; and Washington, *Writings* (Fitzpatrick), 17:449–50.

Samuel Huntington to George Washington

Sir,   Philadelphia February 1, 1780
  I am honour'd with your Excellency's favours of the 26, 27, & 29
ulto. which have been laid before Congress.[1] Enclosed you will receive
an Act of Congress of the 31 Ulto[2] (a Copy of which is transmitted to
Governor Livingston) Expressing the high sense they entertain of
the attachment and Zeal of the Magistrates and Inhabitants of the
State of New Jersey in the Common Cause and their ready and
effectual Exertions in furnishing provision for the Army under your
Excellencies Command.
  I have the honour to be, with the highest respect, your Excelly's
hble Servt,   Sam. Huntington President

RC (DLC: Washington Papers). In a clerical hand and signed by Huntington.
  [1] Huntington is actually acknowledging two letters from Washington of January 26
and two of January 27, all of which had been laid before Congress the previous day.
JCC, 16:111. The letter of the 29th is apparently one directed to Elbridge Gerry, who
had been corresponding with the general on the subject of recruitment for the Continental Army. See PCC, item 152, 8:333–35, 371–81; Washington, *Writings* (Fitzpatrick),
17:443–47, 449–52, 462–64; and Elbridge Gerry to Washington, January 12, 1780.
  [2] See the preceding entry.

James Lovell to Samuel Adams

Feb. 1st. —80
  Not a Line of Information from you respecting the Vermont
Business. Certain Men are here from the Grants to support its Inde-
pendence and offer to come into the Union but not to submit the
Question of their Existence as an independent State.[1]   J.L.

RC (NN: Adams Papers).
  [1] This day Stephen Bradley, Jonas Fay, and Moses Robinson laid before Congress a
copy of their credentials as agents of the "free and independent State" of Vermont,
together with "a vindication" of their territorial claim to the "Grants" region being
contested by New Hampshire, New York, and Massachusetts, and "Vermonts appeal
to the candid and impartial World," a publication explaining Vermont's claims and
readiness to form "an equitable Union with the other independent States of America."
The significance of their appearance this day was that February 1 had been set as the
date for reopening congressional hearings on the claims to the region by New
Hampshire, New York, and Massachusetts, whose legislatures had been asked the
preceding September "to pass laws expressly authorizing Congress to hear and determine all differences between them relative to their respective boundaries." None of
the three was prepared to proceed with such hearings at this time, however, although
the delegates of each expressed alarm at Vermont's pretentions to independent statehood and remained firmly resolved to have the issue treated simply as a dispute
between existing states of the union, out of which no new states could be created
without their consent.
  Congress' task was even further complicated by the appearance on February 7 of
agents representing "towns in the northern district of the New Hampshire Grants, on

both sides of Connecticut river," Peter Olcott and Bezaleel Woodward, whose memorial of that date demonstrated that the inhabitants of the disputed territory were far from united in their claims. The same day, New Hampshire formally announced, through newly arrived delegate Samuel Livermore, its readiness to proceed with the congressional inquiry agreed upon the previous September, and the delegates from both Massachusetts and New York indicated a similar readiness as soon as they received formal authorization from their states, which they expected soon.

The Vermont agents, however, had already announced their intention to return home, and weeks elapsed before Massachusetts and New York were prepared to proceed with the hearings, by which time Congress was experiencing difficulty maintaining the representation of 12 states—9 in addition to the 3 parties to the dispute—as required by Congress' previous pledge. As a result, efforts to open the Vermont hearings failed repeatedly, and although the subject was taken up briefly on May 23 and 29 and June 1 and 2, Congress finally resolved on June 9 to postpone hearings until "the second Tuesday in September next." See *JCC*, 16:116, 130–33, 222, 273, 17:448–53, 471, 481–85, 499; PCC, item 40, 311–24; and *Records of the Governor and Council of the State of Vermont*, E. P. Walton, ed., 8 vols. (Montpelier: J. & J. M. Poland, 1873–80), 2:235–47. See also John Jay to George Clinton, September 25 and October 5, 1779; Nathaniel Peabody to John Langdon, February 7, notes 5 and 6; New York Delegates to George Clinton, February 9, note 1; and Lovell to Adams, March 9, 1780, note 1.

James Lovell to Joseph Ward

Dear Sir   Feb 1st. 1780
    Your kind Wishes for my Prosperity sent from Morris Town the 28th of last Month reached me yesterday; and though they were manifested just at this Time on mistaken Facts, yet I flatter myself they spring out of a Source of long–settled Friendship.

    I am only one of four *in Nomination* for the Service *in France* mentioned by you. As to your Idea of a secretarial Place *here* for forgn. Affairs; it is wanted by some here but I conceive there can be little Benefit from such an Institution, unless the Officer has a Seat in Congress. What would he be with that Seat more than a member of the Comtee. of foreign Correspondence called a Comtee of foreign Affairs?

    I shall be attentive and warm whenever I shall perceive an Opening to promote the Benefit of the United States in Conjunction with your private advantage, persuaded that your enjoyment of the latter will be always sweetned in Proportion to the Progress of the former.[1]

    Yr. Friend & humble Servant,   James Lovell

RC (ICHi: Joseph Ward Papers).
[1] Col. Joseph Ward, who had lost his position as commissary general of musters when his department had been abolished on January 12, was appointed commissary general of prisoners on April 15, 1780. *JCC*, 16:47, 366.

George Plater to Thomas Sim Lee

Sir.   Philadelphia February 1st 1780.

At Mr. Holker's Request, who waited on me this Morning, I have the Honor to forward to your Excellency the inclosed.[1]

The Enemy on Staten Iland have returned Lord Sterling's Visit, burned some Houses near Elizabeth's Town, & taken three or four Officers & about sixty privates Prisoners; having surprized the advanced Posts. I have the Honor to be with the most perfect Respect, Yr Excellency's, most obt. & very hble Sert,   Geo. Plater

RC (MdAA: Red Books).

[1] Not found, but probably related to Maryland's seizure of flour and wheat purchased by Jean Holker's agents in the state and Congress' January 17 resolution recommending that the confiscated provisions be restored, for which see Samuel Huntington to Lee, January 18, 1780, note.

Charles Thomson to the States

Sir   Secretary's Office Feby 1st. 1780

I now enclose you the journals of Congress which will Compleat the set for your State to the first of January 1780. Hereafter they will be printed in monthly Pamphlets which shall be regularly sent.[1]

I take the liberty of reminding you of the request in my letter of 20th Novr. last to which I have not been honored with an answer. The request therein Contained is not suggested by idle curiosity but a desire of promoting public Utility and the cause of America.

I am, Sir, with due respect, Your humble servt.   Cha Thomson

RC (R–Ar: Letters to Governors). Addressed: "His Excellency The Governor of Rhode Island &c." This was a circular letter, of which texts of those sent to seven states have been located.

[1] For publication data concerning Thomson's enclosures and subsequent issues of the journals referred to here, see *JCC*, 15:1462, 18:1237.

Samuel Huntington to Titus Hosmer, William Paca, and George Wythe

Sir   Philada Feby 2. 1780

By the enclosed Acts of Congress of the 15 & 22 Ulto herewith enclosed together with your Commission you will be informed that Congress have constituted & established a Court of appeals for the final Trial & determination of all appeals from the Courts of Admiralty in the several States in Cases of Capture, and that you are elected one of the Judges of that Court.[1]

By reason of the present State of the Currency the Salary of the Judges is not yet fixed, yet there is no doubt their Salaries will be decent and satisfactory; at present twelve thousand dollars is to be advanced to each of them for support that they may immediately enter upon the Business of their Office.

The first Session is to be held at Philadelphia as soon as may be to hear & determine the Causes already appealed, and afterwards at such times and places as they shall Judge most for the public good any where between Williamburgh & Hartford inclusive. I hope the Business may not employ so much of your time as to interfere with your other Engagements and deprive the public of your Service in this important Station, as it may be in the power of the Court to state the Time of their session convenient for themselves without Injury to the public.[2]

I have only to add, the Election of the Judges was with great unanimity, and I trust will give Satisfaction to all the States.

I am Sir, with much respect & Esteem, your hble Servt,

S. H. President

LB (DNA: PCC, item 14). Addressed: "The Honble George Wythe Esquire. N.B. The same verbatim to Messrs. Paca & Hosmer."

[1] *JCC*, 16: 61–64, 79. For the creation of the Court of Appeals, see Samuel Holten's Diary, January 15, 1780, note.

[2] Congress received Paca's acceptance of this appointment on February 9; Hosmer's on May 4. Wythe declined the appointment, and Cyrus Griffin was named in his stead on April 28. Griffin signified his acceptance almost immediately. See *JCC*, 16:143, 254, 322, 326, 366, 397, 411; and PCC, item 59, 3:23–26, item 78, 10:251–54, 12:17–18, 24:183–86.

Samuel Huntington to the Chevalier de La Luzerne

Sir,   Philada Febry 2 1780

You will receive herewith enclosd a copy of the report of the Committee appointed to receive the Communications from the Minister of France.

And also an Act of Congress of the 31 Ulto. containing their Answer, that the whole may be laid before you in one view.[1]

I have the honour to be &c,   S. H. Pt.

LB (DNA: PCC, item 14). Addressed: "The Minister of France."

[1] La Luzerne had submitted a memorial to Congress on January 25 affirming France's determination to prosecute the war in America with vigor in 1780 and seeking a commitment from Congress to prepare with similar energy for the forthcoming campaign. The document had been referred on the 26th to a committee of seven, which immediately arranged a conference with him. The committee presented the results of that meeting on the 28th and subsequently submitted reports to Congress on January 31 and February 2, the second of which concerned a second confer-

ence with La Luzerne. See *JCC*, 16:87–89, 102–9, 111–16; and PCC, item 25, 1:173–78, 181–96. For La Luzerne's reports to the foreign minister of France, the comte de Vergennes, concerning his relations with Congress at this time, see Archives du ministère des affaires étrangères: Correspondance politique, États–Unis, 11:88–113, 147, 150–62, 171, 184–206; and "Abstracts of political correspondence relating to United States in the Ministry of Foreign Affairs, France," Canada, Public Archives, *Report, 1912*–13 (Ottawa: 1913–14), pp. 211–13. See also William E. O'Donnell, *The Chevalier de La Luzerne: French Minister to the United States, 1779*–1784 (Bruges: Desclée de Brouwer, 1938), pp. 80–81, 100–101.

Samuel Holten's Diary

[February 4–5, 1780]
4. Friday. I wrote to Mrs. Holten (no. 99).[1] The medical come. met in my Chamber.[2]
5. Saturday. Mr. Livermore arrived here from New Hampshire.[3] Very cold.

MS (MDaAr).
[1] Not found.
[2] One of the concerns of the medical committee during this meeting may have been Dr. William Brown, physician general of hospitals of the middle department, who according to Holten's diary also "spent the evening" on February 2 with Holten.
[3] Samuel Livermore took his seat in Congress on Monday, February 7. *JCC*, 16:129.

William Churchill Houston to John Jay

Sir,   Philada. 7 February 1780.
    It is not simply from being a Member of the Committee of Foreign Affairs that I take the Liberty of troubling you; my Curiosity to have Access to all the Sources of Knowledge in publick affairs, is a further Apology. For this I confess I have a boundless Thirst and Eagerness.
    A Vessel, lately arrived to the Eastward, reports to have spoken with the Confederacy on the Coast of France, and I indulge myself with the Confidence that you are safely arrived there, and have also reached the last Stage of your Destination: for your Success at which it must be the Inclination, Interest and Duty of every good American to pray.
    The general Complection of Affairs here is favourable. The Subject of Finance constitutes our principal, if not only, Embarrassment. To this, I know, your early Attention will be turned, and, it is to be hoped, strenuous Efforts at Home, with the Assistance of our Friends abroad, will in a little Time surmount it. No military Event of much Notice has taken Place since the unsuccessful Attempt upon Savanna in Georgia by the allied Forces under Count D'Estaing and General Lincoln, in which we were so unfortunate as to lose the gallant Count Pulaski, with other brave Officers and a Number of Men.

From this however the Enemy have not derived any Advantage besides keeping Possession of the Town and a small Scope around it, for they have not occupied one other Post more interiour in that Country. I believe they Suffered severely. By Dispatches, dated 23 December last, from Augusta, the present Capital of Georgia, and received the 3d instant we are informed that the Government of the State, for some Time dormant or rather annihilated, is again organized and in Operation.[1] George Walton, Esqr. I think formerly known to you, is Governour; the legislative and Executive are in plenary Exercise of their Several Duties; and Delegates are appointed to Congress, though not yet arrived here. The Sentiments of the People are resolute and decided; Measures are taken to recruit their Troops, and the Conclusion of their Letter to Congress is, that "in the Fall and wreck of the Union only, and total Extirpation of their State, will they fall and perish." A large Embarkation took Place at New York about Christmas, said to be six or eight Thousand confidently reported and believed to be destined to the Southward. Sir Henry Clinton and Lord Cornwallis have both sailed, and General Knyphausen commands in New-York. This is the Intelligence, but whether Sir Henry is gone with the Troops or to Europe is not ascertained, nor have we heard any Thing of the Fleet since it sailed. Many suppose that the Weather which was uncommonly stormy for some Time after their Departure, must have altered their Course by the West-Indies. To put the Southern Army in Condition to oppose so formidable a Force, the whole North Carolina and Virginia Troops have been detached from hence, and Bodies of Militia called in the Southern Country. The Arrival of these Succours as soon as was calculated and as early as they may be wanted is a Matter of some Doubt from the extraordinary and continuing Rigour of the Winter. It is clear the Enemy mean to bend a pointed Effort against the Southern States, and if possible to pare us down by trying this Extreme; but, I hope, they will find other Use for their Time and Hardihood than plundering and desolating the Country, as in multiplied Instances they have heretofore done. Accounts from the Floridas, which seem to wear every Mark of Credibility, except that they do not come through the official Line of Communication, say that the Forces of His Catholick Majesty are in Possession of the Town and Garrison of Pensacola, and that Operations against St Augustine are well forward. Land-passage being at this Time extremely scarce, difficult and tedious, you will probably have pretty near as early authentick Intelligence in Europe, as we here. As to Navigation, the Delaware has been shut up since the 20th December last, and a Passage for loaded Waggons more than a Month. The News, if true, will draw deep in our Favour.

The Main Army is hutted for the Winter in the vicinity of Morriston in New Jersey: a strong Garrison under the Orders of General MacΓougall is at West point. General Heath commands the Posts at the Highlands; and a small Garrison occupies Rhode Island since it was evacuated by the Enemy. The Papers sent by the Committee of foreign Affairs will give you the other current News.

Governour Livingston and Family are well by Letters lately from him. The Vermont Business just come on. My best Compliments to Mrs Jay, and believe me your Excellency's most obedt Servant,

Wm Ch Houston

RC (NNC: Jay Papers). Endorsed by Jay: "Recd. 27 June 1780."
[1] For Congress' response to the reestablishment of government in Georgia, see Samuel Huntington to George Walton, February 14, 1780. For the prolonged hiatus in Georgia's representation in Congress, see these *Letters*, 12:297–98 n.2.

Samuel Huntington to Jonathan Trumbull, Sr.

Sir,   Philadelphia Feby 7 1780

I am honoured with your Excellencies favour of the 27th Ulto with the Act of Assembly enclosed. The Grant they have been pleased to make me is very acceptable and claims my Acknowledgement.

The vigorous exertions of the State of New Jersey to provide for the late Necessities of the Army are such as have done much honour to the Magistrates & Inhabitants of that State, and provided a plentiful temporary supply.[1]

I may with propriety acquaint your Excellency with reason to expect that the plan of operation for the ensuing Campaign will be on the part of our Ally, as should call forth our most vigorous Exertions & *Cooperations* to expel the Enemy from the United States and put a period to the War.

The Measures adopted by Congress for recruiting the Army for the next Campaign allready too long delayed will be forwarded in a few Days and I hope may reach you before the Assembly rises.[2]

We have undoubted Intelligence that an Expedition against Pensacola was forming at the Havannah, the last fall, and have recent Accounts & reports that they are now in possesion of that place & have made the Garrison prisoners consisting of about Nine hundred Men but of this Success we have no official Intelligence. An Express is Just arrived from Georgia which brings the above report respecting Pensacola but knows not how the Intelligence arrived there though the Capture of the place was publicly talked of there. By this Express we received letters from the Governor & Assembly in Georgia assuring us they meant to defend themselves and support the common Cause to their utmost.

We can as yet obtain no Intelligence of the British fleet which sailed from New York the 26 of Decemr, supposed to be destined for South Carolina or Georgia, & begin to hope that Providence has directed them to depart the Coast. The Severity of the frost in these parts and as far Southward as I have heard is greater than hath been known these forty Years.

I have the honour to be, with every sentiment of respect, your Excellency's hble Servt,   Sam. Huntington

Feby 8 Another Express is Just arrived from Genl Lincoln. The following is an Extract from the Generals Letter dated Charles Town S. Carolina, Decemr 22, 1779.[3]

"Before this reaches you, you will doubtless hear that the Spaniards have been up the river Mississippi and possessed themselves of the English Settlements on that River and that they made nine hundred prisoners, That about the Beginning of this month they [left] Havannah with a Respectable Fleet with Troops for Pensacola or Augustine,[. . . .]"

Yours ut supra,   S. Huntington

RC (Ct: Trumbull Papers). In a clerical hand and signed by Huntington.
[1] See Huntington to William Livingston, February 1, 1780.
[2] See Huntington to the States, February 10, 1780.
[3] A December 22 letter from Benjamin Lincoln to the committee for corresponding with the southern department, which was read in Congress on February 7, is in PCC, item 158, fols. 309–12, but it does not contain the extract quoted by Huntington. *JCC*, 16:129–30.

Samuel Huntington to George Washington

Sir,   Philadelphia Feby 7th 1780
I do myself the honour to forward the enclosed letter from Genl Lincoln address'd to your Excellency.

As Major Lane the Express charged with this letter was late a Prisoner in Savannah, and your Excellency must be anxious to know the State of the Prisoners in the southern Department, I have examined him on that Subject and taken his information in writing which is herewith enclosed, yet hoping you may find in Genl Lincolns Letter a more accurate Account of the Matter.[1]

I have the honour to be, with the highest respect, your Excy's hble Servt,   Sam. Huntington

RC (DLC: Washington Papers). In a clerical hand and signed by Huntington.
[1] Huntington apparently enclosed a letter to Washington from Benjamin Lincoln of December 23, 1779, and a statement signed by Maj. Joseph Lane, Jr., concerning his recollection of the status of prisoners of war in the southern department. Lane explained that there had been a "general" exchange of noncommissioned officers and privates, which had left the British indebted 106 men, but only a "partial" exchange of officers, which had left a few Americans unexchanged. These included Col. Samuel Elbert and assistant commissary Mordecai Sheftall, plus five others he knew by name and a few he could only vaguely remember. A transcript of Lincoln's letter is in the Sparks Collection, MH–H; an extract from it concerning the enemy's claim that Elbert should be exchanged as a brigadier, which was appended to a copy of Lane's "information," is in the Washington Papers, DLC.

Nathaniel Peabody to Woodbury Langdon

My Dear sir   No 8.   Philada. Febry. 7th 1780
I had not the happiness of Receiving a line from you this last Post the last I Reced. was No. 4 which I Noticed last week.[1] Mr. Livermore arrived here the 5th.[2] Puts up in the Chamber You left. Mr. Folsom Lodges at A Mrs Marshals, but where it is, or how he lives I am unable to inform.

The affair of Bradford is frequently agitated but we have come to no dicision upon the matter as Yet, though I think we shall in a few days when I am apprehensive the conclusion will be agreable to my wish.[3]

The Vermont affair has not come on but will soon.[4] Ira Allen has been going to and fro in the Earth and walking up & down in it, ever since the Month of November last and I am informed Jos. Fay & a Col. Robertson from the Grants is in the Citty, but I have not seen Fay.[5] A Col. Olcott and Mr. Woodword are now here and there views appear to me verry agreable.[6] I am of opinion they by no means wish to be seperated from the state of N.H. N.Yrk. with their usual industry will exert every nerve to bring their purposes to pass—but what will be the isue is to me uncertain.

The state will soon be called upon to fill up their Regiments so as to compleat about 1200 Men,[7] and also to furnish their proportion of supplies, for the Army, that we may be in a situation to carry on a Vigorous campaign the ensuing Year, or to Negociate to advantage if peace should be proposed.

The convention is now siting here, who were to have considered the limitation of prices but have not come to a conclusion as Yet.[8] The spaniards have made considerable progress among the English settlements upon the River Misisippi—taken 900 British Troops &c[9]—no news of the fleet since they left N York nor from Europe a late date—except fresh terminations of the friendly dispositions of the Christian & Catholic Kings—and their willingness to Cooperate with Us in carring on the War. Notwithstan[din]g the high price every thing bears here, Bills meet with a dull sale. I have proposed to contribute our proportion of the public Expence by building ships &c. What think you of this and at what rate can they be built in sterling money? I would write my mind of men and things with more freedom, but I understand many letters from Congress have of late fallen into bad hands &c. with expectation of obtaining the secrets of Congress so that outward bound letters must be cautiously wrote.

I was in great hopes to have been relieved by Mr. Livermore but find I am not, and nothing but the cause of my country and the advice of my friends (among whome I have placed not a little dependance upon your opinion) Could have induced me to crucify my interest, &   by Tarrying here through the winter, and I must beg your influence that I may be relieved verry Early in the spring as I shall absolutely if alive within about eight weeks from this time at furtherst. I shall not fail to write to you, and hope for returns.

Please to make my Compliments agreable to Your lady, to Mr. Speaker & his lady & all honest friends.

I am Dear Sir at 4 Clock in the morning, Your most Obedient and verry Humble servant,   Nathl. Peabody

FC (PPL: Pemberton Red Book). In the hand of Peabody and endorsed: "To Judge Langdon. Copy. Feby—80."

¹ Not found.

² Samuel Livermore presented his credentials to Congress this day. *JCC*, 16:129.

³ Peabody was apparently referring to an effort to remove John Bradford as naval agent and head of the Eastern Navy Board. It was undoubtedly to Bradford that Langdon was referring in a December 21, 1779, letter to Peabody when he discussed the prospects for removing "a certain Agent . . . which you mention is likely (and which must be done or we are ruined)." Roberts Collection, PHC. Bradford, however, remained in office.

⁴ See James Lovell to Samuel Adams, February 1, 1780, note.

⁵ For the activities of Ira Allen in behalf of Vermont statehood at this time, see James B. Wilbur, *Ira Allen, Founder of Vermont, 1751–1814* (Boston: Houghton Mifflin Co., 1928), pp. 144–52. Although Allen was in Philadelphia at this time, he was apparently acting fairly independently of his fellow agents, Stephen Bradley, Jonas Fay, and Moses Robinson, who submitted representations to Congress on February 1 and 7, but who had already left to return home. Peabody's disparaging reference to Allen is doubtless to the fact that he used his trip to Philadelphia as an opportunity to visit leaders in New Jersey, Delaware, Maryland, and Pennsylvania in a missionary campaign to develop support for Vermont's stand before Congress. Some of his accounts for expenses incurred in this endeavor (including £922.8 "Spent in a Journey to Maryland and Attending Congress with J. Fay, Mr. Robinson and S. R. Bradley"), as well as a few of those for Bradley, Fay, and Robinson for expenses on their Philadelphia mission, are in "Orders on the Treasurer," vol. 8, Vt–PR.

⁶ That is, Peter Olcott and Bezaleel Woodward, representatives of the "towns in the northern district of the New Hampshire Grants, on both sides of the Connecticut river, " who were opposing Vermont's pretentions to independence and establishment of the territory's boundary at the Connecticut River.

⁷ New Hampshire's actual quota as voted by Congress on February 9 was 1,215. See *JCC*, 16:150; and Samuel Huntington to the States, February 10, 1780.

⁸ The Philadelphia convention for limiting prices met this evening and came to a number of resolutions. The commissioners also met briefly the following evening before adjourning "to the fourth day of April next." See William Ellery to William Greene, February 15, 1780, enclosure.

⁹ Peabody was apparently referring to the Spanish capture of Baton Rouge, Manchac, and Natchez in Spetember 1779, news of which arrived in letters from Gen. Benjamin Lincoln that were read in Congress this day. *JCC*, 16:129–30.

Nathaniel Peabody to William Whipple

Dear Sir,   No. 14.   Philada. Febr. 7th. 1780.

I was favoured this evening with your agreable favour of the 27 of Decr. and am much Obliged to you for part of the information Contained in your letter but am unhappy to find you are not more inclined to accept of the Appointment at the Admiralty Board.[1] Your Observations with respect to the Expense of living here is distressingly true, however I am Certain Congress fully Expect to make Such Allowances as will be adequate to the Expence of living. And it is not in your Power to Compensate for the Disadvantages which will Necessarily attend that very important department upon your refusal. In Short it is my opinion that our having the Naval Department upon a Sure or respectable footing depends exceedingly upon your acceptance. Mr. Livermore is in the Chamber over your Room, And I was in hopes to have been releived by him but find I am not. His appointment as Delegate Expires in a *very few days*![2] I imagine much sooner than it will be possible to finish the Vermont affair which has not Come under Consideration yet. Their agents are here. Colo Olcott and Mr. Woodward are also in the City & not in favour of Vermont if I Can Judge Right.

By letters from Genl Lincoln we learn that the Spaniards are warmly engaged in reducing the British Settlements upon the River Mississippi, have taken 900 Prisoners—&c &c.

The State of New Hampshire will Soon be requested to fill their Regts in the Continental Army to the amount of about *1200* men in all, and also to furnish their Quota of Supplies in kind, as the only probable means of Supporting a proper Army in the field, Next Campaign. No time ought to be lost by the States, for effecting So important an End, The Same exertions are Necessary whether we expect *peace* or *War* and I think the Latter most probable notwithstanding the plausable declaration of Some Gentlemen who wish for a *peace* &c even At the Expence of every thing we ought to hold Dear & Sacred. No late News from Europe, except Some friendly Communications from the minister of france &c.

Please to make my Compliments agreable to your lady, And believe me to be most Sincerely Your Friend & most obedient And very Humble Sevt,   Nathl Peabody

N.B. I inclose a number of Journals Lest the others Should have miscarried.

RC (NhHi: Langdon–Elwyn Family Papers).

[1] In his December 27, 1779, letter to Peabody, a transcript of which is in the Burnett Papers, DLC, Whipple had stated that: "I am happy to find you have taken some measures towards a Reformation of the Nav[al] department and hope that Commission will be filled with men much better qualified for the business than I am. However, it will be time enough for me to give my answer when I have Official information of the appointmt And am made acquainted with the plan." For Whipple's appointment and decision to decline a seat on the new Board of Admiralty, see Samuel Huntington to Thomas Waring, November 27, 1779, note 3.

[2] Samuel Livermore's appointment expired on March 1. *JCC*, 16:129.

Oliver Ellsworth to Jonathan Trumbull, Sr.

Sir,   Philadelphia, Feby. 8th. 1780
    No intelligence or communication has been had from Europe
since I had the honor of addressing your Excellency last.[1] The following is the substance of what material has since that time been received
from the Southward.
    Governor Walton, of Georgia, writes the 15h of Decr.[2] that their
Assembly were then sitting at Augusta, had appointed Delegates to
Congress, were arranging their force, securing their frontiers, &
providing to cooperate in the expulsion of the Enemy.
    General Lincoln, also writes from Charlestown, the 19h & 22d of
the same month that the Enemy remained queit—that a Ship with
military Stores from Philadelphia had very seasonably arived—that
the four continental Frigats ordered there from the Eastward had
also arived & brot. in with them a british Privateer of 16 Guns—&
were in his opinion, in addition to the french marine their before,
sufficient to secure their bar from insults & to keep open the communication of supplies. That the Spaniards had been up the Missisippi
& taken possession of the british settlements & made 900 prisoners.
And that a considerable Naval force with 4,000 Troops on board,
sailed from the Havannah the begining of Decr. for Pensacola or
Augustine or both—which however the british Army affected to
disbelieve, & had sent no reinforcements to either of those posts—&
were in expectation of the arival of Troops from New York.
    There is every reason to beleive, Sir, that Spain will make a serious
diversion in the Florida's; to which perhaps we can have no objection,
provided she does not extend her views on the Missisippi beyond the
Latitude of 31, nor to an exclusive navigation of that river.
    The Convention at this place, have concluded to adjourn to the 1st
Tuesday of April, & to give notice thereof to Virgina that she may
then send commissioners if she thinks proper or otherwise let her
determination be known.[3]
    I have the honor, to be, Sir, with great Esteem & Respect, your
Excellency's most obedt. hum Servt.   Oliv. Ellsworth

RC (Ct: Trumbull Papers).
[1] See Ellsworth to Trumbull, January 30, 1780.
[2] This day another summary of recent southern intelligence was also transmitted to
Connecticut, from which the following passage was printed in the February 29 issue
of the *Connecticut Courant and the Weekly Intelligencer,* under the heading "Extract of a
letter from an honourable member of Congress to a Gentleman in this town [Hartford],
dated February 8."
    "No very late intelligence from Europe: in general her affairs and politics wear a
promising aspect on ours.
    "Our affairs to the southward, though critical are not desperate—Georgia is not yet
conquered, her Assembly were sitting at Augusta the 15th of December, arranging
her force, providing for her frontiers, and with aid, to expel the enemy—have

appointed delegates, and conceived a letter to Congress in the stile of a Roman Senate.

"Charlestown was also safe the 22d of December, with shipping, French and American, sufficient it is apprehended to secure the harbour and keep open a communication for supplies.

"The Spaniards have been up the Missisippi and taken possession of the British settlements and made 900 prisoners. An expedition took place at the Havannah the beginning of December against Pensacola or Augustine, or both, the success of which is not yet known."

[3] For the Philadelphia convention to regulate prices, see William Ellery to William Greene, February 15, 1780.

Elbridge Gerry to Joseph Ward

Dear sir,   Philadelphia 8th Feby 1780

The Board of War have reported on your Letter relative to Subsistence for the Officers of your late Department, & You will probably receive by the post the Resolution of Congress thereon.[1] Nothing is done respecting Pay for the two Officers who have not served eighteen Months, & I think it adviseable for them to state in a Memorial to Congress, their Services whilst acting under You, & the Hardship of being so unfavorably distinguished from the other Officers.

I remain sir with Esteem your Friend & very hum sert,

E Gerry

RC (ICHi: Ward Papers).

[1] See Samuel Huntington to Ward, January 14, 1780.

James Lovell to Samuel Adams

Febry 8 —80

Mr. Lowell, whose Opinion *has had* weight with me, expressed himself when here against the Delegates communicating to any Individual of the respective Assemblies of their States what they did not think right to deliver officially to the Govern—but Laws of Secresy are so imposed at Times in Chesnutt Street that Communications can only go to Colleagues without *glaring* Criminality. I am sure it would be best for the Governmt. of every State in the Confederacy to know what we know here. We must cut Throats another Year at least, and we ought to do it vigorously. F & S[1] will persist in strenuous Cooperation for the Purpose of *securing our* Independce. and *indemnifying themselves.*[2] An armed mediation is not improbable, in which Case the last mediatorial Offers of Spain may be taken up again so that Britain ought not at the End of the next Campaign to hold Possession of any Part of the Territory of the U.S. Our Enemies do not meet with Countenance in Europe yet, but some Powers there may be *obliged* by *secret* Treaties, on certain Events, to interfere against our Interests, tho' unwillingly; disagreable Terms of Peace or additional Force against us & our Allies may therefore become a necessary Alternative.

F is extremely desirous that we should put matters upon such a footing in regard to Spain that a *lasting* Alliance may be formed; and hints at 4 Points

1. A precise & invariable western boundary to the U.S.
2. The exclusive Navign. of Mississipi to S.
3. The Possessn. of the Floridas
4. The Lands on the left or eastern Side of the Miss. On the first F thinks we should go no farther west than was permitted by the royal Proclamn. of 1763.

On the 2d. she thinks we have no Right because we have no Territory situated *on* the River.

On the third as it is probable S. will conquer the Flordas during this war every Cause of Dispute between us & her should be removed.

On the 4th that the Lands lying on the East Side which were prohibited by the Proclamation abovenamed to be settled by the then Provinces are the Property of the Kg. of Engld. and proper Objects against which Spain may proceed for a *permanent Conquest.* S conceives that these States have no Right to those Lands not having *possessed* them nor having a Claim in the Right of the Sovereign whose Govt. we have abjured.[3] On this last we shall assuredly differ— the others are all in a fair Train. We are standing stiff for Mass. that she shd. not be still overburthened by Quota of Troops. We have the Ratio of Sepr. 76 preferred to March 79, but still it is not right; however it will not, I fear, be altered at this very *critical & late* hour of providing for a vigorous Campaign. 6,070 will be requested from you in a day or two. I do not know that we can possibly get an Army unless Mass. perseveres in furnishing what I know she has judged her *Dis*proportion.[4]

Our Frigates are well into Charlestown Harbour with 5 or 6 french ones. The Stores also are arrived there from hence. You will see a Paragraph of Lincolns Letter in Today's paper. I am told *our* Frigates took other Prizes than the 16 Gun Privateer. I did not chuse to say any Thing of the Frigates in the Gazette.[5]

Yrs. affectly,   J L

[*P.S.*] Majr. Osgood will be on his Way home in a day or two.

RC (NN: Adams Papers).

[1] That is, France and Spain.

[2] From this point, Lovell proceeded to discuss Congress' response to the January 25 memorial from the chevalier de La Luzerne, which was the subject of two conferences with the French minister and produced a number of proposals adopted on January 31. See Samuel Huntington to La Luzerne, February 2, 1780, note.

[3] In his recent conferences with a committee of Congress, La Luzerne had explained and defended the Spanish position on claims to western lands, the Floridas, and navigation of the Mississippi, largely out of desire to curb American expansionism

and avoid arousing expectations that could jeopardize cooperation between Spain and the United States against the common enemy. In so doing, he aroused suspicions among some delegates, although he generally worked to avoid the openly partisan involvement of his predecessor, Conrad Alexandre Gérard, whose behavior had previously embarrassed French interests. From his reports to Vergennes, it is clear that he believed that he had not swayed the Americans, and thus this initial exchange of views became his last official discussion with Congress of Spanish-American interests. Convinced that Americans would not relinquish their western claims, he concluded that Spain should simply continue her conquests in the southwest, ultimately forcing the Americans to recognize a fait accompli. To this end the Spanish agent, Juan de Miralles, also released an account of recent Spanish victories on the lower Mississippi, which appeared in the *Pennsylvania Gazette* on February 23 under the heading: "Account of the operation and advantages acquired by His Catholic Majesty's arms, under the command of Brigadier General Don Bernardo De Galvez, Governor of the province of Luciana, against the English situated on the river Mississippi. . . ."

La Luzerne's representation of Spanish interests to Congress has been discussed in William E. O'Donnell, *The Chevalier de La Luzerne, French Minister to the United States, 1779–1784* (Bruges: Desclée de Brouwer, 1938), pp. 100–103; and in his February 11 and March 13 dispatches to Vergennes, Archives du ministère des affaires étrangères: Correspondance politique, États-Unis, 11:184–206, 270–76. Miralles' reports to José de Gálvez of February 1 and 15, March 12, 1780, discussing these developments are in Audiencia de Santo Domingo, Legajo 2598, Archivo General de Indias, Seville.

Concerning the effect of his publication of news of the victories of Bernardo de Gálvez, the following passage from Miralles' March 12 dispatch is especially interesting. "Although reports of the Spanish conquests on the Mississippi River were well received at first, later several members of Congress displayed some displeasure, as have other private citizens who planned to settle there. I have managed to convince them of the absurdity of their ideas, when they did not possess the smallest part of that territory, when they had not been able to hold what they had conquered in February of 1778 nor much less to retake it from the English, because the fortifications which the English had enlarged and the forces they maintained there combined to make it impossible. I believe that the members are aware of these facts, although they may have flattered themselves that they could have in the future mounted efforts great enough to capture that territory and join it to their possessions on the Ohio River, and I think they know that the Spanish conquest deprives them of any basis for claiming freedom of navigation on the Mississippi although that realization is more painful to them." Aileen Moore Topping translation, Manuscript Division, DLC.

[4] At this point in the margin, Lovell wrote the following troop quota figures, which are identical to those adopted by Congress on February 5, except for Rhode Island and Pennsylvania, whose quotas were actually 810 and 4,855, respectively.

"N.H. 1215, M. 6070, R.I. 860, C. 3238, N.Yk. 1620, N.J. 1620, P. 4805, D. 405, M. 3238, V. 6070, N.C. 3640, S.C. 2430, [*total*] 35,211."

See *JCC*, 16:126; and Samuel Huntington to the States, February 10, 1780.

[5] That is, the *Pennsylvania Gazette*.

Nathaniel Peabody to Josiah Bartlett

My Dear Sir,   No. 22.   Philada. Feby 8th. 1780

Your obligeing favour of the 27th of Decr.[1] Came to hand last evening And you may Depend upon my investigating the matters you refer to without loss of time, and Shall advise you of the true State of Facts So far as I Shall be able to obtain them.

Mr Livermore arived here last Saturday, in good time as the Vermont affair is Soon to Come on before Congress.[2] Vermont refuse to refer the Decision of the Matters in dispute to be determined in the mode prescribed by the Resolves of Congress. What operation that will have in the premises in unCertain—there Agents are here with Powers to Support their Independance and Enter into the Union, But not being Clothed with a weding Garment Can they be received, or even heard by Congress.

Agents are here from the Inhabitants on both Sides of Connecticut River, who Seem to be in favour of the State of New Hampr. which is not a Disagreable Circumstance in our favour.

Congress are about to Call upon the Several States, to fill up their Battallions in the Continental Army and to furnish their respective Quotas of Supplies for the Army, and no time ought to be Lost to accomplish So important an undertaking, as much will Depend upon the Exertions of the People, in preparing for the next Campaign. A prospect of pursuing the war with Success, or Negociateing a *peace* to advantage Demand the Same Noble Exertions on our part. The Quota of men to be Compleated by N. Hampr. will be about *1200* men in all.

We have nothing recent from Europe except Some friendly Communications made by the Minister of France, respecting the Intentions of the Christian & Catholic Kings in Cooperating with us the Ensuing Campaign.[3]

Our finances Still remain in a Deranged Situation which Greatly Embarrasses every public proceeding.

Bills of Exchange meet with a Dull Market—and we Can promise our Selves but Little from the Sale.

I Should be extreemly well pleased to hear how you proceed in the State of N. Hampr. with respect to Public affairs.

But hope to be at home very early in the Spring and beg your influence that a member may be Sent on to releive me as Soon as Possible or Else the State will be left with but one member in Congress.

I am Dear Sir, Your Sincere friend most obedt. & very Humbl Servt,   Nathl Peabody

RC (PHC: Roberts Collection).

[1] No December 27, 1779, letter from Bartlett to Peabody has been found, but in a December 25 letter, which may have been the letter referred to here, Bartlett asked Peabody to check Continental Treasury records about $100,000 that was supposedly sent to New Hampshire in 1778 but apparently had not been received. Bartlett Papers, NHi (microfilm).

[2] Samuel Livermore's appointment as a delegate expired on March 1, however, and since hearings on "the Vermont affair" were postponed until long after that date he had no opportunity to play a meaningful role in those debates. For New Hampshire's act authorizing Congress to make determinations concerning the state's claims to the region, which Livermore presented upon his arrival on February 7, see *JCC*, 16:131–33.

[3] See the preceeding entry.

Roger Sherman to Philip Turner

Sir,[1]   Philadelphia 8th Feb. 1780
I received your Letters of the 25th of Novr. & 27th of January. The enclosed Papers contain the late resolutions of Congress respecting the officers of the General Hospital, the medical Committee have not reported any alterations in the arrangement.[2] Congress have appointed three Inspectors to make the necessary reformations, & retrenchments in the several staff departments, & to report any new arrangements that they may Judge expedient.

The Gentlemen appointed are General Schuyler, Genll. Mifflin & Colo. Pickering, they are to consult the Commander in chief on the subject.

I have some expectation that we shall soon introduce a stable medium of Trade & reduce the Pay of officers & men to the old standard.

We lately received a Letter from General Lincoln from Charlestown in S. Carolina, he writes that three of our Frigates & another armed vessel are safely arrived there from Boston, that they took a 16 Gun Privateer Brig, on their passage, that there are 6 French Frigates there—& they have heard nothing from the forces that sailed from New York. That the Spaniards have taken the English Settlements on the River Missippi, and nine hundred Prisoners— That a strong Spanish Fleet with 4000 Troops sailed from Havana the beginning of December last destined against Pensacola or St. Augustine, or both. The General Assembly of Georgia were sitting at Augusta in that State and are preparing to defend the State, they have lately appointed Delegates which are expected soon to arrive at Congress.

The winter has been very severe in this part of the Country the snow about two feet deep on a level at a little distance from hence.

I am with due regard, Your humble servant,

                                              Roger Sherman

Tr (DLC: Peter Force Collection). Endorsed: "A true Copy from the original letter in the possession of John Turner Wait, Esqr., Norwich Town, Conn. Henry Stevens Jr."
[1] Philip Turner (d. 1815) was surgeon general of the Continental Hospital Eastern Department. See these *Letters*, 6:405, 607.
[2] Sherman's references are somewhat obscure. The enclosed "late resolutions" respecting officers of the Continental hospital may have been those of October 27 and November 20, 1779, concerning clothing and subsistence for the medical department; and his reference to the medical committee's failure to report "alterations in the arrangement" may pertain to Congress' November 22 resolve directing the committee to "arrange" various resolutions and amendments respecting the hospital department "as may make the whole consistent with and conformable to the alterations made by Congress in the original system." More recently the medical committee had proposed a half-pay plan for officers of the department, but it seems unlikely that Sherman had this recommendation in mind at this time. See *JCC*, 15:1213–14, 1216, 1294–97, 16:10–12.

Samuel Holten's Diary

[February 9–10, 1780]
Feby. 9. Wednesday. Congress agreed to resolutions for filling up the army.[1] No news.
10. Thursday.[2] I dined with the Honorable R. Morris Esqr. No post come in.

MS (MDaAr).
[1] See Samuel Huntington to the State, February 10, 1780.
[2] This day Holten also wrote the following brief note to the Board of Treasury, which the board immediately acted upon and Congress endorsed on the 11th. See *JCC*, 16:154.
"I shall consider my-self under obligation if you'l report to Congress a resolution in my favor for 5,000 dollars, for which sum, the state I've the Honor to represent will be accountable." Holten Papers, DLC.

William Churchill Houston to Benjamin Franklin

Sir,   Philada. 9 February 1780.
I take the Liberty of troubling you with the enclosed Letters to put them in the Way of reaching the several Persons to whom they are addressed, being assured you will excuse it.

A Plan at this Time lies before Congress for establishing regular Packets to France[1] which bids fairer to be attended with Success and Execution than any hitherto attempted or projected. It is to be hoped when this is carried into Effect, the Court of France will adopt a similar Measure. The Connection and Intercourse between the two Nations require such an Establishment, and will also be greatly promoted by it. Should this take Place, the Committee of Foreign Affairs will not find it so difficult to communicate constantly with the Gentlemen who manage the Interests of the Union abroad. It is to be lamented that so great a Slackness has prevailed in this respect hitherto, it being indeed difficult to find Conveyances every Way suitable, but the proper Improvement has not been made in many Cases even of such as offered.

I have no Wish to increase Your Excellency's Labour of Correspondence, but beg Leave to mention that I would willingly endeavour to make your Intelligence more frequent, if agreeable to you, being satisfied that the publick Interest may derive Advantage from the regular Communication of Facts though unattended with reflections.

By Dispatches dated 22 December last from General Lincoln[2] at Charlestown in South Carolina we are informed that the Enemy are quiet in the Town of Savanna and it's Environs, and have not made any Irruptions into the Country as was apprehended. From this I am led to believe that they suffered more deeply than we supposed when the Town was attempted by the allied Forces under the Command of Count D'Estaing and General Lincoln. It is also mentioned that the Spaniards have attacked the English Settlements on the Mississippi, and made nine Hundred Prisoners, and that an Expedition from the Havanna was shortly expected to proceed against Pensacola or St. Augustine. A large Detachment is ordered from the main Army in New Jersey into the Southern Country, so that in all Probability Things will go well there. Vigorous Preparations are making on our Part for the ensuing Campaign. The Enemy since the Evacation of Rhode-Island possess only York-Island and the two adjacent, and have about the End of last Year embarked six or eight Thousand Men for the Southward or the West-Indies, perhaps both.

I beg Leave to request, Sir, you will be so good as to procure me tha Nautical Almanack[3] for 1780 and 81 published in London under the Direction of the Comisioners of Longitude and which, I suppose, can be had in Paris. It is not to be bo't here, and I had rather give any Price than be without it. I will answer your Bill to any Person in this City, and acknowledge the Kindness by any Services in my Power.

I am, Sir, Your Excellency's most obedt Servant,

William Ch Houston

RC (PPAmP: Bache Collection).

[1] The Board of Admiralty's February 1 plan for establishing three packet boats that would sail between Philadelphia and Nantes on a bimonthly basis is in *JCC*, 16:117. It was apparently never acted on.

[2] Lincoln's letters of December 19 and 22 to the committee assigned to correspond with the southern department was read in Congress on February 7, 1780, and referred to the Board of War and the Committee of Intelligence. *JCC*, 16:129–30.

[3] That is, *The Nautical Almanac and Astronomical Ephemeris*, published annually since 1767.

New York Delegates to George Clinton

Sir,   Philadelphia 9th Feby 1780.

The Great interest which our State have in the speedy determination of the controversy between it, & the neighbouring States, as well as their own refractory subjects in the North eastern Counties, lead us to take the earliest opportunity of laying before you all that has passed in Congress relative to that business, & to represent the disagreeable situation in which we are placed by being unfurnished with the act of Submission, & the necessary materials for defence.[1]

We have ordered the papers to be copied, & shall enclose them together with the enteryies of them on the journal.[2] You will not be surprized that we made no motion upon the occasion, & contented ourselves with general declarations, & a succesful opposition to their being committed, which was very much laboured. Had we done otherwise we shd. necessarily have brought on the question—have your legislature agreed to submit the matter? Are your ready for trial? As both must have been answered in the negative, it would have put it in the power of the Other States, & even of the People upon the grants, to insist upon an immediate hearing agreeable to the terms of the resolutions of Congress. We do not chuse to dwell upon the embarrassing & distressed situation to which the delay of Genl. Scot & Mr. Duane have reduced us. We could have wished to have had the benefit of their assistance in a matter of so much moment to the State, or at least, if deprived of that by any unforeseen accident, to have been possessed of such materials as would have enabled us to exert our poor abilities in her behalf.

We do ourselves the honour to enclose your Excellency the only paper which we have recd. upon the subject. You will judge how far this could be serviceable to us. As it may be of some consequence to know the disposition of our antagonists We will endeavour to give you all we can collect here. Masachusets seems to be indifferent about their claim. New Hampshire extreamly anxious to have a determination, but more so to come to some amicable settlement by which they may preserve to themselves such towns as wish to be with them, on the east side of the mountains, & to relinquish all on the West side *absolutely* together with those on the east side which wish to be connected with New York. The people who have the power on the grants are firmly determined as far as we can collect, to opposition by arms. From this State of facts we are unanimously of opinion, that agents shd. be appointed to conclude some agreement with New Hampshire, and to form a treaty with them for the restoration of peace and good order in that part of the government. The Issue of an appeal to arms considering the dispo[si]tion of our own people, of those on the grants, & in the eastern States, will we conceive be very doubtful, the Country turbulent & unquiet, & the expence of the force necessary to subdue it beyond our abilities. Nor can it be of importance to have subjects whose natural connection is with another State, the Mountains opposing an insuperable bar to their commercial intercourse with New York.

These sentiments we have taken the liberty to submit to your Excellencys consideration, if you shall think them worthy your attention you will communicate them to the Legislature. We also enclose the result of a months conference of delegates from different states in convention.[3] We thought it proper in order to avoid all censure, that one of us shd. attend, & assure them of the disposition of our State to do all that was required of them upon this subject.

We must most earnestly recommend it to our Legislature to take immediate measure for informing themselves accurately of the quantity of flour, grain, & hay, taken for the use of the army, under the Laws of our State, since the first of August last, as it may be of the utmost moment to them. A report now laying before congress for quotas in kind for the use of Army, & remitting two thirds of the tax to be raised to the State which shall furnish it.[4] If this shd. pass & we should be able to make it retrospect we are confident that it will appear that we have already furnished all that will be demanded, we are anxious to be furnished with this account, & the prices at which taken as soon as possible. The papers which we enclose contain all the little news of this Place. We are Sir, With the greatest respect & esteem, Your Excellency's Most Obt. Hum. Servt.

Wm. Floyd

Robert R Livingston

Ezra L'Hommedieu

RC (MiDbEI). Written by Livingston and signed by Livingston, Floyd, and L'Hommedieu.

[1] A reference to the fact that the delegates had received no word of New York's response to Congress' September 24 appeal for enactment of a law, proposed by John Jay, authorizing Congress "to hear and determine all differences" concerning claims to the "country called New Hampshire Grants." See Jay's letters to Thomas Chittenden and to George Clinton, September 25, and to Clinton, October 5, 1779.

[2] The enclosed "papers" and "enteries of them on the Journal" concerning the New Hampshire Grants are in Clinton, *Papers* (Hastings), 5:483–90. For the status of the congressional hearings on the New Hampshire Grants, see James Lovell to Samuel Adams, February 1, 1780, note.

[3] See William Ellery to William Greene, February 15, 1780.

[4] A report of "the committee for estimating supplies," which is in the hand of Robert R. Livingston, was brought before Congress this day, but Congress postponed action on it. The report had emanated from a committee of states appointed on January 17 to resolve objections to an earlier report of the original committee appointed to set the states' provisions quotas. This February 9 report was then debated from February 16 to 25, before agreement was reached on allowable prices and the quotas assigned to each state.

For the development of this requisition system, see *JCC*, 16:68, 143–46, 168, 171–73, 175–78, 182–84, 186, 188–89, 191–94, 196–201; and Erna Risch, *Supplying Washington's Army* (Washington: U.S. Government Printing Office, 1981), pp. 230–34. See also Samuel Huntington to the States, February 26, 1780.

North Carolina Delegates to Richard Caswell

Sir   Philadelphia Feby 9th. 1780

You will before this arrives have received Some resolutions of Congress for recruiting [an] army,[1] a business of the highest Importance at all times, but now peculiarly Interesting, by Reason of the Critical Situation of public affairs, which requires the next campaign to be prosecuted with Such Vigor as may entirely expel the Enemy from every part of the united States. We are persuaded that the advantages arising from Such decisive Success are obvious to every one in the general assembly and scarcely think we have occasion to add any other Suggestions to excite their most vigorous and expeditious exertions for preparing a formidable force to take the field as early as possible, but we cannot Suppress our Opinion which we have formed *on good grounds*, the restoration of Peace, and the future tranq[uility] of the United States, and particularly those to the Southward, in a great measure depend on the Compleat expulsion of the Enemy by the Operations of the current year.

The Proportions of the Several States are far from being estimated by any precise or Satisfactory rule; and you will perceive a resolution for an equitable adjustment of the expence attending the raising and providing for Such Troops as shall be found to be beyond the due proportions.

The Ideas we have of the Circumstances of the State we have the honor to represent determined us to endeavour to obtain a resolution for making all the Efforts of the States for raising men, whether as regulars or Militia, a Common expence.[2] We remembered the vast Sums disbursed by the State and vast expences incurred in calling out militia and making extraordinary exertions in a War whose object is common, and whose Operations have been, perhaps, less threatening to her than to her Neighbors. We also foresaw, that She must make Still greater Exertions in Consequence of the Enemy having pointed their hostilities principally against the Southern States, and we deem it our duty, especially as doubts were thrown out in debate, to take the Sense of Congress, directly, on the Question in order that the General assembly may be fully informed, on a Subject So Interesting to their Constituents. We have failed in our motion as you will See by the inclosed Extract from the Journals. The States who voted against it are very Apprehensive of very great, and perhaps unnecessary expence being the Consequence, if Such a resolution were it to have restrospect, but Seem to have no matterial objection to its future Operation. As our State is much Interested in the retrospective operation, we did not chuse to move it in that form without more particular Instructions from the State.[3]

Your Excellency's Ob. Servts.,   John Penn

Thos. Burke.

Allen Jones.

RC (Nc–Ar: Governors' Papers, Series II). In the hand of Thomas Burke. Tr (*N.C. State Records*, 15:334–35).

[1] See Samuel Huntington to the States, February 10, 1780.

[2] For Burke's amendment to a motion made by Oliver Ellsworth, which Congress considered on February 6 and rejected on the ninth, see *JCC*, 16:127–28, 146–49.

[3] Remainder of text taken from Tr.

Samuel Huntington to the States

Sir,   Circular   Philadelphia Feby 10. 1780

Your Excellency will receive herewith enclosed an Act of Congress of the 9th Instant ascertaining the number of men exclusive of Com-

missioned Officers for the Continental Army the next Campaign to
be 35,211 which Congress deem necessary for the service of the
present Year the Quota of each State being specified in the Act.[1]

You will observe that all the Men belonging to each State respectively now in the public service and whose time of Service does not
expire before the last day of September next, whether they compose
the battallions in the line of the several States, those of the additional
Corps including the guards, the artillery & horse, or the Regimented
Artificers in the department of the Quarter Master General and
Commissary General of Military Stores are to be credited to their
respective States and accounted as part of their Quotas and each
State is required to furnish their respective Deficiencies of their
Quotas as above stated on or before the first Day of April next.

You may expect to receive as soon as possible from the Commander in Chief or his order,[2] an accurate return of the Troops
now in service belonging to the state which will ascertain the deficiency to be furnished by the States respectively agreeable to the Act
inclosed.

As the Quotas apportioned to each State may be supposed not to
be exactly Just you will observe Congress have made provision to pay
the Expence any State hath incurred or may incur by furnishing
more than their Just proportion of men.

It is recommended to each State respectively in the strongest Terms
punctually to comply with this requisition by furnishing their respective Quotas of Men compleat without loss of Time.

Many powerful motives too obvious to need enumeration conspire
to urge the propriety, policy, & necessity of having a respectable
Army ready to take the field early in the spring.

Vigorous exertions and a respectable Army in the field are the
most sure means to prevent the necessity of another Campaign on
the one hand, or on the other to crown it with the desired success
and put a period to the Contest upon honourable Terms.

I have the honour to be &c,   S. Huntington President

LB (DNA: PCC, item 14).
[1] For Congress' adoption of the resolves transmitted with this letter, whose substance was contained in a Board of War report submitted on February 1 and debated
on February 2, 4, 5, 8, and 9, see *JCC*, 16:117–21, 123, 125–28, 141, 146–51.
[2] See the following entry.

Samuel Huntington to George Washington

Sir,   Philadelphia Feby 10. 1780

Your Excellency will receive herewith enclosed the Copy of an Act
of Congress of the 9th Instant requiring that for the ensuing Campaign the States furnish by drafts or otherwise on or before the first

day of April next the deficiencies of their several Quotas so as to make the number of men exclusive of Commissioned Officers for the Continental Service 35,211 for the present year, the particular Quotas to each State being assigned by the Act except Georgia which under its present Circumstances is separately considered.[1]

You will please to observe that all the men whose times of Service do not expire before the last Day of September next are to be counted toward the quotas of the States to which they respectively belong, whether they compose the Battallions in the line of the several States, or the additional Corps or departments mentioned in the Act.

As I am sensible of your Excellencies Anxiety on Account of the delay of this business allready, it is needless to mention the propriety of transmitting to the several States an accurate Account of their respective deficiencies without farther loss of time.[2]

Similar Copies of the Act enclosed are forwarded to all the States except Georgia and Congress have under Consideration a general Regulation to make provision in future if necessary to recruit the army annually in the month of January.

I have the honour to be, with every sentiment of Respect, your Excy's hble Servant,   S. Huntington President

P.S. Your letter of the 30 Jany hath been duly received.[3]

RC (DLC: Washington Papers). In a clerical hand and signed by Huntington.
[1] See the preceding entry.
[2] For Washington's circular letter to the states of February 20 written in compliance with this resolve, see Washington, *Writings* (Fitzpatrick), 18:35–37. As he had explained to Congress on February 17, however, he could not immediately supply every state with accurate and current returns because of "the remote and dispersed situation of many Corps," and therefore regretted that the Board of War had not originally formed "an Estimate (though it had not been as exact as might be wished)" of the men to be furnished by each state simply to avoid delays. The board's explanation of why this approach had not been followed was simple: to avoid giving "pretexts for procrastination to dissatisfied States." Furthermore, it was obvious that the states were more likely to comply with an appeal from Washington than from any congressional agency, and that certain "embarrassments" could probably be avoided if the commander in chief would communicate directly with the states. For Washington's February 17 letter to Congress and Richard Peters' response for the Board of War, see Washington, *Writings* (Fitzpatrick), 18:20–21; Burnett, *Letters*, 5:44; and the Washington Papers, DLC.
[3] This letter is in PCC, item 152, 8:385, and Washington, *Writings* (Fitzpatrick), 17:468.

Robert R. Livingston to John Jay

Dear John   Philadelphia 10th Feby 1780
    I have just steped out of Congress to let you hear by this opportunity that your friends in this part of the world are well & not unmindful of you & to acknowledge the rect of yours from Reedy Island[1]

which after long & wearysome peregrenations reached me three days ago at this place.

The Cypher it contains is not sufficiently intricate to be in any wise relyed on, if the conveyance by which this is to go shd. be delayed I will inclose one that you may venture to express your most hidden thoughts in. If not we will continue the use of yours till a better is established.

The Winter has been so uncomly severe here—as to exclude all foreign intelligence, & for some time all commerce between the several States. Chesapeek, Delaware, & New York bays, together with the Sound, are all frozen so as to bear loaded carts & it is asserted that the Ice extends some miles into the sea. One hardly knows how to communicate information to a person so far removed from us, if we mention nothing but what is new in this part of the world we omit many things which may possibly not have reached the others, And by writing transactions which have passed long since, we run the hazard of obliging you to read what some more punctual correspondent has communicated before. However as the last is the least evil, I will venture to inform you that Sir Henry Clinton sailed from New York with the light infantry & Granadiers of the whole army, & most of the cavalry, & so many other troops as made the whole number about 7000 men. He left the Hook the 26th Decr two days after which came on a most violent North East Storm accompanied with rain & snow. This was followed by North Westerly Winds, & the most extreme cold wheather that has been known in this climate. As several vessels foundered at their anchors within the Hook, we cannot but promise ourselves that this fleet have suffered severely by it, many of them being very probably lost & the remainder driven in a shattered condition to the West Indies. What gives weight to this conjecture is, that neither the Enemy nor we have had the least intelligence of them since their departure, tho we have great reason to believe that they were designed for North & South Carolina, And had they arrived within the usual time I think we must have had intelligence from thence. You have doubtless recd. information of the operations of the Spanish troops in the Missisipi where they have dispossessed the British of several posts & are as we are informed preparing a strong force at the Havanah to make an attempt upon St. Augustine, or Pensicola, which has very probably succeeded by this time, we having no accounts from Charlestown latter than the 22d Decr. at which times the enimies army under Provost still remained at Savannah. I am thus particular because I conceive every information from that quarter of the world may be particularly useful to you in your present situation, & I am fearful that you do not get all you shd from the committee for foreign Affairs of which I have at present the honor to be a member, and which I am labouring to get disolved in order to apoint a secretary for that department. Tho' I know that our little differences of sen[timent] can be of no great momment to you, yet I can not help telling you that Coll. Lawrance having refused to accept his appointment, we have been for some time endeavouring to supply his place. The Candidates Lovel, Morris, Hamilton & Coll Steward. The first had six votes on three different ballotings, the second five.[2] As both parties were fixed the matter rests till some other expedient can be fallen upon. The Minister of france has done me the honor to express the warmest wish that I should go to his court, and as I am absolute in my determination not to fill the present vacantcy, he proposes to his friends to appoint a resident as my desire to go abroad is extreamly languid.[3] I have done nothing to promote this design, & I am inclined to think that its novelty will be a good *osstensible* reason with many for not going into the measure tho' some embrace it very warmly—there is a method in which I could affect it, but then I shd. place {Lov[e]l [in a] situation which will give him too [m]uch influence over foreign negotiations},[4] a thing by all means to be avoided. We have determined to make the greatest exertions this campaign & have called upon the respective States for their quotas of thirty five thousand men which is to be the number of our troops for the ensuing season & who may in a few days in the Northern States be encreased to twice that number if required to act upon any sudden emergency. While we anxiously wish for peace we see no other road to it but such as our arms invent for us. This much for news and politicks. There is one other subject on which I might enter but it requires both more paper and more leisure than I have left. Let me then bid you adieu after requesting you to divide my best wishes with the partner of your heart & my other friends which you carried from hence & believe me to be, Yours Most sincerely,

Rob. R. Livingston

RC (NNC: Jay Papers). Endorsed by Jay: "Recd 27 June 1780."

[1] Jay's October 25, 1779, letter to Livington, written "On Board the Confederacy near Reedy Island" just before he sailed for Spain, is in Jay, *Papers* (Morris), 1:665–66.

[2] No actual votes for the secretary's post are recorded in the journals.

[3] John Mathews proposed "appointing a resident, instead of a secretary to the Minister Plenipotentiary at the Court of Versailles" on February 15, but Congress did not formally act on the motion until April 17, when it was rejected. Only New York and South Carolina supported the measure. *JCC*, 16:168, 371–72.

For James Lovell's view of the appointment of Livingston as a "resident" in France, see Lovell to Samuel Adams, February 16, 1780. See also Livingston to Jay, December 22, 1779.

[4] This passage was written by Livingston in the cipher sent to him by Jay in the October 25 letter cited in note one above. Because Livingston used the cipher somewhat casually, some material has been supplied in brackets to provide a more readable text.

Samuel Huntington to
the Marquis de La Rouerie

Sir   Philada Feby 11. 1780
   Your letter of this day is received[1] and agreeable to your request I
herewith return such of the papers you mention as are come to my
hands, if there be any others which you desire they are in the hands
of Mr Secretary Thomson I suppose who will with pleasure furnish
you with them on application.
   Enclosed you will receive an Act of Congress of the 10th Instant
Expressing their high sense of your merit, & granting you leave of
absence for six months after the End of the next Campaign agreeable to your request.[2]
   I am Sir your hble servt

LB (DNA: PCC, item 14).
   [1] This letter is not in PCC.
   [2] Col. Charles Armand-Tuffin, marquis de La Rouerie, had long sought promotion
to the rank of brigadier, and the Board of War had supported his application in a
January 18 recommendation that Congress had referred to Washington for his opinion.
When Washington opposed the promotion on the ground that it would arouse discontent among other deserving officers, Armand shifted ground and requested assignment to the southern department and the merger of his corps with that of the late
Casimir Pulaski, proposals that Washington promptly endorsed. And he simultaneously requested permission to return to France for six months leave at the end of
the campaign, a face-saving maneuver that avoided the difficulty he had gotten
himself into in 1779 when he had withdrawn a previous threat to resign over failure
to obtain a promotion. See *JCC*, 16:72, 78, 151, 187; PCC, item 148, 1:21–24, item
152, 8:375–78, 393–98, item 164, fols. 404–6; Washington, *Writings* (Fitzpatrick),
17:450–52, 497–98; these *Letters*, 12:22; and Samuel Huntington to Washington,
January 21, 1780.

Elbridge Gerry to
the Massachusetts Board of War

Gentlemen   Phila Feby 12. 1780
   Inclosed is a Copy of a Letter wch. I have lately recd from Lieuten-
ant Osgood Carlton respecting Money which he advanced to Capt
John Harris. The latter passing thro this City in July last on his
Return from Captivity informed me that he had commanded a Vessel employed by you at the Time of his being taken by the Enemy &
was without the Means of defraying his travelling Expences. Mr.
Carlton being at the same Time in the City & entrusted with the
Conveyance of a large Sum of Money to the Loan Office in Boston at
my Request advanced Capt. Harris 100 Dollars & stands indebted
for the Same to Appleton. Capt Harris did not inform me of the
Manner in which the Vessel was employed, & as it was natural to
suppose from his general Information that he was in the immediate

Service of the State, I had no Doubt that the Board of War would order the Money to be reimbursed to Mr Carlton & charge it to Capt Harris. If however the Board should think it not expedient I shall in Notice thereof with the greatest pleasure replace the Money & indemnify Mr Carlton who has conducted with politeness on the Occasion. I remain Gent with Respect

FC (MHi: Gerry-Knight Collection). In the hand of Elbridge Gerry.

Samuel Holten's Diary

[February 12, 1780]

12. Saturday, Majr. Osgood sit out for Boston;[1] I wrote to Colo. Hutchinson, Mr. Freeman, Mr. Webster & Mrs. Holten (no. 101).[2] Congress recd. a letter from Mr. Jay.[3]

MS (MDaAr).
[1] For Samuel Osgood's presence in Philadelphia as one of Massachusetts' delegates to the price-regulating convention in which he had served as secretary, see Elbridge Gerry to Samuel Adams, February 15, 1780, note 1.
[2] None of these letters has been found.
[3] The receipt of John Jay's December 20, 1779, letter to Pres. Samuel Huntington, informing Congress of the severe damage to his ship that required their forced landing in Martinique, is not recorded in the journals. A transcript of the letter is in PCC, item 110, 3:17-18; and Wharton, *Diplomatic Correspondence*, 3:432-33.

Samuel Huntington to Thomas Jefferson

Sir   Philadelphia Feby 12. 1780[1]

Your Excellency will receive herewith enclosed an Act of Congress of the 11th Instant authorizing the Executive Power of Virginia to examine the Accounts charged against Colo Bland while in Command at Charlotte-Ville by the Deputy Commissary General of Purchases & Issues and make such allowances in his favour as they deem Just & proper &c from the peculiar Situation of his Command.[2]

I have the honour to be with the highest respect, your Excy's hble Servt,   Sam. Huntington President

RC (MHi: Washburn Collection). In a clerical hand and signed by Huntington.
[1] This letter is dated February 11 in the presidential letterbook. PCC, item 14, fol. 297.
[2] Congress adopted this resolve in response to a January 26 recommendation from Washington, who explained that Col. Theodorick Bland had been promised a supplemental table allowance upon accepting command of the detachment assigned to guard the Convention Army at Charlottesville, Va., as "the incidental expences of detached or separate commands are always considerable," and in this case "more than commonly so." Washington had intervened in this matter at the urging of Governor

Jefferson, who had explained in a December 16 letter that Bland's claims for additional table expenses had been disallowed by the commissaries in Virginia, who were on the point of seizing his property to reimburse the Continent. Although Jefferson had succeeded in delaying their proceedings, he acknowledged that congressional action would ultimately be required to do justice to Bland. See *JCC*, 16:153–54; Jefferson, *Papers* (Boyd), 3:228–29, 265; and Washington, *Writings* (Fitzpatrick), 17:430, 445–47.

Huntington also sent a copy of this resolve to Bland in a brief letter of this date. PCC, item 14, fol. 296.

Samuel Huntington to George Washington

Sir,   Philadelphia 12 Feby 1780

You will receive herewith enclosed an Act of Congress of the 11th Instant respecting the State of Georgia, with an Extract of the Minutes of Council of the State of Georgia soliciting the Exchange & Promotion of Colo Elbert who was made Prisoner by the British in Georgia. This Officer though a Colonel in the Continental Army is a Brigadier in the Militia of the State of Georgia and the Enemy claim a Brigadier in Exchange for him.[1]

I have the honour to be, with the highest Respect, your Excy's hble servt,   Sam. Huntington President

RC (DLC: Washington Papers). In a clerical hand and signed by Huntington.
[1] For Georgia's recommendation that Col. Samuel Elbert be exchanged and promoted, and Congress' February 11 resolve explaining that Elbert could not be promoted but that Washington would be encouraged to secure his exchange, see PCC, item 73, fols. 256–60; and *JCC*, 16:155–56. See also Huntington to Washington, February 7, 1780, note.

James Lovell to Henry Laurens

Dear Sir   Feb. 12th. 1780

I send you Gazettes & Journals officially.

As your Friend, I send my most affectionate Wishes for your Health & Prosperity.

As an American very anxious about our public Cause (too, too much endangered by our vile Currency) I send my earnest Entreaties that you would persist in your Endeavors to serve your Country, though Individually you have Cause of Complaint against Some of the Rulers of our Union for an ungraceful Negligence in matters essential to your Embassy.

The great Points of recruiting the Army and providing Supplies for it, have prevented a Completion of Parts of Business that you wrote about. But I really hope they will speedily be finished & sent forward to you. We shall *certainly* fight another Year. Holland will therefore probably *not* treat of Alliance but will nevertheless place no Obstruction in yr. Way of borrowing Money from Individuals. Spain wants *all the East Side* of Mississipi.[1] Here I think we must absolutely refuse. Her other Wishes are complied with already in the discretionary Powers to Mr. Jay.

I have scratched these few Lines because the prints should not go without being accompanied with my Assurances of affection & Esteem,   Yr. most humble Servant, James Lovell

RC (NN: Emmet Collection). Endorsed by Laurens: "James Lovel 12 February 1780. Received 23d March."

[1] For Spain's interest in the war in America as outlined in the documents recently presented to Congress by the French minister, see *JCC*, 16:87–89, 102–9, 114–16; and Lovell to Samuel Adams, February 8, 1780.

Samuel Holten to the Massachusetts Council

Sir.   Phila. Feby. 14th. 1780, Monday 9 o'Clock A.M.

Mr. Cranch being about setting out to Boston sooner than I expected, affords me ownly time to mention: That, on Saturday last, Congress received a short letter from the Hone. Mr. Jay, dated Marti[nico] Decr. 20th, informing, that off the Banks of Newfound-Land, they lost their masts, sails, &c, and arrived there the day before; And by another letter that came in the same vessel, we understand, that Mr. Gerard, Mr. Jay & family, sailed the 26th of the same month in a french Frigate;[1] so that I hope the delay will not be so great as was feared at first.

By a late express from the state of Georgia, Congress have letters from Governor Walton informing, that, the assembly are again going on with business; by this you may see, it is not in the Power of our enemies to Govern one small state.[2]

I have the Honor to be, with great respect, sir, your most obedient servant;   S. Holten[3]

RC (M–Ar: Revolutionary War Letters). Addressed: "The Honorable The President of the Council of Massachusetts."

[1] This is undoubtedly the "letter from Mr. Bingham" referred to in the Connecticut Delegates' February 15 letter to Jonathan Trumbull, which may be the December 25 letter from William Bingham that was read in Congress on February 14 and referred to the Marine Committee. It is not in PCC. *JCC*, 16:164. Nevertheless, Jay did not leave Martinique until December 28. See Jay, *Papers* (Morris), 1:689.

[2] See Samuel Huntington to George Walton, this date.

[3] Holten also recorded in his diary for this day: "I wrote to the President of the council of Masachusetts per Post & to the Hone. J. Palmer Esqr. by Mr. Cranch." Holten Diary, MDaAr. The letter to Joseph Palmer has not been found.

Samuel Huntington to Benjamin Lincoln

Sir,   Philada Feby 14. 1780
    You will receive herewith enclosed two Acts of Congress of the 11 & 12 Instant.
    The former among other things approving the plan adopted by the State of Georgia for reducing the four Regiments of that State into one, for officering the same, and also the Regiment of Cavalry; and resolving that such Officers as cannot be employed in the line of that State be deemed supernumeraries and entitled to every Privilege with Officers in like Situation.
    This Act of Congress so far as it differs from any former Act relative to the same Subject you may have received you will consider as superseding the former.[1]
    By the other Act of the 12 Instant you will observe Congress have made provision for supplying the military Chest in your Department by such advances as the Governor and privy Council of the State of South Carolina shall be able to make for that purpose from [time] to time.[2]
    I have the honour to be, with much Esteem, your hble Servt.
                                                                  S.H.

LB (DNA: PCC, item 14).
    [1] In a resolve of January 8, Congress had directed that "the four Georgia regiments" be reorganized into no more than two, and empowered Lincoln "to establish some equitable rule for the arrangement of the said officers." On February 3, however, Congress received letters from the governor and the speaker of the assembly of Georgia explaining their recently adopted plan for reducing the four Georgia battalions to one of infantry and one of cavalry. This plan was immediately endorsed by Congress, which in the process also superseded its January 8 resolve on the subject. See *JCC*, 16:26–27, 122, 156; Huntington to Lincoln, January 8; and Huntington to Walton, this date.
    [2] See *JCC*, 16:154, 160. Huntington also enclosed a copy of this resolve with the following letter to South Carolina governor John Rutledge this day.
    "Your Excellency will receive herewith enclosed an Act of Congress of the 12 Instant requesting the Governor and privy Council of the State of South Carolina to advance from time to time to the military Chest such sums of Money being part of the taxes raised in that State for the Use of the United States as they on consulting the Commanding Officer in the Southern Department may find necessary for the public service there, advising the Board of Treasury thereof and for which the State is to be credited." PCC, item 14, fol. 297.

Samuel Huntington to George Walton

Sir,   Philadelphia Feby 14. 1780
    Your letter & also a letter from the Speaker of your Assembly which were forwarded by Capt Clement Nash have been duly received & laid before Congress though Captain Nash was stopped by Illness as he informs me by letter in Virginia.[1]

Enclosed you will receive an Act of Congress of the 11th Instant expressing their sense of the Exertions, firmness & Zeal manifested by the State of Georgia under all their difficulties, and likewise approving of the plan adopted by the State of Georgia for reducing the four Battallions, and having for their Quota the ensuing Campaign one Battallion of Infantry and one of Cavalry.[2]

That the supernumerary Officers be considered as, and entitled to all the privileges of other Supernumeraries in the continental Army.

I am also to inform you that a General Exchange of prisoners is now negotiating and I have informed General Washington of the Case of Colo Elbert which will have due attention paid to it, although Congress cannot at present promote Colo Elbert in the Continental Line.[3]

By the act of Congress of the 12th Instant[4] also herewith enclosed you will observe that a Warrant is issued in favour of the Governor & Executive Council of the State of Georgia on the Treasurer of Virginia for three hundred thousand Dollars and the Board of War are to take the proper Measures to convey the same to Georgia. The other Six thousand Dollars mentioned in the Act are advanced out of the Coninental Treasury here and paid into the hand of John Foster the Messenger whom Capt Nash sent forward from Virginia with the Despatches and who now returns with these.

I have the honour to be with much Esteem and respect, your hble Servt,   Sam. Huntington President

RC (N: Signers of the Declaration of Independence). In a clerical hand and signed by Huntington.

[1] Walton's December 15 letter to Congress and one of November 30, 1779, from Georgia speaker William Glascock are in PCC, item 73, fols. 250–65. Clement Nash's January 23 letter to Congress (written from "Cumberland Court House, Virginia"), in which he explained that ill health was forcing him to entrust John Foster with the delivery of these letters, is in PCC, item 78, 17:103–6. In reply, Huntington wrote the following letter to Nash, a captain in the 3d Georgia Battalion, this date.

"Your letter by John Foster together with the despatches from Georgia have been duly received and laid before Congress, and the same Messenger now returns, charged with this letter, with a number of Despatches of Importance for North & South Carolina & Georgia.

"These Despatches are of such Consequence they must not be delayed one Day and if you are not able to proceed immediately you must see them forwarded with the greatest despatch and Safety so as to prevent any delay or Miscarriage.

"I have procured to be advanced out of the Continental Treasury six thousand dollars and paid to the Bearer John Foster agreeable to your Request, also procured him a pair of Shoes and Saddle bags." PCC, item 14, fols. 300–301.

[2] The letters from Glascock and Walton had been read in Congress on February 3 and referred to a committee consisting of Thomas Burke, Cyrus Griffin, and John Mathews, who submitted a report on the 11th whose recommendations formed the core of the resolves transmitted herewith by Huntington. See *JCC*, 16:122, 155–56; and PCC, item 20, 2:441–42.

[3] For the case of Col. Samuel Elbert, whose exchange and promotion had been recommended by the Georgia Council, see Huntington to Washington, February 12, 1780.

[4] *JCC*, 16:160–61.

Connecticut Delegates to Jonathan Trumbull, Sr.

Sir   Philadelphia Feby. 15th. 1780
   Soon after our last Letter[1] was Sent off, Mr. Samuel Osgood
Arrived here from Boston who together with Mr. Gerry was Authorized to represent the State of Massachusetts in the Convention for
regulating prices, and Mr. Ellery also received a Commission from
the State of Rhode Island, whereupon it was thought Advisable for
the Convention to re-Assemble and after meeting Several times the[y]
came to Some resolutions which we have the Honr. now to transmit
to your Excellency.[2] It is uncertain whether any Measures for limiting prices will be finally Adopted. If the State of Connecticut Shall
think fit to pass a Law for that purpose in compliance with the
recommendation of Congress, We think it would be advisable to
Suspend the operation of it until they are advised that the other
States have passed Similar Laws.[3]
   We hope that Some Measures will be soon adopted for introducing a Stable medium of Trade that will render a limitation of prices
unnecessary.
   Congress received a Letter from Mr. Jay last Saturday, dated at
Martineco the 20th of December, giving an account that they Arrived
at that place the 19th of Decr, That the Confederacy in which they
Sailed had lost all her Masts and rigging and was other wise much
Damaged. By a letter from Mr Bingham We are informed Mr. Jay
and Mr. Gerrard Sailed from thence for France in a French Ship the
26th of Decr.[4]
   We need not Acquaint Your Excellency that the State of Connecti-
cut will not be represented in Congress after the first day of March
next unless a New Delegation arrives.[5]
   We are with great Esteem & Regard, Your Excellency's Obedient,
Humble Servants,   Roger Sherman

                              Oliver Ellsworth

RC (CtY: Roger Sherman Papers). Written by Sherman, and signed by Sherman and
Ellsworth.
   [1] See Connecticut Delegates to Trumbull, January 26, 1780.
   [2] The document transmitted to Governor Trumbull was undoubtedly the same as
that sent this day to Rhode Island, for which see the enclosure to the following entry;
and Trumbull, *Papers* (MHS Colls.), 3:15–17.
   [3] The Connecticut Assembly did pass an act regulating prices in 1780, but it was
apparently not put into effect. *Public Records of Connecticut*, 2:568n.
   [4] See Samuel Holten to the Massachusetts Council, February 14, 1780, note 1.
   [5] The new credentials of the Connecticut delegates were read in Congress on March
1. *JCC*, 16:219.

William Ellery to William Greene

Sir,   Philadelphia Feby. 15th, 1780.

In Consequence of the powers, for meeting a convention for limiting prices, with which the State was pleased to invest me,[1] I joined it; and, after frequent meetings, we came to the resolutions which are herein inclosed. I did not forget to move and urge the convention to recommend to such States as had passed laws laying restrictions on inland trade, or inland embargoes to repeal them; but they did not chuse to come to any determination thereon until they should have decided on the subject of regulating prices, and so the motion is postponed.

For news &c I beg leave to refer your Excellency to Mr Collins's & my joint letter,[2] and am with great respect, Your Excellency's most obedient humble Servant,   William Ellery

ENCLOSURE

In Convention Monday Feby. 7th. 1780

Whereas at a Meeting of the several States of New Hampshire, Massachusetts, Rhode Island & Providence Plantations, Connecticut, & New York holden at Hartford in Connecticut on the 20th of October 1779, It was then resolved that a Convention of Commissioners from the States of New Hampshire, Massachusetts, Rhode Island & Providence Plantations, Connecticut, New York, New Jersey, Pennsylvania, Delaware & Maryland, & Virginia be requested to meet at Philadelphia on the first Wednesday of January then next for the Purpose of Considering the Expediency of limiting the Prices of Merchandize & Produce.[3]

And whereas in Consequence thereof, Commissioners have met in Convention from the States of New Hampshire, Massachusetts, Rhode Island & Providence Planatations, Connecticut, New Jersey, Pennsylvania, Delaware & Maryland.

And whereas, the Assembly of the State of New York has not met since the Adjournment of the Convention at Hartford; but did previously authorize her Delegates to Pledge the Faith of the State for carrying into Effect a general Plan for regulating Prices, if recommended by Congress, & this Convention have the fullest Assurance that the Measures which they may adopt will be agreed to by said State.

And whereas, it is the Opinion of this Convention, that any Measures for regulating Prices, adopted, without the Concurrence of all the States, proposed by the Convention at Hartford might prove ineffectual.

Therefore Resolved, That the President be desired to inform the Governor of the State of Virginia of the Proceedings of this Convention: & request him to give the earliest Notice of the Determinations of said State with Respect to the Appointment of Commissioners to meet this Convention.

Resolved that the State of New York be in like Manner informed of the Proceedings of this Convention, & be requested to appoint Commissioners to meet the same at their Adjournment.[4]

Resolved that a Committee be appointed to form a general Plan for the Limitation of Prices in the several States & Report the same at the next Meeting of this Convention.

Resolved, that the President,[5] Mr. Ellery, Mr. Gerry, Mr. Paca, & Mr. Henry of Pennsylvania be a Committee for the Purpose aforesaid.

Present

New Hampshire	{ Mr Fulsom
	Mr. Peabody
Massachusetts	{ Mr. Gerry
	Mr. Osgood
Rhode Island	Mr. Ellery
Connecticut	{ Mr. Sherman
	Mr. Ellsworth
Pennsylvania	{ Mr. Henry
	Mr. Bull[6]
Delaware	Mr. Vandyke
Maryland	Mr. Henry[7]

Adjourned to Tuesday 6 oClock P.M.

Then Met according to Adjournment [i.e., on February 8].

Resolved, that the Adjournment of this Convention be to the fourth of April next; to meet at the State House in the City of Philadelphia. And it was accordingly adjourned.

Extract from the Minutes. Attest Samuel Osgood Secy.

RC (R–Ar: Letters to Governors). Enclosure (R–Ar). In the hand of Samuel Osgood.

[1] For Ellery's appointment and credentials as a commissioner to this convention, see Staples, *Rhode Island*, p. 269; and *Public Records at Connecticut*, 2:574. For the background of the convening of this body, see Samuel Huntington to the States, November 22, 1779; and Roger Sherman to Andrew Adams, January 7, 1780, note 2.

[2] See Rhode Island Delegates to Greene, this date.

[3] See Samuel Holten to the Massachusetts Council, November 11, 1779, note 3.

[4] Although New Jersey had not been represented at this convention, the state was not included in this call to Virginia and New York simply because such a request had already been directed to the New Jersey commissioners, Silas Condict and Thomas Fenimore, pursuant to a convention resolve of January 29. See *Public Records of Connecticut*, 2:577.

[5] William Moore, the vice president of the Pennsylvania Council.

[6] William Henry and John Bull.

[7] Former Maryland delegate John Henry.

Elbridge Gerry to Samuel Adams

My dear sir,   Philadelphia 15th Feby 1780
    I am much obliged to You for your Favour of the 20th Decr by
Major Osgood, who reached this City the 25th January, & left it for
Boston the 12th Instant. From him You will be able to collect a more
particular Account of the Proceedings of the Convention, than what
is contained in the Papers inclosed,[1] & also some Information respecting Congress, who are at present engaged in leving a Tax in Kind
for the next Campaign.
    I am happy to find that the Children of our late worthy Friend
General Warren are in better Circumstances than what were represented in the proposed Subscription, but am nevertheless desirous
that something may be done for their honorable Support, by
Congress, the State, or private Benefactors. The Intention of Congress will soon be Known, & should the Sense of the State be taken
on the Subject, it may then be ascertained whether any & what
further provission will be necessary for the purpose mentioned. In
Case of a private Subscription I really wish that it may originate in
the State & that We may have an Oppertunity of promoting it; but
cannot consent to joyn in one that in its *Origin* or *Nature*, is disrespect-
ful to the State.[2]

Feby. 18th. I have detained this Letter a Day or two to give You
some Information respecting the L——e of P——a[3] which are laying
the Foundation of what appears to me an undue, indirect, but extensive Influence, &, if so, will require the Attention of the other States;
but the Business of Congress respects Matters of great Consequence
to the three eastern States & will not admit for the present of other
Speculations. My best Respects to Mrs & Miss Adams, the Doctor &
all our other Friends & be assured that I remain sir yours sincerely,
                                                        E Gerry

RC (NN: Adams Papers).
  [1] For Gerry's enclosure, see the preceding entry. He and Samuel Osgood, in their
capacities as Massachusetts commissioners to the Philadelphia convention for regulating prices had already sent a copy of the same proceedings to the president of the
Massachusetts Council with the following brief cover letter of February 11. "Agreeable
to the Commission, with which We were honored to represent the State in the Convention lately held in this city, We embrace the earliest Oppertunity of reporting their
proceedings, & request You to communicate the same." Gerry endorsed his draft of
this letter: "NB. In the Above was inclosed a Copy of the Journals of the Convention
to the present Day." Private collectionn of Mr. Ronald von Klausen, 1985.
  [2] Undoubtedly a reference to Benedict Arnold's effort to raise funds for Joseph
Warren's children, for which see the Massachusetts Delegates to Samuel Adams and
John Hancock, November 19, 1779.
  [3] That is, the Legislature of Pennsylvania. However, the source of the concern
expressed here by Gerry has not been discovered and the legislature's published
proceedings for this period provide no evidence that something was afoot that might
"requir the Attention of the other States."

Samuel Huntington to Lachlan McIntosh

Sir,   Philada Feby 15. 1780
    You will receive herewith enclosed an Extract of two letters, the one from Govr Walton, the other from Mr Glascock Speaker of the Assembly together with an Act of Congress of this Day, by which you will be informed that Congress deem it inexpedient to employ you at present in the Southern Army and that your Service in that Department be dispensed with until the further Order of Congress.[1]
    I am Sir &c,   S.H.

LB (DNA: PCC, item 14).
[1] The letters from Georgia's governor George Walton and speaker William Glascock noted here had been received by Congress on February 3 and referred to committee. The extracts from these letters that were sent to General McIntosh and used to justify Congress' surprising decision to remove him from the southern department without consulting either Washington or the commander of the southern department, Benjamin Lincoln, contained the charge that McIntosh did not enjoy the confidence of Georgians and therefore his presence in a position of command there impaired the state's ability to resist the enemy. As the Georgia Assembly phrased the matter, in the document bearing Glascock's name: "the common dissatisfaction is such, and that founded on weighty reasons, it is highly necessary that Congress would, whilst that Officer is in the service of the United States, direct some distant field for the exercise of his abilities."
    The committee to whom the letters were submitted merely recommended that General Lincoln "be directed to employ Genl McIntosh in the State of South Carolina, or elsewhere out of the State of Georgia," but Congress ignored this recommendation when it debated the committee's report on February 11, and instead adopted four days later the "Act" enclosed to McIntosh. See *JCC*, 16:122, 155–56, 168–70; and PCC, item 20, 2:441–42.
    The singular nature of this action did not become apparent until much later when McIntosh attempted to determine responsibility for his removal, and in the process elicited a formal denial from William Glascock that he had sent the document containing the accusation against McIntosh quoted above. In a May 12, 1780, letter to Congress, Glascock even asserted that McIntosh had been an able officer and "ought to receive the Grateful testimonials of Publick approbation, instead of the malicious insinuations of Private Slander." But it was not until September 6 that Glascock's disavowal was read in Congress, and although a committee was appointed to inquire into the case, Congress was then in no position to conduct much of an investigation as the British were in possession of most of Georgia and South Carolina and had captured McIntosh. After consulting the Georgia delegates then attending Congress— George Walton and Richard Howly, members of the anti-McIntosh group that had originally secured his removal—the committee merely reported that the information available to Congress in February had constituted "sufficient ground" for the general's dismissal, and Congress immediately endorsed the report. McIntosh eventually was vindicated in Congress in 1781 and in Georgia in 1783 after he was released by the British, but the matter was never cleared up to his satisfaction, and the historians who have probed the controversy have not dispelled much of the mystery surrounding the case. See *JCC*, 17:551, 804, 18:861; PCC, item 73, fols. 250–73, item 162, fols. 297, 314–20; Harvey H. Jackson, *Lachlan McIntosh and the Politics of Revolutionary Georgia* (Athens, Ga.: University of Georgia Press, 1979), pp. 115–27; and Alexander A. Lawrence, "General Lachlan McIntosh and His Suspension from Continental Command during the Revolution," *Georgia Historical Quarterly* 38 (June 1954): 101–41. See also George Walton's Memorial, September 7; and Richard Howly's Statement, September 9? 1780.

Robert R. Livingston to George Clinton

Dear Sir   Philadelphia 15th Feby 1780
   It is late & I feel fatigued with the business of the day, Yet I can
not let the Post slip without leting you know the news of the town as
it relates to a friend in whose happiness I know you interest yourself.
We were all very happy the day before yesterday at recg a letter
from Mr. Jay, but on opening we found it dated at Martinique,
where he was driven after loosing all his Masts & Bowsprit, off the
Banks of Newfoundland. He got in to Martinique the 19th Decr and
left it in a french frigate the 26. all well on board. On the day of their
arrival the english fleet from St Lucy engaged a fleet of merchantmen
under convoy of a frigate, & notwithstanding a gallant attempt of
Monsr La Motte Pequet with 3 ships to relieve them took 14 of
them. The English have a decided superiority at sea in the west
Indias, owing to the storm that divided the french fleet. The Minister tells me that he has acc[ount]s from Europe so late as Novr, the
combined fleet was then preparing for sea under Mr Chaffant, Count
D'Olivers being removed from the command,[1] great preparations
were making on both sides to carry on the war with spirit—the
ensuing summer, & very little prospect of a peace.
   I have yet recd no papers from Mr Scott, nor do I hear when he or
Mr Duane are to come on.[2] By this means I am prevented from
availing myself of the Snow to bring Mrs Livingston home, which I
had intended. Her situation will prevent her travelling in any other
way so that I shall be detained in the Jersies till June for which
reason I shall have no objection if I am not dismissed immediately to
continue in the delegation, till I can return if the Legislature shd
think it necessary, you may intimate this to Benson if you think it
proper tho' by no means as a request of mine since I have not a wish
about it.
   I shd be glad to know whether they are like to pass such a support
bill as will enable me to keep my office. My expences this winter and
the oppressive taxes which I am charged render it necessary for me
to look about me, surely they shd think my whole time a sufficient
tax, & give me as much for my services as will discharge them, I ask
no more, or what is still less that they would suffer me to depart in
peace. I have many temptations to fix my self here. But more of that
hereafter. I am Dr Sir, With the highest respect & esteem, Yr Excellencys Most Obt Humble Servt,   R R Livingston

Tr (DLC: George and James Clinton Papers).
   [1] Actually Lt. Gen. Louis-Charles, comte Du Chaffault de Besné, had been named
French fleet commander after Louis Guillonet, comte D'Orvilliers, had resigned the
post, apparently for personal reasons. Jonathan R. Dull, *The French Navy and American
Independence* (Princeton, N.J.: Princeton University Press, 1975), p. 164.
   [2] John Morin Scott first attended Congress on March 6; James Duane did not
resume his seat until May 1. See *JCC*, 16:230, 399.

Rhode Island Delegates to William Greene

Sir,   Philadelphia Feby. 15th. 1780.

Congress have come to sundry resolutions, determining the number of privates of which the army is to consist, and adjusting the quotas of the States; which we suppose are sent to the State;[1] but as it is possible that they may not reach your Excellency so early as this letter, we will just mention that the whole number of privates is to be thirty five thousand, and our quota eight hundred and ten. We objected to the quota assigned to our state, and proposed that it should not exceed seven hundred men; but were not able to procure any reduction. Several other States made similar objections; but it was thought too late to alter the adjustments and set the matter afloat, and so the report stands as it was offer'd by the board of war, only with the qualifying resolution added to it which you will take notice of.

We received a letter last Saturday from Mr. Jay, our minister to the Court of Madrid, informing us that the Confederacy, off the banks of Newfoundland, met with a violent Storm which carried away her masts and Bowspreet, and obliged her to put away for Martinico where she arrived the 19th of December. His letter was dated the 20th. He further advises us that a British Squadron from St Lucia fell in with about 25 french merchant Vessels, under convoy of a frigate, off and bound to Martinico. That the enemy took 14 of them and drove too ashore. Monsieur De le' Mothe Pequet was dispatch'd to persue them as soon as possible, but, his force being inferior to the enemy, it was not in his power to recover the capture.

Mr. Bingham, our agent at Martinico, in a letter of a later date mentions that Mr. Jay sailed in the Aurora frigate for France the 26th of December.

We are told that there are letters in Town from St. Eustatius so late as the middle of January; but not a word of news from Europe.

The Georgians have organized Government, and are determined to hold their State as long as they can. The Seat of Government is at Augusta. The Spaniards have taken possession of the British Settlements on the Mississippi; and a respectable fleet with 4000 troops sailed from Havannah for Pensacola or Augustine, or both the beginning of December. Affairs wear a better aspect to the Southward than they did some time ago. We have not received any intelligence respecting the famous fleet from New York since it sailed.

We have nothing further to add at present but that we are with great respect, Your Excellency's most obedt. humble Servts.

William Ellery

John Collins

P.S. Genl. Lincoln in a letter bearing date Jany. 8th[2] informs that by the last accounts from Savannah he was informed "that the 60th

Regiment was order'd to St Augustine. The enemy seem to be alarmed at the movements of the Spaniards. We do not know yet the fate of Mobille or of Pensacola. There is some reason to believe that they are both in the hands of the Spaniards; this is undoubtedly the report in Savannah. I have it from deserters and Mr. Cowen one of our Offs. who lately left it. What foundation there is for the report or what gave rise to it I know not. I have my doubts with respect to the fact, though I think it my duty & that I may safely give the hint on mentioning my authority." "I am just informed that 6 or 700 of the No. Carolina militia are arrived at Camden." Camden is 126 miles from Charlestown. The No. Carolina Contl. Brigade were pushing on with forced marches.   W E

RC (R–Ar: Letters to Governors). Written by Ellery and signed by Ellery and Collins.
[1] See Samuel Huntington to the States, February 10, 1780.
[2] Lincoln's letter, addressed "to the committee for corresponding with the commanding officer in the southern department," was read in Congress this day but is not now in PCC. *JCC*, 16:167. However, a letter of the same date to General Washington, containing similar intelligence on the capture of Mobile and Pensacola, is in the Washington Papers, DLC.

John Armstrong, Sr., to Horatio Gates

Carlisle 16th Feby. 1780. Expresses his "uneasy feellings and anxious apprehensions, on the distracted & melancholly State of our finances. . . .

"The first, and fundamental remidy is the *Regulation of Prices* through all our States by the publick *Authority of Law.* 2d, a Speedy determined and judicious *Reformation* of mistakes or abuses, in the two great departments *of the Staff*, including in it a *Retrenchment of Expences*, Offices and Officers—and this by the by, cannot in my Opinion be effected otherwise—than by the Several States, or their Commissioners, perhaps best appointed in their respective Counties. 3d, The laying in of certain quantities of Grain, at the expence of the Owners in Such Magazines as may be appointed, for which Carriage a moderate Miliage may be allowed, except in the distance of five miles, The Grain to be delivered at the regulated price, or pass in whole, or in part of the Owners Tax. These measures at Once Simple, regular & virtuous, aided by such taxation as the people can bear, which by the way must be greatly lessened to what it now is—and by Domestick Loans, will by the Divine blessing carry us on until a foreign Loan can have time to Operate. But if these Steps be declined, I dread to mention the approaching consequences. As for the Chimerically refined notions of Finance which some men have thrown out, they must be considered as so many Phantoms. The plain highway of Regulation by Law, appears now by fatal experience & dint of necessity the only rational line of our direction—and however doubtfull may have been that such a Law cou'd not be put in execution, the more disinterested people here are lamenting the delay of this measure, and grieved to hear that very lately Virginia had Sent no Commissio[ne]rs to assist in binding up the bleeding wounds of this Country—Shall they bleed to death, altho' made with our hands! is not this a kind of National Suicide? Shall poor Jersey be constrained to repeal her virtuous Law? have we now any known value annexed to our currency even for the Space of One Week. Is not all rational calculation at an end, and the use of figures become futile—are we not well pictured by a Ship on the Ocean without Helm or Rudder left to the mercy of the waves! But thanks to god only who commands the waves of our political Sea & may yet vouchsafe to take the helm into his Omnipotent hand. He reigns, let every honest heart & genuine Whigg be Glad! A wise & vigorous regulation must prove to our affairs at present as the main spring of a Watch to the wheels—no matter how many lesser amendments are made in our finances or how proper in themselves, if not fixed on this basis, the disease will recur—palliate they may & but a little— Cure they can not, having no radical powers. As to the Merchantile rule or Hackneyed Maxim that Trade only can regulate itself, I can Scarcely Speak of it with patience, but shall only Say that Obstructed as our commerce is abroad by the Enemy, and by Speculators & Monopolizers, perverted at home, that general rule is with us highly exceptionable, and none but the interested or unobservant part of Our Countrymen can with any propriety plead it in opposition to a regulation by Law, which however arduous, is compelled by the present state of affairs and justified by necessity, as is every act, whether National or personal, that has virtue for it's motive & end."

RC (NHi: Gates Papers).

James Lovell to Samuel Adams

Dear Sir   Feby. 16 1780

I wrote yesterday[1] by Post of the Disaster which the *Confederacy* met with near the Banks of Newfoundland when she lost her Bowsprit, masts, Yards and part of her Sails, her Rudder also being split. She however carried her Passengers into Martinique on the 19 of Decr. from whence they sailed again for France in the Frigate Aurora, on the 25th of that same month.

I inclosed you yesterday two Letters from Genl. Lincoln which he wished safe, I had no right to franc the two now inclosed; and besides, I thought that the dividing the four sent to my Care would give a Chance of conveying News from the Southward to the Generals family by the *first* Oppertunity, which is a Thing in doubt between the Post & Express, tho the Post has *now* the Start. The Enemy, at the

Time of the General's Writing (Jan 8th) had got to be allarmed about St. Augustine and were sending some of their Troops from Savanna to that Place. No Sight of the Enemy's Fleet was had at Charlestown 16 Days after sailing from New York. Perhaps the News Paper of this Day may retail the Reports from Virginia of another Kind, a quite contrary one.

Congress has taken so much notice of Govr *Geo Walton's* Complaints about Brig McIntosh as to inform him his Service in the southern Department is dispensed with, conveying to him a Copy of the Governor's Letter and a Paragraph of one from the Speaker of the Georgia Assembly.[2] The Spirit of that State, as it appears in those Letters is excellent. Waltons Letter was directed to you or any of the *old members* from Massachusetts, and Gerry & I have not slighted the fair occasion of cultivating that Confidence which seemed to be placed *now* in a Spirit which some of Brownson's Colleagues did not formerly coalesce with as he did. Govr. Walton says he shall certainly be here in the Spring. I suppose as a Delegate special if not general.

I hope there has been no printed mention of my going abroad. Your News Papers are remarkable lately for more groundless Paragraphs than most others. I have been told of my name, having thus got in. But I am far from Embarking and I own I am pleased, since I find how much Cabal enters into the Business. We are to discuss next Satday the Proposition for appointing a *Resident* with his official Powers to go to France instead of a *Secy* to the Embassy. This will dignify the Place enough for R R Livingston:[3] and I am somewhat inclined to think that our Affairs here make several wish to be away from the fatigue which they cause. I do not like the Scale of Influence abroad should have Weights from New York rather than from some other State. But I shall not encline to stand against R R L in the Nomination for the new Office tho I will always allow myself to stand as a Check upon Gr M——s.[4]

Upon the whole I must begin to think altogether of getting along thro' the War as well as possible upon the old Ground of drudge hard & fare hard too; which is the Lot of most of the faithful in our Cause.

I dare not believe the Paragraph from Virginia, in the Paper inclosed.[5]

I believe I must forward my Accounts to Boston that I may get the Balances of the 3 years back, what was due in 77 would have so cloathed me that I should not need now to spend twice more for one Suit than I sent my Family through all that Year. 70 Dollrs. I pay for worstead Hose.

Yours affectionately,   J L

RC (NN: Adams Papers).
[1] Not found, and in Adams' March 5 reply acknowledging letters recently received from Lovell, none of February 15 is listed. Adams, *Writings* (Cushing), 4:180–81.

[2] See Samuel Huntington to George Walton, February 14, and to Lachlan McIntosh, February 15, 1780.

[3] See Robert R. Livingston to John Jay, February 10, 1779, note 3.

[4] That is, Gouverneur Morris.

[5] Lovell probably enclosed a copy of this day's *Pennsylvania Gazette* which contained an "extract of a letter from York in Virginia" reporting that "the enemy has evacuated Savannah on a certainty."

James Lovell to Benjamin Lincoln

Dear General[1]   Feb. 16. 1780

I have recd. yr. favors up to Janry. 8th and have forwarded regularly the Letters which you inclosed to my Care. You must not expect very regular Answers to them from the Interruptions to Journying caused by the severest Winter we have known since 1740, I mean severe as to Snow chiefly.

We begin to made Shuttle Cocks of as usual when the Enemy are in yr. Quarter. I suspend all Belief but on your Letters, therefore let us have them as often as your greater Business will permit.

You will hear from the Comtee. who receive your Letters,[2] what our State of Finance & Supply of Food & Rayment is or rather is not, Yet we are to look for a vigorous Campaign. I hope the States are rousing from a Sort of Lethargy, and that they will be able to carry on the next Campaign well notwithstanding the ill Appearances of the present moment.

As to Penobscot we hear almost nothing. But it will be taken into the Plans of Opperation for our Army *when recruited.*

So extensive a Continent calls for great Numbers of Defendants & we can find but few though it is a Land of Plenty, unless Avarice will relax a little of its harpy Demands upon our Treasury.

Our State have determined to make good the Pay of their Troops for 3 years back, and have determined a Scale of Depreciation by a mean Ratio on the 4 Commodities of Beef, Indian Corn, Sheeps Wool & Soal Leather taken monthly from Jany. 77 to Jan 80, the last amountg. to 32, 50 [hundreths?][3] for 1. This is turning the Tables upon the Farmers with a Vengeance I think. But yet Farmers must have done it in Court.

I am, likely, to drudge on here another Year, and will be ready for rendering you any Services in my Power but trying to draw you from the Southward till Things look more favorably in that Quarter.

Your affectionate, humble Servant,   James Lovell

[*P.S.*] All our Family join me in Love & Esteem for you.

RC (NN: Emmet Collection).

[1] The recipient of this letter was undoubtedly Gen. Benjamin Lincoln, from whom a letter of January 8 to the "committee for corresponding" with the southern depart-

ment had just been received and read in Congress on February 15. See Rhode Island Delegates to William Greene, February 15, note 2.

[2] That is, "the committee for corresponding with the commanding officer in the southern department."

[3] Lovell wrote what appears to be the word "hundreths" above the line at this point.

Abraham Clark to the New Jersey Assembly

Sir   Philada. Febry. 17. 1780

The Convention for regulating prices have Adjourned till April and I fear the Attempt will prove Abortive, Virginia seems to hang back, no members have attended from thence, and as far as I can learn none have been Appointed, and their Legislature stands Adjourned till May. I shudder at the prospects before us, a Virgorous War to prosecute, while our money reduced almost to nothing, is Still depreciating with rapidity. The Current exchange here between hard money & paper is from 45 to 50 for one. In the Market, a paper Dollar is estimated at present at one penny and will soon be less than a half penny in all probability.

Congress have now under Consideration the Apportionment of Supplies for the Army to be required of each state the present year,[1] One [Our] Quota at present stands at 18000 hundred weight of Beef or pork, 10,000 barrels of Flour, 3,758 bushels of Salt, 3,500 Tons of hay, 30,000 bushels of Corn, Oats or buckwheat.[2] The Estimate of Prices, as follows. Flour 4 1/2 Dollars per hundred, Summer fatted Beef 5 1/2 dollr per neat hundred, fall fatted Do. 6 1/2 dollars, Stall fed killed after Janry. 7 1/2 Dollars, fresh pork 7 dollars per neat hundred; Salted pork 22 dollars per barrl. containing 240 lb. Indian Corn, 3/4 dollar per bushl., Oats 1/2, Rie 1, Buckwheat 2/3 dollar per bushl., best first crop hay 15 dollrs. per Ton, Rum 1 1/2 dollrs. per Gall, Salt 3 dollars per bushl.

For my part I dislike the plan altogether, as purchases ought to be made where most Convenient having regard to the places where they are to be consumed & the prices in the several states which must depend upon the seasons in them, but I am assured the plan is Agreable to the wishes of our Legislature, by whose Opinion I shall Always be governed. The Salt I fear will be procured with difficulty in our state, but as the prices above Are all Estimated in Specie & that Article Set at 3 dollars, I dare not refuse it to our State, Specially as other states wish for that Article and offer to take it from us in exchange for flour or Other provisions at the Estimated prices—but as Salt is much higher estimated than any other Article, I think we may exchange provisions for it to much greater Advantage by private Contractor perhaps, by promoting the Manufactory of Iron on publick Acct. we may procure that Article of Salt in exchange for Iron and save our provisions. In Case our Legislature shall desire to be freed from procuring the Salt by taking upon them the Supply of Other Articles Equivalent in Value as Estimated, by Signifying their pleasure thereon, I am persuaded the matter can be affected.

Thus far I had wrote before Congress took up the business of Supplies this Day. They had before gone through the Quotas and now took into Consideration the Prices as reported by the Comme. and have Agreed to the price for flour as Above mentioned. The next under Consideration was the Price of Beef, this is not finished but will I believe pass agreable to the report—more of us would be willing to Alter some Articles did we not see that it would deraing all we had before done without any Material Advantage, so that the Prices I have mention[ed], tho' only as reported from a Come. from Each state will I believe be Agreed to. Should any material Alteration take place so as to affect our state, we shall Attempt a reconsideration of the Quotas.

I am with all due respects to the General Assembly, your Obedt. & Humble Servt.   Abra. Clark

RC (Nj: State Papers). Addressed: "Caleb Camp Esqr., Speaker."

[1] See Samuel Huntington to the States, February 26, 1780.

[2] New Jersey's quota as stated here by Clark remained the same in the resolve adopted on February 25. Cf. *JCC*, 16:196.

John Fell to Robert Morris

My Dear sir,   Philadelphia Feby 17th. 1780.

Yesterday I had the Pleasure of Receiving your kind favour of the 8th Instt. Per Mr Erskine, and am realy sorry to hear of the very disagreeable situation of our distressd County. Since I Receivd your favour from Mount holly I have never had an oppertunity of writing you or certainly I should have done myself the Pleasure.

You mention the Reform that you hope has taken Place in Philada. For my Part I know of no kind of Reformation, without disapation and extravigance can be deem'd so, to tell you the real truth, I never live'd so disagreeable in all my Life, (*except in the Provost*) and I some times have my doubts which is best. I want to see you exceedingly, do you not intend to come to Philadelphia, if you do, let me know, and if not, I shall do myself the Pleasure of waiting on you at Trenton; I have not yet heard of Mrs Fells arrival at home.

If any inquireing friends at Trenton, Please to Remember me kindly to them; As the Post goes through Trenton twice a Week, I shall now and then ask you how you do. We are now in debate on the Report of the Committee of 12. Respecting the Quotas to be furnish'd per the several States it is, as Reports of this kind usualy are, subject to many amendments, I am under the Necessity of hearing and not speaking. I have got a bad Cold and am so hoarse I can hardly be heard, (Mr. Clark speaks my opinion on the subject).

I am with great Respect, Your Sincar friend,   John Fell

Friday Feby 18th. When I wrote the above, I thought it was Post-day; I am told Mr. Houston is gone this morning to Princeton. He Proposes staying about a fortnight, and when he returns If Posible I will Pay you a visit.

I am as above,   J. Fell

RC (NjR: Robert Morris Papers).

Elbridge Gerry to John Clark

Dear sir,   Philadelphia Feby 17. 1780
    I have only Time to acknowledge the Receipt of your Favour of the 7th Instant, & to inform You that some of the Gentlemen of the Board of Treasury have lately spoken to me upon the Subject of your Petition & appeared desirous of making You a full Compensation for your Services & Expences.[1] As they have done me the Honor of requesting my Opinion on the Matter, I shall confer with them again on this Business & endeavour to have it compleated. I remain sir with Esteem, your Friend & humble sert,   E Gerry

RC (DNA: PCC, item 41).
[1] For Major Clark's petition for reimbursement, see Gerry to Clark, November 16, 1779, note.

Connecticut Delegates to Joseph Reed

Sir,   [February 18, 1780][1]
    The proposition referred to in your Excellency's letter of yesterday,[2] was duly transmitted to the Governor of the State of Connecticut; to which their delegates in Congress have yet received no answer. They are ready, however, to receive any communication relative to the Subject of it, from the Committee of the State of Pensylvania which they may think proper to make, & to attend for that purpose at the council chamber this evening at 6 o'Clock, or such other time as may be more convenient for the Committee.
    We are, Sir, with much respect, Your Excellency's most obedt, humbl Servts,   Roger Sherman,

                                                  Oliver Ellsworth.

MS not found; reprinted from *Pa. Archives*, 1st ser., 8:112–13.
[1] This undated letter was clearly written the day after Pennsylvania president Joseph Reed wrote the February 17 "letter of yesterday" to the Connecticut delegates discussed below.

² In his February 17 letter, Reed had asked the Connecticut delegates to confer with a committee of the Pennsylvania assembly and council concerning Pennsylvania's November 18, 1779, proposal to settle the Wyoming Valley dispute "in the manner directed in" the Articles of Confederation. *Pa. Archives*, 1st ser., 8:111–12.

Although the Connecticut delegates' response to Reed has not been found, their state assembly had already decided to oppose the Pennsylvania offer for the present. Presumably they soon learned of this decision and communicated it to him accordingly. See Roger Sherman to Jonathan Trumbull, December 20, 1779, note 3.

Committee on Appeals Decree

Feby. 19th. 1780.

David Brooks &c. Lib[ellan]ts & App[ell]ees ⎫   On Motion
vs. The Schooner Hope & her Cargo ⎬   for a New Trial
Aaron Lopez Claim[an]t and App[ellan]t ⎭

We the Commissioners appointed by Congress to hear, try and determine all Appeals &c. from the Courts of Admiralty of the several American States to Congress having heard the Petition exhibited on the Part of the Appellees in the above Cause praying that a new Trial might be granted them by this Court upon the said Appeal and having also heard the Arguments of the Advocates as well on the Part of the Appellants as the Appellees abovenamed and taken Time to consider thereof Do thereupon adjudge and decree that the Causes assigned are not sufficient in Law to induce this Court to grant a new Trial and do therefore dismiss the said Petition with Costs And we do hereby assess the said Costs at Eight hundred and forty Dollars which Sum we do adjudge that the Parties Appellee pay unto the said Appellant for his Costs and Charges by him expended in supporting his Appeal and the Sentence heretofore by this Court pronounced thereupon &c.

Tho. M.Kean   Cyrus Griffin

William Ellery   Ezra L'Hommedieu

MS (DNA: RG 267, case no. 28). In a clerical hand, and signed by Ellery, Griffin, L'Hommedieu, and McKean.

¹ For further information on the case of the schooner *Hope*, which was owned by Aaron Lopez of Newport, R.I., see Committee on Appeals Decree, April 10, 1779, these *Letters*, 12:323–24.

Elbridge Gerry to Samuel Huntington

Sir,   Philadelphia Feby 19. 1780

The Decision of Congress yesterday that I was not in Order in requiring the Yeas & Nays on the question of Order respecting the Motion which I had then the Honor to make appears to me to be contrary to the *Rules & Practice* of the House & to deprive me of the privilege of a Member thereof.¹

The *Rules* alluded to, are contained in the 10th & 12th articles of those which were passed by Congress the 26th May 1778.[2]

The *Practice* referred to may be seen in the printed Journals of Congress of the Year 1779, wherein the Yeas & Nays have been taken on Questions of Order as follows: April 22, May 14th & 24, June 8th, July 30th, Octr 30th & Decr 18th.[3]

Having as I conceive clearly shewn that requiring Yeas & Nays on questions of Order is warranted by the Rules & practice of the House, It may be proper to observe, that the following paragraph of a Report Vizt "Beef best grass fed which shall be delivered between the first of July & the 1st of Decr. Shall be 5 1/2 Dollers, per hundred" was under the Consideration of Congress yesterday when I moved "that the paragraph of the Report of the Committee respecting the prices of Articles which were restricted agreable to the late Act of the State of N Jersey, be recommitted, & that the price of Flower is fixed by Congress agreable to the price agreed on by the Convention of the States from New Hampshire to Pennsylvania inclusively, held at N Haven in January 1778 the Committee be directed to adjust the prices of other Articles in the proportions adopted by the Convention"—& that upon a question, whether the Motion was in order, I appealed to the House & required the Yeas & Nays, whereupon the president taking the Sense of the House declared that the calling the Yeas & Nays in this Case was by the House determined to be out of Order.

If the Decision of the House affected me only in a private Capacity, I should not hesitate a Moment to pass it over in Silence, altho my Feelings would be injured by being denied a privilege which other Members under similar Circumstances had enjoyed; but as it affects me in a publick Character, I am reduced to the disagreeable Alternative of giving up what appears to me an important privilege of a Member of the House, or of defending the same against the Determinations of a Body whose Honor I have much at Heart & shall always endeavour to support. The former, I am not authorized to do & therefore I shall defend the privilege to the best of my abilities & leave the State which I have the Honor to represent to do the Rest.

Congress have wisely endeavoured so to frame their Rules, as to give every Member an Opportunity of shewing his Conduct to his Constituents, & I hold this as a privilege essential to the Interest of the publick, & to the Honor of every Member of Congress; for without it should a Majority of the Members at any Time be arbitrary both in principles & practice, which I sincerely hope will never be the Case, they would oblige the others to leave the House, or suffer unmerited Censure.

In the present Case many precedents have been & more may be produced to shew that the Yeas & Nays have been frequently called on questions of Order, some of which have been determined in the Affirmative & others in the Negative; & if the House undertakes to determine on what Motions the question of Order shall be decided by Yeas & Nays, I conceive that their Rules will only serve as Cobwebs to catch Flies, or in other words as pretexts to enable a Majority, if arbitrary, to bring on the Journals such part of the Conduct of each Member as they may think proper, & thus put a favorable Appearance on their own unjustifiable proceedings, whilst they stigmatize those of the Minority, however wise or vertuous.

I think it peculiarly hard in the present Case, when the paragraph of a Report was under the Consideration of Congress, which as it respected some of the States appeared to me to operate great Injustice, & I made a Motion to prevent it, that the Question of Order should be agitated; that the Decision of the House thereon should preclude me from their Sense on the Motion, & that whatever Reason I may have to suppose that Decision improper, I should be prevented from shewing the Impropriety or even the *Existence* thereof.

The House will probably remember that in a similar Case, when the Report for recruiting the Army was under Consideration, I waved my privilege of appealing to the House on the question of Order, to prevent Altercations on the question of privilege, & afterwards produced to them many of the precedents quoted herein, in Hopes, that by convincing the House of the Facts, all Disputes relative thereto would have been afterwards prevented.

I am unhappy that any part of the present Time of Congress should be spent on a question of Order; I did not agitate it & only required a Decision in the usual Mode.

I shall only add sir, that I think it my indispensible Duty to repeat my Requisition, as a Matter of privilege, that the Sense of the House may be taken by the Yeas & Nays, "whether the Motion which I made Yesterday for recommitting the paragraph of the Report respecting Prices then under the Consideration of the House, was in Order," and I shall be under the Necessity of regulating my Conduct accordingly by the proceedings of the House on this Requisition.

I have the Honor to be sir with Respect your most obed & very humble sert, E Gerry

RC (DNA: PCC, item 78).

[1] Gerry's reference to his having been deprived of "the privilege of a Member," was related to his attempt the previous day to amend proposed resolutions on supply quotas in order to reduce the quota of Massachusetts. The journals do not record Gerry's motion, nor do they record his call for the "yeas and nays." Only the reading of this letter this day, briefly noted, is found in the journals. *JCC*, 16:178.

Although this protest began as a minor one over interpretation of the rules of Congress, it soon became a personal crisis for Gerry when he refused to attend further sessions of Congress until his call for the yeas and nays was honored. And when the delegates reciprocated by refusing to consider his demands until he returned to his seat in Congress, the issue escalated into a significant test of parliamentary privilege.

Congress' failure to respond to this letter led Gerry to write again on February 22, whereupon Congress resolved "that any member thinking his privilege infringed by any thing said or done in the House, ought of right to be heard in his place." Still, Gerry continued to refuse to attend to "be heard in his place," although he wrote again on April 3 defending his position and criticizing Congress' refusal to concede the force of his arguments. On that day also, a motion by George Partridge and Nathaniel Peabody asking that Gerry "be heard" was rejected, but he was given yet another opportunity to compromise and return to Congress on April 15, when a motion by Philip Schuyler and Robert R. Livingston was adopted setting April 17 as the date to take his case "into consideration." Gerry's response on that day declining "to take up the Time of the House with further Observations on the Subject" effectively ended efforts to end the impasse, however, and although he remained in Philadelphia until June 3, Gerry did not attend Congress again until 1783.

See *JCC*, 16:178, 184–86, 324–25, 368–69; Gerry's letters to Huntington of February 22 and April 3 and 17, 1780; and George A. Billias, *Eldbridge Gerry, Founding Father and Republican Statesman* (New York: McGraw-Hill Book Co., 1976), pp. 85–86. For another incident involving the withdrawal of a delegate from Congress under somewhat similar circumstances, see these *Letters*, 9:403–7, 501–2, 508–10, 525–39, 548.

[2] See *JCC*, 11:534–35. Rule 10 reads: "While a question is before the House, no motion shall be received, unless for an amendment, for the previous question, to postpone the consideration of the main question, or to commit it."

Rule 12: "When a question is about to be put, it shall be in the power of any one of the states to postpone the determination thereof until the next day, after which, it shall not be again postponed, but by order of the house."

[3] See *JCC*, 13:490–91, 499–500, 14:589–92, 637–43, 701–8, 902–9, 15:1226–29, 1394–96.

Samuel Holten's Diary

Feby 19. 1780

Saturday. We had an Account from Genl. Washington respecting some damage done by the enemy at white plains.[1]

MS (MDaAr).

[1] Washington's February 14 letter to President Huntington, which was read in Congress this day, reported an enemy attack on Lt. Col. Joseph Thompson's detachment of the 10th Massachusetts Regiment near White Plains, which on the basis of early accounts seemed "unfavourable in the issue." See *JCC*, 16:176; and Washington, *Writings* (Fitzpatrick), 18:8–9.

Samuel Huntington to George Washington

Sir,   Philadelphia Feby 21. 1780

Your Excellency's Letters of the 8th, 14th, & 17th Instant have been received and laid before Congress.[1]

Enclosed you will receive a Memorial from Capt Ebenr Greene one of the Hostages at the Cedars and an Act of Congress of the 19th Instant referring the Memorial to the Commander in Chief to take such Measures relative to those Hostages as he shall Judge most expedient.[2]

I have the honour to be, with perfect Esteem, your Excy's hble
servt,   Sam. Huntington President

RC (DLC: Washington Papers). In a clerical hand and signed by Huntington.

[1] Only the first two of these letters are in PCC (item 152, 8:401–6), but all three are
available in Washington, *Writings* (Fitzpatrick), 17:501–2, 8:8–9, 20–21.

[2] Ebenezer Greene was one of four captains retained as hostages—until "the like
number of British Prisoners" should be delivered in exchange—when the American
prisoners taken at the Cedars had been released in June 1776. Although he had been
released on parole in 1777 by Gen. William Howe, he had recently been called to
return to captivity by Gen. Henry Clinton as one of the many preliminary moves
taken in preparation for arranging a cartel with Washington. In a February 15, 1780,
memorial to Congress (which is in the Washington Papers, DLC), Greene had sought
the interposition of Congress to prevent his return, but at the recommendation of the
Board of War, Congress simply referred the matter to the commander in chief. In his
March 6 response, Washington explained that he would do what he could to effect
Greene's exchange, as he had attempted repeatedly, but that the decision "will rest
with the Enemy." In any event, Greene apparently remained on parole until February
1782. See *JCC*, 16:170–71, 176–77, 187, 209; and Washington, *Writings* (Fitzpatrick),
14:289n.15, 18:93.

John Collins to Nathanael Greene

Dear Sir   Philadelphia, February the 22, 1780
I Received yours of the 18th yesterday & will Endeaver to give all
the information I Can, at present.

I have not heard any mention, of your Resignation Since my Return
to Congress, Nither have I heard of any New Arrangement in, your
Department nither do I think their Will be any done. European
News we have none, and as to Peace, I Can onely give you my
opinion, which is we Shall have no Peace this year, and my reasons
for it is, Spain are not yet Ready for a Peace, they will Conquer the
Floredies and the Eastern banks of the Massicipi and will have to
Sittle with Congress how far they Shall extend East, this is onely my
Opinion and the idea I have, of what Spain will Clame. They undoubt-
edly will take Special Care to keep the united States from their
Maxican Dominions and Shut all the world but them selves out of the
Bay of Maxico and leave the Floradies and what they may obtain
East of the Massicipi a wilderness to prevent the united States from
giting too near their Strong Box; from the above you may Colect my
ideas of Peace and the views of Spain.

As to money maters I Can onely Say I hear dayly Complaints of
the poverty of the treasury. We are now on the Report of the
Committee for Settling the propotion Each State Shall Supply for
the Support of the Armey. If anything heave up Relateing to your
Department I Will give you timely notice.

I am With Great Regard your friend & humbe Servt,
                                          John Collins

NB Anything in my Power to inform you that Relates to you or your Department you may Enquier with great freedom.

RC (MiU–C: Greene Papers).

Elbridge Gerry to Samuel Huntington

Sir,   Philadelphia 22d Feby 1780

I am informed by some of my Collegues, that Congress have not yet considered the Letter which I had the Honor of addressing them the 19th Inst. containing a Remonstrance against their Decision of the preceeding Day, which I conceived had deprived me of an essential privilege of a Member of the House.[1] The Reason assigned for this is, that some Gentlemen objected to my Mode of proceeding as unparliamentary, & said, that a Member who supposes his privileges Invaded, should remonstrate in his place & may there be heard.

I know of no Resolution of Congress for governing their proceedings by Rules of parliament, neither will they apply in general, or in the present Case. Nevertheless, I shall readily attend Congress, if they think it expedient, but cannot consent to take my place for these amongst other Reasons; *that* I have not the privilege in *Congress* of other Members, & *that* every Member, by the Rules of the House may require my Voice upon any question agitated & put whilst I am in Congress, in answering which I shall betray my Cause. When Disputes respecting privilege are not between Congress & a Member, the latter may complain in his place without these Inconveniences.

I conceive that the privilege contended for, is an essential one, &, that without it, a Member cannot discharge his Trust. Congress have viewed it in this Light, or I presume they would not have ingrafted it into the Confederation;[2] & twelve of the States are of the same opinion, or they would probably never have ratified it, without objecting to the Article establishing this privilege.

Several Days have elapsed since my Absence from Congress, during which Time they have proceeded in the important Business under Consideration at the Time of my leaving it. If I ought to be restored to the privilege claimed, Congress will perceive, that in the present Case a Delay of Justice is a Denial of it to the State which I have the Honor to represent so far at least, as I am able to render it Any Services in Congress.

Congress will consider or not consider, my Letter, & grant or refuse my Claim, as to them may seem meet;[3] I am no Way solicitous about the Event, as it respects me personally; but as a Member of the House & Citizen of the united States wish to prevent a Measure which if confirmed by Congress will, as it appears to me, strike at a fundamental principle of the union.

I have the Honor to be, sir with all due respect, your most obedient & very Serv,   E Gerry

RC (DNA: PCC, item 78).
  [1] See Gerry to Huntington, February 19, 1780.
  [2] Gerry is undoubtedly referring to the section of article nine of the Articles of Confederation that states: "the yeas and nays of the delegates of each state on any question shall be entered on the Journal, when it is desired by any delegate." See *JCC*, 19:220.
  [3] Although Gerry's previous protest had not been acknowledged, the present letter immediately led Congress to adopt a resolution declaring "That any member thinking his privilege infringed by any thing said or done in the House, ought of right to be heard in his place." See *JCC*, 16:184–86. This result was then communicated to him at once under cover of the following brief note from President Huntington.
  "Your Letter of this Day was duly received and laid before Congress.
  "I am directed to transmit you the enclosed Act of this Day." PCC, item 14, fols. 310–11.

Samuel Huntington to George Washington

Sir,   Philadelphia 22 Feby 1780
  By a Gentleman just arrived from the Havannah[1] who left that place the 31st of Decemr, I am informed that a Fleet lay in that Port ready to sail with between three and four thousand Troops *supposed* to be destined for Pensacola or Augustine.
  That on their Passage to this Port they fell in on the 7th of January with the fleet that sailed from New York in Decemr as they suppose, some fifty leagues from Land off against Georgia as near as he could judge the weather being foggy, when they discovered their Situation they made their Escape as soon as possible without being able to determine the number of Vessels in the Fleet, their Condition, or Destination.
  I have the honour to be, with the highest Respect, your Excy's hble servt,   Sam. Huntington

RC (DLC: Washington Papers). In a clerical hand and signed by Huntington. Endorsed: "recd 5 March, ans. 6 March 1780."
  [1] Before Washington received this letter he had already received more authentic intelligence from Havana concerning Spanish plans against the Floridas in a February 18 letter from Juan de Miralles, the Spanish agent at Philadelphia, which is in the Washington Papers, DLC. For Washington's February 27 acknowledgment of Miralles' intelligence and the transmittal of it to Gen. Benjamin Lincoln in the southern department, see Washington, *Writings* (Fitzpatrick), 18:55–58.

Ezra L'Hommedieu to George Clinton

Sir,   Philadelphia, February 22, 1780.
  We have for some time past daily expected Mr. Duane or Mr. Scott with the Act of Assembly, and the papers respecting the New

Hampshire Grants. I do not know that the delay on our part hitherto has been attended with any greater disadvantages, than would reasonably be expected. It has encouraged the Vermonts, and is considered by their friends here as a circumstance in their favor.

The Attorney General from New Hampshire[1] is now confined with the small pox by inoculation, and will not likely attend in 8 or 10 days; so that nothing will be done in the business till March, in all probability. The agents from Vermont are gone home without receiving any answer from Congress;[2] those from the East side of the mountain[3] Still continue here waiting for the trial: some gentlemen are going home this week, who are the greatest friends to the proceedings of the people on the Grants, and probably will not return till after the hearing of the cause, which will be no disadvantage to us.

Congress have for some time past been busily employed in forming estimates of Supplies to be furnished by the different States for the ensuing campaign, and fixing prices to the particular articles; which has been attended with much difficulty, as always I believe is the case, when quotas are to be fixed; I expect it will pass in a few days, as the greatest part of the report has been agreed to though 'tis likely some alterations may be made. I enclose you a copy of the supplies required, and the prices as they now stand in which is included the necessary supplies for the Navy twelve months, and the supplies requested by our Allies.[4] I hope this measure if pursued will be attended with the good effects expected from it, at the same time I fear more difficulties will be experienced in carrying it into execution than is at present imagined. If the money should continue to depreciate, as it has lately done here, it will be difficult for the States to furnish their quota of supplies, and pay one third of their tax into the Treasury, as is expected. The exchange of money here is now at 50 for one; it is difficult to assign the reasons for this late depreciation. The emissaries of the enemy by exchanging and raising the price of hard money in a few instances soon fix the rates of exchange in this city, by which every thing else is regulated. A master of a vessel has arrived here from Havannah, which he left the 31st of December, and on his voyage the eighth of Jan'ry saw a large fleet to the Southward of Georgia, which 'tis supposed to be the fleet that sailed from New York or part of them. The River is not yet open here; near twenty vessels 'tis said are arrived below, amongst which some are from France, by which 'tis expected we may receive material intelligence; which if we should, I shall not fail to communicate to you.

I have the honor to be, Sir, your most obedt. servt.

Ezra L'Hommedieu

Tr (MH–H: Sparks Collection).

[1] That is, Samuel Livermore.

[2] That is, Stephen Bradley, Jonas Fay, and Moses Robinson. See James Lovell to Samuel Adams, February 1, 1780, note.

[3] Peter Olcott and Bezaleel Woodward.

[4] Enclosure not found, but for the quota resolutions adopted by Congress on February 25, see Samuel Huntington to the States, February 26, 1780.

Nathaniel Peabody to Meshech Weare

Sir,   No.   Philada. Feby 22d. 1780

I have the honr to inclose you the Transactions of the late Convention of Commissioners from the Eastern States held in this City for the purpose of considering sundry matters relative to a limitation of prices &c.[1]

The Commissrs. were of opinion the difficulties and Embarrassments attending a measure so important in its Consequences, Especially at this time when Virginia which is a very large trading Country, was not represented in Convention nor having communicated their sentiments upon the Subject, were such as would sufficiently apologize for the manner in which the Convention proceeded.

Nothing recent from Europe worth your Notice except that measures are adopted by France and Spain for Carrying on a Vigorous Campaign the ensuing year. I dread the Consequences of calling upon the States for such aid and assistance in the present deranged state of our finances, as will enable us to Cooperate with our Allies in Carrying on the War with success or procuring a permanent & advantageous Peace.

Congress are making out apportionments, and Estimates for men and Supplies, which if I augur right will cost some time and Trouble or Else their Calculations will by no means Suit the meridian of N. Hampr.[2]

You will also find inclosed the Copy of Charges exhibited by Colo Hazen against I Tichener and *Others* as also an account when and where the enquiry is to be made.[3] I Concieve it my duty to give this information that the State might have oportunity to add their assitance if Necessary, to investigate those fradulent practices.

I have the Honr. to be Sir with the most entire Consideration of Esteem Your Honrs. most obedient and very Humle Servt,

Nathl Peabody

RC (Nh–Ar: Weare Papers).

[1] For the "Transactions of the late Convention," see William Ellery to William Greene, February 15, 1780, note 1.

[2] For New Hampshire's quotas "for men and supplies," see *JCC*, 16:150, 196; and Samuel Huntington to the States, February 10 and 26, 1780.

[3] Col. Moses Hazen, commander of the 2d Canadian Regiment, had filed complaints of corruption against three staff officers at Coos, N.H.—Isaac Tichenor, deputy commissary of purchases, Jacob Bayley, deputy quartermaster general, and Matthew Lynes, deputy commissary of issues. Courts-martial were ordered by General Washington for Tichenor and Bayley, and a court of inquiry for Lynes. See Washington, *Writings* (Fitzpatrick), 17:229–30, 18:91, 98–100.

Samuel Holten's Diary

[February 23–25, 1780]
23. Wednesday. The Hone. the medical come. met in my chambr. The weather is cold.
24. Thursday. Congress sit late, upon very important matters.[1] The weather is cold. I wrote to the council of Massachusetts.[2]
25. Friday. I wrote to Mrs. Holten (no. 105).[3] Congress called upon the states for large supys.

MS (MDaAr).
[1] Congress was considering "the report of the committee for estimating supplies." *JCC*, 16:191–94.
[2] Not found.
[3] Not found.

James Lovell to George Washington

General Washington,   Philada. Feb. 23d. 1780
From Expressions in some of your Excellency's Letters to Congress and in one lately to Baron Steuben I conceive that you imagine us more regularly informed than we have actually been about European Affairs—particularly about our Interests in France.[1]
The Correspondence with our Ministers at foreign Courts passing especially under my Eye & Finger, I wish you to be persuaded that I will not omit giving you any Information in my Power from time to time which I can judge may conduce either to your Ease in the Formation of military Plans, or to your Relief under Anxieties about Supplies expected from Europe.
With the latter View, I was putting some Facts together to warrant a Conclusion that our Letters to the King of France, and Invoices to our Minister there had arrived on the 19th of September.[2] Luckily however I am not left to Inferences, a Packet having come to my Hand from Doctor Franklin dated September 30th in which he mentions the Receipt & consequent Presentation of those Letters & Invoices: He signifies only his *Hopes* of obtaining all or a great Part of the Articles.[3] But the Minister of France here had some Weeks ago known under a Date of October from Versailles that Supplies were certainly ordered, tho' it was not clear till now that such Order was posterior to a precise Knowledge of our Wants being conveyed to the King.
This is the only Letter received from Doctor Franklin since one of May 26 last year which came to hand Augst. 17th following.
Doctor Lee under Date of Decr. 8th from Paris[4] has covered the King of England's Speech to his Parliament on November 25th and Sir Joseph York's Memorial to the States General of Holland on the

26th both which you will see in the Gazettes of Philada. They are uncommonly modest. I do not however conclude that England is without any Friends in Europe merely because no mention is made of them in the Speech from the Throne. For, those should not be boasted of as Friends on one Side who mean to step out soon as Mediators between contending Parties. Nor is it good Policy to fore-arm a Foe by publishing well founded Expectations of new Aids.

The Stories of the Display of our 13 Stripes in Holland may be perhaps pleasing to certain Classes here, but I have some Proofs that Things have been conducted rather in Conformity to Dutch Politics, and in a Manner that will be productive of more solid Benefit than the Pleasure of indulging the little proud Affections of our rising Navy.[5]

I am, with much Esteem, Your Excellency's Most humble Servant,

James Lovell

RC (DLC: Washington Papers).

[1] Precisely which of Washington's letters Lovell had in mind remains unclear, but the "one lately to Baron Steuben" may have been his February 8 letter explaining that he could not complete plans for the forthcoming compaign "without a more intimate knowledge of our resources of finance than I at present possess and without ascertaining whether our allies can afford a squadron for an effectual cooperation on this Continent." Steuben, who had been sent to Philadelphia in mid-January to confer with Congress on "the numerous evils and unavoidable embarrassment that must attend our opening the Campaign before we are prepared," undoubtedly also used the occasion to express Washington's long-standing desire to be "more regularly informed."

In his March 4 reply to Lovell, Washington acknowledged that he was "fully persuaded that no intelligence on your part will be withheld, that may be considered as essential or assisting in the discharge of the duties of my station." See Washington, *Writings* (Fitzpatrick), 17:407–8, 504–6, 18:70.

[2] See John Jay to the King of France, July 10; and Committee for Foreign Affairs to Benjamin Franklin, July 16, 1779.

[3] Benjamin Franklin's September 30 letter was read this day in Congress. See Lovell to Franklin, February 24, 1780, note 1.

[4] Arthur Lee's December 8, 1779, letter to the Committee for Foreign Affairs was also read in Congress this day. See *JCC*, 16:186; PCC, item 83, 2:300–301; and Wharton, *Diplomatic Correspondence*, 3:419.

[5] These "Stories" concerned John Paul Jones' entry into the Texel in Holland with the *Serapis*. See Gerard W. Gawalt, ed. and trans., *John Paul Jones' Memoir of the American Revolution* (Washington, D.C.: Library of Congress, 1979), pp. 41–44.

Maryland Delegates to Thomas Sim Lee

Sir,   Philadelphia Feb. 23d 1780.

We herewith forward to your Excellency the Act of Congress relative to furnishing the Officers with Cloathing—& in Compliance with your Requisition, moved that you might have Permission to draw on the Continental Treasury in the State for reimbursing such Supplies. The Congress declined to give their Opinion upon the

Subject, & commited it to an especial Committee; when they report, we shall not fail to give you the Result of this Deliberation—in the mean Time, we think, no ill Consequence can attend drawing on that Fund for the above Purpose.[1] We have the Honor to be with the highest Sentiments of Respect, Yr Excellency's most obt. & very hbl. Servants,

Geo Plater

James Forbes

RC (MdAA: Red Books). Written by Plater and signed by Plater and Forbes.

[1] In order to implement Congress' November 25, 1779, resolution calling upon the states to provide officers of the Continental line with clothing at prices proportional to their pay, Governor Lee had requested the Maryland delegates to seek permission "to draw on the Continental Treasury of this State to reimburse the money that may be expended" in purchasing clothing for Maryland officers. Apparently fearful that the state meant to divert a portion of its monthly quota that "was intended for defraying the public Expences upon a Certain calculation," Congress found it "inexpedient" to comply with Lee's request. See *JCC*, 15:1304–6, 16:188, 190–91; and PCC, item 70, 1:343–47.

Committee for Foreign Affairs to Benjamin Franklin

Sir,   (duplicate)   Feb. 24th. 1780

I forward the Gazettes to Boston for you as usual without knowing when they will find a Passage. Your Letter of Decr. 30 and one from Doctor Lee of Decr. 8th came to hand two Days ago,[1] yr. prior being May 26 recd. Augst. 17th.[2] I hope you have got News Papers from me often, tho' I have written few Letters.

The commercial Committee are impressed with your Sentiments respecting Draughts. They are a meer Name at present.[3] I hope that Branch will for a Time be connected with the Admiralty Board till a new Arrangement can be formed to be executed by Persons not Members of Congress. We are about calling on the States according to the Staples so that the Prospect of suitable Remittances is enlarged. This Plan is consequent upon the Resolve of Decr. 14th.

I am with great Respect, Sir, Your Friend & humble Servant,

James Lovell

[*P.S.*] The Chevalier dela Luzerne has expressed to me an Anxiety because we do not correspond by Cypher. I early communicated to you from Baltimore a very good one tho a little tedious like that of Mr. Dumas. I inclose a Sample at this Time.[4]

RC (PPAmP: Franklin Papers). Written and signed by Lovell, and endorsed by him: "Cypher. To be sunk in Case of Danger."

[1] Lovell inadvertently wrote "Decr. 30" instead of September 30, the correct date of Franklin's letter, which was read in Congress on February 23. A duplicate copy of it, received in May, is in PCC, item 82, 1:137; and Wharton, *Diplomatic Correspondence*, 3:354.

1	c	o	r	1	
2	d	p	s	2	
3	e	q	t	3	
4	f	r	u	4	
5	g	s	v	5	
6	h	t	w	6	
7	i	u	x	7	
8	j	v	y	8	
9	k	w	z	9	
10	l	x	&	1	
11	m	y	a	2	
12	n	z	b	3	
13	o	&	c	4	
14	p	a	d	5	
15	q	b	e	6	
16	r	c	f	7	
17	s	d	g	8	
18	t	e	h	9	
19	u	f	i	1	
20	v	g	j	2	
21	w	h	k	3	
22	x	i	l	4	
23	y	j	m	5	
24	z	k	n	6	
25	&	l	o	7	
26	a	m	p	8	
27	b	n	q	9	

I use only the 9 first figures; both sides num'd

I had a thought to use only the 9 first figures, but then a cypher to use only the 9 first figures is added to the Intricacy

c	o	r	1
c	r	o	2
o	c	r	3
o	r	c	4
r	c	o	5
r	o	c	6

Let the Alphabet be regularly Squared. Agree upon any number of the perpendicular Columns, which you may change as often as you please – referring to any number of Letters in any Epistle known to have been received – as for Instance, suppose, the 3 first Letters of the 8th, 12th &c Word of mine of such and such a Date –

Should this come safely you need only mark y.r Reply with one of the Figures of the Transpositions above to determine me what is the Key.

James Lovell's Instructions in the Use of Diplomatic Ciphers

[2] The irregularity of communication with American ministers in Europe was also discussed by William C. Houston, another member of the Committee for Foreign Affairs, in his February 9, 1780, letter to Franklin.

[3] Why Lovell stated that the Commercial Committee was a "meer Name at present" is not clear. The committee, which had been reestablished on December 14, 1778, had met almost daily in 1779 according to the diary of John Fell. Cyrus Griffin, Cornelius Harnett, and James Searle were the attending members of the committee. It had on occasion been criticized for nonperformance of its duties, and had even been known to apologize to correspondents for tardy answers to their letters. See, for example, John Jay to General Washington, April 26; and Committee of Commerce to Oliver Pollock, July 19, 1779.

Since Fell, Griffin, and Searle were attending Congress and met the three-man committee quorum requirement, the committee was technically able to function at this time, although it may have been ineffectual in its actions.

[4] For the cipher enclosed by Lovell, see illustration.

James Lovell to Samuel Adams

Dear Sir   Feb. 24, [1780]

Besides the Journals of Jany. 1780 I send you two Pamphlets containing the Treaties between us and France in the Language of both Countries.[1] When the Sheets were partly struck off order was given that they should not go into the Journals for other Reasons than because they were badly printed, badly, owing the Want of Accents. I made the Printer complete a few of the Treaties as he had got the last Proof corrected before the Decission to leave the Sheets out of the Journal. Any Person who understands french may with a Pen make the Accents; and some Gentlemen in every state will wish to have the Treaties in the Language in which they were originally composed. And though the commercial one was printed authoritatively in France yet the political one never was I believe unless as translated from the English in our News papers.

Send the Paper to Mrs. A———. You will see that we have at last got some Intelligence from Europe.[2] I mentioned to you that the Retalliation & the Poole had arrived in France Sept 19. They are now in this River. By Doctr. Franklin's Letter of Sept 30 to me, We know he *had* presented ours of July with the Invoices to the King, And tho' no definitive answer had been then given to the Doctr. yet the Chevr. Luzerne some Weeks ago had notice from Versailles of Octr. date that the Supplies were ordered; But the Chevr did not know till he saw my Letter that the order was posterior to the King's precise Knowledge of our Wants.

We are bogueing in Congress much divided upon a Report consequential of our promise made Decr 14.[3] It is impossible to be accurate but crying Iniquity may be avoided. The two great Rocks are. Shall we *now* state the prices at which the similar articles shall be credited to all the States? Shall we do it in *spanish Dollars*. Would or would not the last totally destroy our Paper, that very Paper with wch. the States must purchase.

Whatever we do we ought soon to do, or we shall frustrate the Views of our Allies who have pointed out to us plainly that we should be decisively vigorous this Campaign.

Whether we do or do not fix the Prices *now* it would be wise in the Rulers of our State to cast about how they shall procure certainly and most œconomically

56,000	Cwt of Beef
12,126	Bushels of Salt
195,628	Galls. West Indian Rum

so as to furnish the whole in the Course of the year, the first partly on hoof & partly in Barrels.

Pork may be given in Lieu of Beef.

Continental Rum for W. India with the stipulated allowances if any are stipulated or if not at equitable odds.

As to the Greatness of the Tax it should be considered we went on Years without any. What signifies calling for that which is nought?

If the millions called for will not produce the Quota of Supplies double or treble millions must be had. And the States will get them with ten times the œconomy that our commissarial Legions would.

Let every Man that has a Tongue preach to bring about a vigorous Campaign.

Excuse my slovenly Manner. I am really in want of two pair of Hands. I am alone again on the meek Comtee. of for. Affairs, Mr. Livingston & Mr. Houston being like their predicessors gone for a Season.[4]

A Lee writes to the Comtee. of a Paris date Decr. 8 [a] few Words to cover The King of Englands Speech & Yorks memorial,[5] tollerably modest Things. But we ought not, as Arthur does, to conclude that England has no Friends in Europe because the Speech is silent on that Head. It would be wrong to hold up as Friends Those who may soon appear as Mediators. Or if any mean to take an armed active Part the Antagonist should not be forewarned.

I own that I conclude from the Speech that England knows of a Certainty that she shall be befriended; And I believe she has been advised to say nothing of America by some intentional mediators.

The tickling Story of the Stripes hoisted in Holland may have its Run But I have some Proofs that matters have been conducted more agreably to dutch Politics; and [In] a Way that will produce more sol[i]d Good than the Pleasure of indulging the proud Affectations of an rising Navy.   J L

RC (NN: Adams Papers).

[1] For the publication of the Franco-American treaties, see also Lovell to Horatio Gates, March 4, 1780.

[2] Lovell undoubtedly wanted Adams to send Abigail Adams a copy of the *Pennsylvania Packet* of February 24, which contained extracts from the latest letters from Europe as well as King George III's November 25 speech to Parliament and Sir Joseph Yorke's November 26, 1779, memorial to the States of Holland.

[3] The "promise made Decr. 14" was Congress' resolve of that date specifying that the states would in future be called upon to furnish their quotas in provisions "and other supplies for carrying on the war . . . at equitable prices." See *JCC*, 15:1377; and Samuel Huntington to the States, February 26, 1780.

[4] Lovell's statement was somewhat presumptuous, because William C. Houston did not leave Congress for any extended period in 1780 and Robert R. Livingston left Congress in April for only a month while his child was born.

[5] See Lovell to George Washington, February 23, 1780, note 4.

John Collins to Nathanael Greene

Dear Sir   Philadelphia, Feby the 26, 1780

I Wrote you the 22 instant. Their had been then no mention of your affairs but on the 23 the Reports of treasury ware Read, and two warrants on the Treassury passd. in favour of your Deputy which I make no doubt you have Recived account of before you Recive these,[1]   and mention was made About Regulations but were dropd. untill the incloasd plan was finished, and we had learned what affect it would have on the publick & your Department. It passed the finishing Stroak the 25 and will, be Emeaditly Sent to the differant States,[2] I must Confess it appears to me like takeing a leap in the dark and Crouding the Ship through a Strait amongst Rock and Sholes in a thick fog, we may Run the Ship a Shoar, or She may *poke* through; I have incloased the plan And you will Judge for yourself.

At all times when your leisure will permit a line from you Will be agreeable.

I am With unfaind. Regard yours,   John Collins

RC (MiU–C: Greene Papers).

[1] Congress had approved warrants of $250,000 and $1.5 million in the name of Charles Pettit, assistant quartermaster general. *JCC*, 16:189–90.

[2] See Huntington to the States, this date.

Samuel Huntington to David Oliphant

Sir,   Philada Feby. 26. 1780

You will receive herewith enclosed an Act of Congress of the 25th Instant directing you to make monthly Returns to the medical Committee agreeable to the Resolution of Congress of the 7th of April 1777, and cause Duplicates thereof to be delivered monthly to the Commanding Officer for the Time being in the southern Army.[1]

I am Sir with Esteem & Respect, your humble servt,   S. H.

LB (DNA: PCC, item 14).

[1] *JCC*, 16:204. Adoption of this resolve directing Dr. Oliphant, director general of hospitals in South Carolina, to make returns to the medical committee and the com-

manding officer of the southern department represented a victory for Oliphant, who had been resisting the claims of William Shippen, Jr., to have such reports submitted to his office as director general of the medical department. For the background of this dispute, see Henry Laurens to Benjamin Lincoln, September 24, 1779, note 3.

Huntington also sent copies of this resolve with brief cover letters of this date to director general Shippen and to South Carolina governor John Rutledge. PCC, item 14, fols. 302–3.

Samuel Huntington to the States

Sir,　　　　Circular　　　　　　　　Philadelphia Feby 26, 1780

Your Excellency will receive herewith an Act of Congress of the 25th Instant, by which the several States are called upon to procure their respective Quotas of Supplies for the ensuing Campaign in the Articles and Quantities specified in the Act.[1]

Congress in assigning the Quotas have endeavoured to suit the Circumstances and Conveniency of each State as far as possible.

You will observe that the prices affixed to the several Articles are in Spanish milled Dollars and the accounts are to be kept and finally Settled in like Currency as a fixed Standard in order that equal Justice may be done to all the States and to prevent the great Inequality of Prices which hath happened in some Instances in different States and places for Articles of the same kind and Quality.

As it is not in the power of Congress at present to determine the just Quota of each State they have made provision in this as in former acts that Justice shall be done to each State in the final Settlement of their Accounts.

It is supposed that each State will chearfully take upon themselves to furnish, Collect and deposite the provisions and Articles assigned to them respectively, which being done will supersede the necessity of purchasing Commissaries and Quarter masters in the several States.

In order to enable the States the more easily to comply with this Act you will observe they are excused from paying in the Continental Treasury two thirds of the Monies which they were called on to raise monthly for the use of the united States by the Resolution of the 6th of October last.[2]

Congress have thought it expedient to form the Estimate of Supplies as large as would be necessary for the most vigorous Exertions in any Case that may be with probability supposed; but as the Scene of Action may change or from a Variety of other Causes and unforeseen Events the Quantity of Supplies necessary to be furnished by all or any of the States cannot be reduced to a Certainty, it is expected the Commissary General will give due notice to the several States of the kind and quantity of Articles wanted from time to time that they may [be] collected or deposited at the places assigned by the Commander in Chief.[3]

The Importance and Necessity of a substantial Compliance with this Act of Congress are so obvious that nothing farther seems necessary to be added to excite the most vigorous Exertions on the part of the several States to carry the same into Execution.

I have the honour to be &c,									S.H.

LB (DNA: PCC, item 14).

[1] See *JCC*, 16:196–201. Formulating a reliable and equitable system for ensuring delivery of supplies from the states to the Continental Army had been the greatest problem challenging Congress for months, and the February 25 "Act" transmitted herewith by Huntington had been debated daily since February 16. It had its origins in the collapse of the Continental fiscal system and Congress' consequent decision of December 14 to requisition specific supplies directly from the states, and its details had been threshed out in a committee of 13 appointed on January 17 to adjust state quotas to current price levels as equitably as possible. For the immediate background of the work of this committee, see New York Delegates to George Clinton, February 9, 1780, note 3. See also Huntington's letters to Certain States, to Thomas Johnson, and to William Livingston, December 15, 1779.

Georgia, which was exempt from the quotas set at this time because of the British invasion of the state, was not sent this letter, but Huntington wrote the following brief one to Gov. Richard Howly on February 29 for the general information of Georgia officials.

"You will receive herewith enclosed an Act of Congress of the 25th Instant calling on the several States for their respective Quotas of Supplies for the ensuing Campaign.

"Although Georgia is omitted under her present Circumstances I have thought proper to transmit you the Act for Information; and that your State may conform thereto as far as they shall be able to afford Supplies." PCC, item 14, fol. 306.

[2] That is, Congress hereby reduced the total monthly cash quotas of the states from $15 million to $5 million. See Huntington to the States, October 9, 1779.

[3] See Huntington to Washington, February 29, 1780.

James Lovell to Samuel Adams

Dear Sir									Feb. 28th. [1780][1]

The Report which I hinted at, to you in my last, has passed, and will doubtless be officially sent by the Post Tomorrow.[2] But, as Mr. Fessenden may get early to Boston, I inclose a Sketch which I made use of during the Debates. I do not chuse seperately from my Colleagues to descant upon the Principles of the Report. But I entreat that you would use your utmost Eloquence to promote this Business & every other essential to a *vigorous Campaign.* And I must confidentially entrust you with an Anecdote to prompt yr Zeal. The Chevalr. De la Luzerne, from the purest motives and a most cordial anxious Concern about the Affairs of America & the Alliance, was writing a circular Letter to the Govrs. & Presidts. of the respective States by way of friendly Stimulus, but his Delicacy led him to inclose his Sentiments to the Presidts that the Opinion of the Delegates might be had.[3] The *Letter* was a very good one, but the *measure* was not agreable, for several Reasons which an *old Veteran,* as you have been tautologically called, will easily conceive, at least upon casting yr. Eye over the 6th Article of the confederation. I own that I felt no zeal of Jealousy on this Occasion. But since the Matter has been agitated & delicately quashed. I hope there will not hereafter be any Room to say that Congress have not Influence with the States nor chuse to let the minister of France try his. He certainly has a Right to *treat* with particular States *thro'* Congress by the sd. 6th Article, in Implication. Surely then he may in that Chanel *exhort* & *stimulate* to the Fulfillment of measures recommended by Congress. However, This being not the Question now, I recur to my Entreaty that you would be earnest in promoting all measures for a *vigorous* Campaign. Tho' we were enjoyned Secresy; yet the minister had no Idea that the *Governments* of the States should not know that there is some probability of an *armed* Negociation; when, the Proposals made last yr. by Spain *may* be again advanced. The Enemy therefore should not be allowed to hold any Parts of the United States on the Day of Cessation of Hostilities. We may be assured of the Resources of the Realme of France being used for the Purposes of grand Diversions in our Favor as well as Cooperations here if we get into a Condition for Vigor.

The order for this Day was to determine where we shall move to. That is put off for a Fortnight. I am well satisfied we shall not move at all.[4] Another order for this day was a report upon the Letter from our State; put off till Tomorrow It will cause much debating for I will strive to have something definite; whereas the Report touches only the charging all past Advances & Encreases of Pay as Deductions in the States Account against the Officers & Men. But it ought to be known whether the whole is to be a continental Expence.[5]

I add herewith an Extract of the ministers Communications.[6] I give it to you as a Secret & no Secret to make the most judicious use of in yr. Power. I only say it is not a News Paper Business.

Yrs. affectionately, J L

29th. Mr. Brailsford arrived this morning & has delivered a Letter with Instructions about the Penobscot affairs[7] & Col. Allen the Agent.[8]

Fessenden has dilly-dallied and will be chopping & changing on the Road therefore I send all by Post which I intended by him.

RC (NN: Adams Papers).

[1] Lovell omitted the year from the dateline and the letter was incorrectly endorsed in an unidentified hand "J. Lovell, Feb. 28. 1778," but its content clearly indicates it was written in 1780.

[2] See Samuel Huntington to the States, February 26, 1780.

[3] This "circular letter to the Govrs. & Presidts. of the respective States" is not mentioned in the journals, but the chevalier de La Luzerne reported to Vergennes in a March 10, 1780, letter that several members of Congress had asked him to write an inspirational leter to the state executives urging greater efforts to raise supplies and taxes. He also reported that he abandoned the plan after other delegates objected to his communicating directly with the state governments. Archives de ministère des affaires étrangères: Correspondance politique, États-Unis, 11:73. See also Lovell to Adams, March 17, 1780.

[4] Lovell proved to be correct. After postponing a decision from February 28 to March 13, Congress voted to postpone the decision indefinitely. The issue of removal was resurrected, however, on March 27, but the delegates rejected specific motions to move either to Hartford or to Trenton and finally postponed its "further consideration," while refusing to repeal the original December 3, 1779, resolution declaring their intent to leave Philadelphia at the end of April. See *JCC*, 16:211, 255, 291–93. See also John Fell to Robert Morris, December 3, 1779, note 4.

[5] See the Massachusetts Delegates to the Massachusetts Council, March 1, 1780.

[6] See Samuel Huntington to La Luzerne, February 2, 1780.

[7] See James Lovell to Samuel Adams, April 9; and Massachusetts Delegates to the Massachusetts Council, April 17, 1780.

[8] That is, Col. John Allan, Massachusetts' agent in Nova Scotia.

James Forbes to Thomas Sim Lee

My Dear Sir, Philadelphia Feby 29th 1780

I have your favour of the 18th Ulto. have not wrote you for a long time, owing to the iregularity of the post, And my expecting to leave this every week, And indeed the events of both Health & Spirits, both of which I have in a grate measure lost, by my long & close confinement to business & want of exercise.[1] The Inclosed Letter for our Legislature[2] you will Please to have deliverd, it is to request that a representation may be sent forward, & another Delegate appointed in my place, at all events I am determind to leave this by the middle of next month. The Letter for Diggs Incloses Letters from the Doctr from Tenerieff, Allso a Certificate of his Exchange, which I have got don by being at the Board of Admirality.

Mr. Dickinson is still in Deleware. I wrote him to let me know his lowest price for the Coach but have not received an answer, have no prospect of geting you a pair of Horses. I have sent you the weekly papers for this month, no news but what you must have heard. I ever am, Dr sir, Your affectionate, James Forbes

[*P.S.*] I recd yours by Doctr Brown & immediately forwarded your Letter to Richmond.

RC (MdHi: Lee, Horsey, and Carroll Papers deposit, 1985).

[1] Forbes, whose last vote was recorded the previous day, soon stopped attending Congress altogether because of ill health. He last collaborated with George Plater on a delegate letter to Governor Lee on March 7 and he received his final committee assignment on March 10. Forbes died the 25th. See *JCC*, 16:218, 243, 273, 277, 285–86; and Samuel Holten's Diary, March 25, 1780.

[2] Not found.

Samuel Huntington to George Washington

Sir Philadelphia Feby 29th 1780

You will receive herewith enclosed a Letter from Genl Irwine of the 23d of January and an Act of Congress of this Day referring the same to the Commander in Chief to settle the Claim of Genl Irwine respecting Rank.[1]

You have also enclosed an Act of Congress of the 25th Instant, calling on the several States to procure their respective Quotas of Supplies for the ensuing Campaign.[2] You will please to observe the Articles except Tobacco are to be collected and deposited in each State in such place as the Commander in Chief shall Judge most convenient.[3]

It is most earnestly to be desired that the several States may exert themselves and procure such Suplies and Magazines as may relieve the Quarter master and Commissary General from their Embarrassments, and prevent any future Distress in the Army for Want of provision.

I am favoured with yours of the 23d Inst enclosing Gaines Newspaper.[4]

I have the honour to be with the highest respect, your Excy's hble servt,   Sam. Huntington President

RC (DLC: Washington Papers). In a clerical hand and signed by Huntington.

[1] The enclosed letter from Gen. William Irvine is in the Washington Papers, DLC. Irvine's complaint about his seniority had been referred to the Board of War on January 29, and the board had simply concluded that Washington should "be authorized to direct the necessary enquiry into General Irvine's claim, and finally settle the same." *JCC*, 16:110, 215. For Washington's March 6–8 response to this directive and the results of the enquiry concerning Irvine's rank, see Washington, *Writings* (Fitzpatrick), 18:94, 19:112, 138.

[2] See Huntington to the States, February 26, 1779.

[3] For Washington's March 26 circular letter to the states "fixing the places of Deposit in each State" and the proportions of specific requisitioned supplies to be delivered from time to time at each depository, which he formulated in response to this congressional resolve, see Washington, *Writings* (Fitzpatrick), 18:159–60, especially note 69.

[4] This letter is in ibid., p. 45; and PCC, item 152, 8:423–26. Washington enclosed the February 21 issue of Hugh Gaine's *New-York Gazette* because it contained "his British Majesty's speech and several other Articles of European intelligence."

Robert R. Livingston to John Stevens

Dear Sir   Philadelphia 29th Feby. 1780

I was much mortified at not finding you at Trentown—which was my principal inducement to take that rout; I was detained the whole day at the Ferry & did not get here till yesterday noon after a very irksome journey. The news of this place is contained in a paper which I enclose & which you will do me the favor to transmit with the Letter to Polly.[1] We have a report from Maryland & Virginia that the enimy have arrived at Savannah but nothing directly to Congress. A ship with Hessians seperated from the fleet has fallen into our hands. She was very much shattered so that we may infer from it that the rest of the Fleet have suffered greatly. You will find that

America has effectualy fought the battles of Ireland, so that we shall
have the honour of establishing the freedom of other nations while
we are throwing off our own yoke. I am, Dr. Sir Af., Your Most Obt
Hum. Servt.   Robt R. Livingston

RC (NjHi: Stevens Papers).
[1] Livingston's letter to his wife, Mary (Polly) Stevens, the daughter of John Stevens,
has not been found.

North Carolina Delegates
to Richard Caswell

Sir,   Philadelphia Feby. 29th 1780.
    You will receive, from the President of Congress, sundry Resolu-
tions which are the result of much deliberation; and such as the
Necessity of our affairs, rather than choice, has determin[ed] us to
adopt.[1] This Necessity arises from the state of our circulating
currency; and from the impossibility of having recourse to further
Emissions of paper on public Credit. The Currency is no longer
capable of procuring any given quantity of Supplies; because, it is
impossible to say what quantity of it will be Necessary for purchasing
the Commodities required, whose prices rise beyond any imaginable
proportion; and the press, being once shut up, cannot again be
opened with any prospect of affording relief.
    The only resources, now, for furnishing the Supplies for the war,
are the Contributions of the States, and what may be obtained by
loans. The latter, after many trials, is found to yield but little aid,
and that little, extremely burthensom to the Community. The former is the true and unfailing fountain of the Strength of a Nation,
especially, a free One. But it is not in the power of Congress to call
them forth, otherwise than by Requisitions to the Several States;
and, if the States fail to comply, it will be utterly impossible to carry
on the war.
    While Congress could raise supplies by means of Emissions on
public Credit, a failure of Exertions in any one or more of the States
would not have been fatal. But, since that can no longer be done, it is
unquestionably clear that a failure in any State, who furnishes Considerable Supplies, might be attended with Consequences, in the last
degree ruinous to the Cause we are engaged in; and which is now
happily drawing to a glorious conclusion. In a word, Sir, the Exertions of Congress are no longer competent; and, unless the States
exert themselves, the Cause is utterly lost; and we shall be left in a
situation the most wretched among human beings—that is, exposed
to all the Oppressions and Insults of enraged, Victorious, and avari-
cious Tyranny.

It is much to be wished that the Contributions could be made in money, so as to answer the Exigencies of the war. Such a mode would be most easy in Execution, tho, perhaps, not equally easy and beneficial to the whole, for that part of the Community, which is near the prinicipal Scenes of Action, would be able to demand, and have, a greater proportion of the public money for their produce; and, of Course, pay their quotas with much greater ease than those more remote. So that, not only the difficulty of Contributing would be unequal, but the quantity of Contribution would be unequal also. Contributions in money must be always subject to this inequality, until some mode can be fallen upon for estimating the quotas in proportion to the value of the produce of labor; but this cannot be effected during the War.

There is another objection to Contributions in money, at the present period, which renders it altogether ineffectual.

So urgent, and incessant are the demands of the public, for Necessaries to support an Army, which must disband if not daily supplied, that those who pay taxes have it in their power to insist on any price they please, and, no doubt, will demand higher in proportion to the Tax they expect to pay. This alone is Sufficient to render the taxes unequal to the Supplies. But if to the force of this principle be added the force of that attention which each Individual has to his own Interest, and always determines the Seller to take advantage of the Necessity of the buyer, the force, also, of the abusive System of public purchasing, which, So long as our Necessity continues cannot be corrected, and of the fluctuation which the Events of War always produce in the hopes and fears of men, when all these, Sir, are added, their united Operation will render it impossible to make any given Sum of our Money represent a given quantity of any Commodity. Indeed we find, by experience, that all calculations of this kind are vain. For tho' the States should tax to the amount of all the Money in circulation, the urgency of the public demands, and the avarice of Individuals, would raise the prices to so enormous an heighth, before it could be collected, that the money would go but a very little way in purchasing supplies: so that tho' the Community should be oppressed by Taxes, the Necessary Articles for carrying on the war could not be obtained.

The contributions of the States must necessarily be in the Specific commodities wanted for the Support of the war. The powers of Government which the States possess enable their magistrates to procure them by a variety of Means. They can be obtained on certificates redeemable at a Succeeding Assembly; for which redemption, a tax can be calculated, because, the purchase is previously made, and the price known; and the holder can discharge the Tax by those very certificates. Some can cause them to be collected by Specific Contribution; and Some, we hope, can obtain them by that most desireable mode of contracting. But, we need not suggest the various modes; and our Anxiety for the Success of this most Necessary Measure, has carried us into the mentioning those few we have Suggested, not any opinion that the general assembly will have Occasion for our Advice in a matter, to which their own wisdom is, infinitely, more competent.

We call it, Sir, a most Necessary Measure. We will venture to repeat that it is indispensible. We cannot See any thing that can be adopted, in lieu of it, that promises, even the most distant prospect of relief, and we hope from it, for many Essential advantages to the united States in general, and to our own in particular. As to the last, we shall only say that our Industry will be applied for the discharge of our part of the public burthens, at the Same rate with that of the other States, which our local disadvantages would prevent were we to pay in money only. As to the former, we hope the Measure will remove the public Necessity by the provision of Magazines previous to the want of them, that the Supplies, being furnished by all, and the remote coming in aid of those more near, will prevent that excessive demand, and excessive advantage taken of the public, which were the Consequences of procuring them only in the Neighborhood of the Army. That the evil of a numerous Staff department, established in such a manner as to enhance the most ruinous abuses, will be entirely removed. In a word Sir, will give us plenty of Supplies, without incurring heavy public debts; without giving partial advantages; without causing partial burthens; without leaving us exposed to the abuses of peculation, or danger to our affairs from the precarious Subsistance of our army. If these happy effects should flow from it, our resources will be as inexhaustible as our Industry. Money will attain to it's true use and value, for, in Ordinary Commerce, no individual can be under Such Necessity as the public who are maintaining a War for their very Existence. If prices of Necessaries continue high, those who want them must retrench in the use of them; or increase their Industry to enable them to purchase. The product of that Industry will no where find that Necessity which, at present, every one finds in the public. The market of high prices must be sought among the affluent, who will thus contribute to the support and increase of Industry, but, even among those, prices will find limits beyond which they cannot go; and commerce will so regulate itself[2] that even paper money, will find a Certain fixed value as the general representative of Industry—an Event which may in vain be looked for, so long as the Necessity of the public is Suffered to Continue, by neglecting or failing to foresee and provide for the demands before they arrive.

On perusing the report it will be found that Congress have allowed liberal prices for every Article and all as Near as Could be in the same Proportions. The Prices of the year Seventy four were assumed from the best Information that could be obtained, and fifty per cent were added in Consideration of the particular Circumstances of the

War. The whole indeed will operate as a loan from the Staple States to the whole union of which they must afterwards be charged with their proportions And be creditors for the Surplus. The States who have not Staples, or fail to Supply, will be debtors to the whole Union. It will easily appear to you that it was Necessary to fix the prices in Specie because nothing that is fluctuating could measure either the whole of the amount of Supplies or the several [propo]rtional parts, and Consequently nothing else [could be] adopted for doing Justice to the whole or to each. You will find the quotas assigned to North and South Carolina far beyond what is their Supposed proportion but the prospect of a vigorous Campaign in the southern States, the probability of great Armaments being there employed, the impossibility of Supplying them with provisions from any other States, with other reasons which will occur to you, determined the Delegates of those States to assume the quotas as they now are, and induced Congress to make the requisitions. The Same Considerations will explain the reasons for assigning the different Commodities as they appear in the Resolves. We shall only observe that North Carolina assumed the flower because South Carolina could furnish none, and the Troops from Virginia and North Carolina cannot be Subsisted upon rice. We will now Sir dismiss this subject first praying leave to press its importance in the most Strenuous Manner on the State General assembly.

RC (Nc–Ar: Governors' Papers). In the hand of Thomas Burke. FC (Nc–Ar: Governors' Papers). In the hand of Thomas Burke.
    [1] See Samuel Huntington to the States, February 26, 1780.
    [2] Remainder of RC missing; text taken from FC.

Oliver Ellsworth to Samuel Lyman

Dr sir.   Philada. March 1. 1780
    I am this day favoured with yours of the 7th of Feby.
    What the State of our finances will be three months hense? is indeed to me a hard question. I will as soon as it shall be in my power forward you the result of the deliberations of Congress on this Subject. In the mean time I am not disposed to advise you to any speculations in money, but rather to confine them to the Girls till more certain times open.
    You will glean from the enclosed papers most of the European intelligence recd. by the late arrivals.
    You may now put this in the fire.
    I am D sr., yr obed. hume servt.   O Ellsworth[1]

RC (MeHi: Fogg Collection).
    [1] Ellsworth also wrote a brief letter this day to his wife Abigail:

"I hope you had a good weding & a good partner & rejoice to hear that you have yet victuals enough to eat, & are like to have a resting spell 'till the snow is gone. I shall immediately look for mitts & will also purchase a gown for Sabra if on enquiry I think it can be had cheaper here than at Hartford. Have written to Smith to deliver you the flour immediately & hope you will not suffer 'till I come which will be as soon as possible tho' I am unable precisely to fix the time."   Ellsworth Papers, CtHi.

Oliver Ellsworth to Jonathan Trumbull, Sr.

Sir,   Philadelphia, March 1. 1780.
    The enclosed papers to which I beg leave to refer your Excellency contain most of the intelligence received from Europe by the late arivals. Mr. A Lee in his Letter of Decr. gives it as his opinion that England would receive some aid from Holland but from no other quarter. Doctr. Franklin in his of the same month informs that the Invoices he had lately received from Congress of Cloathing &c for the Army to a very considerable amount had been laid before the ministry & were like to be complied with.[1]
    I have the honor to be, with the highest Esteem, your Excellency most obedt. hum Servt.   Oliver Ellsworth

RC (Ct: Trumbull Papers).
[1] Ellsworth is referring to letters from Arthur Lee of December 8 and from Benjamin Franklin of September 30, 1779. See James Lovell to Washington, February 23, notes 3–4; and Committee for Foreign Affairs to Franklin, February 24, 1780, note 1.

Thomas McKean's Memorial

                                                         Philadelphia, March 1st. 1780
    The Memorial of Thomas McKean, a Member for the State of Delaware, most humbly sheweth,
    That your Memorialist on the 19th day of November last delivered to a certain Samuel Young, Master and Commander of the Letter of Marque Ship called the Lady Washington, bound on a voyage from Philadelphia for St. Eustatia, eight full setts of Bills of Exchange, drawn by Francis Hopkinson Esquire Treasurer of Loans for the United States, and countersigned by Samuel Patterson Esquire Continental Loan Officer for the Delaware State, on the Commissioners or Commissioner at Paris, numbered from 1721 to 1728 inclusive, for thirty dollars each, in favor of your Memorialist, being for one year's interst due to him on the 10th day of September last for fifteen hundred pounds lent to the United States; in order to purchase some articles for him at St. Eustatia.
    Your Memorialist further sheweth, that about the same time the Honoble. David Finney Esquire delivered to the said Samuel Young seven Loan-Office Certificates, signed by Michael Hillegas Esquire

Treasurer of the United States and countersigned by Thomas Smith
Esquire Continental Loan-Officer for the State of Pennsylvania, to
be disposed of for his use at St. Eustatia aforesaid numbered and
dated as follows, to wit, No. 2442, 2443, 2444 and 2445 for 1,000
dollars each, dated February 11th. 1779, and No. 2548 for 1000
dollars, dated February 15th. 1779, No. 5426 for 500 dollars dated
Feby. 11th. 1779, and No. 5501 for 500 dollars, dated Feby 10th.
1779. That the said Samuel Young sailed from Philadelphia about
the beginning of December last on board the said Ship for St. Eustatia
aforesaid, and on the fourth day of said month was captured by the
Roebuck man of war, belonging to His Britannick Majesty and commanded by Sir Andrew Snape Hammond, when he threw the Bills
of Exchange and Loan-office Certificates before described over-
board, before the Enemy took possession, and the same were lost in
the Ocean. All which facts your Memorialist is ready to prove when
and where Congress shall direct; he therefore requests that the Bills
and Certificates afsd. may be replaced by the proper officers, on a
suitable Indemnification being given to the United States.[1]
    And Your Memorialist will pray &c.   Tho M:Kean

MS (DNA: PCC, item 41). Written and signed by McKean.
    [1] McKean's memorial was read in Congress this day and referred to the Board of
Treasury. The board's recommendation to replace the lost bills as requested was
adopted by Congress on April 5. See *JCC*, 16:220, 331–32.

Massachusetts Delegates
to the Massachusetts Council

Sir,   Philada. the 1st of March 1780
    We have been honored with your Letter of the 13th of January
last signed in the Name & Behalf of the General Assembly, and
enclosing one of the same Date to Congress;[1] and we embrace the
earliest Opportunity of transmitting a Resolution which They have
passed in Consequence thereof.[2] We shall immediately apply to the
Quartermasters General, the Paymaster Genl., the Cloathers Genl.
and the Commissary Genl. of Military Stores for an Account of all
the Money & other Articles supplied by their several Departments to
the officers & Soldiers of the Massachusetts Battalions & Corps.
From That it will be easy to extract what is to be charged to them
respectively. But we are of Opinion, from the confused State of the
public Accounts, that this Business will be delayed, unless a proper
Person is sent by the State to attend each of the Staff Officers aforesd.
and assist, if necessary, in making out the Accounts now requested.
    We perceive "it is the Expectation of the State that all the Expences
(being in their Nature only a Fulfilment of the original Engagement
of Congress to their Army to pay them a certain Sum as Wages) will

be charged by Congress to the Debt of the United States and to the Credit of that State." And, in Compliance with the Desire of the Honble. Assembly to know "whether this Matter has been settled here or considered, and what our Apprehensions of it are," We beg Leave to inform them that we do not recollect any Act of Congress which settles the Matter; but, we conceive they have no Intention of conducting it agreable to the Expectation of the Assembly. This Opinion is founded on the Debates of Congress previous to their passing the Resolutions of the 17th of Augst. last;[3] as well as on their late Resolve of the 9th of February respecting "the reasonable Expence" incurred by any State "in raising more than its just Proportion of the Troops serving in the Army."[4] And we apprehend it is the Intention of Congress that the Expence of making good the original Contract to the Officers and Soldiers shall be defrayed by each State so far as it respects "their just Proportion of the Troops actually serving in the Army from time to time."

We shall pay a particular Attention to the Instructions of the General Assembly respecting their Expenditures in the Penobscot Expedition,[5] and the other Matters contained in their Letter of the 9th of February[6] recd. the 28th and we shall give them the earliest Information of the Measures of Congress on those important Subjects.

We have the Honor to be, with every Sentiment of Respect for the General Assembly and, Yourself, Sir, Your most obedient, and Very humble Servants,   E. Gerry   James Lovell

                                        S Holten   Geo Partridge

P.S. Inclosed is a Copy of the Letter[7] which we shall send to the several Officers of the Staff for their respective Accounts.

RC (M–Ar: Revolutionary War Letters). Addressed: "The Honorable Jeremiah Powell Esqr. President of the Council of Massachusetts Bay." Written by Lovell and signed by Lovell, Gerry, Holten, and Partridge.

[1] The Massachusetts Council's January 13 letter to Congress, seeking information on prices in order to adjust military pay "according to the rate of Depreciation," is in PCC, item 65, 1:420–22. Since it was widely recognized that adjusting the pay of soldiers to the pace of inflation was necessary to maintain recruitment needs, Massachusetts had moved the previous February to assure her troops "that there should be no failure of a just Settlement & Payment at the End of War agreeable to the true value of their first Engagement." But no understanding had been reached on whether such added costs would be borne primarily by the state or by the Continent collectively, and most delegates seemed to assume that the issue could be postponed to the general financial settlement that would follow the end of the war. In its letter of January 13, the Massachusetts Council had left the matter rather vague, and Congress' response to their query failed to clarify this issue, although as the Massachusetts delegates explained in the present letter, "we conceive they have no Intention of conducting it agreable to the Expectation of the Assembly." For James Lovell's concern that the operation of the Massachusetts act would work a hardship on the state, see also his letters to Benjamin Lincoln, February 16, and to Horatio Gates, March 4, 1780.

[2] On February 29 Congress had resolved that: "all grants and allowances" made by Congress to Continental soldiers "in addition to their pay, rations or bounties, since

the first day of January, 1777 (except for extra services, or expences in special cases) were made in consideration of the enhanced prices of the necessaries of life, in consequence of the depreciation of the paper currency, and ought to be accordingly considered in making good the original contract." *JCC*, 16:217–18. Pres. Samuel Huntington officially transmitted this resolve to the council under cover of a brief letter of February 29. PCC, item 14, fol. 311.

[3] See *JCC*, 14:974–76.

[4] *JCC*, 16:149.

[5] See Massachusetts Delegates to the Massachusetts Council, April 17, 1780, note 4.

[6] Apparently a letter to the Massachusetts delegates rather than to Congress. It is not in PCC.

[7] Not found.

Rhode Island Delegates to William Greene

Sir,   Philadelphia March 1st. 1780.

This will be accompanied by the substance of a System, which lately passed Congress, for supplying the army. An exact copy will be transmitted by the President.[1] We are now upon a plan for giving stability to our money. As soon as any measures shall be agreed on We will give your excellency the earliest intelligence.

Some time ago Congress had a conference with the minister of France, at his request,[2] by a Committee; when, among other things, he informed us that there was no prospect of a peace this spring, that France and Spain were making preparations for a powerful diversion and that it was expected on our part that we should exert ourselves with vigour this campaign. That successful operations would hasten and facilitate negotiations of peace &c &c. This is the substance of what we think ourselves now at liberty to communicate.

We have lately received a letter from our minister at Paris; but not a word of news, saving that our Invoices for cloathing and military Stores had just arrived, and that he was encouraged to think that our application would meet with success.

The King of Britain's speech is more moderate than usual; but he is still determined it seems to prosecute the war with vigour. It is our duty to be prepared to resist his efforts, and to regain the possession of such parts of the United States as the enemy have taken from us, if we can. This we should be able to effect if we had a naval force superior to that of the enemy; but our own naval force is weak and what force our ally will have in America the ensueing campaign we know not. Count De Estaing with 12 sail of ships are gone to France. It is said that on his passage he had taken a 64 gun-ship and a frigate but I believe this account is uncertain. We presume that their places will be supplied, because we cannot conceive that our Ally will leave the W. Indias exposed.

No certain intelligence hath yet come to hand relating to the famous York fleet. They have been seen at sea. Yesterday a letter was received by a merchant in this place from one of his captains who had just

arrived in Chesapeak from the W. Indias, informing him that in lat:
28 long: 68 he had come across a transport which was one of that
fleet, that had been wrecked by a storm & that he had taken out the
men and left her. That Clinton & Cornwallis were on board the fleet
and that it was .bound to Georgia.

Inclosed will be a news paper which will give you all the flying
news.

We are with great respect, Yr Excellency's most obedt. servants,

William Ellery

John Collins

RC (R–Ar: Letters to Governors). Written by Ellery, and signed by Ellery and Collins.
[1] See Samuel Huntington to the States, February 26, 1780.
[2] See Samuel Huntington to La Luzerne, February 2, 1780.

Samuel Holten's Diary

[March 3–4, 1780]

3. Friday. Congress agreed to recommend to the states to set apart
the last Wednesday in April next as a day of Fasting & prayer.[1] I
wrote to the hon. Caleb Cushing Esqr.[2]

4. Saturday. Congress recd. a packet from France this day,[3] by the
way of Boston. No news material.

MS (MDaAr).
[1] Holten had made the motion to set aside a "day of fasting, humiliation and
prayer," but he was not one of the committee of five appointed to prepare the
recommendation to the states. *JCC*, 16:225.
[2] Not found.
[3] The journals record receipt of the following letters from this packet. From Benjamin Franklin, October 4 and 17, 1779; from Arthur Lee, September 19 and October
13 and 21; from Ralph Izard, September 29; from Lafayette, October 7; and from
Jonathan Williams a memorial and accompanying accounts of unknown date. *JCC*,
16:226–27. Although the letters from Franklin of October 4 and from Lafayette of
October 7 are endorsed by Charles Thomson, "Read March 3, 1780," they are entered in the journals under March 4.

Samuel Huntington to Horatio Gates

Sir,   Philadelphia March 3, 1780

Your letter of the 17th Ulto with the Intelligence therein referred
to enclosed; hath been laid before Congress and referred to the
Board of War.[1]

Nothing farther as yet hath been done thereon.

I have the honour to be, most respectfully your hble servt,

Sam. Huntington President

RC (NHi: Gates Papers). In a clerical hand and signed by Huntington.
[1] In his February 17 letter to Congress, written from his home "Travellers Rest, Berkeley County, Virginia," and "enclosing two papers of intelligence from Canada," Gates had spoken of the desirability of possessing that province and concluded that "I have that confidence in the Wisdom of [Congress] . . . to believe, that they will adopt every measure to Facilitate the Success of an Expedition, of such amazing benefit, not only to them, but Their High Allies." See *JCC*, 16:205; and PCC, item 154, 2:202–3. No response of the Board of War to this intelligence and recommendation has been found.

James Lovell to Horatio Gates

Dear Sir   Feb. [i.e., March] 4th. 1780[1]
It is only because Col. Bull was so obliging as to promise to call on me this morning for a Letter, that I now take up my Pen, for it is impossible for me to write with any Deliberations, having two Expresses to attend to immediately. Yr. Favor of Feby 17th with L's[2] Instructions are on my Table. Verily I cannot conceive he acted from any other Principles than what he avers; and I ought in Charity for Congress to suppose that the Word Protection will fairly admit of the Ideas usually annexed to "*Aids* by Treaty" otherwise their Honors have been over free in the Use of it during the Honey Moon of our late interesting Alliance. However I will consider this matter a little more maturely. You will really be surprized when you [get] to See L's last Letter to Congress. I did not imagine he would write so confessionary an Epistle to any Potentate on Earth. His first is published Jany. 10th, his 2d will be in the Feby Journal.

I did not know but some Persons might chuse to have by them the Treaties in French, the Language in which they were originally drawn up; therefore I made the Printer bind a few of the Sheets which he had struck off, but was forbidden to insert in the 4th Vol. of the Journals; you can accent them with a fine nibbed pen.[3] The Printer had no Tipes for that Purpose.

P.M. I was interrupted this Morning by the Arrival of a large Mail from France by the Mercury after a long Passage.[4] We had later News before. I hope we shall get Supplies of Arms & Amunition early. There is the fairest Prospect. Indeed, we could make out pretty well with our own Magazines. We could by the 1st of May get ready 10,000 including 1600 Queen Ann's, which would serve at West Point. But, the Money! General, the Money! Speculators are 8 times over match for us. As to Massachusetts God knows where they will find the Cartloads; but they have determind to make good the original Contract of Congress with both officers & Men for 3 years back; and to be governed in future by the same Scale which regulates them for the Past—the monthly Average of the Prices of Beef, Indian Corn, Sheeps Wool, and Sole Leather.

I think I mentioned to you some time ago that we ought to be guarding against an Event *not improbable* which is an armed Negociation wherein the Terms offered by Spain last year *may* be again renewed by others as reasonable proposals vizt. Each to hold what they possess on the Day of the Commencement of a long Truce. France & Spain will make powerful combined Diversions to favor us if they should not be also able to cooperate in these Parts.

It is reported that Sr. Henry was not heard of at Carolina on the 10th of February.

The Express who brought my Packet in 14 days from Boston tells me that as he passed thro' Connecticutt he was told that Genl. Putnam had been taken off by a Fit of some Kind, but whether Convulsions or Apoplexy he could not remember.[5]

Our Boston Papers rarely come to hand of late, and are chiefly Advertizements when they do reach us. As I am uncertain whether I shall *print* what Doctr. Franklin mentions of Portugal, I give it to you in Extract.[6]

Passy Octr. 4. 79

"Portugal seems to have a better Disposition towards us than heretofore. about 30 of our People taken & set ashore on one of her Islands by the English were maintained comfortably by the Governer during their Stay then furnished with every Necessary, and Sent to Lisbon; where, on Enquiry to whom Payment was to be made for the Expence they had occasioned, they were told that no Reimbursement was expected, that it was the Queen's Bounty who had a Pleasure in showing Hospitality to Strangers in Distress. I have presented Thanks, by the Portugaise Ambassador here, in Behalf of the Congress. and I am given to understand that probably in a little Time the Ports of that Nation will be open to us as those of Spain."

Arthur Lee was in Paris Decr. 8th.[7] I doubt not he is now on his Way to America, for there is Reason to think Mr. J. Adams arrived soon after that Date. I fear he will never get any Redress from Deane who will take Care to miss him in both Countries.

The Letter which I forward is from Count Montford,[8] as I judge by the handwriting & Size resembling several others which have been opened. He meant well in what he has published though there is nothing very smart or substantial in it. He had a hard boat to steer if he means again to appear as an Officer in America. He has met with some considerable Windfalls on the Decease of a Grandfather & Sister. Conway has a Regiment.

I have Dispatches to prepare in Consequence of the new arrival this morning, which addition to the Labors announced when I first took up my Pen must plead my Excuse for not noticing particularly what have written heretofore about Canada & other Subjects.

Present my affectionates to Mrs. Gates & your Son; and continue to treat me as sincerely your Friend & humble Servt.

James Lovell

RC (NHi: Gates Papers).

[1] Lovell clearly misdated this letter, because he mentions at least three events in it that occurred after February 4, and the letter from Benjamin Franklin quoted at length was read in Congress on March 4. An extract from Lovell's letter is printed under the date February 4 in Burnett, *Letters*, 5:25.

[2] That is, Charles Lee, whose dismissal from the army is discussed at Samuel Huntington to Lee, January 14, 1780.

[3] See also Lovell to Samuel Adams, February 24, 1780.

[4] See Samuel Holten's Diary, March 3–4, 1780, note 3.

[5] Gen. Israel Putnam had suffered a "paralytic stroke" in December 1779 that ended his military career, although he lived until 1790. *DAB*.

[6] The following extract is from Benjamin Franklin's October 4, 1779, letter to John Jay, which was read in Congress this day.

[7] Arthur Lee's December 8, 1779, letter to the Committee for Foreign Affairs was read in Congress on February 23. *JCC*, 16:186.

[8] Count Julius de Montfort, who had resigned a majority in Casimir Pulaski's corps in early 1779. See these *Letters*, 9:767n.1 and 11:500.

New Hampshire Delegates to Meshech Weare

Sir   Philada. March 4th. 1780.

We have the Honr. to transmit you Some extracts from the Communications lately made by the Minister of France,[1] respecting the disposition and probable Intentions of the Several Powers in Europe, by which it will appear Necessary for the States to exert every political Nerve in preparting for a most Vigorous Campaign the ensuing Year; as well to co-operate with our Allies, if Necessary, in offensive Measures, as for the defence of these States. We have no other recent intelligence from Europe worth Communicating.

Our finances tho' much deranged, are rather upon the recovery.

We heartily regret the Necessity of asking such extraordinary Aid, and efforts from our fellow Citizens as Congress have by their late resolves, with Great reluctance, been obliged to do.

The Spirited & Patriotic exertions of the State upon former occasions gives us reason to hope they will not reject the proposed Measures.

Every one here has a Psalm and a Doctrine in finance—and whenever any important Conclusions can with Certainty be Drawn Shall lose no time in Transmitting the Intelligence.

We have the Honr. to be with great Esteem your Honrs. Most Obedt. & very Humble Servts.   Nathl. Folsom

                                        Nathl. Peabody

P.S. The last Wednesday in April next will be appointed as a day of Fasting &c.[2]

RC (Nh–Ar: Weare papers). Written by Peabody and signed by Peabody and Folsom.

[1] See Samuel Huntington to La Luzerne, February 2, 1780.

[2] See Samuel Holten's Diary, March 3–4, 1780, note 1.

John Fell to Robert Morris

Dear sir, Philada. March 5th. 1780

Yesterday I was favour'd with yours of the 1st & 2d Instt. relateing chiefly to the truely distresting situation of our unhappy State. Your feelings on this occasion, may in some measure make you senseable of what ours must be hear, When the dispatches from so many quarters and departments, all breathing their different complaints and wants, requires great fortitude indeed, to bear up, under the weight. As I am engaged, I am not willing to speak, but Assist with my slender Shoulder to the Yoke though I am fearfull it will not avail much.

Look which way you will every thing seems to wear a bad aspect, I would not be understood to mean by the looks or actions of the People hear, for it is quite the reverse, disappation and extravigence of all kinds are beyond conception. The dress now of the Ladies in Paying their Visits is quite equal, to the dress of the Ladies that I have seen in the Boxes in the Playhouses in London, and their dress in general even along the Streets, Resembles in a great degree, the Actresses on the Stage. I suppose from these Reflections you will conclude, I write like an Old fellow, who cannot make Proper allowances, but I ashure you that is not the Case. I never had any of them scruples about dress when it was done with Propriety. Our extravigence is even look't on abroad with contempt. Yesterday a Letter from Dr Franklin was read,[1] wherein he expresses his sorrow, for what he hears of us, in that Respect, and says he has a Proof of it, by the Bills drawn on him for the Interest of the Certifficates, which he understands is chiefly orderd to be laid out in the Purchase of Tea and other triffling articles of extraviegence.

Congress has been some time in a Committe of the whole to consider a Report of a Committee on Supplies for the Treasury,[2] That the States be calld upon to make Provision for sinking by Taxes, Loans, Exchange or otherwise in the course of the Present Year their quotas now in circulation viz. New Hampshire &c &c 200,000,000 Million. Each State to be charg'd in debt for its Quota in Spanish Milld dolls. at the Exchange of 40 for 1 with Interest at 6 Per Cent Per Annum and be Credited in Spanish Milld dolls at the same Rate of exchange for said Bills as they shall be brought to be destroyed, NB now I have begun I believe it will be less trouble to give you the whole then to curtail it.

That it be reccomended to the States as the Bills are drawn out of circulation to emitt Bills on their own Credt. redeemable in Specie within 7 Years not exceeding on any Acct the quotas of 10,000,000 Dolls' not to be Isued more than 1/20th Part so fast as the other Bills shall be brought in to be destroyd and that they establish funds for the Redemption of the Bills they shall Emit.

I grow tired giving you the whole as I do not like any Part of it. As to the different States Emitting their own Bills I do dislike exceedingly, as I am sure that would be Productive of the greatest confusion. As to the Specie Plan, I should have no objection to if it were Practible or Posible to comply with it, but where is New Jersey to get her Part of 500,000 dollars in Specie for her Quotas. I imagine there is as little Specie in that State as any, one reason they have had more Prisoners with the Enemy, which has been a great drain to their friends of all the hard stuff they could get, another reason with me is from their Vicinity to New York, there has been a great European Trade carried on which has been another drain. However you will agree with me, that it is much easier to find fault than to Propose any thing new that will answer the end. As to Projecting Schemes on financing I have no Pretentions that way; If any thing new offers to morrow on this subject I will let you know.

I have two affairs in New Jersey that I want your advice about. One is about the Estate of Henry Caylor deceasd and the other Jos Forman, of whom I have a Mortgage of some Land, I beleave near Allen Town, I think the Papers are in the hands of Henry Waddell Esqr. I wish you would repeal that wicked Tender Law, though I had a hand in the making of it, for instance if I was to attempt to Recover either of the above I suppose they would Pay me off immediately; I have done my endeavour in Congress to get a requisition to the States to Repeal or revise the Law, the Opposition think it has done all the hurt it can, and that now only Tories will benifitt by it. I cannot see it in that light, however there is a Report from a Committee now on the Table on the subject, and was Postponed to take up the Plan now before us.

Now I much want your advice and friendly assistance with regard to [My]Self. As I can safely say, and that without flattery there is no Person in New Jersey in whose opinion I have a greater Esteem. Money you know is the Principle mover. I should be glad to know how I am to recover £500 which I have spent last Year more than my allowance, in absolute necessary Expences, only the Taylors Bill for making One Coat & Breeches, and some Shoes all the rest such expences as were dayly wanted and not One Botle of Wine nor One Shilling spent in Tavern. This Year is to be £20. will that be more then 20 dollars last Year. I doubt it much, however I hope you will write me on the subject and your opinion of the Propriety of my Resigning As I am too much Reduce'd to be able to live hear at my Own Expence. However notwithstanding all these complaints I have given orders for a Cask of Madeira Wine that will hold about 5 Galls. and Cost £50 a Gall, What do you think of that. (I hope it will be better then taking Bark.)

What is your opinion of Justice and the faith of the Nation with regard to realizeing the money, would it be right that a Countryman that makes you Pay 60 Dolls for a Turkey in the market, and at the same time tells you it is only 60 Pence should have his money realized, Or the Butcher that sold his fatt Cow, Yesterday at 20 Dollors a Pound, in that case his Cow would be worth as much as One of the Grand Moguls Eliphants. Or the Landlord that was paid last week for the Rent of a house £300 at the moderate Excha[nge] of 55 for 1. Or the Lawyer who asks you £100 Sterlg for a fee or in Contl at the Exchange. And yet on the other hand there are doubtless many instances were justice only requires it. I expect I shall tire you out before you have read all my nonsense, but I have not done yet.

What think you of The Honble Silas Condict being appointed Quarter Master General.[3] Quere would not his Friend General Winds have understood the Business as well.

I have not heard from Petersfield in several weeks & I am greatly distressed on the Account; If I had a Horse I believe I should be tempted to goe to see what was become of Mrs Fell and Son Peter. A number of Vessells have come up Yesterday and to day, what Effect it will have on the money I know not, but it seems to be agreed on all hands that money is very scarce hear at Present, A very droll circumstance of One of the Vessells from Cadiz, having along Passage and bad weather had been oblidged to throw her Guns over Board, came up with a Snow of 10 Guns which he boarded and took, and after getting the Guns on Board his own Vessell, he took a Brig, both said to be valuable Cargoes, The Watchman say it is Past 10 o Clock, time to goe to Bedd, so Adieu, Good night.

Monday morning [i.e., March 6]. I forgot to tell you last night, when I was out I heard there was letters come from So Carolina on the 10th Feby no account then of the arrival of the British Fleet.

On Saturday Congress agreed not to draw any more Bills on Europe till further orders;[4] I have been uniform in opposing the Plan of drawing Bills from the first time it was mentiond for several reasons.

P.M. This day has been taken up chiefly in dispatches from Major [General] Lincoln dated the 31st Jany.[5] He says on hearing of the Fleet on the Coast he sent out two frigates, who went and lookt in the River at Georgia where they see 5 Ships which they took to be line of Batle, One of which had an Admirals flag and I think about 14 Sail of other Vessells, but on seeing the Ships, Prepairing to make Sail they made the best of their way to Charlestown agreeable to their orders, they took 2 or 3 Vessells with 40 Dragoons and some Officers. One of the Vessells had had 45 Horses on Board, but had thrown 43 Over Board. 1000 of the No Carolina Militia were arrived and the Express who did not leave Charlestown till the 7th February says General Hogan with his Continental Troops, and Coll Washington with his horse were about 100 Mile off on their way and that several Vessells had arriv'd at Charlestown before he came a way from St.

Eustatia with stores &c for the Garrison. If this Letter is not long enough acquaint me in your next.

I am with great Respect Your Real friend,   John Fell

RC (NjR: Robert Morris Papers).
[1] See Samuel Holten's Diary, March 3–4, 1780, note 3.
[2] The "committee for supplying the treasurer," which had been appointed on February 14, had submitted a report that was taken up on March 2 in committee of the whole together with a report of the committee "for apportioning the quotas of bills of credit to the different states." The two reports thereafter became the focus of congressional debate on fiscal policy, which occupied the delegates on March 2, 3, 9, and 13–18 and provided the foundation for the landmark resolves adopted on March 18 repudiating the Continental dollar. These authorized the states to meet their cash quotas by submitting old bills to the Continental treasury at the rate of 40 to 1, and provided for the limited emission of new paper issues as the old bills were retired. See *JCC*, 16:41, 164, 205–8, 216–17, 223–24, 242–43, 255–56, 259, 261–67; and Samuel Huntington to the States, March 20, 1780.
[3] New Jersey governor William Livingston had recommended that Condict be appointed quartermaster general should Nathanael Greene resign his post. See Robert R. Livingston to William Livingston, March 20, 1780.
[4] See *JCC*, 16:228.
[5] According to the journals the Benjamin Lincoln letter read in Congress on March 6 was dated January 29, 1780. Later in the day, however, Congress did consider a Henry Laurens' letter dated January 31. *JCC*, 16:230, 234. For Lincoln's letter, see Samuel Huntington to Lincoln, March 6, 1780.

Samuel Holten's Diary

[March 6, 1780]

6. Monday. I wrote to the President of the Council of Massa Bay, to the Hone. J. Cushing.[1] We have accts that the enemy are arrived in Georgia.[2]

MS (MDaAr).
[1] For Holten's letter to the Massachusetts Council, see the following entry; his letter to John Cushing has not been found.
[2] See Samuel Huntington to Benjamin Lincoln, this date, note.

Samuel Holten to the Massachusetts Council

Sir.   Philadelphia March 6th. 1780.

I had the honor of addressing you a few days since with my colleagues upon public business, which I hope came safe to hand.[1]

The British King has not thought proper to mention America in his late speech; I am at no loss how to acct. for it in my own mind, for if he had observed upon the state of this Country as being in rebellion, I have no reason to think it wou'd be likely to answer a valuable purpose for him, at the several Courts in Europe at this day. His holding up his own immediate danger (no doubt) he apprehended wou'd be more likely to prevail with some of the powers in Europe to assist him, at least, to become mediators; and if they should, and the terms proposed by them cou'd not be complied with by Congress and her ally, the mediating powers would join with him in the war; altho' he may have no expectation of subjugating America, yet he will be very loth that we should continue sovereign & independent, or treat with us as such, and if he should be brought to treat with America as Independent; I suppose he will insist upon holding such parts of the united states, as his armies may be then in possession of; If this may be considered as the state of our national affairs in Europe, it must appear evident that all the exertions in our power ought to be made to drive the enemy from every part of these states.

The enhanced prices of all the necessaries of life, the great demands for money, and the exhausted state of the public treasury, greatly embarrasses our affairs; how far it is in the power of the Honble. Court to assist Congress, or what sums of money the good people can pay in, is best known to their immediate Representatives; But surely these are matters that require the greatest care & attention, as well as exertions.

By letters from General Lincoln dated the 31st of January,[2] which came to hand this day, we are informed that the enemy have arrived in force, in the state of Georgia, but have no particulars as to their numbers; It is supposed to be the Fleet that sailed from New York some time since.

Congress have resolved to recommend to the several states, to set apart the last Wednesday in April next, as a day of fasting, humiliation and prayer.

I have the Honor to be, with the highest sentiment of respect, Sir, your most obedient servant, S. Holten

RC (M–Ar: Revolutionary War Letters). Addressed: "The Honorable The President of the Council of Massachusetts Bay."
[1] See Massachusetts Delegates to the Massachusetts Council, March 1, 1780.
[2] Undoubtedly a reference to the January 29 letter from Lincoln that was read in Congress this day. See Samuel Huntington to Lincoln, this day.

William Churchill Houston to Robert Morris

Dear Sir, Philadelphia 6 March 1780

Looking over my File of unanswered Letters I am really ashamed to find how deeply I have [suf]fered my self to fall in your Debt. Your several obliging Favours of December 19 and 26 and 8 February last and 1 March instant are now before me, and if it is in my Power to keep my Hand to the Paper without Interruption for an Hour, I will endeavour to pay, in Quantity at least. It was my Intention to have lessened the Amount on my return from Princeton, but found the Court of Admiralty had detained you at Allenton; and being afraid that the Ice from above would interrupt the Passage at Howell's Ferry, the only one near, which was passable, I was fain to get [here on?] Monday Morning.

I have not failed duly to warn Congress that the whole, and much less two Thirds, of our Tax will not buy the Supplies for the Army, which must come from the State. They are not insensible of this, but they do not wish to make Exceptions, lest others, who will not have the same Reason, should wish to retain the Whole of their Tax, and it is not unknown to you how absurd People can and will argue when themselves are interested. You may rest assured that not only the whole will be given up, if necessary, but Money will be advanced if in our Power, and to me it is clear that if the Army keep their present Position it will be wanted, e[speciall]y if the Crops are good the coming Season. But from the States at a Distance from the Operations of the War, little will be wanted, except for marching Troops, unless it be of such a Nature as will bear distant Transportation. The Clothing and Sutlery furnished the Troops I find by Mr. Kelsey run very high, and it seems that when the Clothier General, this last Distribution, came to examine the Continental Stock and what each State had procured, he said New-Jersey came nearer to clothing their Troops than most of the other States after adding what Share he had for them, so that I believe we got Little or Nothing from him. This is a great Credit to us, but runs away with our Money and still the whole Brigade is not fully furnished. [It is] to be hoped that our Militia will not be so expensive to us as it has been, the Enemy being weaker at New-York, and the Army in the Vicinity of our Lines throughout a considerable Extent of them, and I have always thought that a smaller Number than we have employed generally, especially if a Proportion of them were active Horse, would answer the Purpose as well as more.

The Vermont Business which was to have come on 1st February ulto has been staved off, as New-York and Massachusetts-Bay were not fully prepared. New York is now ready, and as Massachusetts will probably wave their Claim, or dispute it afterwards with the prevailing Party of the two, the matter is ordered to come on Tomorrow without further postponing. Three Agents from Vermont attended on the 1st of February, but as they claimed to be admitted to support their Pretensions in the Capacity of a free and independent State, and did not submit the Matter on other Grounds, agreeably to the Resolutions of Congress of 14 September last, they staid but a little Time and then returned. I am with you in Apprehensions that this Contest will be extremely troublesome before it is issued, though I do not think that quite all those who are now peaceable and obedient Subjects of the *new State* will choose to carry the Matter to Extremities. One Thing surprises me in the Delegates of New York, and I cannot help reminding them of it now, and then, they talk of the Vermont-people as Great-Britain does of us, that not a third of the People are in the Interest of the new Government, that two Thirds or three fourths are friendly to New York. This is either pretended putting the best Face on the Matter, or is a fond Deception. It is a childish Idea that a Majority in any Country, where Equality of Condition and Improvement prevails, should be governed by a Minority. I almost venture to say it cannot happen anywhere, but in this Case I am certain. Many however may turn about and prefer returning to the Jurisdiction of New York before going to Blows, and in this respect I have some little Hopes. But should they generally persist as strongly as many of them seem to intend, it is not the Power of the State of New-York that can compose the revolt without serious Bloodshed. It may be possible to end the Matter amicably. New-York certainly offers generous Terms, peaceable Possession to every Man of what he has as a Farm and Habitation without Challenge or Incumbrance, and I think if they had offered this sooner, the Animosity [would] never have burned so strongly, nor run to such a Length. I approve these Terms of New-York, but I will remember what I thought some years ago, that if I were oppressed by a Set of Land-jobbers and Aristocratical Gentry as those People were, I would die in the last Ditch rather than succumb to it.

Mr. Clark has been with us since the 25th of January last.[1] I flatter myself that he will not be beside the Point in Matters respecting the Confederation, for I often hear him say that though he thinks the State of publick Affairs requires it's ratification, and postponing it to the Arrival of Peace will leave the States in Danger of a dreadful Separation, yet as to the leading Objections which New Jersey has made to it, they are clearly right, and ought to be contended on every Occasion when the general Good will be promoted by it. I write in Confidence, and take the Liberty to say on what you mention as to former Connections, that the old Leaven is not altogether gone from among us though it rarely appears, and a very desirable Harmony prevails in Congress at present. It is mortifying to recollect how much Time those Animosities have cost. I am of the same Opinion I was when I wrote to the Legislature early after my coming to Congress, which you will see on the Files of the Assembly; and as I feel myself entirely neutral as to Party in every Respect, I am determined to be on my Guard as long as I have a Part in the repre-[sentation], and to support that Character against every Bias, on Subjects of the Nature referred to.

As to the Question mentioned in yours of the 19 Decr. last and more particularly pursued in that of the 8th ulto, it is a Matter on which, all Things considered, the Decision is very difficult. Whether we had better contend for our Right to the Proceeds of what were called the Crown-lands on *United* or *Confederated* Ground?[2] The Reasons you give for taking the former in Preference before the latter are solid, but as usually happens in such Cases the other Side is not without Somewhat to say. I am still in the Situation I was when I wrote you first, undecided and querying. I am not of Opinion that the Confederation guarantees to the States any Bounds, and much less Bounds which they may claim *ad Libitum* without any formal Decision or Control. In our United State no Measure can be taken for the Circumscription, with any Tolerable Prospect of Success; I am convinced of this from the Temper I have seen discovered in Discussions of the Subject in Congress, and Claims are set up which I am well persuaded cannot be countenanced by any Documents in the Hands of the Claimants: but confederated, I must take the Liberty of saying Congress of Right might bring any State to shew their Grounds of Claims and decide whether the Union ought to recognize and defend the Extent to which they go. It is doubtless a Defect in the Confederation that no Mode is laid down for deciding between the United States and any one of them, in a Matter of this Kind, as well as between any two or more States where a Difference subsists as to Boundary; but this must be taken as inc[. . .to the?] Constitution of the Confederation, it being clear to me that there is within the Limits of the whole Confederacy Lands to which no particular State can shew any Title: and if there is one Mile square there may be a Million, and as no Right can subsist without a remedy of obtaining it, it is proper to make the Search, and to take the means for doing so. Suffer me to state three or four Particulars. 1. The *United* States are not in Capacity to take or hold Lands. They are associated for Defense and carrying on the War. Do the Acts and Instructions of the several States from which the Deputies come extend to any other Object but this, and those collateral and necessarily incident to it? And on this Footing I have ever opposed all Propositions for purchasing real Property as a Congress, and particularly in a late Instance in which a Proposal was made to sell to the Union the Estate upon which the Fortifications at West-point are erected.[3] 2. Pursuing this Idea were there a Territory acknowledged to [. . .] be out of the ownership or Claim of any particular State in the Union, are the United States assembled in Congress constituted or authorised to dispose of it? Or had they a Claim to Land or Territory in any State are they a Person or Body politick to pursue it? In my View, they are at present [under a] mere temporary Association, confederated they would stand on different Ground. 3. You see by the Act I sent you of 19 February last, passed in the State of New-York,[4] that there is a Disposition in that State to have their Limits ascertained, and in Order to satisfy the Discontents of many of their Sister-states they may be disposed to do what is reasonable. Their Example may be followed by other States, and though it may be said this will be more likely to be the Case before the Completion of the Confederation than after; as seems to be your Opinion; I confess it does not strike me, but that there will be a better Disposition to it then than now, while Jealousy and Irritation is so apt to take Place, and no Person Seems to feel any Security that if they give up a Part the rest will be Secured to them by a solemn federal guaranty. 4. It seems clear to me that Virginia, the Carolinas and Georgia will find their Interest in deserting a Part of their present Pretensions, and agreeing to a moderate Boundary for the Sake of interesting the rest of the Union to support them, or if they claim the Continuance of the Jurisdiction they will be inclined to relinquish the Property. It is not unknown to you that there is an extensive Territory on the Western Parts of those States which was heretofore of disputed Right between Great Britain and The Family Compact. I am not [sure] whether France or Spain, probably France who releas[ed] to Spain. The Crown of Great Britain in 1763 by Proclamation forbid the Location or Settlement of those Lands, and it is beyond a Doubt that if the Spaniards were disposed they might set up a Claim to them. In such Case Nothing but the Interest of the Union could avail to produce a relinquishment, and no rational thinking Person could expect that this would be cordially interposed for the exclusive Emolument of two or three States. However these Things I say to you in Confidence, and beg you will receive them under an Injunction of the closest Discretion. I could add somewhat further, but you would disapprove of my hinting at Matters which are not Mature for the Light. You will not mistake me, and set it down as my Opinion that it would be best first to confederate and then move in the Prosecution of our right. I had much rather the latter were done first, but my Idea is that the former would not render the latter altogether impracticable, and shut up every Prospect of Justice. That right will some how or other take Place, I am clear; because our Pretension is *just*. I am but a young Man, and younger in publick Business than in Life, but this I have observed, not only in reading but in Experience, that right and Truth do finally prevail, and on this idea my Confidence is rested. Persons of the best Wisdom and Forecast wish a Circumscription of Boundaries to take Place.[5]

RC (NjR: Robert Morris Papers).
[1] New Jersey delegate Abraham Clark had presented his credentials to Congress on January 25. *JCC*, 16:84–85.
Houston did not write this letter at a single sitting. The abrupt change in subject matter at this point and the physical appearance of the sheet upon which he began this section indicate that he wrote it at a later date, undoubtedly after March 7 but before the 13th. This is also apparent from his reference below to having already sent Morris a copy of the New York act concerning its western boundaries, which he enclosed with a letter to him of March 7. See note 4 below; and Houston to Morris, March 7, 1780. The conclusion of the letter is clearly dated "March 13th," for which see Houston to Morris, March 13, 1780.
[2] For their earlier exchanges on the western land issue, see Houston to Morris, November 27, 1779.
[3] This proposal does not appear in the journals of Congress.
[4] The New York legislature's February 19, 1780, act "to facilitate the completion of the Confederation" by limiting its western boundaries was presented to Congress on

March 7 and referred to a committee of Thomas Burke, Samuel Holten, and Roger
Sherman. No further action was taken on the measure until a report was made to
Congress on June 30. *JCC*, 16:236, 17:580. The act is in PCC, item 67, 2:250–53; and
JCC, 19:208–9. For Houston's transmittal of it, see Houston to Morris, March 7, 1780;
and note 1 above.
  [5] For the continuation of this letter, see Houston to Morris, March 13, 1780.

Samuel Huntington to Thomas Jefferson

Sir,   Philadelphia March 6. 1780
  You will receive Herewith enclosed an Act of Congress of this Day
requesting the Governors of Virginia, North, & South Carolina, to
use their utmost Exertions in filling up their Continental Battallions,
and in the mean Time to raise a Body of Militia to supply the Places
of the Battalions.[1]
  From the Intelligence your Excellency must have received from
the southern Department it is presumed the Necessity of reinforcing
the Southern Army hath called forth the Exertions of Virginia and
the more southern States.
  Your Excellency's Dispatches of the 9th ultimo has been received
and laid before Congress.[2]
  I have the honour to be with great respect your Excellency's hble
servant,   Sam. Huntington President

RC (Vi: Continental Congress Papers). In a clerical hand and signed by Huntington.
  [1] For the adoption of this resolve to reinforce the southern army, see *JCC*, 16:234;
and the following entry.
  Huntington also enclosed this resolve with similar letters of this date to the governors of North Carolina and South Carolina. PCC, item 14, fols. 307–8.
  [2] For Jefferson's February 9 letter concerning Virginia's boundary dispute with
Pennsylvania, see Jefferson, *Papers* (Boyd), 3:286–89; and Huntington to Jefferson,
December 30, 1779.

Samuel Huntington to Benjamin Lincoln

Sir,   Philadelphia March 6. 1780
  Your Letter of the 29th January hath been received and laid before
Congress this Day; they are disposed to lend every Aid in their
Power for the Defence of Charles Town and the southern Depart-
ment.
  Enclosed you will receive an Act of Congress of this Day request-
ing the States of Virginia, North and South Carolinas, to use their
utmost Exertions in filling up their Continental Batallions, and in
the mean Time to supply their Place with Militia.[1]
  You will also observe the Treasury are Directed to report the
proper Measures for supplying the military Chest of the southern
Army.

I hope before this comes to Hand, you may receive such Reinforcements as shall enable you to defend Charlestown and cover the Country so as to prevent further Incursions of the Enemy.

I am Sir with great Respect and Esteem your humble Servt,
                                        Sam. Huntington President

RC (NcU: Preston Davie Collection). In a clerical hand and signed by Huntington.

[1] Lincoln's January 29 letter reporting the arrival of an enemy fleet off the coast of Georgia and the vulnerability of South Carolina to immediate attack is in PCC, item 158, fols. 313–15. The enclosed resolve, adopted on motion of South Carolina delegate John Mathews, requested these recruiting measures to augment the southern army under Lincoln's command as soon as possible, but anticipating that compliance would consume several months went on to specify "that, in the meantime, the said states be requested to raise a body of militia, to join and serve in the southern army until the first day of January next, unless sooner relieved. . . ." *JCC*, 16:234. See also Committee of Congress to Lincoln, March 7, 1780.

Samuel Huntington to William Livingston

Sir,   Philada March 6. 1780

Your Excellency will receive enclosed an Act of Congress of this Day recommending to the Legislature of New Jersey to take Measures for the Payment of the Accounts arising for Supplies lately furnished to the Army in Consequence of the Application of the Commander in Chief, in the mode which they may judge most conducive to the Relief of those who have furnished them including the same in account against the United States subject to Examination as other Charges.[1]

I have the honour to be &c &c,   S.H.

LB (DNA: PCC, item 14).

[1] Congress adopted this resolve in response to a Board of Treasury report which explained that simply as a practical matter supplies recently collected in New Jersey "can be more conveniently paid and settled under the direction of the State than in any other mode." See *JCC*, 16:235–36.

Philip Schuyler to Samuel Huntington

Sir   Philadelphia March 6th. 1780

In the letter which I had the honor to address your Excellency on the 15th ult. from Saratoga I purposed personally to have explained myself to Congress on the Subject of the Appointment of the 21st of January last[1] but reflecting that notwithstanding the entire confidence I entertain of the honor and candour of every Individual member of Congress It is nevertheless possible that thro want of perpescuity in Expressing myself or misapprehension in others, what I may verbally deliver on the Subject may be unintentionally Construed or repeated in a sense widely different from my Intentions, this Consideration Induces me to Convey my determination in writing.

Every reflection Sir, I have made, since the receipt of Your Excellencys letter of the 24th January, on the appointment mentioned In It has Confirmed the conclusion I very Early drew that I could not Consistently with my honor and reputation accept of any employment under Congress In a Station rather less honorable or less Important than that which I once had the honor to hold, And when the Circumstances which led to my quitting the Army shall recur to Congress, I trust they will acquiesce In the Justness and propriety of this determination on my part.

I do not mean Sir to Convey the most distant Idea that I Sollicit a restoration to the rank and place I held In the Army; It is true that I quitted It with reluctance and that I have often since Comented that I was drove to the necessity of doing It. Yet the delicacy I entertain with respect to the feelings of others who might possibly conceive themselves Injured by a perfect restoration of my rank, Added to other Considerations have Induced me to lay aside every wish for a reappointment. But Sir as I am Incapable of witholding any Services my Country may deem me Capable of rendering, as a reform In the Civil departments of the Army is of the highest necessity and as Congress have thought proper to apply to me for my Aid on the Occasion permit me to tender them an offer of my services as a member of their house on a Committee to Consult with the Commander In Chief and the heads of the several civil departments of the Army, and to Adopt such Measures as will have a probable tendency to compleat the great Object of the resolution of the 20th January; As a member of such a Committee I should Esteem It my duty to visit every part of the Continent for the purpose of Introducing good order and a proper œconomy and Should deem myself fully rewarded for every possible exertion In the Success of the business and the Approbation of Congress.

I am, Sir very respectfully, Your Excellencys most Obedient Huml. Sert, Ph. Schuyler

RC (DNA: PCC, item 153).

[1] For Schuyler's appointment with Thomas Mifflin and Timothy Pickering as a commissioner to conduct an inquiry into the expenses of the staff departments, and his February 15 reply declining the appointment, see Huntington to Thomas Mifflin, January 24; and Huntington to Schuyler, January 24, note.

Committee of Congress to Benjamin Lincoln

Sir.   Philadelphia March 7. 1780
    The reason why we have not answered your letters of the 18 & 21
of Decr. is, that the board of war (to whom they were committed)
informed us, that they had fully done so.[1]
    Yours of the 31 January we received the 5th Inst. announcing the
appearance of the enemy off your coasts.[2]
    A Copy of the act of Congress, respecting the Co-operations of the
Spaniards with you in the reduction of Savanna and St. Augustine,[3]
has been transmitted to the Governor of the Havannah, & make no
doubt from the favourable dispositions manifisted by that Court,
that every assistence will be afforded on their part, that they can
consistently render us.
    We flatter ourselves when the experiment comes to be made, that
the Frigates will find an easy & safe birth, at the entrance of the bar,
every risque ought to be run in the attempting it, for it is only in this
position we apprehend, that they can be essentially servicable.
    We hope to have as frequent intelligence from you, as you can
conveniently furnish us with—to facilitate which, we shall endeavour
to get established a regular cha[nel] of communication, as we conceive it to be essentially necessary, at this important crisis of our
affairs in your quarter, to have frequent & regular intelligence from
you.
    We have nothing new to communicate to you from hence. Wish-
ing you a successful Campaign, We are Sir, With the highest Esteem
& Regard, Yr. most Obedt. servts.
                                        Jno. Mathews, Chr.
                                        In behalf of the Committee

RC (MH–H: bMS Am 1649.8). Written and signed by John Mathews.
[1] Lincoln's letters of December 19 and 22, 1779, rather than "the 18 & 21 Decr.,"
were presented to Congress on February 7 by the committee "appointed to correspond with the commanding officer in the southern department." The letter of the
19th, which was returned to the committee, is not in PCC. That of the 22d was
referred to the Board of War and committee of intelligence. See *JCC*, 16:129–30; and
PCC, item 158, fols. 309–12. For the February 12 report of the board of war, specifying the steps to be taken for supplying the forces of the comte d'Estaing, see *JCC*,
16:163.
[2] For Congress' official response to this letter, see Samuel Huntington to Lincoln,
March 6, 1780.
[3] For this December 16 act of cooperation, see Committee at Headquarters to
Congress, December 7, 1779, note 1.

William Churchill Houston to Robert Morris

Dear Sir,   Philada. 7 March 1780
I yesterday began a Letter to you but by Reason of constant Inter-
ruption and Business, have not finished it.[1] I enclose you in the
Mean Time an Act of the Legislature of New York[2] which was this
Morning read and referred to a Comittee, from which I am willing
to expect some good Consequences. You will communicate it to the
House, and believe me, dear Sir, your obedt and obliged hble
Servt.   William Ch. Houston

RC (NjR: Robert Morris Papers).
[1] See Houston to Morris, March 6, 1780.
[2] See ibid., note 4.

James Lovell to Abigail Adams

Tuesday March 7 1780 3 o Clock P.M.
The Post but now arrived will be again on his Way in an Hour. I
retire therefore from a Circle of public Debate, to acknowledge, at a
Side-Window, your *Favor* of February 13th this moment unsealed. I
admire the Remarks. Be persuaded, lovely Moralist, to indulge me
with a Sight of what occasioned them—"Passages of Letters of January 6th & 18th."[1] I shall be much chagrined if you do not comply.
Mutilated as to Names, inclosed without Comment under a bare
Superscription to me there will be no Renewal of "Hazard." You
have said "they *shall* pass the Ordeal." Let *me* perform your Vow. It
will be done religiously, you may depend upon it. My Head & Heart
have known no Moment in which Esteem for Mrs. Adams has not
been joined with their Affection for Portia. And, if my Pen has been
untrue to that Union, may a Whitlow punish the Fingers that moved
it! I am not yet competent by Recollection to venture any Thing
further, in Arrest of your Judgement, than a mere Hint, suggested
by the last Line of your Quotation respecting Wit. While, in Winter I
speak to Virgin Portia, only about the keen Air of the Days and the
Comfort of my domestic Fire-side; may I not, to married Lucretia,
take Notice of the lonesome tedious Nights, and lament a Separation
from my own faithful mate? Am I to expect a double Answer? Yea
for a Shepherd, Nay for a "Senator." I could not rest satisfied without some Explanation; yet every Word that is papered frustrates
more & more my Wish & I hope yours for an Oblivion of the Whole,
so far as relates to any third Person. I am sure something is wrong. I
am anxious to know the Degree. I deprecate the Continuance of the
Impressions under which you wrote. I would not have a Monument
remain either of my real Deficiency of Respect for you or of your

Conception of such a Thing. Therefore this Scrawl must be devoted as the 3 others have been.[2]

The new Minister is much esteemed. Mr.Laurens has only a Clerk with him, as he means to change in Europe as he may find Occasion on account of Languages. I am pledged to go if chosen, but I have not nor will I utter a Word that shall seem like soliciting. My Inclination is against going. I foresee much Vexation in the Undertaking. I am enraged at the Publication you speak of, tho' no one here has yet seen it.[3] I have heard of it from Mrs. L & from a Friend at Portsmouth.

A Vessel that sailed from hence 14 days after Mr. Gerard, got to France in 25 days; so that I am led to hope the *Sensible* fell in wth. the same Winds, sailing about the same time.

The Letters by the Mercury were some time prior in date to what we had before recd.

As to the Pages of —78 which began the year,[4] they were forwarded by Mr. Gerard. I have continued —79 under Enclosures to Mr. S. Adams so as that you should also see them unless a Vessel was on the Point of Sailing. I am momentarily in Expectation of being able to give you News of the Arrival of your Husband. It is a favorable Circumstance that we have not yet heard of him Via New York.

With respectful Affection, I am Madam, your humble Servant,

J L

RC (MHi: Adams Papers). Adams, *Family Correspondence* (Butterfield), 3:294–96.

[1] Actually January 13 not "18." For Lovell's allusion, see his letters of January 6 and 13 to Abigail; and Adams, *Family Correspondence* (Butterfield), 3:273–74.

[2] At this point Lovell left one-half page blank.

[3] In her February 13 letter to Lovell, Abigail stated that she had read a newspaper report concerning "a probability of your going abroad," which Lovell had once hinted when his name was being mentioned for the post of secretary to the American mission in France. Ibid., p. 274.

[4] That is, pages of the printed journals of Congress for 1778.

Maryland Delegates to Thomas Sim Lee

Sir, Philadelphia, March 7th 1780.

We are honor'd by your Excellency's Favor of 18th last.[1] The Minister of France knows very well, however wrong he may have deemed the Measure, that the Seizing the french Flour was to releave the exceeding great Distress of the Army, & we have never understood, or even heard it suggested, that the Conduct of the State was imputed to any other Motive. We have no Reason to think that he doubts the Attachment of Maryland to the Alliance, & have heard him express Pleasure at the Receipt of your Excellency's late Letter, which he says is fully satisfactory. We have set before him, in the clearest Point of View we cou'd, the Extent of your Powers, which will not permit the suspension of any Law, without an Exception for that Purpose, & that it is your Duty to see all Laws executed in the utmost Extent; of all which he appears fully persuaded. The Consequences which he mentions to have imparted to one of us were, that as he found the Supplies were uncertain, & not to be depended upon, even after being purchased & stored, he cou'd not, under such Uncertainty, invite a french Fleet to our Coast. We have ever esteemed it our Duty, & hoped we had discharged it, to communicate to the Governor & Council, in Recess of Assembly; all Matters of Importance acted upon in Congress which may relate to Maryland; therefore are at some Loss for the Meaning of your last Paragraph, as we know of no Matter of Importance, relative to the State lately discussed which has not been forwarded—there is indeed a Report of a Committee on the Application of Mr Holker for three thousand Barrels of Flour over & above the Quantity last assigned, which, when passed, we shall not fail to communicate.[3] We have the Honor to be with the most perfect Respect, Yr Excellency's most obt. & very hum. Servants,   Geo Plater

James Forbes

RC (MdAA: Red Books). Written by Plater and signed by Plater and Forbes.

[1] Lee had written to the Maryland delegates on February 18 regarding the purchase of clothing for Maryland troops, for which see Maryland Delegates to Lee, February 23, 1780. The letter to which the delegates are replying here, however, is a February 17 letter from Lee relating to Maryland's seizure of flour purchased by the French agent of marine Jean Holker, for which see *Md. Archives*, 43:89–90; and Samuel Huntington's letters to La Luzerne and to Lee, January 18, 1780.

[2] For the Maryland Council's February 17 letter to La Luzerne, see *Md. Archives*, 43:88–89.

[3] See Samuel Huntington to Certain States, March 11, 1780, note 1. In addition, Maryland was also sent an emergency appeal for flour for the Continental Army by the Board of War this day, since New Jersey was already nearly "exhausted by its Exertions for the Supply of the Troops this Winter." See *Md. Archives*, 43:444.

Frederick A. Muhlenberg to Joseph Reed

Sir,   [March 7, 1780]

Mr. Melsheimer,[1] formerly Chaplain to a Regiment of Dragoons in the british Service, having made Application to me, I beg Leave to assure Your Excellency that I have known him well ever since he has been in this State, & have always found him to be a true Friend to American Liberty, & desirous of remaining in this Country. He has to my certain Knowledge sacrific'd his little All, together with every Prospect of future Promotion in his native Country. He has hitherto officiated in some small Congregations near Lebanon, Lancaster County but unfortunately for him, was some Time ago suspected of interfering in an old Dispute between the Members of, the German Luth. Congregation at Lebanon, which occasioned one Party of them to apply to the Honble Judge Atlee, to have him removed. He assures me, he never meddled either with one or the other Party, and is willing to bind him self not to interfere in their Church Disputes, nor to officiate there, unless by the unanimous Consent of both parties.

I ask Pardon for drawing Your Excellencies Attention from more important Concerns, & have the Honour to be, with the most perfect Esteem & Regard, Your Excellencies most obedient & very humble Servt, F.A. Muhlenberg

RC (PU: Rosengarten Manuscripts). Endorsed: "1780 March 7th. From F.A. Muhlenburgh."

[1] Friedrich Valentin Melzheimer had been a chaplain in a Brunswick regiment of mercenaries with the British army. His relations with the Muhlenbergs and the Lutherans of Pennsylvania can be traced in the journal of Muhlenberg's father, Henry Melchior Muhlenberg, *The Journals of Henry Melchior Muhlenberg*, trans. Theodore G. Tappert and John W. Doberstein, 3 vols. (Philadelphia: Muhlenberg Press, 1942–58), 3:266, 301, 303, 377, 745, 751.

Philip Schuyler to George Washington

Dear Sir Philadelphia March 7th 1780

I arrived on Sunday but did not take my seat In Congress until this morning as I deemed It prudent previously to adress them on the Subject of their appointment of the 21st January which I did by letter Copy whereof I have the honor to Inclose for Your Excellency's perusal.[1] I believe there is a determination not to Accept of any Services I may be able to render them In the line In which I have offered them, many here Affect not to see the propriety of the distinction I have drawn, but I shall be satisfyed If the Candid and Ingenous, who are not Always a majority In or out of doors, shall discover that It is not one, without a difference.

The measure I proposed to Gen. Greene the moment before I parted with him I learnt on my arrival had Already been decided upon as unnecessary,[2] and I was Confidentially advised that It would be In vain to urge It, I must therefore forbear, however Strongly Impressed with Its Importance.

I do not advise you of the Intelligence from Carolina as Gen. Lincoln will probably be more full on the Subject than I can be. The minister has a letter from an agent In which he Informs the former that part of the british were destined *pour les Antilles*.

I believe It will be necessary for Gen. Greene to adress Congress very pointedly on the Subject of the Waggoners as I find a disposition In many to have them drawn from the Army.[3] The reasons why they should not, If Even the Army would after all be Sufficiently in force, will be Obvious to him, and I wish him to Adduce them fully, to Corroborate what I shall deliver on the Subject before his letter arrives.

Our Finances are Compleatly deranged, a Committee of the whole have had them under Consideration for some time before my arrival, they have been on the business to day,[4] without making any progress. It seems a paradox that the whole should be more Incompetent than a part but I am So perfectly persuaded of It, that I shall Strive to get It referred to a few, I have thrown together my Ideas on the Subject, how they will be accepted I must leave to time tho I believe some good would result If they were adopted.

Be so Good as to Intreat Your Lady to Accept of my best respects and to believe that I am most Sincerely with those Sentiments of Affection & Esteem which afford an Ingenous mind the most Sensible of all Satisfactions.

Your Excellency's Most Obedient Hu Servt,   Ph. Schuyler

RC (DLC: Washington Papers).
   [1] Schuyler enclosed a copy of his March 6 letter to Samuel Huntington.
   [2] The "measure" Schuyler had proposed to Quartermaster General Nathanael Greene has not been discovered.
   [3] Congress did not establish new regulations for the wagonmaster and wagoneers until July 15, 1780, when it adopted new regulations for the entire quartermaster general's department. See *JCC*, 17:615–35.
   [4] Schuyler's testimony that Congress debated "Our Finances" this day in committee of the whole should be taken seriously, even though Secretary Thomson's journal entry for March 7 contains no hint of such proceedings. Cf. *JCC*, 16:236–38. Congress had opened debate on the subject on March 2, and the journals do indicate that it was taken up in committee of the whole on March 3, 9, 13, 14, 15, 16, 17, and 18.

Samuel Holten's Diary

[March 8–9, 1780]
   8. Wednesday. I ⟨attended⟩ met the medical committee. Colo. Pickering dined with us, & Colo. Nicholos. Nothing new.
   9. Thursday. Congress have been in a Committee of the whole on finance. This evening a woman was taken as a thief in this house.

MS (MDaAr).

Samuel Huntington to Baron von Steuben

Sir,   Philadelphia March 8. 1780
   I have the Pleasure to transmit you the Act of Congress inclosed of the 7th Instant by which you will be informed they have been pleased to allow you the Sum of two hundred & fifty Louis D'Ors in Bills of Exchange for reimbursing your Expences in coming to America,[1]

And also to order the further Sum of five hundred & forty six Louis D'ors to be advanced to you in Bills of Exchange on Account.

I have the honour to be, with Sentiments of Esteem & Regard, your hble servant,   Sam. Huntington President

RC (NHi: Steuben papers). In a clerical hand and signed by Huntington.

[1] Congress adopted the enclosed March 7 resolve for compensating Steuben pursuant to a February 28 recommendation of the Board of War, for which see *JCC*, 16:204, 215–16, 231–33, 237. For the baron's efforts to put his private finances in order and to cope with the staggering depreciation of Continental currency, see also John M. Palmer, *General von Steuben* (New Haven: Yale University Press, 1937), pp. 223–24.

Samuel Huntington to John Benezet

Sir,   Philada March 9. 1780

By the Act of Congress of the 8th Instant herewith enclosed you will be informed they have directed that Bills of Exchange be drawn on the Honble John Jay Esquire to the Amount of five thousand Pounds Sterling and forwarded to Mr Wm Bingham or delivered to you his Agent, to discharge in part the Debts due from the United States to Mr Bingham.[1]

And also that Congress have been pleased to grant Leave to Mr Bingham to return to Philadelphia agreeable to his request.[2]

I am Sir &c &c,   S.H.[3]

LB (DNA: PCC, item 14).

[1] This action marked the settlement of a long-standing claim against the Committee of Commerce that William Bingham, Continental agent at Martinique, had been actively pursuing since the preceding September. John Benezet (d. 1781), a Philadelphia lawyer who was married to Bingham's sister Hannah, had been representing his brother-in-law in this proceeding. See *JCC*, 15:1036, 1384, 16:190, 241; PCC, item 90, 1:172–79; and Robert C. Alberts, *The Golden Voyage: The Life and Times of William Bingham, 1752–1804* (Boston: Houghton Mifflin Co., 1969), pp. 70–73, 78–81, 86–87, 101.

[2] Bingham boarded ship to return home to Philadelphia from Martinique on March 30, 1780, long before he learned of Congress' adoption of this resolution. Alberts, *Golden Voyage*, pp. 81–82, 86.

[3] This day Huntington also wrote a brief letter to William Smith, former delegate to Congress and Continental agent at Baltimore, enclosing a resolve of March 6 concerning payment of interest on Continental loan office certificates issued in the state of Georgia. Smith had appealed to Congress for relief because the collapse of government in Georgia had made it impossible to collect interest on such certificates, which he had recently received in payment on a business transaction. By Congress' resolve of the sixth, Smith was advised that the government was "now again in operation," and since interest could only be paid "by the person who is possessed of the books of the office" the certificates would have to be presented at the Georgia Continental loan office. See *JCC*, 16:231; and PCC, item 14, fol. 312, item 78, 20:503–6.

Samuel Huntington to George Washington

Sir   Philadelphia March 9. 1780

Your Excellency will receive herewith enclosed an Act of Congress of the 8th Instant, recommending to the States of Virginia, North, and South Carolina to have in readiness to act as the Operations of the Campaign shall require a Body of five thousand Militia, or State Troops over and above their Quotas of Continental, and to be called into actual Service whenever the Commanding Officer in the southern Department shall deem it necessary.[1]

Your Excellency will also observe the discretionary Directions given to make such Detachment from the Troops under your immediate Command as their Strength and Circumstances will permit to reinforce the southern Army.[2]

You have also enclosed an Act of the 6th Instant requesting the Exertions of Virginia and the two Carolinas in filling up their Battallions &c.[3]

It were much to be desired we could obtain a more accurate Knowledge of the number and Strength of the Enemy to the Southward and their intended Operations.

I have the honour to be, with the greatest Respect, your Excy's hble servt,   Sam. Huntington President

RC (DLC: Washington Papers). In a clerical hand and signed by Huntington.

[1] JCC, 16:239–40.

[2] Washington was reluctant to detach troops to the southern department in keeping with this "discretionary" request until he was better informed of the enemy's intentions for the 1780 campaign, but on April 2 he informed Congress that despite the risk involved in weakening his main army, he was placing "the Maryland line and the Delaware Regiment under marching Orders immediately," and he asked assistance in arranging their transportation southward of the Delaware River. See PCC, item 152, 8:487–91; and Washington, Writings (Fitzpatrick), 18:197–200.

[3] For these measures to reinforce the southern department, see Huntington's letters to Thomas Jefferson and to Benjamin Lincoln, March 6, 1780.

James Lovell to Samuel Adams

Dear Sir   March 9. 1780

Be so kind as to place with the Navy Board the Letters for France and forward to Mrs. A Adams those for her.

By some fatality the Letter of our Court of Decr. 2d never reached Congress but in a Copy two days ago: Nor had a Line from you or any body else come to the Delegates on the Subject.[1] The next Post will probably convey a Proclamation for Fasting &c. on the last Wednesday of April. New York presses Congress hard upon the Resolves in regard to Vermont but I believe there will be much parrying. The plain Truth is the People of the Grants gave assurances to our half Comtee. that visited them last Summer,[2] of a Will-ingness to submit to a Decision of Congress. New York did the same. We asked others to follow. The Grant People now refuse. New York & N.H. are desirous of our going on. 3 States cannot vote, two are represented by members not here in Sepr. & Octr: Ellery & Burke who *will not* believe they have any right whatever to discuss the Independce. of Vermont. Others with the Discussion 10 years off. Thus stands the Matter. But I heartily wish to know what Mass. has to say. They were "disconted [discontented] with the" Decission of the King in Council of 1739.[3] So they were with the Navigation Act of an hundred years & more. Did they ever signify that between 1739 and the breaking out of this War.

Col. R H Lee, Doctr. Wetherspoon and Genl. Roberdeau present their Compliments.

The Letters bro't by the Mercury contained nothing so new as we had before recd. I donot think it proper to *publish* from Dr. F—— that Portugal is very friendly and that her Ports may be shortly opened to us.[4] Yrs. affectionately,   Jas. Lovell

[*P.S.*] The Bearer has blank Commissions for the State directed to the president of the Council, but I believe without a Letter of Advice. I recd. them from our Messenger Patten to be sent by the first oppy.

RC (NN: Adams Papers).
[1] In September Congress had called upon Massachusetts, New Hampshire, and New York "to pass laws expressly authorizing Congress to hear and determine all differences between them" relative to Vermont, pledging in return to open hearings on the subject on February 1, 1780. Lovell is referring here to the Massachusetts Council's December 2 response to that appeal, which was finally received by Congress with the council's letter of February 7. See PCC, item 65, 1:416–18, 424–25; John Jay to Thomas Chittenden, September 25; and Massachusetts Delegates to the Council, October 4, 1779.

For Adams' explanation of Massachusetts' slow response to this appeal, see Adams, *Writings* (Cushing), 4:180–81, 183–87.
[2] For the activities of the "half Comtee" that went to Vermont in June 1779 to evaluate prospects for a congressional settlement of rival claims to the region, see Committee of Congress to Samuel Minott et al., June 23, 1779, note 2.
[3] Lovell is referring to the "Order in Council" of December 27, 1739, which estab-lished the boundary between Massachusetts and New Hampshire. It is summarized in *NYHS Collections*, 3 (1870): 110. In his March 25 reply to Lovell, Adams explained that "They were discontented with the Decision in 1739, and I think afterwards directed their Agent Mr Bollan to manifest it to the King in Council." Adams, *Writings* (Cushing), 4:184.
[4] A reference to Benjamin Franklin's October 4, 1779, letter to Congress. See Lovell to Horatio Gates, March 4, 1780, note 6.

John Collins to Nathanael Greene

Dear Sir   Philadelphia March the 10th. 1780
I have nothing of Consequence to inform you. The Committee appointed to take into Consideration your letter, Reported a day or

two past, you w[ill] be Requested to Continue in your office of Qu [M.] General. The Commitioners to Regulate the D[epart]ments of the army are here, a Committee of Congress Consisting of three Are appointed to Join them [in] their Consultations. The Report of the Commi[ttee] on your letter is Referd. to them, and what they may Produce is uncertain.[1] I Shall not be very particular as I am informd. by Mr Mitchell y[ou] are Expected in this City in a day or two.

I Shall be Glad to See you And hope you w[ill] Calmly Reflect before you Resine your Post.

My kind Regard to your Lade & all my Good Frie[nds].

I am With friendly Reg[ards], yours,   John Collins

NB. The Commit. is but this afternoon appointd.

RC (MiU–C: Greene Papers).
[1] See Samuel Huntington to Greene, March 16, 1780.

Samuel Holten's Diary

[March 10–11, 1780]
10. Friday. I met the committee on Finance twice this day. No news.

11. Saturday. I was with the come. of Finance the chief of this day. I dind with the minisr.[1]

MS (MDaAr).
[1] That is, the chevalier de La Luzerne.

Samuel Huntington to
the Chevalier de La Luzerne

Sir,   Philada March 10. 1780
I have been honoured with your Letter of the 8th Instant, with the Intelligence therein referred to received from Le Comte de Vergennes and M. Gerard which you was pleased to communicate all which has been laid before Congress.[1]

The Regard and Affection his most Christian Majesty has been pleased to testify towards these United States in granting the Request respecting the Officers in the Department of Engineers[2] is very pleasing and satisfactory.

The kind Offices of M. Gerard and the Commandant at Martinique are very acceptable and claim particular Notice as evident Proofs of the Friendship and regard which delineate the national Character of our good Allies.[3]

I have the honour to be &c &c,   S. H.[4]

LB (DNA: PCC, item 14).

[1] La Luzerne's March 8 letter to Congress, and the enclosed extract from the comte de Vergennes' September 25, 1779, letter to him, granting permission to four French officers to remain in the service of the Continental Army, are in PCC, item 95, 1:76–83. Vergennes' letter is in Archives du ministère des affaires étrangerès: Correspondance politique, États-Unis, 10:39.

[2] That is, Louis Le Bègue Duportail, Jean-Baptiste de Gouvion, the chevalier de Laumoy, and Louis de La Radière. For their request for permission to remain on leave from the French army to continue as Continental Engineers, see these *Letters*, 11:493–94.

[3] La Luzerne had reported that Conrad Alexandre Gérard had secured permission from the commander of Martinique "for the frigate *Confederation* [*i.e., Confederacy*] belonging to Congress, the same sources and facilties as are enjoyed by his majesty's own vessels. But there are no materials for masts, and as this vessel has been dismasted, Mr. Gerard knows no other means of hastening her repairs than that of sending masts to him from Boston or any other part of the continent where Congress can procure them." The information was immediately referred to the Board of Admiralty. See *JCC*, 16:244; and a translation of La Luzerne's letter in Wharton, *Diplomatic Correspondence*, 3:540–41.

[4] This day Huntington also wrote brief letters to David Avery, "Chaplain to the late [Ebenezer] Learnards [Massachusetts] Brigade," and Col. John Bailey, his commanding officer, communicating Congress' acceptance of Avery's resignation. See *JCC*, 16:225–26; and PCC, item 14, fols. 313–14, item 78, 1:345–48.

Samuel Huntington to Certain States

Sir   Philada March 11. 1780

Your Excellency will receive herewith enclosed an Act of Congress of this Day wherein the States of Maryland, Pennsylvania and Connecticut are respectively requested to deliver Mr Holker Agent for the Royal Marine of France certain specified Quantities of Flour, and other Provisions on or before the first Day [*of May next*] for the Use of the Marine of France,

Which Articles are to be considered as part of the Quotas of Supplies called for from those respective States, by the Resolution of the 25th of Feby last.[1]

As this Provision is wanted to supply the Fleet of our Ally in America, it is not doubted the several States will readily comply with the request of Congress.[2]

I have the honour to be &c,   S.H.

LB (DNA: PCC, item 14). Addressed: "The President of Pennsylvania. N.B. The like to the Governors of Maryland & Connecticut."

[1] In a letter to Congress of January 31, the Board of War had forwarded two letters from Jean Holker concerning difficulties he was still encountering in attempting to obtain provisions for the French navy. These were referred to a committee on February 1, which submitted a report on March 2. This report was immediately recommitted, however, and a revised report was submitted on March 6, which was debated on the 11th. The March 11 resolutions herewith enclosed to Connecticut, Maryland, and Pennsylvania concerning provisions to be procured in these states were adopted essentially as recommended by the committee on the 6th. See *JCC*, 16:116, 222, 231–32, 251–52; and PCC, item 19, 3:147–48, item 148, 1:41–44, 51–52. For the

resolution of February 25 referred to here, see Huntington to the States, February 26, 1780.

[2] Huntington also sent a copy of these resolves this day with the following brief cover letter to Jean Holker. "You will receive herewith enclosed an Act of Congress of this Day by which you will be informed of the Measures they have adopted, not only for replacing the flour which hath been borrowed of you; but also for supplying you with a farther Quantity of flour and other Provisions for the use of the Royal Marine of France." PCC, item 14, fol. 314. See also Huntington's letters to La Luzerne and to Thomas Sim Lee, January 18; and Maryland Delegates to Lee, March 7, 1780.

Samuel Huntington to Benjamin Lincoln

Sir,   Philadelphia March 11. 1780

You will receive herewith enclosed four Acts of Congress of the 25th February and the 6th, 8th, & 11th Instant marked No. 1, 2, 3, & 4.[1]

Congress while they are disposed to give every necessary Aid in their Power for the Defense of the southern States by reinforcing the Army under your Command confide in your Wisdom and Prudence that no unnecessary Burthen or Expence will be created by calling out more of the Militia than the Exigency of the Case may at any Time require.

I have the honour to be, with Sentiments of Esteem & regard, your hble servant,   Sam. Huntington President

RC (CSmH: HM 22638). In a clerical hand and signed by Huntington.

[1] For these resolves, see *JCC*, 16:196–201, 234, 239–40, 252. Huntington's clerk wrote the following descriptions of these items in the margin of the letter, but they have been lined out.

"No 1. Act for specific Supplies."
"No 2. Calling for reinforcements."
"No 3. of Militia in Virginia &c."
"No 4. for Qr Master, Muster & Commissary southern Army."

Samuel Huntington to
Thomas Mifflin and Timothy Pickering

Gentlemen,   Philadelphia March 11. 1780

By the Act of Congress of the 10th Instant herewith enclosed you will observe That upon General Schuyler's declining to accept his Appointment, the other Commissioners are empowered to proceed in the Business committed to them, and a Committee of Congress are appointed to confer &c with the Commissioners on the Subject matter of their Appointment.[1]

I am with Sentiments of Esteem & respect, Gentlemen, your hble servant,   Sam Huntington President

RC (DNA: RG 93, M859). In a clerical hand and signed by Huntington.
[1] *JCC*, 16:244. For the developments that preceded the adoption of this resolution, see Huntington to Thomas Mifflin, January 24, 1780, note 1.

Samuel Huntington to George Washington

Sir,   Philadelphia March 11 1780[1]
Your Excellency will receive herewith enclosed two Acts of Congress of the 10th & 11th Instant.

The former containing Regulations for the Payment of Arrears due, or to become due to the Soldiery for cloathing pursuant to the Resolution of Congress of the 16th of August last,[2]

The latter empowering the Commander in Chief to make the most salutary Regulations possible for modifying the Practice of taking Men from the Regiments to act as Servants to Officers with certain Regulations respecting Servants that may be hereafter enlisted or retained by Officers.[3]

Your Excellency will also herewith receive a Copy of the Sentence of the Court Martial on the Trial of Major General Arnold with an Act of Congress of the 12th of February confirming the same.[4]

I have the honour to be, with the highest Respect, your Excy's hble servant,   Sam Huntington President

RC (DLC: Washington Papers). In a clerical hand and signed by Huntington.
[1] This letter is dated March 12 in the presidential letterbook. PCC, item 14, fol. 316.
[2] See *JCC*, 14:970–71, 16:245–47. Huntington also sent copies of this clothing resolve with brief March 11 letters to the clothier general, James Wilkinson, and to the paymaster general, William Palfrey. PCC, item 14, fol. 315. Furthermore, the enclosed March 10 "Act" partially described here by Huntington actually contained a second resolve, which declared "That no allowance of pay, rations or subsistance, ought to be made to any person after he ceases to be in office." This second resolve was sent by Huntington to the commissary general of issues Charles Stewart on March 17. PCC, item 14, fol. 318.
[3] *JCC*, 16:250.
[4] For Congress' confirmation of Benedict Arnold's court–martial sentence, which carried by a vote of 11 states to 1, only Thomas Burke, Robert R. Livingston, and John Mathews dissenting, see *JCC*, 16:120–21, 135, 153, 161–62. Considering the heat generated by Pennsylvania's charges against Arnold in January 1779, which were the focus of the court-martial whose sentence was hereby confirmed by Congress, the paucity of comment by the delegates concerning this decision is striking. The delay of nearly a month in sending this congressional vote to Washington is also somewhat puzzling. Washington's March 20 response to this letter from Huntington and the public announcement of this verdict in his general orders of April 6, 1780, which he phrased with great caution and sensitivity to Arnold's feelings, can be found in Washington, *Writings* (Fitzpatrick), 18:127–28, 222–25. For the origins of this case and Congress' response to the charges originally brought against Arnold, see these *Letters*, 11:522–23, 12:178–80, 248–53, 329–30. See also *Proceedings of a General Court Martial . . . for the Trial of Major General Arnold . . . Published by Order of Congress* (Philadelphia: Francis Bailey, 1780), Evans, *Am. Bibliography*, no. 17,047, which Huntington subsequently enclosed with his March 29 letter to Washington.

Philip Schuyler to Jacob Cuyler?

Dear Sir,[1]   Copy No. 2   Philadelphia March 11th. 1780

I arrived here on Sunday, on Monday I advised Congress, that I could not consistent with my honor serve under the appointment they had been pleased to make.

The other Commissioners were ordered to proceed in the business, but intimations having been given that my Aid was necessary, a Committee was appointed and I put on it. As this does not comport with my Ideas of propriety I continue to refuse. Men of Sentiment approve my firmness and delicacy, others are chagrined but dare not drive me to a pointed explanation, which I will never give otherwise than in writing, that my Constituents and all my Countrymen may see my Principles.

The subject of Finance has for some time past engrossed the attention of Congress in a Committee of the whole, but paradoxical as it may seem, that a part should be more competent than the whole, it has been thought necessary to refer the business to a lesser Committee, composed of Burck, Elsworth, Holtn, Haustin [Houston], Livingston and Scuyler, a Report will probably be compleated by Monday, my object is a fixture of the present Circulating Medium at a given ratio calling it in, speedily destroying it, a new Emission quoted to States and sent forth on permanent funds, the Quantum to be emitted to be proportioned to the periodical destruction of the present Bills, the new ones to bear a Specie Interest payable at their redemption or in bills on France at the option of the holders. I believe the reports will bear this Complexion, but what transformation it will undergo in the House is impossible to determine, as every Man wishes to be thought a Financier and must have his Ideas. It will probably be like Joseph's coat a composition of patches party coloured.

I can say nothing yet about Your Department, a few days will enable me to do it, and You will have the necessary communications, as far as shall be in my power to afford them, the Vermont business is not yet on the Tapis.

If my Financing Ideas should prevail our State will be able to extricate itself out of its difficulties without continuing the Burden of Taxes, Provided always that our Legislature will be prudent and decisive, and that Men of considerable property will do their duty; altho I am amongst the middling Class of these, I propose to rob them all of the honor of being the first to set a good example; this is perfectly Enigmatical at present to You, and so it must continue, until I am at liberty more fully to explain myself. You that love Your Country shall follow me, at least I will give You an opportunity of doing it at the Risque of our property, may be a little, but the Sacrifice will be glorious, and perhaps too our Countrymen may honor us with the all endearing name of true and Virtuous patriots. That You, I, and all like us, and all our more distressed Fellow Citizens

may truly deserve that pleasing appellation is my sincerest wish, my
fervent prayer, Adieu, my friend, and believe me to be sincerely
such,   Ph. Scuyler

Tr (PRO: C.O. 5, 110:101–2). Endorsed: "Rebel Intercepted Letters No. 1 and 2
taken at Paramus the 23d of March 1780 (No. 1) In Major Genl. Robertsons of 26
March 1780."
    [1] The intended recipient of this letter may have been Jacob Cuyler, deputy commis-
sary general of purchases at Albany and a correspondent of Schuyler's. William
Smith, the loyalist former chief justice of New York, stated in his journal for March
30, 1780, that "The Governor [*i.e.,* Gen. *James Robertson*] produced this Day to the
Council at Mr. Elliot's an intercepted Letter of Philip Schuyler's (I believe) to Jacob
Cuyler, a Commissary at Albany, for the Wrapper was lost; and another from Francis
Lewis to his Son Morgan Lewis. He intended, he said, to cause them to be published
in the News Papers." William Smith, *Historical Memoirs from 26 August 1778 to 12
November 1783 of William Smith . . .,* ed. William H. W. Sabine (1958; reprint ed., New
York: Arno Press, 1971), p. 247; and Milton M. Klein and Ronald W. Howard, eds.,
*The Twilight of British Rule in Revolutionary America: The New York Letter Book of General
James Robertson, 1780–*1783 (Cooperstown, N.Y.: New York State Historical Association,
1983), p. 82nn.9–10. Schuyler's letter, with another captured at the same time, from
Francis Lewis to Morgan Lewis of the same date, was printed by James Rivington in
the *Royal Gazette,* April 1, 1780.

John Fell to Robert Morris

Dear sir,   Philada. March 12th. 1780. Sunday.
    I wrote you last week, of great expectations, of a Plan for fixing
the Quotas and supplying the Treasury &c. After several days spent
in a Committee of the whole, it was agree'd to recommit all the
Papers to a Committee of 6 who have not yet Reported.[1] There is a
Phraise often made use of that we are Pretty near the End of the
tether, that realy appears to be too much the Case. However if we
can hold out a little longer we have a hope in Pro[v]idence yet for
Yesterday a Committee brought in a draft of a proclamation for a
Fast &c on Wednesday 26th of April, which was Read;[2] I thought
there was an omition and moved for an amendment, which was
inserted, but it seems I Laugh'd at the time, for which Mr Clark
seemd much displeasd with me, however he got up and said he
thought some of us, acted like Infidells (I suppose he meant me).
Tomorrow is the day fixt for Congress to determine, whether they
will adjourn from Philadelphia. It is also the order of the day (but I
do not remember wheth[er] I wrote you last week). The great and
Important day, big with the Fate of the People, of the New Hampshire Grants (Alias the State of Vermont) Neither of which I imagine
will come to any thing determinate. Yesterday a Report of a Committee, for Reccomending to the several States, the Revising or Repealing the Tender Law as it is calld,[3] And though I was one that gave
my Assent to it, I think it has been Productive of more mischief in its

Effects, then any one Act that ever was Past, I can speak from woefull experiance.

P.M. Monday 5 OClock [*March 13*]. The Adjournment of Congress, and the State of Vermont (as some would have it,) were both Postponed, to take up a Report from a Committee on Finance, which was Read and afterwards went in to a Committee of the whole, but as it will take some time to digest I shall say no more on the subject at Present. I am with great Esteem, Your Real friend & Humble Servt,   John Fell

NB Eastern Post not come in yet.

RC (NjR: Robert Morris Papers).
    [1] For the report of this committee, see the following entry. For the fiscal resolves adopted by Congress on March 18, see Samuel Huntington to the States, March 20, 1780.
    [2] *JCC*, 16:252–53.
    [3] The report of the committee "respecting tender laws" had been referred to the "Committee on Finance." *JCC*, 16:253.

Philip Schuyler to George Washington

Dear Sir   Philadelphia March 13 [12]th 1780[1]
    Since my last the business of Finance has been Committed agreable to my wish. Livingston, Holten, Houston, Elsworth, Burke & Schuyler were appointed. They have put the finishing hand to the business this day. I sincerely wish the Supposed Sanctity of the day may have An Influence on the deed, the report will be delivered to Morrow.[2] The Great Object In view is Speedily to Call out of Circulation the present circulating medium, to give It In the Interim a permanent Value by assigning a certain proportion to Each State for the purpose of redemption, to Emit new Bills on State Credit and to fund them on Specific and permanent taxes laid as a farther Security In case of the failure of a particular State to pledge the faith of the Confederacy, and to Issue them In a limitted proportion to those now In circulation and as these Shall be destroyed, so as that their shall never be of old at 40 for 1 and new at par above ten million In Circulation—the New to bear Interest payable In Specie at the End of Six Years or Annually by bills on france.
    Altho Congress found me determined not to Accept any office which would carry the appearance of my being their Servant they had the Indelicacy to appoint me one of a *Committee* to assist Gen. Mifflin & Mr Pickering for the purpose mentioned In the resolution of the 20th January. I am determined not to Commit my reputation on a Business which I foresee from the Manner In which It will be Conducted, will neither redound to the honor of the Agents or the

Service of the public, to say not a word of the Indelicacy with respect to others.[3]

This moment a rumour prevails that the British have landed In the Vicinity of Charles town out of fifty transports and that these movements Indicate an Attack on that place, I shall do myself the honor to advise you more fully tomorrow If I can.

I am Dr Sir Most Affectly, Your Ex. Obed. Hu Serv,

Ph. Schuyler

RC (DLC: Washington Papers).
[1] Although Schuyler dated this letter "March 13th," he apparently wrote it on Sunday, March 12. Not only does Schuyler refer in the body of the letter to the "Supposed Sanctity of the day," but he states that the "report will be delivered to morrow" and the journals record that the report on finance was read on Monday, March 13. *JCC*, 16:255.
[2] The report of the fiscal committee to which Schuyler had been appointed on March 9 was read in Congress on March 13 and referred to committee of the whole. *JCC*, 16:243, 255.
[3] See Schuyler to President Huntington, March 6; and Schuyler to Washington, March 7, 1780.

Samuel Holten's Diary

[March 13, 1780]

13. Monday. The post is not come in. Congress has been in a come. of the whole on Finance.

MS (MDaAr).

William Churchill Houston to Robert Morris

March 13th [1780]

You see a Sample of my Mode of Corresponding. I return to close my Letter to you after the Lapse of a Week. You will excuse it however when I inform you that every waking moment of that Time I have been totally immersed in attending to a subject of the first Magnitude to the Union, the State of the Paper Currency. I have, I take the Liberty to say, faithfully attended a Committee appointed to that Duty from which my Mind has not been detached even while I have slept. I earnestly hope the Legislature will not rise till they hear from us on this Subject. The report is going through a Committee of the whole, and I hope this week will finish and put it into your Hands. I hope good things from [it] if the States will join [. . .] Support, without whom what is Congress?

I wrote the Governour and the Speaker pretty fully relative to the Accep·ance of Certificates in the Payment of Taxes,[1] if it can possibly be avoided it is dangerous to meddle with it, and if at all, I would avoid the printed ones in the Quarter-Master's Department, because it must derange the settlement of his Accounts, and may be attended with great mischeifs, and perhaps double Payments.

What you write me in yours of the 1st instant really surprises me. A requisition for so large a Quantity of Forage is rather suspicious. The General must have been misinformed, or Biddle[2] cannot have the Orders he announces. I am afraid strange Practisings and Artifices are made Use of by some who do not wish well to Alterations in the Systems of the Departments. I have this Day been informed there is a large Quantity of Forage at Coryell's Ferry, and also at a Mill in Spotswood quite within the reach of the Enemy. I do not know how to account for many Things which I see, notwithstanding I have not [any] intention but Charity.

If there is any Thing left in New Jersey which can be of Use to the Army, I hope you will have it in the Way of being drawn out. Pennsylvania is really very slow, though I hope when they do begin they will do Something. Is your purchasing Law of 25 December last to be revised this Sitting? It is my sincere *Opinion* that one Purchaser in a County is quite enough, and that more will do Mischief instead of Service; and this one ought to be restricted to his County. There is a very deserving Man I wish were employed as a Purchaser in the County of Middlesex, I am intimately acquainted with him and know him to be a Man of Education, Parts and Business. In the Turns of the Times he is out of Employment and therefore would attend solely to this. I mean Jonathan Baldwin, Esqr of Princeton and believe he is not altogether unknown to you. I never was fond of recommendations, but I should not hesitate to recommend him.

We have no authentick News from the Southward since the 6 February when all was well. Reports tell us that Charlestown is taken, and Porto Rico in the West Indies. These I regard as idle Tales. If it is so we [had] not Time to know it nor have they [. . .] but my Fears are not unalarmed about the Events of that Quarter.

My good Friend, I wish I had Time to say a thousand things more to you, but you will excuse me, oppressed with Care and worn down with Fatigue but always at your Command,

William Ch Houston

RC (NjR: Robert Morris Papers). A continuation of Houston to Morris, March 6, 1780.

[1] Not found.

[2] That is, Foragemaster General Clement Biddle.

Robert R. Livingston to James Duane

Dear Sir   Philadelphia 13th March 1780
I should think myself very blamable if I had deservedly incurred
the censure of neglect. But give me leave to assure you that nothing
has hitherto prevented my enjoying the pleasure of a regular correspondence with you but the greater pleasure which I had every
reason to expect in seeing you here, since I thought the matter had
been so determined when I left you And there never was a time in
which your abilities could have been more extensively useful.
Our suffering the 1st of February to pass off without being prepared for the contest has necessarily put it off sine die,[1] but we have
now got it the first in order after the business of finance, which at
present engages our whole attention & in which by a bold & vigorous
exertion I hope we shall be able to Do something effectual. Tho' not
without incurring the censure & raising the clamours of many who
are more attentive to their own interest than that of the community.
We have accounts (tho not officially) that the enimy have landed
about 30 miles from Charlestown their numbers unknown. As their
fleets have suffered extreamly by the storm we have great reason to
hope that many of them will not arrive at their intended haven.
I congratulate you upon the spirit of your countrymen on the
other side of the Atlantick. They owe us much and I have great
reason to beleive that they will now repay the debt. One of the
members of the house of commons began his debate speech with
"We turn our backs upon England & our face towards America."
Come on soon or let me hear from you often. I am Dear Sir, with
great esteem, your Hume Servt.   Robt R Livingston

RC (NHi: Duane Papers).
[1] Congress had resolved the previous September to reopen debate on the New
Hampshire Grants claims on February 1. See James Lovell to Samuel Adams, February 1, 1780, note.

Nathaniel Peabody to Meshech Weare

Sir,   Philada. 13th March 1780
You will doubtless have the resolutions of Congress respecting the
Quotas of men and Supplies, to be furnished by the respective States,
officially transmitted[1] to you previous to the receipt of this Letter
and on the 4th Instant the delegates of N Hampr. did themselves the
Honr. of inclosing you Extracts from Communications lately made
by the Minister of France;[2] as also the answer Congress made to
those Communications—by all which you will be able to form Some
Idea of the Necessary Measures to be taken for the ensuing Campaign, as also the Situation, and views of the *Allied Powers.*

The Numbers of men assign'd for New Hamp. to furnish is about one 6th part more, in my opinion, than would be their Just Quota. Yet as Congress did on the 9th ulto Resolve "That the reasonable expence any State hath incur'd or may incur by raising and having in the Continental Army more than what shall hereafter appear to have been their Just proportions of the Troops Actually serving in the Said Army from time to time, Shall be allowed to Such States & Equitably adjusted in a final Settlement of their account with the United States" the Injury will not be so great, or in other words, a prospect of future Justice will make the present Grievance more Tolerable.

As to the apportionment, and prices, of supplies, appear to me an Object of Very Great magnitude and ought to be thoroughly investigated—Tho' I cannot say the amount of Supplies alloted to New Hampr. to furnish, Estimated at the rates affixed to them, very far exceeds their due proportion, Yet I must Confess I feel no Small degree of Anxiety when I take a short retrospect of the various manners *practiced* in order to obtain those resolutions Especially that for affixing prices; which must evidently appear to every impartial person, well acquainted with the rates at which those articles were formerly or are at the present day, usually Sold in the Various parts of the Continent respectively Calld upon to furnish the same, it was by no means founded upon those Just and impartial principles of equallity & reciprocity which ought, at all times, to Govern in every important decision, as being the only Sure means of Cementing the Union of these States, or whereby a Nation can ever rationally expect to be *Exalted*.

The ratio by which those prices in *Specie* were pretended to have been determined was for all Articles of American produce at 50 per Cent advance upon the prices Such articles were usually Sold for at the places of delivery, in the respective States in the year 1774—And Articles Imported from foreign ports in the same proportion with a reasonable additional Allowance for the Charge and risk of Importation.

Let us now examine how far this Rule has been observed? Indian Corn in the Southern States was formerly Sold at from 21 to 24 90ths of a Dollar per Bushel, it is now rated at 67 1/2 90ths which instead of being 50, is 200 per Cent advance. Rye, Oats, and Many Other Articles of short forage nearly in the same proportion! The price of the best first Crop hay at the Market was formerly about 6, or 7 Dollars per Ton, it is now rated at more than Cent. per Cent.[3] advance above the former prices. The price of Merchantable flour in this City was formerly about Two Dollars per Cwt, Tho it was often Lower, Now rated at 4 Dollars & 1/2, which is 125 per Cent advance, but enough has been said to shew that Such States, whose distance from the Theatre of *War*, or other Circumstances, will not Admit of furnishing their proportions of these and many other articles rated in a Similar manner, will be Charged in a Specie Account from *100* to 150 per Cent advance above the former prices upon an average. And it ought to be here Observed the various articles were assigned to the respective States previous to affixing the prices.

Let us now pay a Short visit to the Eastward, Say New Hampshire. Their delegates Consented to the article of beef, or other meat Equivalent Supposing it possible to furnish that Article. They also Consented to Some part of the Article of Rum, not doubting but the price of both Articles woud be rated in Just proportion, with other Articles of Supplies Calld for, and in hopes as the Sea Port there was open, it might be in the Power of the State to furnish at lest a part of the Rum, but at the same time, they were the rather induced to Consent to that article, for want of ability to furnish others, and more Necessary Supplies, and apprehending, also, that a failure in furnishing this Rum, would not be attended with so disagreable Consequences to the public, as a failure in many other Articles of Supplies, And of course the State would Escape the most pointed Censures Consequent upon such neglect though unavoidable.

But to the point—It is now time to enquire how and in what manner that State is to discharge it Self from the enormous Debt brot. upon her by Consequence of the high, and unequal, prices affixed as aforsd? By furnishing grass fed beef at 5 & 1/2 Dollars per Hundred wt. I mention Grass fed because those who woud wish to keep their Cattle till after the first of December for a higher price must begin to feed with Corn and other dry forrage, by reason of the Winter Setting in, at least a month earlier there, than in Connecticut and the States to the Southward—which will be Such an additional & partial Expence I expect very little beef will be furnished from that State after the 1st of November.

The price of Good beef at that Season of the Year was heretofore usually about four Dollars per Hundred wt.—And is now rated at five and a half Dollars per Cwt. which is not 40 per Cent advance from the Old price. And as to the Rum though I by no means pretend to be Master of Merchantile affairs Yet I will Venture to assert that no Man can import that article, at this day, by exporting flour at the price affix'd, so as to be able to Sell the Rum here under about 2 Dollars & 3/4ths or three Dollars per Gallon, if he can for that. The present rule of barter here, is from a Gallon to a Gallon & a half of rum for one hundred of flour, hence it is obvious that my calculation upon this Article is well founded. And that New Hampshire must furnish Supplies at a very Great loss, when compared with the allowances made for most part of the articles to be furnished by other States, or Else be Charged in an immoderate Specie Debt to the United States, upon interest, that will not only far exceed their Just proportion of the Necessary Expence of furnishing such Supplies but their ability to discharge! The loss that New Hampshire will Sustain upon a moderate Calculation by the unequal manner in which those prices are affixed upon the Supplies, Call'd for the Current Year will amount at least to 50,000 Dollars in Specie while other States differently Circumstanced will gain in proportion to your Loss, and which mode if Continued but for a few years will entirely mortgage the State. Upon this view of Things you will pardon me if, as a Citizen, I venture to express my Sentiments upon a Subject So vastly important in its Consequences And which so Essencially effects the Interest of a State I have the honr to represent.

And hope it will not be conceived that I have the most distant wish to retard or discourage the State from furnishing all the Supplies in her power, As the existence of the Army and Support of the Cause of America very much depends upon the immediate & vigorous exertions of the several States. Nor ought there to be any responsibility in Congress for the Consequences in Case of a failure. My only Aim by this representation is to give you the Ideas I have upon the Subject, and if possible to induce the State to take Such measures in furnishing the Supplies Call'd for as may reserve to the State or her Delegates in Congress the full and indisputable right, and Power, at any future period when our public affairs will admit of investigating the Subject and endeavouring to obtain a redress of the Grievance and Compensation of the injury Complained of, in such sort that no Act the State may adopt respecting the Subject may by any Construction whatever be deemed an acquiesscence in the System adopted by Congress before alluded to, for furnishing Supplies for the army.

It has Incessantly been my most Ardent wish and aim, that Congress would fall upon Some Eligible Mode for freeing the public from the intolerable burden, they have for a long time been groaning and Travelling under even untill now in Supporting Legions of Continental Sinecures who appear in Swarms like Locusts, upon the Land of Egypt, and not only draw Numberless rations; but are in every other respect rioting upon the blood and Treasures of the virtuous Citizens (if any Such there be) in these united States.

By making calculations upon indisputable documents in my possession I am with astonishment Convinced that there is not one moment to be lost in retrenching public expenditures—loping off every Exuberance in order to introduce a more œconomical System. It will be in vain for these States, in future, to attempt Sustaining the burdens She has but too long been Crouching under. And I have good reason to hope some spirited and vigorous measures will immediately be adopted for effecting so desirable an object.

Tho' in the present Situation of our public affairs, and the deranged State of our finances the Expenditures must be nominally very large, in order to prosecute the war with Success, or negotiate for *peace* with any Tolerable degree of policy or advantage.

However, the present prospect in my private opinion promises no other alternative than abject Slavery on the one hand, or on the other, to exert every Nerve, to Carry on the War, with redoubled vigour the ensuing Campaign, and I hope No Citizen of these States will hesitate in his Choice a single moment.

I have the Honr. to be Sir, with the most entire Sentiments of Esteem, Your Honrs. most obliged obedt. And very Humble Servt.

Nathl. Peabody

P.S. Mr. Livermore is determined to Set off for N. Hampr. as soon as the Travelling will permit and will be able to give full information upon many important matters.

RC (Nh–Ar: Weare Papers).
[1] See Samuel Huntington to the States, February 10 and 26, 1780.
[2] See New Hampshire Delegates to Weare, March 4, 1780.
[3] That is, Centum per Centum, or 100 percent.

Samuel Holten to Joseph Palmer

My dear Sir.[1]   Philadelphia March 14th. 1780
Your favor of the 2d ultimo came to hand the 7th instant, & please to accept my thanks for the same & for the inclosures; and as you have been pleased to leave it to me, respecting laying the extracts before Congress, I think it would not be advisable at present, for such are their engagements at this time, in Financing & other important matters, that I shou'd fear they wou'd not give that attention to the same as the subject requires. It would give me sensible pleasure to converse with you upon our national affairs; but I think there wou'd be an impropriety in committing to writing such important matters if I was under no restraint.

It gives me real concern for the good people, when I hear of their complaints, yet it shou'd be remembered that Congress have no interest seperate from theirs and take a part with them in their best hopes & recommend nothing but what they consider as absolutely necessary, & that our all under God depends upon our exertions at this time; dear Sir, permit me to say, that by your letter it appears to me, as if you was not fully sensible of our distressed situation; It wou'd give me great satisfaction did I think by all our exertions of every kind; that we shou'd be able to bring in to the field the next campaign an Army (absolutely) necessary for our protection & support them when there; so far are my ideas from paying off any part of the national debt, even if the recommendations of Congress are fully complied with.

Some time since Congress allowed some bills to be drawn on Spain & Holland; But have very lately ordered that no more be drawn 'till their further order.

I am sorry my late letters had not come to hand,[2] as I am sensible I am not wanting in numbers, tho' in every thing else, & am thus far willing to stand indebted.

The winter has been more severe here than I ever knew in New England. The Bridge of ice over the Delaware continued more than two months.

I am, Dear Sir, your most obedient.

FC (PPIn). In the hand of Samuel Holten.
[1] Joseph Palmer has been identified in these *Letters*, 1:333n.2.
[2] No prior letters from Holten to Palmer have been found.

Samuel Huntington to the States

Sir,   Circular   Philadelphia March 14. 1780
Enclosed your Excellency will receive a Recommendation of Congress to the several States to set apart Wednesday the 26th of April next as a Day of Fasting, Humiliation and Prayer.[1]

With great respect I have the honour to be &c &c,

                                                        S.H.

LB (DNA: PCC, item 14). Addressed: "Circular. N.B. The like to Genl Washington."
[1] For Congress' March 3 resolve setting aside a fast day, and March 11 adoption of a proclamation declaring its purposes and prescribing the manner of its observation, see *JCC*, 16:225, 252–53.

Samuel Livermore to Meshech Weare

Dear sir   Philadelphia March 14. 1780
I have been now five weeks in this city, my time in Congress expired the last of Feb. Nothing is yet done about Vermont but delay from time to time. Massa. Bay is not ready And they with Connecticut & Rd. Island I believe are all Vermonters, against us behind the curtain. However I dont give it up: on the other hand the prospect looks better & better. I think we shall make something very grand out of it: but perhaps not at this time. My being out of Congress is very detrimental, every thing is transacted behind my back in a manner.

As to news it is much in favour of America from every quarter. The Spaniards it is said have taken the english settlements on the missisippi. The fleet that saild from NYork for Georgia, & Carolina are dispersed by storms, very few arived the 7th Feb, which is the latest account we have from thence. Ireland seems to be on the point of a revolution.

The state of our currency is unfavourable the talk of exchange between paper & silver, sixty for one. Beef is sold 5, 6, & 8 dollers a

Samuel Livermore

pound, and other things in proportion. Expences are beyond imagination.

Congress have in hand a plan for setting the mony on a better footing whether it will succeed I cant tell. The plan is to emit 10 million Dollers to carry an interest of 6 per Ct. per An. to be paid in solid coin. This will it is thought make the paper as good as hard mony. 5 miln. of this is to redeem all the present currency at 40 for one, the other 5 million is to carry on the war. The plan is warmly supported & as warmly opposed. There are other plans, but all are for making mony to Carry an interest, to be paid in silver.

I am happily through the small pox and hope to be on my way home by the last of March. I hope this will find you and your family and friends well.

I am Sir with the highest esteem, Your most obedient humble Servant.   Samuel Livermore

P.S. I was innoculated the 10th Feb. and by the 26th I went all over the city in a manner as well as ever.

RC (MHi: Weare Papers).

John Mathews to Horatio Gates

Dear sir,   Philadelphia March 14th. 1780

I received your very obliging and friendly favour yesterday, & embrace this earliest opportunity of acknowledging it.

It contains matter of high importance and truly deserving the serious consideration of that body of which I am a member. Your observations instantly flashed conviction on my, before, bewildered senses. They at once evince the experienced soldier, & deep Politician, & I return you, Sir, my most sincere & hearty thanks for them. But alas! either from the obstinacy, or something worse, of the men I have to deal with, I have very little hopes of stimulating them to any acts that will tend to the salvation of those devoted Countries. Were an angel from heaven to perch on the back of the Presidents Chair & proclaim the immediate annihilation of the southern states, unless something vigorous, & effectual was done, & even point out the mode, I sincerely believe, as soon as he had taken his flight, & the surprise had subsided, they would just sink again into the same torpid State in which he found them. As a proof of this, I will beg leave to inform you of what passed yesterday. I received your letter just as I was going to the house. I took the first opportunity after I got there, of informing them, that I had a few hours before received a Letter from a Gentleman for whose opinion I entertained a very high respect, & whose information was to be relyed on. And stated the contents of your letter, as matter of information & not opinion, thinking, by giving it this turn, to attract their serious attention.[1] I thought myself well justifyed in doing so, as your opinion had as much weight in my mind as if you had told me, it was founded on information, you had received from Genl. Clinton. I then took the liberty, by your permission, of proposing the plan of operations for the Southern Campaign, agreeable to your Ideas. I was asked, "from whom & whence I had my information, & whether I knew this person to be a Whig." I answered I was not at liberty to say from whom, or whence, I had my information, it was enough for them to be told it was undoubted. That the person was as good a Whig as any in that house. They for a little while seemed to be alarmed, & I thought disposed to act like the Guardians of the *United States*. But as soon as selfishness, and the apprehension of danger to *these* States, from the adoption of such a plan, had repossessed their minds, every art & contrivance was made use of, to silence the just demands of the Southern States for support, & the business was at last got rid of by the old, stale trick of proposing a Committee to go to Camp to consult with the General. This I rejected with indignation, too well knowing its tendency—that is, merely to save appearances, without the least intention of doing anything.[2] Thus you'll see, my Dr. sir, how little is to be hoped from the best plan that human genius can invent, whilst mens minds are warped by self-interest, & the danger is at a distance. You, Sir, have taken an active, & brilliant part in & know most circumstances relative to this revolution & your abilities enable you to draw just conclusions from what I am going to say. In the beginning of this war, whilst the efforts of the enemy were pointed to the reduction of the Northern States, men were drawn from every State in the Union (except So. Carolina & Georgia, whose local circumstances you well know would not admit of it) for the defence of those States in danger, & some of the people of the Southern States, undertook a march of 1000 miles, & underwent the fatigues of it with cheerfulness to effect so laudable & so desirable a purpose, & those that did not send men contributed their aid of money &c with great good will, & an affectionate zeal, & would have with alacrity done any thing in their power towards the support of the common cause. How the Scene is changed. The war is most evidently transfered from the Northern to the Southern States, & in my opinion their conquest there, are meant to be solid & permanent. Then have not those States, now the theater of war the same right to expect, the support of the United efforts of the other states? Should not the Grand army be now employed there, as it has heretofore been here? It may be said the enemy have still a formidable force at N. York, it's my belief they will be much obliged to us, to let them alone, if so, they will not disturb us, besides are not the troops of Six States sufficient, with the powerful Militia these Countrys afford, to keep the enemy within their lines.[3] Undoubtedly I also could write a Volume on this Subject but I am afraid I have already tried your patience. Therefore will for the present relieve you, And subscribe myself with much Esteem & regard, Dr. sir, yr. most Obdt. servt.

Jno Mathews

P.S. I have wrote in great haste & must beg you to excuse inaccuracies.

RC (NHi: Gates Papers).

[1] In his March 7 letter to Mathews, Gates had expressed his conviction that the British court had resolved "to remove the Theatre of the War into the Southern States" and had urged Mathews to propose, in his own name, offensive operations against the British garrison at New York and Clinton's army in South Carolina. Fearing the reaction of "parties" in Congress should the delegates learn that he had proposed such a plan, Gates counseled Mathews "to keep my Letter intirely to yourself." Gates Papers, NHi.

[2] Although these proceedings are not recorded in the journals, Philip Schuyler reported in his March 22 letter to Nathanael Greene that a plan to appoint a committee to confer with the commander in chief had been "moved but without effect" on an unspecified date. Mathews' testimony indicates that the motion was probably offered on March 13.

Earlier attempts to send a committee to camp had proven equally unsuccessful. The January 8 and 10 motions of Robert R. Livingston and Elbridge Gerry, which are discussed at Committee of Congress to Washington, January 11, note 1, eventually culminated in a February 19 Board of War recommendation that a committee be appointed to "repair immediately to Head quarters." *JCC*, 16:110, 178–80. Another Livingston recommendation of January 19 resulted in the appointment of Schuyler and two outside commissioners, Thomas Mifflin and Timothy Pickering, the latter two of whom eventually submitted on March 27 a lengthy plan to reform the departments, for which see Samuel Huntington to Mifflin and Schuyler, January 24, to Mifflin and Pickering, March 11, and to Nathanael Greene, March 16, 1780. It was not until April 6, however, that Congress, faced with the added threat of unrest in the army, adopted yet a third Livingston motion and created a committee to consult with the commander in chief on needed reforms, for which see Congress' Instructions to the Committee at Headquarters, April 6–13, 1780.

[3] Drafts of Gates' March [i.e., April] 3 reply to this letter as well as one of "May 1780" estimates of Sir Henry Clinton's troop strength, are in the Gates Papers, NHi.

John Armstrong, Sr., to Joseph Reed

Carlisle 15th March 1780. "I have at some length lately wrote my Colleagues in Congress on the propriety & necessity of a limitation of prices by Authority, being daily more & more convinced, of the expedience of that measure—and that we have not another, possessed of sufficient energy & requisite dispatch, for the recovery & progress of our affairs—which are too important at this crisis to be risqued on the operation of Slow or doubtful measures—nor have I any doubt but that the law if heartily & any how generally is gone into, will operate & have effect, as beside the requisitions of candid & disinterested men, even those who are much less so, begin to be alarmed at the near approaches of a total stopage of the circulation of the money, & earnestly wish for some certainty respecting it's value, of which at present they have next to none. The topicks of argument in favour of this measure, must often have appeared to your excellency, arising not only from the necessity of the case, from publick & private utillity, but also from the baleful consequences which but too easily present themselves under the want of it. So numerous are the offspring of these different sources of argument, and so plain, that in writing to any wise & good man, I must check the variety of pointing them out, lest I shou'd abuse his time, or tacitly impeach his observation. Nor are political arguments (tho' fully sufficient) the alone Supporters of the doctrine of a general limitation in the present hour, as those of a moral nature also fall into the consideration, altho' we hope there will be no occasion for their publick appearance.

All the Objections I have yet seen to a regulating law, appear to be inconclusive—an idle refinement on civil rights & lethargick timidity, make up the best half of them—nor can the past efforts of the Massachusets-bay be thought Sufficient, being without the present pulse of necessity, the sanction of Congress, or the knowledge of concurence in any other State; no wonder then, that their efforts proved abortive. A crafty evasion or elusion of the Law, is the stronghold of it's opposers—to this disease, no doubt corrosives must be applyed—let them do it at the risque of something considerable (but much less so than the safety of their country), perhaps the loss of Ears that refuse to hear, or some quick Sensation to an unfeeling hand. In circumstances like ours, to call the above an Arbitrary Law, is rather a reproach than a Compliment to government, the ultimate design whereof is the Safety and happiness of the whole. There is also a different line of regulation incumbent upon Congress and equally necessary with that which respects the States as mentioned on the other side. The reformation of abuses & retrenchm't of all unnecessary expences is a great & Salutary work, indeed Some observant men of my acquaintance say it ought to be done previous to a limitation of prices, that it wou'd greatly contribute to the effect of that Law, and is the least encouragement the States can have for their trouble in making & vertue in executing it, that after all, their property be not totally embezled thro' want of System and Economy. This is perfectly my own Opinion with this difference, that instead of either of these means taking any remarkable lead of the other in point of time, they ought to run hand in hand, but in the order of things the regulation or limitation of prices as the only basis of every other amendment shou'd first be known, for until some certain value is affixed to the currency, Congress have no rule whereby to fix their Salleries, nor to make any other useful alteration with effect. I have used the name of Congress in this business of reformation, but well know they cannot do it to publick satisfaction; neither is it possible for the Commander in Chief of our Army, and except his advise in some particular cases & information in others, it is a shame to put it upon him, and what I hope in it's full extent he will not undertake. In short the States or their Executive Councils & they only are competant to this business—and some candid inspectors to make report, or other useful intelligence must at least be had from every County—this is not only essential to the gaining of facts, but by it the people will see that a reformation is intended; for at present chagrin prevails so far, as to excite hard surmises & very disagreeable opinions. The business in question therefore clearly involves two Ideas—the one that it be rightly done, the other that as far as possible the body of the populace have evidence that it is so. By this means confidence in our publick councils may be restored—unanimity & alacrity excited—the best means these, of Securing our future efforts & payment of the publick debt. Congress Ought fully & explicitly to authorize the States in the business above (as I have lately hinted to my Colleagues) and cannot be too early in advising the publick, that they will thoroughly inspect and reform such abuses as have been but too Obvious even to vulgar sight. If any Such resolution as this shou'd be made in Congress, I cou'd wish it dispersed in a number of hand-bills as the News-papers have not a general extent—considering it not only as a mean to animate the hopes of the people, but a good preparative to the limitation of prices by Law, especially if Congress shou'd think proper to express such desire. . . .

You must be puzled at the Alterations & new State-quotas talked of in Congress, of which I had a hint from Mr. Bryan—but no probable progress, nor uniformity of procedure, under any alteration whatever, can I possibly see short of a known or fixed value to our money—at least for some time. It is amazing to see how some otherwise judicious men, will venture to go on, and expect to succeed in the great business of America, without any rational foundation-data, or given point! it is more than any Mathematician on Earth ever pretended to. General Green I hear is a sanguine asserter of the saving efficacy of deep Taxation, that alone is his infallible Nostrem—A deep delusion, a Shameful error. Taxation to the present demands of America is like the Gentlemans Dinner to his appetite, what he had was good, but neither enuff nor half enuff."

[*P.S.*] Some time ago I wrote Mr. McClane,[1] that I cou'd not possibly attend Congress sooner than the begining of May & the prospect of a late Spring but farther confirms that determination—but hope that a Supplement to the Bill, may have passed this last Sessions—not in the addition of Dollars but of Delegates.

RC (NHi: Reed Papers).
[1] Pennsylvania delegate James McLene.

Cyrus Griffin to John Morgan

[Ca. March 15, 1780][1]

In addition to the Ideas mentioned previously respecting Dr Shippens being an proper object of a Citation under the Resolution of Congress I would offer that after Dr Shippen was formally arrested by his Excellency and other Notices being given him here to attend at the testimony of the Deponents it will appear that he treated those Notices with the same silence & Contempt as he did the former. Does it not naturally follow from this that Dr Shippen had no thought of objecting against the Legality of his being Cited to appear at the testimony of [. . .] at the Time—as he treated the like Notices when he was formally Arrested by His Excellency in the same Manner as he did those when he was not—& does [*this*] not induce an Idea that the present Objections would not have been stated had it not been to procrastinate & Delay the Tryal.

RC (DNLM: Morgan Collection). In Griffin's hand, though not signed. The contractions and abbreviations used by Griffin in this cryptic note have been expanded.

[1] This undated note was evidently part of a larger exchange between Griffin and Morgan carried on while Morgan was gathering evidence to prosecute Dr. William Shippen, director general of the medical department, for which see Whitfield J. Bell, "The Court Martial of Dr. William Shippen, Jr., 1780," *Journal of the History of Medicine*, 19 (1964): 218–38. In December Morgan had secured from Congress a resolution permitting the gathering of depositions from witnesses in noncapital court-martial cases "provided the prosecutor and person accused are present at the taking of the same, or that notice be given of the times and places of taking such depositions to the opposite party four days previous thereto." *JCC*, 15:1409. He immediately notified Shippen of his scheduled interviews and itinerary, but Shippen refused to accompany him. On January 5, 1780, while Morgan was traveling, Shippen was formally placed under arrest and informed of the charges against him by the judge advocate. Subsequently, in early February, Morgan again notified Shippen that he would be gathering depositions in Philadelphia, and again Shippen ignored the notice. The day after his trial opened on March 14, however, Shippen moved to strike from the record depositions that Morgan had submitted on several grounds, among them that he had not been arrested or informed of the charges when the depositions were taken, a point at variance with the facts. See Bell, "Court Martial," pp. 226–28. It was the logical inconsistency in Shippen's argument that Griffin addressed in this note to Morgan, written, in all probability, on or shortly after March 15. That Griffin had been cooperating with Morgan for some time seems clear from a December 30, 1779, letter of Morgan to Griffin enclosing a request to Congress of that date for copies of a number of Shippen's letters and hospital returns. Morgan Collection, DNLM.

Ezra L'Hommedieu to George Clinton

Sir,   Philadelphia, March 15, 1780

We were honored with your favor by General Schuyler, who arrived here the day after Genl. Scott, since which time we have not been able to bring on the business of the New Hampshire Grants, although it has been the order of the day for some time past; the attention of

Congress being almost entirely taken up, in endeavoring to establish their finances and prevent a further depreciation, which in these parts is at the rate of 60 for 1, with respect to specie, and much higher when compared, with the necessaries of life. The plan before the house is generally, to call in all the money in about one year by taxes and destroy it, to be received in taxes at the rate of forty for one in specie. As fast as the old money comes in, new issues in the proportion of 20 for 1, for the purpose of purchasing supplies or other expenditures of the war; each State to appropriate funds for the redemption of the new money, and for the payment of the interest in specie. I expect the plan will be finished this week, and will be immediately sent to the different Legislatures. The enclosed letters, though dated the 2nd of December were not received by the President till the last of last week, which makes some suspect they were antedated;[1] as their delegates declared a few days before that they had no advice from the State respecting the controversy and that they would not put in any claim. There is no doubt but they design if possible to cause delays and had rather the independence of those people should be admitted, than they should be under the jurisdiction of New York. I depend that next week this business will be taken up,[2] and after passing a resolution against the independence of the Grants, a Court will be formed for the hearing of the parties that are ready. 'Tis likely New Hampshire and we can [3] agree on the persons for the Court, which will save much time, although 'tis not likely they can suddenly be convened. As we have so many members from our State here, and the expense of living is so enormous, I think it will be prudent for me to return, which I conclude to do as soon as the travelling will admit, which I trust will meet with your approbation. The Act of Assembly for limiting the boundaries of the State was agreeably received by a great majority of the States and was referred to a special Committee to report thereon;[4] which will be done soon as they find the House have time to receive it.

I have the honor to be, Sir, your most obed. and very humble Servt.   Ezra L'Hommedieu

Tr (MH-H: Sparks Collection).

[1] L'Hommedieu is referring to Massachusetts' December 2, 1779, response to Congress' appeal for authorization to make a determination on claims to the New Hampshire Grants, for which see James Lovell to Samuel Adams, March 9, 1780, note 1. L'Hommedieu's enclosure is in Clinton, *Papers* (Hastings), 5:394–96.

[2] The New Hampshire Grants question was again taken up on March 21, but consideration was immediately postponed, "nine states, exclusive of those who are parties to the question, not being represented in Congress." See *JCC*, 16:273; and New York Delegates to George Clinton, May 21, 1780, note 3.

[3] Blank in Tr.

[4] See William Churchill Houston to Robert Morris, March 6, 1780, note 4.

Massachusetts Delegates
to the Chevalier de La Luzerne

Sir,   Philadelphia 15th March 1780

We were honored yesterday with your Letter informing Us of the favorable Light in which his most christian Majesty has been pleased to veiw "the Reception You met with from the Council & State of Massachusetts during your Residence in Boston"; And We are impressed with a grateful Sense of your friendly Disposition in acquainting his Majesty of the Zeal & Efforts of that State "in the common Cause."

We shall embrace the earliest Opportunity of transmitting this Information to the Legislature of the State,[1] & have every Reason to believe that it will be highly pleasing to them, as We assure You sir, it is to their Delegates.

Any Civilities that could have been offered on the part of the State, would in our opinion be but feint Representations of their Attachment to & Affection for your illustrious Sovereign, or of their Friendship & Esteem for his Minister; & be assured sir, that nothing can be more endearing than the Disposition you have manifested, in thus cultivating a reciprocal Confidence between his Majesty & the State.

We conceive ourselves authorized to say, that the Inhabitants of Massachusetts will use their utmost Efforts for bringing the present War to a speedy & happy Issue, & that the vigorous Exertions of our great Ally would operate as a powerful Motive, if any was wanting to produce this Effect.

We have the Honor to be sir, with every Sentiment of Respect, Your most obed & most hum servts,

E Gerry	J Lovell
S Holten	Geo Partridge

Tr (M–Ar: Revolutionary War Letters). Written and endorsed by Elbridge Gerry: "Copy of a Letter from the Delegates of Massachusetts to the Minister of France." Enclosed with the following entry.

[1] For La Luzerne's March 14 letter to the Massachusetts delegates, see the following entry.

Massachusetts Delegates
to the Massachusetts Council

Sir,   Philadelphia 15th March 1780.

We have the Honor to inclose You for the Information of the General Assembly, a Copy of a Letter which We have lately received from the Minister of France, and of our answer to the same:[1] We submit it to the Consideration of the Hona. Assembly, whether it will not be expedient to prevent a Publication of both,[2] & remain with the greatest Respect, Sir, your most obedt & very hum servants.

E. Gerry   James Lovell

S. Holten   Geo. Partridge

ENCLOSURE

Gentlemen   Philada: the 14th of March 1780
I did not fail to inform his Majesty of the Reception I met with from the Council and the State of Massachusett during the Time I was in Boston. He was highly gratified by the Mark of Attachment which you were pleased to manifest to him upon that opportunity in the Person of his Minister. He charges me to express his Satisfaction to the Representatives of the People of your State, and I eagerly seize this Occasion to acquaint you Gentlemen that I do not suffer the King to be uninformed of their Zeal and patriotic Dispositions nor of the Efforts which they propose to make for the Support of the common Cause, and I have not the least doubt but this Information will be fully as agreable to him as the former.

I have the honor to be with the most perfect attachment, Gentlemen, Your most humble and Most obedient Servant,

Le Che dela Luzerne

RC (M–Ar: Revolutionary War Letters). Written by Gerry and signed by Gerry, Holten, Lovell, and Partridge. Addressed: "Hona. Jeremiah Powell Esqr. President of the Council of Massachusetts Bay." Enclosure (M–Ar). In the hand of Lovell and endorsed by him: "Translation."
[1] See the preceding entry.
[2] The delegates' objection to such publication was undoubtedly related to their opposition to La Luzerne's efforts to establish direct contact with the states, for which see James Lovell to Samuel Adams, February 28 and March 17, 1780.

Roger Sherman to Jonathan Trumbull, Sr.

Sir   Philadelphia 15th Mar. 1780
I have the Honr. to transmit to your Excellency An Extract of a Letter from the Council of the State of Massachusetts Bay respecting the Making good to the Officers and Soldiers of the Army the original Contract. And a resolution of Congress in Answer thereto,[1] Also a Paper containing a recommendation for a general Fast.[2] Congress have for Some time past had under consideration a plan for calling in the outstanding Bills of Credit and introducing a Stable Medium of trade. It has been Several times debated & recommitted—it was resumed Yesterday in a Committee of the whole, and the principal parts of it pretty unanimously Agreed to. I expect it will be compleated to day or to Morrow.[3] The Assembly of this State are waiting

only for the completion of it. I have Not time to State it to Your Excellency, as Major Blackden by whom I Send this, is waiting, but it is Similar to what I communicated in a former Letter[4] with Some Improvements, we have no late news from Europe or the Southern States. I have the honor to be with great respect, Your Excellency's Obedient humble Servant,   Roger Sherman

RC (Ct: Trumbull Papers).
  [1] Sherman undoubtedly enclosed an extract of the Massachusetts Council's January 13 letter to Congress and the February 29 resolution adopted by Congress in response, for which see Massachusetts Delegates to the Massachusetts Council, March 1, 1780.
  [2] See Samuel Huntington to the States, March 14, 1780.
  [3] See Samuel Huntington to the States, March 20, 1780.
  [4] Not found.

Samuel Holten to John Kettell

                                             Philadelphia, March 16th, 1780
Dear Mr. Kettell.[1]   (Front Street)
    Before this reaches you, the spring will be opening fast, and as I do not expect to be at home before the last of May, a few lines by way of advice may not be amiss, as I put the greatest dependence upon you in my absence, respecting my Family affairs & little farm.
    I consider it allmost unnecessary to mention anything to you, respecting how to improve the Land, and I am but poorly acquainted with my own private affairs; while the war continues all the produce of the earth will be in very great demand: and the Seasons in our Country are very uncertain, sometimes cold & wet & at other times hot & dry, so that the ground you plant should be some of it low, & some dry, because mising of a crop at such a time as this wou'd be very distressing, for it might not be to be purchased for love nor money; In the first place, I advise you to Sow with Barley & Flax all the ground you have in hills, because that can be done without dung & the barley will be ripe soon in the year. Then consider how much you can dung & where you can get the dung on easiest & what sort of land it is, whether wet or dry, and put your dung on accordingly, much depends upon the sowing & planting the grain; some Land should be sowed or planted much sooner than an other, always consider whither the ground is warm enough, when you are about sowing or planting, and you should take great care in puting the corn into the ground, so that it may be the most likely to come up. I should suppose you could raise Potatoes, Beans, &c, &c, &c, where you can't well raise corn, no land that is rich should remain unimproved at such a day as this. The next thing is hay; I am sensible if you follow the foregoing advise, you can cut but little English hay. But you must cut all the hay you possibly can of all sorts, the meanest will make dung & the dung will make corn, and you must carefully

save all the straw, stalks & husks for this will keep cows, don't forgit to sow plenty of turnip seed, among the Flax and corn. You will take care to keep the Cattle below untill the feed is good above, and then the lower Swamp must be moved late.

Wool is of great value, & I hope you keep much the same number of sheep as when I left home.

There is danger of the corns being greatly destroyed by birds & otherways about the time it comes up; please let me know how your hay holds out, this tedious winter.

The first business upon a farm in the Spring is the beating the dung to pieces in the Field & pasture, if you have time.

Congress have appointed the last Wednesday in April next, as a day of Fasting, humiliation & prayer throughout the States. Give my kindest love to Mrs. Kettell & your little son; and also to Polly & Sally, when you see them.

Yours affectionately,   S. Holten.

P.S. I inclose you a paper which contains the weight of a very large Cow, lately killed in this city; I have often seen her, & have eat some of the beef.

RC (MSaE: Fowler Manuscripts).
[1] John Kettell (d.1801), a resident of Danvers, Mass., was a lieutenant in the Massachusetts militia and later served as a Danvers selectman. Harriet S. Tapley, *Chronicles of Danvers (Old Salem Village), Massachusetts, 1632–1923* (Danvers: Danvers Historical Society, 1923), pp. 73, 111, 253.

William Churchill Houston to the Managers of the United States Lottery

Gentlemen   Philadelphia 16 March 1780

The enclosed Letter[1] has been sent to me by Governour Livingston, and the Bearer mentioned a Direction to me to open it, that the Governour might be advised whether any Thing further was necessary. I do not comprehend why this was requested of me, and send it you just as I received it. The managers are the only Judges how far it is adequate. I have heard Nothing of the Tickets, but suppose they are in the Possession of the Governour to be forwarded as soon as Conveyance offers.

I am Gentn Your most obedt hble Servt,
                                        William Ch Houston

RC (Donaldson, Lufkin & Jenrette, New York, N.Y., 1975).
[1] Not identified.

Samuel Huntington to Nathanael Greene

Sir,   Philadelphia March 16. 1780[1]
Congress have determined to call on the States for Quotas of necessary Articles to be laid up in Magazines ready for the public Exigencies, and on the Exertions of the States they must rely. But as some time must intervene before Supplies in this Way can be brought into use and before any new Arrangements of the Quarter master Generals Department can be compleated, they think it inexpedient that you should resign and they wish you to continue making every possible Exertion for forwarding the Preparations for the next Campaign by every means which may be in your Power.

Nothing can be more desireable to Congress than to have it in their Power to put the public Officers in a Condition to perform their Contracts and to compleat the necessary Preparations. They are sensible of the Importance of those assigned to your Office and of the Causes whence those Difficulties arise. But they have not been able to avail themselves of the resources of these States to such a Degree as to be entirely effectual though they know them to be abundantly sufficient for the Purposes of a vigorous Defence of our Country. The Arrangements made for calling them out to public Use will necessarily take some time in the operation. The Congress hope that Taxes will shortly be productive of Money sufficient to pay off all the Contracts made in the mean time for Supplies and to that Use the first Application thereof shall be appropriated. Congress desire as soon as possible to be furnished with a list particularly stated of all the Debts due from your Department.

With regard to your Deputies and Assistants, Congress have under Consideration a new Arrangement of your Department which will be soon compleated.[2]
I am Sir &c,   S.H.

LB (DNA: PCC, item 14).
[1] This letter was drafted by Thomas Burke, chairman of a committee originally appointed on December 17, 1779, to respond to a letter from Greene of December 12, and to which his letter of February 16 was also subsequently referred. Burke's draft had been reported to Congress on March 4. See *JCC*, 15:1389, 16:184, 228–30.
[2] Plans for "a new Arrangement" of the quartermaster department were being prepared by delegates Roger Sherman and Allen Jones (Philip Schuyler had refused to serve on the committee), in collaboration with commissioners appointed for this purpose, Thomas Mifflin and Timothy Pickering. Their report, primarily the work of Mifflin and Pickering, was submitted to Congress on March 27, at which time the committee was ordered to confer with Greene "on the subject." See *JCC*, 16: 243–44, 293–311; and Philip Schuyler to George Washington, March 22, 1780.

Medical Committee to the Board of Treasury

Gentlemen.   Philadelphia March 16th. 1780.
Your letter of yesterday to the medical committee[1] has been con-
sidered by them, and I have to acquaint you, that they have not
discharged any persons from the Hospitals, but are informed by Dr.
Bond assistant Depy. Directr. that a number of "the juniors & mates"
have resigned, & that, "there is about 12,000 dollars due to them;"
The come. can't but take notice that it is more then a fortnight Since
they recommended to your Honl Board,[2] that you wou'd "report to
Congress a resolution for one hundred thousand dollars in favor of
Jona. Potts Depy. Directr. for which he is to be accountable," but it
don't appear to them, that you have taken said recommendation into
consideration; unless your letter mentioned above can be considered
in this light.
I am, in the Name & behalf of the committee, your most obedient,

FC (DLC: Holten Papers). In the hand of Samuel Holten. Addressed: "The Hone.
The Board of Treasury."
[1] Not in PCC.
[2] This previous communication has not been found, but on "application of the
Medical Committee," Congress ordered the issuance of two warrants on March 18,
"in favour of Jonathan Potts, purveyor general of the hospitals," totaling $46,900. See
JCC, 16:260.

William Ellery to William Vernon

Dear Sir   Philadelphia M[arc]h 17th 1780
I have received your letters, but until that time had not heard of
the letter you referred to;[1] or if I had it made so little impression on
my mind that I had intirely forgot it. There are throughout that
anonymous letter so many strong marks of malice & revenge that I
am confident the author had something more in view than giving
information from a regard to the public good; and I have no doubt
that He is some disappointed Officer, or some one who wishes to
become a member of the Navy board. Of this opinion I find the
marine committee were when they first received it, and in that light
it is viewed by the Admiralty board to whom I read your letter which
respected it. If I could think of any method by pursuing of which
there would be probability of investigating the Assassin, I would
persue it with ardour, and give up to you the villain when detected;
but it appears to me idle to attempt to discover any thing without
some clue. A man who means to stab in the dark will involve himself
in such obscurity as not to leave one single ray of light by which he
may [be] found. The miscreants who too frequently knock down and
rob people in the streets of this city chuse the darkest nights to

perpetrate their hellish purposes in, and I do not recollect that one of them has yet been taken, but I presume they will proceed until embolden'd by their crimes they become less thoughtful of their security, and so expose themselves to detection. In like manner the vile Assassin of the reputation of the eastern Navy board, finding that his attempt hath not succeded, and imagining that he is not watched by them, may prompted on by malice or envy make other attempts until he shall be discover'd. I think that the best way is to let him go on digging his own Pit.

I am sorry that my letter to Mr. Schweighauser[2] did not arrive seasonably for the packet which sailed in January. I hope it will go in the Active. The badness of the roads & the dilatoriness of the Posts have made any distant communications very slow indeed. Your letters of the 22d of January and the 10th of February were a long time coming. The roads will soon grow better and I hope the warmth of Spring will make the riders more active.

The Bugbear expedition as you call it I am afraid will turn out to be something very serious. Part of the fleet have arrived of[f] Georgia and there is no doubt but that Charlestown is their object. I wish we may be able to hold it. It is said that the naval force there is sufficient to guard the passage to it by water. I wish it may prove so and that the force by land may be sufficient to defend it on the land side but I confess I am not without my fears.

There is no prospect of peace at present. What this campaign may produce I dont know, that altogether depends upon the good or ill success of our Arms and that of our allies. Our depretiating currency is at present our worst enemy. We are about calling it in by taxes, destroying it, and substituting another in its room; but of this you will hear more hereafter.

Give my regards to Mr. Warren, your Son & Mr. Brown and believe me to be your friend,　　　　　W. Ellery

RC (RNHi: Navy Board Papers).
[1] Ellery and William Vernon were undoubtedly referring to the same anonymous "letter," criticizing the Eastern Navy Board to which Vernon was a member, that was discussed in Elbridge Gerry to James Warren, January 25; and James Lovell to Samuel Adams, January 28, 1780, note 2.
[2] Not found; but see Ellery to Schweighauser & Dobree, March ? 1780.

Samuel Holten to John Hancock

Dear Sir.　　　　　Philadelphia March 17th. 1780

The disordered state of our Finances, & want of money in the Public Treasury, has greatly embarrassed our affairs & has for sometime past engaged (nearly) all the attention of Congress, several methods have been proposed for consideration, but that which seems most likely to take place (at Present) is a number of resolutions reported by a come. of the whole, some of the out lines of which I will indeavour to give you (viz.) all the bills now in circulation to be brought in by taxes, & the several states to receive new bills at 40 for one on interest, funded on the credit of each state, to the amount of their quota's (subject to a revisal hereafter) the new bills & specie to be received for taxes at the rate of the above exchange, & no more of the new bills to be emitted than 10,000,000 dollars & to issue no faster than 1 for 20 of the old as they come in, said new bills to be redeemed in specie in Six years after the present, & the annual interest to be paid by bills drawn on our commissioners in Europe if desired, the united states however to be bound for the redemtion of the bills in case of any failure of a State.

I believe this or something like it, will soon pass in Congress,[1] and it is a matter of such great importance that it will require the immediate attention of the several states therefore I can't but hope our Court will not rise before they hear further from Congress.

It is my wish that the contents of this epistle, may not go beyond particular friends at present.

I have had the Honr. of writing to the Court, with my colleagues which I expect will go by this Post, covering copies of a letter from the Minisr. of France, to the delegates of Massachusetts & our answer:[2] It is my desire as well as my colleagues that the said letters be not published to the world, for many reasons we can conceive of that would not be adviseable to commit to writing. I am, my dear Sir, with great respect, your most obedient servant,

FC (Donaldson, Lufkin & Jenrette, New York, N.Y., 1975). In the hand of Samuel Holten.

[1] For the fiscal resolves finally adopted by Congress on March 18, see Samuel Huntington to the States, March 20, 1780.

[2] See Massachusetts Delegates to the Massachusetts Council, March 15, 1780.

James Lovell to Samuel Adams

Dr sr.   Friday March 17. 1780

You will recollect what I told you of the wish of the minister to write to the several States.[1] He readily quitted the Scheme. But you will find he has taken an Occasion thro' us to speak to our State. I had sketched a Reply to him more *general* than what you will see transmitted;[2] but I own the Example of Delegates from other States on various Occasions is a great Argument in favor of the *particular* manner which the Opinion of my Colleagues decided. It is not however necessary to *publish* that we are as partial as they.

A Gentleman of high rank in this City is told from Holland Decr. 29th That Mr Temple is coming out with the following proposals to

Congress.³ "G. Britain will acknowledge the Independce. of all the States except Sth. Carola. & Georgia & the Province of Main wch. are to be given to Great Britain. Mr. T is to be allowed to draw for whatever Sums of Money he thinks proper." The following were offered by the British King and rejected by Mr. T——. "The U.S. to join their Arms wth G.B. *against Spain*. If this cannot be obtained, the sd. States not to *assist Spain* against G Br. If this shd. be rejected then the best Terms possible on this Head to be made".

I cannot say what Credit is to be given to this Information but I know the Hint will make you watch & put Things together as they turn up tending to prove or disprove the Story now told.

I suppose you are convinced that nobody can tell what Value *common Consent* will from day to day put upon our continental Bills. 300 for one may be demanded next Week; tho' it is evident that there is not enough now for the Prices current. Something must immediately be done I hope we shall decide Tomorrow; And I doubt not the States will provide Funds. Pensylvania is most earnestly engaged in providing for her Quota. It behoves our State to be looking about for her Foundation whether in Plate or Lands or both. But I shall lose the Post if I do not drop any further Explanation.

Yrs.   J L

RC (NN: Adams Papers).
¹ For this reference to the chevalier de La Luzerne, see Lovell to Adams, February 28, 1780, note 3.
² See the letters of the Massachusetts Delegates to La Luzerne and to the Massachusetts Council of March 15, 1780.
³ This rumor that John Temple was bringing new peace offers from Britain proved to be false, although he did return to Boston in October 1781 for a sojourn of two years. For his previous unsuccessful attempt at diplomacy in America, see these *Letters*, 10:553–55, where he is also identified.

Nathaniel Peabody to Meshech Weare

Sir   Philada., Friday 3 ck. P.M. 17th March 1780.

I have only time to observe that Congress have this moment received the following information,¹ and may probably be depended upon as to Substance—viz. "Mr. Temple is comming out with the following propositions to Congress. G.B. to acknowledge the Independance of all the States except So. Carolina & Georgia, and that part of Massa bay Call'd the Province of Maine, this together with So. Carolina & Georgia to be given to G Britain. Mr. Temple to be allowed to Draw for whatever Sums of money he pleases. The following propositions were offered by the B. King & rejected by Mr Temple viz the United States to Join their Arms with G. Britain a[gains]t Spain—if this Cannot be obtained—the Said States not to assist Spain against Britain—if this shoud be rejected then to make the best Terms on this Head he Can.

"This intelligence Comes from Holland to a Gentleman of high rank in this City by a letter dated 29 Decr 79."

The post waiting. I have the Honr to be with great Esteem your most Obedt. & very Humble Sevt.   Nathl. Peabody[2]

RC (Nh–Ar: Weare Papers).
[1] See the preceding document, note 3.
[2] Peabody endorsed his draft of this letter, which is in Nh–Ar, Miscellaneous Revolutionary Documents, and *N.H. State Papers*, 17:389–90: "Wrote Letters much of the same Tenor & Date to Col. Bartlett & to Speaker [John] Langdon. Copy of Letters Sent to President Weare, Col Langdon and Col. Bartlett, Mar. 17. 1780. Communication respecting Temple."
To his letter to Josiah Bartlett, however, Peabody added the following final paragraph: "The 200,000 Dollars Charged to the State July 1778 was without foundation. Shall give the particulars—the mistake is rectified." Bartlett Papers, NhD.

Samuel Holten's Diary

March 18 [1780]

Saturday. Congress agreed to call in all the paper currency by taxes. I wrote to General Lincoln.[1]

MS (MDaAr).
[1] Not found.

William Churchill Houston to the New Jersey General Assembly

Sir,   Philada 18 March 1780

I have the Honour to enclose you the Proceedings of a General Court-martial, held for the Trial of Major General Benedict Arnold on various Charges exhibited against him by the President and Supreme Executive Council of the State of Pennsylvania.[1] I could obtain but a single Copy otherwise I should have sent one for each House.

I must take the Liberty here to repeat what I have a few Minutes ago requested in a hasty Letter,[2] that the Legislature will sit so long as to attend to the Subject of the Resolutions of to-day which that Letter encloses; and shall hope to be allowed to lay before them my Thoughts upon those Resolutions as soon as I have Time to commit them to Paper.

I am, Sir, with much respect, your obedt. and very hble sevt,

William Ch. Houston

RC (NN: William Livingston Papers). Addressed: "His Exly the Presidt of the Council, and the Honble the Speaker of the Assembly, New Jersey."

[1] For Arnold's court-martial and the published *Proceedings* that Houston enclosed, see Samuel Huntington to Washington, March 11, 1780, note 4.

[2] Not found, but the "Resolutions of to-day" enclosed in it were undoubtedly the fiscal plan that was sent in the letter of Samuel Huntington to the States, March 20, 1780.

Samuel Huntington to George Washington

Sir,   Philadelphia March 19. 1780

I do myself the honour to transmit your Excellency the enclosed Intelligence No 1 & No 2 this Moment received from Charles Town South Carolina.[1]

And have the honour to be, with the highest respect, your Excellency's hble servt,   Sam. Huntington

RC (DLC: Washington Papers). In a clerical hand and signed by Huntington.

[1] These consisted of: "No. 1," an extract from Benjamin Lincoln's February 22 letter to Congress; and "No. 2," a February 25 letter identified by its endorsement—"The express who brings this Says it is an Extract Taken from the late President Laurens in Charles Town which he saw Copied off." Both reported the recent arrival of a large British expedition under the command of Sir Henry Clinton just south of Charlestown. Washington Papers, DLC. Lincoln's letter is in PCC, item 158, fols. 325–30. It was read in Congress with two earlier ones from the general on March 20. *JCC*, 16:269.

John Mathews to Benjamin Lincoln

Dear sir   Philadelphia March 19th 1780

The Committee have nothing new to communicate,[1] therefore do not write by this opportunity.

I most anxiously wait for the arrival of Mr. Kinloch,[2] or some Express, to get some information of your situation, and the movements of the enemy, for we have received no account, from your quarter since the 29th Jany. announcing the appearance of the enemy off our coast.[3] We have had a variety of reports here respecting them, but on which not the least dependence is to be placed. I think it cannot be many days longer before we must hear from you. I should take it as a particular favour if you could contrive to get the inclosed letter to Miss Wragg.[4] It is of great importance to me, & respects my private affairs, The management of which, in the situation the Country is, must devolve entirely on her, as every man, who had any concern in them must either be in the field, or probably in a much worse situation. Mr. John Allen Walter, of Collo. Harry's light horse, I believe, can give you the best information where she is. If you cannot get it safe to her, I must trouble you to inclose it, & return it to me again.

I beg pardon sir for giving you this trouble, but I knew of no one, to whom I could so properly give it at this time as I conclude the enemy are either before or in the town, in either event, all my friends are rendered incapable, of complying with my request, because they are either shut up in the town, or are in the hands of the enemy. And I conclude you will be in the field. And Majr. Lucas, who is the bearer of this, will come directly to Headquarters. I most sincerely wish you better success than I expect to hear of, for, knowing your circumstances, my expectations on this head are small.

Believe me to be, Dr. General, with the most sincere Esteem, Yr. most Obedt. serv.   Jno. Mathews

RC (PHC: Roberts Autograph Letters Collection).
[1] That is, the committee to correspond with the commanding officer of the southern department. Mathews, as chairman, had last written to Lincoln on March 7.
[2] South Carolina delegate Francis Kinloch, who had been elected February 1, 1780, and took his seat in Congress on March 25.
[3] See Samuel Huntington to Lincoln, March 6, 1780.
[4] Not found. Mathews' correspondent may have been a sister of his wife, Mary Wragg Mathews, but little is known about Mary's siblings. Walter B. Edgar et al., eds., *Biographical Directory of the South Carolina House of Representatives* (Columbia: University of South Carolina Press, 1974–), 2:732–33.

Philip Schuyler to George Washington

Dear Sir   Philadelphia March 19th 1780
Since my last nothing new has been received from the Southward. The report which I mentioned to have prevailed of serious Indications on the part of the british to attempt the reduction of Charlestown begins to lose Credit with many. I however cannot believe that so Capital a force would have been Sent to That Quarter merely to hold their Ground In Georgia.

Advices tho not official have been received two days ago via Holland that Mr John Temple was to repair to these states Charged with propositions to Congress from the Court of London, The Substance of which are an acknowledgment of our Independance, provided they retain Canada In all Its Extent, that we Ceed South Carolina and Georgia, and what they Call the province of Main, now part of the Massachusetts State, and that they also retain Acadia with Its dependencies—to leave us at Liberty to fulfil our Engagements with france but to Observe a perfect neutrality with respect to them, & Spain.

The report on Finance is agreed to without any Material Alteration from what I think I Stated in a former letter.[1]

The Committee appointed to Arrange the Civil departments in Conjunction with Messrs. Mifflin & Pickering have not yet reported,[2] as I refused to Attend I can only Judge of what It will be from the

Ideas which Some of the Gentlemen have Communicated on the Subject, & which are not Consonant to mine.

My best respects Attend Mrs Washington, be pleased to Convey them with my Complements to the Gentlemen of the Family.

I am Dear Sir Most Affectionately and [. . .] Your Excellencys most Obedt, Humble Servant,   Ph. Schuyler

RC (DLC: Washington Papers).

[1] See Schuyler to Washington, March 13, 1780.

[2] For the work of this committee, see Samuel Huntington to Nathanael Greene, March 16, 1780, note 2.

Connecticut Delegates to Jonathan Trumbull, Sr.

Sir,   Philadelphia March 20th, 1780

The President will transmit to your Excellency the resolutions of Congress for Sinking the continental Bills of Credit and issuing New Bills on the credit of the Several States,[1] which We hope will be approved by your Excellency & the Honorable the General Assembly.

It was judged impracticable to carry on the war another year with the present currency—and no other plan has been proposed that appeared So likely to relieve us from the Embarrassments of a fluctuating currency as that which has been adopted by Congress. The depreciation here has been at the rate of Sixty for one and in the Southern States from forty to fifty. Neither the Scarcity or the Collection of taxes have had any effect to appreciate, or fix, its value. 'Tis apprehended that the New Bills will be effactually Secured against depreciation, from the Smallness of the quantity to be in Circulation, the funds provided for their redemption, the Shortness of the period, and the payment of an annual Interest.

The preparing them under the direction of the Board of Treasury, and the insurance of payment by the United States in case any State Shall by the events of the war be rendered incapable of redeeming them, will give them a currency through out the United States, and be a Security against Counterfeits.

This emission of Bills will not only introduce a Stable Medium of Trade—but increase the revenue, The amount of five millions of dollars equal to Specie. The Six tenths of the Bills to be emitted will enable the States to purchase the Specific Supplies called for by the resolution of the 25th of February last, and the remaining four tenths will Supply the continental Treasury for Paying the Army &ca, while the States are collecting in the old Bills by taxes. And although it is recommended to collect in the Continental Bills by Monthly Assessments it may be expedient to give the people an opportunity of paying the whole at one payment. It may also be expedient for the States to allow New Bills to be exchanged for the old, that the old may be drawn out of circulation as Soon as possible to prevent further imposition by counterfeits and if there Should be a Scarcity of money people might be allowed to pay their rates in provisions to be delivered at the magazines at the prices fixed by Congress. The New Bills will be prepared and forwarded to the States as Soon As possible.

We hear that the Honorable Assembly have ordered a New Emission of Bills.[2] We beg leave to Submit to Your Excellency whether it will not be expedient to Stop the issuing of them, and immediately adopt the plan recommended by Congress. We Should be Sorry to have that fail of the good effects expected from it by any Act or omission on the part of the States.

The Same proportions are kept up in the present requisitions as in the resolution of the 7th of October last, Wherein Connecticut is rated much too high, but hope that wont prevent her compliance at least to the amount of her quota, which would be about one twelfth part, in case none of the States were disabled by the events of the war from raising their quotas. Perhaps her quota in present circumstances, would be more than one eleventh part of the whole—repeated Assurances have been given by Congress that those States which do more than their proportion Shall be equitably compensated.

There is a report before Congress for fixing the rate in Specie at which the loan office certificates Shall be paid.[3]

It is expected that a new regulation of the Quarter Master's and other Staff departments will Soon be established on the most Economical plans whereby much expence will be Saved. They will be Accommodated to the late regulation of making the purchases by the States. The prices of the Specific Articles to be furnished by the States were estimated at about 50 per cent above the prices in 1774. They include all expences of purchasing and delivering them into the Magazines. The motives for Adopting that measure were, the rendering the Supplies more certain and equable among the States, and to prevent frauds & abuses. And the aid of the States in procuring Supplies was found to be absolutely necessary.

By a Letter from General Lincoln of the 22d Ultimo we are informed that part of the British forces that left New York were Landed on St Johns, & James's Islands, near Charles town the Numbers not Assertained, but he thinks there is a good prospect of making a Successful opposition to them.[4] Mr. Lawrence expected to Sail for Europe the 26th of Feby.

We are, with the greatest respect, your Excellency's humble Servants,   Roger Sherman

Oliver Ellsworth

RC (Ct: Trumbull Papers). Written by Sherman, and signed by Sherman and Ellsworth.
[1] See the following entry.

[2] Connecticut's recent act "for supplying the State Treasury with such Sums as shall be necessary for the Exigencies of this Government . . .," which authorized the immediate emission of "forty thousand pounds, lawfull money, in bills of publick credit," is in *Public Records of Connecticut*, 2:477–81.

[3] The report of the committee "respecting the payment of the principal and interest of loan office certificates" had been delivered on February 17, but no action had been taken. Roger Sherman, who had originally offered the motion on this subject on January 4 and was a member of the committee that prepared this report, successfully moved on March 21 to have the report recommitted to the committee, with Philip Schuyler replacing the incapacitated James Forbes. A new report was submitted on March 25, which was debated on March 28 and thereafter intermittently. When agreement continued to elude the delegates, the report was returned on May 2 to yet another committee, which brought in a report on June 20 that finally resulted in the adoption of a plan of depreciation on loan office certificates on June 28. See *JCC*, 16:12, 171, 273, 287–88, 313, 315, 318, 320, 374–75, 388–90, 393, 403, 17:441–42, 455–57, 538, 542, 544–48, 563, 565–69; Sherman to Jonathan Trumbull, March 28; William Ellery to William Greene, April 18, note 6; and Ezekiel Cornell to William Greene, June 27, 1780.

[4] See Samuel Huntington to George Washington, March 19, 1780, note.

Samuel Huntington to the States

Sir,   Circular   Philada March 20. 1780

Your Excellency will receive herewith enclosed an Act of Congress of the 18th Instant calling upon the several States to bring in the Continental Currency by monthly taxes or otherwise, as shall best suit their respective Circumstances, in proportion to the Quotas, assigned to each State, by the resolution of the 7th of October 1779, and making provision for other Bills to be issued in Lieu thereof, under the regulations and restrictions mentioned in the Act.[1]

This Act is the result of much Labour and Deliberation, as the happiest Expedient that could be adopted to extricate these States from the Embarrassments of a fluctuating Medium and at the same time in some Measure afford the necessary Means for supporting the ensuing Campaign.

You will readily perceive the Importance of this Measure and the indispensible necessity of unanimity in the States in conforming thereto.

It is requested that there may be no Delay in taking this Act under Consideration, and that the Assembly if not sitting may be convened as soon as possible for that purpose, and that the Laws which may be enacted in pursuance thereof be transmitted to Congress without Delay.

The new Bills will be struck under the Direction of the Board of Treasury and sent to the several States in due proportion.

You have also enclosed an Act of Congress of this Day recommending the revision of such Laws as may have been passed making the Continental Bills a Tender in Discharge of Debts &c.[2]

I have the honour &c,   S.H.

In CONGRESS, March 18, 1780.

THESE United States having been driven into this juſt and neceſſary war, at a time when no regular civil governments were eſtabliſhed, of ſufficient energy to enforce the collection of taxes, or to provide funds for the redemption of ſuch bills of credit as their neceſſities obliged them to iſſue, and before the powers of Europe were ſufficiently convinced of the juſtice of their cauſe, or of the probable event of the controverſy, to afford them aid or credit; in conſequence of which, their bills encreaſing in quantity beyond the ſum neceſſary for the purpoſe of a circulating medium, and wanting at the ſame time ſpecific funds to reſt on for their redemption, they have ſeen them daily ſink in value, notwithſtanding every effort that has been made to ſupport the ſame; inſomuch that they are now paſſed by common conſent in moſt parts of theſe United States at leaſt ⁱⁿ below their nominal value, and ſtill remain in a ſtate of depreciation, whereby the community ſuffers great injuſtice, the public finances are deranged, and the neceſſary diſpoſitions for the defence of the country are much impeded and perplexed : And as, effectually to remedy thoſe evils, for which purpoſe the United States are now become competent, their independence being well aſſured, their civil governments eſtabliſhed and vigorous, and the ſpirit of their citizens ardent for exertion, it is neceſſary ſpeedily to reduce the quantity of the paper medium in circulation, and to eſtabliſh and apportionate funds that ſhall enſure the punctual redemption of the bills : Therefore

RESOLVED, That the ſeveral ſtates continue to bring into the continental treaſury, by taxes or otherwiſe, their full quotas of fifteen million dollars monthly, as aſſigned them by the reſolution of the 7th of October, 1779, a clauſe in the reſolve of the 23d of February laſt, for relinquiſhing two thirds of the ſaid quotas, to the contrary notwithſtanding : And that the ſtates be forthwith called on to make proviſion for continuing to bring into the ſaid treaſury their like quotas monthly to the months of April, 1781, incluſive.

That ſilver and gold be receivable in payment of the ſaid quotas, at the rate of one Spaniſh milled dollar in lieu of forty dollars of the bills now in circulation.

Congressional Resolution of March 18, 1780

LB (DNA: PCC, item 14).

[1] The enclosed "Act" of March 18 officially devalued the Continental dollar at a stroke to one-fortieth of its face value—that is, the $200 million then in circulation was revalued to $5 million—culminating a search for a way out of its fiscal dilemma that had troubled Congress for months. To implement this decision, Congress specified that the paper currency in circulation would be destroyed as states continued to pay their monthly quotas (as assigned October 7, 1779) through April 1781.

However, in recognition that they could not continue to maintain the war effort without additional resources, the delegates resolved simultaneously to issue new interest-bearing bills—up to "one-twentieth part of the nominal sum of the bills brought in to be destroyed," and "redeemable in specie, within six years"—whose obligations would be met by "sterling bills of exchange, drawn by the United States on their commissioners in Europe." This bit of wishful thinking convinced virtually no one, of course, but it was seen by some as a measure to gain time, perhaps against the day when foreign loans or state price limitation measures might halt the spiral of inflation. For the details of this fanciful March 18 resolve, which ran to five printed pages, see *JCC*, 16:262–67. For the context of its adoption and discussion of some of the principal fiscal milestones marking Congress' path to its enactment, see John Jay to the States, September 14, 1779, note 3; John Fell to Robert Morris, March 5, 1780, note 2; and Burnett, *Continental Congress*, pp. 425–27.

[2] A motion offered by Thomas McKean seeking revision of the states' legal tender laws, "making the continental bills of credit a tender in payment of debts and contracts . . . so as to prevent injustice to creditors or debtors," had been referred to committee on February 14. The committee's report, which was read in Congress February 29 and debated March 11, led to adoption of a resolve this day that embodied the essentials of McKean's motion. See *JCC*, 16:165, 217, 253, 269.

Robert R. Livingston to William Livingston

Sir   Philadelphia 20th March 1780
I delayed answering your favour of the 24th Ult. till I had made some inquiries into the matter you mention, I cannot find by them that Genl Green is about to resign his quarter master genlship. If he does I will give you the earliest notice of it. But much as I feel disposed to serve the gent. of whose merit your recommendation is a sufficient proof, I fear that an insuperable objection to it will be found in his not having been in the military line, which seems essentially necessary to qualify him for the place of quarter master Genl. A plan of reformation is now upon the carpet which if it shd go thro' may probably afford room for the exertion of Mr. Condicts[1] abilities in a way equally agreeable to him and free from the objection I mention, in which I should endeavour to serve him. I am Sir with the highest respect & esteem Your Excellency's Most Obt. Hum. Servt.   Rob R. Livingston

RC (NN: William Livingston Papers).

[1] Silas Condict, whose suitability for appointment as quartermaster general was also discussed in John Fell to Robert Morris, March 5, 1780.

James Madison to James Madison, Sr.

Philadelphia Monday March 20th. 1780.

The extreme badness of the roads and frequency of rains rendered my journey so slow that I did not reach this place till Saturday last.[1] The only public intelligence I have to communicate is that the great and progressive depreciation of the paper currency had introduced such disorder and perplexity into public affairs for the present and threatened to load the United States with such an intolerable burden of debt, that Congress have thought it expedient to convert the 200,000,000 of Dollars now in circulation into a real debt of 5,000,000 by establishing the exchange at 40 for 1. And taxes for calling it in during the ensuing year, are to be payable at the option of the people in specie or paper according to that difference. In order to carry on public measures in future money is to be emitted under the combined faith of Congress and the several States, secured on permanent and specific funds to be provided by the latter. This scheme was finally resolved on on Saturday last.[2] It has not yet been printed but will be immediately. I shall transmit a copy to you by the first opportunity. The little time I have been here makes it impossible for me to enter into a particular delineation of it. It will probably create great proplexity and complaints in many private transactions. Congress have recommended to the States to repeal their tender laws, and to take measures for preventing injustice as much as possible. It is probable that in the case of loans to the public, the state of depreciation at the time they were made will be the rule of payment, but nothing is yet decided on that point. I expect to be more at leisure to write fully by next post. Yrs. &c. &c.

James Madison Junr.

RC (DLC: Madison Papers). Madison, *Papers* (Hutchinson), 2:3.

[1] Madison, who had been elected to Congress December 14, 1779, presented his credentials this day. *JCC*, 16:268.

[2] See Samuel Huntington to the States, this date. For a lengthy essay that Madison had recently written on the general subject of "Money," which he was apparently prompted to draft as a result of his election to Congress, see Madison, *Papers* (Hutchinson), 1:302–10.

Massachusetts Delegates
to the Massachusetts Council

Sir, Philadelphia 20th March 1780

Since the Receipt of your Letter of Febry. 9th the Attention of Congress has been so engaged with the Affairs of the Army & Finance, as to preclude an Oppertunity of making any propositions respecting the Expenditures of the State in the Penobscot Expedition, but We hope this Business will not be much longer delayed.[1] The Resolution mentioned in your Letter would be useful on this Occasion, & not being able to find it in the Journals, after the most careful Examination thereof, We are under the necessity of requesting You to point it out. We are nevertheless convinced of the Justice of the Claim, & shall prefer it to Congress by the earliest Oppertunity, being sir with great Respect your most obedt. & very humble Servts.

E Gerry   James Lovell

S. Holten   Geo. Partridge

RC (M–Ar: Revolutionary War Letters). Written by Gerry, and signed by Gerry, Holten, Lovell, and Partridge. Addressed: "Hona. Jeremiah Powell. Esqr. president of the Council of Massa. Bay." Endorsed: "In Council April 8, 1780. Read & sent down with Several Papers Accompanying. John Avery, D Scy."

[1] For Massachusetts' application for Continental reimbursement of expenses for the Penobscot Bay expedition, see James Lovell to Samuel Adams, April 9; and Samuel Huntington to the Massachusetts Council, April 14, 1780.

William Shippen, Sr., to Richard Henry Lee

Dear Sir,   Philada. March 20h 1780.[1]

I reced your Favor of the 19th Feby inclosing a Note for Tho Paine Clerk of our Assembly wch I delivered. We hear from Carolina that the Troops to the amount of 8000 are arrived & Landed, some on Johns Island, some on James's Island & some elsewhere, a number of their Ships much shattered, some 3 foundered, all their Horses lost. That one 64 Gun Ship & 2 or 3 smaller appear off the harbour. Sulivan says that if they delay their motion 2 or 3 Weeks he hopes to be prepared for them, that he has expected the Virginia Troops 18 Months not arrived the 24th Feby. Mr Laurens was to sail for Statia the next day. The Vessel wch John Adams sailed in arrived at Corunna in 18 Days. I wish I could inform you of a prospect of an honorable Peace but I guess the fluctuating state of our Finances will encourage our obstinate Foes to struggle hard to prolong the war, by the inclosed imperfect sketch of our present System passed yesterday you'l see how unequal we are to the work. The Credit of our Money is so low that it is absolutely necessary to attempt something.

If I have the pleasure to see your Sons in Philada. on their way to Virginia I shall observe your directions.

I have wrote you several times by the Post & directed agreably to your advice but I dont find you have reced any of my Letters.[2] Inclosed is a Letter from D Scudder, Young Madison one of your Delegates came into Congress yesterday. I cant find any good Sonchong Tea but have bot you one pound very fine Hyson at a Guinea but how to send it I know not. Best Compts to Mrs. Lee & Famy.   W. Shippen

[*P.S.*] I sent you an account of the Numbers of Lottery Tickets long ago & that your Interest on certificate is to be paid in Virginia but have not met with a Safe hand by whom to send it to you.

RC (ViU: Lee Family Papers).
[1] Shippen may have actually written this letter on March 21, as he writes below that "Young Madison . . . came into Congress yesterday," and James Madison first attended Congress on Monday, March 20. *JCC,* 16:268.
[2] The last letter from Shippen to Lee that has been found is dated June 22, 1779.

John Collins to Nathanael Greene

Dear Sir,   Philadelphia March the 21st 1780
I Received yours of the l9th this after noon, would incloased you this days papers—but make no doubt you will Receive it per post in which you will find what accounts we have from Carolina. European News we have but little none but what has been published, we may expect another Campain Except the Irish affairs diverts our Enemies from it, and if they Should, it will be happy for this Countrey.
The Committee for Regulating the Quartermasters and Commissarys Department have Given in their Report but it has not as yet been Read.[1] I will send you a Copy as soon as it is. You Say you are Exceeding Sick of your departmt and wish to get out of it if it Could be don in Charrector, I make no wonder at it, for I know it must be extreem troublelsom, I am not able at preasent to give you any advice, but would Readley do it if I Could, but I Will make this Observation, Popularity once lost justly or injustly, is not easely Regained by the best of men. You Are in the prime of life, let not a little dificoty Discorage you, if I Can be of any service to you you may depend I will Serve you as far as is in my power.
Congress has finished their plan of finance. I Will Send you the Scheem per next post. We have going on the plan Adopted by the New England States to git Rid of their Oald tener. A Silver Dollar is to pay 40 paper Dollers for taxis, And as the money now in Circulation is paid in, it is to be Distroyed, and new money isued Carring 5 Per Cent intrest. I hope the Scheem will answer as well as it did in New England, but the Event must be left to time.
I have not had one line from Rhode Island Since I left it. Should be Glad to hear how the people at Large Relish my leaveing the State in the maner I left it. My Respect to your Lady, I am With Regards yours,   Jno Collins

RC (MiU–C: Greene Papers).
[1] The report was read in Congress on March 27, whereupon the committee was ordered to "confer with Major General Greene, Q.M.G. on the subject." *JCC,* 16:293–311.

Samuel Livermore to Meshech Weare

Dear sir   Philadelphia March 21st. 1780.
Our plan of Finance has at length passed the Congress; but not
just as I expected. As it is lengthy & you will have it officially transmitted[1] I need not copy it. It keeps up the idea of forty for one; but
as it proposes sinking the whole paper Currency in six years, I fear
the burthen will prove too great; it depends on the several states
adopting the plan by Acts of Assembly for that purpose, which it is
thot will not be complid with.
  Vermont business hangs by the eyelids, Masa. Bay not ready, I am
tired of waiting & must set out as soon as travelling will permit.[2]
  The Carolina News is in the enclosed papers to the 25th Feb. I am
anxious for the event. However we are in high spirits, as the attack is
far short of what the enemy intended. Genl Lincoln I hope will be
able to keep the ground.
  I am Your most obedient humble servant.
                                        Samuel Livermore

RC (MHi: Weare Papers).
[1] See Samuel Huntington to the States, March 20, 1780.
[2] Livermore, whose delegate credentials had expired the last day of February, left
Philadelphia on April 8. Samuel Holten's Diary, April 8, 1780. MDaAr.

James Lovell to Abigail Adams

                                          March 21st. 1780
I most sincerely rejoice with you[1] on the safe Arrival of Mr. Adams
in Spain after so short a Passage tho' attended with some Hardships.
  In addition to the News in the Prints I venture, upon some confidential assurances from the worthy Genl. Lincoln, to excite your
Hopes as to our affairs in that Quarter.
  It is recommended to redeem the continental Currency at 40 for 1
and to model the Tender Laws equitably. It is a Thing of uncertain
Event and the Balance of Blessings and Cursings consequent cannot
shortly be fixed. It is one of those Decisions about which much very
much may and will be said on both sides. I believe that most of those
who said nay here on the Determination were glad it was carried
against them. I cannot see how the Continent can suppose that Congress has any separate Interest to guide their Determination on this
inportant Point.
  Yrs. affly.,   J Lovell

RC (MHi: Adams Papers). Adams, *Family Correspondence* (Butterfield), 3:314.
[1] The recipient of this letter is incorrectly identified as John Adams in Burnett,
Letters, 5:85.

James Lovell to Samuel Adams

Dear Sir   21st of March [1780]
The News Papers are not so full on the Subject of Carolina affairs
as what I now convey to you from the best Authority.[1] You will use it
for the Satisfaction of the honble. Council but not neglect Attention
to the confidential Manner in which the discreat General wrote it.
He is no Vaunter. You will find we have been forced, by the enormous artificial Depreciation added to the natural, to come to a decisive Recommendation about the Redemption of the present nominal
Debt at an equitable Ratio and consonant Measures as to the Tender
Laws. If our People of Mass. are paying as the People of Pensylv.
They will be glad to have some Bound set to a cruel Fluctuation.

I am astonished whenever the Post arrives to find I have not a
single Line from you, in particular that you have not been minute
about Vermont or the *Resolve* of Congress on which the Penobscot
Expedition was founded.[2] There is no great Task in finding Resolves
of a quite contrary Spirit, but my Eyes and Head have suffered in
Search of what is possitively asserted in a Letter from our State of
Feb. 9th. I wish one of the 4 Delegates there had pointed to the Date,
I do not comprehend Mr. Ward in that Number.

We can only go upon the Reason and Justice of the Mass Claim to
be reimbursed.

I find nothing more favorable than the 1st Resolve at the Head of
the 25th Page of the 1st Vol. the bottom of Page 101 with the Top of
126—near the Bottom of 127 in regard to N Carolina.[3]

The 4th Paragraph Page 171 is agst. us also the 2d Resolution
from the Bottom of 235 and what relates to the River Delaware. I
shall be much ashamed to find that I have overlooked so important a
Resolve if it really exists.

I wish my very good Friend Doctor Jose Gardner may have from
you Genl. Lincoln's Letter to deliver to Mrs. L after he has read it,
that it may be put with other Papers in her Possession. The Doctr.
has much affection & Esteem for Lincoln as well as Anxiety for the
public Cause.

Yr. sincerely   J L

[*P.S.*] Compliments to Majr. Osgood wh[om] I find was arrived alive
in Boston prior to Feb 28.

RC (NN: Adams Papers).
[1] Lovell undoubtedly enclosed copies of letters from Gen. Benjamin Lincoln, whose
February 11, 14, and 22 letters had been read in Congress on March 20. *JCC,* 16:269.
[2] Lovell's meaning is obscure, but he may have been referring to a congressional resolve of May 21, 1778, opposing an immediate attempt against Nova Scotia but
leaving the prospect open for the future. "If however," the resolve concluded, "any
concurrence of circumstances should sooner render success in this undertaking
probable . . . the honourable council of Massachusetts bay should be empowered at

continental expence to furnish the inhabitants of Nova Scotia with a force, not exceeding two regiments, to assist in accomplishing the purpose." *JCC*, 11:518. For the transmittal of this resolve to Massachusetts, see these *Letters*, 9:734.

[3] Assuming that Lovell was using the 1777 edition of the journals, the resolutions referred to here and in the following paragraph, concerning Continental reimbursement for certain state expenses, are those of October 8, 1774; May 15, June 23 and 26, July 18, November 4, 1775; and June 13 and 14, 1776.

New York Delegates to George Clinton

Sir, Philadelphia, March 21. 1780.[1]

We do ourselves the honor to refer your Excellency to some important resolutions which passed Congress on Saturday, and will be transmitted to you by the President;[2] whether their effect will be such as we wish, time alone can discover. Our hopes are sanguine; as the minutes of Congress will shew that we unanimously concurred in them, we think it proper to lay before your Excellency our reasons, not only as a justification of our conduct to our constituents, if contrary to our expectations the measure should not meet with their approbation, but in order to explain more fully the principles upon which the determinations of Congress were formed. The continued and rapid depreciation, notwithstanding the pressure of taxes, which was severely felt in many places; the increased demands of the Army, in consequence of that depreciation; the exhausted state of the public treasury; the utter impossibility of procuring a supply in any other way, adequate to the demand by taxation, even if the people could have submitted to have their burthens doubled upon them, called aloud for some firm and decided alteration in our system of finance. In vain we endeavored to borrow in aid of the taxes, the monied interest availing themselves of our necessities refusing to lend, though we offered them near fifty per cent advance on sterling bills. This evil increased upon us every day, and loans become more difficult when the depreciated state of the currency reduced the relative quantity below what was necessary as a medium of commerce, in which situation of things no person would lend unless upon such a premium as would be sufficient to indemnify him for the capital drawn from trade; and even then only slowly, and in Small quantities, as the necessities of the public daily giving him hopes for more advantageous terms.

In this situation nothing was left us but some firm and decided measure, or public bankruptcy and ruin. We flatter ourselves the part we have taken will do justice to individuals as far as it can be done with safety, and enable the public to make those exertions on which the happiness of its members depend. The farmer will acknowledge the propriety of a measure which compels him to pay to the public no more than the value of what has been received to his use, and the money holder if he reasons justly, will be satisfied with the real worth of the commodity with which he purchased that money, instead of a visionary wealth which every hour diminishes in his hands, and which must have vanished into air, as the cause on which it was borne could no longer be supported. The continuation of the tax to the amount required, though desirable and to be complied with if possible, must however be limited by the situation of every State. Perhaps with us it may be advisable after the establishment of funds, to take in part of the old by exchange for the new emissions in order to lighten the tax; perhaps too it might be advantageously funded upon our confiscated estates and back lands. The resolution to receive specie and the new bills at 40 times the nominal value of the bills of credit now in circulation is founded upon a belief that that is about the average value at which it was received by the present possessors of them: this may indeed bear hard upon individuals, but in so great a work it cannot but be, that private interests must yield to public utility. It may be asked, what will secure the new emissions from depreciation? We answer, first the reduction of the whole debt to so moderate a compass as to render the payment of it easy; second, the funds on which they are to be issued, which it is expected will be sufficient to convince the creditor of the public that his money rests on a firm basis. These are the only securities a community can give, and these have always been sufficient, if a State did not either outrun its resources, or neglect to apply them to the maintenance of public credit. We flatter ourselves the State will see the necessity of such established system of taxation as will enable the public creditor to calculate the value of his security, without which a paper credit must always fluctuate. Besides the advantages which we have already stated as the probable consequences of this measure, and those more obvious benefits that arise from throwing off an unjust and cumbrous load of debt which threatened for ages to clog the industry of our people. From having some fixed standard by which to ascertain the pay of our officers, civil and military—from checking the idleness and dissipation which a fluctuating medium always occasions, and from banishing their baneful spirit of jobbing and speculation—which disordered Finances and a heavy public debt never fail to give birth to.

We had reasons arising from the peculiar situation of our State which attached us to the measure. We had little room to hope that Congress would make us those allowances in the liquidation of the public debt, which as we conceived, our distresses entitled us to; since, though they acknowledged the weight of our present burthens, yet they seemed to Suppose (and perhaps with some degree of justice) that our future resources were fully sufficient to enable us to bear any proportion of the debt, which by the terms of the confederation could be imposed on us. Had they therefore under this impression adopted any system of appreciation for which taxation was the basis, our State would have been unable to tax in proportion to its neighbors, would necessarily have fallen a sacrifice to that appreciation. From this evil we are now happily secured, since whatever time our necessities may oblige us to take for the redemption of the public debt, we are assured that the value of money cannot increase to our ruin.

We have dwelt thus long upon this subject, because we are sensible that a measure in which numbers are interested must have many difficulties to struggle with, and impressed with its necessity and importance, we wish to bespeak for it the support and patronage of the State.

The business of the Grants still drags on heavily; at present we are prevented from proceeding by the sickness of one of the representatives from Maryland, whose absence breaks up the Congress,[3] if agreeable to the spirit of the resolutions of Sept'r last, the States that are interested in the controversy should stand aside. We shall omit no opportunity of bringing it on, when a convenient season offers.

We have the honor to be with the highest respect and esteem, your Excellency's most obt. humble Servts.

Jno. Morin Scott	Ph. Schuyler
Wm. Floyd	Robt. R. Livingston
	Ezra L'Hommedieu

Tr (MH–H: Sparks Collection). FC (NHi: Robert R. Livingston Papers). In the hand of Robert R. Livingston.

[1] Although Sparks' transcript of the RC of this letter is dated March 21, Livingston's draft is dated March 20. There are no major variations between the texts.

[2] See Samuel Huntington to the States, March 20, 1780.

[3] This day Congress resolved that consideration of claims to the New Hampshire Grants "be postponed, nine states, exclusive of those who are parties to the question, not being represented in Congress," a consequence of the illness of James Forbes, who died on March 25. *JCC*, 16:273.

Rhode Island Delegates to William Greene

Sir,   Philadelphia May [i.e., March] 21st. 1780.[1]

In our last letter we informed your excellency that the haughtiness of Great Britain had determined her to try her strength another campaign.[2]

It is unnecessary to say that it behoves the United States to be fully prepared to resist her greatest efforts; but it is our duty to tell you plainly that unless immediate and essential relief is given to our embarrassed finances it will be impracticable. The sinews of war must be braced, and more regular and more ample supplies bro't into the Treasury than it hath received for months past or our military preparations must cease and the most pernicious consequences ensue.

Congress have long seen with alarming apprehensions the crisis to which a continued depretiation of our paper currency would one day reduce our affairs.

They have given frequent and faithful warnings to the several States; and have exerted every power on their part to avert the impending mischief; but to little or no purpose. The evil, like an uncontrouled torrent hath advanced on with rapid progress, and now threatens to overwhelm us. Under these circumstances Congress have thought it necessary to adopt a new plan of finance; and have accordingly come to the decisive resolutions which we now have the honour to inclose to you.[3]

The main objects of them you will readily perceive are; by one operation to give an establishment to the paper medium, to realize the nominal debt of the United States, and find supplies for the treasury.

We have taken the liberty to point out very briefly the objects of the Plan referred to and the necessity which compelled Congress to adopt it. We will only subjoin that if it should meet the approbation of our legislature, we hope that they will immediately make the necessary provisions for carrying it into effectual execution.

In a letter lately written by Mr Ellery to the Lieut. Governor[4] he mentioned the substance of a letter received not long since from Dr. Franklin, and also transmitted the translation of a letter from the King of France to Congress; and at the same time desired his Honour to communicate them to your Excellency and the Genl. Assembly, with an apology for our not writing to Government.

Since that we have received no intelligence from Europe or any other quarter. We are in daily expectation of hearing something from the Southward. We have received no advices from thence later than the very beginning of February, and they only announced the arrival of part of the British fleet off Georgia, without particularizing their number or the number of troops aboard. Indeed it could not be ascertained.

Inclosed is a resolution of Congress of the 29th of February last,[5] which may be of use in the settlement with the continental Officers & Soldiers of our State. Congress have passed resolutions recommending a revision of their tender Laws &c. of which we will also transmit a copy if one can be procured before the post goes out.[6]

Since writing the foregoing Congress have received a letter from Genl. Lincoln of the 22d of February.[7] In which he observes "The uncertain events of war will not authorize an assurance of success; but I think if my requisition of 2000 militia from the country is complied with, and General Hogan with our other expected succours, arrive time we may flatter ourselves with the probability of an effectual opposition." The intelligence in the paper respecting the Enemy &c at the Southward is good, and renders it unnecessary to copy

anymore of Genl. Lincoln's Letter. We are [*with*] the greatest respect,
Yr Excellency's most obedt. Servts   William Ellery

                                                  John Collins

RC (R–Ar: Letters to Governors). Written by Ellery, and signed by Ellery and Collins.
[1] Internal evidence indicates that this letter was written in March, the bulk of it
before or on the morning of March 20, the date Congress read the letter from
Lincoln mentioned by Ellery in the concluding paragraph. That paragraph was obviously written shortly after Lincoln's letter arrived. John Collins, who signed the letter,
left Philadelphia the week of May 10.
[2] See Rhode Island Delegates to Greene, March 1, 1780.
[3] See Samuel Huntington to the States, March 20, 1780.
[4] Ellery's letter to Jabez Bowen has not been found.
[5] *JCC*, 16:217–18.
[6] See Samuel Huntington to the States, March 20, 1780, note 2.
[7] See Samuel Huntington to George Washington, March 19, 1780.

Philip Schuyler to Nathanael Greene

Dear Sir   Philadelphia. March 22d 1780
    Yesterday I was favored with Yours of the 18th Instant.
    On the first day I took my seat In Congress I enquired what
Measures had been adopted towards a plan for the Military operations of the Campaign, finding none and being Informed that the
propriety of Sending for General Washington and you had Already
been Agitated and deemed unnecessary, I waved saying any thing
on the Subject, and Advised the General of It,[1] Stating at the Same
time the line of Conduct which I had persued with respect to the
Appointment they had made me as one of their Commissioners to
Arrange the Civil departments of the Army. That letter his Excellency had not received when Yours was written but as I am Informed
It went by a Safe Conveyance from hence, It is probably before this
come to hand and the General will advise you of Its Contents. Since
writing that letter the necessity of a Conference with the General
and You appeared to me to have Increased And It was moved but
without Effect.[2] This I forgot to advise his Excellency of In my last
and Intreat you to do It for me.[3]
    There never my Dear Sir Since the Commencement of the Con-
test was an hour In which as It appears to me our Affairs were more
Critical, and perhaps our Councils were never weaker, our Exertions less and torpor Greater. I have fruitlesly rang every Change on
this Subject but despair of Inducing measures which have a tendency to extricate us from the present distresses & which Surround
us on all quarters.
    Assailed on the one Side by duty And Affection to my Country, on
the other by those Sensations which cannot permit me to Join in
wounding the feelings of those I Esteem I am agitated by a Dillemma

the most disagreable possible, that You have been treated with Indelicacy and disrespect I am unhappily too well aware of, that my assent to the offensive measures has never been given You will believe, that I have proposed a line of Conduct on their part which promised to make Attonement I assure you of. I have depricated the Idea of appointing others to form a System for Your Conduct In the department which You Conduct, and have repeatedly recommended to give you power without limitation In the business and all that Confidence which It is for the public Interest you Should have, and without which no man Can Effectually Serve It. What will be done to morrow when the report of the Committee and Commissioners is made I cannot say, I shall be totally Opposed to the *Enacting* of any System whatever, even If I should approve the principles of the System, for I wish You to be perfectly free of every Shackle; If they enter Into my Views former Sins will In a great Measure be done away and I shall In that case not think It Inconsistent with my feelings to recommend, or with Yours to Continue Your Attention to the Important department. If you can Continue without a Sacrifice of reputation, you will Conceive It Your duty so to do both from public & private Considerations. In the last I allude Specially to our friend the General, what must be his Situation with a New Man and most probably an Incompetent one, In a department the head of which, must of necessity be Confidentially trusted on a variety of Occassions.

I am happy to find Your Sentiments on the Subject of the new adopted mode for Obtaining Supplies so perfectly coincident with mine, I have more than once openly and without reserve declared that It would draw In Its train the [ruin?] of the Army. Letters from Colo. Blaine already tend to verify the Assertion, and many members begin to think with me on the Occasion. Perhaps It will Introduce a reformation; that It may, and that Such measures may be adopted as will Secure us Your Services I most Earnestly wish and will most strenuously Contend for. Let me Intreat you to take no hasty decided measure; Your Country is in danger, Your Genral & Your friend In distress, and Your friends here feel for both of You. Adieu. I am Dr Sir with truth & Esteem Your most Obedt, Hu Servant,   P. Schuyler

RC (MiU–C: Greene Papers).
  [1] See Schuyler to George Washington, March 7, 1780.
  [2] Schuyler was undoubtedly referring to the effort made on March 13 to appoint "a Committee to go to Camp" that was reported by John Mathews in his March 14 letter to Horatio Gates. The journals do not mention these unsuccessful proceedings.
  [3] See Schuyler to Washington, March 13, 1780.

Philip Schuyler to George Washington

My Dear Sir   Philadelphia March 22d 1780
   Yesterday I had the happiness of Your Excellencys favor of the
18th Instant.[1]
   I find by enquiry at the Office that my first letter was not forwarded by the Conveyance I Intended It should but was sent by a
Subsequent one, It is therefore probably by this time reached you.[2]
   As Gen. Lincolns dispatch to you will probably contain what he
has Communicated to Congress I thought It needless to trouble You
with a Copy of the latter.
   I do not recollect If advised You that the propriety of a Conference with Your Excellency had a second time been Insisted on, and
that the Same opinion as on the first was prevalent.[3]
   Messrs. Sherman and Jones are to morrow to report the System
they In Conjunction with Gen. Mifflin & Mr. Pickering have formed
for Conducting the Civil departments of the Army.[4] I am afraid
(from what I have learnt) It will not only be Inadequate but If
adopted wound, or rather give additional Soreness to the wounds
already given the Q.M.G. As I dont Conceive In our present Circumstances that any System however Judiciously Compiled can apply I
shall do my endeavour So far to overturn the proposed one as that If
even good. It shall only go as recommendatory. This may probably
make some atonement for the Indelicate Inattention which Gen.
Greene has Experienced. I have Intreated him to take an hasty
decided Step and have taken the liberty to point at the Consequences
of a Change In that department at this Conjuncture.
   Communications on paper are more exposed from, than to the
Army. It may therefore be proper for Characters In particular Situations not to be particular unless where there is the greatest Certainty
of safety In the Conveyance, I mention this least You should attend
from your Politeness to more than I Expect, a bare Acknowledgement that a letter has been recevd will Suffice the *friend*.
   I am Dr Sir, most truly Your Excellency Obedient Huml Servant
&c,   Ph. Schuyler

RC (DLC: Washington Papers).
   [1] Washington's March 18 letter to Schuyler has not been found.
   [2] See Schuyler to Washington, March 7, 1780, to which Washington responded on
March 22. Washington, *Writings* (Fitzpatrick), 18:137–38.
   [3] See the preceding entry, note 2.
   [4] The report was submitted on March 27. *JCC*, 16:293–311.

Connecticut Delegates to
Jonathan Trumbull, Sr.

Sir,   Philadelphia March 23d. 1780
We are honored with your Excellency's dispatches of the 10h
Instant, by Brown, and shall pay due attention to the several matters
and instructions therein communicated.[1]

In particular, with regard to debts due in Connecticut for Beef
purchased under the late Commissary general Wadsworth, we shall
again urge in Congress as we repeatedly have done the necessity of
furnishing money to discharge them. But, Sir, there have been many
and urgent calls for money which it has been impossible for Congress with a nearly exhausted treasury to comply with; and the same
difficulties will remain so long as the several States are dilatory in
collecting their quotas of money, or when collected apply it to other
purposes than the payment of Continental warrants.

The reduction of the Battalions in the continental army, is a matter now before Congress, but is attended with difficulties. Tho'
œconomy pleads strongly in favour of the measure, yet it is doubtful
whether there will be sufficient time to adjust and settle an intire
new arangement of the Army before they may be called to take the
field; and as every new arrangement is also found to be a new source
of discontent, it is the opinion of some to postpone this reduction
until there shall be fewer other causes of discontent in the army than
at present. It has also been observed that should the Battalions not
be reduced at this juncture, yet considerable savings may be made,
by the several States forbareing to fill up vacanies in their respective
lines, which are already numerous should they not become more so.
Our endeavours however shall not be wanting to carry our instructions upon this head into effect.

It is with pleasure we observe from the acts transmitted to us, that
on the great and embarrased subject of the publick finances the
leading sentiments of the assembly of Connecticut are much the
same as on full discussion have been assented to in Congress. And
we entertain the more confidence from this consideration that the
measures which Congress after so much deliberation have recommended will meet that concurrence and support from all the legislatures of these United States as is essential to attaining the ends
therein proposed.

Congress have judged it expedient to continue Jesse Brown an
Express rider until their late establishment of posts shall have taken
its effect and their further orders shall be given.[2]

By a Delegate from South Carolina just arived[3] we learn that
Charlestown was safe on the 1t Instant—that the enemy who had
occupied the adjacent Islands had appeared for some days motionless—that the Garrison were in good spirits—that the North Caro-

lina Brigade of Continental troops had arived—& that the Virginia line were met on their march tho' at the unexpected distance of four hundred miles.[4]

We have the honor to be, with the highest respect, your Excellency's most obedt. humbl. Servants,   Roger Sherman

Oliv Ellsworth

RC (Ct: Trumbull Papers). Written by Ellsworth, and signed by Ellsworth and Sherman.

[1] Jonathan Trumbull's March 10 letter to Congress requesting a review of Connecticut's troop quota and the retention of Jesse Brown as a postrider, was read in Congress on March 22. See *JCC*, 16:275; and PCC, item 66, 2:170-71. His letter of the same date to the Connecticut delegates is in Trumbull, *Papers* (MHS Colls.), 3:17-19.

[2] Governor Trumbull's request to retain Brown as an express had been referred to the Post Office Committee. The committee's report recommending adoption of the governor's request is in the hand of Roger Sherman. See *JCC*, 16:275, 282-83; and PCC, item 20, 1:259-60.

[3] Francis Kinloch, who took his seat in Congress on March 25. See *JCC*, 16:285; and John Mathews to George Washington, March 24, 1780.

[4] Ellsworth apparently sent this same information to another Connecticut correspondent at about this time, since a similar paragraph was printed in the *Connecticut Courant and the Weekly Intelligencer* on April 4 with additional "Extracts of Letters from an Hon. Member of Congress to a Gentleman in this Town [Hartford], dated 22d and 24th March."

"No very late letters, from Europe—Charlestown was safe the 25th of February: the enemy were approaching it from island to island, and had got upon James's Island, which is the nearest, and within half a league of the town. The garrison were in good spirits; and the General trusted, if the aid he had called for from the country seasonably came in; to make effectual defence.

"It appears from deserters and prisoners, that the enemy suffered exceedingly going from New-York; several of their ships foundered, many were damaged, some taken, and some missing; and they have scarce a horse left for their artillery or any other purpose.

"By a Delegate just arrived from South Carolina we learn that Charlestown was safe the 1st instant, and the enemy remained in the same situation as on the 25th of February and motionless. The North-Carolina Brigade of Continental troops had arrived: The Virginia Line were also on the march, though at so great a distance that they cant have arrived yet."

The following "Extract of a letter from an Hon. Member of Congress from this State, dated Philadelphia, March 22d, 1780" also appeared in the same issue of the *Courant*, but it was probably the work of Samuel Huntington or Roger Sherman.

"The measures taken by the Assembly of our State, I think, are wise and judicious, and founded on the same principles as the plan adopted by Congress, which was a considerable time under consideration before it was compleated; and if it is adopted by the several States, I make no doubt, but that it will relieve us from all the evils of a depreciating currency in future . . . . It gives me great pleasure to see the coincidence of councils in Congress, and the State I have the honor to represent."

Oliver Ellsworth to Jonathan Trumbull, Sr.

Sir,   Philadelphia, March 23, 1780

Permit me as a private citizen to express my wishes that the late resolutions of Congress on the subject of finance, may meet your

Excellency's approbation and support. Your Excellency must have long seen with alarming apprehensions the crisis to which a continued depreciation of the paper currency would one day reduce our affairs. It is now, Sir, just at hand. Without more stability in the medium & far more ample supplies in the treasury than for months past, it will be impossible for our military preperations to proceed, & the Army must disband. The present moment is indeed critical, & if let slip the confusion & distress will be infinite. This, Sir, is percisely the point of time for the several Legislatures to act decidedly & in a manner that the world will forever call wise. It is now in their power by a single operation to give a sure establishment for publick credit, to realize the publick debt at its just value, &, without adding to the burdens of the people, to supply the treasury. To furnish one common ground to unite their exertions upon for the accomplishment of these great purposes, your Excellency will easily percieve to be the spirit & design of the resolutions above referred to. They speak a language too plain to need any comment. I will only add concerning them that they have been the product of much labor & discussion; and tho' some States may have reason for thinking they are not the best possible, yet they are the best Congress could agree upon; and should they be rejected I confess I do not well see on what ground the common exertions of the several States are to be united and continued hereafter.

Your Excellency will forgive me the very great freedom of this Letter, and permit me the honor of subscribing myself, with the highest Respect, your Excellencys most obedt. humbl Servt,

Olivr. Ellsworth

RC (Ct: Trumbull Papers).

Oliver Ellsworth to Jeremiah Wadsworth

Dr. sir   Philada. March 23. 1780

I was last week favord with your Letter of the 20h of Feby— And shall with great pleasure nominate Mr. Trumbul to the office you mention when ever there shall be a door open for it.[1] At present there is some hesitancy about making the appointment, some imagining that more than a secretary is there wanting.

I am not surprised at the ill success of Col. Blain,[2] nor to find that the new proposed terms of service in his department are thot. too scantily—his & others representation will doubtless procure a revision of the establishment with some amendments.

As to the Bills on Spain & Holland, an order passed some time since Directing the board of Treasury to suspend the sale of them 'till further orders—it being found that the bills would fetch more than they were selling at. Perhaps further orders may be given at least respecting the bills already forwarded to Connecticut—of which you will have notice as soon as may be.

A Petition from sundry Creditors of your late Department, with the sanction of our assembly is come forward & will be immediately laid before Congress & I hope such measures will be taken thereon as to right & justice appertain.

Some late resolutions have passed Congress respecting the currency, which I have enclosed to Mr. Lyman³—as they are lengthy & I have not time to copy them have desired him to furnish you with the perusal of them. Something farther is under consideration respecting the Loans— the result of which I will send you as soon as it shall be ready for publication.

I am, Dear Sir, with much respect & Esteem, your obed. huml Sevt.   Oliver Ellsworth⁴

[P.S.] Exchange at abt. 60.

RC (DSoC).
¹ In the absence of Wadsworth's letter, we can only conjecture that Wadsworth had recommended Jonathan Trumbull, Jr., as secretary to the American minister in Paris. Trumbull was later nominated as a special envoy to France on December 9, 1780, but John Laurens was unanimously elected to the post. JCC, 18:1138, 1141.
² Col. Ephraim Blaine had replaced Wadsworth as commissary general of purchases in December 1779.
³ Ellsworth's letter to Samuel Lyman has not been found. The resolutions enclosed were doubtless the landmark fiscal resolves of March 18.
⁴ Ellsworth also wrote a brief note this day to his wife, Abigail, discussing the "mighty smart" look of his new blue velvet breeches. Ellsworth Papers, CtHi.

Samuel Huntington to
Certain States and Continental Officers

Sir,   Philadelphia March 23. 1780

Your Excellency will receive herewith enclosed an Act of Congress of the 21st Instant,

Recommending to the governments of the several States to suspend making new Appointments of Officers in the Regiments of their respective Lines except where the Commander in Chief, or Commanding Officer in the southern Department shall deem such Appointment indispensibly necessary.

The Design of this Act is to aid the Intentions of Congress in retrenching the supernumerary Officers as soon as Circumstances will admit without doing Injury or Injustice to the Officers.¹

By the Act of Congress of this Day which is also enclosed, your Excellency will observe Jesse Brown is to be continued an Express rider, and I presume Notice will be given whenever it is thought proper he should be discharged from that Service.²

I have the honour to be &c,   S.H.

LB (DNA: PCC, item 14). Addressed: "Governor Trumbull. N.B. The same (excepting the last paragraph) to New York, Rhode Island, Massachusets Bay, New Hampshire, General Washington & Genl Lincoln." Huntington also sent the first two paragraphs of this letter to New Jersey governor William Livingston. Livingston Papers, NN.
[1] JCC, 16:272–73.
[2] See Connecticut Delegates to Jonathan Trumbull, this date, note 2.

Charles Thomson to Jonathan Trumbull, Sr.

Sir   Philada. March 23 1780

I am honoured with your letter of the 10th instant accompanied with sundry state papers for which I thank you and shall have them deposited in the office.[1] My view is to have as compleat a collection of the public papers of every state as I can deposited here, Where the delegates from the several states may have access to them And as the governments are new and doubtless many experiments must be made in legislation before they can reach perfection, I would wish to have the first essays as well as those perfected by experience. The former may to a legislator in another state be almost as useful as the latter. They may serve as landmarks & teach him the folly of repeating or attempting a similar law in his own state, & thus by the experience of one a benefit may redound to all.

I now enclose you the Journal of Congress for Feby last and am, with due respect, Your excellency's most obedient humble Servt,

Cha Thomson

RC (Ct: Trumbull Papers).
[1] For Trumbull's March 10 letter to Thomson, enclosing "a Copy of the Original Confederation of the first Inhabitants of this State, dated in 1638 . . ., the Charter of King Charles the second . . . Dated in 1662 . . ., and the Act approving the Declaration of the Independance of these United States, passd in October 1776," see PCC, item 66, 2:127–55. For the secretary's request for these and other state papers, see Thomson to the States, November 20, 1779.

Samuel Holten to Joseph Palmer

Dear Sir,   Philadelphia March 24th 1780.[1]

I have been favored with yours of the 17th ulto. with the enclosures one of which I have forwarded (without charge) to Mr. Hudson & the other I shall inclose, as Mr. Cranch has left this City.

The deranged state of our Finances & want of money in the public Treasury has greatly embarrassed our affairs, & for some time past engaged (nearly) all the Attention of congress, but a few days since they went into a number of resolutions respecting the same, and as they may not come to hand before this, I will endeavor to give you some of the outlines (vizt.)[2]

I am wholely unacquainted, "of the price of Epsom salts," but will make some inquiry as I have oppertunity (if it should not slip my memory) & let you know.

By the last account from Genl Lincoln, I think it is likely that the enemy have attacked Charlestown before this time but I hope sir Harry will have reason to repent of this undertaking.

I am, my dear Sir, with great respect, your most obedient

FC (DLC: Holten Papers). In the hand of Samuel Holten.

[1] Congress did not convene this day. As Holten explained in his diary entry for March 23: "Congress have adjourned to Saturday, tomorrow is good Friday." MDaAr.

[2] Holten left several lines blank at this point in the FC.

Samuel Holten to James Sullivan

Dear Sir,[1]   Philada. March 24th 1780.

I have been favored with yours of the 23d ulto. It was delivered me in Congress at the very moment we were debating about taking up the business to which it refers,[2] and it strengthened me in my opinion upon finding it so exactly agreed with yours and I had not only given it as my Judgment, but that I believed it to be the mind of my constituents; The resolutions of Congress that passed in Sepr. last respecting this affair[3] wou'd have been far from being unanimous (in my opinion) if it had not been expected that these people wou'd have submitted the whole matter to Congress, but they have absolutely refused so far as respects their being an independant state. Congress have ownly determined as yet that the affair be not taken up 'till nine states are present inclusive of the states supposed to be intended and you may be assured that when it shall again come before Congress, it will engage all my attention, & I believe I may venture to say the same of Congress.

The deranged state of our Finances & want of money in the public Treasury has greatly embarrassed our affairs, & for some time past engaged (nearly) all the attention of Congress but a few days since they came into a number of resolutions respecting the same, which I expect will be sent forward by the bearer of this, & to which I beg leave to refer you. It gives me some concern about our new proposed constitution when I consider how very difficult it must be to git two thirds of the people to like any one form. I wou'd make some remarks upon the report of the come. did I not consider it as too late, supposing it has passed in convention with many alterations. By the last accounts from Genl. Lincoln, I think it is likely that the enemy have attacked Charlestown before this time, but I hope sir Harry will have reason to repent of this undertaking.

I am, my dear Sir, with great respect, your most obedient.

FC (DLC: Holten Papers). In the hand of Samuel Holten.
[1] James Sullivan has been identified in these *Letters,* 4:75n.1.
[2] The status of the New Hampshire Grants was clearly "the business to which it refers."
[3] That is, the resolves of September 24, 1779. See John Jay to Thomas Chittenden and to George Clinton, September 25, 1779.

John Mathews to George Washington

Sir,   Philadelphia March 24th. 1780
    Mr. Kinloch, One of the Delegates of South Carolina arrived here yesterday in Twenty three days, from that place. He says the British troops were in the same position as on the 25 of February (as your Excy. has already been informed) Genl. Hogan had arrived with the No. Carolina Brigade. Genl. Woodford on the 11 Inst. was 380 miles distant from Chs. Town. Genl. Scott, had at last proceeded for that place alone. The troops that were under his Command remained at Petersburg without the least appearance of moving. The lines of Chs. Town were compleated & the harbour well secured by a respectable Naval armament, & wanted nothing to render it almost impregnable, but a larger body of men, than they then had, or had any prospect of soon obtaining, for its defence. It was the general opinion when he came away, that the enemy had met with material losses at Sea, either in men, or some of their capital Store ships, which caused their inactivity, as they had been possessed of the principal part of the ground they then occupied for twenty one days. Genl. Lincoln commanded in Chs. Town & Genl. Moultrie at a post 24 miles from the town (Bacon's bridge, an important pass on Ashley river) with a body of between 400 & 500 horse, & a few Infantry.
    The inactivity of the enemy in So. Carolina, the arrival of the Roebuck, with the transports from thence, at New York, seems to countenance the opinion, of the enemy's being unprepared for an attack, & which may probably not take place before the return of those Ships from N. York. In this event it will give time for the Virginia troops to get up, which will be a most fortunate circumstance. I thought it advisable to give Your Excy. this information as it may lead to your obtaining some usefull intelligence from a certain quarter.
    I have the Honour to be, with great Respect, Yr Excys most Obedt. servt.   Jno. Mathews

RC (DLC: Washington Papers).

Committee of Commerce Certification

Philadelphia 25 March 1780.
Commercial Committee, 27 March 1779
Having this day received a set of Bills of Exchange dated in Philadelphia the 12th Instant Signed by John Chevalier, Mary Chevalier, Adrian Renaudet all Executors to the Estate of Peter Chevalier deceased; Together with Joseph Bullock, directed to Messrs. Duff & Welch Merchts. in Cadiz drawn for the sum of Nineteen hundred & Sixty pounds Sterling Money, payable to the Order of us the undersigners Members of the Commercial Committee of the Honble. Congress

We do hereby promise to pay to the said John Chevalier, Mary Chevalier, Adrian Renaudt & Joseph Bullock the sum of Forty seven Thousand & forty Continental Dollars when it shall be made appear to the Commercial Committee of the Continental Congress that the above mentiond Bills are duely honoured & paid. Witness out hands in Philada. the day and year abovementioned.

Signed   Fr. Lewis

John Fell

J. Searle

We the Subscribers do Certify that the above is a true Copy of an Entry in the Books of the Commercial Committee of Congress made by direction of the said Committee on the twenty seventh day of March 1779. And we do further Certify That some Short time after the above date Mr. Adrian Renaudet in behalf of the Estate of Peter Chevalier deceased applied to the Committee of Commerce requesting them to pay the within mentiond sum of Forty Seven Thousand & Forty dollars, but the Committee did not comply with the said request.[1]

Fra. Lewis, late Member of
the Commercial Committee
James Searle

MS (DNA: PCC, item 31). In the hand of James Searle, and signed by Searle and Francis Lewis.

[1] John Chevalier and Adrian Renaudet had petitioned Congress on January 27, 1780, for payment of the £1,960 sterling, or its equivalent, furnished to the Committee of Commerce by Peter Chevalier in March 1779. At that time it had been agreed that $47,040 in Continental currency would discharge the committee's obligation, which was to be defrayed as soon as confirmation had been received that the bills of exchange had been drawn in Cadiz, but payment of the debt in the greatly depreciated Continental dollar of 1780 would obviously involve a great loss to Chevalier's heirs. When offered a treasury order for $47,040 in the Continental currency of January 1780, Chevalier's executors protested, and the matter was referred to the Committee of Commerce on January 29. When the committee was unable to reach a decision on the relief to be afforded the petitioners, they submitted a second petition

on February 28, which was referred to the Board of Treasury. An endorsement on
this petition indicates that on March 22 the board decided to postpone their decision
"until further Proofs appear," suggesting that the present certificate was prepared by
Searle for the board's use. Nevertheless, no action was taken at this time, and in May
Searle prepared a second document for the board certifying the facts in the case, for
which see Committee of Commerce Certification, May 12, 1780. The board reported
favorably on the petitioners' claim on May 22, and Congress thereupon ordered that
a warrant be issued "for the sum of eight thousand seven hundred and eleven dollars,
specie, in bills of exchange drawn on the honorable John Jay" to satisfy the claim.
JCC, 16:110, 220, 17:444–45; and PCC, item 41, 2:90–91, 102–3.

Samuel Holten's Diary

[March 25, 1780]
25. Saturday. The Hone. Mr. Forbes a member from the state of
Maryland deceased.[1] I dined with the minister of France.

MS (MDaAr).
[1] For James Forbes' declining health, see Forbes to Thomas Sim Lee, February 29,
1780. The delegates resolved this day to attend his funeral "in a body . . . to-morrow
evening," and to "continue in mourning for the space of one month." *JCC*, 16:285.

Samuel Huntington to George Wattson

Sir,   Philadelphia March 25. 1780
Your Letter of the 5th of February last I have received respecting
the Capture of the Greyhound, I suppose by a number of American
Sailors who carried her into Cape St Nicola Mole.
This Matter has been communicated to me before your Letter
came to hand by the Minister of France.
A Copy of that Communication with Copies of the Proceedings of
Congress consequent thereon you have enclosed which will be suffi-
cient to enable those Seamen to receive the whole Avails of the Prize
to which they are justly entitled by the Resolutions of Congress.[1]
I am Sir &c &c &c,   S.H.

LB (DNA: PCC, item 14).
[1] See *JCC*, 15:1356, 1372, 16:283. Wattson's letter to President Huntington, dated
"Cape Francois Hispaniola, Feb 5th 1779 [i.e., 1780]," is in PCC, item 78, 24:195–97.
In it Wattson stated some of the facts "respecting the Capture of the Greyhound,"
and represented that he was writing "In Behalf of Elisha Carpenter, Robert Wiley,
Comfort Buckley, John Wood, & Benjamin Wiley." For the communication from the
minister of France concerning this case, see Huntington to La Luzerne, December 8
and 11; and Massachusetts Delegates to the Massachusetts Council, December 15,
1779.

Thomas McKean to Richard Henry Lee

Dear Sir,   Philadelphia, March 25th. 1780.
Your esteemed favor of the 15th last month, with the extracts from your much injured brother's letter to the President of Congress, and the copy of Doctor Berkenhout's letter to yourself, inclosed, came safe to hand.[1] Next to the approbation of my own conscience, it has always been my wish to obtain that of the wise & good, and I confess I am happy in having yours. I flatter myself the time will shortly come, when the honest laborers in the cause of freedom & their country will at least meet with the reward of being known, and when also the double-dealing artful pretenders will be discovered.

There has been a virtuous band in Congress from the beginning of the present contest, but they were never so few, or so much opposed as just after you and your good brother left us. In the Winter & Spring of 1779 there was a cabal, whose views I could not fathom; there were some possessed of restless spirits, and who endeavored to set member against member, and the Congress against the States, particularly Pennsylvania and those of New-England, and the States agt. Congress. Every artifice was used to instill prejudices against all our foreign Ministers and Commissioners, particularly your *brothers*; and I really believe, if I had not in April last gone off the Bench into Congress, in the face of a vote of the Assembly of Pennsylvania, that they would have been recalled without exception. My fears were, that at that critical period, when it had been propagated in Europe; and some uneasiness discovered on that score by the court of France that we were listening to overtures from Great Britain, a change of men might have implied a change of measures, and given some countenance to the reports; and for this reason I thought it wrong to recal any Gentleman in such a conjuncture. The vote was taken with respect to Doctor Franklin, and being determined in the negative, it was postponed as to the rest until I was absent on the circuit.[2] Places were sought after by some, and vacancies were necessary for the purpose of obtaining them, but I could not think this was the only thing in contemplation; tho' I may have been mistaken, as harmony seemed to be restored in some measure upon the appointments of Messrs. Jay and Carmichael. The death of Mr. Drayton, and the considerable change about that time of the members, several of them not having been re-elected, left us pretty quiet ever since, tho' prejudices still too much prevail.

When I reflect on the assiduity, the zeal, the fidelity, the abilities and patriotism of Doctor A. Lee, I cannot help deploring his fate, and reprobating the ingratitude of Congress; but, Sir, it is with pleasure I can assure you that he has many unshaken friends still remaining in that Body, who have never seen him, and who esteem him only for his public virtues. I profess myself one of these, and he has at least *my* warmest thanks for his substantial services rendered to my country.

I cannot think it any reflection on a Gentleman's heart, that he has been mistaken in entertaining too good an opinion of another, nor am I at all surprized that even you should have been led into an error with respect to Doctor Berkenhout after perusing his letter and knowing his insinuating address: but I shall say no more on this head, as I am really appologizing for myself.

The deranged state of our finances has given us infinite trouble and concern; A new plan has been adopted, which is published in the News-Papers, to which I shall refer you—if it can be carried into execution it will be a great relief to us; and I see nothing else left but for every Whig to exert himself in its support.

There is no great prospect of peace, tho' the late intelligence from Europe is otherwise favorable. I suspect, that Mr. Temple (who came over in 1778 with Doctor Berkenhout) will shortly venture here again with propositions (perhaps secret) to acknowledge the Independence of the States, except South Carolina & Georgia, and that part of Massachusetts, formerly called the Province of Main, on condition of our neutrality between Britain & Spain—he is to have power to draw on two merchants in London of his own nomination ad libitum.[3] This is not mere conjecture or report; but it may not be attempted to be carried into execution, as I think, upon the least reflection he must despair of success. Can they suppose that these States will be so perfidious to one another, or to the auxiliary of the Ally—that they are so corrupt—so base? Can they be taught to believe, that a virtuous people can grow so extremely wicked by a war of five years continuance? Nemo repente fuit turpissimus.[4]

I am, my dear Sir, with the most perfect esteem, Your most obedient humble servant.   Tho. Mc:Kean

RC (PPAmP: Lee Papers).

[1] Lee's February 15 letter to McKean is not in the Lee Family Papers, ViU microfilm, but the enclosed "extracts" were undoubtedly Arthur Lee's *Extracts From a Letter Written to the President of Congress* [February 10, 1779], 500 copies of which Richard Henry had had printed in Williamsburg and had been distributing. See Evans, *Am. Bibliography*, no. 16,319; and Richard Henry's letters of January 18 to Samuel Adams, of January 22 to Jonathan Trumbull and to Roger Sherman, and of April 24, 1780, to Arthur Lee, in Lee, *Letters* (Ballagh), 2:168, 172–73, 176.

[2] For McKean's role in the April 22, 1779, vote against the recall of Benjamin Franklin, see these *Letters*, 12: 368–69. See also McKean to John Adams, November 8, 1779.

[3] For rumors concerning John Temple's new peace mission, see James Lovell to Samuel Adams, March 17, 1780, note 3.

[4] That is, "Corruption comes by degrees." Juvenal *Satires* 2.83.

James Madison to Thomas Jefferson

Dear Sir   Philadelphia March 27th. 1780
   Nothing under the title of news has occurred since I wrote last
week by express[1] except that the Enemy on the 1st. of March remained
in the neighbourhood of Charlestown in the same posture as when
the preceding account came away. From the best intelligence from
that quarter there seems to be great encouragement to hope that
Clintons operations will be again frustrated. Our great apprehensions at present flow from a very different quarter. Among the
various conjunctures of alarm and distress which have arisen in the
course of the revolution, it is with pain I affirm to you Sir, no one
can be singled out more truly critical than the present. Our army
threatened with an immediate alternative of disbanding or living on
free quarter, the public treasury empty, public credit exhausted, nay
the private credit of purchasing Agents employed I am told as far as
it will bear, Congress complaining of the extortion of the people, the
people of the improvidence of Congress, and the army of both. Our
affairs requiring the most mature & systematic measures, and the
urgency of occasions admitting only of temporary expedients and
those expedients generating new difficulties. Congress from a defect
of adequate Statesmen more likely to fall into wrong measures and
of less weight to enforce right ones, recommending plans to the
several states for execution and the states separately rejudging the
expediency of such plans, whereby the same distrust of concurrent
exertions that has damped the ardor of patriotic individuals must
produce the same effect among the States themselves. An old System of finance discarded as incompetent to our necessities, an untried
& precarious one substituted and a total stagnation in prospect
between the end of the former & the operation of the latter. These
are the outlines of the true picture of our public situation. I leave it
to your own imagination to fill them up. Believe me Sir as things
now stand if the States do not vigorously proceed in collecting the
old money and establishing [funds?] for the credit of the new, that
we are undone; and let them be ever so expeditious in doing this still
the intermediate distress to our army and hindrance to public affairs
are a subject of melancholy reflection. Genl Washington writes that a
failure of bread has already commenced in the army; and that for
any thing he sees it must unavoidably increase.[2] Meat they have only
for a short season and as the whole dependance is on provisions now
to be procured; without a shilling for the purpose, and without
credit for a shilling, I look forward with the most pungent apprehensions. It will be attempted I believe to purchase a few supplies
with loan office Certificates, but whether they will be received is
perhaps far from being certain, and if received will certainly be a
most expensive & ruinous expedient. It is not without some reluc-

tance I trust this information to a conveyance by post, but I know of no better at present, and I conceive it to be absolutely necessary to be known to those who are most able and zealous to contribute to the public relief.

March 28. Authentic information is now recd. that the Enemy in their passage to Georgia lost all their Horse,[3] the Defiance of 64 guns which foundered at sea, three transports with troops, although it is pretended these troops and the men of the Defiance were saved, and 1 transport with Hessians of which nothing has been heard. By a letter from Mr. Adams dated Corunna 16 Decr. there seems little probability that Britain is yet in a humour for peace.[4] The Russian Ambassador at that Court has been lately changed, and the new one on his way to London made some stop at Paris whence a rumor has spread in Europe that Russia was about to employ her mediation for peace. Should there be any reality in it, Mr. Adams says it is the opinion of the most intelligent he had conversed with that the independance of the United [States] would be insisted on as a preliminary: to which G.B. would accede with much greater repugnance than the cession of Gibraltar which Spain was determined to make a sine qua non.

With respect and regard I am, Dr Sir, yrs. sincerely
                                                    James Madison Jr

RC (DLC: Madison Papers). Madison, *Papers* (Hutchinson), 2:5–7.
    [1] Not found.
    [2] Washington's letter of March 17, expressing his "apprehensions on the score of our Provision supplies," was read in Congress March 21, 1780. See *JCC*, 16:274; and Washington, *Writings* (Fitzpatrick), 18:121–22.
    [3] This "authentic information" was transmitted to Congress in Washington's letter of March 23, which was read this day. See *JCC*, 16:288–89; and Washington, *Writings* (Fitzpatrick), 18:145–46.
    [4] John Adams' letters of December 11 and 16, 1779, reporting his safe arrival in Spain aboard the badly leaking *La Sensible* and the early information he had gathered on European affairs, were read in Congress on March 27, for which see *JCC*, 16:288–89; PCC, item 84, 1:227–34; and Wharton, *Diplomatic Correspondence*, 3:422–23, 427–28.

Oliver Ellsworth to Jonathan Trumbull, Sr.

Sir,   Philadelphia, March 28. 1780.
    It has been much expected in Europe that Russia would offer herself as a mediator betwen the belligerent powers there. Good authority now assures us, that if she does one of the ultimata that she will insist on is that America remain independant and that she also wishes Gibralter to be ceeded to Spain. She has lately changed her minister at the court of London. The new one on his way was three weeks at Paris. Letters are received from Mr. Adams in Spain the 11th & 16th of Decr. He acknowledges politeness and civilities greater

than has been usually shewn to strangers in that Kingdom, and found also that orders had been issued from the King for his subjects to treat all Americans as their dear friends. Mr. Adams was proceeding on his way to France by land. His travels it is to be hoped will not only be attended with information to himself but with utility also to the publick.

Advice is had from General Clintons Headquarters as late as the 4th Instant that his principal force was then on James's Island and was preparing to possess Stono Ferry—that the Defiance a 64 gun Ship foundered at Sea on their passage from New York as did also three transports, the men it is given out were saved—that one Transport with Hessian Troops there had been no account of—that all their Cavalry were lost and other damages sustained.

Less pleasing but not less necessary to be known is the information I will further take the liberty [to] add. It is that the continental treasury is now empty. This has been nearly the case for some weeks. The consequence is that the continental agents have not only discontinued their purchases, but cannot move forward the little supplies they have on hand; and the army are again in want. Nor does it yet appear when either the army or Treasury will be supplied by the several States. Surely, Sir, they do not expect the war to be carried on without means, nor can they mean to let it drop here. Does it not then behove them to adopt effectual measures for drawing forth their resources, and that without a moments delay? Can it, Sir, be the design of Heaven, that has roused us to exertions thus far, and armed mighty nations for our support and brought us within sight of the promised rest to leave us after all to destruction, and to lament also the best blood of our land as spilt in vain? I trust not.

Mr. Sherman will leave Congress in a few days and as he will be present with the general assembly when they meet he will be able more fully than a letter can do to give the necessary information of the State of our publick affairs. I hope his place in Congress will be soon supplied & mine also.

For further news of the day I beg leave to refer your Excellency to the enclosed papers. And have the honor to be, with great respect, your Excellency's, most obedt. hume. Servt.   Oliver Ellsworth[1]

RC (CtHi: Trumbull Papers).
[1] Ellsworth also wrote a brief letter this day to his wife, Abigail, expressing regret that he would not be able to return home soon. Ellsworth Papers, CtHi.

Samuel Holten to Samuel Adams

Dear Sir.   Philada. March 28th. 1780
    I enclose a draft of a Bill publishd. by order of the General Assembly of Pennsylvania.[1]

The delegates from Mastts. agreeable to their instructions made a full representation to Congress respecting the Penobscot affair & proposed Several resolutions, which after some consideration were committed, & it is my opinion the reasonable expences of that expedition will be paid by Congress.

The Hone. Mr. Forbes decd. on Saturday last.

I am, my dear Sir, with sincere respect, your most obedient

FC (DLC: Holten Papers). In the hand of Samuel Holten.
[1] Holten undoubtedly enclosed a copy of the "Act for funding and redeeming the Bills of Credit of the United States of America, . . . founded on the Act of Congress of the 18th instant," which the Pennsylvania Assembly had ordered printed before its second reading, and which appeared in the March 25 issue of the *Pennsylvania Packet* and also circulated as a handbill.

Samuel Holten to William Gordon

My dear Sir.   Philadelphia March 28th. 1780.

When I did myself the pleasure of addressing you last,[1] I had tho'ts of leaving Congress soon after, & I think mentioned that as my last epistle, but the season wou'd not admit of it & so great are my present engagements that it is still uncertain when I shall have the opportunity of paying you my personal respects & I consider myself as under obligation for past favors 'tho' I am not behind in numbers.

When we engaged in this War with Britain, what wou'd be our greatest difficulty we shou'd have to encounter was unknown to the best politicians, but from experience we find that the depreciation of our currency is attended with very distressing consequences, by deranging our Finances & greatly embarrassing the public affairs, & for some time past engaged (nearly) all the attention of Congress, but about a week since they came into a number of resolutions respecting the same, which I suppose will come to hand before this, and it gives me some satisfaction to hear that they are generally approved of by the good people here, and I conclude my virtuous countrymen in New England will not be wanting in their exertions to carry the same into effect.

By the last accounts from Genl. Lincoln, I think it is likely that the enemy have attacked Charlestown before this time, but I hope Sir Harry will have cause to repent of this undertaking. I expect we must have another Campaign & much greater exertions (I apprehend) are necessary than the people in general are Sensible of.

I am, Sir, with Sincere respect your most obedient.

FC (PPIn). In the hand of Samuel Holten.
[1] See Holten to Gordon, December 7, 1779.

Samuel Holten to Azor Orne

Dear Sir.[1]   Philadelphia March 28th. 1780

Your great attachment & constant exertions in the great cause of our country can't but indear you to all her true friends, that, has the pleasure of your acquaintance, and in this light I ask leave to address you in addition to personal respect.

It wou'd give me pleasure to converse (freely) with you upon our national affairs (particularly) in Europe, but I think there wou'd be some impropriety in committing such important matters to writing if I was under no restraint; However of this you may be assured that things are agoing on there as well as can be expected, considering all circumstances; yet I expect we must have an other campaign & much greater exertions (I apprehend) are necessary than the people in general are sensible of.

When we engaged in this War with Britain, what wou'd be our greatest difficulty we shou'd have to encounter was unknown to the best politicians, but from experience we find that the depreciation of our currency is attended with very distressing consequences, by deranging our Finances & greatly embarrassing the public affairs, and for sometime past engaged (nearly) all the attention of Congress, but about a week since they came into a number of resolutions respecting the same, which I suppose will come to hand before this, and it gives me some satisfaction to hear, that, they are generally approved of here; and I conclude my virtuous countrymen in New-England will not be wanting in their exertions to carry the same into effect, for much under God depends thereon.

By the last accounts from Genl Lincoln, I think it is likely the enemy have made an attack upon Charleston (So. Carolina) before this time, but I hope sir Harry will have cause to repent of this undertaking.

The affair respecting the charges of the Penobscot expedition is now under consideration of a come. of Congress.

It lays upon my mind that you are not at this time a member of the honl. Court (which I'm sorry for) and that prevents my mentioning some other important matters which respects the business of the assembly.

I am, my dear sir, with great respect, your most obedient

FC (DLC: Holten Papers). In the hand of Samuel Holten.

[1] Azor Orne (1731–96), Marblehead, Mass., merchant and militia colonel, had been a longtime member of the Massachusetts legislature. See George A. Billias, *Elbridge Gerry, Founding Father and Republican Statesman* (New York: McGraw-Hill Book Co., 1976), pp. 29, 38, 41, 44, 47–49, 52.

James Lovell to Samuel Adams

Dear Sir   March 28th. 1780

By your Favor of the 5th received Yesterday I find a very unpleasing Circumstance to excuse your long Silence: I had attributed it altogether to public Occupations.[1] I hope that your Health is fully restored by this Time. We have had a very trying Winter for the Constitution of any one advanced to the Afternoon of Life even if his Body was not like yours exposed to the natural Effects of a daily intense Application of your Mind to very important and intricate State Subjects.

We are really in Pain here continually about Supplies of every Kind. No Man can tell what will be the Event of the Measures recommended to the States. It lays with the Farmer to say whether he will at any Rate furnish the Army. He may see now that his Labors are not mortgaged for Generations to make Silver & Gold of That which by general Consent has been reduced to meer Rags a second Time. The whole daily Allowance which you mention will not here purchase two Pounds of Mutton,[2] the Price of that Article being from 13 to 15 Dollars Per lb. Indeed, Sir, I am totally unable to go on at this Rate. For if I could do without any Cloathing myself will my whole Income give Food alone to my Dependents? Yet they look for Raiment also from my Labors.

You will have Accounts from your military Officers in regard to the Wants of the Army. Transportation is the grand Difficulty at this Period. Our public Horses have been starved for Want of Forage tho' there has been given to that Department almost Paper enough to litter the whole Number.

By Mr. Partridge I shall send my Accounts, his Expenditures being a just Test of mine lately; and as to former Time the moderate Footing will be sufficent.

I hope to have another and better Opportunity of writing this Week by Mr. Adams Express from Doctr. Foster.

The Southern Post is not in, but Col. Lee was lately well & sent his regards to you.

Yr. affectionate humble Servant,   James Lovell

[*P.S.*] The Paragraph in the Paper respectg. Clinton's mishaps is from good Authority though Genl. W——n desired it might not be authenticated here in print.[3]

RC (NN: Adams Papers).

[1] In his March 5 letter to Lovell, Adams had explained that he had been spending his time "partly in my sick Chamber and partly in our Convention for forming a Constitution." Adams, *Writings* (Cushing), 4:180–81.

[2] In the same letter, Adams informed Lovell that he had been allowed "Twenty five Dollars per Day and Expenses" for his service as a delegate in 1779, so "that you may judge whether the Allowance for Time & Service is raisd in Proportion to other things." Ibid.

[3] In his March 23 letter to Congress reporting heavy damage suffered by the recent British expedition en route to South Carolina from New York, Washington warned that "this intelligence comes to me, through a channel which makes me wish there may not be an Official publication, though it may be otherwise mentioned without reserve." Washington, *Writings* (Fitzpatrick), 18:145. Lovell's enclosure was undoubtedly the March 28 issue of the *Pennsylvania Packet*, which contained the "paragraph" alluded to here.

Roger Sherman to Jonathan Trumbull, Sr.

Sir   Philadelphia Mar. 28th. 1780

We had two Letters Yesterday from Mr. John Adams giving an account of his, and Mr. Dana's Arrival in Spain, that they were very kindly and politely received.

That he makes no doubt but that Mr. Jay will be immediately received in his public Character on his Arrival at the Court of Madrid. He thinks there is no prospect of a Peace till after the Next Summers Campaign.

The Assembly of this State is adjourned 'till the tenth of May after Ordering an Emission of Bills to the amount of £100,000 & publishing a Bill for carrying into execution the resolutions of Congress of the 18th instant respecting the currency, their session had been long & Some of the members were gone home. I believe their Adjournment will not occasion much delay as the new Bills they have ordered will furnish their purchasers with money to procure the Supplies for the Army & may be recknoned as part of the quota they were to emit Agreable to resolution of Congress.

The report for Assertaining the value of the loan office certificates is to be taken into consideration to day,[1] a report was made Yesterday by Commissioners for a new arrangement of the Quarter Masters department, and for forwarding the Supplies procured by the Several States, to the Army.[2] We have no news from the Southward but what is included in the Paper enclosed. I expect to return home next week.

I am with great respect, your Excellency's Obedient, humble Servant.   Roger Sherman

RC (MHi: Miscellaneous Bound Collection).
[1] For a discussion of this report, see Connecticut Delegates to Trumbull, March 20, 1780, note 3.
[2] See *JCC*, 16:293–311.

William Ellery to George Washington

Sir,   Philadelphia March 29th 1780

I received a letter from Gove. Greene by the last post informing me, that the General Assembly of the State of Rhode-Island &c,

which I have the honor to represent in Congress, had passed a
resolve at their Session held on the fourth Monday of last month, for
raising eight hundred and ten men including those already raised in
Col Greene's and Col. Angel's regiments, that he had at the request
of the Genl. Assembly written to your excellency, desiring that one
of those regiments might be stationed in the State, the ensueing
campaign, and expressing his wishes that, if I should find it necessary,
I would also address you on this occasion.[1]

I know not what arguments he hath urged on this subject; if I did
I am sensible that I could not add a new one, nor enforce what he
hath said; but as I esteem his desires as commands, your excellency
will give me leave to suggest such reasons as voluntarily offer themselves to my mind. These are—the exhausted and exposed state of
our republic, the vigorous exertions it is making to complete its
continental battalions which will draw off a large number of its men,
and the great injury and expense which must accrue from keeping
up a body of militia for its protection and defence. These considerations are obvious and appear to me to be important. I hope your
Excellency will view them in the same light, and be induced to comply with the request of the legislature; in expectation whereof and
with the highest sentiments of respect, I am, Yr Excellency's most
obedt. Servt.   William Ellery

P.S. Your Excellency hath doubtless heard of Mr. Adams's arrival
in Spain. He writes from thence, that the Court of Madrid were
disposed to receive a minister from these States to acknowledge our
independency and enter into treaties with us.   W.E.

RC (PHi: Gratz Collection).
   [1] Gov. William Greene's March 8 letter to Ellery, in which he explained that he was
appealing to Washington to station a regiment of Rhode Island troops in the state for
its defense, is in Staples, *Rhode Island*, p. 276. His letter of the same date to Washington is in the Washington Papers, DLC.
   In his responses to Greene and Ellery, Washington avoided rejecting their appeals
directly but strongly hinted "the improbability" of being able to comply with their
request. See Washington, *Writings* (Fitzpatrick), 18:172–73, 241–42.

Samuel Huntington to George Washington

Sir   Philadelphia March 29. 1780
   I have been honoured with your Excellency's Favours of the 6th,
8th, 17th, 20th, 23d, 26th & 27th Instant—and laid them before
Congress.[1]
   Have received no later Intelligence from the southern Army than
that which you was pleased to communicate.
   Your Excellency will herewith receive a printed Copy of the Pro-
ceeding of the Court Martial on the Trial of Majr Genl Arnold[2] and

also an Act of Congress of this Day by which you will be informed
that Genl Du Portail is directed to repair with all possible Despatch
to the southern Army.[3] I have the honour to be with the most perfect Respect your Excy's hble servt,

Sam Huntington President

RC (DLC: Washington Papers). In a clerical hand and signed by Huntington.
[1] These letters are in PCC, item 152, 8:427–30, 435–38, 451–66, 471–74; and
Washington, *Writings* (Fitzpatrick), 18:92–94, 121–22, 127–28, 145–46, 152–56,
163–64. Washington's letters of March 6 and 8 are actually a single letter begun on
March 6 and completed on the eighth.
[2] See Huntington to Washington, March 11, 1780, note 4.
[3] This decision was taken in response to Washington's March 27 recommendation
to send Gen. Louis Le Bègue Duportail, chief engineer of the Continental Army, to
the southern department immediately to assist in the defense of Charleston. *JCC*,
16:316.

Abraham Clark to William Livingston

Sir   Phila. March 30. 1780.
There is now Stored at or near Squan a quantity of Blankets
designed for the use of the Army; These with other Articles of
Cloathing are under the direction of the board of War till put under
the care of the Clothier general. How and from whence those blankets came to the Above place, I am not Able to inform your
Excellency, but it appears they are of British Manufacture and on
that Account liable to seizure, and it is said that a Number of the
Inhabitants of New Jersey having knowledge of the said goods and
determind to Avail themselves of the Law Authorizing Seizures in
case of their Removal, This embarrasses the board of War. The Law
eluded to impowers the Commander in Chief of the Army or your
Excellency to grant pass ports for the safe conveyance of any goods
even in case they Actually come out of the Enemies Lines. As those
blankets are the property of the United States, and at this Time
much wanted, the granting a pass port for their safe removal appears
a Necessary and Justifiable measure, for the obtaining which, the
Secretary of the board of War will wait upon your Excellency, which
I presume your Excellency will not hesitate in granting, or Advising
the Commander in Chief of the Army to do it, that the board may
proceed in the business with Safety.[1] I am Sir, Your Excellency's
Obedt. Humble Servt.   Abra. Clark

RC (DLC: Washington Papers).
[1] Clark requested a special passport from Governor Livingston for blankets originally procured in New York City through a special agent of the Board of War under a
plan approved by Congress on December 31, 1779. Livingston enclosed Clark's request
in an April 3 letter to Washington with the explanation that since this was "an affair
wholly relating to the Army, it seems most proper that the passport come from your

Excellency." Washington immediately transmitted the necessary passport to the board.
See *JCC*, 15:1421, 1424; Board of War to Washington, March 30, and Livingston to
Washington and Washington to Livingston, April 3, in the Washington Papers, DLC;
and Washington to the Board of War, April 3, 1780, Washington, *Writings* (Fitzpatrick),
18:212–13, especially note 60.

Elbridge Gerry to Benjamin Lincoln

My dear sir,   Philadelphia 31 March 1780
Being informed late this Evening, that General Duportail is to set
off in the Morning for Charlestown, I shall improve the Oppertunity
of acknowledging your agreable Favour of the 22d Jany,[1] & of transmitting You the latest Intelligence in this Quarter: this is principally
contained in the papers inclosed, which also shew the Measures
taken by Congress relative to Finance. You have undoubtedly seen
the publications respecting the Uneasiness of Ireland, which We
shall hope will increase; altho Lord North has proposed to the british parliament a plan of Accommodation, which in their opinion a
few Years past would not have consisted with the Honor & Dignity
of that august Assembly: but pride often precedes Humility. I shall
put up the Journals from the Date of those transmitted by Major
Rice, & send them by the General, if the package is not too bulky.
I have lately received a Letter from our Friend Mr John Adams,[2]
who after a very short but perilous passage arrived at Ferrol. The
french Frigate Le Sensible in which he was passenger, was so leaky,
that every person on board was under the Necessity of taking his
Turn at the pumps four Times a Day, & She made seven feet of
Water in the Hold in an hour after her Arrival. Mr Adams mentions nothing in particular, excepting the friendly Reception which
he had met with from the Spanish officers, & their warm Attachment to the Cause of America.
By Letters from the Massachusetts I learn that the Convention
have agreed to a Constitution which is to be sent to the Towns &
Districts for their Approbation.
All Eyes are at present towards Charlestown & I am very happy to
inform You, that my Friend General Lincoln has the full Confidence
of his Countrymen(as well Citizens as Soldiers) in this Quarter; &
We have the pleasure of hearing that he is not less esteemed by our
Brethren at the southward. You have hinted something of your
being blamed for not writing, but I can assure You that it was not by
Congress, at least whilst I have been in it or I should have informed
You thereof. I Shall not suggest any thing relative to your Operations,
because I am not a Soldier; nor informed of your Circumstances: &
I am fully persuaded that every Measure will be taken to defend the
City & secure a Retreat if necessary. That Heavens Blessings may
attend You, & crown you with Success & immortal Honor is the most
ardent Wish of Dear sir Your affectionate Friend & most hum ser.
                                                          E. Gerry

FC (MHi: Gerry–Knight Collection). In the hand of Elbridge Gerry.
[1] Lincoln's January 22 letter to Gerry is not in his letterbooks in the Lincoln Papers, MHi.
[2] John Adams' December 11, 1779, letter to Gerry is in Austin, *Life of Gerry*, 1:296–98.

William Churchill Houston to Joseph Ward

Dear Sir,   Philada. 31st March 1780
   There is a Vacancy at present in the Board of Treasury, Mr. Trumbull having declined his Election.[1] It did not occur to me while you were here or I should certainly have consulted you to be put in Nomination. It was Yesterday mentioned in general Conversation, and I have taken the Liberty to inform that you will be nominated,[2] trusting that if the Appointment is not agreeable, you will give me immediate Notice, that neither Congress nor the Treasury may be at any Disappointment. The Election will not be for four or five Days, so that there will be Time to hear from you.
   The Salary of a Commissioner of the Treasury is one of the highest under Congress; but at present, like every other, greatly reduced in Value. This however the Times may mend and Congress do mend. The Business is attentive but not difficult, and with a little Practice becomes abundantly manageable. Should be happy to see Col Ward there, if it might comport with his Inclination and Prospects, and would think it not amiss, unless you wholly avoid the Proposal, to detain a few Days till the Result of the Election is heard, which I shall not fail to communicate. In the mean Time wish to hear from you forthwith.
   I am, with much regard, your very obedt Servant,
                                                    William Ch. Houston

RC (ICHi: Joseph Ward Collection).
[1] See Samuel Huntington to Jonathan Trumbull, Jr., November 12, 1779, and January 3, 1780.
[2] This day Houston's New Jersey colleague, Abraham Clark, placed Ward's name in nomination as a commissioner of the Board of Treasury, a post to which he was not elected. Ward, formerly commissary general of musters, was also nominated this day to replace John Beatty as commissary general of prisoners, a post to which he was elected on April 15, but declined. See *JCC*, 16:319, 366, 17:435.

Samuel Huntington to Benjamin Lincoln

Sir,   Philadelphia March 31, 1780
   Your several Letters of the 8th, 29th January and 11th, 14th, & 22d of Feby have been received and laid before Congress.[1]
   Your Bills drawn upon me are ordered to be accepted and paid by the Board of Treasury as you will see by the Act of Congress of the 23d Instant.[2]

The bearer of this, Brigadier General Du Portail is ordered to join the Army under your Command.[3]

I have the honour to be, with Sentiments of Esteem & regard, Sir, your most hble servant,   Sam. Huntington President

RC (MHi: Lincoln Papers). In a clerical hand and signed by Huntington.

[1] For the receipt of these letters, see *JCC*, 16:167, 230, 269. Lincoln's file copy of his January 8 letter to the "Committee of Correspondence" is in the Lincoln Papers, MHi; the other four are in PCC, item 158, fols. 313–30.

[2] See *JCC*, 16:269, 280–81.

[3] See Huntington to Washington, March 29, 1780, note 3. Gen. Louis LeBègue Duportail, chief of Continental engineers, was also the subject of the following letter of introduction for him from Huntington to South Carolina governor John Rutledge of this date.

"This Will be delivered to your Excellency by Brigadier General Du Portail whom Congress have ordered to join the Army under the Command of Major General Lincoln.

"He is esteemed a brave Officer and skilful Engineer. I take the Liberty to recommend him to your Excellency's favorable notice and hope he may be of special Service in that Department." PCC, item 14, fol. 322.

William Ellery to Schweighauser & Dobrée

Gentlemen[1]   Philadelphia March — 1780

On the 28th of Decr. last I wrote a letter to your Mr. Schweighauser[2] inclosing a letter from my brother Christopher Ellery with sundry bills of exchange and transmitted the same from hence to Boston to be forwarded by the first vessel, there then being no opportunity of sending to France from this place.

Since that I have received your joint letter of the 20th of August last with their inclosures informing me that your house would in future run under the firm of Schweighauser & Dobrée, which I have communicated to my Brother before named.

I now inclose you two Second bills of exchange on our Commissioner at Paris for thirty six dollars each, the first bills of these Setts went inclosed in the Letter I sent via Boston.

The attention of Congress is drawn at present towards So. Carolina & Our last advices from the Southward are that Genl. Clinton with the main body of his army was at James Island which is separated by a river, and is a mile & an half from Charlestown, that on their passage they had lost all their cavalry—that the Defiance a 64 gun ship, and three Transport Ships with troops had founderd at Sea, and that one with Hessian troops was missing. This intelligence is dated the fourth of March last, came through a secret Channel from Genl. Clintons Head Quarters & may be depended upon. Those Losses they acknowledge but we know that they sustained much greater disasters. The French and our frigates and the State Vessels of war in Charlestown harbour it is said are a sufficient defence by

Sea, and the lines & redoubts about the town a sufficient defence by land. Genl. Lincoln who commands there writes us that the troops & inhabitants are in good Spirits and he thinks they will be able to make a successful opposition to the enemy. We are in daily expectation of an account of an attack on Charlestown. As the holding of that place is of considerable importance I cannot avoid being somewhat anxious for its safety. Heartily wishing that we may repulse with disgrace any attempts which may be made on Charlestown, and that our arms and the arms of our allys and friends by Sea & Land may be successful this campaign, and procure us an honorable peace, I am sincerely, your most humble & obedt. Servant,

William Ellery

FC (NNPM: Signers of the Declaration Collection). In the hand of William Ellery.
[1] John Daniel Schweighauser, a merchant and Continental commercial agent at Nantes, and his son-in-law and partner, Peter F. Dobrée. See James Lovell to James Warren, August 13, 1779, note 3.
[2] Not found; but see Ellery to William Vernon, March 17, 1780.

George Partridge to Samuel Adams

Dear Sir   Philadelphia March   1780
    We had the pleasure the last fall to be informd that you had accepted your reappointment as Delegate and would be here this spring.[1] I hope that you will come as soon as travelling is good, certainly our Country needs the Assistance of her best and ablest friends at this difficult Day and the prospects of a better are not very promising while private Interest so absorbs the attention of all Ranks of People that they will damn the currency to make themselves but nominally rich.
    It is to me unaccountable that after the many Efforts which have been made to retrieve the Credit of the currency the evil should not only continue but increase. It has been tho't here impracticable to proceed in the War with the Currency in its present fluctuating State, for let the tax be never so large, the money, by the time it is collected, will purchase very little. Congress have therefore adopted a new plan to remedy these evils which will arrive at your Board by the time this reaches you. I have heard that Connecticut & Virginia have anticipated the measure and agreed to issue money on their own funds redeemable in a short time with Interest.
    I will not venture to predict what the Event of this Measure will be but trust that it will [be] happy should it meet with the approbation of the several Legislatures & the People at Large.
    You will see by the inclosed papers what was the situation of Affairs at the Southward from our latest advices. Genl. Lincoln appears from his private Letters to be in good Spirits and thinks

himself able to make a good Defence should the reinforcements now on their way arrive in season. The North Carolina troops were within 2 or 3 Days march the Virginians some distance behind them.

I purpose to be at Boston about the middle of April as my private as well as some publick concerns make my return home necessary; I the rather mention this as it may affect your preparations for your Journey.

I am Sir with the highest Esteem your most humble Servt.

Geo. Partridge

FC (PHi: Jenkins Collection). In the hand of Partridge and endorsed by him: "Letter to Mr. Adams."

[1] Adams did not return to Congress until June 29, 1780.

INDEX

In this index descriptive subentries are arranged chronologically and in ascending order of the initial page reference. They may be preceded, however, by the subentry "identified" and by document subentries arranged alphabetically—diary entries, letters, notes, resolutions, and speeches. An ornament (☆) separates the subentry "identified" and document subentries from descriptive subentries. Inclusive page references are supplied for descriptive subentries; for a document, only the page on which it begins is given. Eighteenth-century printed works are indexed both by author and by short title. Other printed works are indexed when they have been cited to document a substantive point discussed in the notes, but not when cited merely as the location of a document mentioned. Delegates who attended Congress during the period covered by this volume appear in **boldface type**.

385; inoculated for smallpox, 437, 500; credentials expire, 498; returns home, 527; mentioned, 142, 394, 497

Livingston, Henry Brockholst: appointed John Jay's secretary, 79-80; mentioned, 295

Livingston, Mary Stevens (Mrs. Robert), 451

Livingston, Robert R.: letters from, 240, 260, 285, 294, 296, 375, 402, 407, 421, 450, 493, 523, 529; letters to, 98, 254; ☆ attends Congress, xxi, 220, 277, 445; elected to Congress, xxi, 294; on New York western land claims, 240; recommends Continental intervention in state admiralty proceeding, 240; cost of living, 241; committee for foreign affairs, 260, 444; committee on departmental reform, 266; urged to accept diplomatic post, 295, 409, 425; soothes La Luzerne on flour withheld from French fleet, 296; confers with Pennsylvania on flour crisis, 297; nominated secretary to mission to France, 300; on Virginia sales of western land, 311; proposes Continental Army reduction, 331; nominated to court of appeals, 359; committee on estimates, 404; cipher letter, 409; seeks tax relief, 421; on Elbridge Gerry privilege dispute, 433; opposes Benedict Arnold court martial sentence, 487; finance committee, 488, 490; mentioned, xxvii, 80, 172, 206, 253, 263, 369, 502

Livingston, William: letters to, 47, 52, 101, 134, 135, 168, 210, 216, 218, 261, 268, 270, 282, 350, 352, 383, 386, 405, 446, 473, 498, 521, 523, 539, 555; ☆ corresponds with baron van der Capellen, 67, 323; dismisses supernumerary staff officers, 168; flees British foray, 168; recommends Silas Condict, 466, 523; and Continental lottery, 510; mentioned, 27, 80, 384, 390

Llano, Joseph de, *Tracy* v. *Llano* appeal, 156

Lloyd, Edward: identified, 355; letter to, 353; elected to Congress, xix, 353

Loan office; *see* Continental loan office

Loans, domestic: authorized, 51; mentioned, 230

Loans, foreign: proposal for rejected, 80, 94; mentioned, 90, 120, 230, 370

Locke, Francis, 54

Logwood, 86

London, 463

Long, Nicholas, 54

Lopez, Aaron, *Brooks* v. *Lopez* appeal, 430

Lottery, 526

Lottery managers, letter to, 510

Louis XVI: appoints La Luzerne minister to U.S., 157; exempts Americans from droit d'aubaine, 351; pledges arms for America, 373; petitioned for American supplies, 443; extends leave of French engineers to serve in Continental Army, 484; mentioned, 113, 439, 508, 532

Lovell, James: letters from, 7, 20, 31, 32, 62, 65, 68, 71, 74, 75, 87, 89, 97, 123, 137, 146, 160, 168, 178, 201, 203, 214, 223, 232, 260, 271, 276, 291, 297, 300, 324, 338, 339, 357, 358, 359, 361, 364, 381, 384, 385, 396, 412, 424, 426, 439, 441, 443, 447, 456, 460, 476, 482, 507, 514, 524, 527, 528, 552; ☆ attends Congress, xx, 276; elected to Congress, xx; cipher letters, xxviii, 441–42; candidate for diplomatic post, 32, 143, 271, 276, 278, 280, 291, 295, 297, 385, 409, 477; on Arthur Lee recall, 32; on Silas Deane's expenses, 61; on Du Coudray claim, 62; committee for foreign affairs, 65, 71, 89, 260, 439, 441, 444; and recall debate, 66; suppresses Arthur Lee's resignation letter, 68–69; and Deane-Lee controversy, 75, 359; laments U.S. subordination to France, 138; cost of living, 161, 292, 358, 425, 552; relations with John Hancock, 161; criticizes Washington for neglecting Massachusetts' defense, 178; on Franco-American treaty terms, 202; seeks captors of *Greyhound*, 272; recommends Robert R. Livingston, 300; on George Washington, 359; on Gen. Charles Lee, 362, 460; on peace terms, 396–97; on restructuring of U.S. mission to France, 425; on Massachusetts' depreciation pay, 426; reassures Washington on sharing of foreign intelligence, 439; on Franco-American alliance, 443; on in kind quotas, 444; on La Luzerne's plan to appeal to the states, 447–48; on Vermont controversy, 483; seeks precedents for Massachusetts' Penobscot expenses claim, 528; mentioned, 60, 154, 371

Advisory Committee

Library of Congress American Revolution Bicentennial Program

John R. Alden
James B. Duke Professor of History Emeritus, Duke University

Julian P. Boyd*
Editor of The Papers of Thomas Jefferson, *Princeton University*

Lyman H. Butterfield*
Editor in Chief Emeritus of The Adams Papers, *Massachusetts
Historical Society*

Jack P. Greene
*Andrew W. Mellon Professor in the Humanities, The Johns Hopkins
University*

Merrill Jensen*
Editor of The Documentary History of the Ratification of the
Constitution, *University of Wisconsin*

Cecelia M. Kenyon
Charles N. Clark Professor of Government, Smith College

Aubrey C. Land
University Research Professor, University of Georgia

Edmund S. Morgan
Sterling Professor of History, Yale University

Richard B. Morris
Gouverneur Morris Professor of History Emeritus, Columbia University

George C. Rogers, Jr.
*Caroline McKissick Dial Professor of American History, University of
South Carolina*

*Deceased.

600